Irene C. Fountas & Gay Su Pinnell

The Writing Minilessons Book

Your Every Day Guide for Literacy Teaching

GRADE 1

HEINEMANN
Portsmouth, NH

Heinemann
145 Maplewood Avenue, Suite 300
Portsmouth, NH 03801
www.heinemann.com

Offices and agents throughout the world

The authors and publisher wish to thank those who have generously given permission to
reprint borrowed material: Please see the Credits section beginning on page 579.

Photography: Photo of chef on page 347 by ©Luis Louro/Shutterstock

Library of Congress Cataloging in Publication data is on file at the Library of Congress.
Library of Congress Control Number: 2021935871
ISBN: 978-0-325-11880-2

Editors: Kerry Crosby and Sue Paro
Production: Cindy Strowman
Production Assistant: Anthony Riso
Cover and interior designs: Ellery Harvey and Kelsey Roy
Illustrators: Sarah Snow and Will Sweeney
Typesetter: Sharon Burkhardt
Manufacturing: Erin St. Hilaire

Printed in the United States of America on acid-free paper

1   2   3   4   5   6   MP   25   24   23   22   21
May 2021 Printing

CONTENTS

2 Management

3 Telling Stories

4 Making Books

5 Drawing

6 Craft

7 Conventions

8 Writing Process

Planning Your Writing

Drafting and Revising

Editing and Proofreading

Publishing

Introduction

Welcome to *The Writing Minilessons Book, Grade 1*

To first graders, drawing and writing are new and exciting ways to communicate thoughts, ideas, and plans. To you, children's drawing and writing provide opportunities to watch children grow in amazing ways as they explore written language. Through your teaching, children come to understand the power of putting their ideas on paper. As they learn to live like writers, they notice the world around them and see stories in their every day lives. And now, the journey begins.

Organization of Lessons

You will find two kinds of lessons in this book:

- 25 interactive writing lessons
- 150 writing minilessons

In the interactive writing lessons, you and the children write together as you provide a high level of support. In the writing minilessons, you help children expand what they know about drawing and writing so they can feel like artists and writers. The 25 interactive writing lessons are presented together in Section 1. The 150 writing minilessons are organized across Sections 2–8:

- Section 1: Interactive Writing (IW)
- Section 2: Management (MGT)
- Section 3: Telling Stories (STR)
- Section 4: Making Books (MBK)
- Section 5: Drawing (DRW)
- Section 6: Craft (CFT)
- Section 7: Conventions (CNV)
- Section 8: Writing Process (WPS)

Sections 2–8 contain groups of minilessons, or "umbrellas." Within each umbrella, the minilessons are all related to the same big idea so you can work with it for several days. The umbrellas are numbered sequentially within each section, and the minilessons are numbered sequentially within each umbrella. Each writing minilesson is identified by section, umbrella, and minilesson. For example, MBK.U1.WML1 indicates the first minilesson in the first umbrella of the Making Books section.

Content of Lessons: The Literacy Continuum

Almost all lessons in this book are based on the behaviors and understandings presented in *The Fountas & Pinnell Literacy Continuum: A Tool for Assessment, Planning, and Teaching* (Fountas and Pinnell 2017). This volume presents detailed behaviors and understandings to notice, teach for, and support for prekindergarten through middle school, across eight instructional reading, writing, and language contexts. In sum, *The Literacy Continuum* describes proficiency in reading, writing, and language as it changes over grades and over levels. When you teach the lessons in this book, you are teaching for the behaviors and understandings that first graders need to become proficient readers and writers over time.

Organized for Your Children's Needs

We have provided a suggested sequence of lessons for you to try out and adjust based on your observations of the children. The sequence in Figure I-1 provides one path through the lessons. If this is your first time teaching minilessons, you may want to stick to it. However, once you become familiar with this book and the children's needs, choose the lessons that meet those needs. You will be able to locate the lessons easily because they are organized into sections. We organized the lessons into sections for these reasons:

1. The children in any given first-grade class will vary greatly in their literacy experiences and development. Lessons organized by topic allow you to dip into the sections to select specific umbrellas or lessons that respond to your students' needs. You can find lessons easily by section and topic through the table of contents.

2. You can teach the lessons that make sense for the children in your class and omit any lessons that would be too advanced or too easy.

3. Writing is a complex learning process and involves many levels of learning—from figuring out the idea to communicate, to thinking about what to draw and write, to the mechanics of getting it on paper. Having the lessons organized by section enables you to focus on the areas that might be most helpful to the children at a specific point in time.

Key Words Used in Minilessons

The following is a list of key terms that we will use as we describe minilessons in the next chapters. Keep them in mind so that together we can develop a common language to talk about the minilessons.

▶ **Umbrella** A group of minilessons, all of which are directed at different aspects of the same larger understanding.

▶ **Minilesson** A short, interactive lesson to invite children to think about one idea.

▶ **Principle** A concise statement of the concept children will learn and be invited to apply.

▶ **Writing** All the kinds of "writing" that first-grade children will do, including drawings, scribbles, approximated writing, and making letters they know.

▶ **Mentor Text** A fiction or nonfiction text in which the author or illustrator offers a clear example of the minilesson principle. Children will have heard the text read aloud and talked about it. Mentor texts can be books you have read to them as well as simple texts that you have written or ones you and the children have written together.

▶ **Text Set** A group of either fiction or nonfiction books or a combination of both that, taken together, help children explore an idea or a type of book (genre). You will have already read the books to them before a lesson. Children will have also made important connections between them.

▶ **Anchor Chart** A visual representation of the lesson concept using a combination of words and images. You create it as you talk with the children. It summarizes the learning and can be used by the children as a reference tool.

The chapters at the beginning of this book help you think about the role of talking, drawing, and writing in first grade, how the lessons are designed and structured, and the materials and resources you will need to teach the lessons.

Suggested Sequence of Lessons

If you are new to first-grade minilessons, you may want to use the Suggested Sequence of Lessons (Figure I-1) for teaching the interactive writing lessons and writing minilessons across the year. This sequence weaves in lessons from the different sections so that children receive instruction in all aspects of writing and drawing throughout the school year. Lessons are sequenced in a way we think will support most first-grade children, but you need to observe what most of your young students are doing as talkers, artists, and writers. Then choose lessons that will lead them forward.

The lessons in this book are sequenced in a way that builds on the sequence of mentor texts used in *Fountas & Pinnell Classroom™ Interactive Read-Aloud Collection* (2018) and *Shared Reading Collection* (2018). It is our intention that whenever possible children will have already seen and heard the mentor texts by the time they are used in a lesson.

Every first-grade class is different, so it is impossible to prescribe an exact sequence of lessons. However, this sequence will give you a good starting place as you begin to teach the lessons in *The Writing Minilessons Book, Grade 1*.

▶ The number of days assigned to each umbrella suggests how many days you will spend on teaching the minilessons in an umbrella. You may want to give children time in between lessons to apply the lesson during independent writing.

- You do not have to teach a writing minilesson every day. We have left room in the sequence for you to repeat or revisit lessons as needed or to spend more time exploring certain kinds of writing depending on the children's interests.

- You want to expose children to a variety of writing and writing techniques early in the year, so you teach quite a few lessons in the first few months. It's also a good idea to revisit and repeat umbrellas. Children will apply the lessons in different ways as they develop their abilities to write and draw across the school year.

Figure I-1: The complete Suggested Sequence of Lessons is on pages 555–571 in this book and in the online resources.

Suggested Sequence of Lessons

Months	Texts from *Fountas & Pinnell Classroom™ Shared Reading Collection*	Text Sets from *Fountas & Pinnell Classroom™ Interactive Read-Aloud Collection*	Reading Minilessons (RML) Umbrellas	Interactive Writing (IW) Lessons*	Writing Minilessons (WML) Umbrellas	Teaching Notes
Months 1 & 2	Monster ABCs The Elephant The Hippo The Giraffe The Flamingo In My Bag Silly and Fun: Poems to Make You Smile	Learning and Working Together: School	MGT.U1: Working Together in the Classroom MGT.U2: Using the Classroom Library for Independent Reading	**IW.1: Making a Name Chart (1 day)** **IW.2: Writing About Our Classroom (1 day)** **IW.3: Labeling the Classroom (1–3 days)** **IW.4: Writing from a Picture (1 day)**	MGT.U1: Working Together in the Classroom, WML1–WML5 (5 days)	If you are using *The Reading Minilessons Book, Grade 1,* you do not need to teach MGT.U1. Both RML and WML establish the same routines. However, be sure to take time to build community in your classroom by asking children to draw and write about themselves as they practice these new routines. The opening page of the writing minilessons umbrella MGT.U1 provides specific suggestions. IW.2 can be taught as a culminating activity. Teach IW.3 in conjunction with RML.MGT.U2.
	Rain, Sun, Wind, Snow: Poems About the Seasons Creep, Crawl, Fly: Poems About Bugs	Having Fun with Language: Rhyming Texts	MGT.U3: Engaging in Classroom Literacy Work, RML1–RML4, RML10	**IW.5: Innovating on a Rhyming Text (1 day)**	STR.U1: Learning About Self and Others Through Storytelling, WML1–WML2 (2 days)	STR.U1 helps children get to know one another and build classroom community while allowing them to orally rehearse their stories before writing. Teach the minilessons in STR.U1 over time so that children have more time to tell stories. Provide time each day for children to tell stories while you teach the next few writing umbrellas.

You do not need *Fountas & Pinnell Classroom*™ *Shared Reading Collection, Interactive Read-Aloud Collection,* or *The Reading Minilessons Book, Grade 1* to teach these lessons. We have included them in this sequence for teachers who use these resources so they can connect and organize reading and writing across the year. If you do not have the texts that appear in the lessons as mentor texts, simply pick similar books and examples from your own classroom library or school library. Characteristics of the books used in the lessons are described in the active learning experience of interactive writing lessons and on the opening page of the umbrellas for the writing minilessons. To read more about using the Suggested Sequence of Lessons to plan your teaching, see chapter 8.

Chapter 1   The Role of Writing in Early Literacy Learning

Writing can contribute to the building of almost every kind of inner control of literacy learning that is needed by the successful reader.

—Marie Clay

LOOK AROUND A FIRST-GRADE CLASSROOM, bustling with the energy of young children. Some children are busy observing, sketching, and writing notes about the latest wonder in the science center. Other children are deep into their research about a topic they love and care about. Still others are off making books. They are writing how-to books, making poetry books, and writing about their favorite memories. Partners read each other their stories and offer suggestions, and the teacher confers with individual writers who are eager to share the latest additions to their writing. The classroom is filled not only with the excitement of exploration but with the tools of literacy (Figure 1-1).

Children in your first-grade classroom are learning to be part of a community of talkers, scientists, mathematicians, artists, readers, and writers. The interactive writing lessons and writing minilessons in this book play an important role in this process. In the lessons, children will draw and write in many different ways for many different purposes across the curriculum (Figure 1-2), both together and on their own. Pieces of writing that the children create as a class will become familiar texts for reading and rereading. Writing and drawing done by individual children can be shared with one another.

First graders live in a literate world, a world filled with print in all sizes, shapes, and colors for different purposes. They notice print all around them—from road signs and store names to cereal boxes and text messages. These noticings lead them to understand that the marks on paper or screens mean something, and they want to try to do their own writing.

When we talk about a first grader's writing, what do we mean? Of course, you will have a range of writers in your classroom from those who are just starting to label their drawings and write simple sentences to those who can write across several pages. No matter where they are on this continuum, most first graders understand that they can communicate a message in pictures and words. You can help them see the power of their messages and stories through your response to their attempts at trying new things in their writing. The interactive writing and writing minilessons in this book will help them see the stories in their lives and help you provide time and space for children to share their stories orally as well as in written form. If they have daily opportunities to write, as guided by the lessons, they will learn to see themselves as writers and artists. We have been astounded at young children's ability to grow in writing over time.

Figure 1-1: First graders are eager to engage in new learning. Their participation in literacy activities supports their reading and writing development.

The center of the wheel reads: Kinds of Writing in *The Writing Minilessons Book, Grade 1*

Surrounding segments: All-About Books, Question-and-Answer Books, How-to Books, Memory Stories, Interviews, Poems, Labels, Story Maps, Letters, Cards, Invitations, Science Observations, Signs, Diagrams, Lists, Class Big Books, Charts, Surveys

Figure 1-2: Children will have opportunities to write and draw in a variety of ways across the year.

Children Grow as Writers over Time

Some children have had more experience with or opportunities for drawing or writing than others, but with your support they can all grow as writers. Figure 1-3 shows a rough progression of early writing that you might see in your classroom. (We don't use the word *stages* because writing development is complex and writers can show more than one element at a time in their approximations.) Although the examples move from left to right, forward progress is not linear. Not every child will exhibit the same sequence, and most children will move back and forth. Use Figure 1-3 to see how your own students' writing is developing. Look for evidence that children are expanding their writing over time.

Children Show What They Know

Children learn differently from one another, but all make progress toward the kind of writing they see in books. Watching first graders write and looking at their writing will show you what they know. Notice whether they

- initiate writing quickly,
- have things to write about,
- choose topics and stories they care about,
- show enthusiasm for their writing,
- draw pictures with details,
- write their names,
- write words with standard and approximated spellings,
- talk about their pictures and messages,
- write words in sentences,
- read what they have written,
- try out new learning in their writing,
- use capitalization and punctuation to clarify their writing, or
- revise, or change, their writing to make it more interesting, more detailed, or clearer.

Figure 1-3: Each child's writing develops differently, but there are patterns of development that you might notice, such as the ones shown in these examples.

LABELING PICTURES WITH NAMES

Early on, children add labels to their drawings. They might write familiar names or high-frequency words (e.g., *mom, dad, me*). The name chart can be used for labeling classmates' names (e.g., *Cielo*).

USING ENVIRONMENTAL PRINT

Children integrate words into their writing from the print they see on the walls of the classroom (as in the case of this counting book), in the stores they visit, and on the food boxes on their shelves.

WRITING SIMPLE SENTENCES

As children begin to form sentences, they combine approximated spelling with the standard spelling of some high-frequency words. They write the predominant sounds they hear, often at the beginning and end of a word. This can be seen in the example that reads, *My family went to grill.*

MY F WM To
GL.

When you notice what children are doing with writing, you can build on their strengths and help them take the next steps in their writing. In Figure 1-4, notice all of the things first grader Andrew is doing in his writing. Also notice areas in which he can grow based on his budding understandings. It is important to note that children take on behaviors and understandings over time. The goal of analyzing children's writing is not to "fix" or improve a particular piece of writing (though you might use one piece to teach one or two important new things) but to give children the tools to move forward with writing over time. Analyzing your students' writing gives you direction for what you might teach to lead writers forward. When you meet students where they are and build on their strengths, they are more engaged and interested in learning how to make their writing more like the books they are reading.

Chapter 8 has information about the tools provided in the online resources to assess your students' writing. *The Literacy Continuum* (Fountas and Pinnell 2017) and the assessment sections in both the interactive writing lessons and writing minilessons will guide your observation of children's writing behaviors and your analysis of their writing pieces. When you take time to talk to your writers and read their writing, you learn what they have understood from your teaching, what they have yet to understand, and what you might teach them next.

WRITING WITH MEDIAL SOUNDS

As children become more comfortable taking risks in their writing, they begin to attempt longer words that they do not know how to spell (e.g., *mountain*). They also begin to include medial sounds and vowels in each word.

> I climd up a mootin.
> It wus not ezey.

EXPANDING WRITING

Children write multiple sentences and combine standard and approximated writing, as in this example: *When we went to the reservoir. It is in Leverett. We went on a path. When we came out we saw it! We had fun.*

> Wen we went to the rezsuvoo. It is in levrit. We went on a path. wen we came out we soa it! We had fun.

WRITING WITH COMPLEX SENTENCES

Children begin to make more craft moves, like including dialogue in their writing. They learn that punctuation helps readers understand the message. Though they still use approximated spelling for unknown words, standardized spelling appears more regularly.

> "Were there" said Aly. "Wow" said Jett. "There's Bret's house but it has no walls" said Aly.

Children Connect What They Hear, Say, and Write

A child's journey to becoming literate begins at birth. Andrew has developed the understandings he demonstrates in Figure 1-4 over many years. As caregivers engage the child in language interactions, the child learns to communicate, and this oral language foundation paves the way for learning about written language—reading and writing. All aspects of children's oral and written language—listening, speaking, reading, and writing—develop together and support each other as the young child emerges into literacy. Any time you and the children write together—whether labels, descriptions, observations, or stories—thinking and talking come first. Children learn that their thoughts and ideas can be put into language, language can be put into writing, and the writing can be read (Figure 1-5).

Figure 1-4: Andrew's story about his broken arm is evidence of what he understands about writing and provides a window into possible next steps for this first-grade writer. The story reads *I was climbing on the monkey bars. I broke my arm. A teacher brought me to the nurse. My mom and dad came to the school to bring me to the hospital.*

Andrew demonstrates an understanding that he can show movement in his drawing. Notice the arrows showing him falling.

Andrew understands how to use speech bubbles to add talking and details to the story. He wrote *There goes Drew* and *Are you ok?*

A strength for Andrew is that he presents his ideas in a logical sequence with a clear beginning, middle and end. He also has chosen a story that is important to him.

Andrew would benefit from telling his story aloud to make sure he included all of the important information. His teacher might also help him use his pictures to write the details of his story (e.g., how he fell off the bars).

Andrew understands that he needs to capitalize the first letter in a sentence as well as the pronoun, *I*.

A next step might be to include his feelings in his memory stories. He doesn't yet know how to expand on the emotional moments of his stories.

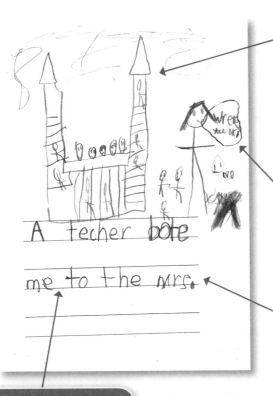

Andrew understands how to draw where the story takes place, including the castle-like play structure at his school. His teacher can build on this understanding to show him how he might also include details about the setting in his writing.

Building on his use of dialogue in speech bubbles, his teacher might introduce how to include dialogue in a story to expand his writing.

Andrew included characters in his story (teacher, mom, and dad). He would benefit from lessons showing how to write details about characters.

Andrew consistently left appropriate space between his words and wrote a combination of upper- and lowercase letters.

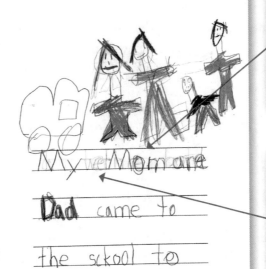

Andrew's writing shows his beginning understanding that names are capitalized even though he didn't get it quite right (he doesn't yet understand that the word *my* changes *mom* and *dad* into common nouns).

Another strength for Andrew is his ability to hear the sounds in words. He is beginning to write consonant clusters like the *br* in *bring* and *broke*. He also controls several high-frequency words including *me, to, the, my*.

The erasure marks on the paper are evidence that Andrew understands writers revise their work. He would benefit from learning to simply cross out instead of erasing to make his work more legible.

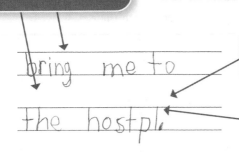

Andrew's writing demonstrates that he has a sense of a story ending with a resolution.

Andrew used periods at the end of his sentences fairly consistently. His teacher might choose to build on this strength to teach him how to use other types of puncutation.

The Contributions of Writing to Language, Literacy, and Learning

As children take on literacy in a joyful way, they grow in oral language, reading, and writing. As they write, they

- Move from thoughts to ideas to language to written representation in images or words
- Link spoken language to written language
- Work on communicating meaningful messages
- Say words slowly to hear the individual sounds in words
- Connect sounds with letters
- Learn how print and the structure of written language works
- Read their writing attempts

Figure 1-5: Contributions of writing to literacy learning

One section of this book is dedicated to telling stories, because for children to be able to write their stories, they first need to be able to tell their stories. By listening to stories read to them and by telling stories themselves (stories from their own lives or retellings of stories from books), children begin to develop an understanding of story structure. We see this in Andrew's simple story about his broken arm. He understands that stories often begin with a problem and end with a resolution. Children develop the ability to use the patterns of language and build strong vocabularies as they listen to and talk about books, ask questions about their classmates' stories, and clarify their own stories for an audience. As they begin to draw and write their oral stories, they have conversations about their writing that deepen their ability to explain their thinking. They learn to put ideas in time order, to elaborate with story details, to develop vocabulary, and to more accurately describe what they want to say.

Children Have Opportunities to Write All Day

In the first-grade classroom, it is important to carve out a dedicated time for writing as well as embed writing opportunities into a variety of daily classroom activities. From the time they enter the literacy-rich classroom, children are engaged in writing. They "sign in" on attendance sheets, answer survey questions on charts, create writing pieces with their class, write explanations for their math solutions, and make sketches of their scientific observations. They talk about what authors do in their books, and they make their own books. Providing first graders with a predictable time to write each day allows them the opportunity to experiment with writing, to make books over time, and to apply their new learning from interactive writing and writing minilessons. Consider setting aside the following times in your day for writing, and think about how you might build writing across content areas and into other established routines (e.g., independent work time) in your classroom.

Shared/Interactive Writing Time During interactive writing, children have the chance to collaborate on a piece of writing as a whole class. You can read in depth about interactive writing lessons in chapter 3.

Independent Writing Time During Writers' Workshop Independent writing time is typically bookended by a writing minilesson and a chance for children to share their writing (Figure 1-6). Children learn about an aspect of writing during a writing minilesson and then have a chance to apply what they learned in that lesson as they write independently on their own pieces for a short period of time. The teacher has the opportunity to confer with individual writers or to work with small groups in guided writing (see page 31 for information about guided writing). Children engage in a variety of writing, especially in making books, which is described in more detail on pages 22–24. The writers' workshop ends with a whole-group meeting in which children share their writing and, if applicable, the ways they used their new learning from the writing minilesson. Chapter 4 describes how the writing minilessons in this book follow and support this structure. Using the Management minilessons will help you establish a productive and engaging independent writing time with your first graders.

Independent Work Time After engaging in an inquiry-based reading minilesson, children participate in a variety of independent literacy activities. They listen to books in the listening center, act out stories with puppets in the drama area, independently read from book boxes, play phonics and word games in the word study center, and/or write in the writing center. During this time, teachers often confer with individual readers as they apply what they learned from the reading minilesson to their independent reading, or work with small groups in a guided reading lesson. As children engage in these literacy activities, they have many opportunities to write. They write about their reading in the listening center, respond to poems in the poetry

Figure 1-6: A writers' workshop structure allows for whole-class learning, individual and small-group guidance from the teacher, independent writing, and whole-class sharing.

Structure of Writers' Workshop

Whole Class	Writing Minilesson	5–10 Minutes
Individuals and Small Groups	Independent Writing Individual Conferences Guided Writing Groups	15–30 minutes (The time will expand as children build stamina across the year.)
Whole Class	Group Share	5–10 Minutes

Work Board

Maya	Derrick	Chase	Jazmine
Brennan	Levi	Maddie	Silas
Yin Chi	Raeesha	Tanaiya	Boyong
Raghad	Jonah	Julian	Uri
Avery	Abdi	Francisco	Sama

Work Time

1. Read a book

2. Listen to a book

3. Work on words

4. Work on writing

Figure 1-7: A work board or a simple list can help you manage children's independent work time.

Figure 1-8: Suggestions for stocking the activity areas of the classroom to encourage writing

center, make observations in the science center, write in response to books in guided reading, and continue their bookmaking in the writing center. Children also use the writing center to write notes or letters to their classmates, make books about things they are learning in science and social studies, or create in ways you might never have imagined. Teachers often manage independent work time with a work board or with a simple list of tasks (Figure 1-7). A list of materials to support writing in each center is shown in Figure 1-8. We provide details for establishing and managing independent work time in both *Guided Reading: Responsive Teaching Across the Grades* (Fountas and Pinnell 2017) and *The Reading Minilessons Book, Grade 1* (Fountas and Pinnell 2019).

Stocking the Activity Centers

Yearlong Activity Center	Materials
Classroom Library	• books in labeled tubs organized by topic, author, illustrator, and kind of book (genre) • covers facing out for easy browsing • labels for the tubs written using shared or interactive writing

Stocking the Activity Centers (cont.)

Yearlong Activity Center	Materials
Writing Center	• pencils, markers, crayons • a variety of paper–different sizes, colors, formats (see online resources) • textured paper for covers • staplers • scissors • glue • premade blank books for bookmaking • sticky notes • white correction tape • name chart and Alphabet Linking Chart • tub of favorite books to help stimulate ideas • additional writing tools: letter stamps and pads, letter tiles, letter sponges, whiteboards, notebooks, notepads, traceable letters, sandpaper letters, stencils
Art Center (This can be adjacent to the writing center in order to share supplies.)	• paper • paints, markers, colored pencils, crayons (in a variety of colors to provide options for different skin tones and hair colors) • glue • scissors • textured materials (e.g., cloth, ribbed paper, tissue paper) • craft sticks • yarn • tub of books with a variety of interesting art (e.g., collage, found objects, paintings)
Word Work (ABCs)	• blank word cards • very simple wall of words nearby (mostly with children's names and a few high-frequency words) • Alphabet Linking Chart and name chart • magnetic letters • games • word cards to sort • cookie trays • index cards with textured names; names with dots indicating where to begin tracing
Listening Center	• listening device • clear set of directions with picture clues • multiple copies of books organized in boxes or plastic bags • clipboards and paper to draw responses to books

Yearlong Activity Centers	Materials
Science Center	• a range of natural items gathered from outside of school (e.g., rocks, shells, leaves, abandoned bird's nest/beehive, snake's skin) • magnifying glasses • writing tools • paper • rulers • pastels and tracing paper for rubbings • nonfiction books with colorful photographs and drawings of subjects such as animals, foods, families, communities • booklet or notebook labeled *Lab Book*

Children Make Important Literacy Connections

Besides having dedicated times for writing, children need to be immersed in a variety of literacy experiences throughout the day so they can make important connections between reading, writing, and word study. In a literacy-building environment, children see print everywhere. They talk and listen to others. They hear books read aloud, learn to read their own books, experience reading and phonics lessons, and write and draw about their reading. They learn about and play with language. They make their own books. All of this supports children's writing development.

Print All Around the Classroom Children live in a world full of print. Just as they see print in their neighborhoods, they walk into a classroom with labels and signs that are meaningful to them. They even participate in making these labels and signs. When you work with children to label parts of the classroom or materials (e.g., window, door, chair, stapler, or paper), you provide a chance for them to produce print that is meaningful and helpful. A word wall that includes children's names provides a helpful resource for the writers in your class. As you introduce high-frequency words (e.g., *the, and, is, I, am, here*), add them to your word wall. Through minilessons, children learn to use the word wall as a tool to help them generate the spelling of unknown words. Keep the word wall active by adding to it regularly. During interactive and shared writing, show children how to use the words on the word wall to spell unfamiliar words (e.g., use the *th* in *then* to start the word *there*) (Figure 1-9).

Figure 1-9: A word wall in first grade starts with children's names and is built over time as you introduce commonly used words.

The Most Important Word Is Your Name Children will quickly learn to read and write their classmates' names. In a first-grade classroom, children see their names all around—on attendance or sign-in charts, on the name chart, on cubbies, on the choice time board, and on a bulletin board display. Their names are displayed on cards that they use to express their opinions on class survey questions that are created together during interactive writing. They learn that familiar names can help them think about how to spell other words (e.g., words that start or end like some of their classmates' names). In some classrooms, a wall has been dedicated to framed self-portraits with children's names written clearly below and to drawings of children's families, inviting all who visit to get to know the children in this special community of learners.

Interactive Read-Aloud and Shared Reading Reading aloud to children is essential. We call it "interactive" because it is so important for children to talk with each other about the books they hear. They also love shared reading with enlarged print books and charts, reading together from the same book, song, or poem (Figure 1-10). Books they read many times become "theirs." Interactive read-aloud and shared reading expose children to a variety of stories, informational books, nursery rhymes, songs, and poems. As children listen to and discuss these books and poems, they hear the way written language sounds and start to notice what other writers and illustrators do in their books. When you spend time pointing out how the illustrator designed the cover, the colors used in the illustrations, an interesting choice of words, or the rhythm of a repeating line, children become aware of the author's or illustrator's craft in a simple and authentic way.

Reading Minilessons, Guided Reading, and Independent Reading Reading minilessons build on the literary understandings developed during interactive read-aloud and shared reading. Children learn more about what illustrators and writers do, how written language sounds, and how stories and information are organized. They learn about the author's message, how

Figure 1-10: Children develop an understanding of story structure, knowledge of how books work, and familiarity with early print concepts through interactive read-aloud and shared reading (shown here).

print and words work, and about different kinds of writing. They participate in shared writing as they work with you to create anchor charts for reading minilessons and learn how to write and draw about their reading. Children grow in all of these understandings as they participate in brief, small-group guided reading lessons in which they read books at their instructional level. Children are also given opportunities throughout the day to read independently. As they engage with a variety of texts independently, children not only apply what they have learned during reading minilessons and guided reading but also make their own discoveries about print, writer's and illustrator's craft, and other literary elements. We have written extensively about reading minilessons and guided reading in *The Reading Minilessons Book, Grade 1* (2019) and in *Guided Reading* (2017). Good teaching in reading is essential to the teaching of writing and vice versa. Interactive writing lessons and writing minilessons help children transfer what they have learned in reading to their own writing. In turn, what they learn about writing will make them stronger readers. It is a deeply reciprocal process.

Writing Across the Curriculum Writing plays an important role in the content areas as well. Children draw and write as they solve math problems and explain their solutions. They record information during science experiments; they sketch and write their observations in the science center; and they write predictions and wonderings about scientific phenomena. Put a set of magnets with different materials in front of first graders, and they will write predictions for what materials the magnet will attract, they will record what happens, and they will ask questions about how these forces work. Writing, along with talking and reading, is one of the vehicles for learning across the curriculum. Encourage your students to make books in science and social studies—for example, a how-to book for conducting a science experiment, an all-about book about something in history or in your community (Figure 1-11), or a lab book of science observations. The interactive writing lessons in this book demonstrate different ways you might show children how to write across the content areas, from IW.11: Labeling a Map to IW.23: Making Scientific Observations. In the Writing Process section, as part of the planning process, there is an umbrella that demonstrates how to observe and write like a scientist.

First graders also have several opportunities throughout the day to write about their reading. Children love to draw to show what they are thinking about a book they have read and can begin to write simple responses after you have modeled how by teaching reading minilessons and interactive writing lessons. You will find several examples of writing about reading in the interactive writing lessons in this book (e.g., IW.6: Making a Story Map). Some first-grade teachers use a reader's notebook as a place to collect their children's writing about reading. The writing minilessons in this book focus on having children write their own original pieces, but writing about reading is still an important part of becoming a writer. For minilessons on writing about reading and how to use a reader's notebook with first graders, see *The Reading Minilessons Book, Grade 1* (2019).

Phonics and Phonemic Awareness

Through interactive writing and writing minilessons, children have several opportunities to begin noticing individual sounds in words (phonemic awareness) and to develop a deeper understanding of the relationship between the letters and sounds (phonics). To further support this learning, many first-grade teachers also provide a specific time for phonics, spelling, and

Figure 1-11: Examples of children's writing across the curriculum

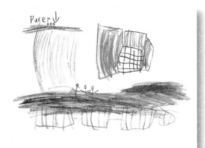

Knox drew a picture and told about the history of his town: *Amherst used to be called the Mill River. The kids walked to school following the river. They get to school following it. The Mill River still exists.*

Knox drew and wrote his observations in the science center: *I see some leaves and some tadpoles and some dirt.*

After listening to *If You Give a Pig a Pancake* by Laura Numeroff, Knox wrote about his reading: *She is eating the pancakes.*

word study lessons (see *Fountas & Pinnell Phonics, Spelling, and Word Study System, Grade 1*, 2017). Through inquiry, children learn key principles about the way words work. Additionally, first graders benefit from opportunities to learn the sounds in words through songs, finger plays, and rhymes. The following list has a few simple ways to help children develop in these areas. Many of these activities could be done in the word work center, during morning meeting, or during circle time.

- Play oral games (e.g., rhyming).
- Incorporate songs, poems, rhymes, and finger plays to help children hear sounds in words.
- Connect sounds and letters to children's own names.
- Demonstrate making words with magnetic letters.
- Use alphabet and letter puzzles.
- Make ABC books accessible.
- Provide games (e.g., picture lotto with letter sounds or rhymes or concepts) and teach children how to play.

Children Love to Make Books

Bookmaking is a powerful way for children to enter into drawing and writing and bring together all of these important literacy experiences. Glover (2009) said it well:

> The reason for making books is simple. Books are what children have the greatest vision for, and having a clear vision for what you are making is important in any act of composition. Young children have the clearest vision for making picture books because that is the type of writing that they have seen most. (13)

Invite your students to make their own books, just like the authors of the books they love (Figure 1-12). Children enjoy using blank books (even as simple as a piece of paper folded in half), but you can also offer any of the variety of optional paper templates for writing from the online resources. The act of making books—we use the term *making* instead of *writing* because some children will protest that they can't write—benefits you and the children in lots of ways.

- Children see themselves as authors, illustrators, and readers (Figure 1-13).
- Children develop feelings of independence and accomplishment at having created something that is uniquely theirs.

- Children begin to take in and try out concepts of writing, such as holding a marker, moving left to right across a page, and making letterforms.

- Children build stamina by working on a book over several days.

- Writing and reading reinforce one another, so as children make their own books, they become more aware of the decisions that authors and illustrators make in their books.

Figure 1-12: Drew shows his understanding of books with his own nonfiction book about a favorite topic, penguins. He included features he has seen in nonfiction books: a cover, a table of contents, fun facts (the writing by the picture on the first page), and boldfaced words for the glossary.

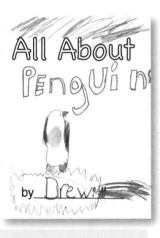

Cover

Table of Contents

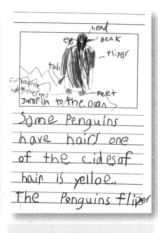

Some penguins have hairs. One of the sides of hair is yellow. The penguins flipper (continues on the next page)

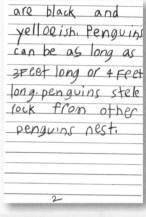

. . . are black and yellowish. Penguins can be as long as 3 feet long or 4 feet long. Penguins steal rocks from other penguins' nest.

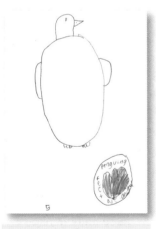

This close-up of a penguin's foot with a caption (lower right) says *Penguins feet are orange.*

Penguins eat fish and shrimp. They have to swim to get their food. The beak (continues on next page)

. . . closes on it's prey and slides and waddles back to feed the baby.

beak–*they eat with it,* **prey**–*it's the animals that try to eat them,* **slide**–*is when they glide on the ground.*

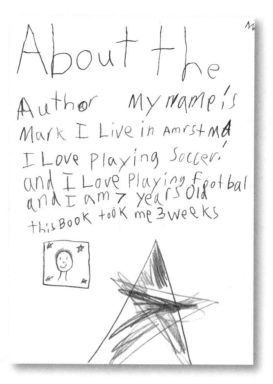

▶ Children learn that reading and writing are similar in many ways (left-to-right direction, top-to-bottom progression, space between words, letterforms, letter-sound relationships).

▶ Children expand their understanding about print, illustrations, and text structure.

▶ The books children write show evidence of what they know about drawing and writing, and you can use that information to decide what they need to learn next.

Some minilessons in Section 4: Making Books get children started in the basics of making books. Other minilessons provide opportunities for children to try making different kinds of books, including how-to books, all-about books (informational books), and memory books.

> Once you treat children as authors and illustrators, and engage them in conversations about how authors and illustrators do things, they notice more and more of those things and wonder how and why authors do them. (Johnston et al. 2020, 14)

In your classroom, offer writing support through shared and interactive writing and writing minilessons so that children can continue to grow as they engage and play with the writing process throughout the day. You'll be amazed at what they discover and learn through their explorations.

Chapter 2 | Inviting Young Children into the Writing Process

The key is that regardless of whether there are words on the page or not, or how approximated the writing appears, the child is conveying a thought through symbols and pictures on a page and is therefore writing.

—Matt Glover

CHILDREN WANT TO BE WRITERS because they become aware of writing in their environment at a very young age. They see others writing, learn its purpose, and start trying to do it on their own. Even a simple grocery list communicates something important to the young child: writing is a useful tool. Take advantage of children's natural curiosity! How do you plan classroom instruction, use language, and provide drawing and writing opportunities in ways that invite these curious young learners into the world of writing?

Young Children Engage in the Writing Process

All writers, regardless of age or experience, engage in the same aspects of the writing process every time they write. Although components of the writing process are usually listed in a sequence, writers can and will use any or all of the components at any point while writing.

- Planning and Rehearsing (Talk about it.)
- Drafting and Revising (Get it down.)
- Editing and Proofreading (Make it better.)
- Publishing (Share it with friends.)

Of course, drawing and reading are fundamental parts of this process, as well, and are especially important for first graders.

Planning and Rehearsing

For children, talk is an important part of planning and rehearsing their writing. They need to be able to form their ideas into oral language before they can attempt to put those ideas on paper. Some of the talk is about children's ideas—*what* they are writing. Some of the talk is about *why* children are writing and for *whom*—the purpose and the audience. When children begin to think about who will read their writing, they are able to ask themselves and each other, "What will the reader need to know? What else should I put in my book to help my reader enjoy and understand it?"

Knowing the purpose for writing often leads to discussions about what type of writing to do and what kind of paper is best for that purpose. For example, if children want to

- say thank you, they might write a note or a letter;
- teach others how to do something, they might write a how-to book;
- create a public service announcement, they might make a poster or a sign; or
- remember an experience or entertain their audience, they might write a story.

In all of these cases, the writer thinks about the purpose, determines what kind of writing will serve that purpose, and then begins to write a message. As you write together as a class with shared and interactive writing, children gradually learn all these connections.

From listening to many books read aloud to them, children learn that writers get their ideas from their own experiences and from what they have learned. Minilessons in the Writing Process section support children in further developing this understanding. When children write personal stories, they discover that they can write about what they have done, what they know or care about, a place they want to remember, or a special object. The possibilities are endless.

Drafting and Revising

At the beginning of the year, most first-grade writing is just getting something down on the paper. We do not expect standard spelling, and drawing is an important way for children to express what they want to say. Young children are pleased to celebrate their early attempts at writing, and it is important for them to feel this power. Talk is especially important for those students whose first language is not English. They need opportunities to rehearse their ideas by telling stories or talking about their ideas before they write. Minilessons in Section 3: Telling Stories invite children to talk in ways that support the process of getting ideas down on paper.

As you guide children in constructing texts, they learn that part of the process of getting something down involves rereading and thinking about each word as part of a larger idea. You can show them how to think what they want to say before they draw or write.

Over the course of the year, children learn more about the way words work, talk about the decisions authors make, and begin to make their own decisions about how to get their ideas down on paper. As children learn more about sounds, letters, and words, they begin to use a combination of standard spelling, particularly of high-frequency words, and approximated spelling in their writing. They start to capture their ideas and messages in both drawing and words.

Children get excited about learning new ways to add to their writing so they can make it more interesting. They learn to reread their writing to make sure it makes sense and to add or cross out when it doesn't (Figure 2-1). The minilessons in Section 8: Writing Process will help you offer guidance in drafting and revising.

EL CONNECTION

When you teach English learners, you can adjust your teaching—not more teaching, but different teaching—to assure effective learning. Look for the symbol above to see ways to support English learners.

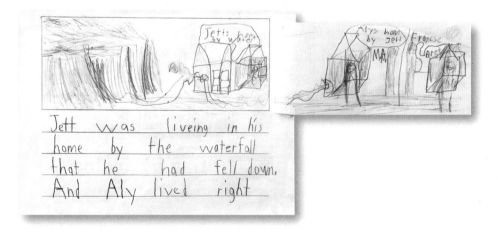

Figure 2-1: Kole taped a paper strip, called a spider leg, to his story to add more details to his picture. He applied a technique taught in a writing minilesson about revision.

Proofreading and Editing

First graders are rapid learners, but most of what they produce early in the year will include temporary, approximated spelling. Sometimes you can't read what they write, but they can usually tell you what their writing says or means. For now, your goal in guiding children to reread and revisit their work is to help them notice what they can do to make their writing and drawings interesting and easy to read. At this point, editing is best demonstrated during interactive writing, as you and the children read and revisit a piece of writing to check whether it makes sense and uses particular aspects of print (e.g., upper- and lowercase letters or punctuation).

As first graders become more familiar with print, you can teach them how to check their own writing for things like spacing between words, the correct spelling of known words, and proper letter formation. If your students are ready, the proofreading checklist, downloadable from online resources, can be a helpful resource to promote independence and ownership over one's writing. They learn the importance of proofreading and editing in making their writing accessible to their readers.

Publishing

When we say "publish" in first grade, we really mean "show it to others." First graders publish or celebrate their writing all the time as they produce group writing with illustrations. Children are invited to share their independent drawing and writing daily as they experiment with new ideas taught through the lessons in this book. Publishing might mean having children type or bind their writing with cardboard or other materials to resemble a book. "Published" books can go into your classroom library for others to check out and read (Figure 2-2). Publishing can also take the form of framing a piece of writing or drawing, displaying it, posting it on a bulletin board, or holding informal writing celebrations. For example, you can have children share their books with another class or with a teacher or administrator, or you can invite families and guests to look at published books. Children have the opportunity not only to celebrate finished pieces but also to celebrate risks taken and new techniques tried.

Children Learn About Writing by Seeing and Doing

Children benefit from seeing examples and demonstrations of drawing and writing before they try drawing and writing on their own. Use modeled, shared, interactive, or guided writing so that children see writing happen

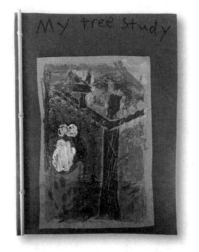

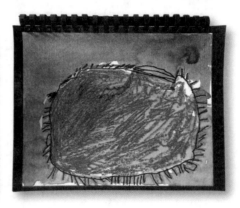

Figure 2-2: You can publish books in a variety of ways. *My Tree Study* is bound with a dowel and a rubber band. *The Hamster* is a simple, stapled booklet, but notice the *Best Story Ever* award that has been drawn on the front resembling awards on published book covers. *How to Make a Water Fountain* is bound with two pieces of cardboard covered in paper. Spiral bound books are also a durable option.

and participate in the process. Let's look at these supportive instructional contexts, all of which lead young children toward independent writing.

Modeled Writing

Modeled writing, which in first grade includes drawing, has the highest amount of teacher support (Figure 2-3). Children see what it looks like to produce a piece of writing as you demonstrate creating a particular type of writing. As you draw and write, talk through the decisions you are making as an artist or writer. Sometimes, you will have prepared the writing before class, but you will still talk about your thought process for the children. Modeled writing or drawing is often used within a writing minilesson to demonstrate what a particular kind of writing looks like and how it is produced.

Shared Writing

In shared writing, use the children's experiences and language to create writing that they can read. Shared writing is used for most of the charts in the writing minilessons. Although you are the scribe who writes the text on chart paper displayed on an easel or whiteboard, children participate by contributing ideas. First, children talk about their experiences and ideas.

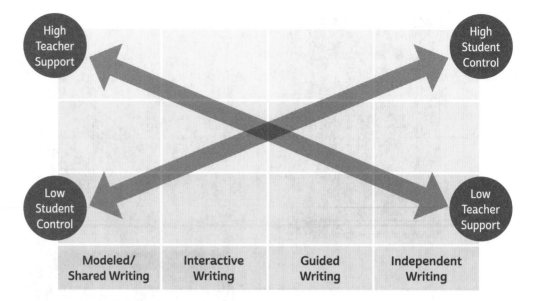

Modeled/Shared Writing	Interactive Writing	Guided Writing	Independent Writing

Figure 2-3: Each instructional context for writing has a different amount of teacher support and student control (from *The Literacy Quick Guide* by Irene C. Fountas and Gay Su Pinnell, 2018).

Figure 2-4: In shared writing, the teacher and children come up with the ideas, but the teacher does all the writing.

Then, you and the children decide together what to say and how to say it. Moving from thoughts or ideas to saying the words to putting the ideas in print (perhaps with a drawing) is a process children need to engage in over and over. The process begins with a plan you make together, and then you move to writing the message word by word as the children observe and talk about the process.

Sometimes you will ask the children to say a word slowly to listen for the sounds and to think about the letters that go with those sounds. It is important for the children to say the word for themselves. Other times, you (with the children's input) will write the word, sentence, or phrase on the chart quickly to keep the lesson moving. Reread what you have written as you go along so that children can rehearse the language structure, anticipate the next word, and check what has been written. The chart then becomes a model, example, or reference for future reading, writing, and discussion (Figure 2-4).

Interactive Writing

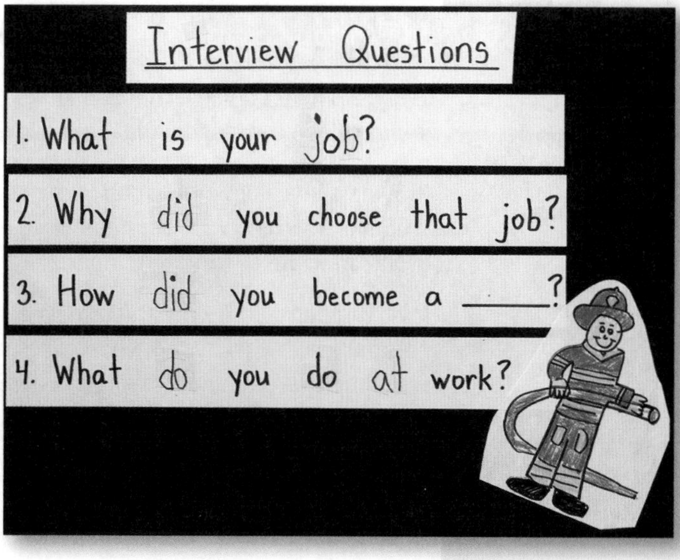

Interactive writing and shared writing are very similar. The only difference is that in interactive writing children "share the pen" by writing letters, word parts, or words (Figure 2-5). Occasionally, while making teaching points that help children attend to various features of letters and words as well as punctuation, invite a child to the easel to contribute a letter, a word, a part of a word, or a type of punctuation. This process is especially helpful to beginning readers and writers because their contributions have high instructional value. Children also participate by helping you add illustrations, though this can be done at a later time.

Figure 2-5: In this example of interactive writing, the teacher did most of the writing but children wrote several high-frequency words that they were learning.

Because interactive writing is such a powerful way to learn about writing across the curriculum, we have dedicated a whole section of this book (twenty-five lessons) to support this learning context. These lessons will help you and your students become familiar with the process and use it for a variety of purposes throughout the day. Note that shared writing is recommended for the first interactive writing lesson (IW.1: Making a Name Chart), but any of the interactive writing lessons in this book can be converted to shared writing lessons if you choose to do all the writing yourself instead of sharing the pen.

Guided Writing

Guided writing allows for differentiated learning in order to address the common needs of a small group of students. By conducting conferences with children and examining their writing, you will determine which students would benefit from small-group teaching. For example, you have introduced a new kind of writing to the whole group but notice that there are a few students who need more support to take on the new learning. Or, you have noticed a few students experimenting with writing poetry and you want to support their new interest. In each case, you can pull a guided writing group together to deepen and expand children's understandings. When the new learning is accomplished, the group is disbanded. Whether you are reviewing or teaching something new that the whole class is not quite ready for, the small-group setting of guided writing allows you to closely observe childrens' writing behaviors and provide specific guidance. Guided writing lessons are brief and focused. Typically a guided writing lesson lasts only ten to fifteen minutes and can take place while the rest of the class is engaged in independent writing (Figure 2-6).

Structure of a Guided Writing Lesson

Teach a Minilesson	Teach a single principle that is useful for a small group of writers at a particular point in time. Keep the lesson brief, and allow student inquiry to drive the learning.
Students Have a Try	Provide a piece of writing, and invite students to apply the new thinking. Support students' learning with additional teaching, as needed. Point out effective applications of the principle by group members.
Students Apply the Principle to Their Own Writing	Invite students to try out the principle using an existing piece of writing or, as appropriate, by beginning a new piece of writing. Students continue to work at the small table as you observe and provide guidance that deepens individual students' understanding of the principle.
Students Share	Invite students to share what they noticed and learned during the lesson. Reinforce the principle, and encourage students to share the next steps they will take in their writing.

Figure 2-6: Structure of a guided writing lesson from *The Literacy Quick Guide* (Fountas and Pinnell 2018)

Independent Writing

When children draw and write for themselves, all their understandings about drawing and writing—literacy concepts, word solving, purpose, audience—come together in a way that is visible. Sometimes they will write about their reading. Sometimes they will write in the content areas (e.g., science or social studies). Sometimes they will write from their personal experiences, and other times they will write about what they know or have learned about a topic through their observations and research. Through their participation in interactive writing lessons and writing minilessons, children take on new understandings. Through independent writing, they try them out. As they happily make books, they learn more about writing and language, which leads to richer talk and discussion in all writing contexts.

Figure 2-7 summarizes the features of modeled writing, shared writing, interactive writing, guided writing, and independent writing. Interactive writing lessons obviously use interactive writing, while writing minilessons might use any one or more levels of support: modeled, shared, and interactive writing. The ultimate goal of both interactive writing lessons and writing minilessons is to support children in developing their own independent drawing and writing.

Levels of Support for Writing	
Type of Writing	**Characteristics**
Modeled	• Whole class or small group • Teacher composes the text [creates and says the sentences] • Teacher writes the print and/or draws images • Used to demonstrate ideas and refer to • Used as a resource to read
Shared	• Whole class or small group • Teacher and children compose the text [create and say the sentences] • Teacher writes what the children decide together • Used to record ideas to read or refer to • Often included in writing minilessons to show something about writing or drawing
Interactive	• Whole class or small group • Teacher and children plan what to write and/or draw • Teacher and children share the pen to write and illustrate the text • Slows down the writing/drawing and allows focus on specific drawing and writing concepts [e.g., space between words, left-right directionality, features of letters and words, techniques for drawing] • The writing/drawing can be used as a mentor text during writing minilessons and as a reference for independent writing • Often used as a shared reading text later
Guided Writing	• Small group • Teacher provides a brief lesson on a single writing principle that children apply to their own writing • Allows for close observation and guidance • Used to differentiate instruction • Teaching might involve modeled, shared, or interactive writing • Similar to a writing minilesson but in a small group setting

Figure 2-7: Choose the level of support that helps you reach your goals for the children. These supports apply to both writing and drawing.

Levels of Support for Writing (cont.)

Type of Writing	Characteristics
Independent	• Individuals • Children decide what to say or draw and then write or illustrate their own texts (mostly through making books) • Supported by side-by-side talk with the teacher • Engages children in all aspects of the drawing and writing processes

Once you get to know the children in your class and understand what they can do on their own and what they can do with your support, you will be able to decide which level of support is most appropriate for a particular purpose. When the processes for each kind of writing are established, you can use them as needed throughout the day.

Chapter 3 | What Is an Interactive Writing Lesson?

Interactive writing is an instructional context in which a teacher shares a pen—literally and figuratively—with a group of children as they collaboratively compose and construct a written message.

—Andrea McCarrier, Irene C. Fountas, and Gay Su Pinnell

IN AN INTERACTIVE WRITING LESSON, the teacher and children play active roles in producing a common piece of writing. Everyone participates in planning what to write and how to say it. Several children help write the planned text by "sharing the pen" at a few selected points.

Children Learn About the Writing Process

Interactive writing lessons are designed to ease children into part or all of the writing process in a highly supported way. McCarrier, Fountas, and Pinnell (2000) describe what goes on when children participate in interactive writing in the following passage:

When children compose [plan] a text, they work on several levels of language at once. They place letters within words, words within phrases, phrases within sentences, and sentences within a longer text. They must first think of meaning in a larger sense and then compose the language. They shift down to put the message into words.

The construction [writing] of the text requires further shifts down the levels of language to attend to specific words, sounds in words, parts of words, and letters.

After using details to write a word, the composer/constructor has to go right back up to the meaning of the larger text to think of the next word to write. The composer/constructor is always climbing up and down the levels of language, from meaning down to the details and then back up to the meaning. (96)

The interactive writing lessons in this book are carefully planned to guide children through the details of writing the text while always thinking about the meaning. It all happens in a very short time. You need only five to ten minutes to write a message or other type of writing with the children. Don't let the lesson go on and on! You can always go back to longer pieces (e.g., murals, class big books), which might be extended across two or three days (Figure 3-1).

Figure 3-1: The children and their teacher planned and wrote the labels for a mural about the ocean after reading books about the ocean.

The Writing Minilessons Book, Grade 1

Children Participate in Real Writing for Real Reasons

The purpose of interactive writing is not simply to practice writing. Children write about their discoveries and the ideas they care about. Interactive writing lessons are richest when they are rooted in real experiences during which children explore, think, and talk. Children who are actively involved in a meaningful experience—reading and talking about books, making something, going somewhere—will have ideas to contribute.

Here's an example of how an active learning experience led to interactive writing. Students in Mrs. Jordan's class read books about planting and growing and were investigating why plants are important. They read *The Dandelion Seed* by Joseph P. Anthony, *Plant Packages: A Book About Seeds* by Susan Blackaby, and *From Seed to Plant* by Gail Gibbons (Figure 3-2). Mrs. Jordan brought in different seeds that varied in size, texture, and shape for

Figure 3-2: Books used for interactive read-aloud can inspire interactive writing.

a seed investigation and discussion. They also planned a small class garden and planted seeds. Together, the class decided to create a how-to book to teach people how to plant their own garden. They used interactive writing to make a list of the materials needed and to write the steps for planting a classroom garden. In science, they tracked the growth of their plants. They took photographs, made sketches, and wrote their observations. As a class, they used interactive writing to make a diagram demonstrating the life cycle of a seed (Figure 3-3) and created a bar graph to show the height of each person's plant. Eventually, Mrs. Jordan plans to use interactive writing to create an invitation

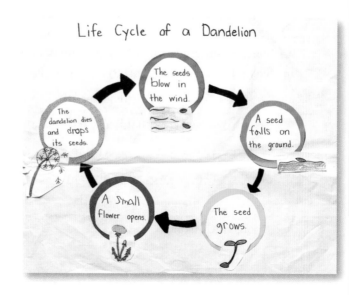

Figure 3-3: In this example of interactive writing, the teacher reinforced children's learning about consonant clusters and using known words to write unfamiliar words. Children wrote *bl* in *blow*, *gr* in *grows*, and *dr* in *drops*. They also used their knowledge of *all* to write *small* and *falls*.

to another class to come see the classroom garden and to learn about plants through a class presentation. They may finish their study by interactively writing a book called *All About Plants* or a memory story about their class presentation. Each experience immerses children in the writing process and the mechanics of writing, moving them forward in their own writing.

A Few Things to Know About Interactive Writing Lessons

Before we take a close look at the individual parts of an interactive writing lesson, here are a few general things to know:

- The interactive writing lessons are stand-alone lessons. They are not grouped in umbrellas like writing minilessons; however, they do build in complexity from the first to the twenty-fifth.

- Lessons can easily be taught out of sequence according to the needs of the class by using shared writing (teacher does all the writing).

- The twenty-five lessons in this book are models for you to use to learn more about the process and structure. Use what you learn about interactive writing to actively involve children in any type of writing in any subject across the day.

- Each lesson is two pages. All lessons follow the structure and routines of an interactive writing lesson (Figure 3-4).

- Each interactive writing lesson is identified with IW plus a number and the lesson name, for example, IW.1: Making a Name Chart.

- The lesson name indicates the type of writing that will be produced in the lesson. The kinds of writing that first graders can be expected to try can be found in the Grade 1 Writing section of *The Literacy Continuum* (Fountas and Pinnell 2017).

Each lesson is carefully designed to promote oral language and talk before any text is written. Children need to learn that they can say what they are going to write. As you move from talking to writing, children might be invited up to the easel or chart to do any of the following:

- Write a known letter (sometimes the first letter of the child's name).

- Use two fingers to "hold" a space while the next word is being written.

- Write a letter that is connected to a sound in the word.

- Write a known word or word part.

- Add punctuation.

- Sign their names.

- Create a quick sketch.

Be intentional about whom you invite to share the pen. Asking too many children to write something or having them write more than they are able to do quickly will slow everything down. Try to choose places that will help your children think and grow. You can write the things you know they already control. Work to keep the writing moving along. Not every child needs a turn to write something in every lesson.

Structure of an Interactive Writing Lesson	
Establish Purpose	Talk together with the children to decide what to write.
Talk About What to Write	Talk together about what to say and how to say it.
Write Together	Invite several children to help you do the writing by contributing a letter, a word, or a part of a word.
Read and Revisit	Reinforce what children are learning (e.g., locate high-frequency words, check the punctuation, or identify words that have consonant clusters or vowel pairs).
Summarize and Invite/Extend	Review the lesson and offer a way to extend the learning.

Figure 3-4: Once you learn the structure of an interactive writing lesson, children become used to the routine, making the lesson run smoothly and keeping it short.

A Closer Look at the Interactive Writing Lessons

While the content of each interactive writing experience will vary, the structure of each lesson is the same. Children will learn the routines, and that means the lesson will be smoother and shorter.

Before the Lesson

Each interactive writing lesson in this book begins with information to help you make the most of the lesson. There are four types of information here:

The Active Learning Experience is the foundation of every interactive writing lesson. Shared classroom experiences provide real opportunities for children to explore, talk, and write. You and the children can take a field trip, conduct a scientific experiment, paint a mural, make something in the creation station (maker space), read a book, or bake a cake. An example of how an active learning experience can lead to a meaningful interactive writing lesson follows.

Active Learning Experience: Take a field trip.

Interactive Writing Possibilities:

> ▶ Write a thank you note to the field trip host.
>
> ▶ Write a memory story about the trip.
>
> ▶ Make and label a map of the place you visited.
>
> ▶ Make a book about the trip.

The topics of these active learning experiences will vary widely depending on your school curriculum and the interests of the children in your class, but we have tried to provide ideas for common activities and experiences for first graders. In many cases, these experiences are also linked to the books in the text sets from *Fountas & Pinnell Classroom™ Interactive Read-Aloud Collection* (2018). These sets of books are grouped by ideas, topics, authors, or type of book. They help children build rich knowledge and language because they have themes that are familiar to first graders, such as school, friendship, and family. If you don't have this collection, we have offered ideas for the kinds of books you might choose to read aloud ahead of the interactive writing lessons.

EL CONNECTION

The active learning experience provides the opportunity to build a shared vocabulary about the hands-on activity. These active experiences are especially good for children who are learning English. Having already had an opportunity to think and talk about the topic, children will find it easier to contribute ideas during the interactive writing lesson.

Goals are based on behaviors from the Grade 1 sections of *The Literacy Continuum*. Interactive writing mirrors the writing process:

> ▶ Composing (planning what to write)
>
> ▶ Constructing (writing the print/drafting)
>
> ▶ Rereading

So, in interactive writing, you can get a lot done in one lesson. You can address several goals. (A writing minilesson, on the other hand, has one focused goal.)

Why It's Important describes how the lesson will support children in their journey as writers.

Assess Learning is a list of behaviors to look for as you observe children during the lesson and when they attempt to apply what they have learned to their own writing. Your observations will inform your decisions about what to teach next.

Interactive Writing Lesson

Under the heading **Interactive Writing Lesson**, you will find a sample lesson. The example includes suggestions for teaching with precise language and open-ended questions that help children think of what to write and then get it down on paper. Each part of the lesson is described below and shown in an annotated lesson in Figure 3-5 (pp. 44–45).

Establish Purpose

Interactive writing lessons begin by talking about the active learning experience, which is the purpose for writing, and about why it is important to write about it. Thinking about your purpose helps in choosing the form of writing, such as a memory story about a class trip.

Talk About What to Write

After deciding on a purpose, spend a short time talking about what to write. Together, think about the message and how it could be said in words. Remember, young children will be thinking about a lot during the short time of the lesson, so don't plan to write too much. A few words, a phrase, or a couple of sentences can be enough to communicate an idea: labels for a picture, the names of a few items on a shopping list, or a few sentences in a thank you note. After you have decided what to write, say it and ask the children to repeat after you. (A writer has to remember the message while writing.)

Write Together

The next part of the lesson provides an example of how you might write the message—sentence by sentence, word by word, letter by letter. When children have the opportunity to plan and write the text with the teacher, they learn much about the way words work, such as the following:

- Words can be broken into syllables to make them easier to write.
- Each word has a vowel.
- Words have connections to other words.

As you write the words in the message, keep the following in mind:

- Help the children connect letters to sounds and make connections to familiar words, particularly to the names of children in the class.
- Have children watch your mouth as you say each word slowly.
- Emphasize sounds but avoid artificially segmenting a word, distorting it so much that children are listening only to the individual sounds instead of the smooth sequence of sounds in a word. (They will have opportunities to segment words in phonics lessons.)

- Say the word slowly and then have children say the word out loud slowly with you and then for themselves. (It is important for them to enunciate the words and listen for the sounds.)

- Clap the syllables in words and help children hear the sounds in each syllable.

- Always write the letters of a word in sequence from left to right.

- Demonstrate how to use known words and word parts to write new words.

- Keep the lesson moving quickly so it will not bog down.

- In one lesson, invite only a few children to do some writing.

Keeping everyone engaged is a challenge! Moving the writing along quickly is the most effective practice, but here are some ways to keep children focused while one child is sharing the pen:

- Have the rest of the children practice writing the letters in the air, on the rug, or in their hands.

- Give the children individual bags with whiteboards and markers so that they can make the letter or word along with the child at the easel.

Many first graders are still developing the ability to distinguish between letters and connect letters to sounds, so at first select teaching points for easy-to-hear sounds. As the year progresses, introduce listening for harder-to-hear medial sounds, such as vowels. Use the following guidelines to be selective and thoughtful about what you ask children to contribute particularly at the beginning of the year:

- Initial and ending sounds are often the easiest to hear, and consonant sounds are generally easier to hear than vowel sounds.

- Avoid asking children to write letters in words that may lead to confusion (e.g., the *o* in the word *one* could be confused with the letter *w*).

- Quickly write harder words that are beyond children's experience.

As children contribute letters, they make connections between the sounds and letters. They also think about the directional movements needed to mechanically write each letter. The Verbal Path for Letter Formation (Figure 7-4) lists the movements a writer uses to make letters. It is referenced throughout this book and is available in the online resources.

While children are focused on making the movements to form letters, they need to keep in mind the purpose they have set and the message they are communicating. That's a lot for first graders to coordinate at once, so your guidance during the interactive writing process is highly valuable.

The process of writing the text is particularly powerful for English learners because in a sense it makes language "stand still." After you have written a word, children are free to reread the sentence to help them remember the next word. It "slows down" processing and makes it easier to focus on the details.

Read and Revisit

As you write words, keep reading the writing in a shared way so children can think about the word to write next. When the writing is finished, reread it together to make sure it makes sense and sounds right. This step provides a model for how to reread for revision and editing.

Rereading also gives you the opportunity to revisit or look back at the text for important teaching about phonics, spelling, and word study. You can have children revisit the text multiple times for different purposes. Here are a few ideas for rereading and revisiting a text:

- ◗ Point to upper- and lowercase letters.
- ◗ Point to the beginning or end of a word.
- ◗ Find a word you know.
- ◗ Find a word that begins like your name or a classmate's name.
- ◗ Find words that begin (end) with the same letter as another word.
- ◗ Find the vowel(s) in a word.
- ◗ Clap the syllables in words.
- ◗ Find rhyming words.

This part of the lesson reinforces some of the teaching you did while writing the text and perhaps even outside of the lesson. The suggestions provided for revisiting the text get more sophisticated over time as children learn more about letters and words. Keep in mind what the children in your class know as you make decisions for how you will have them revisit the text. Use the Writing and the Phonics, Spelling, and Word Study continua in *The Literacy Continuum* to consider other behaviors you might reinforce through this part of the lesson.

Summarize and Invite/Extend

This part of the lesson includes two parts: summarizing the learning and extending the learning. First, help children remember what they learned during the lesson. In IW.15: Writing a Question-and-Answer Book, we remind children that they learned how to write a question-and-answer book and invite them to try writing their own. In addition to this invitation, children will later experience writing minilessons that further extend this lesson by explicitly teaching about different kinds of questions (e.g., repeating questions vs. different questions) and how to research answers.

A Closer Look at an Interactive Writing Lesson

This code identifies this lesson as the thirteenth interactive writing lesson.

Involve children in an **active learning experience** to provide a purpose and some content for writing.

The **goals** of the lesson are clearly identified to support your understanding of what this particular lesson is and why it is important for the children in your classroom.

Look for these specific behaviors and understandings as you **assess** children's learning after presenting the lesson.

Important vocabulary used in the lesson is listed.

Precise language is suggested for teaching the lesson.

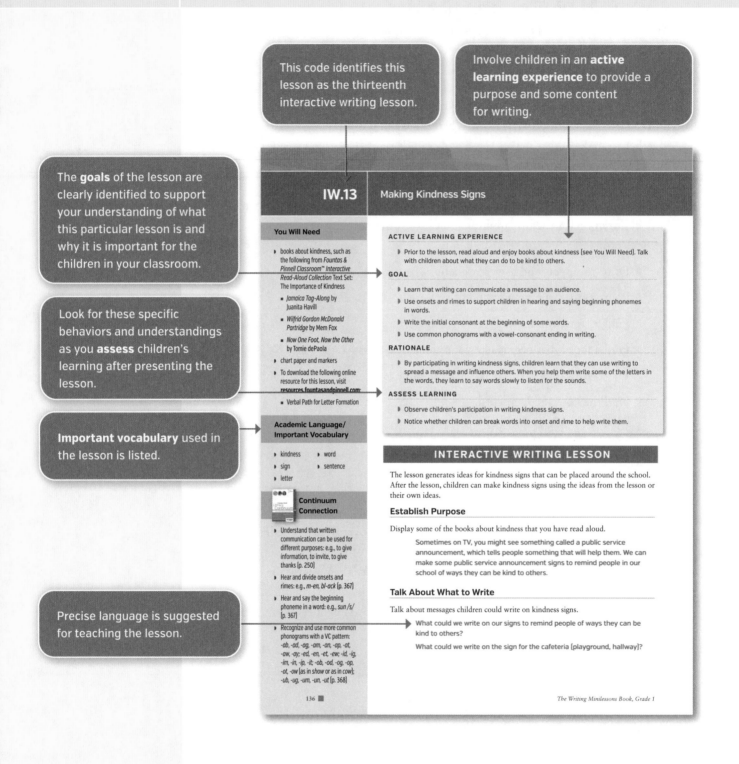

IW.13   Making Kindness Signs

You Will Need

- books about kindness, such as the following from *Fountas & Pinnell Classroom™ Interactive Read-Aloud Collection* Text Set: The Importance of Kindness
  - *Jamaica Tag-Along* by Juanita Havill
  - *Wilfrid Gordon McDonald Partridge* by Mem Fox
  - *Now One Foot, Now the Other* by Tomie dePaola
- chart paper and markers
- To download the following online resource for this lesson, visit resources.fountasandpinnell.com:
  - Verbal Path for Letter Formation

Academic Language/ Important Vocabulary

- kindness
- sign
- letter
- word
- sentence

Continuum Connection

- Understand that written communication can be used for different purposes: e.g., to give information, to invite, to give thanks (p. 250)
- Hear and divide onsets and rimes: e.g., *m-en, bl-ack* (p. 367)
- Hear and say the beginning phoneme in a word: e.g., *sun /s/* (p. 367)
- Recognize and use more common phonograms with a VC pattern: *-ab, -ad, -ag, -am, -an, -ap, -at, -ow, -ay; -ed, -en, -et, -ew; -id, -ig, -im, -in, -ip, -it; -ob, -od, -og, -op, -ot, -ow* (as in *show* or as in *cow*); *-ub, -ug, -um, -un, -ut* (p. 368)

136

ACTIVE LEARNING EXPERIENCE

- Prior to the lesson, read aloud and enjoy books about kindness (see You Will Need). Talk with children about what they can do to be kind to others.

GOAL

- Learn that writing can communicate a message to an audience.
- Use onsets and rimes to support children in hearing and saying beginning phonemes in words.
- Write the initial consonant at the beginning of some words.
- Use common phonograms with a vowel-consonant ending in writing.

RATIONALE

- By participating in writing kindness signs, children learn that they can use writing to spread a message and influence others. When you help them write some of the letters in the words, they learn to say words slowly to listen for the sounds.

ASSESS LEARNING

- Observe children's participation in writing kindness signs.
- Notice whether children can break words into onset and rime to help write them.

INTERACTIVE WRITING LESSON

The lesson generates ideas for kindness signs that can be placed around the school. After the lesson, children can make kindness signs using the ideas from the lesson or their own ideas.

Establish Purpose

Display some of the books about kindness that you have read aloud.

> Sometimes on TV, you might see something called a public service announcement, which tells people something that will help them. We can make some public service announcement signs to remind people in our school of ways they can be kind to others.

Talk About What to Write

Talk about messages children could write on kindness signs.

> What could we write on our signs to remind people of ways they can be kind to others?

> What could we write on the sign for the cafeteria (playground, hallway)?

The Writing Minilessons Book, Grade 1

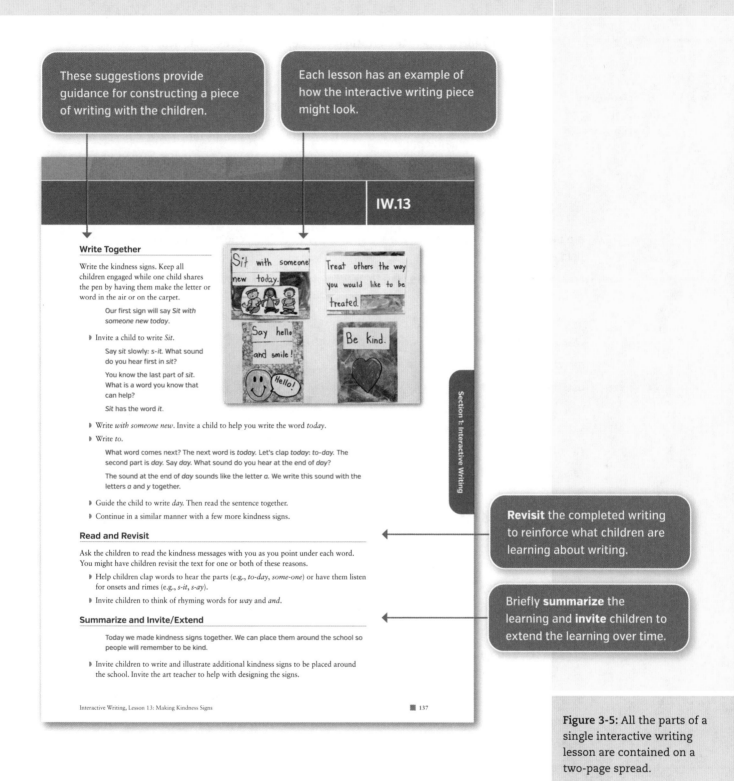

These suggestions provide guidance for constructing a piece of writing with the children.

Each lesson has an example of how the interactive writing piece might look.

IW.13

Write Together

Write the kindness signs. Keep all children engaged while one child shares the pen by having them make the letter or word in the air or on the carpet.

> Our first sign will say *Sit with someone new today.*

▶ Invite a child to write *Sit.*

> Say *sit* slowly: *s-it.* What sound do you hear first in *sit*?
>
> You know the last part of *sit.* What is a word you know that can help?
>
> *Sit* has the word *it.*

▶ Write *with someone new.* Invite a child to help you write the word *today.*

▶ Write *to.*

> What word comes next? The next word is *today.* Let's clap *today: to-day.* The second part is *day.* Say *day.* What sound do you hear at the end of *day*?
>
> The sound at the end of *day* sounds like the letter *a.* We write this sound with the letters *a* and *y* together.

▶ Guide the child to write *day.* Then read the sentence together.

▶ Continue in a similar manner with a few more kindness signs.

Read and Revisit

Ask the children to read the kindness messages with you as you point under each word. You might have children revisit the text for one or both of these reasons.

▶ Help children clap words to hear the parts (e.g., *to-day, some-one*) or have them listen for onsets and rimes (e.g., *s-it, s-ay*).

▶ Invite children to think of rhyming words for *way* and *and.*

Summarize and Invite/Extend

> Today we made kindness signs together. We can place them around the school so people will remember to be kind.

▶ Invite children to write and illustrate additional kindness signs to be placed around the school. Invite the art teacher to help with designing the signs.

Interactive Writing, Lesson 13: Making Kindness Signs   ■ 137

Section 1: Interactive Writing

Revisit the completed writing to reinforce what children are learning about writing.

Briefly **summarize** the learning and **invite** children to extend the learning over time.

Figure 3-5: All the parts of a single interactive writing lesson are contained on a two-page spread.

Effective Interactive Writing Lessons

The goal of interactive writing lessons is to provide a context in which the children experience creating a written piece of text. The activities move them closer to thinking about different ways they might try writing for themselves. Interactive writing lessons are flexible so that you and the children can create any kind of writing. But no matter what you compose and construct together, the characteristics of an interactive writing lesson, listed in Figure 3-6, apply.

Figure 3-6: Characteristics of effective interactive writing lessons

Effective Interactive Writing Lessons . . .

- are **based on a common active, meaningful experience** (e.g., cooking, attending a field trip, reading a book)
- create **a community of learners** who think, explore, play, talk, read, write, and draw together
- establish a **purpose and real reason** for writing
- use drawing and writing for a **variety of purposes** across the curriculum
- are very **brief** and use **explicit** teaching
- use **focused, concise language**
- use **conversation** to support the process
- create a **common text** that can be used for shared reading or as a mentor text for writing
- raise awareness of the writer's and illustrator's **craft**
- develop children's understanding of the **conventions** of writing (capitals, punctuation)
- make **letter-sound connections**
- connect **reading and writing**
- develop young children's **oral vocabulary**
- develop **phonological awareness** (the sounds of language)
- reinforce **how letters and words look**
- are taught at the **cutting-edge of what children can learn** with your assistance
- are **selective** about when the pen is shared
- model **rereading the message** each time a word is added
- make **connections to classroom resources** such as the ABC chart and the name chart
- summarize **new learning**
- invite children to try **drawing and writing on their own**
- provide **documentation** of the understandings of a group of learners
- **differentiate instruction** to meet individual students' needs

Organize for Interactive Writing Lessons

Interactive writing typically takes place with the whole class in the group meeting area, though there are times you may decide to use it with a small group to address a specific need or to provide more intensive support. These small-group lessons can take place in the large-group meeting area or at tables or small-group areas elsewhere in the room. Be sure the children have enough space to sit comfortably. You will need to plan space for children to walk up to the chart, so be sure it is visible and accessible.

Resources

Take some time to think about the materials and resources that will support effective learning opportunities. Make resources such as those listed below available near the meeting area. When limited display space is available, consider using hangers to place charts on a rack. Resources in or near the meeting area might include the following:

- name chart
- Alphabet Linking Chart (Figure 3-7)
- poems or stories for shared reading
- a word wall (with children's names and some high-frequency words as in Figure 1-9)
- classroom labels
- completed or in-progress pieces of interactive writing
- children's independent writing

Materials and Equipment

The chart in Figure 3-8 and the text that follows describe materials to help you make the most of an interactive writing lesson.

Easel An easel that children can reach easily will help them contribute to the writing (Figure 3-9). The slanted surface of an easel is easier to write on than a flat surface. Easels also make it easier for teachers or children to stand to one side to use a pointer with the written text.

Paper Paper selection is surprisingly important. Having a choice of paper affects how children organize their writing and encourages them to be

Figure 3-7: The Alphabet Linking Chart (Fountas and Pinnell 2017) is just one of the helpful resources for shared and interactive writing. An 8 ½" x 11" black-and-white version is available from online resources.

Materials and Equipment for Interactive Writing

Materials and Equipment	Description
Easel	• Sturdy, slanted surface • Accessible height for children
Paper	• White or light-colored unlined chart paper (about 30" x 25"; avoid dark colors) • Light-brown wrapping paper or butcher paper (with a dark black marker) • Large-size construction paper in white or light colors • Sentence strips or card stock cut into word-sized cards
Markers	• Broad-tipped markers that do not bleed through the paper • Dark colors
Correction tape	• One-inch white correction tape • White peel-off mailing labels • Small pieces of paper (matching the color of the chart) applied with a glue stick
Magnetic letters	• Brightly colored plastic magnetic letters organized on a cookie sheet or in a plastic case with compartments
Magnetic drawing board or small whiteboard	• Magnetic or dry-erase board for demonstrating how to write a letter or word
Pointers	• A 48" dowel rod cut in half • Bright or dark color on the tip
Art materials	• Crayons, washable markers, glue sticks, scissors, a variety of paper

Figure 3-8: Materials and equipment for interactive writing

flexible and creative during the writing process. For the easel, chart paper that is wider than it is long works best. A measurement of 30" x 25" is appropriate. Wider paper provides space for more words in each line of print, which allows for more practice of left-to-right movement and spacing of words. Vary between using lined and unlined paper. Unlined paper will give children the experience of organizing space. This is particularly supportive for children who are in the early stages of forming their letters because they do not have to worry about fitting them on the lines. However, first graders will also need practice writing letters on lines. Lined paper including a dashed middle line supports young writers in forming upper- and lowercase letters.

If you have children who need support with word boundaries and word-for-word matching, consider counting the number of words in the sentence you plan to write and either attach a card for each word on the chart paper or add a new card for each new word as you write it. Cut the sentence strip to the length of the word to reinforce children's visual memory of words as long or short.

Use word cards and cut-up sentence strips only temporarily or only with a small group of children who need the extra support. Once children have a good idea of how individual words are defined by space, move away from them so children have the opportunity to write and read words in continuous text on the entire blank surface of the paper.

Figure 3-9: Place an easel similar to this one in the meeting area to use for interactive writing and shared writing.

Markers To make the print easy to read, especially from a distance, use markers in dark colors (e.g., black or blue) on a white or very light background. It is important to write the piece in one uniform color so that the final product looks like a unified text. Using many different colors for the print breaks up the continuous flow and can distract children's attention away from the visual features of the letters and words. Use highlighter tape to draw attention to a particular word or phrase or word part.

Correction Tape Use one-inch correction tape or white mailing labels to cover mistakes—a wrong letter, an uppercase letter instead of a lowercase letter, too little space between words—instead of crossing out or erasing. White tape also allows for quick error correction, which encourages children to take risks because they know how easily a letter or word can be altered (Figure 3-10). We sometimes call it "magic tape"!

Figure 3-10: Word cards help define word boundaries, but use them only as a temporary support. Correction tape shows how easily mistakes can be fixed.

Magnetic Letters Magnetic letters can be used to show how a letter looks or to demonstrate how to spell a word. Organize magnetic letters so that you can find letters that you want quickly and not bog down the lesson. Store the letters

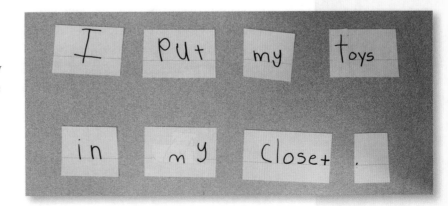

Figure 3-11: A magnetic whiteboard keeps the magnetic letters in place while children practice making words.

alphabetically on a cookie sheet or in a box that has separate compartments for each of the letters. Children can use the letters on a cookie sheet or magnetic whiteboard (Figure 3-11).

Magnetic Drawing Board or Whiteboard A magnetic drawing board has a plastic board with magnetic filings under the surface that can be written on with magnets. Both magnetic drawing boards and dry-erase whiteboards allow you to quickly produce an image for the children—a letter or a word—to help them notice distinctive features. The whiteboard allows you to easily erase a word part, in any location of the word, and you can also underline or circle parts of words.

Pointers Pointer sticks allow you to point crisply under each word and to emphasize left-to-right motion. A pointer is better than your finger because it doesn't block children's view of the print in the same way that your arm or hand does. A helpful suggestion is to color the tip of your pointer to draw children's attention to the part that is placed under the print. We advise against pointers that have embellishments on them such as hands, apples, etc., because such objects can block the view of the print. Teach children where to stand and how to point to the words so as not to block the print.

Art Materials for Children and Downloadable Art Children love the opportunity to illustrate the writing that you have produced together during an interactive writing lesson. Assign children to make the art in the art center during choice time and then attach it to the chart. In some cases, downloadable art is available from online resources. Use downloadable art judiciously. We have provided this art as a time saver for you, but the choices you and the children make will be different. But when it is particularly important for the children to have clear pictures to understand the writing you may decide to use the art provided.

To read more about interactive writing, see *Interactive Writing: How Language and Literacy Come Together, K–2* (McCarrier, Fountas, and Pinnell 2000).

Connect Reading and Writing

Reading books with the children is a shared experience that can be the active learning experience of an interactive writing lesson. The interactive read-aloud lessons in *Fountas & Pinnell Classroom™ Interactive Read-Aloud Collection* (2018) offer suggestions for shared and interactive writing. Many of these suggestions are examples of how you can make strong connections between reading and writing. Figure 3-12 shows how the text sets (collections of books grouped thematically) align with the interactive writing lessons. If you do not have these text sets, there are suggestions for the kinds of books you might want to read to the children prior to the interactive writing lessons so they can be the foundation for the writing.

Figure 3-12: Alignment of *Fountas & Pinnell Classroom™ Interactive Read-Aloud Collection* text sets with interactive writing lessons in *The Writing Minilessons Book, Grade 1.*

Aligning *Interactive Read Aloud Collection* Text Sets with Interactive Writing	
Learning and Working Together: School	IW.1: Making a Name Chart IW.2: Writing About Our Classroom IW.3: Labeling the Classroom IW.4: Writing from a Picture
Having Fun with Language: Rhyming Texts	IW.5: Innovating on a Rhyming Text IW.6: Making a Story Map
The Importance of Friendship	
Taking Care of Each Other: Family	IW.7: Writing About Who We Are IW.8: Writing a Memory Story
Kevin Henkes: Exploring Characters	IW.9: Studying an Author's Writing
Using Numbers: Books with Counting	IW.16: Making a Shopping List
Exploring Fiction and Nonfiction	
Mo Willems: Having Fun with Humor	IW.9: Studying an Author's Writing (repeat with different author) IW.10: Writing with Speech Bubbles
Living and Working Together: Community	IW.11: Labeling a Map IW.12: Writing Interview Questions
The Importance of Kindness	IW.13: Making Kindness Signs
Exploring Nonfiction	IW.14: Writing an All-About Book
Nonfiction: Questions and Answers	IW.15: Writing a Question-and-Answer Book

Humorous Stories	
Nicola Davies: Exploring the Animal World	IW.9: Studying an Author's Writing (repeat with different author)
Journeys Near and Far	
Celebrating Diversity	IW.17: Writing an Invitation IW.18: Taking a Survey
Sharing Cultures: Folktales	
Folktales: Exploring Different Versions	IW.19: Writing an Alternative Ending
Bob Graham: Exploring Everyday Life	IW.9: Studying an Author's Writing (repeat with different author)
Poetic Language	IW.20: Writing a Poem
Understanding the Natural World: Planting and Growing	IW.21: Writing a How-to Book IW.22: Making a Life-Cycle Diagram IW.23: Making Scientific Observations
Using Your Imagination	
Standing Up for Yourself	
Understanding the Natural World: Oceans	IW.24: Making an Ocean Mural IW.25: Writing a Letter
Vera B. Williams: Celebrating Family and Community	IW.9: Studying an Author's Writing (repeat with different author)

Use the Finished Pieces from Interactive Writing Lessons

Children love to revisit the illustrated pieces you have created together and read them again and again. You'll find that children can identify just about every letter or word they have personally contributed! That kind of ownership and engagement is why completed interactive writing texts are so good for shared reading and independent reading. Consider making small copies of some for children to take home to share with their families.

Interactive writing pieces also are useful as mentor texts (examples) for writing minilessons and independent writing. Use an interactive writing lesson to demonstrate a particular type of writing before children try it on their own. Here are some important things to consider as you create interactive writing pieces:

- Keep interactive writing pieces simple and legible.

- Invite children to add illustrations after the lesson to add support to the meaning. You can have children make illustrations in the art center on separate pieces of paper and glue them onto the chart. This process avoids the crowding and space issues that can occur if children try to draw directly on the chart.

- With clear pictures, children can understand the message even if they can't yet read the words.

- Limit the amount of print and drawings that you include on the chart. Too much print and other details can clutter up the piece and make it difficult to read.

- Use the same dark color marker for all of the printing so children see words rather than separate letters. Use correction tape or blank address labels to cover errors so children are reading accurate words.

- Though we value the use of approximated spelling in children's own independent writing, we strongly recommend that the print on the interactive writing pieces reflect conventional spelling and grammar so children have a clear model for their own writing and can read and reread the writing easily.

Turn Interactive Writing Lessons into Shared Writing Lessons

You might choose to change an interactive writing lesson into a shared writing lesson by doing the writing yourself if you are short on time, if you want children to focus more on the content and/or routines of writing together, or if you are creating an important classroom resource that needs to be very clearly legible. In fact, the first lesson in the interactive writing section (IW.1: Making a Name Chart) is actually a shared writing lesson.

Likewise, any shared writing activity becomes interactive writing if children contribute by writing a letter or a word. The writing minilessons in this book rely heavily on shared writing.

Interactive writing lessons allow children the opportunity to participate in the writing process before they try writing on their own. Writing minilessons build on what children have learned through interactive writing lessons, as you will see in the next chapter.

Chapter 4 | What Is a Writing Minilesson?

*Every minilesson should end with students envisioning a new possibility
for their work, and the key to successful minilessons is helping the
group of students sitting in front of us to envision the difference
this lesson might make in their work.*

—Katie Wood Ray and Lisa Cleaveland

A WRITING MINILESSON IS BRIEF. It focuses on a single writing concept to
help children write successfully. A writing minilesson uses inquiry, which
leads children to discovering an important understanding that they can try
out immediately.

Writing minilessons are about ways to make the classroom a community
of learners. They are about telling stories and drawing, both of which are
foundations of writing. They are also about making books, learning about
writer's and illustrator's craft, exploring the conventions of writing, and guiding
children through the writing process. Writing minilessons help children emerge
as readers and writers by thinking about one small understanding at a time.

> In an **inquiry lesson**,
> children engage in the
> thinking and develop the
> thinking for themselves.
> They learn from the
> inside, instead of simply
> being told what to
> understand. *Telling* is not
> the same as teaching.

Six Types of Writing Minilessons

This book has 175 lessons—25 interactive writing lessons and 150 writing minilessons—in eight color-coded sections. The 25 interactive writing lessons are in Section 1, and the 150 writing minilessons are organized within the next seven sections (Figure 4-1):

Management (MGT)	Page 163
Telling Stories (STR)	Page 219
Making Books (MBK)	Page 249
Drawing (DRW)	Page 315
Craft (CFT)	Page 361
Conventions (CNV)	Page 441
Writing Process (WPS)	Page 489

Figure 4-1: The writing minilessons are organized within seven sections.

Minilessons in the Management section help children become a strong community of diverse learners who play and learn together peacefully and respectfully. Most of your minilessons at the beginning of the school year will focus on organizing the classroom and building a community in which children feel safe to share ideas and learn about one another. Repeat any of the lessons as needed across the year. A guiding principle: teach a minilesson on anything that prevents the classroom from running smoothly. In these lessons, children will learn

- routines that will help them work well with their classmates,
- ways they can participate,
- the importance of listening, taking turns, and looking at the speaker when in a group, and
- how to gain an ability to work independently as they learn the structures and routines for playing and writing together in the classroom (including learning about independent writing time, choice time, and the tools of writing).

Minilessons in the Telling Stories section support the oral language component of writing, which is the first step for first-grade children as they move from their thoughts to oral language to drawing and writing their ideas on paper. Listening to stories and telling stories are rehearsals for writing stories. These writing minilessons help children learn that

- they have stories to tell,
- stories can be about things in everyday life, and
- it is important to consider your audience when you tell stories.

These lessons also give children the opportunity to present to their classmates for different purposes. They learn how to retell stories with puppets, tell information they have learned about a topic, and teach each other something they know how to do. Retelling stories helps children broaden their understanding of the elements of story. When they tell information, they learn how to organize their thoughts and take the perspective of their audience. The minilessons in this section address many of the behaviors in the grade 1 Oral Language continuum as well as behaviors from the writing process section of the grade 1 Writing continuum in *The Literacy Continuum* (Fountas and Pinnell 2017).

Minilessons in the Making Books section support children by helping them see that they can make their own books like the authors of the books that they read. The first umbrella, Getting Started with Making Books, is designed to get bookmaking up and running in your classroom. As the year progresses, children begin to explore different types of books they can make. They learn how to

- teach others something they know how to do in a how-to book,
- share stories they have told in a memory book, and
- tell what they know about a topic in question-and-answer and all-about books.

Each time children are exposed to a new kind of book, they expand their understanding of ways they can write and learn more about the way illustrators and authors craft their books. The minilessons in this section address behaviors from across the grade 1 Writing continuum in *The Literacy Continuum*. They address aspects of genre, craft, conventions, and the writing process.

Minilessons in the Drawing section are used to teach children how to draw and use color to represent real life. Drawing is one of the primary ways first graders tell their stories on paper. The minilessons in this section also help children use a variety of materials and techniques to create interesting illustrations for the books they make.

Minilessons in the Craft section help children learn about the decisions writers and illustrators make as they craft their pieces of writing. Through the umbrellas in this section, children explore the way authors use details in their writing to describe the characters and the setting. They look at the ways authors add dialogue to stories and text features to nonfiction writing. They experiment with different ways to start and end their writing and examine the way authors choose words carefully to make their writing interesting and specific. Umbrellas on writing a friendly letter and crafting poetry offer new kinds of writing for first graders to explore and further expand their understandings of craft. The minilessons in this section address the behaviors and understandings in the Craft section of the grade 1 Writing continuum in *The Literacy Continuum*.

Minilessons in the Conventions section help children learn "how print works." They learn, for example, that

- words have space on either side,
- letters and sounds are connected,
- every word has a vowel, and
- words can be broken into syllables.

Other umbrellas in this section touch on properly forming upper- and lowercase letters, using classroom resources to write words, and learning about simple punctuation and capitalization. The lessons in this section address the behaviors primarily in the Conventions section of the grade 1 Writing continuum in *The Literacy Continuum*.

Minilessons in the Writing Process section guide children through the phases of the writing process: planning and rehearsing, drafting and revising, editing and proofreading, and publishing. The minilessons in this section support your students in getting ideas for their writing by teaching them to look for stories in their own lives and in their observations of the world. They also teach first graders to think about why they are writing, whom they are writing for, and what kind of writing will serve their purpose. Minilessons in this section also help children learn how to add to their writing, how to cut and reorganize it, how to proofread it, and, most importantly, how to celebrate it.

Writing Minilessons Are Grouped into Umbrella Concepts

Within each of the seven major sections, lessons are grouped in what we call "umbrellas." Each umbrella is made up of several minilessons that are related to the larger idea of the umbrella. Within an umbrella, the lessons build on each other. When you teach several minilessons about the same idea, children deepen their understandings and develop shared vocabulary. These connections are especially helpful to English learners.

In most cases, it makes sense to teach the minilessons in an umbrella in order. But for some umbrellas, it makes sense to spread the minilessons over time so that children gain more experience with the first idea before moving on to the next. In this book, lessons are placed together in an umbrella to show you how the lessons build the concept over time.

Anchor Charts Support Writing Minilessons

Anchor charts are an essential part of each writing minilesson (Figure 4-2). They capture children's thinking during the lesson and hold it for reflection at the end of the lesson. The chart is a visual reminder of the big, important ideas and the language used in the minilesson. Each writing minilesson features one sample chart, but use it only as a guideline. Your charts will be unique because they are built from ideas offered by the children in your class.

Each minilesson provides guidance for adding information to the chart. Read through lessons carefully to know whether any parts of the chart should be prepared ahead or whether the chart is constructed during the lesson or left until the end. After the lesson, the charts become a resource for the children to refer to throughout the day and on following days. They are a visual resource for children who need to not only hear but also see the information. Children can revisit these charts as they apply the minilesson principles to their writing or as they try out new routines in the classroom. You can refer to them during interactive writing and shared writing lessons and when you confer with children about their independent writing.

EL CONNECTION

Figure 4-2: Constructing anchor charts with and in front of your class provides verbal and visual support for all learners.

Return your writing materials to where they belong.

- Put your materials away quickly and quietly.

Markers

- Put your writing in your folder.

- Put the folder in the basket.

Writing Folders

Some of the art you see on the sample charts is available from the online resources to represent concepts that are likely to come up as you construct the charts with children. The downloadable chart art is provided for your convenience. Use it when it applies to the children's responses, but do not let it determine or limit children's responses. Valuing the ideas of the class should be your primary concern.

When you create charts with first graders, consider the following:

Make your charts simple, clear, and organized. Keep the charts simple without a lot of dense text. Provide white space and print neatly in dark, easy-to-read colors.

EL CONNECTION

Make your charts visually appealing and useful. All of the minilesson charts contain visual support, which will be helpful for all children, especially English learners. Children will benefit from the visuals to help them in understanding the concept and in reading some of the words. The drawings are intentionally simple to give you a quick model to draw yourself. You might find it helpful to prepare these drawings on separate pieces of paper or sticky notes ahead of the lesson and tape or glue them on the chart as the children construct their understandings. This time-saving tip can also make the charts look more interesting and colorful, because certain parts will stand out for the children.

Make your charts colorful. The sample minilesson charts are colorful for the purpose of engagement or organization. Color can be useful, but be careful about the amount and type you choose. Color can support English learners by providing a visual link to certain words or ideas. However, color can also be distracting if overused. Be thoughtful about when you choose to use color to highlight an idea or a word on a chart so that children are supported in reading continuous text. Text that is broken up by a lot of different colors can be very distracting for readers who are still becoming accustomed to using the visual information in print. You will notice that the minilesson principle is usually written in black or a dark color across the top of the chart so that it stands out and is easily recognized as the focus of the lesson. In most cases, the minilesson principle is added at the end of the lesson after children have constructed their own understanding of the concept.

Use the charts to support language growth. Anchor charts support language growth in all children, especially English learners. Conversation about the minilesson develops oral language and then connects oral language to print when you write words on the chart and provide picture support. By constructing an anchor chart with the children, you provide print that is immediately accessible to them because they helped create it and have ownership of the language. After a chart is finished, revisit it as often as needed to reinforce not only the ideas but also the printed words (Figure 4-3).

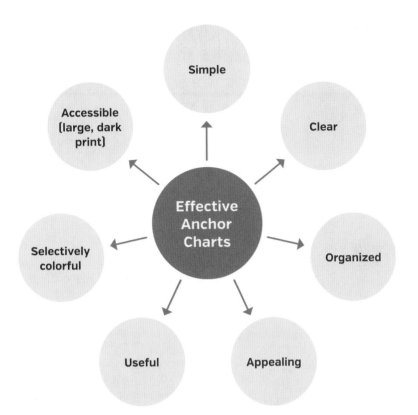

Figure 4-3: Characteristics of an effective anchor chart

Umbrellas and Minilessons Have Predictable Structures

Understanding how the umbrellas are designed and how the minilessons fit together will help you keep your lessons focused and brief. Each umbrella is set up the same way, and each writing minilesson follows the same predictable structure (Figure 4-4). **Use mentor texts that you have previously read and enjoyed with the children** to streamline the lessons. You will not need to spend a lot of time rereading large sections of the text because the children already know the texts well.

A Closer Look at the Umbrella Overview

All umbrellas are set up the same way. They begin with an overview and end with questions to guide your evaluation of children's understanding of the umbrella concepts plus several extension ideas. In between are the writing minilessons.

At the beginning of each umbrella (Figure 4-5), the minilessons are listed and directions are provided to help you prepare to teach them. There are suggestions for books from *Fountas & Pinnell Classroom™ Interactive*

Structure of a Writing Minilesson

Minilesson	• Show examples/provide demonstration. • Invite children to talk. • Make an anchor chart.
Have a Try	• Have children try doing what they are learning.
Summarize and Apply	• Summarize the learning. • Invite children to apply the learning during independent writing time. • Write the minilesson principle on the chart.
Confer	• Move around the room to confer briefly with children.
Share	• Gather children together and invite them to talk about their writing.

Figure 4-4: Once you learn the structure of a writing minilesson, you can create your own minilessons with different examples.

Read-Aloud Collection (2018) and *Shared Reading Collection* (2018) to use as mentor texts. There are also suggestions for the kinds of books you might select if you do not have these books.

A Closer Look at the Writing Minilessons

The 150 writing minilessons in this book help you teach specific aspects of writing. An annotated writing minilesson is shown in Figure 4-6. Each section is described in the text that follows.

Before the Lesson

Each writing minilesson begins with information to help you make the most of the lesson. There are four types of information here:

The Writing Minilesson Principle describes the key idea the children will learn and be invited to apply. The idea for the minilesson principle is based on the behaviors in the grade 1 sections of *The Literacy Continuum* (Fountas and Pinnell 2017), but the language has been carefully crafted to be accessible and memorable for children.

A Closer Look at the Umbrella Overview

A list of minilessons is organized under the umbrella title.

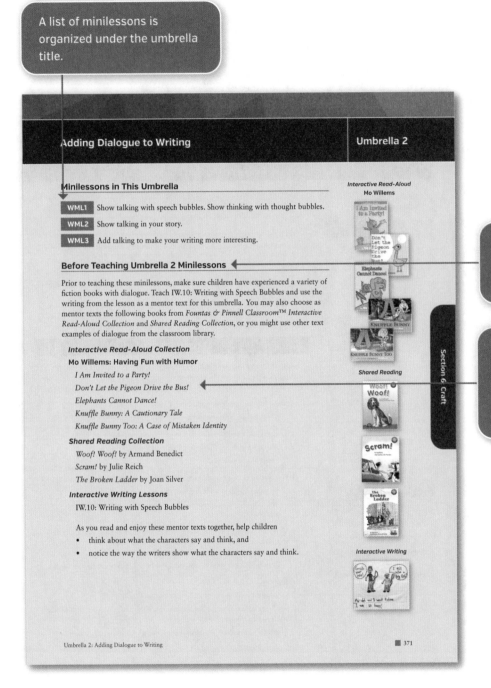

Adding Dialogue to Writing

Umbrella 2

Minilessons in This Umbrella

WML1 Show talking with speech bubbles. Show thinking with thought bubbles.

WML2 Show talking in your story.

WML3 Add talking to make your writing more interesting.

Before Teaching Umbrella 2 Minilessons

Prior to teaching these minilessons, make sure children have experienced a variety of fiction books with dialogue. Teach IW.10: Writing with Speech Bubbles and use the writing from the lesson as a mentor text for this umbrella. You may also choose as mentor texts the following books from *Fountas & Pinnell Classroom™ Interactive Read-Aloud Collection* and *Shared Reading Collection*, or you might use other text examples of dialogue from the classroom library.

Interactive Read-Aloud Collection

Mo Willems: Having Fun with Humor

I Am Invited to a Party!

Don't Let the Pigeon Drive the Bus!

Elephants Cannot Dance!

Knuffle Bunny: A Cautionary Tale

Knuffle Bunny Too: A Case of Mistaken Identity

Shared Reading Collection

Woof! Woof! by Armand Benedict

Scram! by Julie Reich

The Broken Ladder by Joan Silver

Interactive Writing Lessons

IW.10: Writing with Speech Bubbles

As you read and enjoy these mentor texts together, help children

- think about what the characters say and think, and
- notice the way the writers show what the characters say and think.

Interactive Read-Aloud
Mo Willems

Shared Reading

Interactive Writing

Umbrella 2: Adding Dialogue to Writing   371

Prepare for teaching the minilessons in this umbrella with these suggestions.

Use these suggested mentor texts as examples in the minilessons in this umbrella or use books that have similar characteristics.

Section 6 Craft

Figure 4-5: Each umbrella is introduced by a page that offers an overview of the umbrella.

A Closer Look at a Writing Minilesson

The **Writing Minilesson Principle** is a brief statement that describes what children will be invited to learn and apply.

This code identifies this lesson as the first writing minilesson in the second umbrella of the Craft section.

Look for these specific behaviors and understandings as you **assess** children's learning after presenting the lesson.

Important vocabulary used in the minilesson is listed.

Precise language is suggested for teaching the lesson.

WML1
CFT.U2.WML1

Writing Minilesson Principle
Show talking with speech bubbles.
Show thinking with thought bubbles.

Adding Dialogue to Writing

You Will Need

- several mentor texts that have thought and speech bubbles, such as the following:
  - *Woof! Woof!* by Armand Benedict and *Scram!* by Julie Reich, from *Shared Reading Collection*
  - *I Am Invited to a Party!* and *Don't Let the Pigeon Drive the Bus!* by Mo Willems, from Text Set: Mo Willems: Having Fun with Humor
  - class writing from IW.10: Writing with Speech Bubbles
- chart paper prepared with a sentence and drawing of two characters, one with an empty thought bubble and one with an empty speech bubble
- markers
- To download the following online resource for this lesson, visit **resources.fountasandpinnell.com**:
  - chart art (optional)

Academic Language / Important Vocabulary

- speech bubble
- thought bubble
- talking
- thinking

Continuum Connection

- Add thoughts in thought bubbles or dialogue in speech bubbles or quotation marks to provide information or provide narration [p. 256]

372

GOAL

Add speech bubbles to show talking and thought bubbles to show thinking.

RATIONALE

When children notice how writers include speech and thought bubbles in illustrations, they begin to think about ways to use dialogue in their own drawing and writing.

ASSESS LEARNING

- Look for evidence that children understand the purpose of and are trying to use speech bubbles and thought bubbles in their own writing.
- Observe for evidence that children can use vocabulary such as *speech bubble*, *thought bubble*, *talking*, and *thinking*.

MINILESSON

To help children think about including thought or speech bubbles in their own writing, provide an inquiry-based lesson with examples and then model the process. Here is an example.

- Show the class-made writing from IW.10.

  What did we do to show what the characters are saying?

- Engage children in a brief conversation about speech bubbles.
- Show page 5 in *Woof! Woof!* and page 6 in *Scram!*

  What do you notice?

- Help children recognize that speech bubbles point to the speaker's mouth.
- Show pages 12–13 in *I Am Invited to a Party!*

  What do you notice about how Mo Willems used speech bubbles in this book?

- Guide them to identify that because the speech bubbles point directly to the speakers, the reader knows which things Elephant says and which things Piggie says.

  Now think about what Mo Willems did in *Don't Let the Pigeon Drive the Bus!*

- Show and read pages 25–26.

  What do you notice about the bubbles?

- Guide the conversation so children notice the difference between how a speech bubble and a thought bubble are written.

  Why do you think the bubbles look different?

The Writing Minilessons Book, Grade 1

Children try out the new thinking from the minilesson, usually with a partner.

Create **anchor charts** as a useful reference tool and reinforcement of the minilesson principle for children during independent writing.

WML1
CFT.U2.WML1

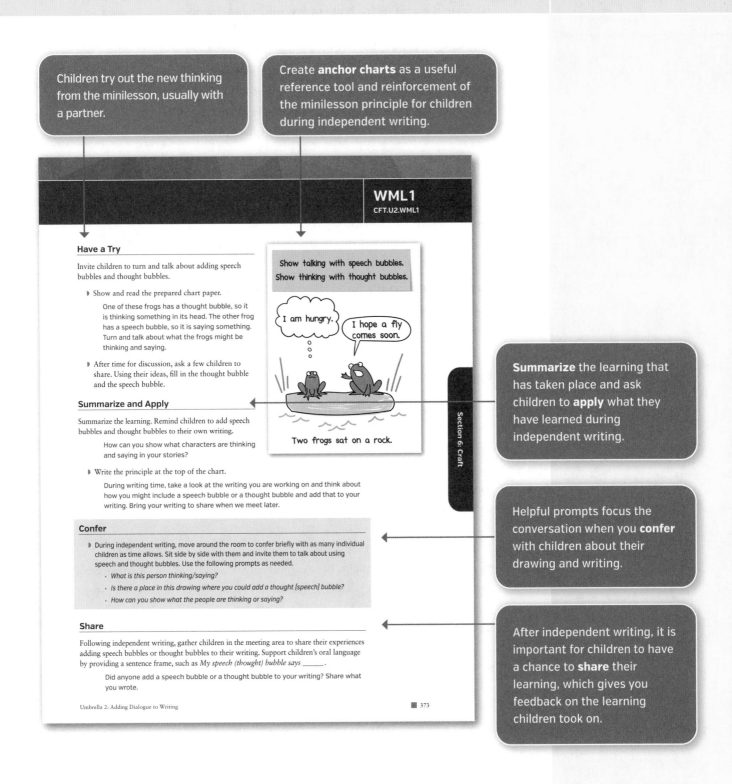

Have a Try

Invite children to turn and talk about adding speech bubbles and thought bubbles.

▸ Show and read the prepared chart paper.

One of these frogs has a thought bubble, so it is thinking something in its head. The other frog has a speech bubble, so it is saying something. Turn and talk about what the frogs might be thinking and saying.

▸ After time for discussion, ask a few children to share. Using their ideas, fill in the thought bubble and the speech bubble.

Summarize and Apply

Summarize the learning. Remind children to add speech bubbles and thought bubbles to their own writing.

How can you show what characters are thinking and saying in your stories?

▸ Write the principle at the top of the chart.

During writing time, take a look at the writing you are working on and think about how you might include a speech bubble or a thought bubble and add that to your writing. Bring your writing to share when we meet later.

Summarize the learning that has taken place and ask children to **apply** what they have learned during independent writing.

Confer

▸ During independent writing, move around the room to confer briefly with as many individual children as time allows. Sit side by side with them and invite them to talk about using speech and thought bubbles. Use the following prompts as needed.

· *What is this person thinking/saying?*

· *Is there a place in this drawing where you could add a thought [speech] bubble?*

· *How can you show what the people are thinking or saying?*

Helpful prompts focus the conversation when you **confer** with children about their drawing and writing.

Share

Following independent writing, gather children in the meeting area to share their experiences adding speech bubbles or thought bubbles to their writing. Support children's oral language by providing a sentence frame, such as *My speech (thought) bubble says _____.*

Did anyone add a speech bubble or a thought bubble to your writing? Share what you wrote.

Umbrella 2: Adding Dialogue to Writing

■ 373

After independent writing, it is important for children to have a chance to **share** their learning, which gives you feedback on the learning children took on.

Section 6: Craft

The minilesson principle gives you a clear idea of the concept you will help children construct. The lessons are designed to be inquiry-based because we want the children to build to this understanding instead of hearing it stated at the beginning.

Although we have crafted the language to make it appropriate for the age group, you can shape the language to fit the way your children use language. When you summarize the lesson, be sure to state the principle simply and clearly so that children are certain to understand what it means. State the minilesson principle the same way every time you refer to it.

The Goal of the minilesson is based on a behavior in *The Literacy Continuum*. Each minilesson is focused on one single goal that leads to a deeeper understanding of the larger umbrella concept.

The Rationale is the reason the minilesson is important. It is a brief explanation of how this new learning leads children forward in their writing journey.

Assess Learning is a list of suggestions of specific behaviors and understandings to look for as evidence that children have absorbed the minilesson concept. Keep this list in mind as you teach.

Minilesson

The **Minilesson** section provides an example of a lesson for teaching the writing minilesson principle. We suggest some precise language and open-ended questions that will keep children engaged and the lesson brief and focused. Effective minilessons, when possible, involve inquiry. That means children actively think about the idea and notice examples in a familiar piece of writing. They begin to construct their understanding from concrete examples.

Create experiences that help children notice things and make their own discoveries. You might, for example, invite children to look at several nonfiction information books, carefully chosen to illustrate the minilesson principle. Children will know these books because they have heard them read aloud and have talked about them. Often, you can use the same books in several writing minilessons to make your teaching efficient. Invite children to talk about what they notice across all the books.

As first graders explore the mentor text examples using your questions and supportive comments as a guide, make the anchor chart with children's input. From this exploration and the discussion, children come to the minilesson principle. Learning is more powerful and enjoyable for children when they actively search for the meaning, find patterns, talk about their understandings, and share in making the charts. Children need to form networks of understanding around the concepts related to literacy and to be constantly looking for connections for themselves.

Children learn more about language when they have opportunities to talk. Writing minilessons provide many opportunities for them to express their thoughts in language, both oral and written, and to communicate with others. The inquiry approach found in these lessons invites more child talk than teacher talk, and that can be both a challenge and an opportunity for you as you work with English learners. However, building talk routines, such as turn and talk, into your writing minilessons can be very helpful in providing opportunities for English learners to talk in a safe and supportive way.

EL CONNECTION

When you ask children to think about the minilesson principle across several stories or informational books that they have previously heard read aloud and discussed, they are more engaged and able to participate because they know the stories and informational books and begin to notice important things about writing through them. Using familiar texts, including some writing that you and the children have created together, is particularly important for English learners. When you select examples for a writing minilesson, choose books and other examples that you know were particularly engaging for the English learners in your classroom. Besides choosing accessible, familiar texts, it is important to provide plenty of wait-and-think time. For example, you might say, "Let's think about that for a minute" before calling for responses.

EL CONNECTION

When working with English learners, look for what the child knows about the concept instead of focusing on faulty grammar or language errors. Model appropriate language use in your responses but do not correct a child who is attempting to use language to learn it. You might also provide an oral sentence frame to get the student response started, for example, *I like the story because* _____. Accept variety in pronunciation and intonation, remembering that the more children speak, read, and write, the more they will take on the understanding of grammatical patterns and the complex intonation patterns that reflect meaning in English.

Have a Try

Before children leave the whole group to apply the new thinking during independent writing, give them a chance to try it with a partner or a small group. **Have a Try** is designed to be brief, but it offers you an opportunity to gather information on how well children understand the minilesson goal. In Management lessons, children might quickly practice the new routine that they will be asked to do independently. In the other lessons, children might verbalize how it might be possible to apply the new understanding to their writing. Add further thinking to the chart after the children have had the chance to try out or talk about their new learning. Have a Try is an important step in reinforcing the minilesson principle and moving the children toward independence.

The Have a Try part of the writing minilesson is particularly important for English learners. Besides providing repetition, it gives English learners a safe place to try out the new idea before sharing it with the whole group. These are a few suggestions for how you might support children during the Have a Try portion of the lesson:

- Pair children with partners that you know will take turns talking.

- Spend time teaching children how to turn and talk. (See MGT.U1: Working Together in the Classroom.) Teach children how to provide wait time for one another, invite the other partner into the conversation, and take turns.

- Provide concrete examples to discuss so that children are clear about what they need to think and talk about. English learners will feel more confident if they are able to talk about a mentor text that they know very well.

- When necessary, provide the oral language structure or language stem for how you want the children to share their ideas. For example, ask them to start with the sentence frame *I noticed the writer* _____ and to rehearse the language structure a few times before turning and talking.

- Imagine aloud how something might sound in a child's writing. Provide children with some examples of how something might sound if they were to try something out in their own writing. For example, you might say something like this: "Marco, you are writing about when you fell off your bike. You could start by drawing yourself on the ground. You could write a speech bubble that says, 'OW!!'"

- Observe partnerships involving English learners and provide support as needed.

Summarize and Apply

This part of the lesson includes two parts: summarizing the learning and applying the learning to independent writing.

The **summary is a brief but essential part of the lesson. It brings together the learning that has taken place through the inquiry and helps children think about its application and relevance to their own learning. Ask children to think about the anchor chart and talk about what they have learned. Involve them in stating the minilesson principle. Then write it on the chart. Use simple, clear language to shape the suggestions. Sometimes, you may decide to summarize the new learning to keep the lesson short and allow enough time for the children to apply it independently. Whether you state the** principle or share the construction with the children, summarize the learning in a way that children understand and can remember.

After the summary, the children apply their new understandings to their independent writing. The invitation to try out the new idea must be clear enough for children but "light" enough to allow room for them to have their own ideas for their writing. The application of the minilesson principle should not be thought of as an exercise or task that needs to be forced to fit their writing but instead as an invitation for deeper, more meaningful writing.

We know that when children first take on new learning, they often want to try out the new learning to the exclusion of some of the other things they have learned. When you teach about speech bubbles, for example, expect to see lots of speech bubbles. Encourage children to try out new techniques while reminding them about the other things they have learned.

Before children begin independent writing, let them know that they can apply the new understanding to any writing they do and will have an opportunity to share what they have done with the class after independent writing. First graders love to share!

Confer

EL CONNECTION

While children are busy independently making books and writing, move around the room to observe and confer briefly with individuals. Sit side by side with them and invite them to talk about what they are doing. In each minilesson, we offer prompts focused on the umbrella concept and worded in clear, direct language. Using direct language can be particularly supportive for English learners because it allows them to focus on the meaning without having to work through the extra talk that we often use in our everyday conversations. Occasionally you will see sentence frames to support English learners in both their talk and their writing.

If a child is working on something that does not fit with the minilesson principle, do not feel limited to the language in this section. Respond to the child in a sincere and enthusiastic way. Remember that the invitation to apply the new learning can be extended another time. This will not be the only opportunity.

General prompts, such as the following, are provided to get children talking so that you can listen carefully to the thinking behind the writing (in using the word *writing* we include *drawing*). Be sure to let children do most of the talking. The one who does the talking does the learning!

▶ *How is your writing going?*

▶ *How can I help you with your writing?*

> What do you think about this piece of writing?

> What do you want to do next in your writing?

> What is the best part of your writing (book) so far?

> Is any part of your writing (book) still confusing for the reader?

> What would you like to do with this writing (book) when it is finished?

Observational notes will help you understand how each writer is progressing and provide purposeful, customized instruction every time you talk with children about their writing (Figure 4-7). You can use your notes to plan the content of future minilessons. You can also take pictures of, scan, or make copies of key pieces to discuss with families.

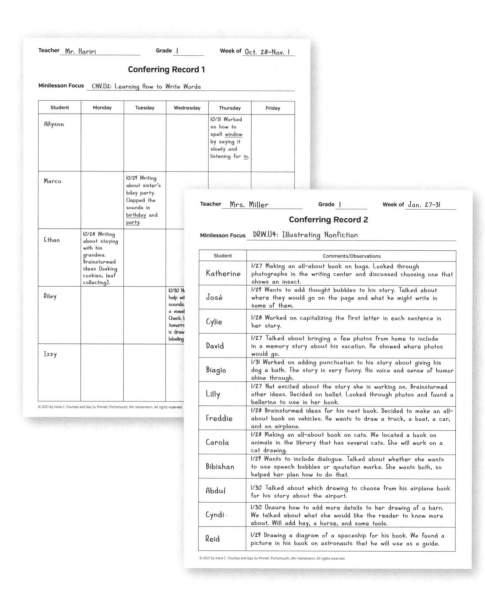

Figure 4-7: Choose one of these downloadable forms to record your observations of children's behaviors and understandings. Visit **resources.fountasandpinnell.com** to download this and all other online resources.

Share

At the end of independent writing, gather children together for the opportunity to **share** their learning with the entire group. During group share, you can revisit, expand, and deepen understanding of the minilesson's goal as well as assess learning. Often, children are invited to bring their drawing and writing to share with the class and to explain how they tried out the minilesson principle. As you observe and talk to children during independent writing, plan how to share by assessing how many children tried the new learning in their writing. If only a few children were able to apply the minilesson principle to their writing, you might ask those children to share with the whole group. However, if you observe most of the class applying the principle, you might have them share in pairs or small groups.

You might also consider inviting children to choose what to share about their writing instead of connecting back to the minilesson principle. For example, one child might share a detail added to make a drawing clearer. Another might share a letter she is writing to her family. Another might read his story to the class.

Share time is a wonderful way to bring the community of learners back together to expand their understandings of writing and of each other as well as to celebrate their new attempts at writing. There are some particular accommodations to support English learners during the time for sharing:

EL CONNECTION

▶ Ask English learners to share in pairs before sharing with the group.

▶ While conferring, help children rehearse the language structure they might use to share their drawing and writing with the class.

Teach the entire class respectful ways to listen to peers and model how to give their peers time to express their thoughts. Many of the minilessons in the Management section will be useful for developing a peaceful, safe, and supportive community of writers.

A Closer Look at the Umbrella Wrap-Up

Following the minilessons in each umbrella, you will see the final umbrella page, which includes a section for assessing what children have learned and a section for extending the learning.

Assessment

The last page of each umbrella, shown in Figure 4-8, provides questions to help you **assess** the learning that has taken place through the entire umbrella. The information you gain from observing what the children can already do, almost do, and not yet do will help inform the selection of the next umbrella you teach. (See chapter 8 for more information about assessment and the selection of umbrellas.)

A Closer Look at the Umbrella Wrap-Up

Gain important information by **assessing** what children have learned as they apply and share their learning of the minilesson principles. Observe and then follow up with individuals in conferences or in small groups in guided writing.

Optional suggestions are provided for **extending** the learning of the umbrella over time or in other contexts.

Figure 4-8: The final page of each umbrella offers suggestions for assessing the learning and ideas for extending the learning.

Umbrella 2	Adding Dialogue to Writing

Assessment

After you have taught the minilessons in this umbrella, observe children as they write letters. Use *The Literacy Continuum* (Fountas and Pinnell 2017) to notice, teach for, and support children's learning as you observe their attempts at reading and writing.

- What evidence do you have of new understandings the children have developed related to dialogue?
  - Do children understand that they can use speech or thought bubbles in their writing?
  - Do they understand how to write dialogue in their stories?
  - Do they use dialogue in order to make their writing more interesting?
  - Are they using vocabulary related to writing dialogue, such as *speech bubble*, *thought bubble*, *talking*, *thinking*, *quotation marks*, *story*, *interesting*, and *purpose*?
- In what ways, beyond the scope of this umbrella, are children thinking about dialogue?
  - Do they have a good understanding of how to use punctuation?
  - Are they beginning to revise their writing?

Use your observations to determine the next umbrella you will teach. You may also consult Suggested Sequence of Lessons (pp. 557–571) for guidance.

EXTENSIONS FOR ADDING DIALOGUE TO WRITING

- If you are using *The Reading Minilessons Book, Grade 1* (Fountas and Pinnell 2019), the minilessons in this umbrella would pair well with LA.U19: Understanding Characters and Their Feelings, LA.U20: Knowing Characters Inside and Out, and LA.U23: Looking Closely at Illustrations.
- As you share other books with dialogue, have children talk about how authors show what characters are thinking and saying.
- Have children engage in readers' theater and then write about the conversations as a way to incorporate dialogue in their stories.
- Talk about using speaker tags (e.g., *shouted*, *whispered*, *cried*, *laughed*) to show how a character says something.
- Gather together a guided writing group of several children who need support in a specific area of writing, such as adding dialogue.

378 *The Writing Minilessons Book, Grade 1*

Extensions for the Umbrella

Each umbrella ends with several suggestions for **extending** the learning of the umbrella. Sometimes the suggestion is to repeat a minilesson with different examples. First graders will need to experience some of the concepts more than once before they are able to transfer actions to their independent writing. Other times, children will be able to extend the learning beyond the scope of the umbrella.

Effective Writing Minilessons

The goal of all writing minilessons is to help children think and act like writers and illustrators as they build their capacity for independent writing and drawing across the year. Whether you are teaching lessons about drawing or telling stories or teaching any of the other minilessons, the characteristics of effective minilessons, listed in Figure 4-9, apply.

Figure 4-9: Characteristics of effective minilessons

Effective Writing Minilessons . . .

- are based on a **writing principle** that is important to teach to first graders
- are based on a **goal** that makes the teaching meaningful
- are **relevant to the specific needs of children** so that your teaching connects with the learners
- are very **brief, concise, and to the point**
- use **clear and specific language** to avoid talk that clutters learning
- stay **focused on a single idea** so children can apply the learning and build on it day after day
- use an **inquiry approach** whenever possible to support active, constructive learning
- often include **shared, high-quality mentor texts** that can be used as examples
- are **well paced** to engage and hold children's interest
- are **grouped into umbrellas** to foster depth in thinking and coherence across lessons
- **build one understanding on another** across several days instead of single isolated lessons
- provide time for children to **"try out" the new concept** before they are invited to try it independently
- engage children in **summarizing the new learning and applying it to their own writing**
- build **important vocabulary** appropriate for children in first grade
- help children **become better artists and writers**
- **foster community** through the development of shared language
- **can be assessed** as you observe children engaged in authentic writing
- **help children understand what they are learning** how to do as artists and writers

Writing minilessons can be used to teach anything from telling stories to drawing pictures to making books and more. Teach a writing minilesson whenever you see an opportunity to nudge the children forward as writers and illustrators.

Chapter 5   Management Minilessons

> *We need a caring classroom community in which multiple perspectives
> are developed and used to think critically and expand learning.
> We need a community in which children come to appreciate the
> value of different perspectives for their own development, in which
> they recognize changes in their own and others' thinking and
> that that difference is the source for the change.*
>
> —Peter Johnston

INDIVIDUALS LEARN BETTER AND HAVE more fun when they have some
routines for working safely and responsibly. The lessons in Section 2:
Management establish these routines. Children learn how to

- listen,

- take turns,

- show kindness to one another,

- draw and write independently,

- share their writing,

- take care of classroom materials,

- use their writing folder resources, and

- use and return materials.

They become independent problem solvers who can work and play as members of a community.

Building a Community of Writers

Writers need to feel valued and included in a community whose members have learned to trust one another with their stories. The minilessons in the Management section are designed to help children build this trust and learn to include one another in discussions and play. The first lesson in MGT.U1: Working Together in the Classroom (WML1: Get to know your classmates) sets the tone for building this community. As children share who they are, where their families come from, what languages they speak, what foods they eat, and what activities they enjoy, they begin to explore their identities and learn about the identities of others. A person's identity influences the way one reads and writes; it impacts the perspective one brings to these literacy experiences. We see this even with our youngest readers and writers. When we celebrate children's unique identities and perspectives, we teach children to value and include one another. This is one of the reasons the share time at the end of independent writing is so important. This time of sharing inspires writing ideas, but it does so much more. It provides a time to celebrate writing and more importantly carves out space to celebrate each writer in the classroom community.

Create a Peaceful Atmosphere

The minilessons in this section will help you establish a classroom environment in which children are confident, self-determined, and kind and in which every child's identity is valued. The lessons are designed to contribute to peaceful activity and shared responsibility. Through the Management minilessons, children learn how to modulate their voices to suit various purposes (silent to outdoor). They also learn to keep supplies in order, help others, listen to and look at a speaker, and clean up quickly and quietly (Figure 5-1).

All of these minilessons contribute to an overall tone of respect in every classroom activity. They are designed to help you establish the atmosphere you want. Everything in the classroom reflects the children who work there; it is their home for the year.

Teach the minilessons in this section in the order that fits your class needs, or consult the Suggested Sequence of Lessons (pp. 555-571). You may need to reteach some of these lessons because as the year goes on you will

Figure 5-1: Characteristics of a peaceful atmosphere for the community of readers and writers

be working in a more complex way. A schedule change or other disruption in classroom operations might prompt a refresher minilesson. Any problem in your classroom should be addressed through minilessons that focus on building a community of learners.

Design the Physical Space

In addition to creating a peaceful atmosphere, prepare the physical space in a way to provide the best support for learning (Figure 5-2). Each umbrella in Section 2: Management will help your first graders become acquainted with the routines of the classroom and help them feel secure and at home. Make sure that the classroom has the following qualities.

▶ **Welcoming and Inviting.** Pleasing colors and a variety of furniture will help. There is no need for commercially published posters or slogans, except for standard references such as the Alphabet Linking Chart (Figure 3-7) or colorful poetry posters. The room can be filled with the work that the children have produced beginning on day one, some of it in languages other than English. They should see signs of their learning everywhere—shared and interactive writing, charts, drawings of various kinds, and their names. Be sure that children's names are at various places

Figure 5-2: Layout of a first-grade classroom

in the room—on tables, on cubbies, on a helper's or "jobs" chart, and on some of the charts that you will make in the minilessons. A framed wall of children's photographs and self-portraits sends the clear message that this classroom belongs to them and celebrates their unique identities. The classroom library should be as inviting as a bookstore or a library. Place books in baskets and tubs on shelves to make the front covers of books visible and accessible for easy browsing. Clearly label the supplies in the writing center so children can see the materials that are available and can access them and return them independently (Figure 5-3). Better yet, have children make labels with you during shared or interactive writing. Children also love to be involved in the naming of the different classroom areas so they truly feel like they have ownership of the classroom. We have seen some classrooms that create space on a low bulletin board with each child's name so that children can choose items to display.

▶ **Organized for Easy Use.** The first thing you might want to do is to take out everything you do not need. Clutter increases stress and noise. Using scattered and hard-to-find materials increases the children's dependence on you. Consider keeping supplies for bookmaking and writing in clearly labeled areas. For example, some teachers organize a writing area where they keep paper, highlighters, staplers, etc. Provide paper and booklets in a variety of different sizes so children can choose the kind of paper they want to use. For example, a simple four-page booklet (two pieces of paper folded in half) or a stapled book folded horizontally can be made and placed in a tray. You might also provide a selection of templates for writing (available from the online resources). Some teachers choose to have children keep the books or other writing projects they are making in writing folders that are stored in the writing center. Others have them in bins located throughout the room so children can easily access their writing without causing traffic jams.

In the first few days of school, children learn how to get supplies and return supplies. Children who choose to make books can get what they need independently and work at their tables. Some teachers choose to have caddies at tables instead of keeping supplies on a shelf in the writing center so that children can spread out and get started right away.

Work areas are clearly organized with necessary, labeled materials and nothing else. Labels with pictures and words as well as an arrow pointing to where the items belong show children exactly what goes where. Some teachers stick a shape on the shelf that matches the bottom of the container (Figure 5-4). Over the course of the year, introduce different kinds of media into the art center and creation station (maker space) so children can experiment with collage, 3D materials, and materials that have different textures.

Arrange furniture to create traffic patterns that discourage running, promote safe movement around the room for all children, and allow for easy access to emergency exits. Be sure that all furniture is appropriate for the children's size/height and that children's work is displayed at their eye level so they can appreciate it.

Figure 5-3: All the materials in the writing center are organized. Each kind of material is kept in a separate, labeled container.

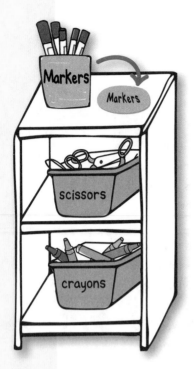

▶ **Designed for Whole-Group, Small-Group, and Individual Instruction.** Interactive writing lessons and writing minilessons are generally provided as whole-class instruction and typically take place at an easel in a meeting space. The space is comfortable and large enough for all children to sit as a group or in a circle. It will be helpful to have a colorful rug. Create some way of helping children find an individual space to sit without crowding one another. (For example, the rug often has squares of different colors.) The meeting space is next to the classroom library so that books are displayed and handy. The teacher usually has a larger chair or seat next to an easel or two so that he can display the mentor texts, make anchor charts, do shared or interactive writing, or place big books for shared reading. This space is available for all whole-group instruction; for example, the children come back to it for group share. In addition to the group meeting space, assign tables and spaces in the classroom for small-group writing instruction. Use low shelving and furniture to define and separate learning areas and to create storage opportunities. First graders need tables and spaces throughout the classroom where they can play and work independently and where you can easily set a chair next to a child for a brief writing conference.

Establish Independent Writing

The second umbrella in the Management section helps you establish independent writing time with your first graders. Through the minilessons in this umbrella, children learn the routines needed to be independent and productive. They learn to get started with their writing quickly and quietly. They increase their stamina and become efficient in storing their writing and materials at the end of writing time. Children will learn that writers are never finished. When they finish making a book, they can start another. At the beginning of the year, keep the writing time short (you may even start with just five minutes of independent time) so they can feel successful right away. Add a few minutes every day until they are able to sustain writing for twenty-five to thirty minutes. Involve the children in setting goals for stretching their writing time and celebrate each time you reach them as a class. You will soon have children begging for more time to do this important work. First graders also begin to see the value of working on a piece of writing over time. They establish important routines like rereading their writing to think what to do next. Through this umbrella, children also learn that writers receive feedback and guidance from other writers. They learn the routines for conferring with a teacher and how to productively share their writing with an audience at the end of independent writing.

Introduce Writing Tools and Resources

The minilessons in the Management section also introduce children to the tools and resources they will need for independent writing. Choose the minilessons from MGT.U3: Using Drawing and Writing Tools that your students need to use tools properly and independently. It might not seem important, but a short lesson on using markers and glue goes a long way in preserving classroom materials and helping children become increasingly independent. There are also lessons to introduce using scissors and a stapler, a new and exciting tool for many first graders. The stapler allows them to add additional information by attaching pages or paper strips to their writing, an important part of revision.

Provide Paper Choices

When you give children the ability to choose from a variety of paper, you teach them to make important decisions as a writer/illustrator. We suggest offering some of the following choices (most available as templates in online resources) throughout the year:

- Paper with picture boxes and lines in varying formats (e.g., picture box on the top/lines on the bottom or picture box on the side with wrapping lines)

- Paper in landscape and portrait layouts

- Paper stapled into booklets (portrait and landscape)

- Paper formatted for text features (e.g., sidebar, table of contents, and materials list)

- Author page

- Dedication page

- Paper in a letter format

Paper choices give children a chance to envision how they want their writing to look. Part of making books is thinking about how you want the print and illustrations to be placed on a page. We have included the lesson MGT.U3.WML3 (Choose your paper) because paper is a tool for writing. However, choosing paper could be introduced or revisited as part of MBK.U1: Getting Started with Making Books.

Introduce the Writing Folder

Your children's writing folders serve two purposes. They provide a place for children to keep ongoing writing projects (e.g., a book they are working on or a letter they are writing) as well as writing they have finished but might want to return to in the future. We suggest using folders with two pockets and fasteners in the middle on which you can place resources for children to use during independent writing (e.g., a personal word list). The minilessons in MGT.U4: Introducing Writing Folder Resources support children in developing an ongoing list of writing ideas, introduce a way for children to record their finished writing pieces, and teach them how to build their own personal word list. These resources give children agency and promote their independence by giving them tools for sustaining their own writing. Templates for these resources are available in the online resources.

The writing folder also helps children view themselves as writers. The record of finished writing pieces gives individual writers a sense of accomplishment and provides a way for you and your students to notice patterns in their writing choices. Use this record and the writing ideas list to help your writers reflect during writing conferences: Are there different kinds of writing they would like to try? Are they choosing topics they care about? Is there a way to write about the same topic in a different way? Consider expanding writing folder resources over time. For example, you could place a list of high-frequency words and a proofreading checklist (both available in the online resources) after teaching the minilessons in CNV.U3: Using Classroom Resources to Write Words and WPS.U6: Proofreading Writing.

Chapter 6

Minilessons for Telling Stories, Making Books, and Drawing

Through their talk, children let us into their worlds, so we listen, pay attention, and continue to carve out space where they can talk their way into stories in the company of an audience who values what they have to say.

—Martha Horn and Mary Ellen Giacobbe

TALK IS WHERE THE WRITING process begins and the way it expands. One section in this book is called Telling Stories and is dedicated to minilessons that "carve out space" for children to talk, share stories, and learn the value of their own storytelling. Once children can tell their stories, they can make a book about them. First graders rely heavily on drawing to put their stories on paper. It is through bookmaking that oral language and drawing come together.

Children need to learn that their everyday lives are a great source for telling and writing stories. First graders have a lot to say, so it is important to give them many chances to be part of meaningful conversation. Providing time to share stories builds a community in which children get to know and respect one another. And children receive an important message: their personal and varied life experiences are unique and highly valued.

Stories We Have Told

Making Pizza by Alejandra

The Butterfly by Danya

My Piano Lesson by Wyatt

Raking Leaves by Amiah

Figure 6-1: Keep a list of stories that children have told to remind them of ideas they can use when they make books.

Telling Stories

All children have stories to tell. The minilessons in the first umbrella of Section 3: Telling Stories focus on different ways children can find the stories in their lives—by thinking about places, people, and things that are meaningful to them. Capture these stories on a chart (Figure 6-1) that children can return to as they move from telling to writing and drawing their stories.

Storytelling is rooted in an individual's family and community, and that might be particularly important when working with African American children (Gardner-Neblett 2015). Several studies have demonstrated that from early on African American children have a wide variety of storytelling styles and tell high-quality stories. It is important to both value and engage a variety of storytelling styles in the classroom. Gardner-Neblett points out that when children are encouraged to engage in storytelling, they have the opportunity to use orally the language that they usually hear and see only in written texts.

When you embrace and celebrate children's storytelling, you support children's development of important literacy understandings that can be applied to both reading and writing. Schools have traditionally taught a familiar European story structure: a beginning, a revelation of the story problem, a series of events, a problem resolution, and an ending. It is important to recognize that there are many different kinds of story structures (Resnick and Snow, 2008). Some cultures string together a series of seemingly unrelated events that ultimately work together to make a point. Others include many characters that are not necessary to the main theme but represent family values and community. Some families tell traditional stories that have been passed down for centuries while others tell current stories about their own family members. In some cultures, traditional stories have an element of fantasy that reveal a deeper truth about life. By recognizing and valuing the different ways children might have learned to tell stories, we can help expand children's understanding of what a story is and how stories work. Through the storytelling umbrellas, children learn to expand their understanding of story and further develop their oral language by

▶ listening to teachers tell their own stories,

▶ hearing classmates' stories,

▶ sharing their own stories and responding to questions about them,

- recreating familiar stories with puppets,

- telling about something they have learned, and

- teaching about something they know how to do.

The Literacy Continuum (Fountas and Pinnell 2017) contains a detailed list of the oral language behaviors important to develop in first-grade children. Every section of this book contains minilessons to support the development of these behaviors. Children learn the routines and conventions of conversation through Management minilessons; they learn how to present their stories orally in the Telling Stories minilessons; and they learn how to share, expand, and discuss ideas for writing through minilessons in the remaining sections. Language is the tool through which all learning is mediated.

Making Books

Weave minilessons for telling stories in between minilessons about making books because storytelling and bookmaking go hand in hand. That's why in the sequence we suggest teaching the minilessons in the first storytelling umbrella over the course of a few weeks. This allows children time in between minilessons to tell their stories, make books about their stories, and then tell more stories. The more stories they tell, the more ideas they have for books.

In the first umbrella in Section 4: Making Books (MBK.U1: Getting Started with Making Books), first graders are invited to make books. As children make books, refer them to the story charts you created with the class to record the stories they have told. Revisiting these charts helps children remember their stories and understand that they can write and draw about them. After this initial exposure, children are introduced in more depth throughout the year to the different kinds of books they can make, such as how-to books, all-about books, and memory books.

In all cases, they can go back to the stories they have told and not only write about those stories but use them as seeds to grow other books. For example, Kyle told a memory story about building a water fountain in his backyard with his grandfather. He also made a how-to book titled *How to Make a Water Fountain.* Later, when all-about books are introduced, he might write a book all about the different fountains he has seen. Eventually, he may want to write a poem about water fountains. When children learn to tell their own stories, they learn about themselves, what they love, and who they are. They are learning how to put themselves on the pages of a book.

Drawing

Drawing is important! Minilessons about drawing help writers tell stories in their books. Ray and Glover wrote that one of their core beliefs is that children do not need to "get ready" to be readers and writers, but rather they are already readers and writers (2008, xvii). Our job is to nurture them and encourage them to grow.

The umbrellas in Section 5: Drawing are designed to nurture children's ability to tell stories across the pages of a book. They also help you and your children take a close look at illustrator's craft—the decisions illustrators make to communicate their ideas. Through these lessons, children's drawings become increasingly representational and detailed.

The first umbrella of Section 5: Drawing focuses on making self-portraits, which can then be used in a class book during interactive writing (IW.7: Writing About Who We Are) or framed and put on your wall to welcome people into your classroom. Through this umbrella, children learn that shapes are the building blocks for making a face. They look in a mirror to see the shapes that make up their faces and practice drawing them. They think about details like whether their hair is curly or straight, long or short. In the next lesson, they learn about adding detail through color. As they think about the color of their skin, hair, and eyes, they notice that their classmates are unique and special in their own ways.

The second umbrella (DRW.U2: Learning to Draw) builds on the understanding that shapes help you draw people. The minilessons focus on how to draw a body in different positions, how to show where a story takes place, and how to draw people consistently on each page.

When you teach drawing, you are also nurturing children's development of writing. As children develop their ability to draw representationally, they begin to add details that capture more of their story in both pictures and words. They become more aware of the way illustrators use their drawings to communicate ideas. For example, Asher didn't just draw where his story takes place. He also showed the passage of time through his series of drawings (Figure 6-2).

There is no doubt Asher learned this technique from an illustrator like Bob Graham. Careful examination of mentor texts in the Drawing minilessons show children how to look at the illustrations in books with an illustrator's eye. Asher has learned to make his words and his drawings work together to convey an idea. He used words and pictures to create the suspense of waiting for five days. In DRW.U3: Adding Meaningful Details to

Figure 6-2: Asher drew a repeating image of a house with a sun in a series of mini-scenes to show the passage of time.

Illustrations, minilessons focus on many of the craft moves illustrators make such as using color to show feelings, drawing motion and sound lines, and using perspective to make something look close or far away. The more children learn about drawing, the more they learn about the process of revising their writing. They get excited to add new details to their pictures after talking about their stories and learning new illustration techniques. This in turn impacts the details they add to their writing.

The minilessons in DRW.U4: Illustrating Nonfiction help children expand their thinking about illustrations beyond drawing characters and settings. They learn that illustrations can be used to show factual information through detailed drawings, diagrams (Figure 6-3), and photographs. Children love experimenting with different media (e.g., cut paper, found objects, or fabric) to make their illustrations interesting for their readers.

Through the last umbrella in Section 5: Drawing (U5: Making Pictures Interesting), children learn that they can borrow techniques used by writers and illustrators, such as collage, textured materials, flaps, and pop-ups (Figures 6-4-1 and 6-4-2) in their own writing.

Figure 6-3: Drew made a diagram for his book *All About Penguins.*

Figure 6-4-1: Daniela used collage to capture a scene from Kevin Henkes's book, *Sheila Rae, the Brave.*

Children need time to tell their stories, experiment with making books, and learn ways to draw their ideas. It is our hope that the lessons in these three sections—Telling Stories, Making Books, and Drawing—will work together to help you nurture the writers in your classroom so they can share the important information and stories in their lives.

Chapter 7

Minilessons for the Study of Craft, Conventions, and Writing Process

One of our primary goals is for children to be self-directed writers who have the ability to follow their own intentions. We want children to be engaged for reasons beyond the fact that they are required to write. We want them to choose projects because they want to entertain their friends or share what they know about a topic or convince someone to do something. Without the ability and opportunity to find authentic writing projects, it will be more difficult for them to become truly self-directed.

— Matt Glover

FOR CHILDREN TO BECOME ENGAGED in the writing process, they have to care about their writing. Teachers of writing know that children are more engaged when they are able to make choices about their writing. Choice comes in many forms. Writers choose the length of their writing, their topic, their purpose, their audience, the kind of writing they will do, and how they will craft it. They make choices about where to put things on the page, how to punctuate a sentence, what to revise and edit, and whether to ultimately publish a piece of writing. If we want to develop authentic writers in our classrooms, we have to provide time, space and instruction for even our youngest children to engage in these decisions. The umbrellas and minilessons in the last three sections of this book, Craft, Conventions, and Writing Process, set the stage for you to develop writers who make these decisions, have a sense of agency, and care deeply about their writing work.

Applying Craft, Conventions, and Writing Process Minilessons

The umbrellas in the Craft, Conventions, and Writing Process sections can be used in several ways. They are perfect for dipping into when you notice that your children are ready for or in need of a certain lesson. For example, let's say you noticed that several of your students are starting to organize similar information together in their nonfiction books and know they would benefit from learning about headings. So, you decide to teach the Craft minilesson on headings or the entire Craft umbrella CFT.U7: Adding Text Features to Books.

Alternatively, you might choose to simply follow the Suggested Sequence of Lessons (pp. 555–571), which weaves the umbrellas from these three sections across the year. Children can apply their new learning about craft to books in a single genre they are all working on (e.g., all-about books) or to books in whatever genres individuals have chosen to work on. Whichever way you decide to use these lessons, be thoughtful about whether your children are writing something that will allow them to try out the minilessons. There are some umbrellas in the Craft section that are more easily applied to certain kinds of writing. For example, you might want to introduce CFT.U2: Adding Dialogue to Writing when children are writing memory stories because they can probably imagine what was said at the time of their stories. If they have difficulty applying new learning to their current writing, consider inviting them to revisit finished work in their writing folders. There are several umbrellas in the Craft, Conventions, and Writing Process sections that can be applied across all kinds of writing (e.g., CNV.U5: Using Capital Letters or WPS.U4: Adding Information to Your Writing).

Another thing to consider when you ask children to apply the minilessons from these three sections is where the majority of students are in their writing process. If most children are just starting a new piece of writing, you might teach WPS.U2: Getting Ideas for Writing. If many children are working on revising their work, you might teach a Craft lesson or a lesson from the drafting and revising part of the Writing Process section. If you want to engage children in editing their work, choose an umbrella from the Conventions section or one of the editing umbrellas in the Writing Process section. Whenever you decide to teach these minilessons, think of it as adding tools to your writers' toolboxes. For many students, you will hand them the right tool at exactly the right time. But others will tuck that tool away and use it when they are ready.

Studying the Craft of Writing

What do we mean when we talk about the craft of writing with first graders? Young children appreciate writer's craft way before they know what it is. They laugh at Mo Willems's speech bubbles with silly fonts and clever punctuation, they are entertained by Cynthia Rylant's beautiful word choices, or they know how to turn to the exact page they want in a Gail Gibbons book because they have figured out how the book is organized. Through the talk that surrounds interactive read-aloud and shared reading, first graders know a lot about the craft of writing. Craft minilessons take this budding knowledge and pull back the curtain on the decisions authors make to create books that are interesting and exciting to read.

The minilessons in the Craft section are based on the behaviors and understandings in the Craft section of the grade 1 Writing continuum in *The Literacy Continuum* (Fountas and Pinnell 2017). It is important to note that minilessons that teach these behaviors and understandings are not limited to the Craft section of this book. There are minilessons that address aspects of craft built into the Making Books section because craft is part of creating a book (e.g., telling your memory story in a sequence or organizing your all-about book). The Drawing section contains minilessons that address illustrator's craft (e.g., how to draw with perspective or how to create a feeling with color). Even minilessons in the Conventions section have an aspect of craft to them. For example, capitalization and punctuation have to do with the conventions of writing, but writers also use punctuation and capitalization to communicate their ideas and voice (e.g., using multiple exclamation points to indicate excitement or using all caps to indicate yelling). Whenever writers make decisions about their writing, they are making craft moves. The minilessons in the Craft section allow you to focus specifically on the following aspects of craft, which can be applied across a variety of genres:

Organization

This aspect of craft includes the structure of the whole text—the beginning, the arrangement of ideas, and the ending. In CFT.U4: Exploring Different Ways Authors Start Books and CFT.U5: Exploring Different Ways Authors End Books, you lead the children through an inquiry process using mentor texts to discover how they might try different beginnings and endings in their own writing. Children also learn the structure of a friendly letter in CFT.U8: Writing a Friendly Letter and how the structure of poetry is different from other kinds of writing in CFT.U9: Crafting Poetry. In CFT.U7: Adding Text Features to Books, they learn that they can use text features (headings, sidebars, and tables of contents) to organize their information for their readers. All these minilessons help children learn how to organize and arrange their ideas as writers while also contributing to their understandings as readers.

Idea Development

Idea development is how writers present and support their ideas with examples and details. For first graders, this means thinking about the details they can add to describe where their stories take place and what their characters are like. Through the use of mentor texts and shared writing in CFT.U1: Writing with Details, children learn how to add these details and show specific examples for their ideas.

Language Use

This aspect of craft addresses the way writers use sentences, phrases, and expressions to describe events, actions, or information. As your first graders grow in their ability to write words, they can turn more of their attention to using language that sounds like the language in books to describe their ideas. Notice how Julianne used a phrase she learned from reading folktales to start her own story (Figure 7-1). Children also begin to notice how authors use dialogue in speech bubbles and in text. CFT.U2: Adding Dialogue to Writing supports children as they experiment with this new way of using language in their stories.

Word Choice

Word choice matters. A writer's choice of a specific word can change the whole meaning of a sentence. For example, consider the difference between writing *The woman strolled down the road* and *The woman sprinted down*

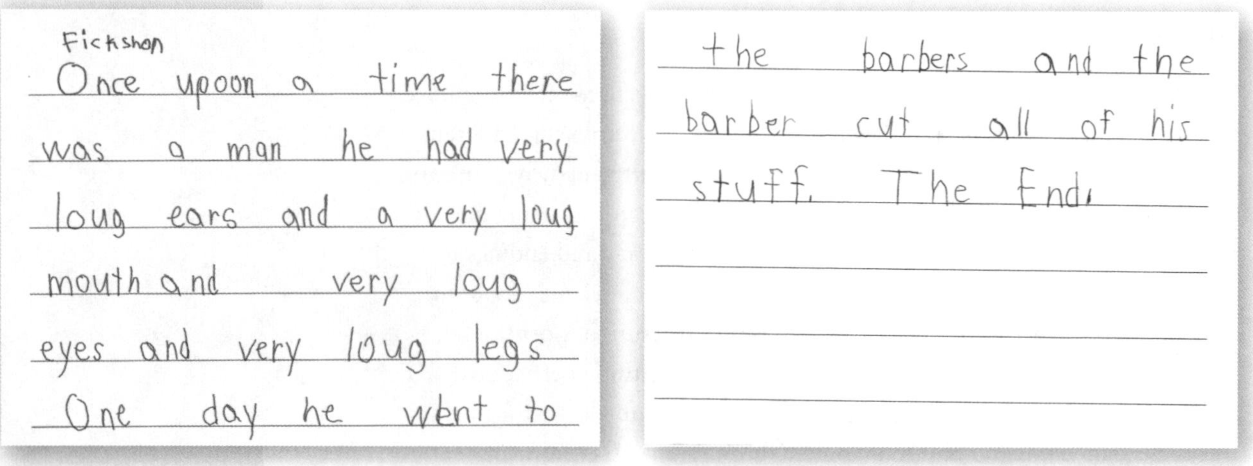

Figure 7-1: Julianne has clearly been inspired to use language she has read in books. She started with a traditional folktale introduction, *Once upon a time.* The repetitive use of the word *long* also resembles the language found in traditional tales.

Fickshon
Once upoon a time there was a man he had very loug ears and a very loug mouth and very loug eyes and very loug legs One day he went to

the barbers and the barber cut all of his stuff. The End.

The Writing Minilessons Book, Grade 1

the road. In the first sentence, we understand that the woman must feel pretty relaxed to be strolling along. The latter conveys much more urgency; we wonder what caused her to hurry. First graders quickly pick up on the importance of word choice once they are taught to pay attention to it. You can begin planting the seeds for this in your interactive read-aloud and shared reading lessons. As you read, linger on a few important words, think aloud about why the author chose them, repeat a word, and simply comment how much you love the author's choice of words. When you heighten children's awareness of how carefully writers choose words, they begin to think about their own word choices (Figure 7-2). One umbrella, CFT.U6: Making Powerful Word Choices, is dedicated to supporting children in taking these early understandings about word choice and applying them to their own writing. Poetry is another powerful place to talk about word choice. In CFT.U9: Crafting Poetry, children learn how to use their senses to help them select descriptive words.

Figure 7-2: Diego wrote a fiction story called *The Lost Day* about a boy named Do who lost his basketball uniform. After searching for and not finding it, Diego wrote *He was disappointed*. Diego's specific word choice shows that he has learned to choose descriptive words to communicate his message: The character is not just sad; he is disappointed.

Voice

It is through the writer's voice that readers get a sense of the author's feelings and passion for a story or topic. Voice is a writer's unique style. The voices of first graders often naturally shine through their writing pieces. They have unique ways of seeing the world, and the way they use their words often conveys this perspective. When children are encouraged to share their feelings in a story or to write the way they talk, they learn important lessons about voice. Voice is also very closely linked to the conventions of writing. When children learn to punctuate their writing with exclamation points, question marks, and even more sophisticated punctuation, their voices become even stronger (Figure 7-3). We will talk about this more as we turn our attention to the Conventions section.

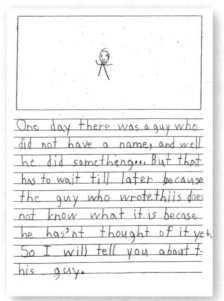

Figure 7-3: The voice of first grader Yosef shines through in this short introduction to his story. He understands that he can use punctuation (ellipses) to create a humorous pause. His voice also comes through as he talks directly to the reader: *So I will tell you about this guy.*

Teaching the Conventions of Writing

Conventions and craft go hand in hand. They work together to communicate meaning. A writer can have great ideas, understand how to organize them, and even make interesting word choices. But the ideas can get lost if the writer doesn't form letters correctly, spell words in recognizable ways, or use conventional grammar and punctuation. For writing to be valued and understood, writers need to understand the conventions of writing. Sophisticated writers might play with these conventions and sometimes break the rules for their use, but they are aware that they are making an intentional decision to do so.

Teaching conventions to first graders can be tricky. Approach it with a spirit of inquiry and discovery. Children are more motivated to use conventions when they see the rewards of others being able to read and understand their writing. Avoid being so rigid in your teaching of conventions that children are afraid to take risks. First graders should celebrate their efforts to spell a new word. How limited and boring their writing would be if they used only the words they knew how to spell! The minilessons in the Conventions section are designed to strike a balance between teaching children to write clearly while making them comfortable to take risks with their new learning. The minilessons in this section are based on the behaviors and understandings in the Conventions section of the grade 1 Writing continuum in *The Literacy Continuum*; however, just like craft, the conventions of writing are not limited to this section. There are aspects of conventions woven into the interactive writing lessons, Making Books minilessons, Craft minilessons, and Writing Process minilessons. The Conventions section, in conjunction with these other sections, address the following conventions of writing:

Text Layout

For first graders, text layout might mean making sure that there is space between their words and that they are writing left to right on a line (see CNV.U1: Using Good Handwriting). In interactive writing, you can introduce children to the idea that they can change the size of the print or use bold print or underlining to convey meaning. Learning about text layout also means learning about where to place print and pictures on a page, including placement of headings and titles. When you introduce a variety of paper templates (available in the online resources) that show a variety of ways to lay out a page, you teach them that writers make important choices about where they place print and pictures.

Grammar and Usage

For first graders, grammar and usage are best taught in the context of writing. For example, children experience how to use past, present, and future tenses as they participate in shared and interactive writing. They learn how to use adjectives, adverbs, prepositions, and conjunctions in the act of writing. The more children are engaged in writing and translating their talk into writing, the more experience they will have in using grammar. In later grades, they will more explicitly learn about the rules of grammar. For now, they learn and internalize the conventions of grammar as they read, talk, and write.

Capitalization

In many cases, first graders are still figuring out the difference between upper- and lowercase letters. The first minilesson in CNV.U5: Using Capital Letters supports children in noticing this difference. They also learn that capital letters are used for names, titles, and the first word in a sentence.

Punctuation

First graders learn that punctuation makes their writing readable for others. CNV.U4: Learning About Punctuation helps children understand that punctuation also communicates how the reader should read the sentence (e.g., an exclamation point indicates excitement or surprise). This beginning understanding of the role of punctuation provides a foundation for children to see punctuation as a way to craft their messages. Writers communicate voice with punctuation. They communicate emotions—excitement, fear, sadness, confusion. Punctuation is inextricably linked with the craft of writing. When first graders learn the conventions of punctuation, they begin to notice how authors use it in their books. They notice that Piggie is worried when Mo Willems places an exclamation point at the end of a sentence. They know Elephant is confused when there is just one question mark in a speech bubble. Writing minilessons make children curious about what writers do and eager to imitate what they notice in their own writing.

Spelling

As first graders acquire knowledge of letters, sounds, and words, they use a combination of approximated spelling and conventional spelling in their writing. Encourage children to write the words they know quickly and accurately and to use a range of strategies to make their best attempts at words they do not know. In CNV.U2: Learning How to Write Words, children learn to say words slowly and listen for all the sounds. They learn to break words into syllables to write them, to include a vowel in every word, and to use what they know about words to help them spell other words. Through CNV.U3: Using Classroom Resources to Write Words, children learn how to use the name chart, ABC chart, word wall, and their own personal word lists to generate the spelling of new words. Each of these minilessons is intended to be generative so children can apply the principles to writing words they do not yet know how to spell.

These minilessons should accompany a strong phonics, spelling, and word study component in your classroom. The two umbrellas on spelling in the Conventions section are not meant to be your students' only instruction in spelling. They are meant to reinforce and supplement what you are teaching in your phonics, spelling, and word study instruction and help children transfer what they are learning to their writing. It is also important to recognize the role of interactive writing in supporting first graders in learning how to write words. Each time you ask children to share the pen, you help them to think about the connections between letters and sounds and bring them directly into the process of constructing words using the strategies explicitly taught in these two writing minilesson umbrellas. The Conventions minilessons, interactive writing lessons, and phonics, spelling, and word study lessons you teach all work together to bring children closer to spelling conventionally and making their writing clear to their readers.

Handwriting and Word Processing

Besides being important for legibility, effective handwriting also increases writing fluency so the writer can give more attention to the message and less attention to the mechanics of writing. The minilessons in CNV.U1: Using Good Handwriting support children in developing writing fluency. These lessons, particularly WML3, are generative and can be used to introduce how to write different letters in the alphabet. In this umbrella, as well as in most interactive writing lessons, we use specific language for how to form letters. The language comes from a resource called Verbal Path for Letter Formation (Figure 7-4), which is available in the online resources. When you consistently use the same direction words, you help children internalize the directions and support early attempts at letter formation.

You can also find an online resource that shows with numbered arrows the strokes for writing each letter. Consider including this resource in your children's writing folders as a reference

Figure 7-4: Use the language of the Verbal Path for Letter Formation consistently to support children in making letters.

Verbal Path for Letter Formation

Sometimes it helps children to say aloud the directions for "making" a letter. This "verbal path" helps them to understand the directional movement that is essential. In addition, it gives the teacher and child a language to talk through the letter and its features. Here, we suggest language for creating a verbal path to the distinctive features of letters.

Lowercase Letter Formation

a — pull back, around, up, and down	n — pull down, up, over, and down
b — pull down, up, around	o — pull back and around
c — pull back and around	p — pull down, up, and around
d — pull back, around, up, and down	q — pull back, around, up, and down
e — pull across, back, and around	r — pull down, up, and over
f — pull back, down, and cross	s — pull back, in, around, and back around
g — pull back, around, up, down, and under	t — pull down and cross
h — pull down, up, over, and down	u — pull down, around, up, and down
i — pull down, dot	v — slant down, up
j — pull down, curve around, dot	w — slant down, up, down, up
k — pull down, pull in, pull out	x — slant down, slant down
l — pull down	y — slant in, slant, and down
m — pull down, up, over, down and up, over, and down	z — across, slant down, across

Verbal Path for Letter Formation: Lowercase Page 1

(Figure 7-5). These minilessons are not intended to replace any handwriting curriculum you already have in place. Feel free to modify these minilessons so they are consistent with the handwriting curriculum you use. Avoid confusing children with conflicting ways of cueing the formation of letters. The paper choices available in online resources provide lines with dashes to support children in their letter formation, but feel free to use the paper templates that are consistent with your school's handwriting program.

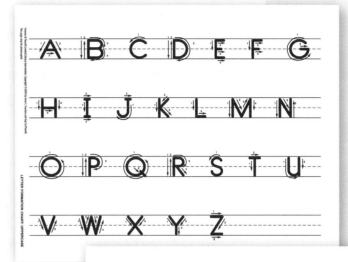

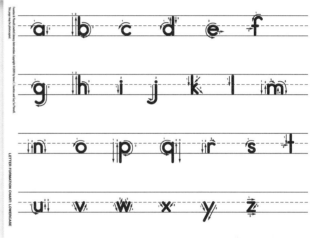

Children will also need to learn keyboarding skills to increase their writing fluency. One way to support children's development of keyboarding skills is to on occasion offer the option of "publishing" a piece of writing on a computer. Figure 7-6 shows a book that has been "published" on the computer. Unlike most of the other published pieces in this first-grade classroom, the teacher and student worked together to polish the piece of writing. In most other cases, published pieces have been edited but are not perfect. They reflect the child's current

We put the cap of the box back on. The box was from the waterfall. We took a picture of it! My dad said, "Let's take a picture!" I said, "Cheese!"

My family ate outside after we finished putting the waterfall away.

Figure 7-5: Use the online resources Letter Formation Chart: Uppercase and Letter Formation Chart: Lowercase to demonstrate how to form letters efficiently.

Figure 7-6: On occasion, first graders can type their writing as one way to "publish" their pieces. You can help them make important decisions about where to place their writing and pictures on a page.

understandings. Mrs. M. offers the chance to publish on the computer a couple of times a year and places the published books in her classroom library. In the next section on the writing process, we discuss other ways you might choose to publish a text.

Engaging Children in the Writing Process

After children have experimented with making books, use Writing Process umbrellas to emphasize that when authors make books, they make important decisions and sometimes change those decisions to improve their books. These umbrellas introduce children to the phases of the writing process, described in detail in chapter 2 (pp. 25–28). They are based on the behaviors and understandings in the Writing Process section of the grade 1 Writing continuum in *The Literacy Continuum*. The umbrellas in the Writing Process section specifically introduce children to

- getting ideas for their writing,

- choosing their purpose, audience, and genre (i.e., the kind of writing they want to do)

- making their writing interesting,

- adding, reorganizing, and deleting writing to make it more focused, organized and interesting,

- proofreading for spacing, proper letter formation, and spelling of known words to make their writing clearer for readers, and

- celebrating their writing by making their books ready for others to read, publishing them in a variety of formats, and sharing risks they have taken in their writing.

So many things contribute to young children's development in writing. When you surround children with literacy activities and print, provide them with time to write, encourage their efforts with enthusiasm, and gently guide them through writing minilessons, you create the right conditions for first graders to grow into confident, engaged writers. With a choice of interactive writing lessons and seven types of writing minilessons, how do you decide which lesson to teach when? Most of your decisions will be based on your observations of the children. What do you see them doing on their own? What might they be able to do with your help? What are they ready to learn? Chapter 8 offers guidance and support for making those decisions.

Chapter 8

Putting Minilessons into Action: Assessing and Planning

With assessment, you learn what students know; the literacy continuum will help you think about what they need to know next.

—Irene Fountas and Gay Su Pinnell

THE INTERACTIVE WRITING LESSONS AND writing minilessons are examples of teaching that address the specific behaviors and understandings to notice, teach for, and support in *The Literacy Continuum* (Fountas and Pinnell 2017). Goals for each lesson are drawn from the sections on Writing; Writing About Reading; Phonics, Spelling, and Word Study; and Oral and Visual Communication. Taken together, the goals provide a comprehensive vision of what children need to become aware of, understand, and apply to their own literacy and learning about writing. Each lesson lists Continuum Connections, which are the exact behaviors from *The Literacy Continuum* that are addressed in the lesson.

Figure 8-1 provides an overview of the processes that take place when a proficient writer creates a text and represents what children will work toward across the years. Writers must decide the purpose of their text, their audience, and their message. They think about the kind of writing that will help them communicate the message (e.g., functional writing such as a list or a letter). They make important craft decisions, such as how to organize the piece, what words to use, and how they want the writing to sound. While keeping the message in their heads, writers must also consider the conventions of writing, such as letter formation, capitalization, punctuation, and grammar. They work through a writing process from planning and rehearsing to publishing. All lessons in this book are directed to helping writers expand their processing systems as they write increasingly complex texts.

Figure 8-1: The writing wheel diagram, shown full size on the inside back cover, illustrates how the writing process encompasses all aspects of writing.

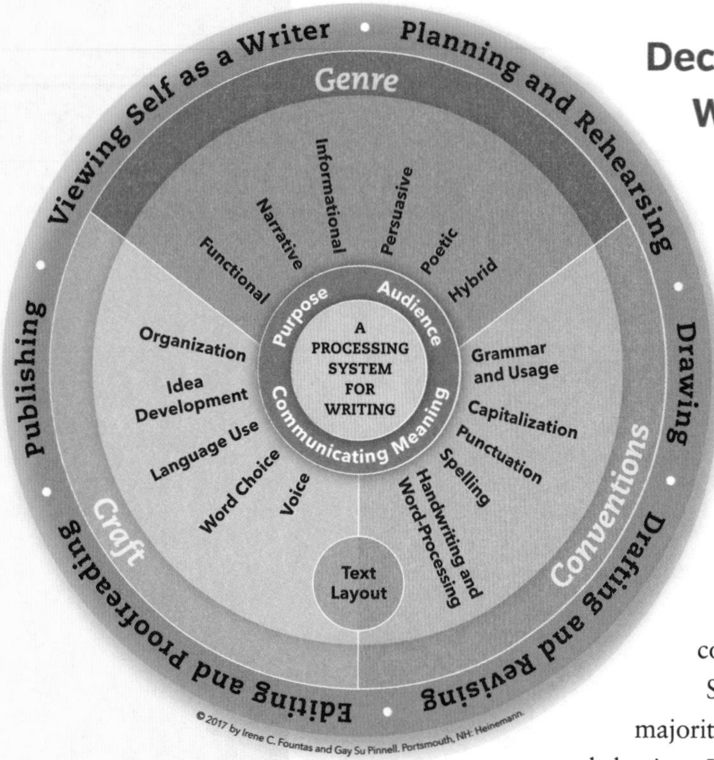

Decide Which Interactive Writing Lessons and Writing Minilessons to Teach

You are welcome to follow the Suggested Sequence of Lessons (discussed later in this chapter and located in the appendix). However, first look at the children in front of you. Teach within what Vygotsky (1979) called the "zone of proximal development"— the zone between what the children can do independently and what they can do with the support of a more expert other (Figure 8-2). Teach on the cutting edge of children's competencies.

Select minilessons based on what you notice the majority of your class needs to learn to develop writing behaviors. Here are some suggestions and tools to help you think about the children in your classroom, the main resource being *The Literacy Continuum* (Fountas and Pinnell 2017):

▶ **Use the Writing continuum** to observe how children are thinking, talking, and writing/drawing. Think about what they can already do, almost do, and not yet do to select the emphasis for your teaching. Think about the ways you have noticed children experimenting with drawing and bookmaking. Observe children's contributions and participation during interactive writing lessons and writing minilessons. Use the Writing Process section to assess how children are developing their own independent writing process.

- Are they volunteering ideas when you talk about what to write?

- Do they demonstrate confidence in trying to write part of a word on the chart when invited during interactive writing?

- How are children applying some of the things they are learning during writing minilessons to independent writing?

The Writing Minilessons Book, Grade 1

The Learning Zone

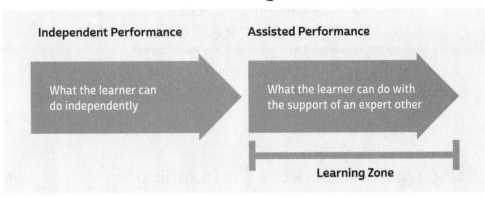

Figure 8-2: Learning zone from *Guided Reading: Responsive Teaching Across the Grades* (Fountas and Pinnell 2017)

◗ **Scan the Writing About Reading continuum** to analyze children's drawing and writing in response to the books you have read aloud. This analysis will help you determine next steps for having them respond to the books and poems you read together.

◗ **Review the Phonics, Spelling, and Word Study continuum** to assess what the children understand about early concepts of print (e.g., understanding the difference between pictures and print, directionality of print, or word boundaries). This section will also help you evaluate children's phonological awareness, letter knowledge, and understanding of how to write words. These insights will help you make important choices about when to invite children to contribute during interactive writing lessons.

◗ **Consult the Oral and Visual Communication continuum** to help you think about some of the routines children might need for better communication between peers, especially as they share their writing with one another. You will find essential listening and speaking competencies to observe and teach for.

◗ **Record informal notes** about the interactions you have while conferring or the interactions you see between children as they write and play during choice time. Look for patterns in these notes to notice trends in children's drawing and writing. Use *The Literacy Continuum* to help you analyze your notes and determine strengths and areas for growth across the classroom. Your observations will reveal what children know and what they need to learn next as they build knowledge about writing over time. Each goal becomes a possible topic for a minilesson. (See Conferring Record 1 and Conferring Record 2 in Figure 4-7.)

◗ **Consult district, state, and/or accreditation standards.** Analyze the suggested skills and areas of knowledge specified in your local and state standards. Align these standards with the minilessons suggested in this book to determine which might be applicable within your classroom.

Chapter 8: Putting Minilessons into Action: Assessing and Planning

■ 101

▶ **Use the Assessment sections** within each lesson and at the end of each umbrella. Take time to assess the children's learning after the completion of each lesson and umbrella. The guiding questions on the last page of each umbrella will help you to determine strengths and next steps for your first graders. Your notes on the online resources shown in the next two sections will also help you make a plan for your teaching.

Use Online Resources for Planning and Teaching

The writing minilessons in this book are examples of how to engage first-grade children in developing the behaviors and understandings of competent writers as described in *The Literacy Continuum*. To help you plan your teaching, use any of the various forms provided in the online resources (resources.fountasandpinnell.com).

The forms shown in Figure 8-3 will help you plan each part of a new interactive writing lesson or writing minilesson. You can design a lesson that uses a different set of example texts from the ones suggested in this book, or

Figure 8-3: Use these downloadable forms to plan your own interactive writing lessons and writing minilessons.

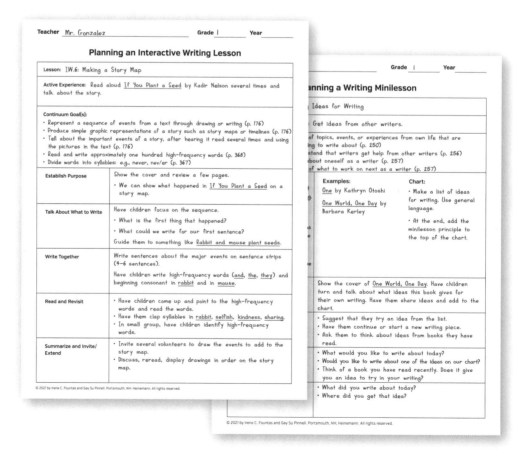

Curriculum Plan: Interactive Writing/Writing Minilessons

Month February	Interactive Writing/Writing Minilessons	Comments/Observations	✓ or Date
Week 1	MBK.U6: Making Question-and-Answer Books WML1: Notice the kinds of questions in question-and-answer books. WML3: Write different questions for your topic. WML4: Find answers to questions you don't know.	They enjoyed adding punctuation. Work with Bibishan, Carola, and David in small groups to distinguish "." from "?". 2/7: Skipped WML2. They are very interested in using internet for research. Set aside more time to assist and have Mrs. R. work with individuals.	
Week 2	WML5: Write a question-and-answer book. DRW.U5: Making Pictures Interesting WML1: Make your book fun to read. WML2: Use found objects to create art for books.	2/10: Teach CNV.U2 (say words slowly to listen for sounds) to Lilly, Abdul, and Ethan in guided writing group to assist with question-and-answer books. 2/12: Skipped WML3. Art teacher did collage. Children enjoyed the found objects.	
Week 3	WPS.U1: Thinking About Purpose and Audience WML1: Think about your purpose. WML2: Think about your audience. WML3: Think about the kind of writing you want to do. IW.16: Making a Shopping List	2/19: Meet with Marco, Reid, and Izzy to help them decide what type of writing to do. 2/20: Children loved IW.16. They want to make their own shopping lists.	
Week 4	CFT.U4: Exploring Different Ways Authors Start Books. WML1: Start your book with talking. WML2: Start your book with a feeling. WML5: Start your book with an interesting fact.	2/27: Skipped WML3 for now. Will do later. Skipped WML4 (children frequently begin with a question already).	

Figure 8-4: Use this downloadable form to make notes about specific interactive writing lessons and writing minilessons for future planning.

you can teach a concept in a way that fits the current needs of the children. The form shown in Figure 8-4 will help you plan which lessons to teach over a period of time to address the goals that are important for the children.

The minilessons are here for you to teach according to the instructional needs of your class. Do not be concerned if you do not use them all within the year. Record or check off the lessons you have taught so that you can reflect on the work of the semester and year. You can do this with the Interactive Writing and Writing Minilessons Record (Figure 8-5).

Meet Children's Needs and Build on Their Strengths

If you are new to interactive writing and writing minilessons, you may want to adhere closely to the suggested sequence, but remember to use the lessons flexibly to meet the needs of the children you teach and to build upon their strengths. Base your decisions about when or whether to use certain lessons on what you notice that children can already do, almost do, and not yet do.

Figure 8-5: Interactive Writing and Writing Minilessons Record for Grade 1

Interactive Writing and Writing Minilessons Record for Grade 1

Interactive Writing Lesson Number	Lesson Title	Notes	✓ or Date
	SECTION 1: INTERACTIVE WRITING		
IW.1	Making a Name Chart	IW.1: Use IW to make a job chart. Use name chart as a reference for name cards.	9/4
IW.2	Writing About Our Classroom		9/11
IW.3	Labeling the Classroom		9/9
IW.4	Writing from a Picture	IW.4: They loved this! Repeat in small groups with photos from this week's field trip.	10/7
IW.5	Innovating on a Rhyming Text		9/18
IW.6	Making a Story Map	IW.6: Nova, Yosef, Carola, Liam want to draw the events on paper. When they finish, have it available so others can read it.	10/1
IW.7	Writing About Who We Are		10/15
IW.8	Writing a Memory Story	IW.8 Use as a mentor text for MBK.3: Making Memory Books.	10/23
IW.9	Studying an Author's Writing		10/30
IW.10	Writing with Speech Bubbles	IW.10 Work with Izzy, Reid, and Lan in a guided writing group. Focus on high-frequency words.	1/4
IW.11	Labeling a Map		1/18
IW.12	Writing Interview Questions		1/25
IW.13	Making Kindness Signs	IW.13 Children will work with art teacher to make kindness signs for around the school.	12/10
IW.14	Writing an All-About Book		1/14
IW.15	Writing a Question-and-Answer Book		2/3
IW.16	Making a Shopping List	IW.16 Engaging. Children want to draw items and make their own shopping lists.	2/20

▶ Omit lessons that you think are not necessary.

▶ Repeat lessons that you think need more time and instructional attention. Or, repeat lessons using different examples for a particularly rich experience.

▶ Move lessons around to be consistent with the curriculum that is adopted in your school or district.

Consider using the analysis tool in Figure 8-6 along with *The Literacy Continuum* after you have taught the minilessons in a few umbrellas. We suggest using this tool, or one of the other assessment tools offered in the online resources, to focus on one or two pieces of a student's writing. Set aside time to analyze the writing of five students a day. By the end of the week, you will have a snapshot of what the children understand and what they do not yet understand. Use Guide to Observing and Noting Writing Behaviors (Figure 8-7) quarterly as an interim assessment. This observation form comes in two versions, one for individuals and one for the whole class.

Analyzing Student Writing for Planning

Use *The Literacy Continuum* and the Assessment section at the end of each umbrella you have taught to analyze a student's writing for evidence of writing behaviors and understandings.

Name: Xavier   Grade: 1   Genre: Memory Story   Date: 1/24

Umbrellas Taught: MBK.U4: Making Memory Books, CNV.U5: Using Capital Letters, DRW.U2: Learning to Draw

	Strengths	Next Steps	Plan (IW, WML, GW, IC)
Genre	• Tells a personally meaningful story. • Tells a story in a sequence. • Pictures and writing match.	• Review how writers add feelings to their stories.	• GW: Bring together Habso, Talib, Linus, Alejandra, and Xavier to review adding feelings to writing.
Craft	• Uses speech bubbles. • Presents ideas clearly—beginning, middle, and end. • Drawings have details and show movement.	• Work on expanding details about setting and characters. • Spend time telling stories orally. • Show how to include dialogue in a story.	• WML: Teach CFT.U1: Writing with Details to whole class. • IC: Show how to include dialogue in his writing.
Conventions	• Uses capitals and periods in sentences. • Says words slowly to listen for sounds. • Has several simple high-frequency words in control: I, my, on, the, was, to, a.	• Talk about different ways to punctuate a sentence. • Needs to learn how to use known words to write unknown words.	• GW: Meet with Xavier, Joe, Ari, Melissa, and Sam to review using known words to write other words. • WML: Address punctuation later CNV. U4: Learning About Punctuation.
Writing Process	• Gets ideas from his life experiences. • Revised last page to make clearer (erasure marks). • Added speech bubbles.	• Remind him to cross out instead of erasing.	• IC: Talk about crossing out vs. erasing.

IW: Interactive Writing   WML: Writing Minilesson   GW:

© 2021 by Irene C. Fountas and Gay Su Pinnell. Portsmouth, NH: Heinemann. All rights reserved.

Guide to Observing and Noting Writing Behaviors—Individual Student
Grade 1

Student:

Behaviors

Genre

Make

Writ... ques...

Writ...

Make

Writ...

Expe...

Craft

Writ...

Tell...

Writ... stor...

Writ...

Desc...

Desc...

Com...

Inclu...

Use...

Add...

Add...

© 2021

Guide to Observing and Noting Writing Behaviors—Whole Class
Grade 1

Date: 1/17

Write students' names/initials and the date when each student consistently demonstrates this behavior.
Use this form quarterly if possible to assess your entire class.

Behaviors and Understandings	Mari	Elvio	Carine	Aaeesha	Ellie	Aayan	Akira	Elijah	Mark	Omar
Genre										
Make picture books (with pictures and/or words)	11/14	11/14	11/14	11/14	11/14	11/14	11/14	11/14	11/14	11/14
Write a variety of information books (all-about books, question-answer books)										
Write books to teach how to do something (how-to books)										
Make memory books	1/17	1/17	1/17	1/17	1/17	1/17	1/17	1/17	1/17	1/17
Write a simple friendly letter										
Experiment with writing poetry	1/17	11/14	1/17	1/17		11/14	1/17	11/14		1/17
Craft										
Write the author's name and a title on the cover	11/14	11/14	11/14	11/14	11/14	11/14	11/14	11/14	11/14	11/14
Tell stories in first person about own experience	11/14	11/14	11/14	11/14	11/14	11/14	11/14	11/14	11/14	11/14
Write across several pages with all pages related to the same story or topic	11/14	1/17	11/14	11/14	11/14	11/14	11/14	11/14	1/17	11/14
Write a story that has a beginning, a series of events, and an ending	11/14	1/17	11/14	11/14	11/14	11/14	11/14	11/14	1/17	11/14
Describe where a story takes place	11/14			11/14			11/14			
Describe the characters or people in a story	11/14	1/17		1/17	1/17	1/17	1/17			1/17
Communicate the main points intended for readers to understand	11/14	1/17	11/14	1/17	1/17	1/17	1/17	11/14		1/17
Include facts and details in information writing				1/17	1/17	1/17	1/17	1/17	1/17	1/17
Use pictures and words to show feelings	11/14	1/17	11/14	11/14	11/14	11/14	11/14	11/14	1/17	11/14
Add speech and thought bubbles	11/14	1/17	11/14	1/17	11/14	1/17	11/14	1/17	11/14	1/17
Add dialogue to a story	1/17						1/17			

The Writing Minilessons Book, Grade 1 **Page 1**

Patterns and trends across students' writing will help you plan what to address through whole-group minilessons, small-group guided writing lessons, or individual conferences. Not only will this allow you to be responsive in your teaching, but it will also give you a sense of how to build upon each student's strengths. Consult the Suggested Sequence of Lessons when necessary to decide if you want to wait to teach a particular umbrella, but don't be afraid to be responsive to your learners. You can always repeat or skip lessons if you have decided to teach them before they come up in the sequence.

Understand the Suggested Sequence of Lessons

The Suggested Sequence of Lessons (pp. 555–571 and also in online resources) is intended to establish a strong classroom community early in the year, work toward more sophisticated concepts across the year, and bring together the instructional pieces of your classroom. The learning that takes place during interactive writing lessons and writing minilessons is applied in many situations in the classroom and so is reinforced daily across the curriculum and across the year.

Because many interactive writing lessons and writing minilessons use mentor texts as a starting point, the lessons are sequenced so that they occur after children have had sufficient opportunities to build some clear understandings of aspects of writing through interactive read-aloud, shared reading, interactive writing, and shared writing. From these experiences, you and the children will have a rich set of mentor texts to pull into writing minilessons.

The Suggested Sequence of Lessons follows the suggested sequence of text sets in *Fountas & Pinnell Classroom™ Interactive Read-Aloud Collection* (2018) and books in *Shared Reading Collection* (2018). If you are using either or both of these collections, you are invited to follow this sequence of texts. If you are not using them, the kinds of books children will need to have read are described on the first page of each umbrella (for the writing minilessons) and in Active Learning Experience (for the interactive writing lessons). Figure 3-12 shows how the text sets in *Fountas & Pinnell Classroom™ Interactive Read-Aloud Collection* connect to and support the interactive writing lessons.

The text sets in the *Interactive Read-Aloud Collection* are grouped together by theme, topic, author, or genre, not by skill or concept. That's why in many minilessons, we use mentor texts from several different text sets and why the same books are used in more than one umbrella.

We have selected the most concrete and clear examples from the recommended books. In most cases, the minilessons draw on mentor texts that have been introduced within the same month. However, in some cases, minilessons taught later in the year might draw on books you read much earlier in the year. Most of the time, children will have no problem remembering these early books because you have read and talked about them. Sometimes children have responded through art, dramatic play, or writing. Once in a while, you might need to quickly reread a book or a portion of it before teaching the umbrella so it is fresh in the children's minds, but this is not usually necessary. Looking at pictures and talking about the book is enough.

In many cases, writing minilessons use pieces you have written with the children during interactive writing lessons. It is very supportive for children to experience an interactive writing lesson about a particular type of writing before they experience specific writing minilessons because they will have more context for understanding.

Use the Suggested Sequence to Connect the Pieces

To understand how the Suggested Sequence of Lessons can help you bring these instructional pieces together, let's look at a brief example from the suggested sequence. In month 5, we suggest reading the text set Exploring Nonfiction from the *Interactive Read-Aloud Collection*. In reading minilessons, children are engaged in studying the characteristics of nonfiction text. One of the suggestions for extending learning after the Exploring Nonfiction text set is to do research on a topic of interest and then write about it. (You do not need any specific books in this text set; use any set of nonfiction books available.) In IW.14: Writing an All-About Book, the class uses what they have learned about sharks to make an all-about book with facts about sharks on each page. Later, the class-made all-about book—along with books from the *Interactive Read-Aloud Collection* and *Shared Reading Collection*—becomes a mentor text in MBK.U5: Making All-About Books. These mentor texts help children learn specific understandings about making an all-about book, such as writing about the same topic on every page, learning to put information in your own words, and thinking about how to get your readers interested in your topic (Figure 8-8).

By the time this umbrella appears in the sequence, children will have already had lots of experience making books through some of the other umbrellas in Section 4: Making Books (e.g., MBK.U1: Getting Started with Making Books and MBK.U2: Expanding Bookmaking) and will be ready to experiment with this new kind of writing during independent writing.

Interactive read-aloud and shared/interactive writing experiences give children the background that helps them go deeper when they experience minilessons on specific topics. They are able to draw on their previous

Connecting All the Pieces

Read aloud and enjoy a nonfiction text set with the children.

Use interactive writing to make a class nonfiction all-about book.

Teach writing minilessons on specific aspects of all-about books.

Have children make their own all-about books.

Figure 8-8: The Suggested Sequence of Lessons helps you connect all the pieces of your classroom instruction and leads to children's own independent writing.

experiences with texts to fully understand the concepts in the minilessons. They can then apply this learning to their own independent writing and bookmaking. The Suggested Sequence of Lessons is one way to organize your teaching across the year to make these connections.

Add Interactive Writing Lessons and Writing Minilessons to the Day in Grade 1

After deciding what to teach and in what order to teach it, the next decision is when. In *Fountas & Pinnell Classroom™ System Guide, Grade 1* (2018), you will find frameworks for teaching and learning across a day. Using those schedules and the information in this book as guides, think about when you might incorporate interactive writing lessons and writing minilessons as a regular part of the day in first grade. One suggestion is to provide a dedicated time each day for independent writing, which begins with a writing minilesson and ends with a share (Figure 1-6). Interactive writing can take place at any time of the day. Ideally, we recommend carving out a dedicated time each day for interactive writing, but if you are short on time, consider substituting interactive writing for a writing minilesson on certain days.

First graders thrive on structure, organization, and predictability. When you set routines and a consistent time for interactive writing and writing minilessons, you teach children what to expect. They find comfort in the reliability of the structure. Children write joyfully when they know they can count on time to experiment with and explore drawing and writing. They delight in knowing that what they have to say is valued. Interactive writing lessons and writing minilessons are opportunities to build on the joy and enthusiasm children bring to all that they do in the classroom setting.

November 12

Dear Bunnies,
We know that you are upset
but you can still do many fun things.
You can have a dance party or play with
your toys. You can also draw a beautiful
picture. We hope you have
snow day!
Love,
1DLP

INTERACTIVE WRITING ALLOWS children the opportunity to experience what it's like to be a writer before they become proficient writers themselves. With interactive writing, you are the guide. You guide the children as they think about what to write and help them express their ideas in language. Then you write together, sharing the pen wth the children at selected points of learning value. The lessons in this section offer examples of the kinds of writing you and the children can do together. Each sample lesson is structured to take you and the children through the process of interactive writing.

1 Interactive Writing

You Will Need

- a name card for every child
- chart paper or a large piece of card stock
- red and black markers
- long, thin pointer
- To download the following online resource for this lesson, visit **resources.fountasandpinnell.com**:
  - Verbal Path for Letter Formation

Academic Language/ Important Vocabulary

- name
- letter
- first
- last
- capital

Continuum Connection

- Use a capital letter at the beginning of a familiar proper noun (p. 255)
- Recognize and talk about the sequence of letters in a word (p. 367)
- Understand and talk about the concept of a word (p. 367)
- Understand and talk about the fact that words are formed with letters (p. 367)

ACTIVE LEARNING EXPERIENCE

- Prior to the lesson, make a card for each child with the first letter in each name written large enough so that children can glue tissue paper onto it. Invite children to write the remaining letters in their names themselves. Place the cards in alphabetical order.

GOALS

- Understand that a word is made up of distinct letters.
- Recognize one's name.
- Use a capital letter at the beginning of one's name.

RATIONALE

- When children learn to look at print, they start to recognize words that are important to them, like their names or letters and letter sequences in their names. Some may even recognize classmates' names. Comparing a specific aspect of a familiar word—such as a name—with that aspect of other names and words helps children understand that they can use their knowledge to organize how they look at words.

ASSESS LEARNING

- Notice if children understand that words are formed with letters.
- Notice if children can recognize their names and are using a capital letter at the beginning of their names.

INTERACTIVE WRITING LESSON

We recommend that you write the names on the name chart so that the letters are legible enough to be used as a resource for children to see how their names look and to learn to recognize letters within a word.

Establish Purpose

Refer to the children's name cards (see Active Learning Experience).

> Your name is a word, and a word is made up of letters. Today we are going to make a name chart so that you can see how your name looks and how your friends' names look. I'll write each name with a capital letter at the beginning.

Talk About What to Write

Talk about what you will write on the name chart.

- Point to the child whose name comes first in alphabetical order.

> Who is this? Yes, this is Aisha. Clap Aisha's name with me.

> The first letter in Aisha's name is *A*. *A* is the first letter in the alphabet, so *Aisha* will be the first name we put on our name chart.

Write Together

Make a name chart.

▶ Write *Aisha* on the chart, using red for the first letter and black for the remaining letters. Invite Aisha to trace the letter *A* with her pointer finger while the other children write the letter in the air following the Verbal Path for Letter Formation.

> Slant down, slant down, across.

> Point under your name, Aisha, and we will all read it together.

▶ Continue this process in alphabetical order. This may be extended to another day depending upon the number of children in the classroom.

Read and Revisit

Read the names with the children as you point under them. You might have children revisit the name chart for one or more of the following reasons.

▶ Invite children to observe that some of the names begin with the same letter. Draw a line around the names that begin with the same letter.

▶ Invite children to point to the first and last letters in their names.

▶ Invite children to observe the same letter in more than one name and in more than one position.

▶ Invite children to count the letters in their names.

Summarize and Invite/Extend

Summarize the lesson. You might also decide to extend the learning.

> You can look at the name chart to know how to write your name and the names of your friends. Remember that a name begins with a capital letter.

▶ Display the name chart near the meeting area so that you and the children can use it whenever you do shared or interactive writing.

▶ Provide plenty of opportunities for children to work with their names (e.g., match a name card to the name chart, use a finger to trace the first letter, find names in other places in the room).

▶ Use interactive writing to create a job chart with the children. They can refer to the name chart to make name cards to insert next to the jobs.

Aisha	Isaac
Alejandra	Jayden
Ben	Jordan
Carmen	Kate
Chris	Malik
Daniella	Marla
Eliza	Michael
George	Mr. Saunders
Gretchen	Sanjay
Hadley	Sarah
	Zane

You Will Need

- familiar books about school, such as the following from *Fountas & Pinnell Classroom™ Interactive Read-Aloud Collection* Text Set: Learning and Working Together: School:
  - *Elizabeti's School* by Stephanie Stuve-Bodeen
  - *David's Drawings* by Cathryn Falwell
  - *First Day Jitters* by Julie Danneberg
  - *Jamaica's Blue Marker* by Juanita Havill
- chart paper and markers
- To download the following online resources for this lesson, visit **resources.fountasandpinnell.com**:
  - Alphabet Linking Chart
  - Verbal Path for Letter Formation
  - chart art (optional)

Academic Language / Important Vocabulary

- classroom
- community
- letter
- word
- period
- sentence

Continuum Connection

- Draw and write for a specific purpose (p. 255)
- Recognize and point to the distinctive features of letter forms (p. 367)
- Hear, say, and clap syllables: e.g., *farm, be/fore, an/i/mal* (p. 367)
- Recognize and use high-frequency words with one, two, or three letters: e.g., *a, I, in, is, of, to, and, the* (p. 368)

ACTIVE LEARNING EXPERIENCE

- Prior to the lesson, read and discuss books about school, such as those from Text Set: Learning and Working Together: School. Teach MGT.U1: Working Together in the Classroom. Then talk with children about how they can help each other learn and work together well in the classroom community.

GOALS

- Understand that writing has a purpose.
- Recognize and point to distinctive features of letters.
- Recognize and use high-frequency words with one, two, or three letters.

RATIONALE

- When children work together to write about a positive classroom community, they learn that writing has an authentic purpose. Because they are active participants in creating the text and sentences are reread while writing, they will be interested in reading it and take ownership over the content.

ASSESS LEARNING

- Notice whether each child takes part in writing about an ideal classroom community.
- Observe whether children can identify some features of letters.
- Notice whether children can recognize and use some high-frequency words.

INTERACTIVE WRITING LESSON

This lesson is designed as an interactive writing lesson. Alternatively, you might choose to do all the writing yourself (shared writing). Keep the completed class agreement displayed so children can refer to it often.

Establish Purpose

Show the covers of the books about school you have read aloud.

> Think about the books we have read and the ways we have worked and learned together in the classroom. What can you do to make our classroom community a good place for all of us to work and learn together?
>
> Together, we can write about our classroom community.

Talk About What to Write

Talk about and plan what to write about the classroom community.

> What is one thing you can do to help your classmates and to make the classroom community a good place to learn together?

- Ask several children for suggestions. Guide the conversation as needed.

Write Together

Write a title and text describing a classroom learning community. While one child shares the pen, engage others by having them make the letter in the air or on the carpet in front of them.

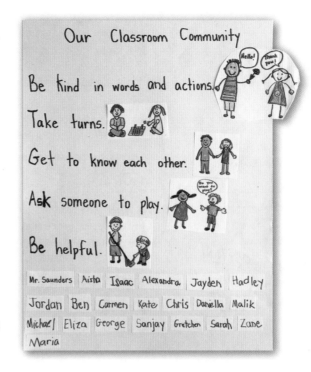

) Write *Be*. Point under the word as you read it with children to help them anticipate the next word. Invite a child to write *k*.

> The next word is *kind*. Say *kind* with me. Listen for the first sound. What sound do you hear?

> The first sound is /k/. The letter that goes with that sound is *k*.

) Point to the letter *k* on the ABC chart.

) Write *ind* and the rest of the sentence. Pause before the word *and*.

> The next word is *and,* which is a word you know. Who can write *and* quickly?

> What goes at the end of the sentence to show that the sentence is finished?

) Finish writing the sentence and then reread it together.

) Repeat the process of composing and writing several more sentences. Invite two or three more children to add letters for easy-to-hear sounds at the beginning or end of words, such as the *T* in *Take*, the *G* in *Get*, or the *k* in *Ask*.

Read and Revisit

Ask the children to read Our Classroom Community with you as you point under each word. You might have children revisit the text for one or more of the following reasons.

) Invite children to identify features of letters (e.g., tall/short, round/straight, pointed).

) Have the children say and clap syllables in two-syllable words (e.g., *someone*, *helpful*).

Summarize and Invite/Extend

Summarize the lesson. You might also decide to extend the learning.

> Today we talked about how to make our classroom community a good place to learn. Later, we will add our names to show that we all decided on these ideas.

) Use the names on the bottom of the chart to help children practice recognizing their names (e.g., match name cards, find names that have the same letter).

You Will Need

- several book bins from the classroom library
- five blank labels for bins
- markers
- To download the following online resources for this lesson, visit **resources.fountasandpinnell.com**:
  - Alphabet Linking Chart
  - Verbal Path for Letter Formation

Academic Language / Important Vocabulary

- label
- word
- letters
- sound

Continuum Connection

- Say words slowly to hear a sound and write a letter that represents it (p. 255)
- Attempt unknown words through sound analysis (p. 255)
- Attempt unknown words using known word parts and letter-sound knowledge (p. 255)
- Use simple resources to help in spelling words or check on spelling (word walls, personal word lists) (p. 255)

ACTIVE LEARNING EXPERIENCE

- Prior to the lesson, give children ample time to explore the classroom. Point out areas of the classroom and name objects in those areas that you will eventually label (e.g., point out the book bins in the library area).

GOAL

- Understand the purpose of labels.
- Slowly articulate unknown words and record sounds in sequence.

RATIONALE

- When you engage children in writing labels for the classroom, they begin to take ownership for the management of their own print-rich classroom. Labels expose children to writing and reading with purpose, promote letter and word recognition, and offer visual cues to the location of objects.

ASSESS LEARNING

- Observe for evidence that children understand labels.
- Listen to children say words slowly. Can they hear and identify the initial sound?

INTERACTIVE WRITING LESSON

This lesson is designed as an interactive writing lesson in which you and the children will compose the text together and share the pen. Alternatively, you might choose to do all the writing yourself (shared writing).

Establish Purpose

Review what children have learned about the classroom.

> You had a chance to explore the classroom and to see where things are. Today we will write labels for the book bins in our classroom library. The labels will help you choose books to read and know where books belong after you read them.

Talk About What to Write

Plan what to write on the labels. Help children decide on labels for about four book bins.

- Show the contents of a book bin.

  > What label would tell about the books in this bin?

  > Let's write *Weather* on the first label.

Write Together

Write the labels. Invite several children to share the pen. Engage the others by having them try the letter in the air or on the carpet in front of them.

▶ Say the word *Weather*, accentuating the first sound, /w/. Then have children say *Weather* with you.

>**What sound do you hear first in *Weather*?**
>
>***Weather* begins with /w/, and the letter that goes with that sound is *W*. Notice we're starting with a capital letter.**

▶ Invite a child to write the *W* on the label. Together, locate *W* on the ABC chart, name chart, or word wall.

>**To make the letter *W*, slant down, up, down, up.**

▶ Continue to slowly articulate the word and record the remaining letters in sequence. Read the label together slowly while you point under the letters.

▶ Repeat this process for the remaining labels, inviting children to add letters for easy-to-hear consonant sounds, such as *S*, *B*, and *C*. Make connections to the ABC chart, name chart, or word wall. Use the verbal path as necessary to guide letter formation.

▶ If the word has more than one syllable, such as *Colors*, have the children clap the syllables as you write each part separately.

Read and Revisit

Ask the children to read the labels with you as you point under each word. You might have children revisit the labels for one or both of the following reasons.

▶ Point to a word that begins with a certain letter.

▶ Ask one or more children to point to a word on the ABC chart or name chart that begins with the same letter as the word on a label.

Summarize and Invite/Extend

Summarize the lesson. You might also decide to extend the learning.

>**Today we wrote labels for our classroom library. When you do your own writing, remember to say the word slowly and write the letter for the sound you hear.**

▶ Continue labeling items in the classroom library and other areas of the classroom across several days and as new items are added. Have children illustrate the labels.

You Will Need

- a photograph or picture attached to chart paper
- sentence strips
- marker
- long, thin pointer
- To download the following online resources for this lesson, visit **resources.fountasandpinnell.com**:
  - Alphabet Linking Chart
  - Verbal Path for Letter Formation

Academic Language / Important Vocabulary

- picture
- begins
- middle
- end
- space
- sound

Continuum Connection

- Place words in lines, starting left to right, top to bottom (p. 254)
- Attempt unknown words using known word parts and letter-sound knowledge (p. 255)
- Generate ideas or topics for writing (p. 256)
- Recognize and use high-frequency words with one, two, or three letters: e.g., *a, I, in, is, of, to, and, the* (p. 368)
- Recognize and use high-frequency words with three or more letters: e.g., *you, was, for, are, that, with, they, this* (p. 368)

ACTIVE LEARNING EXPERIENCE

- As you read books aloud, support children in noticing how the words tell about what is happening in the pictures. Prior to the lesson, gather photographs, including some taken of class activities. Encourage children to talk about what is happening in the pictures.

GOAL

- Use a picture to generate ideas for writing.
- Identify space between words.
- Say a word slowly to hear sounds in sequence, and write letters for the sounds.
- Recognize and use the high-frequency words *you, was, for, are, that, with, they,* and *this*.

RATIONALE

- A picture is something concrete that children can talk about and write about. The oral rehearsal helps children create meaning through talk and then translate that to print on the page. It also helps them begin to bring depth to their writing.

ASSESS LEARNING

- Notice how actively children talk about what is happening in a picture.
- Notice if children use the name chart and the ABC chart to make connections to other words.
- Observe for evidence that children can write predominant sounds in some words.

INTERACTIVE WRITING LESSON

Use any photograph or picture from which children can generate ideas for writing. You and the children will compose the text together and then share the pen. Alternatively, you might choose to do all the writing yourself (shared writing).

Establish Purpose

Display several picture books you have read with the class.

> A picture can give you ideas for writing. Today we are going to look at a picture together and decide what to write about it.

Talk About What to Write

Talk about the children's ideas to plan what to write about a photograph or picture.

> What do you notice in this picture? Let's talk about that.

> What could we write about that?

- Help the children reframe their thoughts into two or three simple sentences. Have children say the sentences with you while you point to where they will be written.

Write Together

Invite several children to share the pen by writing a letter, a group of letters, or a word. Keep the others engaged by having them look for the letters on the ABC chart, name chart, or word wall.

▶ Repeat the first sentence slowly with the children. Invite a child to write *We*.

> The first word is *We*. It starts with a capital letter because *We* is the first word in the sentence. *We* is a word you know. Let's say the sentence again to hear which word comes next.

▶ Say *saw* and have children say it with you and listen for the first sound.

> What sound do you hear first in *saw*?

▶ Have a child write *s*. Finish writing *saw* and then write *cows*.

▶ Ask a volunteer to write the known words *at the*.

▶ Model how to use known letters and words to spell an unknown word.

> Say *farm* slowly to hear the first sound. What letter comes first in *farm*?

> The next sound rhymes with *car*. I will write it.

> Say *farm* and listen for the last sound. The last sound in *farm* is /m/. Find a word on the name chart or ABC chart that has the same sound.

▶ Have children use the word *the* to write *They*. Supply the *y*. Continue by having children write letters for easy-to-hear sounds such as *gr* and the final *s* in *grass*.

Read and Revisit

Read the sentences with children as you point, using a pointer, under each one. You might have children revisit the text for one or both of the following reasons.

▶ Point to some high-frequency words (*we, at, the, they*).

▶ Point to a word that ends in *ing*.

Summarize and Invite/Extend

Summarize the lesson. You might also decide to extend the learning.

> A picture can give you ideas for something to write about.

▶ Encourage children to talk about further details they could write about.

ACTIVE LEARNING EXPERIENCE

▸ Read and enjoy books with rhythm and rhyme, such as *Mrs. McNosh Hangs Up Her Wash*, enough times that children can read or recite it along with you. Have each child create an animal rhyme drawing in the art center or during art class prior to this activity (e.g., fish on a dish, cat in a hat, poodle eating a noodle). Attach each drawing to a large piece of paper.

GOALS

▸ Hear and generate rhyming words.

▸ Write high-frequency words conventionally.

▸ Say words slowly to hear and record the initial sound.

RATIONALE

▸ When children innovate on a text, they reinforce early concepts of print, such as letter formation, saying words slowly to listen for consonant sounds, and recognizing high-frequency words. For this lesson, the text of the story will be changed slightly to use the pattern _____ *hangs up the* _____, with two new rhyming words inserted at the end.

ASSESS LEARNING

▸ Observe for evidence of children's ability to hear and generate new rhyming words.

▸ Notice whether children can write high-frequency words.

▸ Observe whether children can recognize and write letters for beginning consonant sounds.

INTERACTIVE WRITING LESSON

Tailor the sentence to fit your class, for example, *She hangs up . . .* or *"Your Name" hangs up. . . .* Use the term you prefer, *uppercase* or *capital*. Later, attach the sentence strips to the pictures and hang them on a clothesline.

Establish Purpose

Revisit a rhyming book, such as *Mrs. McNosh Hangs Up Her Wash*.

> Writers can use books as ideas for writing. We can write our own version of *Mrs. McNosh Hangs Up Her Wash* using the animal rhyme drawings you made.

Talk About What to Write

Talk about how to plan a new version of the text.

> _____ drew a dog on a log. Later, I will hang this picture. What could we write that would sound like the book we read?

▸ Guide children to compose a sentence pattern that can be repeated for each picture. Have children repeat the sentences so that they have the pattern in their heads.

Write Together

Begin writing the new text. As one child contributes a word or letter, engage the others by having them use the verbal path, ABC chart, or word wall to write the letters in the air with their fingers.

▶ Say the sentence with children.

> The sentence begins with *She*. *She* is a word you know.

▶ Invite a child to write the word *She*.

> *She* begins with an uppercase *S* because it is at the beginning of the sentence. Write *She* quickly.

▶ Say *hangs* with children to listen for the first sound. Invite a child to write *h*.

> For lowercase *h*, pull down, up, over, and down.

▶ Continue writing the text for each picture. Ask volunteers to contribute a few easy-to-hear consonants and known high-frequency words. Challenge children to write words such as *dog* and *fish* using what they know about *log* and *dish*.

▶ Read each sentence after completion, emphasizing the words that rhyme and pointing back to the drawing it represents. Continue with other pictures and rhymes.

Read and Revisit

Ask the children to read the sentences with you as you point under each word. You might have children revisit the text for one or both of the following reasons.

▶ Have them find *S* and *s*. Talk about how both have the same shape, but one is tall and one is short.

▶ Reread a sentence and ask children to identify the rhyming words. Frame the two words and ask children what they notice.

Summarize and Invite/Extend

Summarize the lesson. You might also decide to extend the learning.

> Today we wrote our own version of a rhyming story by using your animal drawings.

▶ Keep the pictures on the clothesline so children can read around the room. This activity can be added to the work board.

Section 1: Interactive Writing

You Will Need

- a story with a simple plot, such as *The Giant Jam Sandwich* by John Vernon Lord and Janet Burroway, from *Fountas & Pinnell Classroom™ Interactive Read-Aloud Collection* Text Set: Having Fun with Language: Rhyming Texts
- sentence strips
- a large sheet of butcher paper
- marker
- To download the following online resource for this lesson, visit **resources.fountasandpinnell.com**:
  - Verbal Path for Letter Formation

Academic Language/ Important Vocabulary

- story map
- letter
- word
- sentence

Continuum Connection

- Represent a sequence of events from a text through drawing or writing (p. 176)
- Produce simple graphic representations of a story such as story maps or timelines (p. 176)
- Tell about the important events of a story, after hearing it read several times and using the pictures in the text (p. 176)
- Divide words into syllables: e.g., *never, nev/er* (p. 367)
- Read and write approximately one hundred high-frequency words (p. 368)

ACTIVE LEARNING EXPERIENCE

- Prior to the lesson, read a story aloud that has a clear order of events, such as *The Giant Jam Sandwich*. Children should have heard the story more than once and had a chance to discuss it.

GOAL

- Understand that the important events of a story happen in sequential order.
- Hear and say the beginning phoneme in a word.
- Read and write high-frequency words.
- Hear, say, and clap syllables.

RATIONALE

- By participating in making a story map, children begin to understand that the events in a story happen in sequential order. When you help them write about the sequence of events, they learn to say words slowly to listen for the sounds.

ASSESS LEARNING

- Observe the accuracy of children's retellings of the story.
- Notice whether children can write some high-frequency words.

INTERACTIVE WRITING LESSON

This lesson is based on *The Giant Jam Sandwich*, but any story with a clear, sequential plot could be used. Spread the writing across one or two days, depending on the attention span of the children in your class.

Establish Purpose

Briefly revisit *The Giant Jam Sandwich*.

- Show the cover of *The Giant Jam Sandwich* and review a few pages.

  We can show what happened in *The Giant Jam Sandwich* on a story map.

Talk About What to Write

Plan a few sentences to write on the story map.

  Think about what happened in the story. What is the first thing that happened?

  What should we write for our first sentence?

- Have children say the sentence with you so they can anticipate what to write.

Write Together

Write sentences about the major events in the story. Invite several children to share the pen by writing high-frequency words. Engage the others by having them make the words in the air or on the carpet.

- Say each word as you write *Four million wasps flew*.

  What is the next word in our sentence?

  Say and clap *into*. The two parts of *into* are words that you know. Who can write *into*?

- Write the rest of the sentence yourself. Read the sentence together.

- Repeat the process to write two or three more sentences. Invite different volunteers to write high-frequency words such as *the* and *they* or easy-to-hear beginning or ending consonants, such as *t* in *town*, *m* in *made*, or *s* in *sandwich*.

Read and Revisit

Read the sentences on the story map with the children. You might have them revisit the story map for one or both of the following reasons.

- Invite the children who wrote words to point to and read the words they wrote.

- Invite the children to clap the syllables in multisyllable words, such as *into*, *million*, *villagers*, and *sandwich*.

Summarize and Invite/Extend

Summarize the lesson. You might also decide to extend the learning.

  Today we made a story map for *The Giant Jam Sandwich*. You can use the story map to tell the story.

- Distribute drawing paper and crayons. Review the events on the story map and assign two or more children to draw each of the events. When the drawings are finished, read the story map with children so that the pictures can be placed in the right order.

- Make the completed story map available for children to read on their own.

You Will Need

- children's self-portraits (see Active Learning Experience)
- paper for making a big book
- markers
- long, thin pointer
- To download the following online resources for this lesson, visit **resources.fountasandpinnell.com**:
  - Alphabet Linking Chart
  - Verbal Path for Letter Formation

Academic Language / Important Vocabulary

- uppercase letter
- lowercase letter
- syllable/word part

Continuum Connection

- Think about the people who will read the writing or might like to read it and what they will want to know (p. 255)
- Say words to break them into syllables to spell them (p. 255)
- Write some words with consonant letters appropriate for sounds in words (beginning and ending) (p. 255)
- Use a capital letter at the beginning of a familiar proper noun (p. 255)
- Look for ideas and topics in personal experiences, shared through talk (p. 256)
- Recognize and use high-frequency words with one, two, or three letters: e.g., *a, I, in, is, of, to, and, the* (p. 368)

ACTIVE LEARNING EXPERIENCE

- Have children each draw a self-portrait (see DRW.U1: Making a Self-Portrait). Use the portraits to help children get to know one another by having them show their portraits and share something about themselves that other people would want to know.

GOAL

- Say words to break them into syllables and to listen for and record consonant sounds in sequence.
- Write and then locate high-frequency words with two or more letters.

RATIONALE

- A classroom community functions best if its members know each other well and value each other. Creating a class big book will help children learn something about each other so that they can make connections and conversation. In writing the book, children also learn to break words into syllables and to listen for and record consonant sounds in sequence.

ASSESS LEARNING

- Observe whether children actively participate in writing a class book.
- Notice if children break words into syllables to listen for consonant sounds in sequence.
- Look for evidence that children can write and read some high-frequency words.

INTERACTIVE WRITING LESSON

Use the self-portraits and the oral language from the Active Learning Experience as the basis for the writing. Have children help write their own pages. Use the term you prefer, *uppercase* or *capital*. Depending on the number of children in the class, the book could take several days to finish.

Establish Purpose

Remind children how they made self-portraits and then shared the portraits along with something about themselves.

> When you shared your self-portrait, you also told something about yourself. We could make a book about all of us and call it *We Are Special*.

Talk About What to Write

Talk about what will go on the pages of the book.

> When Juste shared his self-portrait, he shared that he is from Uganda and that he is new here. How can we say that?

- Have children repeat the sentences before they are written.

Write Together

Write the first page of the book. As one child contributes a letter or word, keep the others engaged by having them form the letter (or word) in the air.

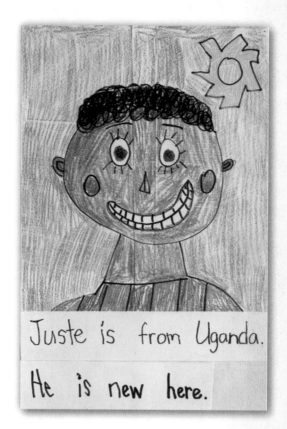

▶ Ask Juste to write his name. Connect the name he is writing to the name chart. If he cannot write his whole name, ask him to write the first letter in uppercase.

> **A name begins with an uppercase letter.**

▶ Ask Juste to write *is*. Continue writing the sentence and pause before a word with an easy-to-hear beginning, ending, or syllable sound that the child will help write.

> **Say *Uganda* slowly with me. Let's clap that. How many parts or syllables does it have?**
>
> **What letter goes with the sound at the beginning?**
>
> ***Uganda* is the name of a country, so it begins with an uppercase *U*.**

▶ Have a child write *U*. Say each syllable slowly as you finish writing *Uganda*.

> **Let's read what has been written so far so we can remember what comes next.**

▶ Have Juste (or other children) write high-frequency words they are learning (e.g., *He*, *is*) or easy-to-hear sounds (e.g., *n* in *new* and *her* in *here*).

Read and Revisit

Read the sentences with children as you point, using a pointer, under each word. You might have children revisit the text for one or both of the following reasons.

▶ Ask children to find high-frequency words such as *he* and *is*.

▶ Review how to clap out longer words and listen for the sounds in each part.

Summarize and Invite/Extend

Summarize the lesson. You might also decide to extend the learning.

> **Today we began a book about how each of us is special. We will add more pages another day.**

▶ Provide time for children to work with high-frequency words that are just right for them. They can use magnetic letters to build, mix, and fix those words.

You Will Need

▶ a familiar book about a memory, such as *The Relatives Came* by Cynthia Rylant, from *Fountas & Pinnell Classroom™ Interactive Read-Aloud Collection* Text Set: Taking Care of Each Other: Family

▶ children's drawings of a shared class memory (see Active Learning Experience)

▶ chart paper and markers

▶ long, thin pointer

▶ To download the following online resources for this lesson, visit **resources.fountasandpinnell.com**:

  ▪ Alphabet Linking Chart

  ▪ Verbal Path for Letter Formation

Academic Language/ Important Vocabulary

▶ memory   ▶ sound

▶ remember   ▶ letter

▶ experience   ▶ sentence

Continuum Connection

▶ Understand that writers may tell stories from their own lives (p. 250)

▶ Understand that a story can be a "small moment" (description of a brief but memorable experience) (p. 251)

▶ Understand and talk about the concept of a sentence (p. 367)

▶ Identify words that end the same and use them to solve unknown words: e.g., *chin, main* (p. 369)

▶ Identify rhyming words and use them to solve unknown words: e.g., *down/clown/drown* (p. 369)

ACTIVE LEARNING EXPERIENCE

▶ Have children draw pictures of a shared experience (e.g., field trip, visit to a local park, class activity). This lesson is based on a class field trip to a science museum. Also read aloud and enjoy several books in which memories are shared, such as *The Relatives Came*.

GOALS

▶ Understand that a story can be a "small moment" within a bigger memory.

▶ Understand the concept of a letter, a word, and a sentence.

▶ Use known words to help you spell an unknown word.

RATIONALE

▶ When you teach children to write about a class memory, they learn that they can write stories from their own lives, and that they can use words to share memories and experiences.

ASSESS LEARNING

▶ Look for evidence that children understand the idea of a small moment.

▶ Notice whether children understand the concept of a letter, a word, and a sentence.

▶ Observe children as they write. Do they use known words to write unknown words?

INTERACTIVE WRITING LESSON

In addition to focusing on concepts of writing, this lesson also incorporates specific talk around deciding what to write. Several prompts are given to support children. A child's drawing of a shared experience is used to inform the writing.

Establish Purpose

▶ Show *The Relatives Came*. Talk about how the book tells about a memory of relatives coming for a visit.

> We can write memory stories about things we remember, too, like our trip to the science museum.

Talk About What to Write

Engage children in specific talk to decide what to write about the museum trip.

▶ Use children's drawings to prompt discussion. Help them focus on one particular part of the field trip rather than the entire event.

> What is one part of the field trip that you really liked? We can write about that.

> Who can add to what _____ said?

> What else do you remember about that?

Write Together

Using children's suggestions, write sentences about the field trip. Ask several children to contribute a word or a letter. Engage the others by having them form the word or letter on the carpet or in the air.

> The first word is *We*. *We* is a word you know.

▶ Ask a volunteer to write *We*. Continue writing the sentence and pause before a word with an easy-to-hear beginning and/or ending sound that a child will help write.

> Say *museum* slowly with me. What sound do you hear at the beginning? What sound do you hear at the end?

> The first and last sounds in *museum* are the same: /m/, like the first and last sounds in *mom*. What letter goes with that sound?

▶ Use the verbal path to guide a child to write the *m* at the beginning. Write the middle letters. Finally, have the child write the *m* at the end.

▶ Continue writing the next sentences, having children contribute letters for easy-to-hear sounds and familiar high-frequency words.

▶ Model aloud the process of using known letters and words to spell new words.

> The next word is *fun*. Up here, we wrote the word *sun*. How should we write *fun*?

▶ Have a volunteer come up to write *fun*. Finish writing the sentence.

Writing a Memory Story
We went to the science museum.
There was a show about lightning.
The guide told us that a lightning bolt is hotter than the sun.
We had fun on the field trip.

Read and Revisit

Using a pointer, read the sentences with children as you point under each word. You might have children revisit the text for one or both of the following reasons.

▶ Have volunteers point to letters, words, and space between words.

▶ Reread the text and talk about which of its parts are sentences.

Summarize and Invite/Extend

Summarize the lesson. You might also decide to extend the learning.

> Today, you can make your own memory story. You can make your story a book.

▶ Use the writing from this lesson as a mentor text when children learn more about memory stories (MBK.U3: Making Memory Books).

You Will Need

- several familiar books by a single author, such as Kevin Henkes
- chart paper and markers
- long, thin pointer
- To download the following online resources for this lesson, visit **resources.fountasandpinnell.com**:
  - Alphabet Linking Chart
  - Verbal Path for Letter Formation
  - masking cards

Academic Language / Important Vocabulary

- author
- sentences
- technique
- bold
- italics

Continuum Connection

- Notice and write about elements of the writer's craft: word choice, use of literary elements (p. 177)
- Notice a fiction writer's use of repetition, refrains, rhythm using interactive or shared writing (p. 177)
- Recognize and use beginning (ending) consonant sounds and the letters that represent them (p. 367)
- Understand and talk about the concept of a letter (word) (p. 367)
- Locate the first and last letters of words in continuous text (p. 367)

ACTIVE LEARNING EXPERIENCE

- Prior to the lesson, gather a text set from an author that the class has previously read and studied, for example, Kevin Henkes. Children's familiarity with the books will help them think and talk about the author's craft techniques. If you have *The Reading Minilessons Book, Grade 1* (Fountas and Pinnell 2019), see LA.U2: Studying Authors and Illustrators.

GOAL

- Notice the techniques that writers use to make their writing interesting.
- Recognize and use beginning and ending consonant sounds and the letters that represent them.
- Use the initial letter in a name to make connections to other words.
- Understand the concept of first and last letters in continuous text.

RATIONALE

- Noticing techniques authors use when writing books allows children to become aware of possibilities for their own writing. They begin to read like a writer, becoming cognizant of an author's craft and recognizing similarities across books.

ASSESS LEARNING

- Observe what children notice about an author's writing.
- Notice if children recognize and use beginning and ending consonant sounds and the letters that represent them.
- Notice if children use letters in one word or name to make connections to other words.

INTERACTIVE WRITING LESSON

In addition to focusing on studying an author's writing, this lesson also incorporates specific talk around deciding what to write. Children's noticings about a selection of books by the same author will be used to inform the writing.

Establish Purpose

Display several books by a single author, such as Kevin Henkes.

> Let's talk about what Kevin Henkes does to make his writing interesting.

Talk About What to Write

Talk about what to write about how Kevin Henkes makes his writing interesting, such as repeating words and sentences and styling print in bold and italics.

> What do you notice about Kevin Henkes's writing?

- Help the children think of simple sentences to describe the author's techniques. Have them say the sentences with you.

Write Together

Write the sentences. Invite several children to share the pen by writing a letter, a group of letters, or a word. Keep the others engaged by having them make letters in the air or on the carpet.

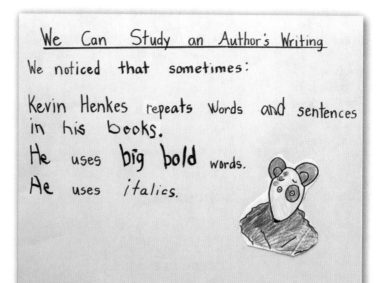

- Write a heading at the top of the chart. Then repeat the first sentence slowly with the children.

- Write *Kevin Henkes*.

    Clap *repeats*. Say the first part, *re*, and listen for the beginning sound.

    Repeats starts like *ring* on the ABC chart. What letter is that?

- Have a child write the letter.

    To write *r*, pull down, up, and over.

    Say *repeats* slowly again. What do you hear next?

- Use the verbal path to guide a child to write *e*. Write the rest of the word.

- Write quickly the words that children can already write or the word parts that would be too difficult. Invite children to write high-frequency words that they are learning (*he*, *and*, *in*) and the letters for easy-to-hear initial, medial, and ending sounds, such as in *big* and *bold*. Some children may be able to link the word *look* to *book*.

Read and Revisit

Read the sentences with children as you use a pointer to point under each word. Have children revisit the text for one or both of the following reasons.

- Have several children find the longest (shortest) word and count the letters.

- Ask several children to use a masking card to show the first and last letter of a word.

Summarize and Invite/Extend

Summarize the lesson. You might also decide to extend the learning.

> **We noticed how an author makes his writing interesting.**

- Continue to write sentences for any additional noticings children might have. For example, sometimes Henkes uses speech bubbles.

- When children write books, encourage them to try the techniques they have noticed.

Section 1: Interactive Writing

You Will Need

- several books with speech bubbles, such as those from *Fountas & Pinnell Classroom™ Interactive Read-Aloud Collection* Text Set: Mo Willems: Having Fun with Humor

- a book that lends itself to speech bubbles, written by a child

- a copy of a page from the child's book, enlarged on chart paper

- markers

- long, thin pointer

- To download the following online resources for this lesson, visit **resources.fountasandpinnell.com**:

  - Initial Consonant Cluster Linking Chart

  - Verbal Path for Letter Formation

  - Alphabet Linking Chart

  - High-Frequency Word List

Academic Language / Important Vocabulary

- speech bubble
- bold print
- underline

Continuum Connection

- Use underlining and bold print to convey meaning (p. 255)

- Add dialogue in speech bubbles or quotation marks to provide information or provide narration (p. 256)

- Recognize and use two consonant letters that represent one sound at the beginning of a word: e.g., *change*, *phone*, *shall*, *thirty*, *where* (p. 367)

- Say a word slowly to hear the sounds in sequence (p. 369)

ACTIVE LEARNING EXPERIENCE

- Read and discuss books that include speech bubbles (see You Will Need) and bold print. Have children write their own books. Encourage them to try out these techniques.

GOAL

- Learn that speech bubbles show what the characters are saying.
- Understand what *bold print* means.
- Recognize and use two letters to represent one sound.
- Hear and record sounds in sequence in unknown words.

RATIONALE

- Discussing how authors use speech bubbles helps children learn to include dialogue in their own writing to make a story more interesting.

ASSESS LEARNING

- Look for evidence of what children know about speech bubbles and bold print.
- Notice if children recognize and use two letters to represent one sound.
- Observe children as they say words slowly to listen for sounds and record letters in sequence.

INTERACTIVE WRITING LESSON

This lesson is designed as an interactive writing lesson in which you and the children will share the pen to add speech bubbles and dialogue to a child's writing.

Establish Purpose

Revisit several Mo Willems books and show pages with speech bubbles.

> How does Mo Willems show that a character is speaking?
>
> A shape like this pointing to a person's mouth is called a speech bubble. A speech bubble tells you what a person is saying. You can use speech bubbles in your writing.

Talk About What to Write

Plan how to add speech bubbles to a child's writing.

- Hold up a book made by a child in the class that lends itself to dialogue. Invite the child to talk about what is happening in the picture and think about dialogue.

  > Michael and his dad are in the picture with fishing poles. Turn and talk to your partner. What might they say to each other?

- Help children form short sentences that fit inside a speech bubble. As you repeat the sentences, point to where you will write and then draw speech bubbles.

Write Together

Begin writing. As one child shares the pen by writing a letter or word, keep the others engaged by having them write the letter or word in the air or on the carpet with a finger.

▶ Repeat the first sentence slowly with the children.

> **What word will we write first? Remember we can't write too big because we have to fit the whole sentence in a speech bubble.**

▶ Guide children to say *Grab* slowly, listen for the four sounds, and, one at a time, identify the letter for each sound. Invite a child to write *Grab*.

> **Read *Grab* with me slowly and think about what word comes next. I'll write *your*. Look, it starts with the word *you*.**

▶ Have children say the word *pole* slowly and listen for the three sounds in sequence. Have a child write *pol*. Add the final *e*.

▶ Draw a speech bubble around the first sentence. Then repeat this process for the second speech bubble. Have children say the sentence with you. Guide them to write *cat* in *catch* and then the four letters that represent the three sounds in *fish*.

Read and Revisit

Read the speech bubbles with children as you point under each word. You might have children revisit the text for one or both of the following reasons.

▶ Talk about the bold print in Mo Willems' book. Make the word *big* bold.

▶ Talk about how two letters can go together to make a new sound (e.g., *sh*, *ch*).

Summarize and Invite/Extend

Summarize the lesson and invite children to include speech bubbles in their own books.

> **Today we added speech bubbles to a page in Michael's book. He can work on the other pages on other days. You can add speech bubbles to your books, too.**

▶ When children add speech bubbles to their own writing, have them write the words first and then draw the bubble.

You Will Need

- chart paper and markers
- word cards for labels
- tape
- To download the following online resources for this lesson, visit **resources.fountasandpinnell.com**:
  - Initial Consonant Cluster Linking Chart
  - Alphabet Linking Chart
  - Verbal Path for Letter Formation

Academic Language / Important Vocabulary

- map
- label
- word
- first
- middle
- last

Continuum Connection

- Understand that a writer or illustrator can add a label to help readers (p. 250)
- Understand that a label can add important information (p. 250)
- Recognize and say consonant clusters that blend two or three consonant sounds (onsets): *bl, cl, fl, gl, pl, sl, br, cr, dr, fr, gr, pr, tr, sc, sk, sm, sn, sp, st, sw, tw, qu; scr, spl, spr, squ, str* (p. 367)
- Understand and talk about the fact that a noun can refer to more than one person, place, or thing: e.g., *fathers, towns, toys* (p. 368)
- Say a word slowly to hear the sounds in sequence (p. 369)

ACTIVE LEARNING EXPERIENCE

- Talk with children about the communities that they belong to, including the school community. Take children on a walk outside on the playground. Then work together to make a map of the playground. Labels will be added in this lesson.

GOALS

- Learn that labels add important information.
- Recognize and say consonant clusters that blend two sounds.
- Say words slowly to hear the sounds in sequence.
- Understand and talk about plural nouns.

RATIONALE

- When children learn that labels give more information to a drawing, they recognize that they can add labels to their own drawings to help explain what they represent. They learn that the pictures and writing together create one clear message.

ASSESS LEARNING

- Look for evidence of what children know about labels.
- Listen to children say words slowly. Can they hear the sounds? Do they write letters in sequence?
- Look for evidence that children understand that when letters are put together they make one word, and that the plural of a word refers to more than one thing.

INTERACTIVE WRITING LESSON

This lesson is designed as an interactive writing lesson in which you and the children will compose the text together and share the pen. Alternatively, you might choose to do all the writing yourself (shared writing).

Establish Purpose

- Show the map of the playground.

  How can we make our map more helpful for other people to use?

  We can add labels to tell what is on our playground, like the slide.

Talk About What to Write

Talk about and plan what labels to add to the map.

  Let's talk about the parts of our playground map. What labels could we add?

Write Together

Label the map. Invite several children to share the pen by adding a letter or a group of letters. Keep the others engaged by having them practice making the letter in the air or on the carpet.

> Here is the slide. Say *slide* slowly. What two sounds do you hear at the beginning?

▶ Choose a child to write *sl* on a word card. Continue to say the word slowly and ask the child to record the predominant sounds.

> What letter would we add to make the word look right?

> There is a silent *e* at the end, as in the word *like*.

▶ Point to the swings on the map.

> Say *swings* slowly and listen for the first two sounds you hear. What letters go together to make the two sounds? Let's look at the consonant clusters chart.

▶ Ask a child to write *sw* on a word card. Record *ing* yourself.

> There are two swings, so I'll write *s* to make the word *swings*.

▶ Continue by having children say words slowly and write the letters for sounds that will expand their ability to write new words.

Read and Revisit

Ask the children to read the labels with you as you point under each word. You might have children revisit the text for one or both of the following reasons.

▶ Have children point to a word that starts like *swim* and a word that starts like *slow*.

▶ Have children find the singular words and tell how to make them plural.

Summarize and Invite/Extend

Summarize the lesson. You might also decide to extend the learning.

> Today we labeled the map of our playground. You can label your drawings.

▶ Invite children to write about things that happened in different places on the map.

Interactive Writing, Lesson 11: Labeling a Map

You Will Need

- books about community, such as the following from *Fountas & Pinnell Classroom™ Interactive Read-Aloud Collection* Text Set: Living and Working Together: Community

  - *The Night Worker* by Kate Banks

  - *A Bus Called Heaven* by Bob Graham

  - *Be My Neighbor* by Maya Ajmera and John D. Ivanko

- chart paper and markers

- To download the following online resource for this lesson, visit **resources.fountasandpinnell.com**:

  - Verbal Path for Letter Formation

Academic Language/ Important Vocabulary

- letter
- word
- question
- interview

Continuum Connection

- Ask questions and gather information on a topic (p. 256)

- Understand and talk about the fact that some letters represent vowel sounds (p. 365)

- Recognize and read known words quickly (p. 369)

- Identify rhyming words and use them to solve unknown words: e.g., *down/clown/drown* (p. 369)

ACTIVE LEARNING EXPERIENCE

- Prior to the lesson, read and discuss books about community (see You Will Need). Discuss the various jobs that people in a community may hold.

GOAL

- Understand that writers write for a purpose.
- Understand that writers ask questions to get information about a topic.
- Hear, identify, and write short vowel sounds in familiar words.

RATIONALE

- By participating in writing interview questions, children understand that they can use writing to gain information and learn more about a topic. When they help write some of the words in the questions, they learn to say words slowly to listen for the sounds.

ASSESS LEARNING

- Observe children's participation in composing and writing interview questions.
- Look for evidence of what children understand about interview questions.
- Notice whether they can identify and write some short vowel sounds in familiar words.

INTERACTIVE WRITING LESSON

The purpose of this lesson is to prepare children for interviewing guest speakers about their careers. The lesson is designed as an interactive writing lesson. Alternatively, you might choose to do all the writing yourself (shared writing).

Establish Purpose

Display some of the books about community that you have read aloud.

> Some members of our community (or neighborhood) are going to visit our classroom. You will interview them about their jobs. When you interview someone, you ask questions. Today we will write interview questions to ask people about their jobs. Our list will help us remember what to ask.

Talk About What to Write

Talk about what to write for the first interview question.

> When special guests come to our classroom to talk about their jobs, what information will you want to find out first?

> We could ask *What is your job?* Say that with me.

Write Together

Write the interview questions. While one child shares the pen, engage the others by having them make the letter in the air or on the carpet in front of them.

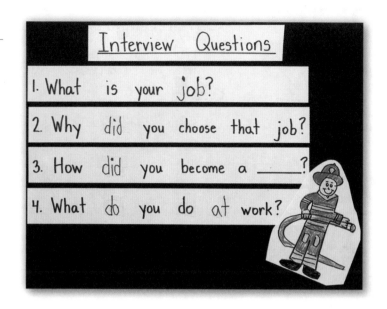

▶ Write a title and then *1. What is your* on chart paper.

> **What is the next word in our question?**
>
> **Say** *job*. **What sound do you hear first? What letter is that?** *Job* **starts with the letter** *j*, **like** *John* **and** *jar*.

▶ Invite a child to write *j*.

> *Job* **has the /o/ sound in the middle. I will write the letter o.**

▶ Have children say *job* again and listen for the last sound.

▶ Invite a volunteer to write the *b* in *job*. Use the verbal path to guide her, if needed.

▶ Explain that you are ending the sentence with a question mark because it is a question. Read the question together.

▶ Talk about what other questions children will want to ask. Repeat the process to write them, inviting children to contribute words they know and can write quickly, such as *did*, *do*, *you*, and *at*.

Read and Revisit

Ask the children to read the interview questions with you as you point under each word. You might have children revisit the questions for one or both of the following reasons.

▶ Invite children to point to a word that rhymes with, for example, *Bob (job)*.

▶ Have children locate known words quickly (e.g., *is, you, at*).

Summarize and Invite/Extend

Summarize the lesson. You might also decide to extend the learning.

> **Today we wrote interview questions together. We will ask our special guests these questions when they come to our classroom.**

▶ After children interview the speakers, help them write thank you letters to the speakers.

▶ Use interactive writing to write about what the class learned about different jobs.

You Will Need

- books about kindness, such as the following from *Fountas & Pinnell Classroom™ Interactive Read-Aloud Collection* Text Set: The Importance of Kindness
  - *Jamaica Tag-Along* by Juanita Havill
  - *Wilfrid Gordon McDonald Partridge* by Mem Fox
  - *Now One Foot, Now the Other* by Tomie dePaola
- chart paper and markers
- To download the following online resource for this lesson, visit **resources.fountasandpinnell.com**:
  - Verbal Path for Letter Formation

Academic Language/ Important Vocabulary

- kindness
- word
- sign
- sentence
- letter

Continuum Connection

- Understand that written communication can be used for different purposes: e.g., to give information, to invite, to give thanks (p. 250)
- Hear and divide onsets and rimes: e.g., *m-en, bl-ack* (p. 367)
- Hear and say the beginning phoneme in a word: e.g., *sun /s/* (p. 367)
- Recognize and use more common phonograms with a VC pattern: *-ab, -ad, -ag, -am, -an, -ap, -at, -aw, -ay; -ed, -en, -et, -ew; -id, -ig, -im, -in, -ip, -it; -ob, -od, -og, -op, -ot, -ow* (as in *show* or as in *cow*); *-ub, -ug, -um, -un, -ut* (p. 368)

ACTIVE LEARNING EXPERIENCE

- Prior to the lesson, read aloud and enjoy books about kindness (see You Will Need). Talk with children about what they can do to be kind to others.

GOAL

- Learn that writing can communicate a message to an audience.
- Use onsets and rimes to support children in hearing and saying beginning phonemes in words.
- Write the initial consonant at the beginning of some words.
- Use common phonograms with a vowel-consonant ending in writing.

RATIONALE

- By participating in writing kindness signs, children learn that they can use writing to spread a message and influence others. When you help them write some of the letters in the words, they learn to say words slowly to listen for the sounds.

ASSESS LEARNING

- Observe children's participation in writing kindness signs.
- Notice whether children can break words into onset and rime to help write them.

INTERACTIVE WRITING LESSON

The lesson generates ideas for kindness signs that can be placed around the school. After the lesson, children can make kindness signs using the ideas from the lesson or their own ideas.

Establish Purpose

Display some of the books about kindness that you have read aloud.

> Sometimes on TV, you might see something called a public service announcement, which tells people something that will help them. We can make some public service announcement signs to remind people in our school of ways they can be kind to others.

Talk About What to Write

Talk about messages children could write on kindness signs.

> What could we write on our signs to remind people of ways they can be kind to others?

> What could we write on the sign for the cafeteria (playground, hallway)?

Write Together

Write the kindness signs. Keep all children engaged while one child shares the pen by having them make the letter or word in the air or on the carpet.

> Our first sign will say *Sit with someone new today.*

❯ Invite a child to write *Sit*.

> Say *sit* slowly: *s-it*. What sound do you hear first in *sit*?
>
> You know the last part of *sit*. What is a word you know that can help?
>
> *Sit* has the word *it*.

❯ Write *with someone new*. Invite a child to help you write the word *today*.

❯ Write *to*.

> What word comes next? The next word is *today*. Let's clap *today*: *to-day*. The second part is *day*. Say *day*. What sound do you hear at the end of *day*?
>
> The sound at the end of *day* sounds like the letter *a*. We write this sound with the letters *a* and *y* together.

❯ Guide the child to write *day*. Then read the sentence together.

❯ Continue in a similar manner with a few more kindness signs.

Read and Revisit

Ask the children to read the kindness messages with you as you point under each word. You might have children revisit the text for one or both of these reasons.

❯ Help children clap words to hear the parts (e.g., *to-day*, *some-one*) or have them listen for onsets and rimes (e.g., *s-it*, *s-ay*).

❯ Invite children to think of rhyming words for *way* and *and*.

Summarize and Invite/Extend

> Today we made kindness signs together. We can place them around the school so people will remember to be kind.

❯ Invite children to write and illustrate additional kindness signs to be placed around the school. Invite the art teacher to help with designing the signs.

You Will Need

- several informational nonfiction books, including at least one about sharks, such as *Surprising Sharks* by Nicola Davies from *Fountas & Pinnell Classroom™ Interactive Read-Aloud Collection* Text Set: Exploring Nonfiction

- paper to make a big book and markers

- To download the following online resource for this lesson, visit **resources.fountasandpinnell.com**:
  - Verbal Path for Letter Formation

Academic Language/ Important Vocabulary

- all-about book
- page
- letter
- word
- sentence

Continuum Connection

- Write books and short pieces of writing that are enjoyable to read and at the same time give information to readers about the same topic (p. 251)

- Select interesting information to include in a piece of writing (p. 251)

- Recognize and use two consonant letters that represent one sound at the beginning of the word: e.g., *change*, *phone*, *shall*, *thirty*, *where* (p. 367)

- Recognize and use long vowel sounds in words and the letters that represent them (p. 368)

ACTIVE LEARNING EXPERIENCE

▶ Prior to the lesson, read aloud and enjoy several informational nonfiction books. Then choose one topic to focus on in particular. This lesson uses sharks as an example, but select any topic that interests the children. Read aloud books about sharks and engage children in a discussion about what they know about sharks.

GOAL

▶ Learn the characteristics of an all-about book.

▶ Listen for and record the letters that represent consonant digraphs.

▶ Hear and identify long vowel sounds in words and the letters that represent them.

RATIONALE

▶ When children write an all-about book, they learn that writing can be used to share information. Children also begin to understand the difference between fiction and nonfiction.

ASSESS LEARNING

▶ Look for evidence of what children understand about an all-about book.

▶ Observe for evidence that children understand that two consonants can represent one sound.

INTERACTIVE WRITING LESSON

This lesson results in a book all about sharks, but make the book about whatever the children in your class have been reading and learning about. Make as many pages of the book as children can manage in one sitting.

Establish Purpose

Display some of the nonfiction books that you have read aloud.

> The authors of these nonfiction books wrote about something they know a lot about. We can write a book about something we know a lot about, too! Let's write a book about sharks. The title could be *All About Sharks*.

Talk About What to Write

Plan what to write on at least the first page of the book. Have children state their ideas, and then ask them how they want to say it. Other pages could be completed later.

> Nonfiction authors keep similar types of information together. On our first page, we can put together information about different sizes of sharks. Then on other pages, we can write something else about sharks. What could we write about the sizes of sharks on the first page of our book?

> How should we say that?

Write Together

Write the text for the all-about book. When you invite one child to share the pen by writing a letter, keep the others engaged by having them form the letter in the air or on the carpet.

> Let's say the first sentence together.
>
> The first word is *Sharks*. Say *sharks*. What sound do you hear at the beginning of *sharks*?
>
> *Sharks* starts with /sh/, which we write with the letters *s* and *h* together. Who would like to write these letters? *Sharks* is the first word in the sentence, so it begins with a capital *S*.

▶ Invite a volunteer to come to the chart to write the letters *Sh*.

> To write an *S,* pull back, in, around, down, and back around. To make an *h,* pull down, up, over, and down.

▶ Finish writing *Sharks*. Have a child hold a space, and then write the next part of the sentence, stopping before the word *shapes*. Help children listen for the vowel sound and identify the letter that goes with it. Invite a volunteer to write *a*.

▶ Finish writing the sentence. Then read the sentence together.

▶ Continue in a similar manner with the rest of the sentences on this page and additional pages. Invite several children to share the pen at selected parts that offer new learning. See an example of a completed book on page 162.

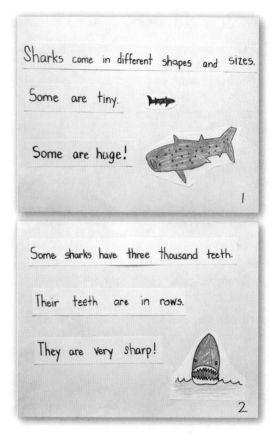

Section 1: Interactive Writing

Read and Revisit

Invite the children to read the all-about book with you as you point under each word. You might have them revisit the text for one or both of the following reasons.

▶ Talk with children about page numbers. Add the page numbers.

▶ Ask children to point to words that contain, for example, the consonant digraph *sh* or *th* or a long vowel sound.

Summarize and Invite/Extend

Summarize the lesson. You might also decide to extend the learning.

> Today we made an all-about book to share what we know about sharks.

▶ Invite children to create a cover and illustrations for the book. Bind the book and number the pages. Make the finished book available for children to read.

You Will Need

- familiar question-and-answer books, such as the following from *Fountas & Pinnell Classroom™ Interactive Read-Aloud Collection* Text Set: Nonfiction: Questions and Answers:

  - *What Do You Do With a Tail Like This?* by Steve Jenkins and Robin Page

  - *A Cool Summer Tail* by Carrie A. Pearson

  - *Best Foot Forward* by Ingo Arndt

  - *Animals Black and White* by Phyllis Limbacher Tildes

- paper to make a big book and markers

Academic Language / Important Vocabulary

- question
- answer
- information
- capital letter
- period
- question mark

Continuum Connection

- Understand how to write a factual text from listening to mentor texts read aloud and discussing them (p. 251)

- Think about the readers (audience) and what they need to know (p. 251)

- Use a capital letter for the first word of a sentence (p. 255)

- Notice the use of punctuation marks in books and try them out in one's own writing (p. 255)

- Hear and say the ending phoneme in a word: e.g., *bed*, /d/ (p. 367)

ACTIVE LEARNING EXPERIENCE

- Read several nonfiction books with a question-and-answer format. If possible, share books that have a variety of formats, including lift-the-flap books. Teach a science or social studies content unit that lends itself to writing question-and-answer books.

GOALS

- Capitalize and punctuate sentences.
- Recognize ending consonant sounds and the letters that represent them.

RATIONALE

- When children learn that some books ask questions and provide answers as a way to give the reader information, they know what to expect from question-and-answer books and can write a book in this format.

ASSESS LEARNING

- Observe for evidence that children understand the format and pattern of a question-and-answer book.

- Look for evidence that children understand how to use capital letters and punctuation marks.

- Observe whether children can hear the first and last sounds in words.

INTERACTIVE WRITING LESSON

The question-and-answer book created in this lesson is about animal parents and babies, but you can choose any science, social studies, or other topic. Save the book to use as a mentor text in MBK.U6: Making Question-and-Answer Books.

Establish Purpose

Use a book such as *What Do You Do With a Tail Like This?* to review the idea of a question-and-answer book and to establish a purpose for writing.

> Together, we can make a question-and-answer book about animal parents and their babies.

Talk About What to Write

Talk about ideas for a question-and-answer book and what the questions and answers could be.

> You have been learning about how animal parents take care of their babies. What would someone want to know about that?

- Talk through the ideas with the children.

> How do you want to say that?

Write Together

Begin writing the question-and-answer book. Invite several children to share the pen by writing a letter or punctuation mark. Keep the others engaged by having them use their fingers to write the letter or punctuation mark in the air.

- Say the question with children. Then review that a sentence begins with a capital letter. Point out that many question words begin with *wh*.

    Who can show where to write *Wh* on the page?

- Ask a child to write the letters *Wh*. Continue writing and pause before *mother*.

    Say and clap the word *mother* and listen for the sound that comes at the end.

- Repeat the word and assist children to identify /r/. Explain that sometimes *e* goes with *r*. Start the word and ask a volunteer to add the *er*.

- Finish the sentence and read the sentence with expression. Assist children in identifying that a question mark is needed.

    A question mark goes at the end of a question. Who can write the question mark?

- Continue writing as many pages as children can manage in one sitting. Invite them to clap multisyllable words and share the pen to write periods and question marks and word parts like *er*, *wh*, *ee*, and *ir*.

Read and Revisit

Ask the children to read the sentences with you as you point under each word. You might have children revisit the text for one or both of the following reasons.

- Practice reading the sentences to reflect the end punctuation.
- Clap words that have more than one syllable (e.g., *father*, *penguin*, *baby*).

Summarize and Invite/Extend

Summarize the lesson. You might also decide to extend the learning.

    Today we wrote a question-and-answer book.

- Work with several children to add illustrations and flaps to hide the answers.
- Invite children to write a question-and-answer book about a science concept.

Section 1: Interactive Writing

You Will Need

- *Jake's 100th Day of School* by Lester L. Laminack, from *Fountas & Pinnell Classroom™ Interactive Read-Aloud Collection* Text Set: Using Numbers: Books with Counting
- chart paper and markers
- To download the following online resource for this lesson, visit **resources.fountasandpinnell.com**:
  - masking card

Academic Language/ Important Vocabulary

- list
- word
- letter
- syllable

Continuum Connection

- Make lists in the appropriate form with one item under another (p. 250)
- Use lists to plan activities or support memory (p. 250)
- Say words to break them into syllables to spell them (p. 255)
- Recognize and talk about the fact that letters can be consonants or vowels (p. 367)
- Recognize and use plurals that add -s: e.g., *books, cars, dogs, farms, mothers, zoos* (p. 368)

ACTIVE LEARNING EXPERIENCE

- Prior to the lesson, read and discuss *Jake's 100th Day of School*. Plan activities for celebrating the 100th day of school in your classroom. One way is to make a 100th-day snack mix. In this lesson, children will write a shopping list for the snack mix.

GOAL

- Understand the purpose and format of a list.
- Say words to break them into syllables to support spelling.
- Recognize and use plurals that add -s.
- Recognize and talk about the fact that letters can be consonants or vowels.

RATIONALE

- Writing a shopping list with children demonstrates that writing has a purpose and is useful in everyday life. Children learn that writing is not just for telling stories–it also has many other purposes, such as recording information you want to remember.

ASSESS LEARNING

- Look for evidence of what children know about a list.
- Notice whether children break words into syllables to spell them.
- Notice whether children know to add -s to nouns to create plurals.

INTERACTIVE WRITING LESSON

This lesson is designed as an interactive writing lesson in which you and the children will compose the text together and share the pen. Alternatively, you might choose to do all the writing yourself (shared writing).

Establish Purpose

Revisit *Jake's 100th Day of School* by Lester L. Laminack in preparation for writing a shopping list.

> Today we will write a shopping list for our snack mix. A shopping list is our list of all the items we need to buy.

Talk About What to Write

Talk about what to write on the shopping list. Add a title to the chart paper.

> One thing that we could put in our snack mix is pretzels. What else could go in the snack mix? What would taste good with pretzels?

- Invite suggestions, agreeing on three to five items for the list. Have children say the items with you.

Write Together

Write the shopping list. Keep all children engaged while one child shares the pen by having them make the letter in the air or on the carpet in front of them.

> We decided that the first thing on our shopping list is *Pretzels.* We can break this word into parts to help us write it. Clap and say *Pret-zels.* What two sounds do you hear at the beginning of *Pret?*

> *Pret* begins with the sounds /p//r/, which we write with the letters *P* and *r* together. Who would like to write the letters *Pr?*

▶ Invite a volunteer to write the letters *Pr.* Then write the rest of the word *Pretzel* yourself.

> This is the word *Pretzel,* which means one pretzel. One pretzel isn't enough. How can we show that we need more than one pretzel?

▶ Invite a volunteer to add the *s.*

> What did we say would be next on our shopping list?

> In a list, each item goes on its own line. *Chocolate chips* goes under *Pretzels.*

▶ Repeat the process to write the rest of the items on the list. Invite children to clap to hear each syllable in multisyllable words. Invite different volunteers to write word parts they may know such as *in* in the word *raisin* and *ow* in *marshmallow* by linking the part to other words they know (e.g., *snow*).

Read and Revisit

Reread the shopping list together, pointing under each word as you read it. You might have children revisit the list for one or both of the following reasons.

▶ Invite children to use a masking card to show consonants or vowels.

▶ Invite children to point to the *s* at the end of each item and explain why it is there.

Summarize and Invite/Extend

Summarize the lesson. You might also decide to extend the learning.

> Today we made a shopping list for our 100th-day snack mix.

▶ Invite children to draw pictures for the shopping list.

▶ After day 100, invite children to write about how they celebrated it.

You Will Need

- books that celebrate diversity, such as the following from *Fountas & Pinnell Classroom™ Interactive Read-Aloud Collection* Text Set: Celebrating Diversity:
  - *Two Eggs, Please* by Sarah Weeks
  - *Whoever You Are* by Mem Fox
  - *My Name Is Yoon* by Helen Recorvits
- chart paper and markers
- To download the following online resource for this lesson, visit **resources.fountasandpinnell.com**:
  - High-Frequency Word List

Academic Language/ Important Vocabulary

- invitation
- letter
- date
- sentence
- word

Continuum Connection

- Understand that written communication can be used for different purposes: e.g., to give information, to invite, to give thanks (p. 250)
- Understand that the sender and the receiver must be clearly shown (p. 250)
- Understand that an invitation must include specific information (p. 250)
- Write notes, cards, invitations, and emails to others (p. 250)
- Change the beginning sound or sounds to make and solve a new word: e.g., *he/me* (change /h/ to /m/), *more/shore* (change /m/ to /sh/), *bright/might* (change /b/ /r/ to /m/) (p. 369)

ACTIVE LEARNING EXPERIENCE

- Prior to the lesson, read and enjoy books with children that celebrate diversity, as suggested in You Will Need.

GOAL

- Understand that you can write an invitation to invite someone to do something.
- Understand that an invitation contains specific information.
- Be able to change the beginning sound to make a new word.

RATIONALE

- Writing an invitation with children demonstrates one of the many useful purposes of writing in everyday life. Children learn that they can use writing to invite people to go somewhere or do something.

ASSESS LEARNING

- Observe for evidence of what children know about an invitation.
- Notice whether children suggest specific information to include in the invitation.
- Look for evidence that children know they can change the beginning letter of one word to make another.

INTERACTIVE WRITING LESSON

This lesson is designed as an interactive writing lesson in which you and the children compose the text together and then share the pen. Alternatively, you might choose to do all the writing yourself (shared writing).

Establish Purpose

Display some familiar books about celebrating diversity.

> We can make a book to celebrate the different foods your families eat. Let's write an invitation inviting your families to bring in a favorite food and a recipe so we can make a recipe book.

Talk About What to Write

Talk with the children about what they want their families to know and what they want to ask them to do.

> What information do our families need to know?

- Work with children to compose a couple of sentences that give the purpose of the invitation. Have children say the sentences with you before writing them.

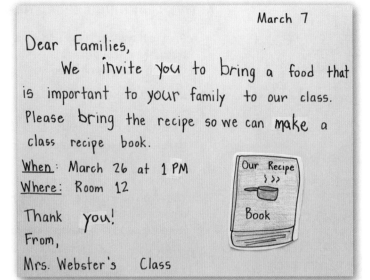

Write Together

Write the invitation. Keep all children engaged while one child shares the pen by having them make the letter in the air or on the carpet in front of them.

> Write the date and the greeting, reading them aloud and explaining their purpose as you write. Then write *We*. Read what has been written so far to help children anticipate the next word.
>
> > The next word is *invite*. Clap it: *in-vite*. The first part is a word you know. It's on our word wall.

> Have a child write *in*. Finish the word and write the words up to *bring*.
>
> > Say *bring* and listen for the two sounds at the beginning. What letters go with those sounds?

> Invite a volunteer to write the letters *br*.
>
> > Let's think about how to write the rest of the word. *Bring* rhymes with *sing,* and I know that *sing* ends with the letters *ing.* So *bring* must end with *ing* as well.

> Write the *ing*. Then continue writing the rest of the invitation in a similar manner. Have children write familiar high-frequency words (e.g., *make, you*) and spell words by making connections to other words (e.g., *you* in *your*).

Read and Revisit

Reread the invitation together, pointing under each word as you read. You might have children revisit the invitation for one or both of these reasons.

> Invite children to point to the different parts of a letter (date, greeting, closing).

> Ask children to find a word that rhymes with, for example, *string* (*bring*), *glass* (*class*), *bike* (*like*), or *cook* (*book*).

Summarize and Invite/Extend

Summarize the lesson. You might also decide to extend the learning.

> > Take home a copy of the invitation. When we get the recipes, we will make our recipe book!

> Help children organize, illustrate, and publish the class recipe book.

Section 1: Interactive Writing

You Will Need

- books that celebrate diversity, such as the following from *Fountas & Pinnell Classroom™ Interactive Read-Aloud Collection* Text Set: Celebrating Diversity:
  - *Two Eggs, Please* by Sarah Weeks
  - *Whoever You Are* by Mem Fox
  - *My Name Is Yoon* by Helen Recorvits
- chart paper and markers
- a name card for every child
- To download the following online resource for this lesson, visit **resources.fountasandpinnell.com**:
  - masking card

Academic Language/ Important Vocabulary

- survey
- word
- sentence
- question

Continuum Connection

- Use periods, exclamation marks, and question marks as end marks (p. 255)
- Use a capital letter at the beginning of a familiar proper noun (p. 255)
- Ask questions and gather information on a topic (p. 256)
- Use known words to help spell an unknown word (p. 369)

ACTIVE LEARNING EXPERIENCE

- Prior to the lesson, read and enjoy books that celebrate diversity. Engage children in discussions about their families' different cultural heritages and traditions. Also, ask the children's parents or caregivers to write the countries their families originated from.

GOALS

- Recognize, talk about, and write letter patterns while spelling unknown words.
- Understand the use of capital letters at the beginning of proper nouns.

RATIONALE

- When you help children make a survey, you demonstrate that they can use writing to record information that they want to remember. As they write the survey question, they learn to use familiar words or word parts to spell unknown words.

ASSESS LEARNING

- Observe children's participation in creating a survey question and chart.
- Notice whether children use known words or word parts to spell unknown words.
- Notice whether children use capital letters at the beginning of proper nouns.

INTERACTIVE WRITING LESSON

This lesson is designed to highlight and celebrate the places the children's families are from. If most or all the families are from the same place, think of another interesting difference.

Establish Purpose

Display familiar books about celebrating diversity.

> Your families come from many different places. It would be interesting to make a survey about the countries your families come from. When you make a survey, you ask people a question and write the answers.

Talk About What to Write

Talk with children about the question they want to ask.

> What question can we ask to find out where your families come from?

> We can ask *What country is your family from?*

- List the countries that children's parents or caregivers wrote down across the bottom of a sheet of chart paper.

Write Together

Write the survey question. Keep all children engaged while one child shares the pen by having them make the letter(s) in the air or on the carpet in front of them.

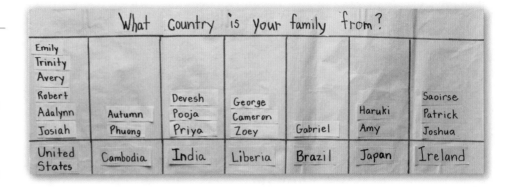

▶ Have children repeat the question with you.

> The first word is *What*. Say it slowly and listen for the sound at the beginning.
>
> Two letters go with that sound: *Wh*.

▶ Invite a volunteer to come to the chart to write *Wh*. Finish the word.

▶ Have children listen for the first sound in *country*. Invite a child to write *c*. Finish the word and write *is*.

> *Your* has a familiar word in it. The first part looks like the word *you*. Who can write the word *you*?

▶ After the child writes *you*, have the class listen for the final sound and identify the letter. Have the child write *r*.

▶ Clap the word *family* with children. Invite a volunteer to write the *y*. Invite the children to say *from* and identify the first two letters.

> What punctuation mark should we put at the end of our sentence?

▶ Give each child a name card. Invite children to attach their name cards to the chart.

Read and Revisit

Ask the children to read the question with you as you point under each word. You might have children revisit the text for one or both of the following reasons.

▶ Invite children to use a masking card to identify capital letters.

▶ Ask the children to use a masking card to find the word parts they used to write new words.

Summarize and Invite/Extend

Summarize the lesson. You might also decide to extend the learning.

> Today, we made a survey about all the places your families are from.

▶ Using shared or interactive writing, help children write about the results of the survey.

You Will Need

- a folktale that you have read recently to the class, such as one of the following from *Fountas & Pinnell Classroom™ Interactive Read-Aloud Collection* Text Set: Folktales: Exploring Different Versions:

  - *Goldilocks and the Three Bears* by Jan Brett
  - *The Gingerbread Man* by Eric A. Kimmel
  - *The Little Red Hen* pictures by Lucinda McQueen

- chart paper and markers
- To download the following online resources for this lesson, visit **resources.fountasandpinnell.com**:

  - Initial Consonant Cluster Linking Chart
  - chart art (optional)

Academic Language/ Important Vocabulary

- story
- ending
- word
- sentence

Continuum Connection

- Compose innovations on very familiar texts by changing the ending, the series of events, characters, and/or the setting (p. 176)
- Recognize and use concept words: e.g., color names, number words, days of the week, months of the year, seasons (p. 368)
- Use known word parts (some are words) to solve unknown larger words: e.g., *in*/*into*, *can*/*canvas*; *us*/*crust* (p. 369)

ACTIVE LEARNING EXPERIENCE

- Prior to the lesson, read aloud and enjoy several folktales with the children (see You Will Need). Take particular note of how the stories end.

GOAL

- Recognize and use two letters that represent one sound.
- Recognize and use concept words.
- Use known word parts to solve unknown larger words.

RATIONALE

- Writing an alternative ending for a familiar story is a way of responding to reading. In this lesson, children think about how familiar characters might act differently and see that their ideas can be written down and read by others.

ASSESS LEARNING

- Observe children's participation in contributing to the alternative ending.
- Look for evidence that children understand that two letters can represent one sound.
- Notice whether children can use a known word to write a new word.

INTERACTIVE WRITING LESSON

This lesson is based on *Goldilocks and the Three Bears*, but any familiar story could be used. (To plan a new lesson, use Planning an Interactive Writing Lesson in online resources. See p. 102.)

Establish Purpose

Display *Goldilocks and the Three Bears* and briefly review the story.

> How does *Goldilocks and the Three Bears* end?

> The author made up that ending. We can write a different ending to make a new story.

Talk About What to Write

Talk about a plan to write an alternative ending to the story.

> What's another way that the story could end?

> Goldilocks could apologize, or say sorry, to the three bears. How can we say that?

> What might happen after she apologizes?

Write Together

Write the text for the new ending. Invite several children to share the pen by writing a letter, a word, or part of a word.

> Let's say the first sentence together.

▶ Write the sentence, having children clap *Gol-di-locks* and *a-pol-o-gized* while you write those words. Stop at the word *three*.

> Say *three* with me. What sound do you hear at the beginning?

> It's the same sound as at the beginning of *thumb*. What two letters go with that sound?

▶ Refer children to the Initial Consonant Cluster Linking Chart. Invite a child to write *th*.

> What sound do you hear next in *three*?

▶ Have the child write *r*. Repeat the process for *e* and then tell children that there are two *e*'s together.

▶ Write the rest of the sentence, having children identify and write *br* in *breaking*.

▶ Say the next sentence with children. Write the sentence, pausing before *became*. Invite a child to write *be*.

> You know a word that can help you write the beginning of *became*. Say *be-came*. What word is that?

▶ Finish the word and then the sentence, inviting a child to write *fr* in *friends*.

Goldilocks apologized to the three bears for breaking into their house. The three bears and Goldilocks became good friends.

Read and Revisit

Read the alternative ending together. You might have children revisit the text for the following reason.

▶ Invite children to identify words that begin the same way (e.g., *the/their*).

Summarize and Invite/Extend

Summarize the learning. You might also decide to extend the learning.

> Today we wrote a new ending for *Goldilocks and the Three Bears*.

▶ Invite children to change the plot, the characters, or the setting in other familiar tales.

You Will Need

- familiar poems with sensory imagery, such as those in *All the Colors of the Earth* by Sheila Hamanaka, *Mud* by Mary Lyn Ray, and *Puddles* by Jonathan London, from *Fountas & Pinnell Classroom™ Interactive Read-Aloud Collection* Text Set: Poetic Language

- chart paper and markers

- To download the following online resources for this lesson, visit **resources.fountasandpinnell.com**:
  - Initial Consonant Cluster Linking Chart
  - Alphabet Linking Chart

Academic Language/ Important Vocabulary

- sound
- letter
- nature
- poem

Continuum Connection

- Understand poetry as a way to communicate in sensory images about everyday life (p. 251)

- Closely observe the world (animals, objects, people) to get ideas for poems (p. 251)

- Use language to describe how something looks, smells, tastes, feels, or sounds (p. 251)

- Use descriptive words (p. 332)

- Recognize and say consonant clusters that blend two or three consonant sounds (onsets): *bl, cl, fl, gl, pl, sl, br, cr, dr, fr, gr, pr, tr, sc, sk, sm, sn, sp, st, sw, tw, qu; scr, spl, spr, squ, str* (p. 367)

ACTIVE LEARNING EXPERIENCE

- Read aloud and enjoy poems and books with poetic language. Discuss the way writers choose interesting words, compare one thing to another, and use descriptive language. Go outside with children and have them sit quietly to observe their surroundings. Have them touch bits of the natural world, such as leaves and rocks. Ask the children what they see, hear, smell, and feel.

GOALS

- Learn about sensory images and descriptive words.
- Listen for and identify the two letters in a consonant cluster.
- Write known high-frequency words quickly.

RATIONALE

- When children write poems, they develop an understanding of the sounds of language and learn that they can make choices about the words they write and where to put them.

ASSESS LEARNING

- Notice whether children understand that words are chosen carefully and placed on a page to create a poem.
- Look for evidence that children can use sensory language.
- Notice whether children can hear and identify the two letters in a consonant cluster.

INTERACTIVE WRITING LESSON

If you have *The Reading Minilessons Book, Grade 1* (Fountas and Pinnell 2019), you might teach LA.U8: Analyzing the Writer's Craft or LA.U22: Analyzing the Way Writers Play with Language as a foundation for this lesson. Here is an example.

Establish Purpose

Revisit page 13 in *All the Colors of the Earth*, page 11 in *Mud*, and page 6 in *Puddles*.

> What do you notice about the words on these pages?

> The words describe how things look, how they sound, and how they feel when you touch them. We can write a poem about the things we observed.

Talk About What to Write

Talk about a plan to write a poem using sensory language and similes.

> What should the title of our poem be?

> How can we describe the leaves?

- Ask children to offer words that describe the leaves. Encourage descriptive words, for example *float* instead of *fall*. Point out how the poem looks on the page.

Write Together

Write a nature poem. While one child shares the pen, keep other children engaged by having them find the letters on the Initial Consonant Cluster Linking Chart or ABC chart.

▶ Write *Leaves* as the title.

> *Leaves* is the title of our poem. The title goes at the top.

> The first word of the poem is *Bright*. Say *bright*. What two sounds do you hear at the beginning?

▶ As children identify the letters using the consonant clusters chart, guide a volunteer to write *Br*. Finish the word.

▶ Continue writing the poem by having children contribute other consonant clusters (*gr*, *cr*, *br*, *fl*, *gr*) or vowel pairs like *ee*, *ow*, *oa*, and *ou*. Write any high-frequency words they already know.

▶ Point out that not all poems rhyme.

Read and Revisit

Ask the children to read the poem with you as you point under each word. You might have children revisit the poem for the following reason.

▶ Ask children to think of rhyming words for some of the words in the poem (e.g., *light/ night/sight*, *down/town*, *boat/coat/goat*).

Summarize and Apply/Extend

Summarize the learning. You might also decide to extend the learning.

> You learned that you can write a poem about things you notice in nature by describing what you see, hear, smell, and feel. You also learned that poems do not have to rhyme.

▶ Have children illustrate the poem.

▶ Encourage children to write nature poems in the writing center. Gather the poems together into a book for the class library.

You Will Need

- books about plants, such as the following from *Fountas & Pinnell Classroom™ Interactive Read-Aloud Collection* Text Set: Understanding the Natural World: Planting and Growing:
  - *From Seed to Plant* by Gail Gibbons
  - *Plant Packages: A Book About Seeds* by Susan Blackaby
- materials to grow seeds
- paper to make a class book
- markers
- To download the following online resource for this lesson, visit **resources.fountasandpinnell.com**:
  - Alphabet Linking Chart

Academic Language/ Important Vocabulary

- how-to
- steps

Continuum Connection

- Understand that a procedural text helps people know how to do something (p. 250)
- Write sequential directions in procedural or how-to books (p. 250)
- Spell approximately one hundred high-frequency words conventionally and reflect spelling in final drafts (p. 255)
- Hear and identify short vowel sounds in words and the letters that represent them (p. 368)
- Use known word parts (some are words) to solve unknown larger words: e.g., *in/into*, *can/canvas*, *us/crust* (p. 369)

ACTIVE LEARNING EXPERIENCE

▶ Prior to the lesson, read and discuss books about plants (see You Will Need). Then give children the opportunity to plant seeds to grow plants that they can observe and write about later (see IW.23: Making Scientific Observations).

GOAL

▶ Use known word parts to write new words.

▶ Say a word slowly to hear and write a letter that represents the beginning, middle, or final consonant sound.

▶ Write known words quickly.

RATIONALE

▶ When you write a how-to book with children, they learn about a functional type of writing that can be used in everyday life to communicate a process.

ASSESS LEARNING

▶ Observe children's use of known word parts to write new words.

▶ Notice whether children say words slowly to hear the sounds.

▶ Notice whether they can write some high-frequency words.

INTERACTIVE WRITING LESSON

The lesson is designed as an interactive writing lesson. Alternatively, you might choose to do all the writing yourself (shared writing).

Establish Purpose

Display some of the books you have read aloud about plants.

> We can write a how-to book to teach other people how to plant seeds.

Talk About What to Write

Talk about what to write in the how-to book.

> First, we need to list the materials that people will need to plant a seed. What are some things they will need?

> First, we will write the materials for planting seeds in a list. Then we'll write the steps on the pages of our how-to book.

Section 1: Interactive Writing

Write Together

Write the text for the how-to book. Invite several children to share the pen.

▶ Write *Materials* and read it aloud.

> What is the first thing people will need? Say *pot*. *Pot* rhymes with *not*. You can use *not* to help you write *pot*.
>
> Who would like to write the word *pot*?

▶ Guide a volunteer to write the word *pot*. Then write *soil*.

> What else do people need? They need seeds.

▶ Invite a child to the chart.

> Say *seeds* slowly. *Seed* has a word part that you know: *see*. How do we change *see* to make it *seed*?

▶ Have the child write *seed*. Add an *s* to make it plural. Invite a child to the chart to help you write *water*.

> Clap *wa-ter*. What sound do you hear at the beginning of *water*?

▶ Invite the child to write *w*. Write *at*. Say *water* again to have children listen for the sound at the end. Have the child write *er*.

▶ Continue in a similar manner to write each step on a page, inviting different children to write high-frequency words (e.g., *put*, *make*) and/or letters to represent easy-to-hear sounds. Other steps might be to make a hole in the soil, put the seeds in the hole, and water the seeds.

Read and Revisit

Read aloud the how-to book together, pointing under each word. You might have children revisit the text for the following reason.

▶ Say a word that rhymes with a word in the how-to book. Have children identify the rhyming word.

Summarize and Invite/Extend

Summarize the lesson. You might wish to extend the learning.

> Today we wrote a how-to book about how to plant a seed. You can write your own how-to book about anything that you know how to do!

▶ Invite children to create a cover and illustrations for the how-to book.

▶ Children will write about their plants in IW.23: Making Scientific Observations.

You Will Need

- at least one book that describes a life cycle, such as *The Dandelion Seed* by Joseph Anthony, from *Fountas & Pinnell Classroom™ Interactive Read-Aloud Collection* Text Set: Understanding the Natural World: Planting and Growing
- chart paper and markers

Academic Language/ Important Vocabulary

- life cycle
- diagram
- word

Continuum Connection

- Use vocabulary appropriate for the topic (p. 254)
- Use drawings to show how something looks, how something works, or the process or change (p. 256)
- Select information that will support the topic (p. 256)
- Recognize and say consonant clusters that blend two or three consonant sounds (onsets): e.g., *bl, cl, gr* (p. 367)
- Use known word parts (some are words) to solve unknown larger words: e.g., *in/into, can/canvas; us/crust* (p. 369)

ACTIVE LEARNING EXPERIENCE

- Prior to the lesson, read and discuss books about plant life cycles (see You Will Need). If children have not already planted seeds and observed them growing, do so now.

GOAL

- Learn that a diagram shows how something looks or how something works.
- Recognize and say the consonant cluster at the beginning of a word.
- Use known word parts to write new words.
- Recognize that the same word part can represent more than one sound.

RATIONALE

- When you make a life-cycle diagram with children, they learn that writing can be combined with images to explain complex processes.

ASSESS LEARNING

- Notice whether children can hear and identify the letters in consonant clusters.
- Observe whether they can use known word parts to write new words.
- Confirm that they understand that some word parts represent multiple sounds.

INTERACTIVE WRITING LESSON

The lesson is designed as an interactive writing lesson. Alternatively, you might choose to do all the writing yourself (shared writing).

Establish Purpose

Display *The Dandelion Seed*.

> In this book, you learned about the life cycle of a dandelion. We can make a diagram showing all that happens. A diagram is a special type of picture that shows the parts of something or how something works. It usually has both words and drawings.

Talk About What to Write

Talk about what to write for each step in the life-cycle diagram.

- Discuss each major step in the life cycle. With children, decide on a sentence to write for each step.

Write Together

Write a title and text for the life-cycle diagram. Invite several children to share the pen.

> Let's say the first sentence together.

▶ Write the first part of the sentence and have children read what you have written to get ready for the next word.

> What should we write next?

> Say *blow* slowly to listen for the two sounds at the beginning. What are the two letters that go with those sounds?

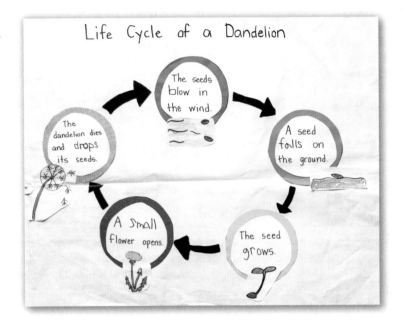

▶ Guide a volunteer to write *bl.* Then write the rest of the sentence yourself.

▶ Invite a child to write the word *falls.*

> What happens next? The next step is *A seed falls to the ground.* Say *falls. Fall* has a word part that you know, *all.* What should we add to *all* to get *fall*? What do we have to add to *fall* to get *falls*?

▶ Continue in a similar manner with the rest of the steps in the life cycle.

Read and Revisit

Read aloud the life-cycle diagram together, pointing under each word. You might have children revisit the text for one or both of the following reasons.

▶ Invite children to find words that have the letters *ow* (*blow, flower, grow*). Ask them if the letters *ow* in the words sound the same or different.

▶ Ask children to identify a new word that they learned how to spell today.

Summarize and Invite/Extend

Summarize the learning and invite children to illustrate the diagram.

> Today we made a life-cycle diagram about the life of a dandelion.

▶ Invite children to illustrate the diagram. You might also help them label parts of their drawings (roots, leaves, etc.).

You Will Need

- books about plants, such as the following from *Fountas & Pinnell Classroom™ Interactive Read-Aloud Collection* Text Set: Understanding the Natural World: Planting and Growing:

  - *From Seed to Plant* by Gail Gibbons

  - *Plant Packages: A Book About Seeds* by Susan Blackaby

- chart paper prepared with a template for a bar graph

- markers

Academic Language/Important Vocabulary

- scientific
- observation
- question mark
- chart
- title
- label

Continuum Connection

- Understand that a label can add important information (p. 250)

- Observe carefully to detect and describe change (growth, change over time in plants or animals, chemical changes in food), and talk about observations (p. 256)

- Add a phoneme to the beginning of a word: /s/ + *it* = *sit* (p. 367)

- Recognize and say consonant clusters that blend two or three consonant sounds (onsets): e.g., *pl* (p. 367)

- Use known word parts (some are words) to solve unknown larger words: e.g., *in*/*into*, *can*/*canvas*; *us*/*crust* (p. 369)

ACTIVE LEARNING EXPERIENCE

- Prior to the lesson, read and enjoy several books about plants (see You Will Need). Right before this lesson, help children measure their plants (see IW.21: Writing a How-to Book) by cutting string or strips of paper equal to the height of their plants. Save the strings or strips of paper to make the chart.

GOAL

- Recognize and say the consonant cluster at the beginning of a word.

- Use known word parts to write new words.

- Talk about the use of question marks.

RATIONALE

- When you record scientific observations with children, they learn to make careful observations and measurements and record what they notice. This process helps children understand that writers have many purposes for writing.

ASSESS LEARNING

- Look for evidence that children understand the purpose of a chart.

- Notice whether children recognize and say consonant clusters.

- Observe whether children are able to use known word parts to spell new words.

INTERACTIVE WRITING LESSON

The lesson is designed as an interactive writing lesson. Alternatively, you might choose to do all the writing yourself (shared writing).

Establish Purpose

Talk about the children's plant measurements.

> You measured your plants to see how tall they have grown. We can make a chart to show how tall your plants are. First, we will write a question.

Talk About What to Write

Talk about what question to ask.

> Think about what we want to know. What question do we want to ask about your plants?

Write Together

Create the chart. Invite volunteers to share the pen.

> Say the question with me.
>
> I will write the word *How*. Who would like to write the next word, *tall*? Say it with me: *t-all*. What word part do you hear at the end of *tall*?
>
> *Tall* has the word part *all*. What do we need to add to *all* to make *tall*?

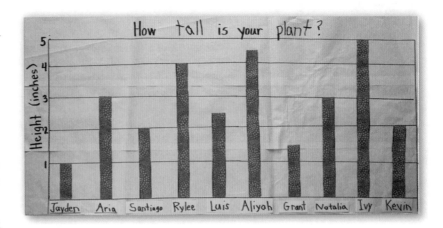

❱ Write *is your*. Then invite a child to write *plant*.

> What's the next word in our sentence?
>
> The next word is *plant*. Say it in parts: *pl-ant*. What two sounds do you hear at the beginning of *plant*? And how would we write the word *ant*?
>
> What do we need to write at the end of our sentence to show that it's a question?

❱ Write a question mark. Then have children glue their precut pieces of string or paper to the chart and write their names.

> When you write your name, you are adding a label to the chart. The labels help the readers know what information the chart shows.

❱ Point to and read the other labels on the chart.

Read and Revisit

Invite the children to read the chart with you as you point under the words. You might have them revisit the text for the following reason.

❱ Invite children to identify words or names with particular word parts (e.g., *in* in *inches*, *ant* in *Grant*).

Summarize and Invite/Extend

Summarize the lesson. You might also decide to extend the learning.

> Today we made a chart to show our scientific observations.

❱ Use interactive writing to write sentences that show conclusions (e.g., *Ivy has the tallest plant; Jayden has the shortest plant*).

You Will Need

- a book about ocean animals and habitats, such as *On Kiki's Reef* by Carol L. Malnor from *Fountas & Pinnell Classroom™ Interactive Read-Aloud Collection* Text Set: Understanding the Natural World: Oceans
- children's drawings (see Active Learning Experience)
- word cards or sentence strips for the labels and captions
- markers

Academic Language/ Important Vocabulary

- mural
- label
- fact
- plural
- vowel

Continuum Connection

- Use new vocabulary from texts when writing to appropriately reflect meaning (p. 178)
- Think about the readers (audience) and what they need to know (p. 251)
- Select interesting information to include in a piece of writing (p. 251)
- Recognize and use plurals that add -s: e.g., *books, cars, dogs, farms, mothers, zoos* (p. 368)
- Say a word slowly to hear the sounds in sequence (p. 369)

ACTIVE LEARNING EXPERIENCE

- Prior to the lesson, read several books about ocean animals and their habitats, such as *On Kiki's Reef* by Carol L. Malnor. Then help children make a list of sea creatures to include in an ocean habitat mural. Have children draw pictures of the animals and paint a blue background for the mural in the art center.

GOAL

- Understand that writers think about what their readers would like to know and find interesting.
- Hear and identify easy-to-hear long and short vowel sounds.
- Recognize and use plurals that add -s.
- Use content vocabulary when writing an informational text.

RATIONALE

- When you help children make an ocean habitat mural, they learn that they can use a combination of writing and pictures to provide information about a topic. They begin to think about what their readers may want to know about a topic.

ASSESS LEARNING

- Observe how children decide what information to include in their writing.
- Notice whether children can hear and identify long and short vowel sounds.
- Observe whether children can form plural nouns with -s.

INTERACTIVE WRITING LESSON

The lesson is designed as an interactive writing lesson. Alternatively, you might choose to do all the writing yourself (shared writing).

Establish Purpose

Display the children's drawings.

> Today we're going to make a mural using your ocean pictures. We will label your animals and write facts about them so readers can learn more about sea creatures.

Talk About What to Write

Talk about what to write for the labels and captions for the mural. Use several of the children's drawings to decide what to write.

> _____, what animal did you draw?

> What is an interesting fact about this animal?

Write Together

Add the drawings to the mural and write labels and captions for them. Invite several children to share the pen.

> Let's begin with _____'s drawing of a sea turtle. I will write the label *Sea Turtle*. What is an interesting fact about sea turtles?

▶ Write the sentence up to the word *five*.

> Say the word *five* slowly.

▶ Ask children to identify the sounds they hear first, next, and last as a child writes the letters for each of the sounds.

> What do you need to put at the end to make it look right?

▶ Write the rest of the sentence.

▶ Add a picture of a coral reef to the mural. Write the label *Coral Reef* and read it aloud. Have children name a fact about coral reefs and compose a sentence to write.

> Let's write *Coral reefs are not plants*.

▶ Write the beginning of the sentence. Then invite children to say *plants* slowly as a volunteer writes the letter for each sound.

▶ Continue in a similar manner with several more sea creatures. Help children identify and write word parts they are learning such as initial and final clusters and vowel pairs.

Read and Revisit

Invite the children to read the text with you as you point under the words. You might have children revisit the text for one or both of the following reasons.

▶ Invite children to identify words with consonant clusters or vowel pairs.

▶ Ask children to identify the number words.

Summarize and Invite/Extend

Summarize the lesson. You might also decide to extend the learning.

> Today we made an ocean mural. As we have time, we will finish the mural.

▶ Encourage children to write labels and captions for pictures in the books they make.

You Will Need

- a familiar book related to caring for the earth, such as *On Kiki's Reef* by Carol L. Malnor, from *Fountas & Pinnell Classroom™ Interactive Read-Aloud Collection* Text Set: Understanding the Natural World: Oceans
- chart paper and markers
- To download the following online resources for this lesson, visit **resources.fountasandpinnell.com**:
  - Alphabet Linking Chart
  - High-Frequency Word List

Academic Language/ Important Vocabulary

- letter
- opinion
- word
- sentence

Continuum Connection

- Write with a specific purpose in mind (p. 250)
- Include important information in the communication (p. 250)
- Use a capital letter for the first word of a sentence (p. 255)
- Use periods, exclamation marks, and question marks as end marks (p. 255)
- Delete the beginning phoneme of a word: e.g., *can, an* (delete /k/) (p. 367)
- Add a phoneme to the end of a word: e.g., *an + d = and* (p. 367)
- Recognize and use contractions with *is* or *has*: e.g., *he's, she's, it's* (p. 368)

ACTIVE LEARNING EXPERIENCE

- Read and have rich conversations about books related to caring for the earth, such as *On Kiki's Reef*. Share People Helping Turtles at the end of the book and talk about how people can make a difference in the world. Walk around the school and talk about ways children might help the earth right at their school or around town.

GOALS

- Learn that a letter can express an opinion.
- Understand the concept of a sentence.
- Understand that sentences begin with capital letters and end with punctuation.
- Write high-frequency words quickly.

RATIONALE

- When children gain inspiration for writing from books they have read, they recognize that they can use writing to share their opinions with others.

ASSESS LEARNING

- Notice whether children understand that writing can be used to share opinions.
- Take note of whether children understand the concept of a sentence and that it begins with a capital letter and ends with a punctuation mark.
- Observe whether children can write high-frequency words quickly.

INTERACTIVE WRITING LESSON

For this lesson, use any book related to caring for the earth. If you have *The Reading Minilessons Book, Grade 1* (Fountas and Pinnell 2019), you might teach WAR.U5: Writing Opinions About Books as a foundation for this lesson. Make sure children understand the two meanings of *letter*.

Establish Purpose

Introduce the idea of writing a letter to share an opinion.

> When we read *On Kiki's Reef*, we shared our thinking about it by talking. Another way to share your thinking is by writing a letter. We can write a letter to a newspaper to share our opinion about taking care of the earth.

Talk About What to Write

Talk about what to write in the letter.

- Have the children focus their thinking on one thing that can be done locally to take care of the earth (e.g., install recycling bins in areas around town).

> What one thing can be done to help take care of our town? How might our letter start?

Write Together

Write the letter. Invite several children to write word parts and new high-frequency words they are learning.

▶ Write the salutation, explaining that it tells whom you are writing to.

> Let's say the first sentence. What type of letter is at the beginning of a sentence?

> In a letter, you begin writing on the line below the greeting, so I will start here.

▶ Start writing the first sentence, asking children to clap *a-bout* as you write it. Invite a child to write *ways*.

> You know the word *day*. How can you use *day* to write *way*?

▶ Add the *s* and finish writing the sentence.

> What punctuation mark goes at the end?

Dear Town,
We read about ways to take care of the earth. We want to help take care of our town. We could put recycling bins in the library. It's important not to waste paper. We hope you'll do this. Please remember don't waste paper!
From,
Room 1A

▶ Say the next sentence with children. Write it, pausing before *take*. Say *take* slowly and have a child write the letters to represent the sounds she hears (*tak*).

> What do you need to add to make it look right?

▶ Continue writing the letter. Invite a child to contribute at selected points that offer learning value.

Read and Revisit

Read the sentences with children, using a pointer to point under each word. You might have children revisit the letter for the following reason.

▶ Invite children to find a contraction and say the two words the contraction represents.

Summarize and Apply/Extend

Summarize the lesson. You might also decide to extend the learning.

> We wrote a letter about taking care of the earth. Today, you can write a letter about another way to help. Someone could add an illustration to the letter.

▶ Revisit a story about friendly letter writing, such as *Dear Juno* by Soyung Pak, from *Fountas & Pinnell Classroom™ Interactive Read-Aloud Collection* Text Set: Journeys Near and Far. Then encourage children to write a letter to a family member or friend.

Interactive writing is a way to provide modeling and support for children as they learn to make their own books. Below is a complete all-about book that shows what is possible when you show children what they can do. Once a class book is complete, it can be used for shared reading and as a mentor text when children make their own similar books.

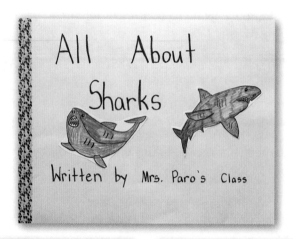

All About Sharks

Written by Mrs. Paro's Class

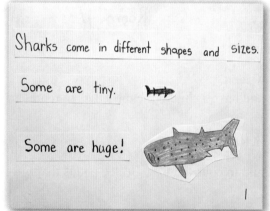

Sharks come in different shapes and sizes.

Some are tiny.

Some are huge!

1

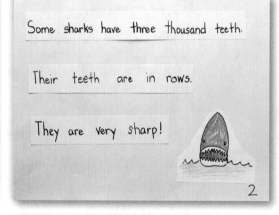

Some sharks have three thousand teeth.

Their teeth are in rows.

They are very sharp!

2

A shark's skin feels rough. It feels just like sandpaper. The rough skin helps the shark swim better.

3

A baby shark is called a pup.
Some baby sharks are about 20 inches long.
A baby great white shark is about 5 feet long!

4

Management

MANAGEMENT MINILESSONS WILL help you set up routines for learning and working together in the classroom. They allow you to teach effectively and efficiently and are directed toward the creation of an orderly, busy classroom in which children know what is expected and how to behave responsibly and respectfully in a community of learners. A class that has a strong feeling of community is a safe place for all children to do their best work and have fun. Most of the minilessons at the beginning of the school year will come from this section.

2 | Management

Minilessons in This Umbrella

School

WML1	Get to know your classmates.
WML2	Use an appropriate voice level.
WML3	Move from one spot to another quickly and silently.
WML4	Turn and talk to share your thinking.
WML5	Listen carefully to each other.
WML6	Do your best work.
WML7	Find ways to solve problems when you need help.
WML8	Take good care of classroom materials.
WML9	Use kind words.

Before Teaching Umbrella 1 Minilessons

This set of minilessons helps you establish a respectful and organized classroom community in which members get to know and understand each other. If you use *The Reading Minilessons Book, Grade 1* (Fountas and Pinnell 2019) and have already taught the first umbrellas in the Management and Literary Analysis sections, you do not need to teach this umbrella.

After teaching each minilesson, provide a drawing and writing activity so that children have something to do for about ten minutes as they apply what they have learned about working together. For example, MGT.U1.WML1 asks children to make an identity web. The web could be continued for another day or two. On subsequent days, children could be asked to draw and write about their families, their friends, what they like to do at home or school, or places they like to go.

We recommend that toward the middle or end of this umbrella you teach IW.2: Writing About Our Classroom. Read books from the classroom library or use books from *Fountas & Pinnell Classroom ™ Interactive Read-Aloud Collection* text sets about what it means to be part of a caring community.

Learning and Working Together: School

A Fine, Fine School by Sharon Creech

First Day Jitters by Julie Danneberg

Jamaica's Blue Marker by Juanita Havill

Section 2: Management

Writing Minilesson Principle
Get to know your classmates.

Working Together in the Classroom

You Will Need

▸ chart paper prepared with a sketch or photo of yourself and a web of details to help children get to know you

▸ chart paper and markers

▸ To download the following online resource for this lesson, visit **resources.fountasandpinnell.com**:

  ▪ chart art (optional)

Academic Language / Important Vocabulary

▸ community

▸ proud

▸ special

Continuum Connection

▸ Sustain a conversation with others: e.g., teachers, family, peers (p. 332)

▸ Enter a conversation appropriately (p. 332)

GOAL

Learn to value one another's unique identities as part of a community of learners.

RATIONALE

When children feel valued for their identities and recognize what makes them unique, they learn to value the special qualities of their classmates. This common feeling creates a rich, interesting classroom community in which children feel comfortable expressing themselves in writing.

ASSESS LEARNING

▸ Observe whether children show an interest in getting to know classmates.

▸ Look for evidence that children value special qualities in themselves and others.

▸ Look for evidence that children can use vocabulary such as *community*, *proud*, and *special*.

MINILESSON

Engage children in a conversation about getting to know and appreciate one another using a web with a sketch or photograph of yourself. Then provide a lesson to help children brainstorm ways they can learn about each other. Here is an example.

▸ Show the prepared chart and read the words to children.

   What do you notice that I have done?

   This web gives information so you can get to know me better. What kinds of things did I share about myself?

▸ As children respond, use a new sheet of chart paper to list general categories.

   What other kinds of things could we talk about to get to know each other?

▸ Continue adding to the list.

   How does getting to know your classmates make the classroom community a good place for writing, drawing, and working together?

▸ Guide children to understand that sharing things that make them proud, special, and unique allows classmates to value each other. Help them understand that when they know each other, they feel more comfortable sharing through drawing and writing.

Have a Try

Invite children to turn and talk to get to know each other.

> Choose one of the things on the chart to talk about with your partner.

▶ After time for discussion, ask a few volunteers to share what they learned about their partner.

Summarize and Apply

Summarize the lesson. Write the principle on the chart.

> Today you learned ways to get to know your classmates so you can enjoy and appreciate each other. During writing time, draw a picture of yourself and add drawings and words to show some of the ways you are special.

▶ Additionally, you might take a photo of each child and place it in the center of a web.

Confer

▶ During independent writing, move around the room to confer briefly with as many individual children as time allows. Sit side by side with them and invite them to talk about making their webs. Use the following prompts as needed.

- *Why is it important to get to know your classmates?*
- *What makes you special?*
- *What is your favorite thing to do when you are not at school?*

Share

Following independent writing, gather children in the meeting area to share something special about themselves.

> What did you draw or write about yourself today? Share something about yourself that makes you proud.

Writing Minilesson Principle
Use an appropriate voice level.

Working Together in the Classroom

You Will Need

- chart paper and markers
- To download the following online resource for this lesson, visit **resources.fountasandpinnell.com**:
  - chart art (optional)

Academic Language / Important Vocabulary

- voice level
- appropriate
- silent
- soft
- normal
- loud

Continuum Connection

- Speak at an appropriate volume (p. 332)

GOAL

Learn to use an appropriate voice level for the activity.

RATIONALE

When you explicitly teach appropriate voice volume, children learn to independently determine the acceptable noise level for various settings and activities, both inside and outside of the classroom.

ASSESS LEARNING

- Observe whether children can identify appropriate activities for each voice level.
- Notice whether children articulate why using an appropriate voice level is important.
- Look for evidence that children use the appropriate voice level for the activity they are doing.
- Look for evidence that children can use vocabulary such as *voice level*, *appropriate*, *silent*, *soft*, *normal*, and *loud*.

MINILESSON

To help children think about the minilesson principle, engage them in conversation about using an appropriate voice level and work with them to construct a reference chart. Here is an example.

- Talk about why you use a soft voice sometimes and a loud voice sometimes.

  One way to help each other do your best work in the classroom is to use an appropriate voice. An appropriate voice is the voice level that is best for what you are doing. For example, when you are playing outside, would you use a soft voice or a loud voice?

  When you are reading and writing, how might your voice sound?

  We can talk about the kind of voice to use by using a number. A 0 voice means you are silent; you are not saying anything.

- Begin a voice level chart to show appropriate voice levels. Write the numeral *0* and the word *silent* along with a speech bubble that says *Shhh*.

  What are times at school when we use a 0 voice?

- As children provide examples, write them on the chart.

- Repeat the procedure for each voice level. Show that a 1 means using a soft voice, a 2 means using a normal voice, and a 3 means using a loud voice.

Have a Try

Invite children to practice using a good voice level with a partner.

▶ Select an activity to engage the children in practicing using an appropriate voice level.

> You can practice using an appropriate voice level for partner work. Look at the chart to help you. Turn and talk to your partner. Use a good voice level to talk about something you like to do.

Summarize and Apply

Help children summarize the lesson. Remind them to speak in the voice level appropriate for the activity.

> Look at the chart. What does it show you about which voice level to use?

> Think about the appropriate voice level to use during writing time. Practice using that voice level as you draw and write.

▶ Keep the voice level chart posted so children can refer to it.

Our Voice Level Chart

0	1	2	3
Silent	Soft	Normal	Loud
Shhh...			!!!
-Working by yourself	-Small-group work	-Whole-group work	-Outside recess
-Independent reading	-Partner work	-Meetings	
-Independent writing/drawing	-Snack	-Read-aloud	
-Hallways		-Shared reading	
		-Interactive writing	

Confer

▶ During independent writing, move around the room to confer briefly with as many individual children as time allows. Sit side by side with them and invite them to talk about voice levels. Use the following prompts as needed.

• Look at the chart. What voice level are you using as you draw (write)?

• Why is it important to use a 0 voice when you are writing?

• When you share your writing with classmates, what voice level will you use?

Share

Following independent writing, gather children in the meeting area to talk about the voice levels they have used so far today.

> Talk about what voice levels you used today. What were you doing?

Writing Minilesson Principle
Move from one spot to another quickly and silently.

Working Together in the Classroom

You Will Need

- three children prepared to demonstrate transitioning
- voice level chart from WML2
- chart paper and markers
- To download the following online resource for this lesson, visit **resources.fountasandpinnell.com**:
  - chart art (optional)

Academic Language / Important Vocabulary

- quickly
- silently
- voice level
- meeting area

GOAL

Learn how to transition from one activity to another in the classroom.

RATIONALE

Setting clear expectations for transitions in the classroom increases time available for learning. These expectations additionally provide a model for how children should move outside of the classroom.

ASSESS LEARNING

- Observe children as they transition from one activity to the next.
- Notice whether children are able to articulate how to act during transitions.
- Look for evidence that children can use vocabulary such as *quickly*, *silently*, *voice level*, and *meeting area*.

MINILESSON

To help children think about the minilesson principle, engage them in a demonstration and discussion of how to transition smoothly between activities. Here is an example.

> There are many different places that you work and learn in the classroom. Sometimes you work in the meeting area. Sometimes you work at your tables.

- Invite three volunteers to demonstrate.

> We are going to watch _____, _____, and _____ walk from the meeting area back to the writing area. Remember to walk quickly (but don't run) and silently.

- After the demonstration, talk about what the volunteers did. As children discuss, record each step of the transition process on chart paper.

> What did you notice about how they moved from one place to another?

- Point to the voice chart.

> Look at the voice chart. What voice level did they use when they moved?

- Ask the volunteers to return to the meeting area.

> Why is it important that they moved quickly and silently and used a 0, that is, a silent voice level?

> Where did they put their hands and feet when they sat down in their spots?

Have a Try

Invite children to practice transitioning from one place to another.

❯ Decide on a signal to indicate the children should transition.

> You can practice moving from one place to another. When I give this signal, please move quickly and silently to your table.

❯ Signal children to move.

> Now, please move back to the meeting area.

❯ Signal children to move.

Summarize and Apply

Help children summarize the lesson. Remind them how to transition from one place to another.

> How should you move from one spot to another?

❯ Write the principle at the top of the chart.

> When it is time to come back to the meeting area after writing time, put your materials away carefully and walk quickly and silently.

Move from one spot to another quickly and silently.

- Walk quickly but do not run.

- Use a 0 voice level.

Shhh...

- Keep hands and feet in your space.

Confer

❯ During independent writing, move around the room to confer briefly with as many individual children as time allows. Sit side by side with them and invite them to talk about transitioning. Use the following prompts as needed.

- *What are you working on today?*
- *What will you draw and write on the next page?*
- *Show how you will move back to the meeting area when you finish.*

Share

Following independent writing, gather children in the meeting area to talk about what they learned today.

> Tell what you learned about moving from one spot to another.

> Why is it important that you move quickly and silently in the classroom?

Writing Minilesson Principle
Turn and talk to share your thinking.

You Will Need

- a child prepared to demonstrate turn and talk

- one or two familiar texts that children enjoy, such as *A Fine, Fine School* by Sharon Creech and *First Day Jitters* by Julie Danneberg, from Text Set: Learning and Working Together: School

- chart paper and markers

- To download the following online resource for this lesson, visit **resources.fountasandpinnell.com**:

  - chart art (optional)

Academic Language / Important Vocabulary

- turn and talk
- listen
- signal
- voice level
- eye contact

Continuum Connection

- Look at the speaker when being spoken to (p. 332)

- Engage actively in conversational routines: e.g., turn and talk (p. 332)

GOAL

Develop guidelines for turn and talk.

RATIONALE

Turn and talk is a routine that provides all children an opportunity to express themselves verbally and engage in conversation with others. It helps children develop thinking and listening skills. Establishing clear guidelines for the routine gives all children numerous opportunities to share.

ASSESS LEARNING

- Observe whether children actively listen to one another when they turn and talk.

- Notice whether children take turns, make eye contact, and use body language to show they are listening.

- Look for evidence that children can use vocabulary such as *turn and talk*, *listen*, *signal*, *voice level*, and *eye contact*.

MINILESSON

To help children think about the minilesson principle, choose familiar texts to provide an inquiry-based lesson. If you haven't read *A Fine, Fine School* with the class yet, substitute any familiar book or read the book to the child who will participate in the demonstration.

- Show the front cover of *A Fine, Fine School*.

  Sometimes when you read a book or draw or write something, you turn and talk to a partner about your thinking. _____ is my partner, and we are going to turn and talk about interesting parts in *A Fine, Fine School*.

  While we turn and talk, notice what we are doing with our bodies and voices.

- Ask the participating child to talk to you about something interesting about the book.

- Briefly model the turn and talk procedure.

  What did you notice about the way we turned our bodies and talked to each other?

- List and sketch (or add the downloadable art for) children's responses on chart paper to create guidelines for turn and talk. If children mention looking at their partners, take into consideration that some children may not be comfortable establishing or able to establish eye contact because of cultural conventions or for other reasons.

  When you share your thinking with a partner, each of you gets to talk.

Have a Try

Invite children to turn and talk to share their thinking with a partner.

▶ Show the cover of *First Day Jitters* or any book that children have heard read aloud.

> Turn and talk to your partner about what you noticed or found interesting.

▶ After time for discussion, ask a few children to share what they did during turn and talk.

Summarize and Apply

Help children summarize the lesson. Write the principle on the chart. Tell children to think about what they could share about their writing during turn and talk.

> Look at the chart. What should you do when you turn and talk to a partner?

> Today you learned that you can share your thinking with others. During writing time today, continue working on writing you have already started or begin something new. Later, you will turn and talk to share with a partner.

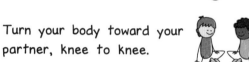

Turn and talk to share your thinking.

Look at your partner.

Wait for your partner to finish talking.

Use a soft voice.

Listen carefully to your partner.

Turn your body toward your partner, knee to knee.

Stop talking at the signal and turn back.

Confer

▶ During independent writing, move around the room to confer briefly with as many individual children as time allows. Sit side by side with them and invite them to talk about how they will share their thinking. Use the following prompts as needed.

- *Look at the chart. What is one thing you will do when you turn and talk?*
- *What would you like to draw or write today that you can share with your partner?*
- *Why is it important to stop talking at the signal and turn to look at me?*

Share

Following independent writing, gather children in the meeting area in pairs. Have them bring their work from today.

> Turn and talk to your partner to share what you worked on today. Look at the chart to remember how to turn and talk.

Writing Minilesson Principle
Listen carefully to each other.

Working Together in the Classroom

You Will Need

- voice level chart from WML2
- chart paper and markers
- To download the following online resource for this lesson, visit **resources.fountasandpinnell.com**:
  - chart art (optional)

Academic Language / Important Vocabulary

- listen
- carefully
- speaker
- politely
- agree
- disagree

Continuum Connection

- Look at the speaker when being spoken to (p. 332)
- Demonstrate respectful listening behaviors (p. 332)
- Listen and respond to a partner by agreeing or disagreeing and explaining reasons (p. 332)

GOAL

Learn expectations for listening during whole- or small-group meetings.

RATIONALE

When you teach children to listen to classmates during whole- or small-group instruction, you promote effective communication and collaboration and support respectful behavior in the classroom.

ASSESS LEARNING

- Observe whether children can explain why it is important to listen to each other and to the teacher.
- Look for evidence that children follow the listening guidelines from the chart.
- Look for evidence that children can use vocabulary such as *listen*, *carefully*, *speaker*, *politely*, *agree*, and *disagree*.

MINILESSON

To help children think about the minilesson principle, engage them in discussing effective listening behaviors and in creating listening guidelines. Here is an example.

> **When one person in the classroom talks, the rest of us listen. What does it look like to be a good listener in our classroom?**

- Guide the conversation to help children talk about what a good listener does. Show the voice level chart from WML2 to help children make the connection between voice level and listening. Prompt the conversation as needed with questions such as the following.
  - *What does your body look like when you are listening?*
  - *When you listen, what are you thinking about?*
  - *When someone finishes talking, how can you respond to show you listened?*
  - *When you are listening, what voice level do you use?*
  - *What do you do when you have a question?*
- As children provide ideas, create guidelines on chart paper for how to be a good listener. If children mention looking at the speaker, take into consideration that some children may not be comfortable with establishing or able to establish eye contact because of cultural conventions or for other reasons.
- Post the chart to help children remember to listen carefully to each other.

Have a Try

Invite children to turn and talk about how to listen carefully.

> Look at the chart. Turn and tell your partner one thing that you will be sure to do the next time you listen to someone.

▶ Ask a few volunteers to share.

Summarize and Apply

Help children summarize the lesson. Remind them to listen carefully to each other.

▶ Write the principle on the chart.

> What are some ways to show that you are listening carefully? Look at the chart to remember.

> Remember to be a good listener when someone else is speaking. You can practice being a good listener when we meet later to share the writing you are working on.

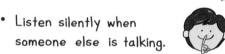

Listen carefully to each other.

- Look at the person who is talking.
- Think about what the speaker is saying. *I thought so too.*
- Say something to the speaker. *I like what you said.*
- Listen silently when someone else is talking.

Section 2: Management

Confer

▶ During independent writing, move around the room to confer briefly with as many individual children as time allows. Sit side by side with them and invite them to talk about listening carefully. As you do, model how to listen carefully. Use the following prompts as needed.

- *Let's talk about what you do when you listen.*
- *Show how your body looks when you are listening carefully.*
- *When someone finishes talking, how will you respond when you agree? disagree?*

Share

Following independent writing, gather children in the meeting area to share their writing and practice listening carefully

> Who would like to share your writing?

> While _____ shares, what will you do to listen carefully?

Writing Minilesson Principle
Do your best work.

Working Together in the Classroom

You Will Need

- four children prepared in advance to demonstrate the principle
- paper, pencils, and crayons
- chart paper and markers
- To download the following online resource for this lesson, visit **resources.fountasandpinnell.com**:
    - chart art (optional)

Academic Language / Important Vocabulary

- best
- focus
- independent

GOAL

Learn to start work promptly and stay focused.

RATIONALE

When you teach children to get to work promptly and stay focused, you promote independence. Setting the guidance to for other children.

ASSESS LEARNING

- Observe for evidence that children can articulate a goal for doing their best work.
- Look for evidence that children are able to stay focused.
- Look for evidence that children understand and use vocabulary such as *best*, *focus*, and *independent*.

MINILESSON

To help children think about the minilesson principle, engage them in a short demonstration of how to do their best work. Here is an example.

- In advance, prepare four children to demonstrate going to their table, taking out drawing/writing materials, starting right away, and staying focused.

    The work you do by yourself is important. Watch as your classmates do their best work.

- Give directions to the four children you have prepared in advance to go to the writing area and start writing or drawing a picture. Have the rest of the class observe for a brief time. Call the four children back to the meeting area, allowing others to observe how they put materials away and then move silently and quickly as they return.

    What did you notice about how your classmates worked?

- Record children's responses on chart paper using general categories. Guide the conversation to help children notice the various ways that the participants did their best work.

Have a Try

Invite children to turn and talk about how they can do their best work.

> Look back at the chart. Think about one thing you do well and one thing you need to practice more in order to do your best independent work. Turn and talk to your partner how you will do your best work. You can start by saying "I am going to try to _____."

▶ After time for discussion, ask a few volunteers to share.

Summarize and Apply

Write the principle on the chart. Remind children to do their best work by reviewing the chart.

> During writing time today, you can practice all the ways to do your best work. You can look at the chart to remember.

Confer

▶ During independent writing, move around the room to confer briefly with as many individual children as time allows. Sit side by side with them and invite them to talk about doing their best work. Use the following prompts as needed.

- *What are you working on today?*
- *How can you do your best work?*
- *What are you doing right now to do your best work?*
- *What will you do when writing time is over?*

Share

Following independent writing, gather children in the meeting area. Ask a few children to talk about how they did their best work.

> Who did your best work today? Tell how you did your best work.

Section 2: Management

WML7
MGT.U1.WML7

Writing Minilesson Principle
Find ways to solve problems when you need help.

Working Together in the Classroom

You Will Need

- chart paper and markers
- To download the following online resource for this lesson, visit **resources.fountasandpinnell.com**:
  - chart art (optional)

Academic Language / Important Vocabulary

- problem solve
- help
- question
- ask
- directions
- emergency

GOAL

Find ways to solve problems independently when help is needed.

RATIONALE

When children learn how to collaborate and problem solve independently, they gain confidence. Their independence also frees you up to work with small groups or individuals without interruption.

ASSESS LEARNING

- Observe whether children are independently trying one or two ideas for problem solving.
- Look for evidence that children are able to get help when you are busy.
- Look for evidence that children understand and use vocabulary such as *problem solve*, *help*, *question*, *ask*, *directions*, and *emergency*.

MINILESSON

To help children think about the minilesson principle, engage them in a discussion of what to do when they need help. Here is an example.

- A few days before this minilesson, notice when and why children ask you for help. Use these observations for the discussion.

  Sometimes when you are working, you may need help. When I am talking to another person or working with a group, I may not be available to help you right away.

  What are some things you can do to get help on your own?

- Record ideas on chart paper. If children have trouble generating ideas, help them think through different scenarios. For example, if they did not understand directions for playing a game, what could they do? Guide them to think of resources in the room they could use and to understand that they could ask a classmate or, as a last resort, you.

- Briefly discuss what an emergency is and that it's okay to interrupt you if there is an emergency.

Have a Try

Invite children to act out and then discuss solving problems.

▶ Invite a few children to act out one or more of the following scenarios:

- *You don't know how to spell a word.*
- *You forgot what to do next.*
- *You forgot the directions for playing a game.*
- *Your pencil broke, and you don't have another.*

▶ After each scenario, ask children to turn and talk with a partner about how they could solve the problem without your help.

Summarize and Apply

Summarize the lesson. Write the principle on the chart. Remind children to think about how to solve problems.

What are some ways you can solve problems when I am busy? When you are working on writing today, try to solve any problems you have by yourself, ask a classmate, or do your best until I am free to help you.

Find ways to solve problems when you need help.

Reread the directions.

Use the word wall.

Ask a classmate in a soft voice.

Ask the teacher when she is not busy.

Confer

▶ During independent writing, move around the room to confer briefly with as many individual children as time allows. Sit side by side with them and invite them to talk about ways to solve problems. Use the following prompts as needed.

- *What can you do if you forget how to write your name on your paper?*
- *What can you do if you are not sure about the directions?*
- *If you want to make a book, but cannot find the paper, what can you do?*

Share

Following independent writing, gather children in the meeting area. Ask a few children to share their experiences solving problems.

Did you solve a problem today? Tell about what you did.

Working Together in the Classroom

You Will Need

▸ two children prepared to demonstrate using classroom materials

▸ chart paper and markers

▸ To download the following online resource for this lesson, visit **resources.fountasandpinnell.com**:

 ▪ chart art (optional)

Academic Language / Important Vocabulary

▸ take good care of

▸ materials

▸ return

GOAL

Learn to take good care of classroom materials and supplies and return them independently.

RATIONALE

When you teach children how to take care of supplies and return them to the correct location, you promote independence. You are also establishing respect for the materials and a process for keeping the classroom community organized.

ASSESS LEARNING

▸ Observe for evidence that children are taking good care of classroom materials.

▸ Look for evidence that children are able to get supplies and return them to the appropriate place.

▸ Look for evidence that children can use vocabulary such as *take good care of*, *materials*, and *return*.

MINILESSON

To help children think about the minilesson principle, engage them in a short demonstration and conversation about caring for materials. Here is an example.

▸ Have a brief discussion about how the materials are organized in the writing center and ensure all children understand what is meant by the term *materials*.

> What are some of the materials you use to draw and write in the classroom?

> Watch _____ and _____ get the materials they need to do their work. Pay attention to what they do with the materials when they finish working.

▸ Provide a few minutes for the children to demonstrate getting and returning the materials. Point out that the places where the materials belong are labeled.

> What did you notice?

> How can your classmates take good care of the materials when they use them?

> What does it mean to take good care of something?

▸ Add responses to chart paper. Show children how to match a materials box to its label on the shelf.

> How should the classroom sound when you are cleaning up? At the end of writing time, return materials quickly and silently to where they belong.

Have a Try

Invite children to practice taking care of classroom materials.

▶ Ask a few more children to model taking out different drawing and writing supplies and returning them.

> Turn and talk to your partner about how they used the materials and what they did when they were finished.

Summarize and Apply

Summarize the lesson. Write the principle on the chart. Remind children to take good care of classroom materials during writing time.

> Today you learned to get, care for, and return materials to the place where they belong so others can use them. During writing time, think about how to take good care of the materials.

> ### Take good care of classroom materials.
>
> • Get your materials.
>
> • Use them carefully.
>
> • Put materials away in the same place.

Confer

▶ During independent writing, move around the room to confer briefly with as many individual children as time allows. Sit side by side with them and invite them to talk about how they are taking good care of the classroom materials. Use the following prompts as needed.

  • *How will you show that you are taking good care of the writing materials today?*

  • *What will you do with the writing materials when you are finished using them?*

  • *Why is it important that each person in our classroom community takes good care of materials?*

Share

Following independent writing, gather children in the meeting area. Ask a few children to share their experiences taking care of materials.

> Put your thumb up if you returned the materials to where they belonged when you were finished.

> Who would like to share what you put away and where you put it?

Writing Minilesson Principle
Use kind words.

Working Together in the Classroom

You Will Need

▸ a familiar book that relates to communication, such as *Jamaica's Blue Marker* by Juanita Havill, from Text Set: Learning and Working Together: School

▸ chart paper and markers

Academic Language / Important Vocabulary

▸ kind words

▸ respect

▸ conversation

Continuum Connection

▸ Use courteous conversational conventions: e.g., *please*, *thank you*, greetings (p. 332)

▸ Enter a conversation appropriately (p. 332)

▸ Listen and respond to partner by agreeing or disagreeing and explaining reasons (p. 332)

▸ Express and reflect on their own feelings and recognize the feelings of others (p. 332)

GOAL

Learn to use language to facilitate discussion, express opinions, and show respect.

RATIONALE

When children use their words in a respectful way to communicate their opinions and feelings, they contribute to a positive learning environment and learn to show empathy and concern for others.

ASSESS LEARNING

▸ Observe whether children use their words to communicate in a positive way.

▸ Look for evidence that children use conventions of polite conversation.

▸ Look for evidence that children understand and use vocabulary such as *kind words*, *respect*, and *conversation*.

MINILESSON

To help children think about the minilesson principle, engage them in a conversation about how to use words in a positive way in the classroom. (If you haven't read *Jamaica's Blue Marker* with the class yet, take a moment to read it aloud now and revisit it in detail later.) Here is an example.

▸ Show the cover of *Jamaica's Blue Marker*.

> The way Jamaica uses her words with Russell is different at the beginning of the book from the way she uses them at the end of the book. Think about how she uses words as I show you a few pages.

▸ Revisit pages 6–7 and then pages 22–26.

> What did you notice about the different ways that Jamaica uses her words?

> Which way works better? Why?

▸ Have a brief discussion about how using words in a positive way helped Jamaica understand Russell and get along with him better.

> What are some kind words that you can say to each other in the classroom?

▸ Guide the conversation to help children talk about using kind and respectful language in the classroom. As they provide suggestions, make a list on chart paper of words and phrases to use to communicate positively.

> These are examples of words that you can use in a conversation to show respect for the person with whom you are talking.

Have a Try

Invite children to turn and talk about using words in a positive way.

> Look at the chart and think about one way you will practice using kind words today. Turn and talk to your partner about that.

▶ After time for a brief discussion, ask a few volunteers to share their thinking.

Summarize and Apply

Summarize the lesson. Write the principle on the chart. Remind children to use kind words in the classroom to have discussions, express opinions, and show respect.

> Today practice using kind words to help make the classroom a place where you can all work together. As you get your writing materials and put them away, look for a chance to say some kind words. For example, if someone hands you your writing folder, you could say thank you. Look at the chart to help you remember ideas.

Use kind words.

Please.

Thank you.

Excuse me.

Hi, my name is_____.
What's your name?

You're welcome.

Do you want to play with us?

We can share.

Confer

▶ During independent writing, move around the room to confer briefly with as many individual children as time allows. Sit side by side with them and invite them to talk about using kind words. Use the following prompts as needed.

- *How can you use words to share what you are thinking?*
- *How can you use words to show respect for your classmates?*
- *Show me how you can ask to share the glue in a kind way.*

Share

Following independent writing, gather children in the meeting area. Ask a few children to share their experiences using kind words.

> How did you use words in a good way today?

> Did anyone say kind words to you?

Assessment

After you have taught the minilessons in this umbrella, observe children in a variety of classroom activities. Use *The Literacy Continuum* (Fountas and Pinnell 2017) to notice, teach for, and support children's learning as you observe their attempts at building a classroom community.

▶ What evidence do you have of new understandings children have developed related to working together in the classroom community?

- Are children showing an interest in getting to know each other?
- Do they use voice levels appropriate for the activity?
- Are they transitioning from place to place quickly and quietly?
- Do they follow the procedures for turn and talk?
- Do they actively listen when someone is speaking?
- Do they start new work right away and stay focused?
- Are they using other resources besides the teacher for help?
- Are they taking good care of classroom materials and supplies and keeping the classroom clean and organized?
- Do you notice that children use kind words to each other in discussions to share opinions and to show respect?
- Are they using vocabulary such as *community, proud, special, voice level, appropriate, meeting area, listen, small group, whole group, turn and talk, best, classmates, goals, focus, directions, word wall, take good care, materials, words,* and *respect*?

▶ In what ways, beyond the scope of this umbrella, are children showing an understanding of building a positive classroom community?

- Do they treat each other with respect?
- Are they ready to follow a work board to know what to do during independent work time?

Use your observations to determine the next umbrella you will teach. You may also consult Suggested Sequence of Lessons (pp. 557–571) for guidance.

EXTENSIONS FOR WORKING TOGETHER IN THE CLASSROOM

▶ From time to time, have children role-play different classroom activities to show how responsible classroom community members act. This is especially important as new students join the class.

▶ Review voice levels before and after an activity.

Minilessons in This Umbrella

WML1 Get started on your writing quickly and quietly.

WML2 Draw and write until the end of writing time.

WML3 Put your writing in your writing folder.

WML4 Reread your writing to think what to do next.

WML5 Talk with your teacher about your writing.

WML6 Share your writing with an audience to get ideas.

WML7 Return your writing materials to where they belong.

Before Teaching Umbrella 2 Minilessons

We recommend that children have the opportunity for independent writing time every day. Learning the routines for independent writing time will help children build self-confidence by achieving a sense of agency and responsibility for their own work while also allowing time for you to work with individual children or small guided writing groups. Introduce the minilessons in this umbrella after children have had time to experiment with making books so that they understand one way to use their time during independent writing and so that they have something to which they can apply the umbrella's principles.

Before teaching the minilessons in this umbrella, organize the classroom writing center to facilitate easy access to materials. Materials may include but are not limited to paper, pens, pencils, crayons, markers, and staplers. As children become familiar with these materials, introduce other materials and tools, such as different kinds of paper, a hole punch, tape, glue sticks, and scissors. Some of the minilessons in MGT.U1: Working Together in the Classroom will provide helpful background for the lessons in this umbrella.

Writing Minilesson Principle
Get started on your writing quickly and quietly.

Establishing Independent Writing

**Establishing Independent
Writing**

You Will Need

▸ a child prepared to demonstrate getting writing materials and starting quickly and quietly

▸ chart paper and markers

▸ To download the following online resource for this lesson, visit **resources.fountasandpinnell.com**:

  ▪ chart art (optional)

**Academic Language/
Important Vocabulary**

▸ writing time

▸ writing folder

▸ quickly

▸ quietly

**Continuum
Connection**

▸ Keep working independently rather than waiting for a teacher to help (p. 257)

▸ Listen with attention and understanding to directions (p. 332)

GOAL

Learn a routine for beginning independent writing quickly and quietly.

RATIONALE

Teaching children to begin independent writing quickly and quietly promotes independence and a sense of responsibility, allows the class to function efficiently, and gives you time to confer with individual children or small groups.

ASSESS LEARNING

▸ Notice whether children get ready for independent writing quickly, quietly, and independently.

▸ Look for evidence that children can use vocabulary such as *writing time*, *writing folder*, *quickly*, and *quietly*.

MINILESSON

Consider assigning children to one of four folder colors and keeping each color in a separate corner of the classroom to alleviate traffic jams when children retrieve their folders. To help children learn the routine for independent writing, engage them in a short demonstration and discussion. Here is an example.

> We will have writing time every day in our classroom. Let's talk about what you expect to do during writing time.

> During writing time, you will learn about writing, spend some time writing on your own, and then come together to share what you wrote.

▸ Invite the child prepared to demonstrate the routine for independent writing to come forward.

> Watch _____ as she gets started on her writing.

> What did you notice about how she got started? What did she do first?

> What could you hear when she went to get her writing folder and materials?

> How quickly did she get started?

▸ Make a list based on children's responses on chart paper.

Have a Try

Invite children to talk to a partner about the routine for independent writing.

> Turn and talk to your partner about how you will get started during writing time.

▶ After children turn and talk, invite a few children to share their responses. Clarify the routine if necessary.

Summarize and Apply

Write the principle at the top of the chart. Read it to children. Summarize the learning and remind children to follow the routine for getting started with independent writing.

> You learned how to get started during writing time. Today you will have a chance to try out what you learned. During writing time today, remember to get started quickly and quietly. Look at the chart if you need help remembering what to do.

Get started on your writing quickly and quietly.

Start quickly and quietly.

Get your writing folder.

Get your materials.

Sit down and begin to draw and write.

Markers

My Story

Confer

▶ During independent writing, move around the room to confer briefly with as many individual children as time allows. Sit side by side with them and invite them to talk about getting started with their drawing and writing. Use prompts such as the following as needed.

- *What materials do you need for your writing today?*
- *What do you want to write about today?*
- *Where did you get the idea to write about that?*
- *What will you write about on the next page?*

Share

Following independent writing, gather children in the meeting area to talk about getting started with independent writing.

> How did you get started during writing time today?

> Why is it important to get started quickly and quietly?

Writing Minilesson Principle

Draw and write until the end of writing time.

Establishing Independent Writing

You Will Need

▸ chart paper and markers

▸ To download the following online resource for this lesson, visit **resources.fountasandpinnell.com**:

  ▪ chart art (optional)

Academic Language/ Important Vocabulary

▸ writing time

▸ add

▸ reread

Continuum Connection

▸ Keep working independently rather than waiting for a teacher to help (p. 257)

▸ Think of what to work on next as a writer (p. 257)

▸ Produce a quantity of writing within the time available: e.g., one or two pages per day (p. 257)

GOAL

Learn how to work independently and build stamina during independent writing.

RATIONALE

Teaching children to write independently and to use all of the time at their disposal allows them to develop as writers and build their stamina for and interest in writing.

ASSESS LEARNING

▸ Look for evidence that children can work independently during independent writing.

▸ Notice whether children work on their writing for the whole independent-writing period.

▸ Look for evidence that children can use vocabulary such as *writing time*, *add*, and *reread*.

MINILESSON

To help children learn to work independently and build stamina during independent writing, engage them in a discussion about using the entire amount of time allotted for drawing and writing. Here is an example.

> You have been learning about what to do during writing time. I've noticed that some of you stop your drawing and writing before writing time is over. What are some things you can do if you think you have finished writing?

▸ Record responses on chart paper. As needed, prompt children to think about actions such as checking the pictures, rereading the words, adding more words or pictures, and starting a new book.

▸ Explain how children will know how much time they have left during independent writing. You might use a timer or tell them what time independent writing will end. Gradually increase the length of the time for writing as children become comfortable with the routine and build stamina.

Have a Try

Invite children to talk to a partner about what they will do during independent writing.

> Turn and talk to your partner about what you will do if you think you've finished writing your book before writing time is over.

Summarize and Apply

Write the principle at the top of the chart. Read it to children. Summarize the learning and remind children to draw and write until the end of independent writing.

> Whenever you think you have finished writing, there is always something more you can do. You can add more words and pictures to your book, or you can start a new book. A writer's job is never finished! Today and every day, remember to keep writing and drawing until writing time is over.

[Chart]

Draw and write until the end of writing time.

Check your pictures.

Reread your writing.

Add words or pictures.

Start a new book.

Confer

▶ During independent writing, move around the room to confer briefly with as many individual children as time allows. Sit side by side with them and invite them to talk about writing to the end of independent writing. Use the following prompts as needed.

- *What did you write and draw about on this page?*
- *Did you reread your writing? Is there anything else you could add to your book?*
- *What do you think you would like to work on next?*
- *You kept drawing and writing all the way until the end of writing time!*

Share

Following independent writing, gather children in the meeting area. Invite them to share how they stayed busy during independent writing time.

> Give a thumbs-up if you wrote and drew until the end of writing time.

> If you decided you were finished with your writing before the end of writing time, what did you do?

Writing Minilesson Principle
Put your writing in your writing folder.

You Will Need

- a child prepared to demonstrate putting writing in a writing folder
- a writing folder for each child
- chart paper and markers
- To download the following online resource for this lesson, visit **resources.fountasandpinnell.com**:
  - chart art (optional)

Academic Language/ Important Vocabulary

- organized
- writing folder

Continuum Connection

- Listen with attention and understanding to directions (p. 332)
- Remember and follow directions with multiple steps (p. 332)

GOAL

Learn to keep writing organized within a writing folder.

RATIONALE

Teaching children to put their writing in a writing folder helps them keep their writing organized and builds a routine for independent writing that makes it easier to write more, confer with other writers, and share writing.

ASSESS LEARNING

- Notice whether children keep their writing organized in a writing folder.
- Look for evidence that children can use vocabulary such as *organized* and *writing folder*.

MINILESSON

To help children learn to use a writing folder, engage them in a short demonstration. Folders with a pocket on each side are preferable. Here is an example.

> When you finish your writing for the day, you can put your writing away in a special place and keep it organized. Why is it important to keep your writing organized?
>
> You have a writing folder to help you keep your writing organized. _____ will show you how to use it.

▶ Invite the participating child to demonstrate how to put writing in a writing folder.

> What did you notice about how _____ put his writing into his writing folder?
>
> The folder has two sides with pockets. Where did _____ put his writing?
>
> _____, why did you put your writing on that side?

▶ Help children understand that one side of the folder is for unfinished writing and the other side is for finished writing.

Have a Try

Invite children to talk to a partner about how they will put away their writing.

> Turn and talk to your partner about what you will do with your writing at the end of writing time. Where and how will you put it away?

▶ After children turn and talk, ask several children to share their responses. Record responses on chart paper.

Summarize and Apply

Write the principle at the top of the chart. Read it to children. Summarize the learning and remind children to put their writing in their writing folder.

> Today you learned where to put your writing when it is finished and when you are still working on it. At the end of writing time today, remember to put your writing in your writing folder. Then bring your folder to the carpet to share.

Put your writing in your writing folder.

My First Bike

Unfinished   Finished

Put unfinished writing in the left pocket.

Put finished writing in the right pocket.

Make sure you can see the front.

Confer

▶ During independent writing, move around the room to confer briefly with as many individual children as time allows. Sit side by side with them and invite them to talk about using their writing folders. Use prompts such as the following if needed.

- *What are you writing about today?*
- *What will you write on the next page?*
- *Are you finished with this book, or will you work on it again another day? Where should you put it?*
- *How will you keep the writing in your writing folder organized?*

Share

Following independent writing, gather children in the meeting area to share how they used their writing folders.

> How did you decide where to put your writing?

> Who would like to show how you put your writing away?

Writing Minilesson Principle
Reread your writing to think what to do next.

You Will Need

- an example piece of writing that you have written
- chart paper and markers
- the children's writing folders
- To download the following online resource for this lesson, visit **resources.fountasandpinnell.com**:
  - chart art (optional)

Academic Language/ Important Vocabulary

- reread
- ideas

Continuum Connection

- Reread writing each day (and during writing on the same day) before continuing to write (p. 256)
- Think of what to work on next as a writer (p. 257)

GOAL

Understand that rereading writing helps a writer remember what to work on next.

RATIONALE

Rereading their writing helps children remember what they were working on so that they can continue writing in a coherent and cohesive manner. It is also the foundation for the process of revision.

ASSESS LEARNING

- Notice whether children reread their writing before revising, adding to, or finalizing it.
- Look for evidence that children can use vocabulary such as *reread* and *ideas*.

MINILESSON

To help children learn to reread their writing, engage them in a short demonstration. Here is an example.

- Display the example piece of writing that you prepared.

  I started writing this book yesterday, and I'm going to continue working on it today. Watch what I do before I add more writing.

- Read aloud the piece of writing. Think aloud about what you might do next as a writer.

  What did you notice about what I did?

  I reread my writing. When you reread something, it means that you read it again. Why do you think I reread my writing before writing more?

  Rereading my writing helped me remember what I wrote yesterday. What did I think about after I reread my writing?

  I thought about what I wanted to write next. I'm going to write the end of the story, and then I'm going to add more details to my pictures.

Have a Try

Invite children to reread their writing and talk about it to a partner.

▶ Distribute the children's writing folders. Direct them to reread their latest piece of writing.

Read your writing aloud to your partner. Then turn and talk about what you will do next.

Summarize and Apply

Summarize the learning and remind children to reread their writing.

What did you learn to do before you continue writing?

▶ Read aloud the principle as you write it at the top of a piece of chart paper. Create a chart with the children to summarize their learning.

Before you start writing today, remember to reread your writing from yesterday. Rereading your writing each day will help you think about what to do next.

Reread your writing to think what to do next.

• Reread your writing.

• Think about what you wrote.

• Think about what to do next.

Should I write more words? Should I add to my pictures?

Confer

▶ During independent writing, move around the room to confer briefly with as many individual children as time allows. Sit side by side with them and invite them to talk about what to they could do next. Use prompts such as the following as needed.

• *The last thing you wrote was _____. What could you write next?*

• *What could you add to your words?*

• *Could you add to your pictures to show more details or make it more interesting?*

• *Is your book finished? What will your next book be about?*

Share

Following independent writing, gather children in the meeting area. Invite several children to share their writing. Ask them whether they reread their writing.

Give a thumbs-up if you reread your writing today.

What did you do next?

How did rereading your writing help you as a writer?

WML5

MGT.U2.WML5

Writing Minilesson Principle
Talk with your teacher about your writing.

Establishing Independent Writing

You Will Need

- a child prepared to demonstrate a writing conference
- chart paper and markers
- To download the following online resource for this lesson, visit **resources.fountasandpinnell.com**:
  - chart art (optional)

Academic Language/ Important Vocabulary

- writing time
- writer

Continuum Connection

- Understand that writers get help from other writers (p. 256)
- Generate and expand ideas through talk with peers and teacher (p. 256)

GOAL

Understand that writers find it helpful to talk about their writing with another person.

RATIONALE

When children reread their writing, they can listen for what they are communicating to others. Helping children understand why and how to talk to you about their writing can give them an audience and help them generate and expand ideas to write and draw more.

ASSESS LEARNING

- Notice how children discuss their writing with you.
- Look for evidence that children can use vocabulary such as *writing time* and *writer*.

MINILESSON

To help children understand why and how to talk to you about their writing, engage them in a short demonstration. Select in advance a child who is willing and able to talk with you about her writing in front of the class. Here is an example.

- Sit on a low chair with the prepared child in front of the group.

  Please read your writing, _____.

- Model some of the language you might use to support the writers in your classroom, such as the following:

  - *I understand that you wrote about going camping with your family.*
  - *I'm wondering what the weather was like when you were camping in the tent.*
  - *You said that it was windy and the tent was moving a bit. Is that something that will help readers understand your story? How could you add that to your story?*
  - *What else could you add to your words?*
  - *What details could you add to your pictures?*
  - *Do you have any questions for me? Is there anything you need help with?*
  - *What will you work on next?*

Have a Try

Invite children to talk to a partner about what they observed.

> What did you notice when _____ and I talked about her writing and drawing? What did she do? What did I do? Turn and talk to your partner.

> ▶ After children turn and talk, invite several children to share their responses. Record responses on chart paper.

Summarize and Apply

Write the principle at the top of the chart. Summarize the learning and remind children that talking about their writing helps them grow as writers.

> Why is it important to talk about your writing?

> Today during writing time, I will sit with some of you just like I sat with _____. You will read your writing to me, and then we will talk about what you want to work on next.

Talk with your teacher about your writing.

Writer	Teacher
• Read your writing aloud.	• Listens to writer read.
• Answer the teacher's questions.	• Asks questions.
• Tell what you will add to your book.	• Says what she is wondering.
• Ask for help if you need it.	• Helps the writer.

Confer

> ▶ During independent writing, move around the room to confer briefly with as many individual children as time allows. Sit side by side with them and invite them to talk about their writing. Use prompts such as the following.

> • I am wondering why _____. Would you like to add something about that?

> • What could you write to help readers understand _____?

> • Talk more about your pictures. Why did you decide to draw _____?

> • How can I help you?

Share

Following independent writing, gather children in the meeting area to share their writing and talk about side-by-side conferences.

> Who talked with me about your writing today?

> What did we talk about?

> Was it helpful? Why?

WML6

Writing Minilesson Principle
Share your writing with an audience to get ideas.

Establishing Independent Writing

You Will Need

- an example book that you have written
- chart paper and markers
- To download the following online resource for this lesson, visit **resources.fountasandpinnell.com**:
  - chart art (optional)

Academic Language/ Important Vocabulary

- audience

Continuum Connection

- Understand that writers get help from other writers (p. 256)
- Speak with confidence (p. 332)
- Look at the audience (or other person) while speaking (p. 332)
- Listen actively to others read or talk about their writing and give feedback (p. 332)
- Form clear questions to get information (p. 332)
- Demonstrate respectful listening behaviors (p. 332)

GOAL

Learn that speaking to an audience about one's writing is a way to get ideas.

RATIONALE

Helping children understand why and how to share their writing with each other helps them generate and expand their ideas, build off of each other's comments, and strengthen their listening skills.

ASSESS LEARNING

- Observe children as they share their writing with each other.
- Notice whether children listen respectfully to their peers and give constructive feedback.
- Observe whether children use peer feedback to develop their writing.
- Look for evidence that children can use vocabulary such as *audience*.

MINILESSON

Before teaching this minilesson, make sure children are familiar with the concepts taught in MGT.U1: Working Together in the Classroom, particularly WML2, WML4, and WML5. To help children understand how to share their writing, engage them in an inquiry-based lesson. Here is an example.

> Writers often share their writing with an audience. An audience is a group of people who watch and listen to what is being shared. Today I am going to share my writing with you. You will be my audience. As I share, think about what I am doing as the writer and what you are doing as my audience.

▶ Read aloud the example piece of writing that you prepared. Use a strong voice, be sure to look at the audience, and show any pictures.

> What did I do when I shared my writing?

> What did the audience do?

▶ As needed, prompt children's thinking with questions such as the following. However, take into consideration that some children may not be comfortable with establishing or able to establish eye contact because of cultural conventions or for other reasons.

- *What kind of voice did I use?*
- *What did I do with my hands?*
- *Where did I (you) look?*
- *How did you show that you were listening to me?*
- *What did you do after I finished reading?*

▶ Record children's responses on chart paper.

Have a Try

Invite children to talk to a partner about why it is helpful to share writing with an audience.

> Why is it helpful to share your writing with an audience? How can this help you become a better writer? Turn and talk to your partner.

▶ After children turn and talk, invite several pairs to share their thinking.

Summarize and Apply

Write the principle at the top of the chart. Read it to children. Summarize the learning and remind children why it is important to share writing with an audience.

> Sharing your writing with an audience can help you get ideas and learn more about how to make your writing interesting. During writing time today, think about how you will share your writing with an audience. When we meet later, some of you will have a chance to share your writing with an audience.

Share your writing with an audience to get ideas.	
Writer	**Audience**
• Read your book aloud.	• Look at the writer.
• Use a strong voice.	• Listen carefully.
• Show the pictures.	• Ask questions.
• Look at the audience.	
• Answer questions.	• Tell what you think.

Confer

▶ During independent writing, move around the room to confer briefly with as many individual children as time allows. Sit side by side with them and invite them to talk about sharing their writing. Use prompts such as the following if needed.

- *What are you writing about today?*
- *Can you read your writing aloud?*
- *What could you add to tell more about _____?*
- *How will you share your book with an audience? What will you remember to do?*

Share

Following independent writing, gather children in the meeting area. Invite several children to practice what they learned about sharing their writing with an audience.

> Who would like to share your writing?

> Does anyone have any questions or comments for _____?

WML7

MGT.U2.WML7

Writing Minilesson Principle
Return your writing materials to where they belong.

Establishing Independent Writing

You Will Need

- two or three children prepared to demonstrate putting away writing materials
- chart paper and markers
- To download the following online resource for this lesson, visit **resources.fountasandpinnell.com**:
  - chart art (optional)

Academic Language/ Important Vocabulary

- writing time
- materials

Continuum Connection

- Listen with attention and understanding to directions (p. 332)
- Remember and follow directions with multiple steps (p. 332)

GOAL

Learn the routine of putting materials away at the end of writing time.

RATIONALE

Teaching children to put away their writing materials helps them create an organized learning environment. This builds the children's independence and allows them to quickly find their materials.

ASSESS LEARNING

- Notice whether children carefully put away their materials at the end of independent writing.
- Look for evidence that children can use vocabulary such as *writing time* and *materials*.

MINILESSON

Before this minilesson, children should already be familiar with the materials in the writing center and how they are organized. If the writing center materials are not yet labeled, teach IW.3: Labeling the Classroom. To help children learn how to put away their writing materials, engage them in a short demonstration. Right before teaching the lesson, ask two or three children to place their writing materials at their writing spots.

> What materials do we have in the writing center?

> Writers keep their materials organized so they can easily find them and start writing quickly and quietly. How are the writing materials organized? How do you know where each type of material belongs?

- Invite the children prepared to demonstrate to pick up the writing materials that they placed at their writing spots and put them away.

> Your classmates will show you what to do at the end of writing time. Watch what they do.

> What did you notice your classmates do?

> How did it sound when they were putting their materials away?

- Record children's responses on chart paper.

Have a Try

Invite children to talk to a partner about what to do at the end of independent writing.

> Turn and talk to your partner about what you will do at the end of writing time.

▶ After children turn and talk, invite several pairs to share their responses.

Summarize and Apply

Help children summarize the learning. Remind them to put away their writing materials at the end of independent writing.

> Why is it important to return your materials to where they belong when writing time is over?

▶ Write the principle at the top of the chart.

> At the end of writing time today, remember to put your materials away. However, if you would like to share your writing when we meet later, bring the writing you are working on. You can put it away later.

Return your writing materials to where they belong.

- Put your materials away quickly and quietly.

- Put your writing in your folder.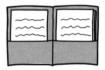

- Put the folder in the basket.

Confer

▶ During independent writing, move around the room to confer briefly with as many individual children as time allows. Sit side by side with them and invite them to talk about what they will do at the end of writing time. Use prompts such as the following if needed.

  - *What should you do at the end of writing time?*
  - *Where are you going to put your finished writing?*
  - *Look for the label that says* Pencils.
  - *Remember to wait for your turn to put your folder in the basket.*

Share

Following independent writing, gather children in the meeting area. Invite several children to share their writing and talk about what to do at the end of independent writing time.

> Who would like to share your writing?

> Where does your writing go at the end of writing time?

Assessment

After you have taught the minilessons in this umbrella, observe children as they prepare for, progress through, and conclude independent writing time each day. Use *The Literacy Continuum* (Fountas and Pinnell 2017) to notice, teach for, and support children's learning as you observe their attempts at reading and writing.

▶ What evidence do you have of new understandings children have developed related to the routines for independent writing time?

- Do children get started on their writing quickly and quietly?
- Are they able to sustain working for the whole independent writing time?
- Is the writing inside children's writing folders organized?
- Do children reread their writing to think about what to write next?
- How are they talking with you about their writing?
- How are they sharing their writing with an audience to get ideas?
- Do they return their writing materials to where they belong?
- Do they understand and use vocabulary such as *reread*, *organized*, *ideas*, *audience*, and *materials*?

▶ In what other ways, beyond the scope of this umbrella, are children getting started with independent writing?

- Are they using drawing and writing tools appropriately?
- Are they writing about their imaginative play?

Use your observations to determine the next umbrella you will teach. You may also consult Suggested Sequence of Lessons (pp. 557–571) for guidance.

EXTENSIONS FOR ESTABLISHING INDEPENDENT WRITING

▶ Teach children to use the resources in their writing folder, such as a list of finished writing, a list of ideas for writing, an ABC chart, a personal word list, guidelines for writing time, and a proofreading checklist. (See online resources for minilessons in MGT.U4: Introducing Writing Folder Resources.)

▶ Show children what to do with their finished pieces when the writing folder gets too full.

▶ When children share, help them progress from statements like "I like your writing" to "The words you used helped me make a picture in my mind of _____."

Minilessons in This Umbrella

WML1 Take good care of the markers and glue.

WML2 Use the scissors carefully.

WML3 Choose your paper.

WML4 Put the stapler on the left and click.

Before Teaching Umbrella 3 Minilessons

When you begin the school year, decide how to organize the writing center. Choose containers for materials and label them with pictures and words. Also label the areas where the containers will be stored. Labeling helps with organization and also helps children recognize words and understand that print carries meaning. Provide space for glue, markers (sorted in sets or by color), scissors, pencils, pens, colored pencils, staplers, staple removers, blank paper of different sizes, and blank paper stapled into booklets. Start with just a few materials to make it easier for children to find the materials they need and return them to the proper location after use. After you teach these minilessons and children have time to gain experience with the materials, you can increase the mix of items, for example, different kinds of paper. Note that there are different formats of books. *Booklets* refers to paper that is either folded or bound to look like a book for reading. Books can also be written across pages and stapled in one corner. Several kinds of paper templates for writing and making books are available in the online resources.

Section 2: Management

Writing Minilesson Principle
Take good care of the markers and glue.

Using Drawing and Writing Tools

You Will Need

- glue sticks

- markers (multiple sets in multiple colors)

- designated, labeled container(s) in the writing center for storing glue sticks and markers

- paper for drawing/gluing

- chart paper and markers

- To download the following online resource for this lesson, visit **resources.fountasandpinnell.com**:

  - chart art (optional)

Academic Language/ Important Vocabulary

- place

- replace

- glue

- markers

Continuum Connection

- Listen with attention and understanding to directions (p. 332)

- Remember and follow directions with multiple steps (p. 332)

GOAL

Learn the routines for using glue and markers.

RATIONALE

You want children to carefully, appropriately, and independently use supplies (such as glue sticks and markers) in the writing center. Children need to be taught explicit steps for using the materials. When they know how to use materials appropriately, they take good care of them so that everyone will have tools for writing and drawing and the need for teacher direction will be minimized.

ASSESS LEARNING

- Notice whether children know where to get the glue sticks and markers, use them properly, and return them.

- Look for evidence that children can use vocabulary such as *place*, *replace*, *glue*, and *markers*.

MINILESSON

Before teaching this minilesson, make sure children have used markers and glue sticks and know where they are stored in the classroom. To help children learn how to use them properly, engage them in a short demonstration.

> What is the first thing you do if you want to use markers to draw a picture?

- Select several markers to use to draw a picture. Guide children through the steps of properly using the markers. As they describe each step, model it with markers.

  > Sometimes when you make a picture, you might want to stick something onto the paper. Talk about how you do that.

- Guide them through the steps of using a glue stick to glue a picture to a piece of paper, modeling as children describe each step.

- Consider using the following prompts to talk about using glue sticks/markers.

  - *Why is it important to turn up the glue stick just a little?*

  - *Why do you put the cap back on after using a glue stick (marker)?*

  - *What do you do when you are finished using a glue stick (marker)?*

  - *Show how you can make the* click! *sound when you put on the cap.*

Have a Try

Invite children to talk to a partner about using markers and glue in the classroom.

> Turn and talk to your partner about some ways you use markers and glue properly in the classroom.

Summarize and Apply

Make a chart to help children summarize the learning. Remind them to take good care of the markers and glue when they work in the writing center.

> What are the important things to remember about using markers and glue?

▶ On chart paper, write each step as children share ideas, guiding the conversation. Highlight the importance of using the right amount of glue, placing the cap on the end when you are using a marker, and hearing the *click!* when replacing caps. Write the principle at the top.

> Today if you make a book or a picture during writing time, you might want to use a glue stick or markers. You can look at the chart to remember the important things about using glue and markers.

<table>
<tr><td colspan="2">Take good care of the markers and glue.</td></tr>
<tr><td>Take the cap off.</td><td>Take the cap off.</td></tr>
<tr><td>Put the cap on the end.</td><td>Turn up the glue a little.</td></tr>
<tr><td>Put the cap on. Click!</td><td>Use a small amount.</td></tr>
<tr><td>Return the markers.</td><td>Turn down the glue.</td></tr>
<tr><td></td><td>Put the cap on. Click!</td></tr>
<tr><td></td><td>Return the glue stick.</td></tr>
</table>

BLUE MARKERS

Click!

GLUE   GLUE

Confer

▶ During independent writing, move around the room to confer briefly with as many individual children as time allows. Sit side by side with them and invite them to talk about taking good care of the markers and glue. Use the following prompts as needed.

- *Show how to move the glue stick up and down.*
- *Why is it important not to push too hard on the paper with a marker?*
- *How do you know the glue stick (marker) cap is on tight?*
- *Where will you put the glue stick (marker) when you are finished?*

Share

Following independent writing, gather children in the meeting area. Ask a few children to share their experiences using glue sticks and markers.

> Tell one step you did when you used a glue stick (marker).

Writing Minilesson Principle
Use the scissors carefully.

Using Drawing and Writing Tools

You Will Need

- a pair of scissors and paper to use for modeling
- scissors (one per child)
- paper for cutting (one piece per child)
- designated, labeled container(s) for storing scissors
- chart paper and markers
- To download the following online resource for this lesson, visit **resources.fountasandpinnell.com**:
    - chart art (optional)

Academic Language/ Important Vocabulary

- draw
- write
- scissors
- carefully
- safe

Continuum Connection

- Listen with attention and understanding to directions (p. 332)
- Remember and follow directions with multiple steps (p. 332)

GOAL

Learn to use scissors safely.

RATIONALE

When children learn to use scissors safely and carefully, they keep themselves and others from getting hurt, develop fine motor skills, and build confidence and independence with writing and drawing projects.

ASSESS LEARNING

- Notice whether children understand the importance of using scissors in a careful, safe way.
- Notice whether they can use scissors appropriately.
- Look for evidence that children can use vocabulary such as *draw*, *write*, *scissors*, *carefully*, and *safe*.

MINILESSON

Before teaching this minilesson, make sure children have used scissors and know where scissors are stored in the classroom. To help children learn how to use scissors properly, engage them in a short demonstration. Here is an example.

- Hold up a pair of scissors.

    What do you know about using scissors?

    Notice the way I use these scissors.

- Model the correct way to sit and hold the scissors and use them to cut a piece of paper. Then, model carefully walking with scissors and properly passing the scissors.

    What did you notice about how I used the scissors?

- As children discuss, include a conversation about safety rules. Using their suggestions, make a list with sketches on chart paper to show how to use scissors in a careful way.

- Pass out a pair of scissors and a piece of paper to each child. Have them practice using the scissors. Ask volunteers to model proper scissor behavior.

- Collect the scissors and return them to the correct spot in the writing center.

Have a Try

Invite children to talk to a partner about using scissors in the classroom.

> Turn and talk to your partner about how you use scissors in a careful and safe way.

▶ Ask a few volunteers to share.

Summarize and Apply

Write the principle on the chart. Read it to the children and summarize the learning.

> You learned to hold the closed scissors by the blades, to point the blades down while walking, and to face the handle away from you when passing scissors.

> Today if you make a book or a picture during writing time, you might want to use scissors. You can look at the chart to help you remember how to use the scissors carefully.

Use the scissors carefully.

 Sit in a chair.

 Cut away from you.

 Turn the handle out to pass the scissors.

 Hold the scissors in a safe way when you walk.

Confer

▶ During independent writing, move around the room to confer briefly with as many individual children as time allows. Sit side by side with them and invite them to talk about using scissors carefully. Use the following prompts as needed.

- *Show how to pass scissors to a classmate.*
- *How do you hold scissors when you walk?*
- *Why is it important to be careful when you use scissors?*

Share

Following independent writing, gather children in the meeting area. Ask a few children to share their experiences using scissors.

> What did you make with the scissors?

> Tell one way that you used scissors carefully today.

Section 2: Management

Writing Minilesson Principle
Choose your paper.

GOAL

Learn that writers choose different paper depending on what they are planning to write.

RATIONALE

Children can begin to feel like writers even before they can use all the conventions of writing. When children learn to think about what kind of paper they might use, they understand that writers choose different paper for different writing activities (e.g., a greeting card, a sign, or a book).

ASSESS LEARNING

▸ Notice whether children recognize that writers select different kinds of paper depending on what they are writing.

▸ Look for evidence that they are selecting appropriate paper for what they are writing.

▸ Look for evidence that children can use vocabulary such as *draw*, *write*, and *paper*.

MINILESSON

Before teaching this minilesson, make sure children are familiar with different kinds of paper (e.g., size, color, thickness) and know where paper is stored in the classroom. You might want to print out a few examples of different paper templates from the online resources. To help children learn to select paper depending on what they are writing, engage them in a short demonstration and inquiry-based lesson. Here is an example.

▸ Show examples of the children's writing on different kinds of paper.

  Look at all of the different kinds of paper you have used for writing. What do you notice?

▸ Have a conversation about the different kinds of paper and why a writer might choose a particular kind of paper. Use the following prompts as needed.

  • *How could you use these small pieces of paper?*

  • *What kinds of writing could you do with a big piece of paper?*

  • *What could you make with these stapled pages?*

  • *How could you use a folded piece of paper?*

  • *What could you use this kind of paper for?*

Have a Try

Invite children to talk to a partner about using different paper for different purposes.

> Look around the room. Turn and tell your partner one kind of paper that you see and what you could do with it.

Summarize and Apply

Help children summarize the learning. Invite them to use different kinds of paper during writing time.

▶ Make a chart to summarize the learning.

> What are some different ways you could use this paper?

▶ Guide the conversation as needed. Write the principle at the top.

> During writing time, choose the kind of paper that is best for your writing. Bring your writing to share when we meet later.

Choose your paper.

Folded paper	• Greeting card • Book
Blank paper	• Letter • Menu
Stapled paper	• Book
Paper in different colors	• Shape book • Pictures • Animal poster
Small pieces of paper	• Sign • Poem

Confer

▶ During independent writing, move around the room to confer briefly with as many individual children as time allows. Sit side by side with them and invite them to talk about choosing paper. Use the following prompts as needed.

• *What kind of paper will you choose to make that book?*

• *What kind of paper might work well for a sign?*

• *What kind of paper might work well for a menu?*

Share

Following independent writing, gather children in the meeting area. Ask a few children to share their experiences using different kinds of paper.

> What type of paper did you use today? Tell how you made your paper choice.

Writing Minilesson Principle
Put the stapler on the left and click.

GOAL

Learn how to properly use a stapler.

RATIONALE

When children learn to use a stapler, especially to add pages to their own writing, they gain independence and agency in making their own decisions about their writing.

ASSESS LEARNING

▸ Notice whether children understand that writers use tools, such as staplers, to add to their writing.

▸ Notice whether they can properly and safely handle a stapler.

▸ Look for evidence that children can use vocabulary such as *stapler*, *firmly*, and *click*.

MINILESSON

Before teaching this minilesson, make sure children have used stapled booklets and know where the staplers are stored in the classroom. Decide whether children will staple once in the left corner or three times along the left side (so the pages open like a book). To help children learn to use a stapler properly and safely, engage them in a short demonstration and inquiry-based lesson. Here is an example.

▸ Hold up a stapler.

  What do you know about using staplers?

  Watch me use this stapler.

▸ Model the correct way to use a stapler by taking multiple pages of paper, lining them up so that the edges are even, keeping your fingers out of the way, and stapling the papers together. Use two hands, one atop the other, and push down firmly.

  What did you notice about how I used the stapler?

  I lined up the pages, I put the pages in the stapler, and I used two hands to push down firmly but not too hard.

▸ Model the way a stapler clicks two times. Then turn the paper over to show children that the staple has gone through.

  How many sounds did you hear?

  Make sure you hear two clicks.

▸ Talk about how they might use the stapler in the writing center: to make a booklet, to staple pages together in the upper left corner, or to add a page to a book. It is best not to remove staples when adding pages; instead, the book will just have more staples. Record the ways on the chart.

Have a Try

Invite children to practice using a stapler.

▶ Pass out a stapler and a piece of paper to each child (or group). Have them practice using the stapler. Ask volunteers to model proper use of the stapler.

> Remember to use two hands and listen for two clicks.

▶ Collect the staplers.

Summarize and Apply

Write the principle on the chart. Read it to the children and summarize the learning.

> Today you learned about handling a stapler in. Today if you work on a book, you might use a stapler to make the book or to add pages.

▶ At first, it is common for children to want to add a page to a book or make a new book just so they get to use the stapler. Provide them this time for a few days to explore using the stapler. Once they are accustomed to using it, they will start to staple only when it is necessary and get back to writing.

Put the stapler on the left and click.

Line up the paper.

Click, click!

Put the paper in the stapler.

Use two hands.

Keep fingers out of the way!

Check the staples.

Confer

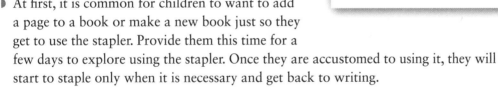

▶ During independent writing, move around the room to confer briefly with as many individual children as time allows. Sit side by side with them and invite them to talk about using a stapler. Use the following prompts as needed.

- *Show how you will use the stapler to make a book.*
- *How will you add more pages to your book?*
- *Remember to turn your paper over to make sure the staples went through the paper.*

Share

Following independent writing, gather children in the meeting area. Ask a few children to share their experiences using a stapler or to demonstrate how they used a stapler.

> Who used a stapler today? Tell about how you used it.

Assessment

After you have taught the minilessons in this umbrella, observe children as they learn to use drawing and writing tools. Use *The Literacy Continuum* (Fountas and Pinnell 2017) to notice, teach for, and support children's learning as you observe their attempts at using drawing and writing tools during independent writing.

▶ What evidence do you have that children understand how to use drawing and writing tools?

- Do they know how to appropriately use glue sticks?

- Do they understand how to take care of markers?

- Do children hold scissors carefully when using them, carrying them, and sharing them?

- Do they select paper that is appropriate for the type of writing they are doing?

- Do children use a stapler properly?

- Do they understand and use vocabulary such as *draw*, *write*, *glue*, *markers*, *scissors*, *paper*, and *stapler*?

▶ In what ways, beyond the scope of this umbrella, are the children using drawing and writing tools?

- Are children making books?

- Are they paying careful attention to how they make their illustrations?

Use your observations to determine the next umbrella you will teach. You may also consult Suggested Sequence of Lessons (pp. 557–571) for guidance.

EXTENSIONS FOR USING DRAWING AND WRITING TOOLS

▶ Repeat the lesson on glue to teach how to use different kinds of glue and applicators (e.g., liquid glue, glue bottle and brush, cotton swabs, paint brushes).

▶ Teach minilessons for other items children use in the writing center or art center. (See Planning a Writing Minilesson in the online resources.)

▶ Introduce different kinds of paper that can be used to spark imagination (e.g., labels and forms, guest check-in sheets, shopping lists, postcards, greeting cards, envelopes, invitations, gift tags).

▶ Provide a demonstration on what to do if there are problems using a stapler (e.g., it is not working, it runs out of staples) or if a page needs to be added in the middle of a book.

Minilessons in This Umbrella

WML1 List your ideas for writing.

WML2 List your finished writing.

WML3 Add to your personal word list.

Before Teaching Umbrella 4 Minilessons

We suggest that children have the opportunity for independent writing time every day. Independent writing time is described on page 15.

Before teaching the minilessons in this umbrella, prepare a writing folder for each child. Folders should have two pockets with fasteners. As you think about how children will organize their writing, consider labeling the pockets *Finished* (possibly with a smiley face) and *Unfinished* (possibly with half of a smiley face). A good idea is to use folders in four or five different colors. Assign children to a color and keep each color in a separate corner of the classroom to alleviate traffic jams when children retrieve their folders. These ideas are introduced in MGT.U2: Establishing Independent Writing, which you may want to complete in advance of this umbrella.

Online resources introduced in this umbrella are described in each minilesson. Add each online resource to the writing folder only as it is introduced. Use books from the following text sets in *Fountas & Pinnell Classroom™ Interactive Read-Aloud Collection*, or use books from the classroom library, including at least one that lists the author's previously published books.

Learning and Working Together: School

First Day Jitters by Julie Danneberg

Elizabeti's School by Stephanie Stuve-Bodeen

Taking Care of Each Other: Family

Papá and Me by Arthur Dorros

As you read and enjoy these texts together, help children

- think about ideas for their own writing,

- notice other books written by the same authors, and

- notice how the accuracy of the spelling and the clear spacing between words makes it easier for the reader to read.

School

Family

Section 2: Management

WML1

Writing Minilesson Principle
List your ideas for writing.

Introducing Writing Folder Resources

You Will Need

▶ a familiar book, such as *First Day Jitters* by Julie Danneberg, from Text Set: Learning and Working Together: School

▶ a writing folder for each child with a My Ideas for Writing chart fastened inside

▶ chart paper prepared with My Ideas for Writing chart (either drawn on or printed out and fastened to the chart paper)

▶ markers

▶ To download the following online resource for this lesson, visit **resources.fountasandpinnell.com**:

  ▪ My Ideas for Writing

Academic Language / Important Vocabulary

▶ ideas

Continuum Connection

▶ Generate ideas or topics for writing (p. 256)

▶ Have a list or notebook with topics and ideas for writing (p. 257)

▶ Listen with attention and understanding to directions (p. 332)

GOAL

Learn how to create and keep an ongoing list of writing ideas.

RATIONALE

When you teach children to gather ideas for writing throughout the day—and make note of these ideas—you help them view themselves as writers and generate and expand their ideas for writing.

ASSESS LEARNING

▶ Observe for evidence of children's ability to create and keep writing ideas in a My Ideas for Writing chart.

▶ Notice if children are drawing on ideas for writing from a variety of home and school experiences.

▶ Look for evidence that children can use vocabulary such as *ideas*.

MINILESSON

In advance of this lesson, prepare for each child a writing folder with a My Ideas for Writing chart fastened inside. Demonstrate thinking about ideas for writing and noting them on the chart. Here is an example, but talk about your own personal stories.

▶ Display the prepared chart paper. Draw a quick sketch of an idea for writing on the first row of the chart.

> Writers are always thinking about ideas they can write about. Over the weekend, I went to the beach with my two sons. I'd like to write about that someday, but right now I am writing a book about my dog. I don't want to forget my idea about the beach trip, so I will write it on this chart called My Ideas for Writing. I can make a quick note and a drawing to remind myself that I want to write about that idea sometime.

▶ Display a familiar book, such as *First Day Jitters*. Prepare to record, in words, an idea for writing inspired by the book. (Children do not need to be familiar with this book.)

> Writers also get ideas for writing from books they read. When I first read *First Day Jitters*, it made me think I could write a book about the first time I met all of you. I will add that to my chart.

Have a Try

Invite children to talk to a partner about writing ideas.

> Sometimes writers get ideas for writing by talking to other writers. Turn and talk to your partner. What is something you might write a book about?

▶ After time for discussion, ask a few children to share their ideas. Add them to the chart.

Summarize and Apply

Summarize the learning. Remind children to use the My Ideas for Writing chart in their writing folders.

▶ Display a child's writing folder open to the My Ideas for Writing chart.

> Writers are always on the lookout for ideas. You don't want to forget your ideas, so you can write them on your own My Ideas for Writing chart in your writing folder.

▶ Write the principle at the top of the chart paper.

> Before you start working on a book, write words about or draw a quick sketch of one or two ideas you have for writing. You will share an idea for writing later.

List your ideas for writing.

My Ideas for Writing

1. Day at the beach

2. First day of school

3. Taking the school bus

4. Going to gym class

Confer

▶ During independent writing, move around the room to confer briefly with as many individual children as time allows. Sit side by side with them and invite them to talk about their ideas for writing. Use the following prompts as needed.

- *What might be an idea you could write about?*
- *What did you do yesterday/over the weekend/last week?*
- *Who are some people in your family? What do you like to do with them?*

Share

Following independent writing, ask children to bring their writing folders to the meeting area. Invite children to share with a partner one idea from their My Ideas for Writing chart.

> Who can share an idea for writing?

WML2

Writing Minilesson Principle
List your finished writing.

Introducing Writing Folder Resources

You Will Need

- several familiar books that include titles of other books written by those authors, such as these:

  - *Elizabeti's School* by Stephanie Stuve-Bodeen, from Text Set: Learning and Working Together: School

  - *Papá and Me* by Arthur Dorros, from Text Set: Taking Care of Each Other: Family

- class books from interactive writing lessons

- a writing folder for each child, with a My Finished Writing chart fastened inside

- chart paper with a version of a My Finished Writing chart drawn on or attached and retitled Our Finished Writing

- markers

- To download the following online resource for this lesson, visit **resources.fountasandpinnell.com**:

  - My Finished Writing

Academic Language / Important Vocabulary

- finished
- completed

Continuum Connection

- Select an appropriate title for a poem, story, or informational book (p. 254)

- Listen with attention and understanding to directions (p. 332)

GOAL

Learn how to keep track of finished writing to reflect on progress across the year.

RATIONALE

A finished writing list allows children to communicate to you when they believe a piece of writing is complete so you can plan further instruction for them. It also allows them and you to reflect on their writing across the year, and it provides information for you when you discuss children's progress in writing.

ASSESS LEARNING

- Observe children's ability to create and maintain a My Finished Writing chart.

- Notice if children are appropriately evaluating the completeness of their writing.

- Look for evidence that children can use vocabulary such as *finished* and *completed*.

MINILESSON

In advance of this lesson, prepare for each child a writing folder with a My Finished Writing chart fastened inside. Display pages from familiar books that list other books written by the same authors. (Children do not need to be familiar with the books mentioned in this lesson.) Then demonstrate tracking the completed interactive writing class books on a chart. Here is an example.

- Display the inside front and back covers of *Elizabeti's School*.

  What do you see inside the covers of *Elizabeti's School*?

  These are other books written by Stephanie Stuve-Bodeen.

- Repeat this process by showing and reading the author note in *Papá and Me*.

  Both of these books have lists of other books that the authors have finished writing.

- Display the prepared chart. Ask children to help you fill in the chart.

  As writers, you can keep track of your finished writing too. What is a book we have finished as a class?

  We can write the titles of our class books on the chart.

Have a Try

Invite children to talk to a partner about other interactive writing class books they could add to the chart.

> Turn and talk to your partner. What are some other books we have finished writing as a class?

▶ After time for discussion, ask a few children to share titles. Add them to the chart.

Summarize and Apply

Write the principle at the top of the chart. Read it to children and then invite them to use the My Finished Writing chart in their writing folders.

▶ Display a child's writing folder open to the My Finished Writing chart.

> Each time you finish a piece of writing, write the title on your My Finished Writing chart in your writing folder.

> Before you get to work on the new book you are writing, take a moment to write on the chart the title of the book you have finished writing.

List your finished writing.

Our Finished Writing

1. Our Classroom

2. Writing from a Picture

3. My Friend

Confer

▶ During independent writing, move around the room to confer briefly with as many individual children as time allows. Sit side by side with them and invite them to talk about their finished writing.

- Take out your finished writing. What is the title of this piece?
- Let's think about the titles of these books [show familiar read-aloud books]. What is this book about? What is the title? You want the title of your book to match what your book is about, too.
- What is your book about? What is a title that matches that?

Share

Following independent writing, ask children to bring their writing folders to the meeting area.

> Share your My Finished Writing chart with your partner.

> It is so interesting to look back at all of the books you have written!

WML3

MGT.U4.WML3

Add to your personal word list.

Introducing Writing Folder Resources

You Will Need

- class-made books from interactive writing lessons

- a writing folder for each child, with My Words chart printed as two-page spreads and fastened inside

- chart paper prepared with a portion of My Words drawn on or attached

- markers

- To download the following online resource for this lesson, visit **resources.fountasandpinnell.com**:

  - My Words

Academic Language / Important Vocabulary

- spell
- personal
- frequently

Continuum Connection

- Use simple resources to help in spelling words or check on spelling (word walls, personal word lists) (p. 255)

- Spell approximately one hundred high-frequency words conventionally and reflect spelling in final drafts (p. 255)

- Use beginning reference tools: e.g., word walls or personal word collections or dictionaries (p. 257)

- Understand that the more accurate the spelling and the clearer the space between words, the easier it is for the reader to read it (p. 257)

GOAL

Learn how to add a new word to a personal word list to use for future reference.

RATIONALE

When you help children develop a list of their own high-frequency words, they can use the list as a reference to support the accuracy, fluency, and speed of their writing.

ASSESS LEARNING

- Observe children's ability to create and maintain a personal word list.
- Notice if children refer to their personal word list when writing.
- Look for evidence that children can use vocabulary such as *spell*, *personal*, and *frequently*.

MINILESSON

In advance of this lesson, prepare for each child a writing folder with My Words fastened inside so that the chart opens in two-page spreads. Consider writing a couple of words on children's lists ahead of time to get them started. Demonstrate adding words to the chart. Here is an example.

- Display several of the books completed by the class through interactive writing and discuss the accuracy of the spelling.

  We have completed quite a lot of writing together. What do you notice about how we spelled the words in those pieces of writing?

  The words are spelled the way they are spelled in books. We could call this book spelling. When you read, you see the words spelled this way. How does the way words are spelled help the reader?

- Display the prepared chart and the online resource My Words.

  The big chart shows part of what you will have on this chart in your writing folder. What do you notice on the chart?

  Each box has a capital and lowercase letter of the alphabet. What do you think you will write in each box?

  When you talk with me about your writing and we notice you use the word *brother* a lot, I could write *brother* on your personal word list so that you can learn to spell it yourself.

- Demonstrate writing *brother* on the chart.

  Where else can you look to know how to write a word?

- Direct children's attention to resources in the room.

Have a Try

Invite children to talk to a partner about other high-frequency words they could add to their personal word lists.

> Turn and talk to your partner. What are some other words you use a lot in your writing that you might want on your personal word list?

▶ After time for discussion, ask a few children to share words. Add them to the chart.

Summarize and Apply

Write the principle at the top of the chart. Remind children to add words to their personal word lists.

▶ Display a child's writing folder open to the My Words pages.

> When you and I talk about your writing, notice if we spend time talking about how to spell some words that you like to use in your writing. Those are the words I can help you write on your personal word list

> You can use tools like a word wall, a dictionary, or your word list to write a word or check your spelling.

Add to your personal word list.

My Word List   Name _____

Aa	Bb	Cc
	brother	
Gg	Hh	Ii

Confer

▶ During independent writing, move around the room to confer briefly with as many individual children as time allows. Sit side by side with them and invite them to talk about their personal word lists. Use the following prompts as needed.

- *What are you working on today as a writer? What is your writing about?*

- *When I read your writing, I notice you write the word _____ a lot. Let's add _____ to your personal word list. That will help you learn to write that word quickly. (Teacher writes word to ensure legibility and spelling.)*

Share

Following independent writing, gather children in the meeting area. Ask several children to share the personal word lists they have started.

> When you aren't sure how to write a word that you use a lot, you can look at your personal word list. Let's look at the words _____ uses a lot in his writing.

Assessment

After you have taught the minilessons in this umbrella, observe children as they prepare for, progress through, and conclude independent writing time each day. Use *The Literacy Continuum* (Fountas and Pinnell 2017) to notice, teach for, and support children's learning as you observe their reading and writing attempts.

▶ What evidence do you have of new understandings children have developed related to the writing folder resources?

- Do children write or draw ideas for future writing?
- Do they add the title of a finished work to a chart in their writing folder?
- Do they add to and refer to a personal word list?
- Do they understand and use vocabulary such as *ideas*, *finished*, *completed*, *spell*, *personal*, and *frequently*?

▶ In what other ways, beyond the scope of this umbrella, are children using and thinking about writing folder resources?

- Are they keeping their writing folders neatly organized and returning them to where they belong?
- Are they talking about their imaginative play with one another as a way to develop new ideas for writing?
- Are they thinking creatively about titles for their finished work?
- Is the accuracy and speed of their writing improving?

Use your observations to determine the next umbrella you will teach. You may also consult Suggested Sequence of Lessons (pp. 557–571) for guidance.

EXTENSIONS FOR INTRODUCING WRITING FOLDER RESOURCES

▶ To help children become independent in what to do next as a writer, remind them to refer to the My Ideas for Writing chart to get them started on the next book.

▶ Create an Our Ideas for Writing chart where the whole class can keep track of ideas for writing about group experiences, for example, field trips, gym or music classes, or science experiments they have done together.

▶ Place a high-frequency words list (use your own or see **resources.fountasandpinnell.com**) in each writing folder. While children should not stop writing every time they think a word might be on the list, they can be taught to refer to it (sparingly) while writing. Or, they can learn to check spelling afterwards. Likewise, you can introduce a proofreading list to the writing folder (see WPS.U6: Proofreading Writing).

Section 3 | Telling Stories

THE LESSONS IN this section build children's oral language and storytelling abilities by reminding them that they can tell stories from their lives. They can tell stories to the class or to one other. They can even use puppets! When children tell stories, it is an oral rehearsal for their writing.

3 | Telling Stories

Minilessons in This Umbrella

WML1   Tell stories about yourself.

WML2   Tell stories about things you did.

WML3   Tell stories about places you don't want to forget.

WML4   Tell stories about things from your Me Box.

Before Teaching Umbrella 1 Minilessons

Prior to teaching these minilessons, provide opportunities for children to hear and talk about stories from diverse authors and with diverse characters. Hearing stories will enable children to understand that people share what they are thinking through language. Include stories from your own life as well. Telling stories will help children rehearse and organize their ideas before putting them on paper.

The focus of these lessons is to help children realize that they can get story ideas from their own lives. It is not recommended that you teach the minilessons within this umbrella consecutively because you will want children to have opportunities to tell their own stories between each of the lessons. Post the charts from these minilessons so that children can use them as a reference for story ideas. For mentor texts, use the books listed below from *Fountas & Pinnell Classroom™ Interactive Read-Aloud Collection*, or choose books from the classroom library that tell stories that are personal to the authors.

Interactive Read-Aloud Collection

Learning and Working Together: School

David's Drawings by Cathryn Falwell

Elizabeti's School by Stephanie Stuve-Bodeen

Shared Reading Collection

Tap, Tap, Tappity-Tap! by Elizabeth Sawyer

Clippity Clop by Susan A. Layne

The Camping Trip by Louis Petrone

Ripples in the Sea by Miriam Glassman

As you read and enjoy these texts together, help children

- talk about what events from their own lives the stories make them think about, and

- imagine what events from an author's life he may have used to decide what to write about.

Interactive Read-Aloud
Learning and Working Together

Shared Reading

Section 3: Telling Stories

Writing Minilesson Principle
Tell stories about yourself.

Learning About Self and Others Through Storytelling

You Will Need

▸ several familiar books about topics that might be personal to the author, such as the following:

  ▪ *David's Drawings* by Cathryn Falwell, from Text Set: Learning and Working Together: School

  ▪ *Tap, Tap, Tappity-Tap!* by Elizabeth Sawyer and *Clippity Clop* by Susan A. Layne, from *Shared Reading Collection*

▸ chart paper and markers

Academic Language / Important Vocabulary

▸ stories

▸ know

▸ special

▸ identity

▸ care

Continuum Connection

▸ Understand that writers may tell stories from their own lives (p. 250)

▸ Generate and expand ideas through talk with peers and teacher (p. 256)

▸ Look for ideas and topics in personal experiences, shared through talk (p. 256)

▸ Use storytelling to generate and rehearse language that may be written later (p. 256)

GOAL

Understand that you can tell stories about what makes you special.

RATIONALE

When children tell stories about what makes them special, they are able to get their ideas out orally before writing them. Telling stories builds classroom community by helping children get to know one another as individuals and appreciate the different experiences of each individual.

ASSESS LEARNING

▸ Notice whether children understand that they can tell a story about themselves.

▸ Listen for evidence that children are using ideas from their own lives to tell stories.

▸ Look for evidence that they can use vocabulary such as *stories*, *know*, *special*, *identity*, and *care*.

MINILESSON

Use familiar stories to engage children in thinking about storytelling. Here is an example.

▸ Read the note about the author on the inside cover of *David's Drawings*.

  Where did the author get the idea for her story?

▸ Guide the conversation so children understand that when she was young, the author used drawing to make friends, just like David did in the story.

▸ Briefly revisit several other books, such as *Tap, Tap, Tappity-Tap!* and *Clippity Clop*.

  How do you think the authors of these books thought of these ideas?

▸ Guide children to realize that the authors probably chose something they knew about from their own lives (e.g., having a passion for drums, working with horses on a farm).

  You can also write about yourself. Tell things that are special about you and make you who you are.

▸ Tell a story that relates to who you are (e.g., your family, where you come from, your home language). The goal is to choose an authentic subject and tell about it, but share only what you are comfortable sharing. This is just an example.

  When I was just a teenager, I moved by myself from a country called Cambodia. I thought I would be moving to a big city, but instead, my new home was in a small farm town. I learned English, but I still speak and write Khmer, which is the language of Cambodia. I now have two countries to love and to call my own.

Have a Try

Invite children to tell a story about something that makes them special.

> Think about something that makes you special. Turn and tell your partner your story.

▶ After time for discussion, ask several children to share their story ideas. Record the ideas on chart paper with a simple sentence and sketch.

Summarize and Apply

Summarize the learning and invite children to tell a story and write about it during independent writing.

▶ Write the principle at the top of the chart. Read it aloud.

> During writing time, you can tell a story about something that makes you special to me or to a partner. Then you can draw and write your story. Look at the chart to help you think of ideas.

Tell stories about yourself.

Shan speaks Mandarin and English.

Hello   Nǐ hǎo.

Ava can cook.

Hope has three cats.

Kai lives with his grandparents.

Grandma Grandpa Kai

Confer

▶ During independent writing, move around the room to confer briefly with as many individual children as time allows. Sit side by side with them and invite them to tell stories about themselves. Use the prompts below as needed.

- *What is something that makes you special?*
- *Tell more about what happened.*
- *What happened next? after that?*

Share

Following independent writing, gather children in the meeting area. Ask several children to share their stories. As they share, add their ideas to the chart.

> Tell a story you were thinking about today.

Writing Minilesson Principle
Tell stories about things you did.

Learning About Self and Others Through Storytelling

You Will Need

- a book that children know that includes familiar experiences, such as *The Camping Trip* by Louis Petrone, from *Shared Reading Collection*
- chart paper and markers

Academic Language / Important Vocabulary

- stories
- ideas

Continuum Connection

- Understand that writers may tell stories from their own lives (p. 250)
- Use storytelling to generate and rehearse language that may be written later (p. 256)
- Generate and expand ideas through talk with peers and teacher (p. 256)
- Tell stories from personal experience (p. 332)
- Tell personal experiences in a logical sequence (p. 332)

GOAL

Understand that you can tell stories about things you have done.

RATIONALE

When children tell stories from their own lives, they practice moving their thoughts into words. Telling stories also supports children's ability to move from oral language to written language.

ASSESS LEARNING

- Notice whether children can choose a topic for storytelling.
- Listen to children's stories. Is there evidence of story structure (e.g., sequence)?
- Look for evidence that children can use vocabulary such as *stories* and *ideas*.

MINILESSON

To help children think about the minilesson principle, use a familiar book and a simple oral story of your own to demonstrate that people tell stories about things they have done. Here is an example.

- Show *The Camping Trip*.

  What story does this book, *The Camping Trip*, tell about?

- Go through a few pages with children and engage them in a conversation about the things Andy and his family did together. Help them realize that the author may have used ideas from his own life in the book.

  This story makes me think about things I have done that I can tell a story about.

- Tell a story about something you recently did with a friend (e.g., volunteered at an animal shelter, sang in a chorus) or something the class did together (e.g., planted seeds, visited a museum). Include some details and a story structure. Consider modeling telling the story across your fingers (tell about the first event on the first finger, the next event on the next finger, and so on).

  You can tell stories about things you have done, too.

Have a Try

Invite children to talk to a partner about an experience from their own lives.

> **Think of something you did with your family or a friend. Turn and tell your partner about what you did.**

▶ After time for discussion, invite a few children to quickly share their stories. After each story, write a quick sentence and make a sketch on chart paper to help children generate ideas for storytelling.

Summarize and Apply

Summarize the learning and invite children to tell stories about their own lives during independent writing.

▶ Write the principle at the top of the chart and read it aloud.

> **During writing time, you can tell your story to me or to a partner. Then you can draw and write your story. Look at the chart to help you think of ideas.**

Tell stories about things you did.

Wei made dumplings.

Logan went to the dentist.

Aliyah helped her aunt sell flowers.

Charlotte found a frog.

Confer

▶ During independent writing, move around the room to confer briefly with as many individual children as time allows. Sit side by side with them and invite them to tell stories about things they did. Use the prompts below as needed.

- *What did you do yesterday (last week, last summer)?*
- *You can write a story about that.*
- *Tell the story across your fingers. Point to the first finger. What happened first?*
- *How will your story end?*

Share

Following independent writing, gather children in the meeting area. Ask several children to share their stories. As they share, add ideas to the chart.

> **Share a story that you told someone today.**

Writing Minilesson Principle
Tell stories about places you don't want to forget.

Learning About Self and Others Through Storytelling

You Will Need

▸ several books about places that are special, such as the following:

- *Ripples in the Sea* by Miriam Glassman, from *Shared Reading Collection*

- *Elizabeti's School* by Stephanie Stuve-Bodeen, from Text Set: Learning and Working Together: School

▸ chart paper and markers

Academic Language / Important Vocabulary

▸ stories

▸ places

Continuum Connection

▸ Understand that writers may tell stories from their own lives (p. 250)

▸ Generate and expand ideas through talk with peers and teacher (p. 256)

▸ Look for ideas and topics in personal experiences, shared through talk (p. 256)

▸ Use storytelling to generate and rehearse language that may be written later (p. 256)

GOAL

Understand you can tell stories about places you have been.

RATIONALE

Teaching children to express their ideas by telling stories about places that are familiar to them helps them understand that the things they know about the world have value. As children tell their stories, help them clarify information and add details by asking questions and restating what you heard.

ASSESS LEARNING

▸ Notice whether children tell stories about places they have been.

▸ Listen for the details that children include in their stories.

▸ Look for evidence that they can use vocabulary such as *stories* and *places*.

MINILESSON

To help children think about storytelling, use books that feature interesting settings and tell an authentic story.

▸ Show pages 2–3 of *Ripples in the Sea*.

> This story is about a girl who goes on a boat in the ocean. This place is special to her.

▸ Show *Elizabeti's School* and read the note about the author on the inside cover.

> The author, Stephanie Stuve-Bodeen, tells a story about a place in Africa called Tanzania. This place is special to her. She shared a story about that place by writing a book.

▸ Orally tell about an authentic place that is special to you. Here is an example.

> A place that is special to me is my grandma's apartment. She lives right across from the subway station, and I always see her waving out her window when I get off the train. When I enter the building, I smell fresh empanadas cooking. My nose guesses whether they will be made from chicken, pork, or beef. When she opens her door, my grandma gives me a marshmallow-blanket kind of hug. My eyes adjust to the bright colors of her handmade art that she weaves from threads in brilliant red, blue, yellow, and orange.

▸ Engage children in a conversation about using a special place to tell a story.

> What did you learn about a place that is special to me?

> What words showed what my grandma's apartment is like?

> Would this place be good to write a story about? Why or why not?

WML3
STR.U1.WML3

Have a Try

Invite children to talk to a partner about places they want to remember.

> When you tell a story about a place that is special to you, tell about what you do there and what the place looks like, smells like, and sounds like. Turn and tell your partner about a place that you don't want to forget.

▶ After time for discussion, invite a few children to share ideas. On chart paper, draw a quick sketch of the place and add the child's name.

Summarize and Apply

Summarize the learning. Remind children they can write stories about places during independent writing.

> What is something you can tell a story about?

▶ Write the principle on the chart and read it aloud.

> During writing time today, you can tell me or a partner a story about a place that is special to you. Then you can make a book about it.

Tell stories about places you don't want to forget.

Mason

Kaylee

Henry

Ruby

Confer

▶ During independent writing, move around the room to confer briefly with as many individual children as time allows. Sit side by side with them and invite them to tell stories about places they don't want to forget. Use the prompts below as needed.

- *Can you add to that idea?*
- *Tell more about that.*
- *Describe how you were feeling when you were in that place.*
- *What did you see (hear, smell, feel) there?*

Share

Following independent writing, gather children in the meeting area. Choose several children to share their stories about places they want to remember. As they share, add story ideas to the chart.

> Tell about a place that is special to you.

Umbrella 1: Learning About Self and Others Through Storytelling

227

Learning About Self and Others Through Storytelling

You Will Need

- Me Boxes for you and for each child or other objects for storytelling
- chart paper and markers

Academic Language / Important Vocabulary

- stories
- Me Box

Continuum Connection

- Understand that writers may tell stories from their own lives (p. 250)
- Generate and expand ideas through talk with peers and teacher (p. 256)
- Look for ideas and topics in personal experiences, shared through talk (p. 256)
- Use storytelling to generate and rehearse language that may be written later (p. 256)
- Gather information for writing: e.g., objects, books, photos, sticky notes, etc. (p. 256)

GOAL

Understand you can tell stories about items that represent important memories.

RATIONALE

When children choose topics from their own lives for telling stories, they learn to value their lives and understand that they have unique stories to tell. Telling stories orally helps children develop their use of language before they write their ideas.

ASSESS LEARNING

- Notice whether children understand that they can share their memories through storytelling.
- Listen to children tell stories about items in their Me Boxes.
- Look for evidence that they can use vocabulary such as *stories* and *Me Box*.

MINILESSON

To help children understand that they can use special items for story ideas, engage them in thinking and talking about items from their Me Boxes. Here is an example.

- Before teaching, have each child prepare a Me Box filled with meaningful objects. Make a Me Box for yourself as well.
- Choose an item to show from your Me Box. Tell a story about the object you have chosen. Here is an example, but tell your own personal story.

  In my Me Box there is a library card. When I was six years old, my dad took me to the library for story time. After the librarian read some stories, my dad told me that this was a special day. He had a big smile on his face as we walked to the desk. The librarian handed me my own library card! I got to write my name on it, which you can see right here. I was so surprised and excited because I could check out my very own books! I saved my first library card to remind me of how happy I felt on that day.

- Engage children in a conversation about the story you told and have them think about what items from their Me Boxes they might tell a story about.

  What did you learn about this item from my Me Box?

  Look at the items in your Me Box. What is an item you could tell a story about?

- Ask a few children to share ideas. Create a chart with a simple sentence and a sketch of the item they have chosen. Post the chart to help children remember ideas they can tell stories about.

Have a Try

Invite children to tell a partner about something from their Me Boxes.

> Choose one item from your Me Box. Tell your partner about that item.

▶ After time for discussion, invite a few children to share. Add new ideas to the chart.

Summarize and Apply

Summarize the learning. Remind children they can write stories about objects in their Me Boxes during independent writing.

> What is something you can tell a story about?

▶ Write the principle at the top of the chart.

> During writing time today, you can tell a story about something in your Me Box to me or to a partner. Then you can make a book about it.

Tell stories about things from your Me Box.

Alba went to a bird show.

Wells made tortillas with his uncle.

Elisa collected shells on the beach.

Darius learned to do magic tricks.

Confer

▶ During independent writing, move around the room to confer briefly with as many individual children as time allows. Sit side by side with them and invite them to tell stories about items in their Me Boxes. Use the prompts below as needed.

- *Tell about this item in your Me Box.*
- *Why did you choose to include this item in your Me Box?*
- *Tell more about that.*
- *Can you add to that?*

Share

Following independent writing, gather children in the meeting area. Have several children share their stories. As they share, add ideas to the chart.

> Tell about something from your Me Box.

Assessment

After you have taught the minilessons in this umbrella, observe children as they engage in storytelling. Use *The Literacy Continuum* (Fountas and Pinnell 2017) to notice, teach for, and support children's learning as you observe their attempts at telling stories.

> ▸ What evidence do you have of new understandings children have developed related to storytelling?
>
> > • Do you find evidence that children tell stories about what makes them special?
> >
> > • Do children tell stories about events and places from their own lives?
> >
> > • Can they develop stories about items from their Me Boxes?
> >
> > • Do they understand and use vocabulary such as *stories*, *know*, *care*, *identity*, *ideas*, *places*, and *Me Box*?
>
> ▸ In what ways, beyond the scope of this umbrella, are children showing readiness for storytelling?
>
> > • Do they show an interest in acting out their stories?
> >
> > • Are they using ideas from stories they have told when making books?

Use your observations to determine the next umbrella you will teach. You may also consult Suggested Sequence of Lessons (pp. 557–571) for guidance.

EXTENSIONS FOR LEARNING ABOUT SELF AND OTHERS THROUGH STORYTELLING

▸ Have children tell their stories to partners, rotating the children so they have opportunities to hear stories from and get to know different classmates.

▸ Invite families to make a Family Box and fill it with items and photos that represent shared family experiences. Children can use those items to tell stories.

▸ After reading several related books (e.g., two versions of a fairy tale), have children tell the stories to each other.

▸ Assign a special topic for telling stories about one's own life (e.g., family traditions).

▸ Post the charts created in these lessons so that children can get ideas for independent writing.

▸ Have children engage in heart mapping (Heard 2016), in which they use a heart cut-out to write memories about people and places that are special to them. They can then choose from ideas within the heart map for storytelling and writing.

Minilessons in This Umbrella

WML1 Speak with a strong voice.

WML2 Look at your audience.

WML3 Tell your story in the order it happened.

WML4 Stay on topic.

Before Teaching Umbrella 2 Minilessons

Before teaching the minilessons in this umbrella, teach STR.U1: Learning About Self and Others Through Storytelling. In addition, give children plenty of opportunities to listen to stories read aloud and told by you and to share stories of their own. Tell various kinds of stories (e.g., about your own experiences, shared class experiences, retellings of familiar stories) and model effective presentation techniques, such as speaking at an appropriate volume and rate, making eye contact with the audience, staying on topic, and retelling events in the correct sequence.

As you share stories together, help children think about what is happening at the beginning, in the middle, and at the end of the story, and notice how the speaker is telling the story.

Section 3: Telling Stories

WML1

Writing Minilesson Principle
Speak with a strong voice.

Learning How to Present Ideas

You Will Need

- an idea for a story or presentation
- chart paper and markers
- To download the following online resource for this lesson, visit **resources.fountasandpinnell.com**:
  - chart art (optional)

Academic Language/ Important Vocabulary

- speak
- strong
- voice
- audience

Continuum Connection

- Talk about a topic with enthusiasm (p. 332)
- Speak with confidence (p. 332)
- Tell stories in an interesting way (p. 332)
- Speak at an appropriate volume to be heard but not too loud (p. 332)
- Speak at an appropriate rate to be understood (p. 332)

GOAL

Speak with confidence and enthusiasm and in a way that can be heard and understood.

RATIONALE

When children understand that the way they speak (volume, rate, etc.) matters, they are better able to communicate their ideas effectively. Telling stories and sharing ideas orally will help them put their ideas into writing later on.

ASSESS LEARNING

- Observe whether children adjust the volume and rate of their speaking as they tell stories.
- Look for evidence that children can use vocabulary such as *speak*, *strong*, *voice*, and *audience*.

MINILESSON

To help children think about the minilesson principle, engage them in an inquiry around how you use your voice when presenting.

- Tell a brief story about a personal or shared class experience (e.g., a recent vacation, a funny thing that happened) or give a short presentation on a topic that will interest the children (e.g., dinosaurs). Model how to speak with appropriate volume, rate, and expression.

  What did you notice about my voice?

  Did I speak too quietly or too loud? too fast or slow?

  Did I sound interested in what I was talking about?

- Guide children to realize that you spoke in a way that they could hear you and understand what you were saying—neither too quietly or too loudly nor too fast or too slowly—and you sounded excited.

  How would you tell someone to speak when presenting ideas or telling a story to an audience? What would you say about how to make your voice sound?

- Record ideas on chart paper.

  When you present your ideas or tell a story to an audience, use a strong voice.

Have a Try

Invite children to tell a partner about something that interests them.

> Think of something you're really excited to talk about. For example, you might want to talk about something fun you did recently or something interesting you read about in a book. Turn and tell your partner about it. Remember to use a strong voice so your partner can hear and understand you.

Summarize and Apply

Summarize the learning and remind children to speak with a strong voice when they present.

▸ Write the principle at the top of the chart and read it aloud.

> The chart tells what a strong voice is like.

> Today during writing time, think of something else that you'd like to talk about. You will have the chance to talk about it to me during writing time or to your classmates when we come back together.

Speak with a strong voice.

- Not too quiet.

- Not too loud.

- Not too fast.

- Not too slow.

- Sound excited!

Confer

▸ During independent writing, move around the room to confer briefly with as many individual children as time allows. Sit side by side with them and invite them to tell stories, present their ideas, or read their writing. Use prompts such as the following if needed.

- *Do you have a story that you'd like to tell? Or a topic that you'd like to talk about?*
- *Try speaking a little louder. I don't want to miss anything!*
- *Can you say that again, this time a little more slowly?*
- *You spoke with a good, strong voice!*

Share

Following independent writing, gather children in the meeting area to practice using a strong voice.

> Who would like to tell a story or share something interesting? Remember to use a strong voice so we can hear and understand what you're saying.

Writing Minilesson Principle
Look at your audience.

Learning How to Present Ideas

You Will Need

- an idea for a story or presentation
- chart paper and markers
- To download the following online resource for this lesson, visit **resources.fountasandpinnell.com**:
  - chart art (optional)

Academic Language/ Important Vocabulary

- audience

Continuum Connection

- Look at the audience (or other person) while speaking (p. 332)

GOAL

Look at the audience (or other person) while speaking.

RATIONALE

When children understand the importance of maintaining eye contact, they are better able to communicate with an audience. This in turn will make them more confident and more motivated to continue telling stories and sharing ideas.

ASSESS LEARNING

- Observe whether children make eye contact with their audience when they tell stories and present ideas.
- Look for evidence that children can use vocabulary such as *audience*.

MINILESSON

To help children think about the minilesson principle, model how to effectively make eye contact with the audience while presenting. Below is an example. However, take into consideration that some children may not be comfortable with establishing or able to establish eye contact because of cultural conventions or for other reasons. Skip or adjust this lesson as appropriate for the children in your class.

- Tell a very short story or give a brief presentation. Be sure to look directly at the children.

  > What did you notice about what I was doing while I was speaking? Where was I looking?

  > Do you think it's important for me to look at you when I speak to you? Why?

- Guide children to realize that when you look at them, they are more likely to look at you and listen to you.

  > When you look at your audience when you are speaking to them, they will be more interested in what you have to say. They will feel that you are talking right to them!

  > Remember to look at your audience when you tell a story or share your ideas. Your audience is the person or the people who are listening.

Have a Try

Invite children to talk to a partner about their favorite hobbies.

> Turn and talk to your partner about what you like to do when you're not at school. Remember to use a strong voice and to look at your audience!

Summarize and Apply

Summarize the learning and remind children to look at their audience when they present.

▶ Write the principle at the top of the chart paper and add an illustration.

> Today during writing time, think of a story that you'd like to tell. It can be a story you read or something that happened to you. You will have the chance to tell your story to me during writing time or to your classmates when we come back together.

Look at your audience.

Confer

▶ During independent writing, move around the room to confer briefly with as many individual children as time allows. Sit side by side with them and invite them to tell you a story. Use the following prompts as needed.

- *Where should you look when you're speaking to an audience?*
- *Say that part again, but this time remember to look at me.*
- *You looked at me while you spoke.*

Share

Following independent writing, gather children in the meeting area. Invite them to practice what they have just learned about presenting their ideas.

> Who would like to tell a story?

> Would anyone like to tell us about someone else's story?

> Remember to use a strong voice and look at your audience.

Learning How to Present Ideas

You Will Need

▸ an idea for a story (e.g., a personal experience or a retelling of a familiar book)

▸ chart paper and markers

▸ To download the following online resource for this lesson, visit **resources.fountasandpinnell.com**:

  ▪ chart art (optional)

Academic Language/ Important Vocabulary

▸ story

▸ order

Continuum Connection

▸ Tell personal experiences in a logical sequence (p. 332)

▸ Present ideas and information in a logical sequence (p. 332)

▸ Demonstrate knowledge of story structure (p. 332)

GOAL

Tell stories in a logical sequence.

RATIONALE

When children understand how to tell stories in a logical sequence, they are better able to tell stories that their audience will understand and enjoy.

ASSESS LEARNING

▸ Observe whether children tell stories in a logical sequence.

▸ Look for evidence that children can use vocabulary such as *story* and *order*.

MINILESSON

To help children think about the minilesson principle, model telling a story in a logical sequence and engage children in a discussion about what they noticed. Here is an example.

▸ Tell a short story about a brief moment in your life or a shared class experience, or retell a familiar story (e.g., a story that you read aloud recently to the class). Hold up a finger for each part that you tell and explain that each part could be a page in a book.

> What happened first in my story?
>
> What happened next?
>
> What happened after that?
>
> What happened last?

▸ Guide children to notice that you told the events in your story in the order they happened.

> I told my story in the order that it happened.
>
> Why is it important to tell a story in the order it happened?
>
> When you tell your story in the order it happened, you make it easier for your audience to understand and enjoy the story.

Have a Try

Invite children to tell a story to a partner.

> Turn and tell your partner a story about something fun you did last weekend. Hold up a finger as you tell about what will go on each page.

▶ Choose one of the stories and show on chart paper each of the major events in order (or use the story about going to school shown on the chart).

Summarize and Apply

Help children summarize the learning. Write the principle at the top of the chart and read it to children. Remind them to tell their stories in the order they happened.

> What did you learn today about telling stories?

> Today during writing time, tell a story to me or to a classmate. Make sure to tell your story in the order it happened. You might choose to make a book about your story. If you do, put one part of your story on each page.

Confer

▶ During independent writing, move around the room to confer briefly with as many individual children as time allows. Sit side by side with them and invite them to tell you a story. Use the following prompts as needed.

- *What happened first in your story?*
- *Then what happened?*
- *What happened last?*
- *You held up four fingers, so you can have at least four pages in your book.*

Share

Following independent writing, gather children in the meeting area. Invite several children to tell their stories.

> Who would like to tell a story?

> Tell the story across your fingers.

Learning How to Present Ideas

You Will Need

- an idea for a presentation about a specific topic
- chart paper and markers
- To download the following online resource for this lesson, visit **resources.fountasandpinnell.com**:
  - chart art (optional)

Academic Language/ Important Vocabulary

- topic

Continuum Connection

- Speak to one topic at a time, and stay on topic (p. 332)

GOAL

Learn to speak on one topic at a time and stay on that topic.

RATIONALE

When you teach children to stay on topic when they are speaking, they are better able to develop their ideas and communicate them with an audience.

ASSESS LEARNING

- Observe whether children stay on topic when they tell stories or present ideas.
- Look for evidence that children can use vocabulary such as *topic*.

MINILESSON

To help children think about the minilesson principle, model how to stay on topic while presenting. Here is an example.

- Give a brief presentation about a specific topic that will interest the children (e.g., the planets in the solar system).

    What topic did I talk about?

    Did I talk about what I had for breakfast?

    Did I talk about my dog?

    Did I talk about my house?

    I didn't talk about any of those things. The only topic I talked about was the planets in the solar system. I talked about that topic the whole time. When you are talking about a topic, remember to stay on that topic the whole time—don't start talking about something completely different.

Have a Try

Invite children to talk to a partner about their favorite foods.

> What are your favorite foods? Turn and talk to your partner about this topic. Remember to stay on topic, and don't talk about anything else besides your favorite foods.

Summarize and Apply

Summarize the learning and remind children to stay on topic when they present their ideas.

▶ Make a chart to summarize the learning. Write the principle at the top and read it aloud.

> Why do you think it's important to stay on topic when you are speaking?

> Today during writing time, think about a topic you would like to talk about. For example, you might want to talk about what you did last weekend or a movie you like. You will have the chance to talk about it to me during writing time or to your classmates when we come back together. You might also decide to write a book about the topic. Remember to write only about the topic in your book.

Stay on topic.

Confer

▶ During independent writing, move around the room to confer briefly with as many individual children as time allows. Sit side by side with them and invite them to talk about the topic of their writing. Use the following prompts as needed.

- *What would you like to talk about?*
- *Does _____ have to do with _____?*
- *Remember to stay on topic. Talk more about _____. You can talk about _____ another time.*
- *You stayed on topic the whole time you were speaking.*

Share

Following independent writing, gather children in the meeting area to present their ideas.

> Who would like to share something with the class? Remember to stay on topic.

Assessment

After you have taught the minilessons in this umbrella, observe children as they tell stories and present their ideas. Use *The Literacy Continuum* (Fountas and Pinnell 2017) to notice, teach for, and support children's learning as you observe their oral communication skills.

▶ What evidence do you have of new understandings children have developed related to presenting ideas?

- How do children's voices sound when they tell a story or present their ideas?

- Do they look at their audience?

- Do they retell events in the order they happened?

- Are they able to stay on topic?

- Do they understand and use vocabulary such as *strong*, *voice*, *audience*, and *order*?

▶ In what other ways, beyond the scope of this umbrella, are children developing their presentation skills?

- Are they sharing their writing with others?

- Do they use their stories to make books?

Use your observations to determine the next umbrella you will teach. You may also consult Suggested Sequence of Lessons (pp. 557–571) for guidance.

EXTENSIONS FOR LEARNING HOW TO PRESENT IDEAS

▶ Give children daily opportunities to share stories and ideas with their classmates.

▶ When children tell stories, prompt them to give more details with questions such as *What did you do after that? How did you feel when that happened? What did it smell/taste/look/sound like? What did you like about that?*

▶ When children listen to stories told by others, ask them questions such as *What happened first in the story? What happened next? What happened at the end of the story? What did you notice about how _____ told his story?*

▶ Have children draw and write about stories or topics that they have shared orally.

▶ Provide models of good presentation skills by inviting speakers to the class to tell a story or present on a particular topic (e.g., the speaker's career) or playing recordings of professionally recorded books.

Mo Willems

Minilessons in This Umbrella

WML1 Use puppets to act out a story.

WML2 Tell about something you have learned.

WML3 Teach others about something you know how to do.

Before Teaching Umbrella 3 Minilessons

The minilessons in this umbrella are designed to give children more opportunities to strengthen their oral language skills and develop vocabulary for presenting both stories and information. These lessons can be spread out over the year to support different kinds of writing the children are working on. WML1 can be taught early in the year to support children's understanding of fiction. WML2 can be taught when the children are working on nonfiction writing, particularly all-about books. WML3 might be taught when the children are working on how-to books.

Before teaching WML1, read and discuss stories that are easy to retell and act out, such as those with few characters, simple plots, and plenty of repetition. For WML1, use the following text from *Fountas & Pinnell Classroom™ Interactive Read-Aloud Collection*, or choose a book that could be acted out with puppets from your classroom library.

Mo Willems: Having Fun with Humor

Elephants Cannot Dance!

As you read and enjoy stories together, help children

- think about what is happening in the story,

- talk about the words, actions, and personality of each character, and

- notice how the illustrations help tell the story.

Section 3: Telling Stories

Writing Minilesson Principle
Use puppets to act out a story.

You Will Need

▶ a familiar story that can be acted out with puppets, such as *Elephants Cannot Dance!* by Mo Willems, from Text Set: Mo Willems: Having Fun with Humor

▶ a child prepared to act out the story with you

▶ stick puppets for each character

▶ chart paper and markers

▶ To download the following online resources for this lesson, visit **resources.fountasandpinnell.com**:

  ▪ Character Puppets

  ▪ chart art (optional)

Academic Language/ Important Vocabulary

▶ puppet

▶ act

▶ character

▶ order

Continuum Connection

▶ Perform plays and puppet shows that involve speaking as a character (p. 332)

▶ Retell familiar stories or stories from texts (p. 332)

▶ Use language from stories when retelling (p. 332)

▶ Demonstrate knowledge of story structure (p. 332)

GOAL

Use puppets to retell a familiar story.

RATIONALE

Retelling familiar stories helps children internalize story structure and language, knowledge that they will use when they write their own stories. Using a visual aid such as a puppet helps them engage more deeply and concretely with a story.

ASSESS LEARNING

▶ Notice whether children can accurately retell the events in a story's plot when they act out the story using puppets.

▶ Observe whether children retell the events in the correct order.

▶ Observe for evidence that children can use vocabulary such as *puppet*, *act*, *character*, and *order*.

MINILESSON

Before the lesson, glue the character puppets from online resources onto craft sticks. With help from a child, use the stick puppets to demonstrate using puppets to act out a story. Here is an example.

▶ Show the cover of *Elephants Cannot Dance!* and read the title. Briefly show a few pages to refresh children's memories of the story.

> We read this fun story about Gerald the elephant and Piggie. Watch what _____ and I do.

▶ With the child who has been prepared beforehand, act out the story (or a portion of it) using the stick puppets. Then ask the other children what they noticed.

> What did you notice about what _____ and I did? How did we tell the story?

> What did we do with the puppets?

> How did we know what to say and how to say it?

> What part of the story did we tell first? What did we tell last? How did we know the order in which to tell the story?

> When you tell a story with puppets, first tell the beginning of the story. Then tell what happens next and after that. Then tell what happens at the end. Tell the story in the same order that the author tells it in the book.

▶ Talk with children about how acting out a story with puppets could make the story come alive and entertain an audience.

Have a Try

Invite children to talk to a partner about how to use puppets to act out a story.

> Turn and talk to your partner about how to use puppets to act out a story. What do you need to remember to do?

▶ After children turn and talk, invite several pairs to share their ideas. Record responses on chart paper.

Summarize and Apply

Summarize the learning. Remind children to tell the story in the correct sequence when they use puppets to act out a story.

▶ Write the principle at the top of the chart. Read it aloud.

> During writing time today, some of you will work with a partner to act out *Elephants Cannot Dance!* using puppets. Remember to tell the story in the same order that it happens in the book and to talk like the characters.

Use puppets to act out a story.

- Say what the characters say.
- Talk like the characters talk.
- Make your puppets do what the characters do.
- Tell the story in the same order it happens in the book.

Confer

▶ While some children are writing, help pairs of children use stick puppets to act out *Elephants Cannot Dance!* Use prompts such as the following if needed.

- *What happens first? How can you show that with your puppets?*
- *Use your puppets to show what the characters do next.*
- *What do the characters say? Let's check the book to make sure.*
- *How does the story end? Can you show that with your puppets?*

Share

Following independent writing, gather children in the meeting area to talk about using puppets to act out a story.

> How did you use puppets today to act out *Elephants Cannot Dance!*

WML2

STR.U3.WML2

Writing Minilesson Principle
Tell about something you have learned.

Presenting with a Purpose

You Will Need

- a prepared brief oral presentation about a nonfiction topic that will interest children
- chart paper and markers
- To download the following online resource for this lesson, visit **resources.fountasandpinnell.com**:
  - chart art (optional)

Academic Language/ Important Vocabulary

- stay on topic
- audience

Continuum Connection

- Make brief oral reports that demonstrate understanding of a simple, familiar topic (p. 332)
- Understand and use words related to familiar experiences and topics (p. 332)
- Speak to one topic at a time, and stay on topic (p. 332)
- Speak at appropriate volume to be heard, but not too loud (p. 332)
- Look at the audience (or other person) while speaking (p. 332)
- Speak at an appropriate rate to be understood (p. 332)
- Answer questions asked by the audience (p. 332)

GOAL

Make a brief oral report about a topic.

RATIONALE

Presenting orally about a topic will help children put their ideas into writing later on. You may want to teach this lesson immediately prior to teaching Umbrella 5: Making All-About Books in the Making Books section.

ASSESS LEARNING

- Observe children as they give brief oral presentations.
- Notice whether children stay on topic and speak at an appropriate rate and volume.
- Observe for evidence that children can use vocabulary such as *stay on topic* and *audience*.

MINILESSON

To help children think about the principle, demonstrate giving a brief oral presentation about a topic and then engage children in an inquiry around what they noticed. Here is an example.

> I would like to tell you about something interesting I learned about nature, or our outside world. Listen carefully, and watch what I do.

- Give a brief oral presentation about nature or another topic that will interest the children (e.g., dinosaurs, sharks, spaceships). Model speaking at an appropriate rate and volume and making eye contact with the audience. Afterwards, ask the children if they have any questions. Then ask the children what they noticed about your presentation.

> Why do you think I chose to talk about _____?
>
> How did my voice sound? Was it a *0, 1, 2,* or *3* voice?
>
> Did I speak fast or slow?
>
> Where did I look?
>
> Did I speak about anything else besides _____?
>
> What did I do when I was done talking about _____?

- Record children's responses on chart paper, generalizing them as necessary. If children mention looking at the audience, take into consideration that some children are not comfortable with establishing or able to establish eye contact because of cultural considerations or for other reasons.

Have a Try

Invite children to talk with a partner about something they learned in class

> We've been talking about _____ in class. Turn and talk to your partner about something you learned about _____.

Summarize and Apply

Help children summarize the learning. Invite them to give an oral presentation about a topic.

▶ Write the principle at the top of the chart. Read it aloud.

> Talk about what you learned today. How do you tell someone or a group about something you have learned?

> Today during writing time, tell a partner about something you have learned. Look at the chart if you need help remembering what to do.

Tell about something you have learned.

- Choose an interesting topic.

- Speak loudly but not too loudly.

- Don't speak too fast or too slow.

- Look at the audience.

- Stay on topic.

- Answer questions.

Confer

▶ Sit side by side with pairs of children and listen carefully as they give oral presentations to each other. Use prompts such as the following if needed.

- *What would you like to tell about? What have you learned about recently?*

- *Tell about what you learned. Remember to stay on topic the whole time.*

- *Can you speak a little bit louder? You don't want the audience to miss anything.*

- *You looked at your audience the whole time you were speaking.*

Share

Following independent writing, gather children in the meeting area and invite a few children to present to the class.

> Today you told a partner something you have learned about _____. Would anyone like to tell the whole class what you learned about _____?

Section 3: Telling Stories

Writing Minilesson Principle
Teach others about something you know how to do.

You Will Need

- a prepared brief oral presentation about how to do something (e.g., plant a seed)
- if appropriate, props or illustrations to support the presentation
- chart paper and markers

Academic Language/ Important Vocabulary

- step
- topic
- audience
- prop
- illustration

Continuum Connection

- Make brief oral reports that demonstrate understanding of a simple, familiar topic (p. 332)
- Understand and use words related to familiar experiences and topics (p. 332)
- Present ideas and information in a logical sequence (p. 332)
- Speak at an appropriate volume to be heard, but not too loud (p. 332)
- Look at the audience (or other person) while speaking (p. 332)
- Speak at an appropriate rate to be understood (p. 332)
- Answer questions asked by the audience (p. 332)
- Use props, images, or illustrations to extend the meaning of a presentation (p. 332)

GOAL

Make a brief oral presentation to teach others how to do something.

RATIONALE

Giving oral instructions about how to do something will help children put their ideas into writing (in a how-to book) later on. You may want to teach this lesson immediately prior to teaching MBK.U4: Making How-to Books.

ASSESS LEARNING

- Observe children as they give oral instructions.
- Notice whether children present information in a logical sequence, stay on topic, and speak at an appropriate rate and volume.
- Observe for evidence that children can use vocabulary such as *step*, *topic*, *audience*, *prop*, and *illustration*.

MINILESSON

To help children think about the principle, demonstrate giving a brief oral presentation about how to do something and then engage children in an inquiry around what they noticed. Here is an example.

- Give a simple, brief oral presentation about how to do something that will interest the class (e.g., plant a seed or make a snack). Include props or illustrations in your presentation. Afterward, invite questions from the audience. Then ask children what they noticed.

  What did I tell you about?

  What did you see and hear me do when I spoke?

  What did I tell you about first? What did I tell you about next? What did I tell you about last?

  When you teach others about how to do something, tell about the first step first, then the second step, then the third step, and so on. This will make it easy for them to follow your directions.

  What did I do to help you better understand how to _____?

  When you teach people how to do something, you can use illustrations or props to show them exactly how to do it.

  What did I do at the end?

- Record children's responses on chart paper, generalizing them as necessary. If children mention looking at the audience, take into consideration that some children are not comfortable with establishing or able to establish eye contact because of cultural conventions or for other reasons.

Have a Try

Invite children to brainstorm potential topics with a partner.

> What are some things that you know how to do? What could you teach other people how to do? Turn and talk to your partner about this.

Summarize and Apply

Help children summarize the learning and invite them to give an oral presentation about how to do something.

▶ Write the principle at the top of the chart. Read it aloud.

> Talk about what you learned today. How can you teach others to do something?

> During writing time today, you will teach a partner about something you know how to do. Look at the chart if you need help remembering what to do.

Teach others about something you know how to do.

- Talk about something that you know how to do.
- Tell the steps in the right order.
- Don't speak too loudly or too quietly.
- Don't speak too fast or too slow.
- Look at the audience.
- Stay on topic.
- Use props or illustrations.
- Answer questions.

Step 1: ⁓⁓
Step 2: ⁓
Step 3: ⁓

Confer

▶ Sit side by side with pairs of children and listen carefully as they give oral presentations to each other. Use prompts such as the following if needed.

- *What is something that you know how to do? Can you teach someone how to do that?*
- *What do you do first? What do you do next? What do you do after that?*
- *Speak a little louder (slower) so that your audience understands every step.*
- *Remember to stay on topic. Only speak about how to _____.*

Share

Following independent writing, gather children in the meeting area and invite a few children to present to the class.

> Who would like to teach all of us something you know how to do?

Section 3: Telling Stories

Assessment

After you have taught the minilessons in this umbrella, observe children as they present stories and information. Use *The Literacy Continuum* (Fountas and Pinnell 2017) to notice, teach for, and support children's learning as you observe their oral communication development.

▶ What evidence do you have of new understandings children have developed related to presenting with a purpose?

- How do children use puppets to act out a story?

- Do they use good presentation skills when they tell about something they have learned?

- Do they use good presentation skills when they teach others how to do something?

- Are they using vocabulary such as *puppet*, *story*, *audience*, *prop*, and *stay on topic*?

▶ In what other ways, beyond the scope of this umbrella, are children ready to develop their writing skills?

- Are they ready to add dialogue to their books?

Use your observations to determine the next umbrella you will teach. You may also consult Suggested Sequence of Lessons (pp. 557–571) for guidance.

EXTENSIONS FOR PRESENTING WITH A PURPOSE

▶ Remind children to use what they have learned about speaking to an audience whenever they share in group meetings.

▶ Have children practice and present a puppet show for a kindergarten class.

▶ Teach minilessons on using props, slides, illustrations, and/or multimedia to support different types of presentations. Consider using Planning a Writing Minilesson (p. 102) to plan your new lesson.

▶ Encourage children to write books using stories, ideas, and topics that they have presented orally.

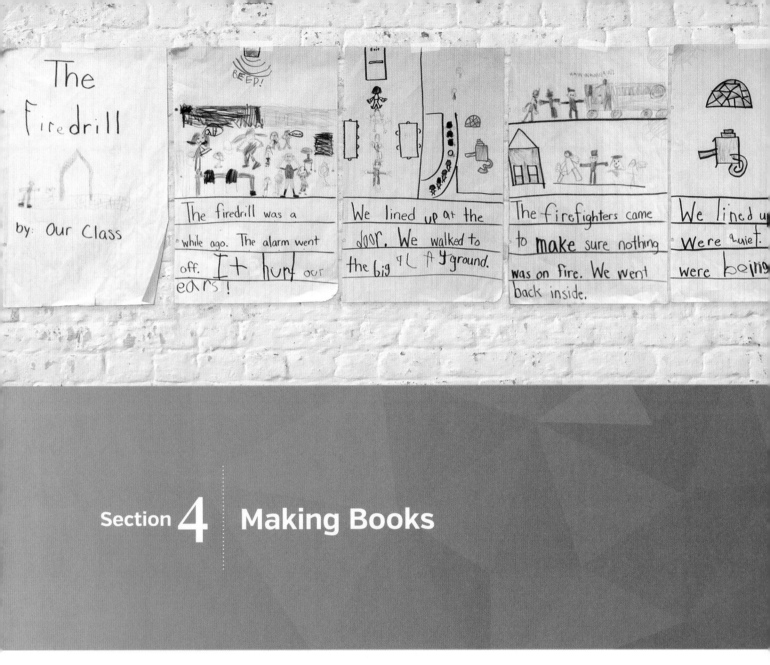

The firedrill

by: Our Class

The firedrill was a while ago. The alarm went off. It hurt our ears!

We lined up at the door. We walked to the big PLAYground.

The firefighters came to make sure nothing was on fire. We went back inside.

We lined up Were quiet were being

Section 4 | Making Books

BOOKMAKING BRINGS TOGETHER children's literacy experiences, such as interactive read-aloud and writing, shared reading and writing, and independent reading and writing. Making their own picture books is a logical next step. The lessons in this section introduce the basics of making books and suggest several kinds of books that children might make.

4 Making Books

Minilessons in This Umbrella

WML1 Make a book with pictures and words.

WML2 Write your name and the date on your book.

WML3 Plan what to put on each page.

WML4 Write labels on your pictures.

WML5 Decide when your book is finished.

Before Teaching Umbrella 1 Minilessons

Children will benefit from having experienced at least some of the minilessons in the Telling Stories section and from having heard and enjoyed a variety of books, such as fiction stories, wordless books, pattern books, and nonfiction books. Use the books listed below from *Fountas & Pinnell Classroom™ Interactive Read-Aloud Collection* and *Shared Reading Collection* as well as the class-made book from IW.7: Writing About Who We Are. Alternatively or in addition, use a variety of books from the classroom library that children have enjoyed.

It's a good idea to make a book of your own to use for the concepts throughout this umbrella. A simple booklet of stapled-together paper with several pages completed is all you need to get started. You will add to the book as you move through the lessons. If children are already writing full sentences or labeling their writing, WML4 may be reserved for children who need additional support. When they make their books, children can use plain paper or any of the paper templates from online resources that are appropriate.

Interactive Read-Aloud Collection
Learning and Working Together: School

First Day Jitters by Julie Danneberg

Elizabeti's School by Stephanie Stuve-Bodeen

David's Drawings by Cathryn Falwell

Taking Care of Each Other: Family

Max and the Tag-Along Moon by Floyd Cooper

Shared Reading Collection

Monster ABCs by Finnoula Louise

Interactive Writing Lessons

IW.7: Writing About Who We Are

As you read and enjoy these texts together, help children notice that

- writers and illustrators make books,
- there are words and/or pictures on every page, and
- writers tell about different things in their books.

Interactive Read-Aloud
School

Family

Shared Reading

Interactive Writing

Section 4: Making Books

Writing Minilesson Principle
Make a book with pictures and words.

Getting Started with Making Books

You Will Need

- a variety of familiar picture, wordless, alphabet, and informational books
- a prepared book of your own
- IW.7: Writing About Who We Are
- charts from STR.U1: Learning About Self and Others Through Storytelling (optional)
- chart paper and markers
- To download the following online resource for this lesson, visit **resources.fountasandpinnell.com**:
  - chart art (optional)

Academic Language/ Important Vocabulary

- author
- pictures
- words

Continuum Connection

- Have ideas to tell, write, draw about (p. 249)
- Create a picture book as one form of writing (p. 254)
- Use words and drawings to compose and revise writing (p. 256)
- Demonstrate confidence in attempts at drawing and writing (p. 257)
- Understand that when both writing and drawing are on a page, they are mutually supportive, with each extending the other (p. 257)

GOAL

Make books using drawing and approximated writing.

RATIONALE

When you introduce children to making books, you help them view themselves as writers and illustrators, which builds their stamina and enthusiasm for writing. They learn the power of their own ideas and that drawing and writing can communicate ideas to others.

ASSESS LEARNING

- Look for evidence that children can distinguish between the pictures and the words in a book and understand that the pictures and words are related.
- Notice evidence that they can use vocabulary such as *author*, *pictures*, and *words*.

MINILESSON

To help children explore bookmaking, use familiar books that have both pictures and print, the class book created in IW.7: Writing About Who We Are, and a book you made yourself (interior pages only; cover will be addressed in WML2). Here is an example.

- Display different types of books, including picture books, wordless books, alphabet books, and informational books.

  Who made these books? What is this person called?

  A person who makes books is called an author.

  What did these authors tell about in their books?

  Authors write about many different things. Some just use pictures. Some tell stories, and some tell information. You can also find books about the alphabet.

  You write books, too. Your books can be about school. You can make an ABC book or a book about something that happened to you.

- Show several pages from a class-made book, such as the one made for IW.7. Point under the words as you read them, and then point to the picture.

  What do you notice on these pages?

  Each page has a picture and some words. The pictures and the words tell what makes each of us special.

- Attach the book you made to chart paper or display it on the easel. Point to the pictures and words.

  Here is a book I wrote. On each page, I drew a picture and wrote the words that go with the picture.

Have a Try

Invite children to talk to a partner about a story they might draw and write. As needed, refer to the charts from STR.U1.

> Talk to your partner about a story you could tell. What pictures will you draw to go with that story? What words will you write?

▶ Listen to partners as they talk. After a few moments, share with the class several ideas as examples.

Summarize and Apply

Help children summarize what they have learned about making books. Then invite them to work on their books.

> What will you include on each page when you make your book?

▶ Write the principle at the top of the chart paper.

> During writing time, get a booklet and think about what to write and draw.

Confer

▶ During independent writing, move around the room to confer briefly with as many individual children as time allows. Sit side by side with them and invite them to talk about their books. Use the following prompts as needed.

- *What is your book about?*
- *Talk more about your story.*
- *What happened first [next, after that]?*
- *What will you draw for that part of the story?*
- *Start here. Write the next word here.*

Share

Following independent writing, gather children in the meeting area. Choose books to share on a variety of topics to show the breadth of possibilities. You don't need to read the books aloud, especially if the approximated writing is hard to decipher. Just share what you know from conferring with the children. Ask a few of the authors to point out the words and pictures in their books.

> This is a story about _____. Here is the picture and here are the words.

Writing Minilesson Principle
Write your name and the date on your book.

Getting Started with Making Books

You Will Need

- several familiar books, such as the following:
  - *First Day Jitters* by Julie Danneberg and *Elizabeti's School* by Stephanie Stuve-Bodeen, from Text Set: Learning and Working Together: School
  - *Monster ABCs* by Finnoula Louise, from *Shared Reading Collection*
- cover for the book you made for WML1
- books children have made or are working on
- markers
- To download the following online resources for this lesson, visit **resources.fountasandpinnell.com**:
  - Verbal Path for Letter Formation
  - chart art (optional)

Academic Language/ Important Vocabulary

- author
- illustrator
- front cover

Continuum Connection

- Write a title and the author's name on the cover of a story or book (p. 254)
- Write name and date on writing (p. 255)

GOAL

Understand that the person who writes a book is the author, and the author's name is on the cover.

RATIONALE

When you teach children that the person who wrote a book is the author and that the author's name is on the cover of the book, they understand they can write their own names on the books they write. This ownership builds their identity as writers. Writing the date helps you and the children observe progress in writing across the year.

ASSESS LEARNING

- Look for evidence that children know that the author is the person who wrote the book.
- Notice whether children can point to the author's name on the cover of a book.
- Observe children's ability to write their names and the date on their books.
- Look for evidence that they can use vocabulary such as *author*, *illustrator*, and *front cover*.

MINILESSON

To support the principle, share a number of books with children to help them notice the author's name on the cover. Consider using enlarged texts so the author's name is large enough for the children to see. Refer to the book you began in WML1. Here is an example.

- Display familiar books, such as *First Day Jitters*, *Elizabeti's School*, and *Monster ABCs*. Read the name of the author while pointing to it on each book.

  > How do you know who wrote the book?

  > Each book has the author's name on the front cover.

- Attach your book to the chart paper or display it on the easel. Write your name on the cover of the book you made.

  > My book has a front cover. Since I am the author of this book, I will write my name on the cover. Watch how I write my name.

  > You will write your name on the cover of the books you make.

- Show the copyright year on the inside cover of *Monster ABCs*.

  > Each book has a date in it that tells you when the book was published.

  > I am going to write the date on my book, too.

- Show children where to find today's date in the classroom. Write the date on the cover of your book. Encourage children to include month, day, and year.

Have a Try

Distribute the books children have written or are working on. Ask them to think about where they will write their name and the date on the cover.

> Show your partner where you will write your name and the date. Or does your book already have your name and the date?

Summarize and Apply

Summarize the learning and remind children to write their names and the date on the books they make.

> You are writers and illustrators. You can make books about lots of different things.

▶ Write the principle on the chart paper.

> To show everyone you are the author, put your name on your book. To remember when you wrote the book, write the date. I will talk to several writers today about their books.

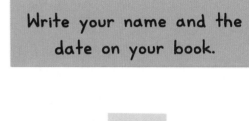

Write your name and the date on your book.

My Trip to the Grocery Store
Ms. Ly
March 10

Confer

▶ During independent writing, move around the room to confer briefly with as many individual children as time allows. Sit side by side with them and invite them to talk about writing their books and making their covers. Use prompts such as the following as needed to support children's writing. For children ready to start a new book, use prompts from WML1.

- *Listen to how I say words to help me. Say the words to help you write the letters. [Refer to the Verbal Path for Letter Formation.]*

- *Use the name chart (ABC chart) to help you.*

- *Write the date here.*

- *Take a look at the date written next to our calendar. Use that to help you write the date on your book.*

Share

Following independent writing, gather children in pairs in the meeting area with their books. Ask partners to share their books with one another, pointing to the name on the cover.

> Point to where you wrote your name and the date on the cover of your book.

> You are the author of your book. Whenever you begin a new book, be sure to write your name and the date on the cover.

Writing Minilesson Principle
Plan what to put on each page.

Getting Started with Making Books

You Will Need

- several familiar picture books, such as *Max and the Tag-Along Moon* by Floyd Cooper, from Text Set: Taking Care of Each Other: Family:
- blank book
- chart paper and markers

Academic Language/ Important Vocabulary

- plan
- across

Continuum Connection

- Tell one part, idea, or group of ideas on each page of a book (p. 254)
- Write and/or draw about one topic on a page or across several pages of a book, including one category of information related to a main topic on every page (p. 254)
- Understand that when both writing and drawing are on a page, they are mutually supportive, with each extending the other (p. 257)
- Understand how writing and drawing are related (p. 257)

GOAL

Plan what to put on each page so the pictures and words match.

RATIONALE

Part of making a book is learning to think about and plan what goes on each page. Learning to tell a story across their fingers helps children realize that a story has many parts and they must make the decision about which part to draw and write about on each page. They also must consider how the pictures and words on each page support one another.

ASSESS LEARNING

- Look for evidence that children know how to plan what goes on each page of their books.
- Notice whether they write about one idea or group of ideas on a page, with pictures that support it.
- Look for evidence that they can use vocabulary such as *plan* and *across*.

MINILESSON

To help children plan what to write on the page of a book, use familiar picture books to show how the authors tell about one part of the story on each page. Here is an example.

- Briefly review what happens in the story *Max and the Tag-Along Moon*. Tell the story across your fingers by pointing to a finger for each part of the story.

    There are many parts to this story. I'll tell the story across my fingers. I'll tell one part of the story and point to one finger. I'll tell the next part of the story and point to my next finger.

    First, the author wrote about Max talking about the moon with his grandfather and then saying goodbye to Granpa. Then he wrote how Max watched the moon—all the way until Max got into bed in his room.

- Plan a story about yourself, using your fingers to indicate the parts. As you tell the story, refer to a page in a blank book for each part, indicating where the words and pictures for that part could go.

    I want to write a book about the picnic I had with my daughter. First, I will write about the food we packed. I can write about that here. I can draw a picture of our kitchen above that. The kitchen is where we packed the food, so the picture goes with the words.

- Repeat this process for a few more pages.

    When you make books, think about the part of the story that you will tell on each page. You may want to tell your story across your fingers first. Put the picture and the words for each finger on its own page.

The Writing Minilessons Book, Grade 1

Have a Try

▶ Invite children to tell a story across their fingers to a partner, perhaps about an activity they did at school that day. Discuss the steps together and write them on the chart.

> Let's talk about how to plan what to put on each page when you write a book. First, you have to think about a story to write. What do you do next?

▶ Write the steps on the chart.

Summarize and Apply

▶ Write the principle on the top of the chart and read it aloud. Remind children to plan what goes on each page of their books.

> Today you will work on a book you have already started, or you will start making a new book. During writing time, I will sit with some writers.

Plan what to put on each page.

Think of a story.

Tell it across your fingers.

Put each part of the story on its own page.

Make sure your pictures match your words.

Confer

▶ During independent writing, move around the room to confer briefly with as many individual children as time allows. Sit side by side with them and invite them to talk about their plans for what to write and draw on each page. Use prompts such as the following as needed.

- *Tell your story across your fingers.*
- *What will you put on the first page? on the next page?*
- *What will you draw for that part of the story?*
- *What words go with that picture?*

Share

Following independent writing, invite children to share their books in pairs or trios or show one book to the whole class.

> How did you decide what to put on each page?

Getting Started with Making Books

You Will Need

- several familiar picture books, such as the following:
  - *Monster ABCs* by Finnoula Louise, from *Shared Reading Collection*
  - *David's Drawings* by Cathryn Falwell, from Text Set: Learning and Working Together: School
- chart paper and markers
- document camera (optional)
- a prepared book or picture of your own to which you will add a label
- To download the following online resource for this lesson, visit **resources.fountasandpinnell.com**:
  - chart art (optional)

Academic Language/ Important Vocabulary

- label
- illustration
- picture
- drawing

Continuum Connection

- Understand that a writer or illustrator can add a label to help readers (p. 250)
- Add words to pictures (p. 250)
- Use words and drawings to compose and revise writing (p. 256)
- Understand how writing and drawing are related (p. 257)
- Take on both approximated and conventional writing independently (p. 257)

GOAL

Understand that labels can tell more about a picture.

RATIONALE

Adding labels of one or more words to tell the reader about a picture is a way children can begin to tell a story as they transition to writing sentences. As they discover that labels enhance the meaning and enjoyment of a book, it will help them be more attentive readers and encourage them to use labels to convey information in their own writing.

ASSESS LEARNING

- Look at the labels children write. Do they tell more about the pictures?
- Notice whether they use labels or short groups of words in their writing.
- Look for evidence that they can use vocabulary such as *label*, *picture*, *illustration*, and *drawing*.

MINILESSON

To help children think about the principle, use familiar picture books to show how the author uses labels or short groups of words to convey meaning. (If children are already writing sentences, this lesson may not be necessary.) Use a document camera, if available. Here is an example.

- Display *Monster ABCs*. Read several pages. Point to the labels as you read.

  In this book, the author wrote a word to go with a picture for each letter of the alphabet.

  This word is called a label. The label tells you about the picture.

- Repeat this process with pages 18 and 26 of *David's Drawings*.

  What do you notice David wrote on some of his drawings? How does that help you know about the pictures?

Have a Try

Show a page of the book or picture you prepared in advance. Demonstrate labeling the drawing.

> Let me show you what I mean. What label could I add to let the reader know what this is a picture of?

▶ Write a label on the picture.

Summarize and Apply

Write the principle at the top of the chart. Read it aloud and remind children to label their drawings.

> Labels tell more about the pictures in a book. When you are writing your own book, be sure to add labels that allow the reader to get more details about the story and enjoy the book even more. I will talk with some of you today to help you think about what labels you can add to your writing.

Write labels on your pictures.

Shopping cart

Confer

▶ During independent writing, move around the room to confer briefly with as many individual children as time allows. Sit side by side with them and invite them to talk about the labels they are adding to their pictures. Use prompts such as the following to help them think about labeling their books.

- *What could you write to help the reader know about the picture?*
- *[Looking at a drawing] What do you want your reader to understand? Write that word (those words) here.*
- *Say the word slowly. Listen for sounds you hear in the first (last) part.*
- *Write that letter here.*

Share

Following independent writing, invite children to share their books with the whole class. As needed, support children's oral language by providing a sentence frame, such as *My label says _____.*

> Who would like to share a book you worked on today?

> Show what you wrote in your book.

Getting Started with Making Books

You Will Need

- the book you prepared for this umbrella
- a child's book and the child prepared to talk about the book
- chart paper and markers
- To download the following online resources for this lesson, visit **resources.fountasandpinnell.com**:
  - chart art (optional)

Academic Language/ Important Vocabulary

- decide
- finished

Continuum Connection

- Think of what to work on next as a writer (p. 257)
- Keep working independently rather than waiting for a teacher to help (p. 257)

GOAL

Understand when a book is finished and when to start another one.

RATIONALE

When you teach children how to decide when a book is finished and what to do next, it builds a foundation for revising and editing their writing (perhaps over several days) and supports them as independent writers.

ASSESS LEARNING

- Observe whether children can evaluate when they have finished making a book.
- Observe whether children know what to do when they have finished making a book.
- Look for evidence that they can use vocabulary such as *decide* and *finished*.

MINILESSON

To help children think about the minilesson principle, use the book you created to demonstrate thinking about whether a book is finished. Here is an example.

- Show and read the book you wrote.

  I'm wondering if my book is finished. What do you think? Why?

  It's not finished. What's missing?

  I could add the end of the story. I could tell what happened after I went to the grocery store.

- Show the child's book.

  Here is _____'s book. It might be finished, but what can she do to find out?

  She can reread her book.

- Record the response on the chart paper.

  When you reread your book, think about whether you told everything that the reader needs to know. If you didn't, you might need to add some words to your book. Besides the words, what else can you check?

  You can check the pictures to be sure that all the important details are there.

- Record responses on chart paper.

Have a Try

Invite children to talk to a partner about what to do when they decide they have finished a book.

> If you have reread your book and checked the words and pictures, what should you do next? Turn and talk to your partner.

▶ Talk about what they should do to start the next book—where to get a new booklet, how to think of an idea, and so forth.

Summarize and Apply

Summarize the learning. Remind children to make sure their books are finished before they start a new book.

▶ Write the principle at the top of the chart.

> Today we talked about how to decide when you have finished making a book. During writing time each day, before you start a new book, look at the chart and think about whether your book is finished. When you are sure, put the book away, get another booklet, and start writing a new book.

Decide when your book is finished.

Reread the book.

Then I went home.

Check the words.

Check the pictures.

Confer

▶ Observe children for a few minutes at the beginning of independent writing. If there are children who get a new booklet immediately, sit side by side with them individually or in a small group and talk more about the principle. Refer to the chart as a way to build independence. Use prompts such as the following as needed.

- *I noticed you are starting a new book. Let's look together at your last book and think about what to do to make sure it is finished.*

- *What can you add to the illustrations to help your reader understand more?*

- *What can you add to your words to help the reader understand _____?*

- *You reread your book and checked the pictures. Now what will you do?*

Share

Following independent writing, invite a few children to share how they decided they were ready to begin a new book. As needed, support children's oral language by providing a sentence frame, such as *I knew my book was finished because _____.*

> How did you know you were finished with your book?

Assessment

After you have taught the minilessons in this umbrella, observe children as they draw and write. Use the behaviors and understandings in *The Literacy Continuum* (Fountas and Pinnell 2017) to notice, teach for, and support children's learning as you observe their reading and writing attempts.

▶ What evidence do you have of new understandings children have developed related to making books?

- Do children understand that they can make their own books?
- Do they write their names and the date on the front cover?
- Are there pictures and/or words on each page of the book?
- Do the pictures match the words on each individual page?
- Are children able to plan what goes on each page?
- Are they beginning to understand what to do when their books are finished?
- Do they understand and use vocabulary related to bookmaking, such as *author*, *front cover*, *pictures*, *words*, *topic*, *illustrator*, and *finished*?

▶ In what other ways, beyond the scope of this umbrella, are children ready to expand their bookmaking experience?

- Are they adding details to their illustrations?
- Are they ready to learn more about how to write words?
- Would they benefit from more experience with storytelling?

Use your observations to determine what you will teach next. You may also consult Suggested Sequence of Lessons (pp. 557–571) for guidance.

EXTENSIONS FOR GETTING STARTED WITH MAKING BOOKS

▶ Help children rehearse their writing by making short videos of them talking about what they want to say. When it's time for children to write, replay the videos to remind them of what they want to write.

▶ Gather several books by someone who both wrote and illustrated the books. Talk about what it might have been like for this person to make the book: *Where did the ideas come from? How long do you think it took to make the book? What did the person do to make the pictures?*

▶ Gather together a guided writing group of several children who need support in a specific area of writing.

▶ Create a chart that lists the titles of the books children have made.

Minilessons in This Umbrella

WML1 Write a title on your cover.

WML2 Write an author page.

WML3 Dedicate your book to someone.

Before Teaching Umbrella 2 Minilessons

The minilessons in this umbrella add to the learning gained in MBK.U1: Getting Started with Making Books. The best time to teach these minilessons is once children are comfortable with the bookmaking routine and you observe them using both standard and approximated spelling. You do not need to teach the minilessons one right after another. Teach them when you observe that the children are ready.

Give children plenty of opportunities to write and draw freely and without constraints. Read and discuss simple books from a variety of genres. Use the following books from *Fountas & Pinnell Classroom™ Interactive Read-Aloud Collection*, or choose books from your classroom library.

Exploring Fiction and Nonfiction

Too Many Pears! by Jackie French

Milk: From Cow to Carton by Aliki

The Last Polar Bear by Jean Craighead George

Going Places by Peter H. and Paul A. Reynolds

Ice Bear: In the Steps of the Polar Bear by Nicola Davies

As you read and enjoy these texts together, help children notice that authors

- write a title on the cover, and

- sometimes include an author's page and/or dedication.

Fiction and Nonfiction

Section 4: Making Books

Writing Minilesson Principle
Write a title on your cover.

You Will Need

- several familiar books, such as the following from Text Set: Exploring Fiction and Nonfiction:
  - *Too Many Pears!* by Jackie French
  - *Milk: From Cow to Carton* by Aliki
  - *The Last Polar Bear* by Jean Craighead George
- chart paper prepared with a book cover (no title)
- marker
- To download the online resource for this lesson visit **resources.fountasandpinnell.com**:
  - chart art (optional)
  - paper templates (optional)

Academic Language/ Important Vocabulary

- cover
- title
- author

Continuum Connection

- Select an appropriate title for a poem, story, or informational book (p. 254)
- Place titles and headings in the appropriate place on a page (p. 254)

GOAL

Write titles using approximated writing on the front cover of books.

RATIONALE

When you teach children that books have titles on the cover and that authors choose the titles for their books, they will learn to add titles to their own books.

ASSESS LEARNING

- Look for evidence that children understand that a title tells what a book is about.
- Notice if children add a title to their own books.
- Observe for evidence that children can use vocabulary such as *cover*, *title*, and *author*.

MINILESSON

To help children think about the minilesson principle, use several familiar books to start a discussion about book titles. Below is an example. When children make their covers, they can use blank paper or the cover page from the paper templates in online resources.

- Display the covers of several familiar books. Point to and read each title.

   The front of a book is called the cover. What is written on the cover of a book?

   The title of the book is written on the cover.

- Display *Too Many Pears!*

   What is this book about?

   Because this book is about a cow that eats too many pears, the author chose the title *Too Many Pears!* What do you notice about this title? Is it short or long?

   A book title usually has just a few words, and it's usually not a full sentence. "Pamela the cow eats too many pears" would be too long for a book title, so the author chose a few words that tell the most important idea: *Too Many Pears!*

- Show the cover of *Milk: From Cow to Carton* and read the title.

   What does the title tell you?

   Why is this a good title for this book?

   The title helps you know what the book is about.

Have a Try

Have children help you write a title for the cover on the prepared chart.

> Here's a book cover that needs a title. If the book was about a spaceship that traveled to the moon, what might be a good title? Turn and talk to your partner about this.

▶ Accept ideas from children and choose one that everyone agrees on. Then discuss where on the cover you should write the title. Write the title.

Summarize and Apply

Summarize the learning and remind children to title their books.

▶ Write the principle at the top of the chart.

> During writing time today, remember to write a title on the cover of your book. Make sure to choose a title that helps your readers know what the book is about.

Confer

▶ During independent writing, move around the room to confer briefly with as many individual children as time allows. Sit side by side with them and invite them to talk about writing titles. Use the following prompts as needed to help children title their books.

- *What is your book about?*
- *What would be a good title for your book?*
- *Remember that a title is usually just a few words, not a whole sentence. How could you make your title shorter?*
- *Why did you choose that title for your book?*

Share

Following independent writing, gather children in the meeting area. Invite several children to share their book covers.

> What is the title of your book, _____?

> What do you think _____'s book is about?

Write a title on your cover.

To the Moon!

Expanding Bookmaking

You Will Need

- several familiar books that have an author page, such as the following from Text Set: Exploring Fiction and Nonfiction:
  - *The Last Polar Bear* by Jean Craighead George
  - *Ice Bear* by Nicola Davies
  - *Going Places* by Peter H. and Paul A. Reynolds
- chart paper and markers
- To download the online resource for this lesson visit **resources.fountasandpinnell.com**:
  - paper templates (optional)

Academic Language/ Important Vocabulary

- author
- author page

Continuum Connection

- Write an author page at the beginning or end of a book that tells details about the author (picture, writing) (p. 254)
- Talk about oneself as a writer (p. 257)

GOAL

Write an author page to share information about yourself.

RATIONALE

Studying author pages and supporting children in writing their own author pages helps children view themselves as writers. It encourages children to take pride in and celebrate their writing and share important information about themselves with their readers.

ASSESS LEARNING

- Look for evidence that children understand the purpose of an author page.
- Notice if children write author pages in their own books.
- Look for evidence that children can use vocabulary such as *author* and *author page*.

MINILESSON

To help children think about the minilesson principle, study author pages in several familiar texts. Engage children in a discussion about the information that authors share about themselves on an author page. Below is an example. When children make their author pages, they can use plain paper or the author page from the paper templates in online resources.

- Read aloud the author information in *The Last Polar Bear*.

  What does this part of the book tell you about?

  What do you learn about Jean Craighead George and Wendell Minor from this part of the book?

- Record children's responses in general terms on chart paper.
- Continue in a similar manner with *Ice Bear* and *Going Places*.

  The information about the author is called the author page. Sometimes the author page will be in the front or back of a book. Sometimes the information is on a back cover or back flap. Why might an author write an author page?

  Knowing a little bit about authors or why they wrote their books can help you enjoy or understand them more.

Have a Try

Invite children to talk with a partner about what they would write on their own author page.

> When you write your own books, you can write an author page to tell readers all about yourself! Turn and talk to your partner about what you might write about yourself on an author page.

> ▶ After children turn and talk, invite several children to share their responses.

Summarize and Apply

Help children summarize the learning. Remind them that they can write an author page in their books.

> What did you learn today about the author pages?

> ▶ Write the principle at the top of the chart. Read it aloud.

> Today during writing time, think about what you'd like your readers to know about you. Write that on an author page. Bring your book to share when we meet later.

Write an author page.

- Other books the author has written
- Awards
- Where the author lives
- Family
- Website
- Why the author wrote the book
- Other job

About the Author

Confer

> ▶ During independent writing, move around the room to confer briefly with as many individual children as time allows. Sit side by side with them and invite them to talk about writing an author page. Use prompts such as the following as needed.
>
> - *What would you like your readers to know about you?*
> - *You could write about why you wrote this book.*
> - *You could draw a picture of yourself on your author page.*

Share

Following independent writing, gather children in the meeting area. Invite several children to read aloud their author pages.

> Who would like to read your author page?

> What did you learn about _____ from his author page?

Writing Minilesson Principle
Dedicate your book to someone.

You Will Need

- several familiar books that have a dedication, such as the following from Text Set: Exploring Fiction and Nonfiction:
  - *Too Many Pears!* by Jackie French
  - *Going Places* by Peter H. and Paul A. Reynolds
  - *The Last Polar Bear* by Jean Craighead George
- chart paper and markers
- To download the following online resource for this lesson, visit **resources.fountasandpinnell.com**:
  - paper templates (optional)

Academic Language/ Important Vocabulary

- author
- dedicate
- dedication

Continuum Connection

- Dedicate a story to someone and write the dedication on the inside of the cover, on the title page or copyright page, or on a page of its own (p. 254)

GOAL

Write a dedication to someone or something that is important to you.

RATIONALE

When children study dedications and think about the reasons authors choose to dedicate a book to someone, they understand that authors are real people who care about and are influenced by others. They also begin to think of themselves as authors and write their own dedications.

ASSESS LEARNING

- Look for evidence that children understand the purpose of a dedication.
- Notice if children write dedications in their own books.
- Look for evidence that children can use vocabulary such as *author*, *dedicate*, and *dedication*.

MINILESSON

To help children think about the minilesson principle, study dedications in several familiar texts. Engage children in a discussion about dedications. Below is an example. When children make their dedication pages, they can use plain paper or the dedication page from the paper templates in online resources.

- Read aloud the author's dedication in *Too Many Pears!*

  Does anyone know what this part of the book is called?

  This is the dedication. What do you think a dedication is?

  In the dedication, the author dedicates the book to someone. Dedicating a book to someone is a way of remembering that person and showing respect and appreciation.

- Reread the dedication.

  The author dedicates her book to Pam Horsey. Why does she dedicate her book to her?

  Maybe Pam Horsey gave the author the idea to write this book.

- Generalize children's responses and record them on the chart paper.

- Read the dedication in the back of *Going Places*. Point out that the dedication is usually in the front of the book, but sometimes it is in the back.

  Why do you think they decided to dedicate it to their teacher?

- Record responses on the chart.

- Continue in a similar manner with *The Last Polar Bear*.

Have a Try

Invite children to talk with a partner about their own dedications.

> Think about the book you're working on or the last book you wrote. Who is the person you would like to dedicate your book to? Why? Turn and talk to your partner about this.

▶ After children turn and talk, invite several children to share their responses.

Summarize and Apply

Help children summarize the learning. Remind children that they can dedicate their books to someone.

▶ Write the principle at the top of the chart. Read it aloud.

> Why do authors dedicate their books to people?

> During writing time today, think about to whom you would like to dedicate your book. Then write a dedication to that person. Bring your book to share when we meet later.

Dedicate your book to someone.

- Someone who gave you the idea for the book

- Someone who taught you an important lesson

- Someone you care about

> **Dedication**
> This book is for Mama, Papa, and our faithful dog, Lucy.

Confer

▶ During independent writing, move around the room to confer briefly with as many individual children as time allows. Sit side by side with them and invite them to talk about writing a dedication. Use prompts such as the following as needed.

- *Did someone give you the idea for this book?*

- *Do you want to dedicate your book to someone special in your family?*

- *You could write a reason that you are dedicating your book to_____.*

Share

Following independent writing, gather children in the meeting area. Invite several children to read aloud their dedications. Support children's oral language by providing a sentence frame, such as *My dedication says* _____ or *I dedicated my book to* _____ *because* _____.

> Tell about the dedication in your book.

Assessment

After you have taught the minilessons in this umbrella, observe children as they draw, write, and talk about their writing. Use the behaviors and understandings in *The Literacy Continuum* (Fountas and Pinnell 2017) to notice, teach for, and support children's learning as you observe their attempts at drawing and writing.

▶ What evidence do you have of new understandings related to bookmaking?

- Do children title their books?

- Can they write an author page about themselves?

- Have they tried writing a dedication?

- Is there evidence that children can use vocabulary related to bookmaking, such as *author*, *title*, *cover*, and *dedication*?

▶ In what other ways, beyond the scope of this umbrella, are children ready to expand their bookmaking skills?

- Are they ready to learn about making different types of books?

- Are they ready to learn how to add more details to their writing?

- Are they ready to add text features to their books?

Use your observations to determine the next umbrella you will teach. You may also consult Suggested Sequence of Lessons (pp. 557–571) for guidance.

EXTENSIONS FOR EXPANDING BOOKMAKING

▶ To help children know which words to capitalize in their titles, consider teaching CNV.U5.WML4.

▶ Encourage children to add more information to their front covers, such as the author's name and an illustration. Help them make back covers that provide information about what the book is about.

▶ During interactive read-aloud, read aloud author pages. Discuss with children the different kinds of information contained within.

▶ Help children add acknowledgments to their books.

▶ Gather together a guided writing group of several children who need support in a specific area of writing.

Minilessons in This Umbrella

WML1 Make a list of stories you remember.

WML2 Tell a story you remember.

WML3 Draw and write your story in the order it happened.

WML4 Say *I* and *we* when you tell a story about yourself.

WML5 Use pictures and words to show how you were feeling.

Before Teaching Umbrella 3 Minilessons

For young writers, understanding that they can make a book about anything they have personally experienced is an important realization. This is the goal of the minilessons in this umbrella. As children choose topics for memory stories, help them narrow the memory by focusing on small moments. You might choose to have children work on one memory story throughout the umbrella and apply these lessons to that one piece, or you might prefer to have them work on several memory stories across the umbrella.

Prior to teaching these minilessons, children should have an understanding of story structure. If you have *The Reading Minilessons Book, Grade 1* (Fountas and Pinnell 2019), lessons included in LA.U19: Understanding Characters and Their Feelings help support children's understanding of how to add emotion to their memory stories. Additionally, it would be useful to teach IW.8: Writing a Memory Story because the text you and the children create in that lesson can be used as a mentor text for these lessons. For other mentor texts, use books that are told in the first person from the classroom library or that you have created with the class. Also consider the following books from *Fountas & Pinnell Classroom™ Interactive Read-Aloud Collection* and *Shared Reading Collection*.

Interactive Read-Aloud Collection
Taking Care of Each Other: Family

The Relatives Came by Cynthia Rylant

A Birthday Basket for Tía by Pat Mora

Papá and Me by Arthur Dorros

The Importance of Friendship

Mr. George Baker by Amy Hest

Shared Reading Collection

In My Bag by Amy Frank

Interactive Writing Lessons

IW.8: Writing a Memory Story

As you read and enjoy these texts together, help children

- connect texts to memories in their lives,

- notice the sequence of story events,

- notice the use of *I* and *we*, and

- talk about what the pictures and words show about how characters are feeling.

Friendship

Shared Reading

Interactive Writing

Section 4: Making Books

WML1

MBK.U3.WML1

Writing Minilesson Principle
Make a list of stories you remember.

Making Memory Books

You Will Need

- several familiar books that tell about memories, such as the following:
  - *In My Bag* by Amy Frank, from *Shared Reading Collection*
  - *Papá and Me* by Arthur Dorros and *The Relatives Came* by Cynthia Rylant, from Text Set: Taking Care of Each Other: Family
- chart paper prepared with a blank sketch of the online resource Ideas for Memory Stories
- markers
- To download the following online resources for this lesson, visit **resources.fountasandpinnell.com**:
  - chart art (optional)
  - Ideas for Memory Stories

Academic Language / Important Vocabulary

- list
- stories
- memory
- remember
- small moment

Continuum Connection

- Think of topics, events, or experiences from own life that are interesting to write about (p. 250)
- Understand how to craft a personal memory story or narrative from mentor texts (p. 250)
- Understand that a story can be a "small moment" (description of a brief but memorable experience) (p. 251)

GOAL

Understand that writers generate ideas for stories from memories that are important to them.

RATIONALE

When children learn that they can make books about personal memories, they realize that their own memories have value and that each child has a unique story to tell. By sharing their memory books children hear about and learn to value experiences and perspectives different from their own, which strengthens the community of writers in your classroom.

ASSESS LEARNING

- Look for evidence of what children understand about small moments.
- Observe whether children can make a list of personal experiences they might write about.
- Look for evidence that children can use vocabulary such as *list*, *stories*, *memory*, *remember*, and *small moment*.

MINILESSON

Use familiar stories to demonstrate that authors write stories to tell about their own memories. Help children focus on one small moment as they brainstorm ideas. Here is an example.

- Show and read the author's note at the end of *In My Bag*.

  The author lets the reader know that she writes about things she remembers. Things that you remember are your memories.

- Revisit page 16.

  Finding the turtle is one small moment she remembers.

- Use other mentor texts about memories to help children focus on one small moment. You may want to use the suggestions below.
  - *Papá and Me* (pp. 9–10): Point out that the author probably wrote about his experiences with his own father. Focus on puddle splashing.
  - *The Relatives Came* (p. 20): Point out that the author probably wrote about her own family memories. Focus on the relatives playing music together.

  To write a memory book, I think about what I remember. I remember a camping trip. That's a big idea. A smaller idea is that I lost my shoes on the trip or that I slept in a tent. Each smaller idea could be a story.

- Show the prepared chart. As you think aloud about your memory, sketch and write about a few small moments related to that memory. This is just one example; choose an authentic memory that is special to you.

Have a Try

Invite children to turn and talk about a memory.

> Think of a memory you have. What is one small moment that was special to you? Turn and tell your partner about the small moment you remember.

▶ Ask a few children to share ideas (e.g., spent a day at the lake, helped build a tree house). Choose a few ideas to add to the blank boxes on the chart. Include a couple of small moments for each idea.

▶ Keep the completed chart to use in the next minilesson.

Summarize and Apply

Summarize the learning and have children make a list of story ideas.

▶ Show a blank copy of Ideas for Memory Stories.

> During writing time, make a list of story ideas using a chart like the one we used today. You will find the chart in the writing center. In each box, draw a picture or write words about something you remember doing. You can tell about a different memory in each box. Remember to think about small moments.

Ideas for Memory Stories

My camping trip:
- losing my shoes
- climbing the trail
- sleeping in a tent

Day at the lake:
- finding a shell
- rowing a boat

Building a tree house:
- using lots of tools
- painting flowers

Giving the dog a bath:
- wet dog running around
- soap and water mess

Confer

▶ During independent writing, move around the room to confer briefly with as many individual children as time allows. Sit side by side with them and invite them to talk about their ideas for memory stories. Use the following prompts as needed to help children expand their thinking.

- *Tell more about this memory.*
- *Which idea will make the best story? Why?*
- *What is one small moment that is special to you?*

Share

Following independent writing, gather children in pairs in the meeting area to share their ideas for memory stories.

> Share the memories you wrote down. Talk about which memory you are the most excited to make a book about.

Making Memory Books

You Will Need

- class memory story from IW.8: Writing a Memory Story
- chart from WML1 with teacher's and children's memories

Academic Language / Important Vocabulary

- tell
- story
- memory
- remember

Continuum Connection

- Tell about experiences or topics in a way that others can understand (p. 254)
- Use storytelling to generate and rehearse language that may be written later (p. 256)
- Tell stories in chronological order (p. 256)
- Tell stories from personal experience (p. 332)

GOAL

▶ Tell the important events in a story orally to an audience.

RATIONALE

▶ Telling a story orally is a rehearsal for writing a story. As children move their ideas into words, they can work out how best to tell the story before committing the words to paper.

ASSESS LEARNING

▶ Notice whether children are telling stories about a memory.

▶ Look for evidence that children can use vocabulary such as *tell*, *story*, *memory*, and *remember*.

MINILESSON

Prior to teaching this lesson, teach IW.8: Writing a Memory Story. Use your own story to model how to tell a memory story. Here is an example.

▶ Revisit the class writing about a memory from IW.8.

What special memory did we write about together?

We wrote about our class field trip to the science museum. The small moment we wrote about was the lightning show.

▶ Display the chart completed in the previous minilesson that lists the teacher's and the children's story ideas.

Here is our chart of memory story ideas. I am going to choose one of my memories from this chart and tell a story about it. To help me think about how to draw and write my story, I'm going to tell it across my fingers.

▶ Choose one of your story ideas and tell a story, modeling how you can tell it across your fingers. You might find the following prompts helpful.

- *The first thing that happened is _____ (point to thumb).*
- *Then, _____ (point to index finger).*
- *Next, _____ (point to middle finger).*
- *After that, _____ (point to ring finger).*
- *At the end, _____ (point to pinky finger).*

Have a Try

Invite children to turn and talk about what they understood from your memory story.

> Turn and talk to your partner about the important things you heard in the memory story I told. Share with your partner if there is anything you wondered about.

▶ After a brief discussion, ask a few volunteers to share ideas.

Summarize and Apply

Summarize the learning and have children tell a memory story.

> During writing time, you can take turns telling a story you remember to a partner. Tell it across your fingers to help you think how you will draw and write the story in a book. Look at the chart to help you think of ideas. After you listen to your partner's story, tell what you understood and what you are wondering about.

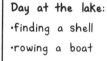

Ideas for Memory Stories

My camping trip:
- losing my shoes
- climbing the trail
- sleeping in a tent

Day at the lake:
- finding a shell
- rowing a boat

Building a tree house:
- using lots of tools
- painting flowers

Giving the dog a bath:
- wet dog running around
- soap and water mess

Confer

▶ During independent writing, move around the room to confer briefly with as many individual children as time allows. Sit side by side with them and invite them to tell memory stories across their fingers. Use the following prompts as needed.

- *What happened first?*
- *What happened next?*
- *Now point to your ring finger and tell what happened.*
- *Tell the story across your fingers. Write what you told on your first finger on the first page.*

Share

Following independent writing, gather children in the meeting area to share their stories.

> Who would like to share your memory story? Tell it across your fingers.

WML3
MBK.U3.WML3

Writing Minilesson Principle
Draw and write your story in the order it happened.

Making Memory Books

You Will Need

▸ familiar books that tell about
  memories in chronological order,
  such as the following:

  ■ *The Relatives Came* by Cynthia
    Rylant and *A Birthday Basket
    for Tía* by Pat Mora, from Text
    Set: Taking Care of Each Other:
    Family

▸ several pages of a memory story
  you have written, attached to
  chart paper

▸ markers

▸ To download the following online
  resource for this lesson, visit
  resources.fountasandpinnell.com:

  ■ chart art (optional)

Academic Language / Important Vocabulary

▸ order

▸ then

▸ after

▸ beginning

▸ middle

▸ end

Continuum Connection

▸ Draw a picture or a series of
  pictures and tell or write about
  them (p. 250)

▸ Tell events in order that they
  occurred in personal narratives
  (p. 251)

▸ Present ideas in a logical
  sequence (p. 254)

GOAL

Understand that the pictures and writing in a story occur in chronological order.

RATIONALE

When children learn that authors tell stories in sequential order, they realize that the order of events in a story matters.

ASSESS LEARNING

▸ Look for evidence that children understand the chronological order of a story.

▸ Notice whether children draw and write memory stories in the order in which they happened.

▸ Look for evidence that children can use vocabulary such as *order, then, after, beginning, middle,* and *end*.

MINILESSON

Use familiar stories plus your own original story to engage children in thinking and talking about chronological order in memory stories. Here is an example.

▸ Ahead of time, write and sketch a simple story in sequential order based on the oral memory story you told in the previous lesson. The story used in this minilesson is just an example.

▸ Show and read page 2 of *The Relatives Came*, helping children notice that the first sentence shows that this story is about a memory. Then, show the first two pages, a few pages from the middle, and the last two pages.

▸ Guide a conversation about the sequence of events in the book, using a few prompts about the beginning, middle, and end of the story such as the following.

  • *Why do you think the author started this story with the relatives packing up their car for the road trip?*

  • *Then what happened? What happened after that?*

  • *Why do you think the author ended this story with the relatives' car parked in the garage after they returned from the road trip?*

  • *How can you tell that the author wrote about the story events in order?*

▸ Repeat if needed with another memory story that is written in chronological order, such as *A Birthday Basket for Tía*.

Have a Try

Invite children to turn and talk to a partner about whether a memory is written in the order it happened.

▶ Show the prepared chart with your memory story.

▶ Read the story across your fingers. Then have children turn and talk about the order of events in your story.

▶ After a brief discussion, ask children to share. As they do, add (or have volunteers add) numbers to the chart to show the story sequence and note that the story is told from beginning to end.

▶ Save this memory story to use in WML5.

Summarize and Apply

Write the principle at the top of the chart to summarize the learning. Remind children to draw and write their stories in the order they happened.

> When you make a memory book, make sure you draw the pictures and write the words in the order the story happened. Bring your book to share when we meet later.

Confer

▶ During independent writing, move around the room to confer briefly with as many individual children as time allows. Sit side by side with them and invite them to talk about their memory stories. Use the following prompts as needed.

- *Tell what happened after that.*
- *What did you do first? What did you do next? What happened last?*
- *Tell the story across your fingers to help you know what goes on each page.*
- *Read your story. Is everything in the right order?*

Share

Following independent writing, gather children in the meeting area to share their stories. Choose several volunteers whose memory books you know are written in sequential order.

> Listen to _____'s memory book.

> How do you know that the drawings and words are in order?

Writing Minilesson Principle

Say *I* and *we* when you tell a story about yourself.

Making Memory Books

You Will Need

- several familiar books that are told in first-person point of view, such as the following:

  - *In My Bag* by Amy Frank, from *Shared Reading Collection*

  - *Mr. George Baker* by Amy Hest, from Text Set: The Importance of Friendship

- IW.8: Writing a Memory Story (optional)

- chart paper prepared with simple sketches of one person and more than one person and sentences with *I* and *we*

- highlighter tape

- marker

- To download the following online resource for this lesson, visit **resources.fountasandpinnell.com**:

  - chart art (optional)

Academic Language / Important Vocabulary

- story
- memory
- yourself
- I
- we

Continuum Connection

- Understand that a story about your life is usually written in first person (using *I* and *we*) (p. 250)

GOAL

Know to use the words *I* and *we* when you tell a story about yourself.

RATIONALE

Teaching children to use the words *I* and *we* when writing a story about themselves helps them recognize that authors choose particular words in order to give information. This reinforces the concept that a memory story is one that is written about an author's own life.

ASSESS LEARNING

- Look for evidence that children can identify the words *I* and *we* in a story.
- Notice whether children use the words *I* and *we* when they write memory stories.
- Notice evidence that children can use vocabulary such as *story*, *memory*, *yourself*, *I*, and *we*.

MINILESSON

Use familiar stories told in the first person to engage children in thinking and talking about writing memory books. Here is an example.

- Show page 5 from *In My Bag*.

  As I read this page from *In My Bag*, listen for the words the author uses to help you know who is telling the story.

- Slowly read page 5, pointing under each word as you do.

  I notice the author uses the word *I* to show who is telling the story. Listen as I read it again and put your thumb up when you hear the word *I*.

- Reread the page. As children identify *I*, add highlighter tape to the word. If the children mention the word *my*, include it in the discussion and add highlighter tape to the word.

- Show page 10 from *Mr. George Baker*.

  While I read this page from *Mr. George Baker*, listen for any words that help you know who is telling the story.

- Guide the conversation so children notice both *I* and *we*, adding highlighter tape as before. Have them discuss how *I* and *we* help the reader know who is telling the story.

- Repeat with the class memory story (IW.8) if it includes the words *I* and/or *we*.

Have a Try

Invite children to turn and talk about the words *I* and *we*. If the children in your class are ready, include *my*, *me*, *us*, and *our*.

▶ Show the prepared chart with the sketches. Read the words as you point to the corresponding drawings.

> Turn and talk about what words help you know who is telling the story.

Summarize and Apply

Help children summarize the learning. Remind them to use *I* and *we* when they write books about themselves.

> What words did we talk about today?

▶ Write the principle at the top of the chart.

> When you work on your memory book today, remember to use the words *I* and *we* when you write a story about yourself. Bring your writing to share when we meet later.

Say I and we when you tell a story about yourself.

I flew the kite. My kite is special to me.

We flew the kite. Our kite is special to us.

Confer

▶ During independent writing, move around the room to confer briefly with as many individual children as time allows. Sit side by side with them and invite them to talk about using *I* and *we*. Use the following prompts as needed.

- *Who is your story about?*
- *How will the reader know who your story is about?*
- *Where can you look to know how to write the words* I *and* we?
- *Where did you use the words* I *and* we?

Share

Following independent writing, gather children in the meeting area to share their memory books.

> Who used the word *I* or *we* in your memory book? Share a page that uses *I* or *we*.

Writing Minilesson Principle
Use pictures and words to show how you were feeling.

Making Memory Books

You Will Need

- a familiar book with pictures that show feelings, such as the following:

  - *The Relatives Came* by Cynthia Rylant, from Text Set: Taking Care of Each Other: Family

- chart paper prepared with a page from a memory story you have written (see WML3)

- markers

- several cut-out arrows to attach to the chart

- glue stick or tape

- To download the following online resource for this lesson, visit **resources.fountasandpinnell.com**:

  - chart art (optional)

Academic Language / Important Vocabulary

- story
- feeling
- show
- tell

Continuum Connection

- Understand that the writer can look back or think about the memory or experience and share thoughts and feelings about it (p. 250)

- Explain one's thoughts and feelings about an experience or event (p. 250)

- Write in an expressive way (similar to oral language) (p. 254)

- Tell a story or give information in an interesting way (p. 254)

GOAL

Understand that the pictures and words in the story can show how you feel.

RATIONALE

Teaching children to add pictures and words to show feelings when making a book helps them learn that authors reveal information in a variety of ways.

ASSESS LEARNING

- Notice whether children recognize that authors show feelings through words and pictures.

- Observe whether children add pictures and words to show feelings in their own writing.

- Notice evidence that children understand can use vocabulary such as *story*, *feeling*, *show*, and *tell*.

MINILESSON

Use familiar stories that have illustrations and words that show feelings to engage children in thinking and talking about making memory books. Here is an example.

- Show the illustrations on pages 9–12 from *The Relatives Came*.

  Take a look at the relatives on these pages. The pictures show many things about how the people are feeling. How do you think they are feeling?

  What makes you think that?

- Guide the conversation to help children discuss the joyful, excited, loving facial expressions and body language, which show that the family members are happy to see each other.

- Read the text on pages 10 and 11.

  What do the words tell you about how the people are feeling?

- Guide the conversation to help children identify language to show how happy, loving, and excited the people feel, such as *They hugged us for hours* and *so much laughing and shining faces*.

  A writer can *show* feelings in the pictures and *tell* feelings in the words.

Have a Try

Invite children to turn and talk about how to show feelings in pictures and words.

▶ Show the chart paper that has been prepared with a page from your memory book. Note that the idea in this lesson is merely an example.

> Here is the end of my story when I was in my tent. How do you think I felt? How do you know? Turn and talk to your partner about that.

▶ After time for a brief discussion, ask volunteers to share.

▶ Choose volunteers to attach arrows to the chart, one pointing to the facial expression (picture) and one pointing to the sentence (words).

Summarize and Apply

Write the principle at the top of the chart. Summarize the learning and remind children to show emotion through pictures and words when they make books.

> When you work on your memory book, add pictures and words that show how you were feeling.

Confer

▶ During independent writing, move around the room to confer briefly with as many individual children as time allows. Sit side by side with them and invite them to talk about conveying their feelings in their memory books. Use the following prompts as needed.

· *How were you feeling? How can you show that?*

· *What words can you add to tell how you were feeling?*

· *Can you add something to your drawing to show how you were feeling?*

Share

Following independent writing, gather children in the meeting area to share their stories.

> Who would like to share the memory book you are working on?

> Share a page that shows feelings and tell about that.

Assessment

After you have taught the minilessons in this umbrella, observe children as they draw, write, and talk about their writing. Use *The Literacy Continuum* (Fountas and Pinnell 2017) to notice, teach for, and support children's learning as you observe their attempts at writing, drawing, and reading.

▶ What evidence do you have of new understandings children have developed related to making a memory book?

- Are children able to make a list of memories?

- Can they tell stories about memories from their own lives?

- Do they draw and write story events in chronological order?

- Are they using *I* and *we* when telling a story about themselves?

- Are they using pictures and words to show feelings when they make books?

- Do they understand and use vocabulary related to making a memory book, such as *list, story, memory, remember, small moment, order, beginning, middle, end,* and *yourself*?

▶ In what ways, beyond the scope of this umbrella, are children making books?

- Do they show an interest in making different kinds of books?

- Are they making connections to books they read and then talking about ideas for writing books about their own lives?

Use your observations to determine the next umbrella you will teach. You may also consult Suggested Sequence of Lessons (pp. 557–571) for guidance.

EXTENSIONS FOR MAKING MEMORY BOOKS

▶ Have children look back at STR.U1: Learning About Self and Others Through Storytelling to remind themselves of stories from their own lives.

▶ If there are several children who need to work on a specific aspect of writing, pull them together into a small guided writing group.

▶ Help children rehearse their writing by making short videos of them talking about what they want to say. When it's time for children to write, replay the videos to remind them of what they want to write.

▶ As you read books together that show emotion through words and drawings, have children talk about the different ways authors and illustrators show feelings.

Minilessons in This Umbrella

WML1 Make a book to teach something.

WML2 Write words and draw pictures to show the order of what to do.

WML3 Write a number for each step.

WML4 Make a list of materials.

Before Teaching Umbrella 4 Minilessons

Prior to teaching these minilessons, make sure children have read some how-to books, engaged in making or doing something that they could teach to others (e.g., preparing a snack or riding a bike), and talked about those activities. Teach IW.21: Writing a How-to Book so that children will have learned something about making a how-to book. The lessons in this umbrella build on that experience, leading children to make books independently. Prepare blank booklets (four to eight stapled pages with a cover) for children to use. You might also want to provide any of the paper templates from online resources that are appropriate. Store booklets and paper templates in the writing center.

Use the class-made book from IW.21 as a mentor text for the minilessons in this umbrella. You may also use the following books from *Fountas & Pinnell Classroom™ Interactive Read-Aloud Collection* and *Shared Reading Collection*, or you might use other how-to texts from the classroom. Recipes from cookbooks and directions on the back of boxes or on websites are other good sources of examples for these lessons.

Interactive Read-Aloud Collection
Understanding the Natural World: Planting and Growing

From Seed to Plant by Gail Gibbons

Plant Packages: A Book About Seeds by Susan Blackaby

Shared Reading Collection

Boomer's Checkup by Aaron Mack

Interactive Writing Lessons

IW.21: Writing a How-to Book

As you read and enjoy these texts together, help children

- notice what the reader can learn from the text,

- talk about how the pictures help the reader learn how to do something,

- notice whether the steps are numbered, and

- notice if the writer included a list of materials.

Interactive Read-Aloud
Planting and Growing

Shared Reading

Interactive Writing

Section 4: Making Books

WML 1

Writing Minilesson Principle
Make a book to teach something.

Making How-to Books

You Will Need

- several books that show how to do something, such as *From Seed to Plant* by Gail Gibbons and *Plant Packages: A Book About Seeds* by Susan Blackaby, from Text Set: Understanding the Natural World: Planting and Growing

- class how-to book from IW.21: Writing a How-to Book

- several examples of different how-to formats, such as a recipe and a set of directions

- chart paper and markers

Academic Language / Important Vocabulary

- how-to book
- teach
- writing
- idea
- drawing

Continuum Connection

- Understand that a procedural text helps people know how to do something (p 250)

- Generate and expand ideas through talk with peers and teacher (p. 256)

- Look for ideas and topics in personal experiences, shared through talk (p. 256)

- Rehearse language for informational writing by retelling experiences using chronological order, describing what they know, or repeating procedural steps in order (p. 256)

GOAL

Think of ideas for making a how-to book.

RATIONALE

When children learn to choose an idea and decide what pictures and words to include in a how-to book, they understand that both pictures and words convey meaning and that they are valued writers who have information to share.

ASSESS LEARNING

- Look for evidence of what children know about how-to books.
- Observe whether children can choose an idea for writing a how-to book.
- Look for evidence that they can use vocabulary such as *how-to book*, *writing*, *drawing*, *teach*, and *idea*.

MINILESSON

To prepare children to make a how-to book independently, engage them in a discussion of how-to texts, including the class book from IW.21: Writing a How-to Book. Here is an example.

- Show the cover and pages 28–29 of *From Seed to Plant*.

    What do you notice on these pages?

- Engage children in a conversation, guiding them to understand that this book shows the reader how to plant and grow bean plants.

- Repeat with pages 15–21 of *Plant Packages*, the class-made book from IW.21, and other how-to examples you have gathered, such as a recipe and a set of directions.

    How-to books teach the reader how to do something, just like these books and examples. What could you teach a reader with a how-to book?

- Ask a few volunteers to respond. Record children's ideas next to their names on chart paper.

Have a Try

Invite children to turn and talk about making how-to books.

> Turn and talk about an idea you have for making a how-to book.

▶ Ask a few volunteers to share ideas. Add new ideas to the chart. Keep the chart posted to help children generate ideas for making how-to books.

Summarize and Apply

Help children summarize what they learned about how-to books. Have children choose an idea and begin making a how-to book during writing time.

> You talked about some ideas you have for making a how-to book.

▶ Write the principle at the top of the chart and read it aloud.

> During writing time, begin making a how-to book to teach the reader how to do something. Look back at the chart if you need ideas.

Make a book to teach something.

Renata How to play the piano

Safal   How to brush your teeth

Oliver   How to draw a shark

Erva   How to ride a skateboard

Estella How to jump rope

Confer

▶ During independent writing, move around the room to confer briefly with as many individual children as time allows. Sit side by side with them and invite them to talk about their plans for their how-to books. Use the following prompts as needed to get children started with their how-to books.

- *What is something you could teach someone to do?*
- *What are you thinking about teaching in your how-to book?*
- *How will your how-to book begin?*

Share

Following independent writing, gather children in the meeting area to talk about making how-to books. As needed, support children's oral language by providing a sentence frame, such as *My book will teach how to _____.*

> What will you teach in your how-to book?

WML 2

MBK.U4.WML2

Writing Minilesson Principle
Write words and draw pictures to show the order of what to do.

Making How-to Books

You Will Need

- a book that teaches how to do something that is *not* written in how-to format, such as *Boomer's Checkup* by Aaron Mack, from *Shared Reading Collection*
- class how-to book from IW.21: Writing a How-to Book
- five pages stapled together for a how-to book
- markers
- sticky notes
- To download the following online resource for this lesson, visit **resources.fountasandpinnell.com**:
  - chart art (optional)
  - paper templates (optional)

Academic Language / Important Vocabulary

- how-to book
- order
- gather
- materials

Continuum Connection

- Understand that pictures can accompany the writing to help readers understand the information (p. 250)
- Use drawings in the process of drafting, revising, or publishing procedural writing (p. 250)
- Present ideas in a logical sequence (p. 254)

GOAL

Learn that words and pictures help readers understand how to do something.

RATIONALE

Learning that writers make choices about what words and illustrations to include in a text and about how to order the information helps children understand that pictures, words, and sequence convey meaning. In the process, they become thoughtful about how they use space and what they place on each page as they make books.

ASSESS LEARNING

- Look for evidence that children understand the significance of sequence in a how-to book.
- Observe whether children's drawings and words show the order of how to do something.
- Look for evidence that children can use vocabulary such as *how-to book*, *order*, *gather*, and *materials*.

MINILESSON

To help children understand the role of words, pictures, and sequence in a how-to book, model the making of a how-to book. Use familiar texts, including the class-made book from IW.21: Writing a How-to Book. Here is an example.

- Show the class-made how-to book from IW.21 to support a conversation about the materials needed, pictures, words, and sequence.

  What do you notice on the pages in this how-to book?

- Then revisit a few pages from *Boomer's Checkup*. Guide the discussion so children understand that the writer tells how to give a dog a checkup and that the book follows the order of Boomer's Chart at the top of each page. Point out that the words and pictures show details of the vet checkup.

  This book teaches about what happens when you take your dog to the vet (an animal doctor is called a vet) for a checkup. Let's think about how to use this information to make a how-to book.

- Display the first page of the prepared book.

  Before you can make or do anything, you have to gather the materials. What should I draw and write on the first page for the first step?

- As children provide suggestions, draw or place pictures and write a sentence under the pictures. (Either draw "pages" on chart paper or attach booklet pages to the easel.) Show children how you can look at the pictures in the book for help in drawing the items.

- Continue for the next steps. (Note: The steps will be numbered in the next minilesson.)

Have a Try

Invite children to revisit the how-to book to check for completeness.

> Take a look at the pages in the how-to book. Are the steps clear? Are they in order? Turn and talk to your partner about whether anything should be changed.

▶ After a brief discussion, ask a few volunteers to share ideas. Make the suggested changes, using sticky notes as needed.

▶ Keep the how-to book for WML3 and WML4.

Summarize and Apply

Help children summarize the learning. Then have them work on making how-to books during independent writing.

> What did you learn today about making how-to books?

▶ Write the principle at the top of the chart paper.

> During writing time, you will start a how-to book or continue working on one you have already started. Bring your how-to book to share when we meet later.

Confer

▶ During independent writing, move around the room to confer briefly with as many individual children as time allows. Sit side by side with them and invite them to talk about the steps in their how-to books. Use the following prompts as needed.

- *How will you begin your how-to book?*
- *What drawing (words) could you make to go with the words (drawing)?*
- *What is the next step?*
- *Are the steps in order?*

Share

Following independent writing, gather children in the meeting area to share their how-to books.

> Choose one page of your how-to book to share.

Making How-to Books

You Will Need

- a familiar how-to book with numbered steps, such as *From Seed to Plant* by Gail Gibbons, from Text Set: Understanding the Natural World: Planting and Growing:
- class how-to book from IW.21: Writing a How-To Book
- the how-to book from WML2

Academic Language / Important Vocabulary

- how-to book
- number
- steps
- in order

Continuum Connection

- Understand that a procedural text often shows one item under another item and may include a number for each item (p. 250)
- Present ideas in a logical sequence (p. 254)

GOAL

Put the steps in a set of directions in the right order and write the number for each step.

RATIONALE

When children learn to number the steps in a how-to book, they recognize that directions and books are read in a certain order. This will help them organize the pages of their own books sequentially.

ASSESS LEARNING

- Notice whether children understand that the steps in a how-to book are in sequential order.
- Look to see whether children number the steps in their how-to books.
- Look for evidence that they can use vocabulary such as *how-to book*, *number*, *steps*, and *in order* (meaning "sequenced").

MINILESSON

To help children think about the minilesson principle, use familiar how-to books to show how steps are often numbered to show the order. Here is an example.

- Briefly revisit pages 28–29 of *From Seed to Plant* and the class-made book from IW.21 and ask children to recall what the books show the reader how to do.

    What do you notice about these pages?

- Guide the children to notice that there are numbered steps that show the reader how to do something (e.g., grow bean plants, plant seeds).

    Some writers use numbers. Other writers do not use numbers, or they might use letters instead of numbers. Some writers don't use either numbers or letters. How have the writers used numbers on these pages?

- Show the first page from the how-to book you made in the previous lesson (how to give a dog a checkup).

    If I wanted to number this first step, what number should I write?

    Why is it important to use number *1* for the first step?

- Continue asking children to identify which number to add to each step. As they do, add the correct number to each step.

- Keep the how-to book to use in the next minilesson.

Have a Try

Invite children to turn and talk to a partner about numbering the steps in a how-to book.

> Turn and talk to your partner about how writers can help the reader by using numbers in a how-to book.

Summarize and Apply

Help children summarize the learning. Then have them add numbers to the steps in their how-to books during independent writing.

> What do some authors do to help you know the order of the steps in a how-to book?

▸ Add the principle to the top of the chart. (If you are using the chart from WML2, you can write the principle on a strip of paper and place it over the previous principle.) Read it aloud.

> When you work on your how-to books during writing time, write a number for each step. Bring your how-to book to share when we meet later.

> **Write a number for each step.**
>
> 1. Gather the materials.
> 2. Weigh the dog on the scale.
> 3. Check the dog's mouth, teeth, eyes, and ears.
> 4. Check the dog's heart and body. Don't forget the paws!
> 5. All done!

Confer

▸ During independent writing, move around the room to confer briefly with as many individual children as time allows. Sit side by side with them and invite them to talk about numbering the steps in their how-to books. Use the following prompts as needed.

- *What step is first? second? third?*
- *What number goes with the first step?*
- *What number will you write for the next step?*

Share

Following independent writing, gather children in the meeting area to share their how-to books.

> Tell about the how-to book you worked on today. How did you decide which number to add to each step?

WML 4

Writing Minilesson Principle
Make a list of materials.

Making How-to Books

You Will Need

- several how-to books that do *not* have a clear list of materials, such as *Plant Packages: A Book About Seeds* by Susan Blackaby and *From Seed to Plant* by Gail Gibbons, from Text Set: Understanding the Natural World: Planting and Growing

- the how-to book from WML2

- a recipe that has ingredients listed (e.g., from the back of a corn muffin box)

- chart paper and markers

- To download the following online resource for this lesson, visit **resources.fountasandpinnell.com**:

  - chart art (optional)

  - paper templates (optional)

Academic Language / Important Vocabulary

- how-to book
- list
- need
- materials

Continuum Connection

- Understand that a procedural text often includes a list of what is needed to do the procedure (p. 250)

- Place items in the list that are appropriate for its purpose or category (p. 250)

- Make lists in the appropriate form with one item under another (p. 250)

GOAL

Understand that sometimes writers include a list of materials needed to complete the instructions in the how-to book.

RATIONALE

Learning how a list of materials is useful in a how-to book encourages children to think about their own writing from a reader's perspective. This process enables them to think about and include necessary and important information in their own how-to books.

ASSESS LEARNING

- Look for evidence that children understand the usefulness of a list of materials in a how-to book.

- Observe whether children include a list of materials in their own how-to books.

- Look for evidence that they can use vocabulary such as *how-to book*, *list*, *need*, and *materials*.

MINILESSON

To help children understand that a list of materials is helpful to include in a how-to book, provide a minilesson using a sample recipe and familiar how-to books. Here is an example.

- Show a recipe and point to the list of ingredients.

  In this recipe, there is a list of materials, or ingredients, you need at the beginning of the recipe. How would this list help you make these corn muffins?

- Show page 1 from the how-to book you made in WML2.

  What materials are needed for a dog checkup at the vet's office?

- Revisit pages 15–16 of *Plant Packages*.

  This book shows how to grow a pumpkin patch, but it doesn't include a list of all the materials that are needed. Why would a list be helpful to someone who wants to grow a pumpkin patch?

- Have a conversation about the usefulness of a complete list of materials.

  If we wanted to make a complete list of materials for making a pumpkin patch, what items would be on the list? Turn and talk with two classmates about that.

- After time for a brief discussion, ask children to share. Use their suggestions to make a list on chart paper.

Have a Try

Invite children to turn and talk to a partner about a list of materials in a how-to book.

▶ Show pages 28–29 of *From Seed to Plant*.

> Turn and talk with your partner about what to put on a list of materials for growing bean plants.

▶ After time for discussion, ask children to share. If needed, explain that some how-to books do not have a list of materials, but if the book is about making something, it probably will have one.

Summarize and Apply

Help children summarize the learning. Then have them make a list of materials in their how-to books.

> What did you learn today about making how-to books?

▶ Write the principle at the top of the chart paper. Read it aloud.

> As you work on a how-to book today, add a list of materials.

Make a list of materials.

Materials to Grow a Pumpkin Patch

garden tools

pumpkin seeds

soil

water

Confer

▶ During independent writing, move around the room to confer briefly with as many individual children as time allows. Sit side by side with them and invite them to talk about making a materials list for their how-to books. Use the following prompts as needed.

- *What materials will the reader need?*
- *Does your list have everything on it?*
- *How will adding a list of materials help the reader?*

Share

Following independent writing, gather children in the meeting area to share their how-to books.

> Who added a list of materials in your how-to book today? Share what you put on the list.

Assessment

After you have taught the minilessons in this umbrella, observe children as they explore making books. Use *The Literacy Continuum* (Fountas and Pinnell 2017) to notice, teach for, and support children's learning as you observe their attempts at reading and writing.

▶ What evidence do you have of new understandings children have developed related to making how-to books?

- Can children explain the purpose of a how-to book?
- Do you notice children's interest in making how-to books independently?
- Do their how-to books contain pictures, numbers, and a list of materials?
- Do they understand and use vocabulary related to making a how-to book, such as *how-to book*, *writing*, *drawing*, *teach*, *idea*, *words*, *number*, *order*, *steps*, *list*, *need*, and *materials*?

▶ In what ways, beyond the scope of this umbrella, are children making books?

- Do they show an interest in sharing their books with others?
- Are they thinking about other topics they might make a book about?

Use your observations to determine the next umbrella you will teach. You may also consult Suggested Sequence of Lessons (pp. 557–571) for guidance.

EXTENSIONS FOR MAKING HOW-TO BOOKS

▶ Have children follow a recipe for a healthy snack that has 3–4 steps and then talk about the steps with a partner. Following this, they can make a how-to book to share the recipe with their families.

▶ Talk to children about things they do at school and encourage them to make a how-to book to teach someone something they have done (e.g., play four-square, play a drum, make a paper boat).

▶ If you and the class read how-to books, directions, or recipes that do not have numbered steps, use sticky notes to add numbers or letters to show the order. Explain that how-to books might or might not have numbers or letters.

▶ Teach children how to add captions to pictures to tell more about the pictures.

▶ As children engage in social studies projects and science activities, use shared or interactive writing to make a list of materials.

▶ Gather together a guided writing group of several children who need support in a specific area of writing.

Minilessons in This Umbrella

WML1 Make an all-about book.

WML2 Write about the same topic on every page.

WML3 Learn about your topic and put the information in your own words.

WML4 Think about how to get your readers interested in your topic.

Before Teaching Umbrella 5 Minilessons

Prior to teaching these minilessons, read aloud a variety of engaging nonfiction books. Teach IW.14: Writing an All-About Book so that children will have learned something about making an all-about book. The lessons in this umbrella build on that experience, leading children to make books independently. Prepare blank booklets (four to eight stapled pages with a cover) for children to use. You might also want to provide any of the paper templates from online resources that are appropriate. Store the booklets and paper templates in the writing center.

Use the class-made book from IW.14 as a mentor text for the minilessons in this umbrella. You may also use the following books from *Fountas & Pinnell Classroom™ Interactive Read-Aloud Collection*.

Exploring Nonfiction

Tools by Ann Morris

Water: Up, Down, and All Around by Natalie M. Rosinsky

What If You Had Animal Teeth!? by Sandra Markle

Surprising Sharks by Nicola Davies

What Do You Do When Something Wants to Eat You? by Steve Jenkins

Interactive Writing Lessons

IW.14: Writing an All-About Book

As you read and enjoy these texts together, help children

- notice that the books communicate information,
- recognize that all of the pages in each book are about the same topic, and
- think about how the authors engage and interest their readers.

Exploring Nonfiction

Interactive Writing

WML 1

MBK.U5.WML1

Make an all-about book.

Making All-About Books

You Will Need

- nonfiction books that provide information about a single topic, such as the following from Text Set: Exploring Nonfiction:

  - *Tools* by Ann Morris

  - *Water: Up, Down, and All Around* by Natalie M. Rosinsky

  - *What If You Had Animal Teeth!?* by Sandra Markle

- the class all-about book from IW.14: Writing an All-About Book

- chart paper and markers

- To download the following online resource for this lesson, visit **resources.fountasandpinnell.com**:

  - chart art (optional)

Academic Language/ Important Vocabulary

- all-about book

- topic

Continuum Connection

- Understand how to write a factual text from listening to mentor texts read aloud and discussing them (p. 251)

- Select one's own topic for informational writing and state what is important about the topic (p. 256)

- Choose topics that one knows about, cares about, or wants to learn about (p. 256)

- Choose a topic that is interesting to the writer (p. 256)

GOAL

Understand that you can make a book to tell what you know about something.

RATIONALE

When children write all-about books, they learn that they can share their knowledge with others. Engaging in bookmaking enables children to use high-level thinking about the process of writing.

ASSESS LEARNING

- Observe children as they write all-about books and talk about their writing.

- Notice whether children can explain why they chose a particular topic to write about.

- Look for evidence that they can use vocabulary such as *all-about book* and *topic*.

MINILESSON

To prepare children to write all-about books independently, engage them in a discussion about nonfiction books, including the class book from IW.14. Here is an example.

- Show the cover and a few pages of *Tools*.

  What does Ann Morris tell all about in this book?

  The topic of the book is tools because that's what the author tells all about.

- Record the topic on chart paper.

- Revisit *Water: Up, Down, and All Around*.

  What does the author tell all about?

  Natalie Rosinsky tells all about water in this book. She knows a lot about water!

- Add to the chart.

- Continue in a similar manner with *What If You Had Animal Teeth!?* and the class-made book from IW.14.

Have a Try

Invite children to talk to a partner about their ideas for writing.

> The chart shows some things that people have written books about. You can write a book about something you know a lot about. What would you like to write about? Turn and talk to your partner about this.

Summarize and Apply

Summarize the learning. Remind children to think about a topic for an all-about book.

▶ Write the principle at the top of the chart.

> Today you learned that in an all-about book the author tells all about a topic, like tools or water.

> During writing time today, choose a topic for an all-about book. It can be something you know a lot about, that you care about, or that you want to learn more about.

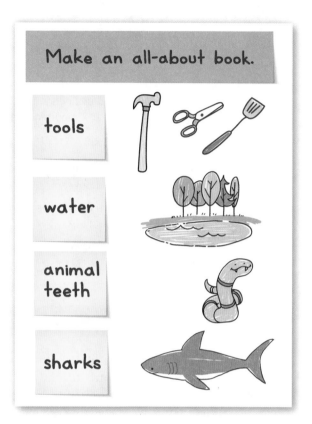

Make an all-about book.

tools

water

animal teeth

sharks

Confer

▶ During independent writing, move around the room to confer briefly with as many individual children as time allows. Sit side by side with them and invite them to talk about their plans for making all-about books. Use the following prompts as needed.

- *What do you know a lot about?*
- *Is there anything that you'd like to learn more about?*
- *Why do you want to write a book about that topic?*
- *What could you write in a book about that?*

Share

Following independent writing, gather children in the meeting area. As needed, support children's oral language by providing a sentence frame, such as *I am going to write about _____ because _____.*

> Who would like to share what you will write about in your all-about book?

> Why did you choose that topic?

Writing Minilesson Principle
Write about the same topic on every page.

You Will Need

- nonfiction books that provide information about a single topic, such as the following from Text Set: Exploring Nonfiction:
  - *Surprising Sharks* by Nicola Davies
  - *Water: Up, Down, and All Around* by Natalie M. Rosinsky
- chart paper and markers
- To download the following online resource for this lesson, visit **resources.fountasandpinnell.com**:
  - chart art (optional)
  - paper templates (optional)

Academic Language/ Important Vocabulary

- all-about book
- topic
- information
- page

Continuum Connection

- Write and/or draw about one topic on a page or across several pages of a book, including one category of information related to a main topic on every page (p. 254)

- Put together the related details on a topic in a text (p. 254)

- Tell one part, idea, or group of ideas on each page of a book (p. 254)

GOAL

Understand that every page in a book is related to the same topic.

RATIONALE

When children understand that all of the pages in an all-about book relate to the same topic, they learn the importance of staying on topic when making their own books.

ASSESS LEARNING

- Listen to children talk about nonfiction books. Do they recognize that all of the pages are about the same topic?
- Observe whether children write about the same topic on every page in their own all-about books.
- Look for evidence that they can use vocabulary such as *all-about book*, *topic*, *information*, and *page*.

MINILESSON

To help children think about the principle, use familiar all-about books to help them notice that all of the pages are about the same topic. Below is an example. When children make their all-about books, they can use blank paper or the paper templates from online resources.

- Show the cover of *Surprising Sharks* and read the title. Show pages 8–9.

  What are these pages about?

- Record children's responses on chart paper. Repeat with pages 13 and 14–15.

  What do you notice about all the pages in this book?

  All the pages in this book are about sharks. Each page gives different information about sharks, but all the pages are about sharks.

Have a Try

Invite children to talk to a partner about what each page in *Water: Up, Down, and All Around* is about.

▶ Show the cover of *Water: Up, Down, and All Around* and read the title. Display pages 4–5, 6–7, and 15 and ask children what each page is about.

> What do you notice about all the pages in this book? What are they all about? Turn and talk to your partner about this.

Summarize and Apply

Summarize the learning and remind children to write about the same topic on every page of their all-about books.

▶ Write the principle at the top of the chart.

> Today you noticed that every page of an all-about book is about the same topic. The pages might give different kinds of information about the topic, but they are all about the same topic.
> During writing time today, start writing your all-about book. Remember to write about the same topic on every page.

Write about the same topic on every page.

Pages 8–9   Dwarf lantern <u>shark</u>

Page 13   Shapes and sizes of <u>sharks</u>

Pages 14–15 A <u>shark's</u> body parts

Every page is about <u>sharks.</u>

Confer

▶ During independent writing, move around the room to confer briefly with as many individual children as time allows. Sit side by side with them and invite them to talk about their all-about books. Use the following prompts as needed.

- *What will you write about on every page of your book?*
- *What will you write about the topic on this page? the next page?*
- *What else can you write about that topic?*

Share

Following independent writing, gather children in the meeting area to share their all-about books.

> Who would like to share the all-about book you worked on today?

> What did you write about on every page of your book?

WML 3

Writing Minilesson Principle

Learn about your topic and put the information in your own words.

Making All-About Books

You Will Need

- familiar nonfiction books, such as the following from Text Set: Exploring Nonfiction:
  - *Surprising Sharks* by Nicola Davies
  - *What If You Had Animal Teeth!?* by Sandra Markle
- chart paper and markers

Academic Language/ Important Vocabulary

- all-about book
- topic
- information
- notes

Continuum Connection

- Ask questions and gather information on a topic (p. 256)
- Take notes or make sketches to help in remembering information (p. 256)

GOAL

Understand how to research a topic and put the information in your own words.

RATIONALE

When you teach children how to research a topic and put the information in their own words, they begin to understand that nonfiction authors do not merely copy information they read elsewhere. Rather, they think about and synthesize information from several sources and add their own personal ideas and style.

ASSESS LEARNING

- Observe children as they gather information for their all-about books. Do they take notes or make sketches to help in remembering information?
- Notice whether children put information in their own words in their all-about books.
- Look for evidence that they can use vocabulary such as *all-about book*, *topic*, *information*, and *notes*.

MINILESSON

To help children think about the principle, model researching a topic, taking notes, and writing the information in your own words. Make sure children understand *notes* as used in this minilesson.

> I am writing a book all about sharks. I want to write a page about shark attacks, but first I need to learn more. Watch what I do.

- Show the cover of *Surprising Sharks* and read the title.

> This book is all about sharks, so I think it will have the information I need.

- Turn to page 29 and read the first paragraph aloud. Pause regularly to take notes or make sketches of relevant information on chart paper.

> What did you see me do?

> I used a book about sharks to learn about the topic. I took notes and drew pictures so I would remember the information for my own all-about book. Now I'm going to write a page for my book, using the information I found.

- Rewrite the information you gathered in your own words, reading it aloud as you write it.

> What did you notice about how I wrote the information?

> I put the information in my own words. When you write an all-about book, you can use other books to learn about the topic, but it's important to write the information in your own words.

Have a Try

Invite children to talk to a partner about how to put information in their own words.

▶ Show the cover of *What If You Had Animal Teeth!?* Read the title and the main text on page 10.

> If you were writing about an elephant's tusks, what would you write? How would you put some of this information in your own words? Turn and talk to your partner about this.

▶ After children turn and talk, invite several pairs to share their ideas.

Summarize and Apply

Write the principle at the top of the chart. Summarize the learning and remind children to research their topic and put the information in your own words.

> Why do you think it's important to write the information you learn in your own words?

> During writing time today, use books or the internet to learn about your topic. You can take notes or draw pictures to help you remember what you learned. Then put the information in your own words.

Learn about your topic and put the information in your own words.

- 500 kinds of sharks
- 30 kinds have attacked people
- eat small fish

Sharks are not as dangerous as you think—unless you're a fish.

There are 500 types of sharks.

Only 30 types have ever attacked people.

Most sharks are happy eating small fish.

Confer

▶ During independent writing, move around the room to confer briefly with as many individual children as time allows. Sit side by side with them and invite them to talk about the information in their all-about books. Use the following prompts as needed.

- *What is the topic of your all-about book? Let's look for a book (or website) about that.*
- *What information do you want to put in your book? You can write it down or draw a picture so you'll remember it.*
- *How can you tell about that in your own words?*

Share

Following independent writing, gather children in the meeting area.

> How did you find information to put in your all-about book?

> Read aloud what you wrote. Is it in your own words?

Writing Minilesson Principle
Think about how to get your readers interested in your topic.

You Will Need

- familiar nonfiction books with a variety of engaging features, such as the following from Text Set: Exploring Nonfiction:
  - *Surprising Sharks* by Nicola Davies
  - *What If You Had Animal Teeth!?* by Sandra Markle
  - *What Do You Do When Something Wants to Eat You?* by Steve Jenkins
- chart paper and markers

Academic Language/ Important Vocabulary

- all-about book
- readers
- interested
- topic

Continuum Connection

- Understand that a writer may work to get readers interested in a topic (p. 251)
- Understand that a writer of a factual text uses words and illustrations to make it interesting to readers (p. 251)
- Think about the readers (audience) and what they need to know (p. 251)
- Select interesting information to include in a piece of writing (p. 251)
- Tell about a topic in an interesting way (p. 256)

GOAL

Understand different ways writers get readers interested in a topic.

RATIONALE

When children notice different ways that nonfiction authors engage their readers, they are likely to try the same techniques in their own all-about books.

ASSESS LEARNING

- Observe children as they talk about nonfiction books. Can they identify different ways that authors get readers interested in a topic?
- Notice whether children experiment with these techniques in their own writing.
- Look for evidence that they can use vocabulary such as *all-about book*, *readers*, *interested*, and *topic*.

MINILESSON

To help children think about the principle, engage children in an inquiry around different ways that nonfiction authors engage readers.

- Show the cover of *Surprising Sharks* and read the title. Read the first two pages (pp. 6–7).

  Do these pages make you want to read the rest of the book and learn more about sharks?

  How does the author get you interested in the topic?

- Record children's responses on chart paper.
- Turn to page 18. Read the first paragraph and the caption about sand tiger sharks. Show the illustration.

  How does the author get you interested in baby sharks?

- Add responses to the chart.
- Show the cover of *What If You Had Animal Teeth!?* Read the title and the first page.

  How does the author of this book get you interested in animal teeth?

  She makes you think about what it would be like if you had animal teeth.

- Read pages 4–5.

  What else does the author do to get you interested in animal teeth?

- Add children's responses to the chart. Draw children's attention to the fun facts and the illustrations of children with animal teeth, if needed.

Have a Try

Invite children to talk to a partner about how another author gets readers interested in a topic.

▶ Show the cover of *What Do You Do When Something Wants to Eat You?* Read the title and the first two pages.

> How does the author make you want to learn more about the octopus? Turn and talk to your partner.

▶ After children turn and talk, invite a few pairs to share their responses. If needed, help children understand that the author makes the readers turn the page to find out what the octopus does.

Summarize and Apply

Summarize the learning and remind children to think about how to get their readers interested in their topic.

> What did we talk about today?

▶ Write the principle at the top of the chart.

> Today when you work on your all-about book, think about how to get your readers interested in your topic. Bring your all-about book to share when we meet later.

Think about how to get your readers interested in your topic.

- Ask questions to make the reader think.

- Choose interesting words.

- Write words in different colors and sizes.

- Draw or choose funny pictures.

- Tell fun facts.

- Make the readers turn the page to find something out.

Confer

▶ During independent writing, move around the room to confer briefly with as many individual children as time allows. Sit side by side with them and invite them to talk about getting readers interested in their topics. Use the following prompts as needed.

- *How can you get your readers interested in _____?*
- *Is there something on the chart that you would like to try?*
- *Do you know any fun facts about _____?*
- *What questions could you ask your readers?*

Share

Following independent writing, gather children in the meeting area to share their all-about books.

> What did you do to get your readers interested in the topic?

Assessment

After you have taught the minilessons in this umbrella, observe children as they explore making books. Use *The Literacy Continuum* (Fountas and Pinnell 2017) to notice, teach for, and support children's learning as you observe their attempts at writing.

▶ What evidence do you have of new understandings children have developed related to making all-about books?

- Are children able to explain what an all-about book is?

- Are they making all-about books on their own?

- Is every page of the book related to the topic?

- Do they put the information they learn into their own words?

- Do they experiment with different ways of getting readers interested in a topic?

- Do they understand and use vocabulary such as *all-about book*, *topic*, and *information*?

▶ In what other ways, beyond the scope of this umbrella, are children exploring bookmaking?

- Do children show an interest in making other kinds of books?

- Are children starting to revise their writing?

Use your observations to determine the next umbrella you will teach. You may also consult Suggested Sequence of Lessons (pp. 557–571) for guidance.

EXTENSIONS FOR MAKING ALL-ABOUT BOOKS

▶ Help children use computers or other technological tools to make all-about books.

▶ Teach children how to add text and organizational features, such as a table of contents, captions, or sidebars, to their nonfiction texts [see CFT.U7: Adding Text Features to Books].

▶ Gather together a guided writing group of several children who need support in a specific area of writing.

▶ When children show an interest in a topic, help them learn more by providing resources and encouraging them to make an all-about book with their newly acquired knowledge.

▶ Invite a nonfiction author to speak to the class about the writing process.

Minilessons in This Umbrella

WML1 Notice the kinds of questions in question-and-answer books.

WML2 Write a repeating question for your topic.

WML3 Write different questions for your topic.

WML4 Find answers to questions you don't know.

WML5 Write a question-and-answer book.

Before Teaching Umbrella 6 Minilessons

Teach this umbrella later in the year so that children have learned about a wide variety of topics and can generate ideas for their question-and-answer books. This umbrella will make children aware of two kinds of question-and-answer books: books with repeating questions and books with different questions. You might choose to have children apply these lessons to one piece, or you might prefer to have them work on several question-and-answer books across the umbrella. Before this umbrella, teach IW.15: Writing a Question-and-Answer Book. The book you make with children in IW.15 will be used as a mentor text in this umbrella.

Prior to teaching these minilessons, gather a variety of question-and-answer books and nonfiction books, both published mentor texts and children's writing. You may also choose the following books from *Fountas & Pinnell Classroom™ Interactive Read-Aloud Collection* and *Shared Reading Collection*.

Interactive Read-Aloud Collection

Nonfiction: Questions and Answers

Animals Black and White by Phyllis Limbacher Tildes

Best Foot Forward: Exploring Feet, Flippers, and Claws by Ingo Arndt

What Do You Do With a Tail Like This? by Steve Jenkins and Robin Page

Shared Reading Collection

Bone Riddles by Ernesta Flores

Zoom In and Out by Amanda Yskamp

Inventions and Nature by Nancy Geldermann

Interactive Writing Lessons

IW.15: Writing a Question-and-Answer Book

As you read and enjoy these texts together, help children

- notice that the books have questions and answers, and

- recognize that all of the pages are related to the same topic.

Interactive Read-Aloud
Nonfiction

Shared Reading

Interactive Writing

Section 4: Making Books

WML1

MBK.U6.WML1

Writing Minilesson Principle
Notice the kinds of questions in question-and-answer books.

Making Question-and-Answer Books

You Will Need

- several question-and-answer books, such as the following:
  - *Animals Black and White* by Phyllis Limbacher Tildes and *What Do You Do With a Tail Like This?* by Steve Jenkins and Robin Page, from Text Set: Nonfiction: Questions and Answers
- chart paper and markers

Academic Language / Important Vocabulary

- question-and-answer book
- topic
- repeating question
- different questions

Continuum Connection

- Understand that a writer may work to get readers interested in a topic (p. 251)
- Learn ways of using language and constructing texts from other writers (reading books and hearing them read aloud) and apply understandings to one's own writing (p. 254)
- Tell one part, idea, or group of ideas on each page of a book (p. 254)
- Tell about experiences or topics in a way that others can understand (p. 254)
- Choose a topic that is interesting to the writer (p. 256)
- Generate ideas or topics for writing (p. 256)

GOAL

Understand that question-and-answer books have one of two kinds of questions.

RATIONALE

When children learn that nonfiction books can be organized to make the information interesting to the reader, and that authors choose topics and what types of questions to ask, they realize that they can decide how to present content in a fun and memorable way.

ASSESS LEARNING

- Look for evidence that children understand that some question-and-answer books have one question that repeats and other question-and-answer books have different questions.
- Notice evidence that children can use vocabulary such as *question-and-answer book*, *topic*, *repeating question*, and *different questions*.

MINILESSON

Before this lesson, children should have heard and read a variety of nonfiction books and they should have experienced making a class question-and-answer book (see IW.15). Use text examples to help them notice types of question-and-answer books. Here is an example.

- Show the covers of two familiar question-and-answer books, one in a *repeating question* format and one in *different questions* format.

  We have been reading different types of question-and-answer books. What are the topics of these books?

- Briefly revisit the topics. Reread the questions on pages 1, 5, and 9 in *Animals Black and White*.

  What question does the author ask?

  The author asks *What am I?* When the same question is asked again and again, it is a *repeating question* book.

- Write on the chart *Repeating Question* with a definition and the question.

- Reread the questions on pages 7, 11, and 16 in *What Do You Do With a Tail Like This?*

  What questions do the authors ask?

  The authors change the question each time. They ask different questions about the animal body parts, such as *What do you do with ears like these?* and *What do you do with eyes like these?* When different questions are asked, it is a *different questions* book.

- Record similar information about *Different Questions* on the chart.

Have a Try

Invite children to talk to a partner about question-and-answer books.

> What topic do you think you might like to write about? Turn and talk about that.

▶ Ask a few children to share ideas. Use one child's topic to get children thinking about types of questions. For example:

> Hannah, if you are going to make a question-and-answer book about dogs, you could have a repeating question, like *What dog is this?* Or, you could have different questions like *What do dogs eat? How many walks do dogs need?*

Summarize and Apply

Summarize the learning. Then have children experiment with ideas.

▶ Write the principle at the top of the chart. Help children understand that the question-and-answer format makes it interesting for the reader.

> During writing time, make a list of topics you could make a question-and-answer book about and write some questions you could ask in your book.

Notice the kinds of questions in question-and-answer books.

<u>Repeating Question</u>— the same question every time

What am I?

<u>Different Questions</u> — a different question every time

What do you do with a tail like this?

What do you do with ears like this?

Confer

▶ During independent writing, move around the room to confer briefly with as many individual children as time allows. Sit side by side with them and invite them to talk about their plans for making their question-and-answer books. Use the following prompts as needed.

- *What topic are you interested in writing about?*
- *What are some questions you might ask?*
- *Will you ask a repeating question or different questions? Why?*

Share

Following independent writing, gather children in the meeting area and ask several volunteers to share the topic they might write about and a few questions they might ask.

> What will you write about in your question-and-answer book?

> What is one question you might write in your book?

WML2

Writing Minilesson Principle

Write a repeating question for your topic.

You Will Need

▶ several question-and-answer books, such as the following:

- *Animals Black and White* by Phyllis Limbacher Tildes and *Best Foot Forward* by Ingo Arndt, from Text Set: Nonfiction: Questions and Answers

- *Bone Riddles* by Ernesta Flores and *Zoom In and Out* by Amanda Yskamp, from *Shared Reading Collection*

▶ chart paper and markers

Academic Language / Important Vocabulary

▶ question

▶ answer

▶ question-and-answer book

▶ topic

▶ repeating question

Continuum Connection

▶ Learn ways of using language and constructing texts from other writers (reading books and hearing them read aloud) and apply understandings to one's own writing (p. 254)

▶ Ask questions and gather information on a topic (p. 256)

▶ Try out techniques other writers and illustrators have used (p. 257)

GOAL

Write a repeating question to explore one kind of question-and-answer book.

RATIONALE

When children learn that using a repeating question is one way to construct a question-and-answer book, they realize that as writers, they can make decisions about the kind of book they will make.

ASSESS LEARNING

▶ Notice whether children can identify a repeating question in a mentor text.

▶ Look for evidence that children decide on a repeating question to use in a question-and-answer book.

▶ Notice evidence that children can use vocabulary such as *question, answer, question-and-answer book, topic,* and *repeating question*.

MINILESSON

Use text examples to help children make a list of some sample repeating questions that they might use in their question-and-answer books. Here is an example.

▶ Revisit the questions on several pages of *Animals Black and White* and *Bone Riddles* (*What am I?*).

> In these two question-and-answer books, what question is asked again and again?
>
> What is that kind of question called?

▶ Begin a list on chart paper with examples of repeating questions that can be used in a question-and-answer book. Add *What am I?* to the list.

▶ Show examples from *Best Foot Forward* (*Whose foot is this?*) and *Zoom In and Out* (*What will you see when you zoom out?*) and ask children to identify the questions.

▶ As children identify the repeating questions, add a generic form of the question to the chart.

▶ Model how you might use a repeating question for a topic. This is one example.

> I would like to make a question-and-answer book that shows different kinds of dogs. If I use a repeating question, I might ask something like *What kind of dog is this?* I could write the question on one page and then make a flap to hide the answer. What are some different types of dogs I could show under the flap for the answer?

▶ Model the repeating question by asking volunteers *What kind of dog is this?* as they suggest a few dog breeds for the answers. Add to the chart, using a generic form of the question.

Have a Try

Invite children to talk to a partner about repeating questions in question-and-answer books.

> What is another repeating question you might use in a question-and-answer book for your topic? Turn and talk about that.

▶ Ask a few children to share ideas. Guide the conversation and add to the chart.

Summarize and Apply

Summarize the learning. Then have children experiment with ideas.

▶ Write the principle at the top of the chart.

> During writing time, think about a repeating question you might use in your question-and-answer book and write it. You might want to write some answers if you know them.

Write a repeating question for your topic.

What am I?

Whose _____ is this?

What will you see when _____?

What kind of _____ is this?

What says _____?

What is a _____?

What color is a _____?

Confer

▶ During independent writing, move around the room to confer briefly with as many individual children as time allows. Sit side by side with them and invite them to talk about their plans for making their question-and-answer books. Use the following prompts as needed.

- *What topic are you thinking about?*
- *What ideas do you have for a repeating question you might ask again and again in your book?*
- *Let's talk about some answers you might use for your repeating question.*

Share

Following independent writing, gather children in the meeting area and ask several volunteers to share the topic they might write about and a few questions they might ask.

> What topic will you choose for your question-and-answer book?

> What is one repeating question you might use in your book?

Making Question-and-Answer Books

You Will Need

- several question-and-answer books, such as the following:
  - *What Do You Do With a Tail Like This?* by Steve Jenkins and Robin Page, from Text Set: Nonfiction: Questions and Answers
  - *Inventions and Nature* by Nancy Geldermann, from *Shared Reading Collection*
- the class question-and-answer book from IW.15
- chart paper and markers
- To download the following online resource for this lesson, visit **resources.fountasandpinnell.com**:
  - chart art (optional)

Academic Language / Important Vocabulary

- question-and-answer book
- topic
- different questions

Continuum Connection

- Ask questions and gather information on a topic (p. 256)
- Remember important information about a topic in order to write about it (p. 256)
- Record information in words or drawing (p. 256)

GOAL

Generate ideas for different questions and write at least two questions about a topic.

RATIONALE

When children learn that using different questions is one way to construct a question-and-answer book, they realize that as writers they can make decisions about their books.

ASSESS LEARNING

- Notice whether children can identify different questions in a mentor text.
- Look for evidence that children can think and talk about different questions that they might use in a question-and-answer book.
- Notice evidence that children can use vocabulary such as *question-and-answer book*, *topic*, and *different questions*.

MINILESSON

Use text examples to help children make a list of some sample different questions to get them thinking about questions they might use in their question-and-answer books. Here is an example.

- Revisit the questions on several pages of *What Do You Do With a Tail Like This?*

  What do you notice about the questions in this book?

- Guide children to notice that each question is different. The questions do not repeat.

- Repeat the process with *Inventions and Nature*.

- To help children think about what readers might want to know about a topic, model a writer's thinking process. Think aloud as you come up with a new question for a mentor text. Use an idea from something the class has learned about. This is one example.

- Reread the class-made question-and-answer book from IW.15.

  I'm thinking about other things a reader might want to know about how animal parents take care of their babies. We learned that mother dogs protect their babies when they are in danger. That is something a reader might like to know about. I am going to add the question *What does a mother dog do when a puppy is in danger?* to the chart.

- Add the new question to the chart.

  What is the answer to this question?

- This question and answer will be used in WML5.

Have a Try

Invite children to talk to a partner about different questions in question-and-answer books.

> Think about the topic you will write about. What are some different questions you might use in your question-and-answer book? Turn and talk about that.

▶ Ask a few children to share ideas. Record on the chart.

Summarize and Apply

Summarize the learning. Then have children experiment with ideas.

▶ Write the principle at the top of the chart.

> During writing time, think about two different questions you might use in your question-and-answer book. Write the questions or draw a picture to help yourself remember your questions.

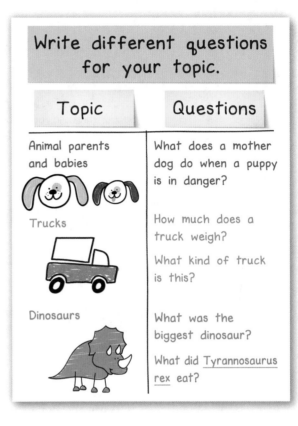

Confer

▶ During independent writing, move around the room to confer briefly with as many individual children as time allows. Sit side by side with them and invite them to talk about their plans for making their question-and-answer books. Use the following prompts as needed.

- *What topic are you thinking about?*
- *What ideas do you have for different questions you might ask in your book?*
- *Tell me what questions you might use and I can write down what you say.*

Share

Following independent writing, gather children in the meeting area and ask several volunteers to share the topic they might write about and a few questions they might ask.

> What topic will you write about in your question-and-answer book?

> What are some different questions you might use in your book?

Making Question-and-Answer Books

You Will Need

▸ several question-and-answer books, such as the following:

- *Bone Riddles* by Ernesta Flores, *Zoom In and Out* by Amanda Yskamp, and *Inventions and Nature* by Nancy Geldermann, from *Shared Reading Collection*

▸ chart paper and markers

▸ To download the following online resource for this lesson, visit **resources.fountasandpinnell.com**:

- chart art (optional)

Academic Language / Important Vocabulary

▸ question-and-answer book

▸ topic

▸ research

▸ internet

▸ interview

▸ expert

Continuum Connection

▸ Ask questions and gather information on a topic (p. 256)

▸ Select information that will support the topic (p. 256)

GOAL

Use resources to find answers to questions for their books.

RATIONALE

When children understand that they can find answers to the questions they have in a variety of places, they gain confidence in gaining access to information and can apply this in their own lives when they have questions or wonderings.

ASSESS LEARNING

▸ Notice whether children can identify resources they can use for finding answers.

▸ Look for evidence that children are trying to find answers to their questions independently.

▸ Notice evidence that children can use vocabulary such as *question-and-answer book*, *topic*, *research*, *internet*, *interview*, and *expert*.

MINILESSON

Use text examples to help children think about how writers find answers to questions they have. Here is an example.

▸ Gather several examples of question-and-answer books on a variety of topics (see You Will Need).

▸ Show the cover and a few pages of *Bone Riddles*.

> What does the author of *Bone Riddles* want you to learn about?

> The writer gives information about animal skeletons. Before making *Bone Riddles*, the writer needed to find answers to the questions she had. Can you think of one place the writer might have looked to find answers to her questions?

▸ Guide children to understand that the author could look in books about animals and their skeletons to learn facts before writing the book. Begin a list on chart paper of ways children can find answers to questions.

▸ Repeat the process using question-and-answer books on several other topics to prompt the conversation. Help children identify other ways to find information (e.g., use the internet, interview someone, ask an expert). Add to the chart list.

Have a Try

Invite children to talk to a partner about how they might find answers to questions for their question-and-answer books.

> What question(s) will you have in your question-and-answer book? Turn and tell your partner your question and talk about where you might look to find answers.

▶ Ask a few children to share ideas. During this conversation, help guide them to identify the question(s) they will be using and at least one place to look for answers.

Summarize and Apply

Summarize the learning. Then have children begin looking for answers.

▶ Write the principle at the top of the chart.

> Writers look in different places to find information to write about. During writing time, look at the question(s) you have about your topic. Think about one way you might find answers to your question(s) and decide how you will do that. Write down your ideas. If you know a place you can look for answers, you can begin looking.

Find answers to questions you don't know.

• Look in books.

• Use the internet.

• Interview someone.

• Ask an expert.

Confer

▶ During independent writing, move around the room to confer briefly with as many individual children as time allows. Sit side by side with them and invite them to talk about their plans for making their question-and-answer books. Use the following prompts as needed.

- *What topic are you writing about?*
- *Let's look in the classroom library for some books about your topic.*
- *Would you like me to help you use the computer to find an answer?*

Share

Following independent writing, gather children in the meeting area and ask several volunteers to share the way they will find answers to their questions.

> What question(s) do you have about your topic?

> How will you find the answer to your question(s)?

Writing Minilesson Principle
Write a question-and-answer book.

Making Question-and-Answer Books

You Will Need

▸ the class question-and-answer book from IW.15, along with the idea for a new question and answer that can be added (see WML3)

▸ several sheets of the same paper used in the class book from IW.15

▸ chart paper and markers

▸ To download the following online resource for this lesson, visit **resources.fountasandpinnell.com**:

  ▪ chart art (optional)

Academic Language / Important Vocabulary

▸ question-and-answer book

▸ topic

▸ page

Continuum Connection

▸ Understand that layout of print and illustrations is important in conveying the meaning of a text (p. 254)

▸ Choose the form of text to fit the purpose: e.g., poem, ABC book, photo book, label book, story with pictures (p. 255)

▸ Consider how the purpose affects the kind of writing (p. 255)

▸ Use words and drawings to compose and revise writing (p. 256)

GOAL

Understand that writers choose the kind of book they want to make and decide where to write the information on the pages.

RATIONALE

When children learn that writers have many choices when they make books, they begin to take ownership over their own writing and gain confidence in making decisions about what and how to write. Children may find it easier to use the repeating question format for the first question-and-answer book they make independently, but providing a choice gives them ownership over the process.

ASSESS LEARNING

▸ Notice whether children understand that writers make choices when they write books.

▸ Observe whether children are making independent decisions about what to write and where to write on the page.

▸ Notice evidence that children can use vocabulary such as *question-and-answer book*, *topic*, and *page*.

MINILESSON

To help children decide on a topic and format for a question-and-answer book and to begin writing, provide an interactive lesson to show options for where to place the information on the pages of their book. Here is an example.

▸ Revisit the class-made question-and-answer book from IW.15 and the new question and answer for the book (see WML3).

> You talked about a new question and answer you might add to this book. On the new page, should the writing go at the top or the bottom? Where should a picture go?

▸ As children provide ideas, begin making a new page for the book. Guide the conversation to help them think about why they are making the decision about where to place the questions and answers.

> How will putting the information in this place help the reader?

> What is another place we could choose to put the information on the page?

▸ Use a new piece of chart paper and lay the page out differently. As needed, repeat the process, using a new piece of chart paper for each variation.

> As a writer, you have choices about the type of question-and-answer book to make. You also have choices about where you will put the information on the page.

Have a Try

Invite children to talk to a partner about question-and-answer books.

> What will be the topic for your question-and-answer book? Will you use a repeating question or use different questions? Turn and talk about that. Tell your partner where you will place the information on the page.

▶ Ask a few children to share ideas.

Summarize and Apply

Summarize the learning. Then have children work on question-and-answer books.

> You learned about different types of question-and-answer books and talked about where information can be placed on a page. During writing time, you may continue working on a book you already started or you may begin a new book.

Confer

▶ During independent writing, move around the room to confer briefly with as many individual children as time allows. Sit side by side with them and invite them to talk about their question-and-answer books. Use the following prompts as needed.

- *What type of question-and-answer book are you making?*
- *Where will you place the information on the page? Why?*
- *Point to the place on the page where you will begin writing.*

Share

Following independent writing, gather children in the meeting area and ask several volunteers to share the question-and-answer books they are working on.

> Who would like to share your question-and-answer book?

Assessment

After you have taught the minilessons in this umbrella, observe children as they explore making books. Use *The Literacy Continuum* (Fountas and Pinnell 2017) to notice, teach for, and support children's learning as you observe their attempts at writing.

▶ What evidence do you have of new understandings children have developed related to making question-and-answer books?

- Are children noticing different types of question-and-answer books, such as books with repeating questions and books with different questions?

- Do they attempt to find answers to questions they do not know by using a book, using the internet, or interviewing an expert?

- Are they making their own question-and-answer books?

- Do they understand and use vocabulary related to making a question-and-answer book, such as *question*, *answer*, *question-and-answer book*, *topic*, *repeating question*, *different questions*, *research*, *internet*, and *interview*?

▶ In what ways, beyond the scope of this umbrella, are children making books?

- Do they show an interest in making a variety of types of books?

- Are they starting to add to, delete from, or reorganize their writing?

Use your observations to determine the next umbrella you will teach. You may also consult Suggested Sequence of Lessons (pp. 557–571) for guidance.

EXTENSIONS FOR MAKING QUESTION-AND-ANSWER BOOKS

▶ Provide assistance as children use a computer or other technological tools to make books.

▶ Gather together a guided writing group of several children who need support in a specific area of writing.

▶ When children show an interest in a topic, help them learn more by providing resources and encouraging them to make a question-and-answer book with their newly acquired knowledge.

▶ Teach minilessons from WPS.U4: Learning About Punctuation as needed.

▶ Help children notice text features in nonfiction books and encourage them to try the features in their own writing (e.g., table of contents, captions). If you are using *The Reading Minilessons Book, Grade 1* (Fountas and Pinnell 2019), see LA.U14: Using Text Features to Gain Information.

Section 5 | Drawing

CHILDREN'S ABILITY TO draw recognizable people and objects develops throughout first grade. In these lessons, children learn that details (e.g., intentional use of color or perspective) and the use of specific kinds of images (e.g., photographs or diagrams) convey meaning to their readers.

5	Drawing

Minilessons in This Umbrella

WML1 Draw your face.

WML2 Color your face so it looks like you.

Before Teaching Umbrella 1 Minilessons

This umbrella is designed to teach children how to draw and paint a self-portrait that reflects realistic skin tones, hair, and eye colors. To do this, children can use hand-held mirrors, which help them study their faces up close and also help them realize that the face drawing should fill the space. The goal is to help children draw themselves so that they look real, so they should be encouraged to use ovals and shapes that represent what they see in the mirror. These minilessons can be applied during independent writing or during independent work time, when children might be working in activity centers (pp. 15–16). We recommend that children use a pencil in the first lesson. Once they have completed the sketch of their faces, we suggest you outline the faces with a thin, black marker so children can see the lines when they paint in the second lesson. The self-portraits made in this lesson can be used in IW.7: Writing About Who We Are.

In order to evaluate faces and how they are drawn, children will benefit from looking carefully at the illustrations of characters in a variety of picture books. Choose books with close-ups and facial features that represent a range of diversity. Read books from your own library, or use books from *Fountas & Pinnell Classroom™ Interactive Read-Aloud Collection* text sets. If you are following the *Fountas & Pinnell Classroom™* sequence, children may have not yet been exposed to all of these titles, but the illustrations can be used to provide examples.

The Importance of Friendship

Leon and Bob by Simon James

Mr. George Baker by Amy Hest

Taking Care of Each Other: Family

Max and the Tag-Along Moon by Floyd Cooper

Papá and Me by Arthur Dorros

The Relatives Came by Cynthia Rylant

As you read and enjoy texts together, help children

- study how the illustrator drew faces,
- notice the illustrator's use of color, and
- notice how each face is unique, just like each child's face is unique.

Friendship

Family

WML1

DRW.U1.WML1

Draw your face.

Making a Self-Portrait

You Will Need

- several picture books that show realistic drawings of people, such as the following from Text Set: Taking Care of Each Other: Family:
  - *Max and the Tag-Along Moon* by Floyd Cooper
  - *Papá and Me* by Arthur Dorros
  - *The Relatives Came* by Cynthia Rylant
- hand-held mirrors (one per child or pair)
- chart paper and black marker
- drawing paper

Academic Language/ Important Vocabulary

- draw
- face
- shape
- self-portrait
- skin

Continuum Connection

- Use drawings to represent people, places, things, and ideas (p. 257)
- Create drawings that employ careful attention to color or detail (p. 257)

GOAL

Draw a self-portrait with details (e.g., eyes, nose, mouth, ears, hair, facial expressions).

RATIONALE

When children understand that writers tell stories in a way that is as real as possible, they learn that making realistic drawings of people is one way to make a story seem real. By learning to draw self-portraits, children observe details and identify shapes to make their drawings more representational. They also learn to celebrate the diversity in human features.

ASSESS LEARNING

- Notice whether children draw the main parts of the face (e.g., eyes, nose, mouth, ears, hair) and include more specific facial details (e.g., eyebrows, teeth).
- Observe how children place facial features on the page.
- Look for evidence that children can use vocabulary such as *draw*, *face*, *shape*, *self-portrait*, and *skin*, as well as words to describe face shapes, facial features, and hair.

MINILESSON

Use this lesson to introduce independent writing or independent work time, depending on your class schedule and when you would like children to draw their self-portraits. You might want to draw your portrait on the same paper that children will use so that you can display all the self-portraits together. Here is an sample lesson.

- Begin the self-portrait by using a black marker. Have children use pencil. Color will be added in the next lesson. For now, focus on features and shapes.

  When you draw a picture of yourself, the drawing is called a self-portrait. Let's look at some books to see how illustrators have drawn people.

- Show page 1 from *Max and the Tag-Along Moon*.

  What do you notice about the way these faces are drawn?

- Prompt the conversation to help children focus on facial shape and features. Repeat with *Papá and Me* (pp. 5–6) and *The Relatives Came* (pp. 21–22).

  To draw my self-portrait, I will study my face in a mirror to think about the shape.

- As you look in the mirror, use your finger to outline the outside of your face. Draw your face shape large enough to take up almost all of the space on the paper.

  Is my hair curly or straight? Long or short?

- Using children's suggestions, draw more facial features.

Have a Try

Invite children to look in a mirror and talk to a partner about the shapes they see.

> Turn and talk to your partner about the shapes you see when you look at your face in the mirror.

▶ Invite a few children to share what they observed. Provide assistance with shape words as needed. Ask children to make the shapes they see in the air with their fingers.

Summarize and Apply

Summarize the learning. Remind children to look carefully at the details in their faces.

▶ Write the principle on the chart. Read it to the children.

> Today you will draw your self-portrait. Be sure to use a pencil. You will add color to your drawing later.

▶ Over the next few days, provide time for children to add more detail.

▶ Save the self-portrait for WML2, where you will teach children to add color to their self-portraits.

Draw your face.

Confer

▶ During independent writing or independent work time, move around the room to confer briefly with as many individual children as time allows. Sit side by side with them and invite them to talk about their self-portraits. Use the following prompts as needed.

- *Look in the mirror. What shape is your mouth (eyes, nose)?*
- *What do you notice when you look closely at your eyes? Where will you draw them on the page?*
- *What shape are your eyebrows? How far above your eyes will you draw them?*

Share

Gather children in the meeting area. Ask a few children to share their self-portraits.

> Talk about how you drew your face. What did you think about?

Writing Minilesson Principle
Color your face so it looks like you.

Making a Self-Portrait

You Will Need

- several picture books that show realistic drawings of people with a variety of skin tones, such as the following:

  - *Leon and Bob* by Simon James and *Mr. George Baker* by Amy Hest, from Text Set: The Importance of Friendship

  - *Papá and Me* by Arthur Dorros and *The Relatives Came* by Cynthia Rylant, from Text Set: Taking Care of Each Other: Family

- hand-held mirrors (one per child or pair)

- self-portraits from WML1

- paints or crayons in a wide variety of colors to represent a variety of skin tones

- drawing paper

Academic Language/ Important Vocabulary

- self-portrait
- color
- skin

Continuum Connection

- Create drawings that employ careful attention to color or detail (p. 257)

GOAL

Add realistic color to a self-portrait.

RATIONALE

Using color in drawings makes them more realistic, so encouraging children to use color in a realistic way when making a self-portrait helps them understand this. They learn to observe details and identify color, as well as to celebrate the wide range of unique skin tones that people have, including themselves and classmates.

ASSESS LEARNING

- Notice the colors children choose for their skin, eyes, and hair.

- Look for evidence that children can use vocabulary such as *self-portrait*, *color*, and *skin*, as well as facial feature and hair description words.

MINILESSON

For their self-portraits, children should use the color they see in the mirror, but that does not take away from how they may describe themselves. Use this lesson to introduce independent writing or independent work time, depending on your class schedule and when you would like children to work on their self-portraits. Here is a sample lesson.

> Today you are going to add color to your self-portrait so it looks like you. Look at how some illustrators have added color to drawings of people.

- Show page 22 from *Leon and Bob*.

  > What do you notice about the colors that the illustrator used to draw Leon and Bob?

- Prompt the conversation to help children focus on the color variations. Repeat with *Mr. George Baker* (p. 8), *Papá and Me* (pp. 3–4) and *The Relatives Came* (pp. 17–18).

- Display the self-portrait you created in WML1, along with paints or crayons so that children can see the wide variety of colors. Use a mirror to look at your face.

  > What color is my skin? Which color best matches my face?

- Add color to the face in your self-portrait. Look in the mirror again.

  > What color should I choose for my hair?

- Have a volunteer choose a color. Paint or color the hair on the self-portrait.

- Continue in this way with the remaining features. If using paint, you might wait a day until the face and hair are dry before repeating the process for other features. It may be easiest to use markers or colored pencils for fine facial features, such as eyelashes and eye color.

Have a Try

Invite children to talk to a partner about the colors they see when they look in a mirror.

▶ Provide a hand-held mirror to each pair of children. Have them talk about the colors they see.

When you use colors in your self-portrait, the drawings look more real. Turn and talk to your partner about the colors you see when you look at your face in the mirror.

▶ Invite a few children to share what they observed. Provide assistance with color words as needed.

Summarize and Apply

Summarize the learning and then have children add appropriate colors to their self-portraits.

▶ Write the principle at the top of the chart paper. Read it aloud.

Today you can paint or color your self-portrait. Try to choose a color that closely matches the colors you see in the mirror. Your self-portrait should look like you.

▶ Over the next few days, provide time for children to add more detail and color. After the self-portraits are complete, children may want to outline features such as eyes, nose, mouth, and eyelashes with black marker or to paint a background.

Color your face so it looks like you.

Confer

▶ During independent writing or independent work time, move around the room to confer briefly with individual children. Sit side by side with them and invite them to talk about their self-portraits. Use the following prompts as needed.

- *Look in the mirror. What paint color closely matches your skin (eyes, nose, mouth, hair)?*
- *What color is your hair?*
- *What other colors do you see when you look at your face?*

Share

Gather children in the meeting area. Ask a few children to share their self-portraits.

Today you celebrated all of the unique skin colors in our classroom.

Share your drawing. How did you decide which colors to use in your self-portrait?

Assessment

After you have taught the minilessons in this umbrella, observe children as they draw. Use *The Literacy Continuum* (Fountas and Pinnell 2017) to notice, teach for, and support children's learning as you observe their attempts at drawing and writing.

▶ What evidence do you have that children understand how to make a self-portrait?

- Are children able to name and draw the shapes of their faces?
- Can they select colors that accurately depict the colors of their faces?
- Do they celebrate the diversity they see in facial features and colors?
- Do they understand and use vocabulary such as *draw*, *shape*, *face*, *self-portrait*, and *color*?

▶ In what ways, beyond the scope of this umbrella, are children showing readiness for drawing?

- Are they using realistic shapes to draw bodies and adding clothing that is appropriate for the person they are drawing?
- Could their illustrations use more details?

Use your observations to determine the next umbrella you will teach. You may also consult Suggested Sequence of Lessons (pp. 557–571) for guidance.

EXTENSIONS FOR MAKING A SELF-PORTRAIT

▶ The self-portraits can be used to make a class big book (see IW.7: Writing About Who We Are). As an alternative, you could frame the portraits and hang them on the walls of the classroom.

▶ Continue discussions about shape and color as children draw other people and objects. Help them focus their attention on objects in the world around them and help them notice shapes and colors.

▶ As you read books with children that have illustrations with facial details, have children talk about what decisions the illustrators made when drawing people.

▶ Have conversations about which illustrations look like real people and which do not, helping children identify which techniques make drawings appear more realistic.

Minilessons in This Umbrella

WML1 Use shapes to draw people.

WML2 Draw people in different positions.

WML3 Draw where your story takes place.

WML4 Add color to your picture.

WML5 Make people look the same on every page.

Before Teaching Umbrella 2 Minilessons

Before teaching the minilessons in this umbrella, read and discuss a variety of picture books with different styles of illustrations and provide plenty of opportunities for children to draw and color without restrictions. It will be helpful for you to have taught the first umbrella in this section (Making a Self-Portrait). If you have *The Reading Minilessons Book, Grade 1* (Fountas and Pinnell 2019), consider teaching a minilesson that focuses on the illustrations of a familiar author (see LA.U2: Studying Authors and Illustrators).

Use the following texts from *Fountas & Pinnell Classroom™ Interactive Read-Aloud Collection* text sets, or choose books from the classroom library that show a variety of illustration styles and techniques.

Learning and Working Together: School

Elizabeti's School by Stephanie Stuve-Bodeen

Jamaica's Blue Marker by Juanita Havill

The Importance of Friendship

Leon and Bob by Simon James

Taking Care of Each Other: Family

When I Am Old with You by Angela Johnson

Using Numbers: Books with Counting

Jake's 100th Day of School by Lester L. Laminack

As you read and enjoy these texts together, help children

- notice and talk about the illustrations,
- share what they notice about the characters,
- notice details in the background,
- notice the illusion of sound and motion, and
- talk about the colors in the illustrations.

School

Friendship

Family

Using Numbers

Section 5: Drawing

Learning to Draw

You Will Need

▸ a familiar book with illustrations of people that can be easily broken down into shapes, such as *Elizabeti's School* by Stephanie Stuve-Bodeen, from Text Set: Learning and Working Together: School

▸ tracing paper, pencils, and a document camera or overhead transparencies and markers

Academic Language/ Important Vocabulary

▸ draw

▸ shape

▸ oval

▸ rectangle

▸ triangle

Continuum Connection

▸ Use drawings to represent people, places, things, and ideas (p. 257)

GOAL

Understand that shapes can be used to draw people.

RATIONALE

By teaching children a way to draw people, you help them draw more easily and more representationally. Helping children draw more easily will assist them in getting more of their ideas onto paper. Helping children draw representationally will help them get more details into their drawings and therefore into their writing.

ASSESS LEARNING

▸ Look for evidence that children are using shapes to draw people.

▸ Notice how children are trying to make their drawings of people look real.

▸ Look for evidence that they understand and can use vocabulary such as *draw* and *shape*, as well as the names of specific shapes.

MINILESSON

Use a mentor text to engage children in a conversation about drawings of people. Select examples that show people facing front. Then model how to use shapes to draw people. Here is an example.

▸ Show page 18 of *Elizabeti's School*.

> What shapes make up Elizabeti's and Pendo's body parts?

▸ Using your finger to trace over the body parts, show how the body can be broken down into oval shapes for the head, torso, upper arms, lower arms, and legs and into circles for the hands. Then quickly sketch the shapes.

> What do you notice about what I have drawn?

▸ Guide children to recognize that you have drawn the basic shapes only, without clothes. Point out that Pendo is taller, so you drew her body with taller shapes.

▸ Have children look at page 18 to discuss the girls' clothing.

> The characters need to have clothes. What shapes do you see?

> Watch as I add their clothes.

▸ Add a piece of tracing paper (or an overhead transparency) on top of the body-part shapes so that they show through. Ask the children for guidance as to what shapes to draw for the clothing (triangle, square, rectangle).

> What else has to be added?

▸ Show how you can smooth out the ovals by tracing along the outer edges to make the limbs. Finish the drawing by adding facial features, hair, hands, and feet.

Have a Try

Invite children to talk to a partner about drawing people.

> Think about the way we drew these characters from *Elizabeti's School*. You can draw any person using shapes. Think about a person or some people you might like to draw. Turn and talk about how you might do that.

Summarize and Apply

Help children summarize the learning and remind them to use shapes when they draw people.

> How can you draw people?

▶ Write the principle at the top of the chart.

> Today during writing time, you will draw a person. Remember to use shapes, like ovals, rectangles, and triangles, in your drawings.

▶ If children in your class are ready, you can show them how they can draw the shapes lightly with pencil and then erase the marks after the clothes are drawn. Otherwise, they can make a finished drawing by placing a piece of tracing paper over the drawing with shapes and use the shapes as a guide.

Use shapes to draw people.

Confer

▶ During independent writing, move around the room to confer briefly with as many individual children as time allows. Sit side by side with them and invite them to talk about their drawings of people. For reference, provide children with a selection of realistic fiction books with detailed illustrations or provide photographs of people. Use prompts such as the following to support children as they draw.

- *Look closely at the illustration (photo). What body shapes do you see?*
- *What shapes do you see in the clothing?*
- *How can you use those shapes in your drawing?*

Share

Following independent writing, gather children in the meeting area to share their drawings.

> Who would like to talk about how you drew a person in your book?

Learning to Draw

You Will Need

- a book with illustrations of people in various positions, such as *Jake's 100th Day of School* by Lester L. Laminack, from Text Set: Using Numbers: Books with Counting

- tracing paper, pencils, and a document camera or overhead transparencies and markers

Academic Language/ Important Vocabulary

- draw
- shape
- position
- oval

Continuum Connection

- Use drawings to represent people, places, things, and ideas (p. 257)

GOAL

Understand that shapes can be placed so as to draw people in different positions.

RATIONALE

Once children understand how to draw people using shapes, they can be taught to place the shapes to depict people in different positions. When children understand this principle, they can draw their stories' characters engaged in any activity or scenario.

ASSESS LEARNING

- Look for evidence that children understand the idea of drawing people in different positions.

- Notice whether children make people recognizable even when they are drawn in different positions.

- Look for evidence that children can use vocabulary such as *draw*, *shape*, *position*, and *oval*.

MINILESSON

Use a mentor text to engage children in an inquiry around drawings of people in different positions and then demonstrate how to use shapes to draw people in these positions. Here is an example.

- Show the cover of *Jake's 100th Day of School*. Turn to page 3 and show the illustration.

  What do you notice about how the illustrator draws people?

  How do you think the illustrator drew the people standing and walking like this?

- Show the illustrations on pages 19–20 and 23–24.

  What do you notice about how the illustrator draws kids?

  You learned how to draw people using shapes, like ovals. You can put the shapes in different places to draw people in different positions.

- Return to page 3 and begin drawing the girl at the front left of the page who is walking but turning to talk to a friend. Start with the head and use ovals for body parts. Explain the positioning of each oval you draw.

- After you draw the shapes, use children's suggestions to finish the drawing on a piece of tracing paper or an overhead transparency attached over the shape drawing.

Have a Try

Invite children to talk to a partner about how to draw another position.

▶ Ask a volunteer to sit (in a chair or cross legged on the floor) in front of the class.

Turn and talk about the shapes you see.

Summarize and Apply

Help children summarize the learning and remind children to draw people in different positions.

What did you learn today about drawing people?

▶ Write the principle at the top of the chart.

Today during writing time, try drawing the same person in two different positions.

Draw people in different positions.

Confer

▶ During independent writing, move around the room to confer briefly with as many individual children as time allows. Sit side by side with them and invite them to talk about the people they are drawing in their books. If possible, provide children with a selection of books or photographs that show people in different positions. Use prompts such as the following to support children as they draw.

· *What do you notice about how the person is standing? What is he doing with his legs?*

· *Where should you put the ovals for the person's legs?*

· *Which way should this oval point? Try to make the leg point in the same direction as the leg in the picture.*

Share

Following independent writing, gather children in the meeting area to share their drawings.

Who would like to show a drawing of a person that you made today?

Tell about what you were thinking as you drew the picture.

Learning to Draw

You Will Need

- several familiar books with detailed backgrounds, such as the following:
  - *Jamaica's Blue Marker* by Juanita Havill, from Text Set: Learning and Working Together: School
  - *When I Am Old with You* by Angela Johnson, from Text Set: Taking Care of Each Other: Family
- chart paper
- black marker
- To download the following online resource for this lesson, visit **resources.fountasandpinnell.com**:
  - chart art (optional)

Academic Language/ Important Vocabulary

- draw
- picture
- take place
- background
- detail

Continuum Connection

- Use drawings to represent people, places, things, and ideas (p. 257)
- Create drawings that are related to the written text and increase readers' understanding and enjoyment (p. 257)

GOAL

Understand that the background in a picture helps the reader understand the story.

RATIONALE

When you draw children's attention to the information that they can learn from the background of an illustration, you help them understand that they, too, can give such information in their own drawings.

ASSESS LEARNING

- Look for evidence of understanding that the background of an illustration has important details.
- Notice children's drawings to see whether they include story information in their backgrounds.
- Look for evidence that children can use vocabulary such as *draw*, *picture*, *take place*, *background*, and *detail*.

MINILESSON

Use texts with backgrounds in the illustrations to engage children in a discussion about what can be learned from an illustration's background, and model drawing a background. Here is an example.

- Show pages 19, 21, and 23 of *Jamaica's Blue Marker*.

  Where does this story take place?

  How can you tell?

- Help children understand that the illustrator shows that the story takes place in a classroom and that it is autumn (October). Guide the conversation to help them notice that on each page the details are related, so the reader knows that the story takes place at the same time period in the same place.

- Show page 5 of *When I Am Old with You*.

  What information does the illustrator show in the background?

  What shapes does the illustrator use to draw the background?

- Help children recognize that the characters are standing on the shore of a lake, about to go fishing in a boat, and that the sky shows that it is a sunny morning.

Have a Try

Invite children to talk to a partner about the background in *When I Am Old with You.*

> Turn and talk about the way the illustrator drew the background. Tell your partner what parts of the picture you think are most important and why you think the illustrator drew them.

▶ After discussion, ask volunteers to share. As they do, sketch the background on chart paper with a black marker. Begin with the basic shapes for the people. Then guide children to focus first on the shapes and the placement of the background on the page before moving on to details.

▶ Save the chart. Color will be added in WML4.

Summarize and Apply

Summarize the learning and remind children to think about the background when they draw.

▶ Write the principle at the top of the chart.

> Today you learned that the background gives the reader information. During writing time, think about what to draw in the background of your pictures.

▶ If the children need more guidance before drawing backgrounds on their own, you might repeat the activity by asking a volunteer to suggest a background for a book he is making. Show children how to choose the most important details and how to sketch them.

Draw where your story takes place.

Confer

▶ During independent writing, move around the room to confer briefly with as many individual children as time allows. Sit side by side with them and invite them to talk about how they are drawing the setting in their books. Use prompts such as the following.

- *Close your eyes and imagine where the story takes place. What do you see?*
- *What can you draw in the background to show where and when the story happens?*

Share

Following independent writing, gather children in the meeting area to share their drawings.

> Who would like to share a picture you drew today? Tell about the background.

Learning to Draw

You Will Need

- several books with colorful illustrations of people and backgrounds, such as the following:
  - *Leon and Bob* by Simon James, from Text Set: The Importance of Friendship
  - *Jamaica's Blue Marker* by Juanita Havill, from Text Set: Learning and Working Together: School
  - *When I Am Old with You* by Angela Johnson, from Text Set: Taking Care of Each Other: Family
- the black line sketch from WML3
- markers, crayons, or paints of different colors (including representations of different skin tones)

Academic Language/ Important Vocabulary

- drawing
- color
- illustration
- illustrator

Continuum Connection

- Create drawings that employ careful attention to color or detail (p. 257)

GOAL

Understand that color in pictures helps the reader understand more about the story.

RATIONALE

As children study the illustrations in the books you share with them, they begin to notice that illustrators use color intentionally. When you talk with them about how illustrators use color, children learn that they can use color in similar ways in their own drawings.

ASSESS LEARNING

- Observe how children use color in their drawings.
- Look for evidence that they can use vocabulary such as *drawing, color, illustration,* and *illustrator,* as well as the names of specific colors.

MINILESSON

Use mentor texts to engage children in an inquiry around color and then demonstrate adding color to a drawing. Here is an example.

- Show page 22 of *Leon and Bob*.

  What do you notice about the colors in this illustration?

  Why do you think the illustrator used so many different colors on this page?

- Show pages 24–25 of *Jamaica's Blue Marker* next to the page from *Leon and Bob*.

  What do you notice about the colors on these pages from *Jamaica's Blue Marker*?

  How did these two different illustrators use color in the same way in these drawings? in different ways?

- Support a conversation about color choice in skin tone, hair, clothing, and background.

  When you choose colors to match the way people and things actually look, your drawings look real.

- Display the black line drawing that was created in WML3.

  To make this illustration look real, it needs some color. What color should I begin with?

- With children's input, add color to the illustration, including skin, clothing, and background. You may decide to show the original illustration on page 5 of *When I Am Old with You* and use similar colors, or you may decide to let children choose colors without looking at the original drawing.

Have a Try

Invite children to talk to a partner about what colors they will use for an illustration.

> **What colors will you add to a drawing you are working on? Turn and talk to your partner about your ideas.**

> ▶ After children turn and talk, invite a few children to share their ideas.

Summarize and Apply

Write the principle at the top of the chart. Read it to children. Summarize the learning and remind children to think about color when they draw.

> **Today during writing time, you will have a chance to work on your books. As you draw pictures for your books, remember to think carefully about what colors to use.**

Add color to your picture.

Confer

> ▶ During independent writing, move around the room to confer briefly with as many individual children as time allows. Sit side by side with them and invite them to talk about adding color to the drawings in their books. Use prompts such as the following.
> - *Why did you choose that color?*
> - *What color(s) would make that look real?*
> - *What colors will you choose to show the time of day (time of year)?*

Share

Following independent writing, gather children in the meeting area to talk about the colors they used in their drawings.

> **Who would like to share a picture you made today?**

> **Tell about the colors in your picture. Why did you choose those colors?**

Learning to Draw

You Will Need

- a familiar book with illustrations of human characters, such as *When I Am Old with You* by Angela Johnson, from Text Set: Taking Care of Each Other: Family
- chart paper
- markers, crayons, or paints of different colors

Academic Language/ Important Vocabulary

- people
- character
- page
- same
- illustration
- illustrator

Continuum Connection

- Use drawings to represent people, places, things, and ideas (p. 257)
- Create drawings that employ careful attention to color or detail (p. 257)

GOAL

Understand that it is important to draw people consistently on every page.

RATIONALE

When characters are drawn consistently throughout a book, readers recognize the characters and are better able to follow the story. When children notice that illustrators draw people consistently, they learn to do the same thing in their own books.

ASSESS LEARNING

- Observe whether children understand the importance of consistency in illustrations.
- Notice whether children draw characters consistently throughout their books.
- Look for evidence that children can use vocabulary such as *people*, *character*, *page*, *same*, *illustration*, and *illustrator*.

MINILESSON

Use a mentor text to engage children in a discussion about drawing people consistently. Then demonstrate doing so. Here is an example.

- Show page 1 of *When I Am Old with You*.

    Who are these people? Look closely at how they are drawn.

- Turn to the last page and point to the boy and his grandfather.

    How do you know who these people are?

    What clues show that this story begins and ends on the same day and in the same place?

- Help children see the consistency in the way the characters, clothing, and backgrounds are drawn throughout the book. Guide them to notice that the characters in their rockers now have on hats and jackets because they have been for a walk.

- Show several pages of the book and have children talk about similarities and differences in how the characters look.

    How do you know the people from page to page are the same characters?

- Begin a simple sketch of a person.

    I'm going to draw a person.

Have a Try

Invite children to talk to a partner about consistency in drawings.

> Now I'm going to draw the same person again, but I'm going to change the drawing a little bit. Let's say that later the same day the weather got cooler. What should stay the same and what might be different?

▶ After children turn and talk, ask a few volunteers to share ideas. Choose a simple way to show how the drawing can show the same person at a different time and the person can still be recognized.

Summarize and Apply

Write the principle at the top of the chart to summarize the learning. Remind children to make people look the same on every page.

> Today you learned that people should look the same on every page. When you work on the drawings in your book today, remember to make people look the same on every page.

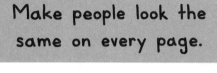

Make people look the same on every page.

Confer

▶ During independent writing, move around the room to confer briefly with as many individual children as time allows. Sit side by side with them and invite them to talk about their drawings. Use prompts such as the following to support children in drawing people consistently on every page of their books.

- *Who are you drawing on this page? Have you drawn this person before?*
- *How will you make this person look the same on every page?*
- *What will you add on the next page to show that it is the same (a different) time of day?*

Share

Following independent writing, gather children in the meeting area to share their drawings.

> Share two pages of your book that have a person who looks the same on both pages.

Assessment

After you have taught the minilessons in this umbrella, observe children as they illustrate their books. Use the behaviors and understandings in *The Literacy Continuum* (Fountas and Pinnell 2017) to notice, teach for, and support children's learning as you observe their attempts at drawing and writing.

▶ What evidence do you have of new understandings children have developed related to drawing?

- Do children notice and use shapes to draw people?

- Are they attempting to draw people in different positions?

- Do they pay attention to how they draw a character throughout a story?

- How well do the backgrounds show where the action is taking place?

- Do children purposefully choose colors to use?

- Do they understand and use vocabulary related to drawing, such as *draw*, *shape*, *color*, *face*, and *background*?

▶ In what ways, beyond the scope of this umbrella, are children drawing?

- Do they know how to find and use drawing and writing tools?

- What kind of detail do they include in their illustrations?

Use your observations to determine the next umbrella you will teach. You may also consult Suggested Sequence of Lessons (pp. 557–571) for guidance.

EXTENSIONS FOR LEARNING TO DRAW

▶ Talk with children about the details they could add to their illustrations to show more about where the story takes place. Encourage children to study the background illustrations in books for ideas.

▶ Have children draw people from the back. Ask a child to model walking away and then have children talk about what they notice before trying to draw a person on paper.

▶ During interactive read-aloud, invite children to notice the background. Talk about how the illustrator had to make decisions about the background—how much to show, what colors to use, how far away things should look, and so forth.

▶ Talk with children about how to use lines to show sound and motion in their drawings.

▶ As you and the children look at picture books, study the illustrations and talk about how illustrators use color. Is it to show things realistically? to convey a mood? to symbolize something in the story?

Minilessons in This Umbrella

WML1   Use colors to show a feeling.

WML2   Draw motion or sound lines to show something moving or making noise.

WML3   Add details to your drawings to give information.

WML4   Draw things big to make them look close and small to make them look far away.

Before Teaching Umbrella 3 Minilessons

In addition to the minilessons in this umbrella, there are other lessons that support children when they draw illustrations. WPS.U4: Adding Information to Your Writing discusses adding details to drawings, giving children a foundation for revising and adding to their work. CFT.U3.WML2 is a general inquiry lesson discussing the decisions that illustrators make.

Give children plenty of opportunities to write and draw freely and to make their own books. Read and discuss enjoyable books with detailed and informative illustrations. Use the following texts from *Fountas & Pinnell Classroom™ Interactive Read-Aloud Collection*, or choose books from the classroom library that the children will enjoy.

Nicola Davies

Journeys

Bob Graham: Exploring Everyday Life

How to Heal a Broken Wing

The Silver Button

"Let's Get a Pup!" Said Kate

Nicola Davies: Exploring the Animal World

Bat Loves the Night

Journeys Near and Far

Dear Juno by Soyung Pak

As you read and enjoy these texts together, help children notice

- how illustrators use color to show feelings,
- the specific details illustrators put into illustrations to support the story, and
- how illustrators make things look close or far away.

Section 5: Drawing

WML1

Writing Minilesson Principle
Use colors to show a feeling.

Adding Meaningful Details to Illustrations

You Will Need

- several texts with illustrations that convey feelings, such as the following from Text Set: Bob Graham: Exploring Everyday Life:
  - *How to Heal a Broken Wing* by Bob Graham
  - *The Silver Button* by Bob Graham
- chart prepared in advance with book titles
- a brief mentor text written in advance (see Have a Try in CFT.U1.WML1 or write a new text)
- markers and tape
- yellow crayons or colored pencils

Academic Language / Important Vocabulary

- feeling
- color
- illustration

Continuum Connection

- Create drawings that employ careful attention to color or detail (p. 257)
- Create drawings that are related to the written text and increase readers' understanding and enjoyment (p. 257)
- Add or remove details to drawings to revise information (p. 257)

GOAL

Add colors to drawings to convey a certain tone or feeling to the pictures.

RATIONALE

When children notice that colors can be used in illustrations to show feelings and help the reader gain deeper understanding of the story, they can begin to try this in their own illustrations.

ASSESS LEARNING

- Observe whether children recognize that color can be used to show a feeling.
- Notice children's use of color to represent a feeling in their own illustrations.
- Observe for evidence that children can use vocabulary such as *feeling*, *color*, and *illustration*.

MINILESSON

To help children think about the minilesson principle, use familiar texts to engage them in noticing how color can be used in an illustration to show a feeling. Here is an example.

- Show the cover of *How to Heal a Broken Wing*. Read and show pages 1–2.

  What do you notice about the colors the illustrator used here?

  Why do you think he used those colors? What kind of feeling do you get?

- Add noticings to the chart. Repeat this process with pages 31–32.

  When you read, notice the colors in the illustrations. Sometimes they are used to tell you more about how characters are feeling. You can use colors to show a feeling when you make books, too.

- Repeat this process with *The Silver Button*, using the page with the soldier hugging his mom, and the page with the mom holding her new baby.

Have a Try

Use a mentor text (e.g., the text from CFT.U1.WML1) to model thinking about how to add color to an illustration to show a feeling.

▶ Show and discuss with the children what is happening on a page in the book you wrote. Invite children to turn and talk to a partner about the color(s) that might represent an appropriate feeling.

> How would you feel about going to get some ice cream?

> If you felt happy or excited, what splash of color(s) might help readers understand those feelings?

Summarize and Apply

Write the principle at the top of the chart to summarize the learning. Remind children to use color to show a feeling in the books they make.

> What did you notice about how color can be used in illustrations?

> Today, reread a story you have written or are working on. Think about how you or the other people in your story feel. Add some color to the illustrations to show that feeling and help your reader understand more. Think about this as you begin new books, too. Bring your writing to share when we meet later.

Use colors to show a feeling.

Colors	How Colors Can Make You Feel	
Gray	• sad • not caring	☹
Yellow Pink Orange	• hopeful • caring • excited • happy	☹ ☺ ☺
White	• happy • hopeful	☺

Confer

▶ During independent writing, move around the room to confer briefly with as many individual children as time allows. Sit side by side with them and invite them to talk about the colors in their illustrations. Use prompts such as the following to support children as needed.

- *What color would help your reader know what you were feeling?*
- *What color are you thinking of adding to your illustration? What feeling will that show to your reader?*

Share

Following independent writing, gather children in the meeting area to share their illustrations with a partner. Then choose several children to share with the group.

> What color did you use to show that feeling?

Writing Minilesson Principle
Draw motion or sound lines to show something moving or making noise.

Adding Meaningful Details to Illustrations

You Will Need

- several texts with illustrations that convey motion and/or sound, such as the following:
  - *"Let's Get a Pup!" Said Kate* and *The Silver Button* by Bob Graham, from Text Set: Bob Graham: Exploring Everyday Life
  - *Bat Loves the Night* by Nicola Davies, from Text Set: Nicola Davies: Exploring the Animal World
- two labeled sticky notes: *Motion Lines* and *Sound Lines*
- chart paper and markers
- To download the following online resource for this lesson, visit **resources.fountasandpinnell.com**:
  - chart art (optional)

Academic Language / Important Vocabulary

- motion lines
- sound lines
- information

Continuum Connection

- Create drawings that employ careful attention to color or detail (p. 257)
- Create drawings that are related to the written text and increase readers' understanding and enjoyment (p. 257)
- Add or remove details to drawings to revise information (p. 257)

GOAL

Add motion or sound lines to show something moving or making noise in a picture.

RATIONALE

When children notice how lines are used in illustrations to indicate motion and sound, they will understand how this technique helps them to enjoy stories more and gain a deeper understanding of the stories. They can then begin to try this in their own illustrations.

ASSESS LEARNING

- Observe whether children recognize that lines can be used to show movement or sound.
- Notice children's use of lines to represent something in their own illustrations moving or making a sound.
- Observe for evidence that children can use vocabulary such as *motion lines*, *sound lines*, and *information*.

MINILESSON

To help children think about the minilesson principle, use familiar texts to engage them in noticing how lines can be used in an illustration to indicate motion or sound. Here is an example.

- Show *"Let's Get a Pup!" Said Kate*. Display and read the two-page spread that begins "Dave was so excited" and the following two-page spread.

  What do you notice about the illustrations?

  Why do you think the illustrator placed those small lines in the illustrations? What do those lines tell you?

- Add a simple drawing to the chart to illustrate motion lines. Invite a child to add the sticky note labeled *Motion Lines*.

Have a Try

Repeat the process with the children, using an example of sound lines from *Bat Loves the Night*. Invite children to turn and talk to a partner about what the lines mean.

▶ Show page 14 and read the italic print. After children turn and talk, add noticings to the chart.

> **What do you notice about this illustration? Why did the illustrator do that?**

> **The curved lines are sound lines. They tell you the bat is making a noise.**

▶ Add a simple illustration to the chart. Invite a child to add the sticky note labeled *Sound Lines*.

Summarize and Apply

Summarize the learning and remind children that they can use sound and motion lines in their own books.

> **What did you notice about how illustrators show movement and sound?**

▶ Write the principle at the top of the chart.

> **As you work on a book today, look for a place to use motion lines or sound lines. Bring your writing to share when we meet later.**

Confer

▶ During independent writing, move around the room to confer briefly with as many individual children as time allows. Sit side by side with them and invite them to talk about how they have shown (or could show) motion and sound in their drawings. Use prompts such as the following as needed.

- *Read your story aloud. Who or what is moving in this part of the story? How can you add motion lines to help the reader understand that?*

- *Read your story aloud. What sounds do you hear in this part of the story? How can you add sound lines to help the reader understand that?*

Share

Following independent writing, gather children in the meeting area with their writing. Invite several children to share their illustrations.

> **How did you use motion or sound lines in your drawings?**

WML3
DRW.U3.WML3

Writing Minilesson Principle
Add details to your drawings to give information.

Adding Meaningful Details to Illustrations

You Will Need

- several texts with detailed illustrations, such as the following:
  - *Dear Juno* by Soyung Pak, from Text Set: Journeys Near and Far
  - *"Let's Get a Pup!" Said Kate* and *The Silver Button* by Bob Graham, from Text Set: Bob Graham: Exploring Everyday Life
- chart prepared in advance with book titles
- markers
- four sticky notes, three labeled *Place* and one labeled *People*

Academic Language / Important Vocabulary

- details
- information

Continuum Connection

- Create drawings that employ careful attention to color or detail (p. 257)
- Create drawings that are related to the written text and increase readers' understanding and enjoyment (p. 257)
- Add or remove details to drawings to revise information (p. 257)

GOAL

Add details to your drawings to give information about the people or the places in the story.

RATIONALE

When children notice details in illustrations, they begin to understand how these details help them to enjoy stories more and gain a deeper understanding of the story. They can then begin to try this in their own illustrations.

ASSESS LEARNING

- Observe for evidence that children recognize that details in drawings give information about the people or places in the story.
- Notice children's use of details in their own illustrations.
- Observe for evidence that children can use vocabulary such as *details* and *information*.

MINILESSON

To help children think about the minilesson principle, use familiar texts to engage them in noticing how details can be used in an illustration to show more about people or places. Here is an example.

- Show the cover of *Dear Juno* and the illustration on page 21. Add responses to the chart paper.

  What details do you notice about the illustration?

  What do the details tell you?

  These details clearly show that the people are in the family room.

- Repeat this process with the illustration of Juno outside by his mailbox on pages 25–26.

- Repeat this process with *"Let's Get a Pup!" Said Kate*, using the page where the family is in the kitchen.

- Repeat this process with *The Silver Button*, using the page with the woman wearing a tracksuit and pushing a stroller.

  What do you notice the illustrator included to help you know more about this person?

  Illustrators think carefully about how to draw the illustrations so that the readers will understand the story. When you draw your illustrations, think about details that will help your reader understand what you are writing about.

Have a Try

Use sticky notes to label the *Place* and *People* examples on the chart.

> Some of the details you noticed tell you more about places in the story and some tell you more about people in the story. Turn and talk to your partner. Which details tell you about people and which about places?

▶ After children turn and talk, place a sticky note that says *Place* on the chart next to the place examples. Do the same for *People*.

Summarize and Apply

Write the principle at the top of the chart to summarize the learning. Remind children to use details in their own books.

> What did you notice about how illustrators use details in their drawings?

> Today, look at the illustrations in a book you have written or are working on. Think of some details you could add to help your readers understand more about your story or topic. Bring your writing to share when we meet later.

Add details to your drawings to give information.

Details	What the Details Tell You	What the Details Describe
Furniture Rug	The people are in the family room.	Place
Warm hat Mailbox Leaves falling	The boy is outside.	Place
Table and chairs Plates and bowls Toaster	The family is in the kitchen.	Place
Sweatband Sneakers Tracksuit	The woman is a jogger.	People

Confer

▶ During independent writing, move around the room to confer briefly with as many individual children as time allows. Sit side by side with them and invite them to talk about adding details to their drawing and writing. Use the following prompts as needed.

- *Read your story aloud. Talk about a person (place) in your story. How can you add details to help your reader understand more about this person (place)?*
- *Where are you thinking of adding details to your illustration? What will they help your reader understand better?*

Share

Following independent writing, gather children in the meeting area with their writing. Invite several children to share their illustrations.

> What details did you use in your drawings? What do they help your reader understand better about the people or places?

Writing Minilesson Principle

Draw things big to make them look close and small to make them look far away.

Adding Meaningful Details to Illustrations

You Will Need

- several texts with illustrations that show perspective, such as the following:
  - *Bat Loves the Night* by Nicola Davies, from Text Set: Nicola Davies: Exploring the Animal World
  - *How to Heal a Broken Wing* and *The Silver Button* by Bob Graham, from Text Set: Bob Graham: Exploring Everyday Life
- chart prepared in advance with book titles
- markers

Academic Language / Important Vocabulary

- illustration
- illustrator
- details

Continuum Connection

- Create drawings that employ careful attention to color or detail (p. 257)
- Create drawings that are related to the written text and increase readers' understanding and enjoyment (p. 257)
- Add or remove details to drawings to revise information (p. 257)

GOAL

Draw things big to make them look close and small to make them look far away.

RATIONALE

Perspective in an illustration can add a new dimension to the story: objects that are large and close tell the reader to pay attention; small objects far away may tell the reader how the object fits into a bigger landscape. As children begin to understand these concepts they can try these techniques in their own illustrations.

ASSESS LEARNING

- Observe whether children recognize that drawing objects big makes them look close and drawing them small makes them look far away.
- Notice children's use of perspective in their own illustrations.
- Observe for evidence that children can use vocabulary such as *illustration*, *illustrator*, and *details*.

MINILESSON

To help children understand the minilesson principle, use familiar texts to engage them in noticing how objects can be drawn to look close or far away and discussing what this helps them understand better about the story. Here is an example.

- Show *Bat Loves the Night*. Turn to page 10.

  Look closely. What do you notice about how the illustrator drew the bat?

  The bat is very small. What does that tell you about where the bat is?

  The bat looks like it is very far away, way up in the sky.

- Repeat this process with pages 1–2 of *How to Heal a Broken Wing*.

  The bird is almost hard to find in this picture! Why do you think the bird looks so small here?

- Repeat this process with page 3.

  How did the illustrator draw the bird this time? What does that tell you?

Have a Try

Use an ordinary classroom object to illustrate how things look larger when they are close and smaller when they are far away.

> ❱ Display an object, such as a marker, close to the children. Then ask a child to display it farther away.
>
>> What do you notice about how the size of the marker looked as _____ moved it across the classroom?
>>
>> When illustrators want an object to appear close, they draw it larger, and when they want it to appear far away, they draw it smaller, like the bat.

Summarize and Apply

Help children summarize the learning. Remind children to think about how they can use perspective.

> What did you learn about illustrations?

> ❱ Write the principle on the chart.
>
>> Today, look at the illustrations in a book you are working on. Make them larger or smaller to help your reader understand more. Bring your writing to share when we meet later.

Draw things big to make them look close and small to make them look far away.

The bat is small. It looks far away.

The marker is big. It looks close.

Confer

> ❱ During independent writing, move around the room to confer briefly with as many individual children as time allows. Sit side by side with them and invite them to talk about perspective in their drawings. Use prompts such as the following as needed.
>
> - *Talk about the story you are writing. What illustrations will you draw for this part of the story? Which of those do you want to seem close to the reader? Draw that large.*
> - *Which part of the illustrations do you want to seem far away from the reader? Draw that small.*
> - *Look at this part of your drawing. Is it close or far away?*

Share

Following independent writing, gather children in the meeting area to share their illustrations with the class.

> How did you make the size of an object tell us more about it?

Section 5: Drawing

Assessment

After you have taught the minilessons in this umbrella, observe children as they draw, write, and talk about their writing. Use the behaviors and understandings in *The Literacy Continuum* (Fountas and Pinnell 2017) to notice, teach for, and support children's learning as you observe their attempts at drawing and writing.

▶ What evidence do you have of new understandings children have developed related to adding meaningful details to illustrations?

- Do children use colors to convey a certain tone or feeling?
- Do they use motion or sound lines to show something moving or making noise?
- What kinds of details do they add to give information about the people or the places in the story?
- Do they use size to show things in perspective?
- Do they notice and use vocabulary such as *feeling*, *color*, *illustration*, *motion*, *sound*, *information*, *illustrator*, and *details*?

▶ In what other ways, beyond the scope of this umbrella, are the children showing an interest in adding meaningful details to illustrations?

- Do they use details when they illustrate nonfiction?
- Are they using speech and thought bubbles?

Use your observations to determine what you will teach next. You may also consult Suggested Sequence of Lessons (pp. 557–571) for guidance.

EXTENSIONS FOR ADDING MEANINGFUL DETAILS TO ILLUSTRATIONS

▶ Use mentor texts to explore how colors change from one page to the next to indicate a change in feeling or the tone of a story.

▶ Makes copies of children's illustrations that use motion or sound lines or that use perspective (these illustrative principles do not require color). Make a display of children's samples as mentor texts to build ownership.

▶ As children write about books they have read, encourage them to think about the specific details they will include about the books in their illustrations.

▶ Gather together a guided writing group of several children who need support in a specific area of writing, such as adding details to their illustrations.

Minilessons in This Umbrella

WML1   Use photographs in your nonfiction book.

WML2   Look at pictures in books and try to include some of the same details.

WML3   Draw diagrams to give information.

Before Teaching Umbrella 4 Minilessons

Read aloud a variety of engaging illustrated nonfiction books about different topics and give children plenty of opportunities to experiment with creating their own nonfiction books. For mentor texts, choose nonfiction books that include photographs, diagrams, and different styles of illustration. Use the following books from *Fountas & Pinnell Classroom™ Interactive Read-Aloud Collection* and interactive writing lessons, or choose nonfiction books from the classroom library.

Interactive Read-Aloud Collection

Exploring Nonfiction

Tools by Ann Morris

What Do You Do When Something Wants to Eat You? by Steve Jenkins

Water: Up, Down, and All Around by Natalie M. Rosinsky

Surprising Sharks by Nicola Davies

As you read and enjoy these texts together, help children

- notice whether each book has photographs or illustrations,
- look closely at the pictures and share details that they notice,
- notice and understand diagrams, and
- discuss how the images help them better understand the book's topic.

Interactive Read-Aloud
Exploring Nonfiction

Section 5: Drawing

Writing Minilesson Principle
Use photographs in your nonfiction book.

Illustrating Nonfiction

You Will Need

- a familiar nonfiction book with photographs, such as *Tools* by Ann Morris, from Text Set: Exploring Nonfiction

- a page from a nonfiction book or chart paper prepared with a photograph and text; cover the photograph

- a collection of other photographs (e.g., taken yourself, printed from the internet, or cut out from magazines)

- marker

Academic Language/ Important Vocabulary

- nonfiction
- photograph
- author

Continuum Connection

- Understand that a writer of a factual text uses words and illustrations to make it interesting to readers (p. 251)

- Understand that writers of nonfiction texts have many ways to show facts: e.g., labels, drawings, photos (p. 251)

- Begin to incorporate illustrations and organizational tools in nonfiction texts: e.g., drawing or photograph with caption or label, map, diagram; table of contents, heading, sidebar (p. 254)

GOAL

Understand that photographs make books interesting and help readers understand more about a topic.

RATIONALE

When children understand why and how authors use photographs in nonfiction books, they learn to study them for details and begin to use them in their own books.

ASSESS LEARNING

- Observe for evidence that children understand the difference between a drawing and a photograph.

- Look for evidence that children understand that the photographs in a nonfiction book provide information about the topic.

- Notice evidence that children can use vocabulary such as *nonfiction*, *photograph*, and *author*.

MINILESSON

To help children think about the minilesson principle, use mentor texts to demonstrate the use of photographs in nonfiction books. Here is an example.

- Display the cover of *Tools* and read the title. Show several pages.

  This nonfiction book has lots of pictures. What do you notice about the pictures in this book? How were they made?

  This book has photographs. Some nonfiction books have drawings, and some have photographs. How are a drawing and a photograph different?

  Why do you think Ann Morris decided to use photographs in her book?

  What do the photographs in this book help you understand?

  Authors use photographs in nonfiction books to help you learn more about the topic of the book. You can use photographs in your books, too.

Have a Try

Invite children to talk to a partner about a photograph in a nonfiction book.

▶ Show a page from a nonfiction book (or one that you have prepared on chart paper). Make sure the photograph is covered. Read the text aloud.

> There is a photograph under this piece of paper. What might it show? Turn and talk to your partner about what you are thinking.

▶ After children turn and talk, invite a few children to share their predictions. Reveal the photograph and talk about how the photograph helps the reader understand the sentence.

Summarize and Apply

Help children summarize the learning. Remind them to use photographs in nonfiction books.

> Why do authors sometimes use photographs in nonfiction books?

▶ Write the principle at the top of the chart. Read it aloud.

> Today during writing time, work on a nonfiction book that you have already started or start a new one. Look to see if there is a page that could use a photograph. Bring your writing to share when we meet later.

Use photographs in your nonfiction book.

People use tools to make food.

Confer

▶ During independent writing, move around the room to confer briefly with as many individual children as time allows. Sit side by side with them and invite them to talk about using photographs in their nonfiction books. Use prompts such as the following if needed.

- *Would a photograph help readers learn more about your topic? What should the photograph show?*

- *Why did you choose that photograph?*

- *How will the photograph you chose help readers learn about _____?*

Share

Following independent writing, gather children in the meeting area.

> Raise your hand if you would like to share a photograph in your nonfiction book.

WML2
DRW.U4.WML2

Look at pictures in books and try to include some of the same details.

Illustrating Nonfiction

You Will Need

- a familiar nonfiction book with detailed illustrations, such as *What Do You Do When Something Wants to Eat You?* by Steve Jenkins, from Text Set: Exploring Nonfiction

- chart paper and markers or crayons

Academic Language/ Important Vocabulary

- nonfiction
- illustration
- drawing
- detail

Continuum Connection

- Understand that writers get help from other writers (p. 248)

- Create drawings that employ careful attention to color or detail (p. 249)

- Create drawings that are related to the written text and increase readers' understanding and enjoyment (p. 249)

- Understand that a writer of a factual text uses words and illustrations to make it interesting to readers (p. 251)

- Understand that writers of nonfiction texts have many ways to show facts: e.g., labels, drawings, photos (p. 251)

GOAL

Use other illustrators' pictures to get ideas for adding details to drawings.

RATIONALE

When children look closely at other illustrators' drawings and copy some of the details they see, they develop their observational skills and create richer, more informational illustrations for their nonfiction books.

ASSESS LEARNING

- Notice how children choose the details to include in their drawings.

- Observe for evidence that children can use vocabulary such as *nonfiction*, *illustration*, *drawing*, and *detail*.

MINILESSON

Demonstrate looking closely at an illustration in a nonfiction book and drawing some of the same details in your own drawing. Here is an example.

- Show the cover of *What Do You Do When Something Wants to Eat You?* and read the title. Show page 19.

  > I'm writing a book about insects, and I want to include a page about hover flies. First, I will draw a picture of a hover fly. I want to make sure my hover fly looks real, so I'm going to look closely at the illustration in this book and draw what I see.

- On chart paper, draw a hover fly similar to the one on page 19. Think aloud as you try to replicate each of the details shown in the illustration.

  > I see that the hover fly in the book has six long, thin legs that are yellow with brown bands. I'm going to give my hover fly legs just like that. Now, I'm going to add two big, round, black eyes like the hover fly in the book has.

- Stop before adding certain details (e.g., the antennas).

Have a Try

Invite children to talk to a partner about what else to add to the drawing.

> What other details should I add to my drawing? Look closely at the hover fly in the book. Are any details missing from my drawing? Turn and talk to your partner about this.

▶ After children turn and talk, invite a few children to share. Complete the drawing using the children's suggestions.

Summarize and Apply

Help children summarize the learning. Remind them to look at pictures to get ideas for their own drawings.

> What did you learn today about drawing illustrations for nonfiction books?

▶ Write the principle at the top of the chart.

> During writing time today, continue working on a nonfiction book you have already started or start a new one. To get ideas for your illustrations, look at illustrations in books. Bring your writing to share when we meet later.

Look at pictures in books and try to include some of the same details.

Confer

▶ During independent writing, move around the room to confer briefly with as many individual children as time allows. Sit side by side with them and invite them to talk about the illustrations in their nonfiction books. Use prompts such as the following if needed.

- *Where could you look for an illustration of a _____ to get ideas for your drawing?*
- *What details do you notice in that illustration?*
- *Can you draw that in your own picture?*

Share

Following independent writing, gather children in the meeting area to share their nonfiction books.

> Did anyone look at an illustration in a nonfiction book to get ideas for your own drawings? What details from the book did you include in your own drawing?

Illustrating Nonfiction

You Will Need

- familiar nonfiction books with diagrams, such as the following from Text Set: Exploring Nonfiction:

  - *Water: Up, Down, and All Around* by Natalie M. Rosinsky

  - *Surprising Sharks* by Nicola Davies

- a simple drawing of an animal that shows the main parts (no color)

- markers

Academic Language/ Important Vocabulary

- nonfiction

- diagram

Continuum Connection

- Use illustrations and book and print features (e.g., labeled pictures, diagrams, table of contents, headings, sidebars, page numbers) to guide the reader (p. 251)

- Begin to incorporate illustrations and organizational tools in nonfiction texts: e.g., drawing or photograph with caption or label, map, diagram; table of contents, heading, sidebar (p. 254)

GOAL

Learn how to draw diagrams to give information.

RATIONALE

When children study diagrams in nonfiction books and think about why the diagrams were included, they learn that they, too, can create diagrams to give more information about a topic.

ASSESS LEARNING

- Observe for evidence that children understand the definition and purpose of a diagram.

- Notice whether children try creating diagrams for their own nonfiction books.

- Observe for evidence that children can use vocabulary such as *nonfiction* and *diagram*.

MINILESSON

To help children think about the minilesson principle, use mentor texts to demonstrate how diagrams can be used to give information. Here is an example.

- Display the cover of *Water: Up, Down, and All Around* and read the title. Show page 20.

  What does this picture help you understand?

  This is a special kind of picture called a diagram. The arrows help you understand that the water cycle is a process that happens over and over again, in the same way each time.

- Display the cover of *Surprising Sharks* and read the title. Show pages 14–15.

  This is another kind of diagram. What information does this diagram give you?

  What are you noticing about diagrams? What is a diagram?

  A diagram is a kind of simple picture that shows how something works or the parts of something. A diagram usually has both pictures and words.

Have a Try

Invite children to talk to a partner about how to make a diagram.

▶ Show a simplified drawing of an animal, such as the hover fly in WML2.

> How is this drawing different from ones you usually see?

> It's a very simple picture of a hover fly that shows just the main parts. There is no color. What words could I add to label the parts? Turn and talk to your partner about this.

▶ After children turn and talk, invite a few children to share their ideas. Label the animal's body parts.

Summarize and Apply

Help children summarize the learning. Remind children that they can include diagrams in their own nonfiction books.

> Why do you think nonfiction authors sometimes include diagrams in their books? Why are diagrams helpful?

▶ Write the principle at the top of the chart. Read it aloud.

> Today during writing time, continue working on your nonfiction book or start a new one. Think about whether you could include a diagram to show the parts of something or how something works. Bring your writing to share when we meet.

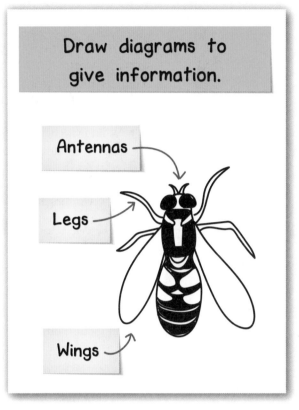

Draw diagrams to give information.

Antennas

Legs

Wings

Confer

▶ During independent writing, move around the room to confer briefly with as many individual children as time allows. Sit side by side with them and invite them to talk about diagrams. Use prompts such as the following if needed.

- *Could you draw a diagram to help readers understand more about your topic?*
- *What could the diagram show?*

Share

Following independent writing, gather children together to share their diagrams.

> Who drew a diagram? What will it help readers learn?

Assessment

After you have taught the minilessons in this umbrella, observe children as they write, draw, and talk about their writing and drawing. Use *The Literacy Continuum* (Fountas and Pinnell 2017) to notice, teach for, and support children's learning as you observe their writing and drawing.

▶ What evidence do you have of new understandings children have developed related to illustrating nonfiction?

- Do children include photographs in their nonfiction books?
- Do they look at pictures in nonfiction books to get ideas for the details in their own drawings?
- Do they create diagrams for their nonfiction books?
- Do they understand and use vocabulary such as *nonfiction*, *photograph*, *detail*, and *diagram*?

▶ In what other ways, beyond the scope of this umbrella, are children working on nonfiction books?

- Are they attempting to write different kinds of nonfiction books?
- Are they trying to add text and organizational features to their nonfiction books?

Use your observations to determine the next umbrella you will teach. You may also consult Suggested Sequence of Lessons (pp. 557–571) for guidance.

EXTENSIONS FOR ILLUSTRATING NONFICTION

▶ Invite children to bring in photographs from home to use in their nonfiction books. You might also consider helping children look online for photographs or take their own photographs.

▶ Help children write captions for the photographs in their nonfiction books.

▶ Discuss other types of graphics in nonfiction books (e.g., maps, charts, and infographics). Invite children to include these types of graphics in their own books.

▶ Gather together a guided writing group of several children who need support in a specific area of writing, such as adding various kinds of illustrations to their books.

Minilessons in This Umbrella

WML1   Make your book fun to read.

WML2   Use found objects to create art for books.

WML3   Use collage to make your pictures interesting.

Before Teaching Umbrella 3 Minilessons

Teach the lessons in this umbrella when they are relevant to the needs of the class, rather than sequentially. Provide plenty of time for children to experiment with each technique before introducing another; this will also help manage the volume of art supplies needed at one time. In addition to the supplies suggested for each lesson, consider having the following available in your art or writing center: googly eyes, felt, fabric scraps, yarn, ribbon, textured paper (e.g., sandpaper), greeting cards, tissue paper, magazines, grocery circulars, and cardboard scraps.

Read and discuss picture books that illustrate a variety of art techniques (e.g., lift-the-flap, cut-outs, pop-ups, collage, mixed media). Use the following books from *Fountas & Pinnell Classroom™ Interactive Read-Aloud Collection* and *Shared Reading Collection*, or choose books from your classroom library that have interesting features.

Interactive Read-Aloud Collection

Exploring Nonfiction

What Do You Do When Something Wants to Eat You? by Steve Jenkins

Nonfiction: Questions and Answers

What Do You Do With a Tail Like This? by Steve Jenkins and Robin Page

Shared Reading Collection

Bone Riddles by Ernesta Flores

The Big Mix-Up by Nicole Walker

As you read and enjoy these texts together, help children

- discuss what makes the books fun to look at, and

- talk about how these techniques make the illustrations interesting.

Interactive Read-Aloud
Exploring Nonfiction

**Questions and
Answers**

Shared Reading

Make your book fun to read.

Making Pictures Interesting

You Will Need

- books with features such as lift-the-flap, fold-out pages, cut-outs, pop-ups, etc., such as *Bone Riddles* by Ernesta Flores and *The Big Mix-Up* by Nicole Walker, from *Shared Reading Collection*

- chart paper prepared to show lift-the-flap, fold-out, cut-out, and pop-up

- glue stick and markers

Academic Language/ Important Vocabulary

- lift-the-flap
- fold-out
- cut-out
- pop-up
- illustrator
- author

Continuum Connection

- Try out techniques other writers and illustrators have used (p. 257)

- Create drawings that are related to the written text and increase readers' understanding and enjoyment (p. 257)

GOAL

Understand that writers and illustrators use lift-the-flap, cut-out, and pop-up features to make books fun to read.

RATIONALE

When you help children notice techniques writers and illustrators use to make their books fun to read, they can experiment with the same techniques in their own work.

ASSESS LEARNING

- Observe children's willingness to try different techniques for making books fun to read.

- Look for evidence that children can use vocabulary such as *lift-the-flap*, *fold-out*, *cut-out*, *pop-up*, *illustrator*, and *author*.

MINILESSON

Use mentor texts to show children techniques for making books fun to read, such as lift-the-flap, fold-out, cut-out, and pop-up features. Here is an example.

- Show the cover of *Bone Riddles* and read the title. Read pages 6–7, inviting a volunteer to lift the flaps.

    How did the author and illustrator of this book make it fun to read?

    They used flaps to hide the answers to the questions. It is fun to lift up the flaps in the book to see the answers hiding underneath.

- Help the children understand how flaps are constructed by attaching a flap to chart paper.

    Glue the flap onto the page like this. Lift it up to see what's underneath.

- Look at *The Big Mix-Up* with children to help them notice the use of fold-out pages, or use any other books from your classroom library that have special features, including cut-outs. Add the features to the chart and discuss how they make the books fun to read.

Have a Try

Invite children to talk to a partner about pop-ups.

- ▶ Display a pop-up illustration in a book or one you prepared for the chart.

    Turn and talk to your partner about what you notice about this illustration. What do you think it's called?

- ▶ After children turn and talk, invite a few children to share their responses. Talk about what makes a pop-up book fun to read.

Summarize and Apply

Help children summarize the learning. Remind them that they can include special features in their own books.

    What are some ways that authors and illustrators make their books fun to read?

- ▶ Write the principle at the top of the chart.

    During writing time today, try doing one of the things we talked about–lift-the-flap, cut-outs, pop-ups, or fold-out pages–in your own book. Bring your book to share when we meet later.

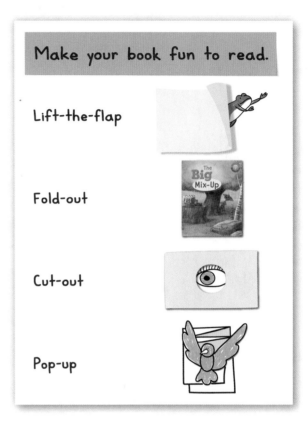

Confer

- ▶ During independent writing, move around the room to confer briefly with as many individual children as time allows. Sit side by side with them and invite them to talk about making their books fun to read. Use prompts such as the following if needed.

    - *Would you like to try adding flaps, fold-out pages, cut-outs, or pop-ups to your book?*

    - *What will you write on the flap? What will you write underneath it?*

    - *What do you want to pop up?*

    - *What materials do you think you'll need to make that?*

Share

Following independent writing, gather children in the meeting area to share what they did to make their books fun to read.

    What did you try today to make your book fun to read?

WML2

DRW.U5.WML2

Writing Minilesson Principle
Use found objects to create art for books.

Making Pictures Interesting

You Will Need

- a book with an illustration made with found objects, such as *What Do You Do With a Tail Like This?* by Steve Jenkins and Robin Page, from Text Set: Nonfiction: Questions and Answers
- chart paper prepared with an outline of a dog
- a collection of found objects, such as feathers, twigs, buttons, leaves, cotton balls, fake fur, and yarn
- glue stick

Academic Language/ Important Vocabulary

- found object
- art
- book
- illustrator

Continuum Connection

- Try out techniques other writers and illustrators have used (p. 257)
- Create drawings that are related to the written text and increase readers' understanding and enjoyment (p. 257)

GOAL

Understand that writers and illustrators use different art materials and objects they have found to make pictures interesting.

RATIONALE

When you help children notice how illustrators use found objects in their art, they can experiment with the same technique in their own artwork.

ASSESS LEARNING

- Notice whether children try using found objects in their illustrations.
- Look for evidence that children can use vocabulary such as *found object, art, book,* and *illustrator.*

MINILESSON

Use a mentor text to show how illustrators may use found objects in their artwork. Then demonstrate using found objects to create a picture. Here is an example.

- Show the cover of *What Do You Do With a Tail Like This?* and read the title. Turn to pages 13–14.

    Look closely at the skunk. How do you think the illustrator made the skunk's white fur?

    It looks like she glued cotton onto her picture to make the skunk's fur look like real fur. Then she took a photo of the picture and put it in the book.

    You can use found objects to make illustrations for your books. Found objects are any objects that you can find, either indoors or outdoors.

- Show the found objects available in the art center.
- Demonstrate how to make a picture using found objects. Display the outline of a dog that you prepared before class.

    I made this drawing of a dog, and now I want to decorate it with found objects. I'm going to glue fake fur to the paper to make the dog's fur. Then I'm going to use buttons to make the dog's eyes.

Have a Try

Invite children to talk with a partner about how to make the dog's tail.

> ❙ Show a few different found objects, such as yarn, leaves, and cotton balls.
>
>> **What object would make a good tail for a dog? Turn and talk to your partner about this.**
>
> ❙ After children turn and talk, invite a few children to share their ideas. Demonstrate gluing some yarn to the dog picture to make a tail.

Summarize and Apply

Write the principle at the top of the chart to summarize the learning. Remind children that they can use found objects to create illustrations for their books.

> **Today during writing time, create an illustration for your book using found objects. We have lots of fun objects in our art center that you can use. Bring your illustration to share when we meet later.**

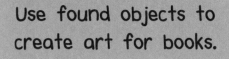

Use found objects to create art for books.

Confer

> ❙ During independent writing time, move around the room to confer briefly with as many individual children as time allows. Sit side by side with them and invite them to talk about their writing and illustrations. Use prompts such as the following if needed.
>
>> • *Talk about your illustration.*
>>
>> • *How could you use found objects to make that?*
>>
>> • *Take a look at the objects we have. Do you see anything you want to use?*
>>
>> • *What could you use to make the bird's beak?*

Share

Following independent writing, gather children in the meeting area to share how they used found objects in their illustrations.

> **Who would like to share an illustration you made using found objects?**
>
> **How did you make that?**

WML3

DRW.U5.WML3

Writing Minilesson Principle
Use collage to make your pictures interesting.

Making Pictures Interesting

You Will Need

- a book with examples of collage, such as *What Do You Do When Something Wants to Eat You?* by Steve Jenkins from Text Set: Exploring Nonfiction
- different colored construction paper cut into the shape of a fish's body, fins, eye, and tail
- chart paper and markers
- glue stick

Academic Language/ Important Vocabulary

- collage
- illustration
- illustrator
- shape

Continuum Connection

- Try out techniques other writers and illustrators have used (p. 257)
- Create illustrations as an integral part of the composing process (p. 257)

GOAL

Understand that writers and illustrators can use collage to make pictures interesting.

RATIONALE

When you help children notice ways that illustrators make their illustrations interesting, they can experiment with the same techniques in their own work.

ASSESS LEARNING

- Observe children's willingness to try different art techniques for their drawings.
- Notice whether children understand how to use collage.
- Look for evidence that children can use vocabulary such as *collage, illustration, illustrator,* and *shape*.

MINILESSON

To help children think about the minilesson principle, demonstrate how to make a collage. Here is an example.

- Show the cover of *What Do You Do When Something Wants to Eat You?* and read the title. Show several pages of the book.

  What do you notice about the illustrations in this book? How do you think the illustrator made them?

  He made the illustrations using collage. Say it with me: *collage*. You can use collage by tearing or cutting pieces of paper and gluing them onto a sheet of paper to make a picture.

- Demonstrate how to make a picture of an animal, such as a fish, using collage.

  I want to make an illustration of a fish using collage. First, I will cut the fish's body out of orange paper. Next I will glue it onto the paper in the place where I want the fish to be.

  Now the fish needs fins and a tail! I will cut the fish's fins and tail from red paper. Who would like to glue them to the picture?

- Invite volunteers to glue the fins and tail to the paper.

Have a Try

Invite children to talk to a partner about how to finish the fish illustration.

> What else does our fish need? Turn and talk to your partner about how we can use collage to finish our picture of a fish. What color and shapes of paper do we need?

▶ After children turn and talk, invite a few pairs to share their ideas. Using children's suggestions, finish the picture of a fish (using a black circle for an eye, for example).

Summarize and Apply

Summarize the learning and remind children that they can use collage in their own books.

> What did you learn today about making your book interesting to read?

▶ Write the principle at the top of the chart.

> Today during writing time, try using collage to make an illustration.

▶ During independent writing, provide children with a variety of materials for collage making, such as paper of different colors and textures, old magazines or catalogs, glue sticks, and scissors.

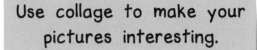

Use collage to make your pictures interesting.

Confer

▶ During independent writing, move around the room to confer briefly with as many individual children as time allows. Sit side by side with them and invite them to talk about making their pictures interesting. Use prompts such as the following if needed.

- *What would you like to make an illustration of today?*
- *How could you make that using collage?*
- *What color paper do you need? What shapes do you need to cut?*

Share

Following independent writing, gather children in the meeting area to share their illustrations made using collage.

> Who would like to share an illustration you made using collage?

> Did you like using collage? Why or why not?

Section 5: Drawing

Assessment

After you have taught the minilessons in this umbrella, observe children as they draw, write, and talk about their drawing and writing. Use *The Literacy Continuum* (Fountas and Pinnell 2017) to notice, teach for, and support children's learning as you observe their attempts at writing and illustrating.

- ▶ What evidence do you have of new understandings children have developed related to how to make pictures interesting?
    - Are children using different techniques (e.g., lift-the-flap, fold-outs, cut-outs, pop-ups) to make their books interesting?
    - Do they use found objects and collage to create art for their books?
    - Is there evidence children can use vocabulary such as *illustration*, *illustrator*, and *author*?
- ▶ In what other ways, beyond the scope of this umbrella, are children ready to expand their bookmaking techniques?
    - Are children attempting to write stories?
    - Are they beginning to write how-to and other nonfiction books?
    - Are they making book covers and including text features?

Use your observations to determine the next umbrella you will teach. You may also consult Suggested Sequence of Lessons (pp. 557–571) for guidance.

EXTENSIONS FOR MAKING PICTURES INTERESTING

- ▶ Invite children to use the techniques they have learned to make a front or back cover for a book.

- ▶ Teach children how to use torn paper and collage to create a border—around a page or illustration or on a cover.

- ▶ Invite children to create a watercolor painting and then tear or cut the painting into pieces or shapes to use for collage.

- ▶ Invite children to experiment with other materials, such as transparent or vellum paper or aluminum foil, and found items like leaves, feathers, discarded maps, pages from books, buttons, or recycled objects.

Once Upon a Time

The Three Billy Goats Gruff

First, the youngest billy goat crosses over the bridge.

"Don't eat me!"

a dry, rocky hill

The Troll said, "Who's that tripping over my bridge."

a river

Main Characters
Who the story is mostly about

Setting
Where and when the story takes place

Plot
The actions or events in the story

Problem
The conflict in the story

Solution
How the problem is solved or fixed

Interactive Writing
After reading many fairy tales, Room selected *The Three Billy Goats Gruff* to ret a bulletin board mural.

Section 6 | Craft

THROUGH THE TALK that surrounds interactive read-aloud and shared reading, first graders learn a lot about the craft of writing. The minilessons in this section take this budding knowledge and pull back the curtain on the decisions authors make (e.g., choosing powerful words, using dialogue) to create books that are interesting and exciting to read.

Minilessons in This Umbrella

WML1 Describe where the story takes place.

WML2 Describe the characters or people in the story.

WML3 Show examples for your ideas.

Before Teaching Umbrella 1 Minilessons

Give children plenty of opportunities to write and draw freely and to make their own books. Read and discuss books with detailed and informative illustrations and descriptive language. Each Have a Try involves adding details to a text that you provide. Write your own text or use the suggestions in the three Have a Try sections. For mentor texts, use the following texts from *Fountas & Pinnell Classroom™ Interactive Read-Aloud Collection*, or choose books from the classroom library that children will enjoy.

The Importance of Friendship

The Magic Rabbit by Annette LeBlanc Cate

Chester's Way by Kevin Henkes

Learning and Working Together: School

Elizabeti's School by Stephanie Stuve-Bodeen

Kevin Henkes: Exploring Characters

Sheila Rae, the Brave

As you read and enjoy these texts together, help children notice and discuss

- how the setting is described,
- how characters or people are described, and
- how examples are used to explain an idea.

Friendship

School

Kevin Henkes

Section 6: Craft

Writing with Details

You Will Need

- books with strong descriptions of setting, such as the following:
  - *The Magic Rabbit* by Annette LeBlanc Cate, from Text Set: The Importance of Friendship
  - *Elizabeti's School* by Stephanie Stuve-Bodeen, from Text Set: Learning and Working Together: School
- a brief mentor text written in advance (see Have a Try)
- piece of paper to be added to your mentor text
- chart paper and markers

Academic Language / Important Vocabulary

- describe
- reread
- details

Continuum Connection

- Provide some descriptive details to make the story more interesting (p. 251)
- Notice craft decisions that the author or illustrator has made and try out some of these decisions in one's own writing with teacher support (p. 251)
- Use modifiers: e.g., *red dress*; *ran fast* (p. 255)
- Observe carefully before writing about a person, animal, object, place, action (p. 256)

GOAL

Include details to describe where a story takes place.

RATIONALE

Readers know only as much about the story as the details the writer includes. When you teach children that writers describe a setting to make a story more interesting and to help the reader navigate a story, they understand that they can try this in their own writing.

ASSESS LEARNING

- Observe for evidence that children understand the importance of describing the setting.
- Look for evidence that children include details to describe the setting in their writing.
- Notice evidence that children can use vocabulary such as *describe, details,* and *reread*.

MINILESSON

Remind children that their writing and drawing should fit together. See DRW. U2.WML3 for a minilesson about drawing the setting. To help children think about the minilesson principle, use mentor texts (published and original) to help them notice that writers use details to describe the setting. Here is an example.

- Show *The Magic Rabbit*. Read the title and page 11.

   What did the author write about here?

   She wrote about where this part of the story takes place. What are some words the author used to tell where this part of the story takes place?

   What do those words help you understand?

   The author helped you understand how the place looks.

- Record that information on the chart paper.
- Repeat this process with page 8 from *Elizabeti's School*.

   These authors used details, like the squirrels and boys and girls laughing, to help you see how the place looks and also how it sounds.

- Record that information on the chart.

   What else might readers want to know about where a story takes place?

- Record the information that children suggest on the chart. Point out that the illustrations also show details about the setting.

   When you write, think about the details you can use in your writing and drawing to describe where your story takes place. Think about what it's like to be in the place.

Have a Try

Discuss with children what details to add to your story. (The story used in this and the next two minilessons is about going for ice cream after playing at a park.)

▶ Read a page from your mentor text: *After we went to the park, we got ice cream*. Write children's suggestions on a piece of paper (attached to the chart) that could be added to your mentor text.

> How can I help the reader understand where this part of my story takes place? What details can I add?

Summarize and Apply

Summarize the learning and remind children to describe where their story takes place.

▶ Write the principle at the top of the chart.

> Before you start your writing today, first reread the writing you already did. Find a page where you show or tell where the story takes place.
> Think about how you might describe it to help the reader understand more. You can write on the page or tape on a strip of paper (spider leg) if you don't have room.

Describe where the story takes place.

- How the place looks

- What you can hear

- What you can smell

- Who was there

We saw a building with a big pink ice cream cone on it.

We heard the door squeak when we opened it.

Someone said, "Can I help you?"

Confer

▶ During independent writing, move around the room to confer briefly with as many individual children as time allows. Sit side by side with them and invite them to talk about where their stories take place. Use prompts such as the following as needed.

- *What words can you write to describe where your story takes place?*
- *What did that place look like? Where could you add that to your story?*
- *What did it sound like at the _____ ? Where could you add that to your story?*
- *You can also add details to your drawings.*

Share

Following independent writing, gather children in the meeting area to share their writing.

> Who would like to share some details you added to describe where your story takes place?

Writing Minilesson Principle
Describe the characters or people in the story.

You Will Need

- books with strong descriptions of characters or people, such as the following by Kevin Henkes::
  - *Sheila Rae, the Brave*, from Text Set: Kevin Henkes: Exploring Characters
  - *Chester's Way*, from Text Set: The Importance of Friendship
- a brief mentor text written in advance (see Have a Try)
- piece of paper to be added to your mentor text
- markers

Academic Language / Important Vocabulary

- characters
- describe
- reread

Continuum Connection

- Provide some descriptive details to make the story more interesting (p. 251)
- Notice craft decisions that the author or illustrator has made and try out some of these decisions in one's own writing with teacher support (p. 251)
- Use modifiers: e.g., *red* dress; ran *fast* (p. 255)
- Observe carefully before writing about a person, animal, object, place, action (p. 256)

GOAL

Write a description of the characters or people in the story.

RATIONALE

When you teach children that writers describe characters or people in a story to help the reader understand them better and make a story more interesting, they begin to try this in their own writing.

ASSESS LEARNING

- Observe whether children recognize that writers describe characters and people in their writing.
- Look for evidence that children can describe characters or people in their own writing.
- Notice evidence that children can use vocabulary such as *characters, describe,* and *reread.*

MINILESSON

Remind children that their writing and drawing should fit together. See DRW.U2.WML5 for a minilesson about drawing people consistently throughout a story. To help children think about the minilesson principle, use mentor texts (both published and original) to help them notice that writers use details to describe the characters. The story used in this and the next minilesson is about going for ice cream after playing at a park. Here is an example.

- Show *Sheila Rae, the Brave*. Read pages 1 and 10–12.

  What are these pages about?

  The author wrote about the main character of the story, Sheila Rae. What do the author's words tell you about Sheila Rae?

  The author wrote to tell you what Sheila Rae is like. She is brave.

- Record the information on chart paper.
- Repeat this process with another text, such as pages 1–2 of *Chester's Way*.

  The author wrote about what Chester does.

- Record the information on the chart.

  What else might you tell about a character in a story?

- Record the information that children suggest on the chart. Point out that the illustrations also show what the characters are like.

  When you write, think about how you describe the characters and people in your stories. Think about what details you can add to your writing and drawing to help the reader understand a character.

Have a Try

Use the text you wrote to help children practice describing a character. Write the thinking on a new piece of paper attached to the chart.

▶ Read a page from your mentor text: *One little boy dropped his ice cream cone.*

> What can I add about the boy that will help the reader understand more?

▶ Record ideas on the new page for your book.

Summarize and Apply

Summarize the learning and remind children to describe characters in their books.

▶ Write the principle at the top of the chart.

> Today, reread the book you are working on. Find a page with one of the characters or people in your story. Think about how you might describe that character to help the reader understand more. Add that to your story. You can write on the page or tape a strip of paper (spider leg) to the page if you don't have room.

> Describe the characters or people in the story.

- What the character is like
- What the character does
- How the character looks
- What the character is wearing

The boy cried.

Tears fell on his red shirt.

"I want more ice cream!" he yelled.

Confer

▶ During independent writing, move around the room to confer briefly with as many individual children as time allows. Sit side by side with them and invite them to talk about the characters in their stories. Use prompts such as the following as needed.

- *Talk about one person in your story. Can you add more words to your story?*
- *What does the character/person look like here? What facial expression does the person have? What is the person wearing? Is that important for understanding this part of the story? How could you add that to your story?*
- *You can also add details to your drawings.*

Share

Following independent writing, gather children in the meeting area with their writing. Read one or two children's descriptions of characters.

> What words help you understand the characters more?

Section 6: Craft

Writing with Details

You Will Need

- books where the author describes an idea through examples, such as the following by Kevin Henkes:
  - *Sheila Rae, the Brave*, from Text Set: Kevin Henkes: Exploring Characters
  - *Chester's Way*, from Text Set: The Importance of Friendship
- a brief mentor text written in advance (see Have a Try)
- piece of paper to be added to your mentor text
- markers

Academic Language / Important Vocabulary

- examples
- ideas
- details

Continuum Connection

- Provide supportive description, details, or examples to explain the important ideas in shared or interactive writing (p. 254)
- Introduce ideas followed by some supportive details and examples (p. 254)

GOAL

Write examples to support ideas.

RATIONALE

When you teach children that writers provide examples in their writing to explain ideas and to help the reader understand the story better, they begin to try this in their own writing.

ASSESS LEARNING

- Observe whether children recognize that writers show examples of ideas in their writing.
- Look for evidence that children can show examples for ideas in their own writing.
- Notice evidence that children can use vocabulary such as *examples*, *ideas*, and *details*.

MINILESSON

Use familiar texts to engage children in thinking about how authors show examples for ideas as a way to add specific details to their writing.

- Review pages 1 and 10–12 of *Sheila Rae, the Brave*.

  When we talked about this book before, you noticed that Sheila Rae is brave. How did the author let you know that Sheila Rae is brave?

- Guide children to understand that the actions that the author described help readers understand that Sheila Rae is brave.

  The author wrote and drew about the idea that Sheila Rae is brave. He wrote examples of the brave things that she does.

- Record examples on chart paper.

- Review pages 1 and 2 of *Chester's Way*. Have a similar discussion about Chester.

  How did the author let you know that Chester does things his own way?

  The first page of the book tells us the idea that Chester has his own way of doing things. How did the writer show how Chester has his own way of doing things? Talk about some examples.

- Record the examples on the chart. Point out that the illustrations show details about the ideas in the writing.

  Giving examples to explain an idea helps the reader understand the story and the character better. When you write, think about how you can use words and drawings to give examples of your idea to help your reader understand more.

Have a Try

Use the text you wrote to help children practice writing examples for an idea. Write the thinking on a new piece of paper taped to the chart.

▶ Read a page from your mentor text: *The boy's mother calmed him down.*

> My idea is that the boy's mother calmed him down. What examples can I add to help the reader understand how the mom calmed the boy down?

▶ Record ideas on the new page for your book.

Summarize and Apply

Summarize the learning and remind children to provide examples for their ideas in their books.

▶ Write the principle at the top of the page.

> Today, reread the book you are working on. Find a page where you share an idea of something in your story. Think about how you might add examples for that idea to help your reader understand more. You can write on the page or on a strip of paper (spider leg) that you can tape on if you don't have room. Bring your writing to share when we meet later.

Show examples for your ideas.

The Idea	Examples
Sheila Rae is brave.	• She stepped on every crack. • She walked backwards with her eyes closed. • She growled at stray dogs.
Chester has his own way of doing things.	• He cut sandwiches the same way. • He got out of bed on the same side.

The mom hugged the boy.
"It's OK. Don't worry," she said.
She bought more ice cream.

Confer

▶ During independent writing, move around the room to confer briefly with as many individual children as time allows. Sit side by side with them and invite them to talk about adding examples to their writing. Use prompts such as the following as needed.

- *Read this part of your story aloud. Listen for ideas you could add examples for.*
- *The idea in your story is _____. What examples could you share to tell the reader more about that?*
- *Talk more about that idea. You could add examples like that to your writing.*

Share

Following independent writing, gather children in the meeting area with their writing. Read a few pieces of writing where they added examples for an idea.

> What examples did you add to your story to help the reader understand your idea?

Assessment

After you have taught the minilessons in this umbrella, observe children as they draw, write, and talk about their writing. Use the behaviors and understandings in *The Literacy Continuum* (Fountas and Pinnell 2017) to notice, teach for, and support children's learning as you observe their attempts at drawing and writing.

▶ What evidence do you have of new understandings children have developed related to writing with details?

- How well do children describe where a story takes place?

- Do they describe the characters or people in a story?

- Are they able to show examples for their ideas?

- Do they notice and use vocabulary such as *setting*, *reread*, *characters*, *describe*, *examples*, *ideas*, and *details*?

▶ In what other ways, beyond the scope of this umbrella, are the children showing an interest in writing with details?

- Are they trying to make their drawings more detailed?

- Are they reading like a writer?

Use your observations to determine what you will teach next. You may also consult Suggested Sequence of Lessons (pp. 557–571) for guidance.

EXTENSIONS FOR WRITING WITH DETAILS

▶ Add a child's description of where a story takes place or of a character to the lesson charts. Using children's writing as mentor texts builds ownership.

▶ Remind children that the words and the pictures in their stories should go together. If you haven't already taught DRW.U3: Adding Meaningful Details to Illustrations, consider teaching some of those lessons now.

▶ Repeat WML3 with nonfiction text examples and children's writing. Consider using Planning a Writing Minilesson (p. 102) to plan the new lesson.

▶ Gather together a guided writing group of several children who need support in a specific area of writing, such as adding details to their writing.

Minilessons in This Umbrella

WML1 Show talking with speech bubbles. Show thinking with thought bubbles.

WML2 Show talking in your story.

WML3 Add talking to make your writing more interesting.

Before Teaching Umbrella 2 Minilessons

Prior to teaching these minilessons, make sure children have experienced a variety of fiction books with dialogue. Teach IW.10: Writing with Speech Bubbles and use the writing from the lesson as a mentor text for this umbrella. You may also choose as mentor texts the following books from *Fountas & Pinnell Classroom™ Interactive Read-Aloud Collection* and *Shared Reading Collection*, or you might use other text examples of dialogue from the classroom library.

Interactive Read-Aloud Collection
Mo Willems: Having Fun with Humor

I Am Invited to a Party!

Don't Let the Pigeon Drive the Bus!

Elephants Cannot Dance!

Knuffle Bunny: A Cautionary Tale

Knuffle Bunny Too: A Case of Mistaken Identity

Shared Reading Collection

Woof! Woof! by Armand Benedict

Scram! by Julie Reich

The Broken Ladder by Joan Silver

Interactive Writing Lessons

IW.10: Writing with Speech Bubbles

As you read and enjoy these mentor texts together, help children

- think about what the characters say and think, and

- notice the way the writers show what the characters say and think.

Interactive Read-Aloud
Mo Willems

Shared Reading

Interactive Writing

Section 6: Craft

WML1

Writing Minilesson Principle
Show talking with speech bubbles.
Show thinking with thought bubbles.

Adding Dialogue to Writing

You Will Need

▸ several mentor texts that have thought and speech bubbles, such as the following:

- *Woof! Woof!* by Armand Benedict and *Scram!* by Julie Reich, from *Shared Reading Collection*

- *I Am Invited to a Party!* and *Don't Let the Pigeon Drive the Bus!* by Mo Willems, from Text Set: Mo Willems: Having Fun with Humor

- class writing from IW.10: Writing with Speech Bubbles

▸ chart paper prepared with a sentence and drawing of two characters, one with an empty thought bubble and one with an empty speech bubble

▸ markers

▸ To download the following online resource for this lesson, visit **resources.fountasandpinnell.com**:

- chart art (optional)

Academic Language / Important Vocabulary

▸ speech bubble   ▸ talking

▸ thought bubble   ▸ thinking

Continuum Connection

▸ Add thoughts in thought bubbles or dialogue in speech bubbles or quotation marks to provide information or provide narration (p. 256)

GOAL

Add speech bubbles to show talking and thought bubbles to show thinking.

RATIONALE

When children notice how writers include speech and thought bubbles in illustrations, they begin to think about ways to use dialogue in their own drawing and writing.

ASSESS LEARNING

▸ Look for evidence that children understand the purpose of and are trying to use speech bubbles and thought bubbles in their own writing.

▸ Observe for evidence that children can use vocabulary such as *speech bubble*, *thought bubble*, *talking*, and *thinking*.

MINILESSON

To help children think about including thought or speech bubbles in their own writing, provide an inquiry-based lesson with examples and then model the process. Here is an example.

▸ Show the class-made writing from IW.10.

> What did we do to show what the characters are saying?

▸ Engage children in a brief conversation about speech bubbles.

▸ Show page 5 in *Woof! Woof!* and page 6 in *Scram!*

> What do you notice?

▸ Help children recognize that speech bubbles point to the speaker's mouth.

▸ Show pages 12–13 in *I Am Invited to a Party!*

> What do you notice about how Mo Willems used speech bubbles in this book?

▸ Guide them to identify that because the speech bubbles point directly to the speakers, the reader knows which things Elephant says and which things Piggie says.

> Now think about what Mo Willems did in *Don't Let the Pigeon Drive the Bus!*

▸ Show and read pages 25–26.

> What do you notice about the bubbles?

▸ Guide the conversation so children notice the difference between how a speech bubble and a thought bubble are written.

> Why do you think the bubbles look different?

The Writing Minilessons Book, Grade 1

Have a Try

Invite children to turn and talk about adding speech bubbles and thought bubbles.

▶ Show and read the prepared chart paper.

> One of these frogs has a thought bubble, so it is thinking something in its head. The other frog has a speech bubble, so it is saying something. Turn and talk about what the frogs might be thinking and saying.

▶ After time for discussion, ask a few children to share. Using their ideas, fill in the thought bubble and the speech bubble.

Summarize and Apply

Summarize the learning. Remind children to add speech bubbles and thought bubbles to their own writing.

> How can you show what characters are thinking and saying in your stories?

▶ Write the principle at the top of the chart.

> During writing time, take a look at the writing you are working on and think about how you might include a speech bubble or a thought bubble and add that to your writing. Bring your writing to share when we meet later.

> Show talking with speech bubbles.
> Show thinking with thought bubbles.

I am hungry.

I hope a fly comes soon.

Two frogs sat on a rock.

Confer

▶ During independent writing, move around the room to confer briefly with as many individual children as time allows. Sit side by side with them and invite them to talk about using speech and thought bubbles. Use the following prompts as needed.

- *What is this person thinking/saying?*
- *Is there a place in this drawing where you could add a thought (speech) bubble?*
- *How can you show what the people are thinking or saying?*

Share

Following independent writing, gather children in the meeting area to share their experiences adding speech bubbles or thought bubbles to their writing. Support children's oral language by providing a sentence frame, such as *My speech (thought) bubble says _____.*

> Did anyone add a speech bubble or a thought bubble to your writing? Share what you wrote.

Umbrella 2: Adding Dialogue to Writing

Adding Dialogue to Writing

You Will Need

▸ several mentor texts with dialogue, such as the following:

- *I Am Invited to a Party!* and *Knuffle Bunny: A Cautionary Tale* by Mo Willems, from Text Set: Mo Willems: Having Fun with Humor

- *The Broken Ladder* by Joan Silver, from *Shared Reading Collection*

▸ chart paper prepared with a sentence and drawing to which dialogue can be added

▸ markers

▸ To download the following online resource for this lesson, visit **resources.fountasandpinnell.com**:

- chart art (optional)

Academic Language / Important Vocabulary

▸ story

▸ talking

▸ quotation marks

Continuum Connection

▸ Use dialogue as appropriate to add to the meaning of the story (p. 251)

GOAL

Understand that writers include dialogue within their stories.

RATIONALE

When children notice how writers use dialogue to reveal information about a character, they begin to think about ways to use dialogue to show character traits and motivations in their own writing.

ASSESS LEARNING

▸ Notice evidence that children are including dialogue in their writing.

▸ Observe for evidence that children can use vocabulary such as *story*, *talking*, and *quotation marks*.

MINILESSON

To help children think about how writers include dialogue in their stories, provide an inquiry-based lesson and model the process for adding dialogue. Here is an example.

▸ Show and read pages 8–11 of *I Am Invited to a Party!*

How did Mo Willems show that Elephant and Piggie are talking?

▸ Briefly review how speech bubbles show that the characters are talking.

▸ Show and read pages 13–14 of *Knuffle Bunny: A Cautionary Tale*.

What do you notice that Mo Willems did to show talking in this book?

▸ Engage children in a conversation to notice the use of both speech bubbles and dialogue within the writing.

Mo Willems used a speech bubble to show what Trixie sounds like when she talks. He used quotation marks to show that Daddy is talking. These are two ways that writers can show that someone is talking.

▸ Show and read page 2 in *The Broken Ladder*.

What do you notice about how Joan Silver showed that someone is talking in this book?

▸ Guide them to talk about the quotation marks, the use of *said*, and the speakers' names.

When different people are talking, you can use a speech bubble to point to the speaker's mouth. Or, you can use quotation marks and write the name of the person who is talking, like Joan Silver did in this book. Say that with me: *quotation marks*.

Have a Try

Invite children to turn and talk about including dialogue in a story.

▶ Show and read the prepared chart paper.

> These two children are sitting in a sandbox. If the children talk to each other, what might they say? Turn and tell your partner.

▶ After time for a brief discussion, ask volunteers to share. Use their ideas to add dialogue, modeling how to use quotation marks and the speakers' names.

Summarize and Apply

Summarize the lesson. Remind children that they can add dialogue to their writing.

▶ Write the principle at the top of the chart. Read it aloud.

> How can you show that characters in your story are talking?

> During writing time, think about what the people might say to each other in the writing you are working on and add some talking. Bring your writing to share when we meet later.

Show talking in your story.

Two children played together.

"Let's build a sandcastle," said Grace.

"I love making sandcastles!" said Caleb.

Confer

▶ During independent writing, move around the room to confer briefly with as many individual children as time allows. Sit side by side with them and invite them to talk about using dialogue in their books. Use the following prompts as needed.

- *What are the people saying to each other?*
- *What can you add to show that people in your story are talking?*
- *How can you show which person is speaking?*

Share

Following independent writing, gather children in the meeting area to share their experiences writing dialogue.

> Who added talking to your writing today? Share what you wrote.

> How did you show that people are talking?

Writing Minilesson Principle
Add talking to make your writing more interesting.

Adding Dialogue to Writing

You Will Need

▸ several mentor texts with dialogue, such as the following:

- *Elephants Cannot Dance!*, *Knuffle Bunny: A Cautionary Tale*, and *Knuffle Bunny Too: A Case of Mistaken Identity* by Mo Willems, from Text Set: Mo Willems: Having Fun with Humor

▸ chart paper prepared with a sentence and drawing to which dialogue can be added

▸ markers

▸ To download the following online resource for this lesson, visit **resources.fountasandpinnell.com**:

- chart art (optional)

Academic Language / Important Vocabulary

▸ talking

▸ interesting

▸ purpose

Continuum Connection

▸ Explain one's thoughts and feelings about an experience or event (p. 250)

▸ Use dialogue as appropriate to add to the meaning of the story (p. 251)

▸ Write in an expressive way (similar to oral language) (p. 254)

▸ Add thoughts in thought bubbles or dialogue in speech bubbles or quotation marks to provide information or provide narration (p. 254)

GOAL

Understand that dialogue should add to the meaning of the story and add interest.

RATIONALE

When children notice how writers use dialogue to reveal a character's feelings and make the writing more interesting, they begin to think about ways to include dialogue in their own writing.

ASSESS LEARNING

▸ Notice evidence that children understand that dialogue should have a purpose.

▸ Observe whether children are using dialogue in a purposeful way.

▸ Observe for evidence that children can use vocabulary such as *talking*, *interesting*, and *purpose*.

MINILESSON

To help children understand that dialogue is purposeful in that it adds meaning or makes the writing more interesting, use mentor texts. Here is an example.

▸ Show and read pages 44–45 of *Elephants Cannot Dance!*

> Elephant says *AND TRIED* again and again on these pages. Why do you think Mo Willems decided to have Elephant say the same thing so many times?

▸ Guide the conversation so children recognize that the writer used talking to show the reader that Elephant is frustrated because he cannot dance and that the dialogue provides more interest than writing *Elephant is frustrated.*

▸ Show and read pages 17–18 of *Knuffle Bunny: A Cautionary Tale.*

> Why do you think Mo Willems wrote what Daddy and Trixie say?

▸ Talk about how Daddy does not understand why Trixie is upset because he does not yet know that they left Knuffle Bunny behind. Trixie is trying to express that there is a problem, so Mo Willems shows that she is crying very loudly to get Daddy's attention.

▸ Show and read pages 35–36 of *Knuffle Bunny: A Case of Mistaken Identity.*

> Why did Mo Willems have Trixie and Sonja saying these words to each other?

▸ Help children understand that the words show how the characters are feeling.

> A writer adds talking to a story for a reason. The writer might want to show how the people are feeling. The writer might want to make the story more interesting. The writer might want to show what is happening in the story.

Have a Try

Invite children to turn and talk about adding dialogue in a purposeful way.

▶ Show and read the prepared chart.

Turn and talk about what these three friends might be saying. Their talking might tell the friends' feelings or what is happening in the story.

▶ After time for a brief discussion, ask a few volunteers to share. Use their ideas to add dialogue.

Summarize and Apply

Summarize the lesson. Remind children to add dialogue in a purposeful way.

What is a way to make your writing more interesting?

▶ Write the principle at the top of the chart.

During writing time, you can add talking to your own writing. Remember to include talking that shows feelings, is interesting, or tells what is happening in the story. Bring your writing to share when we meet later.

Add talking to make your writing more interesting.

The three friends are having a picnic.

"I love picnics," said Eli.

"Me too. What's in the basket?" asked Vivian.

"Let's open it and find out," said Henry.

Confer

▶ During independent writing, move around the room to confer briefly with as many individual children as time allows. Sit side by side with them and invite them to talk about adding dialogue to their books. Use the following prompts as needed.

• *What talking can be added to make the story more interesting?*

• *What could the people in your story say to show what is happening?*

• *How do you show what the people are saying?*

Share

Following independent writing, gather children in the meeting area to share their writing.

Who added talking to your story today? Share what you wrote.

How does the talking show feelings (make the story more interesting, show what is happening in the story)?

Assessment

After you have taught the minilessons in this umbrella, observe children as they write letters. Use *The Literacy Continuum* (Fountas and Pinnell 2017) to notice, teach for, and support children's learning as you observe their attempts at reading and writing.

▶ What evidence do you have of new understandings the children have developed related to dialogue?

- Do children understand that they can use speech or thought bubbles in their writing?

- Do they understand how to write dialogue in their stories?

- Do they use dialogue in order to make their writing more interesting?

- Are they using vocabulary related to writing dialogue, such as *speech bubble*, *thought bubble*, *talking*, *thinking*, *quotation marks*, *story*, *interesting*, and *purpose*?

▶ In what ways, beyond the scope of this umbrella, are children thinking about dialogue?

- Do they have a good understanding of how to use punctuation?

- Are they beginning to revise their writing?

Use your observations to determine the next umbrella you will teach. You may also consult Suggested Sequence of Lessons (pp. 557–571) for guidance.

EXTENSIONS FOR ADDING DIALOGUE TO WRITING

▶ If you are using *The Reading Minilessons Book, Grade 1* (Fountas and Pinnell 2019), the minilessons in this umbrella would pair well with LA.U19: Understanding Characters and Their Feelings, LA.U20: Knowing Characters Inside and Out, and LA.U23: Looking Closely at Illustrations.

▶ As you share other books with dialogue, have children talk about how authors show what characters are thinking and saying.

▶ Have children engage in readers' theater and then write about the conversations as a way to incorporate dialogue in their stories.

▶ Talk about using speaker tags (e.g., *shouted*, *whispered*, *cried*, *laughed*) to show how a character says something.

▶ Gather together a guided writing group of several children who need support in a specific area of writing, such as adding dialogue.

Minilessons in This Umbrella

WML1 Notice the decisions writers make.

WML2 Notice the decisions illustrators make.

Before Teaching Umbrella 3 Minilessons

The minilessons in this umbrella are designed to help children notice elements of author's and illustrator's craft that they can try in their own bookmaking. We do not recommend teaching these two lessons consecutively so that children have time to explore and participate in the inquiry over time. Repeat them throughout the year as children get to know different authors and illustrators.

Read and discuss engaging books with a variety of writing and illustration styles. Give children plenty of opportunities to study multiple books by the same author or illustrator. If you are using *The Reading Minilessons Book, Grade 1* (Fountas and Pinnell 2019), LA.U2: Studying Authors and Illustrators provides a foundation for this umbrella. Consider using the following books from *Fountas & Pinnell Classroom™ Interactive Read-Aloud Collection*, as well as complete text sets of books by Nicola Davies, Mo Willems, and Kevin Henkes, or choose books from your classroom library.

Interactive Read-Aloud

Nicola Davies: Exploring the Animal World

Big Blue Whale

Bob Graham: Exploring Everyday Life

"Let's Get a Pup!" Said Kate

Kevin Henkes: Exploring Characters

Lilly's Big Day

As you read and enjoy these texts together, help children

- notice and discuss interesting examples of author's and illustrator's craft, and
- notice similarities in books by the same author or illustrator.

Interactive Read-Aloud
Nicola Davies

Bob Graham

Kevin Henkes

Section 6: Craft

Writing Minilesson Principle
Notice the decisions writers make.

You Will Need

- several familiar books by authors the children have studied, such as those in Text Sets: Nicola Davies: Exploring the Animal World; Mo Willems: Having Fun with Humor; and Kevin Henkes: Exploring Characters
- chart paper and markers

Academic Language/ Important Vocabulary

- decision
- writer
- author

Continuum Connection

- Notice craft decisions that the author or illustrator has made and try out some of these decisions in one's own writing with teacher support (p. 251)
- Try out techniques other writers and illustrators have used (p. 257)
- Talk about oneself as a writer (p. 257)

GOAL

Notice the craft decisions writers make and try them out.

RATIONALE

When children notice the craft decisions that authors make, they realize that they can try the same techniques in their own writing. They are more likely to experiment with new writing techniques.

ASSESS LEARNING

- Listen to children as they talk about books. Can they identify interesting examples of author's craft?
- Notice whether children try out techniques that they have noticed other writers using.
- Observe for evidence that children can use vocabulary such as *decision*, *writer*, and *author*.

MINILESSON

To help children think about the minilesson principle, guide them to notice the authors' craft decisions in books they know. Here is an example.

- Show several books the children have already heard by a familiar author, such as Nicola Davies.

  We have read several books by Nicola Davies. When we read these books together, you noticed some interesting things about her writing. What did you notice about how Nicola Davies writes?

  Why do you think she does that?

- Record children's responses on chart paper.
- If necessary, guide children to notice specific examples of author's craft. For example, show pages 12–13 of *Just Ducks*.

  What do you notice about how Nicola Davies shared facts about ducks in this book?

  The facts are a smaller print size than the story. Why do you think the writer did that?

- Read pages 26–27 of *One Tiny Turtle*.

  What do you notice about how Nicola Davies described things? What kind of words did she use?

  Why do you think she used a lot of interesting words, like *burst* and *skitter*, when she described things?

- Continue in a similar manner with books by at least two more familiar authors, such as Mo Willems and Kevin Henkes.

Have a Try

Invite children to talk to a partner about techniques they would like to try in their own writing.

> Look at the chart. Which of these things would you like to try in your writing? Turn and talk to your partner about this.

▶ After children turn and talk, invite a few children to share their responses.

Summarize and Apply

Help children summarize the learning. Remind them to try some of the authors' techniques in their own writing.

▶ Write *Read Like a Writer* at the top of the chart. Read it aloud.

> What does it mean to read like a writer?

> Today during writing time, you can start a new book or continue working on one you've already started. As you write, think about the things you've noticed other writers doing and try one of these things in your own writing. You can look at the chart to get ideas.

Read Like a Writer

Author	What does the author do?	Why?
Nicola Davies	Writes facts in a smaller size	So you can tell them apart from the story
	Describes things with interesting words	So you can make a picture in your mind
Mo Willems	Uses speech bubbles	To show what the characters are saying in a fun way
	Uses *italics* and CAPITAL LETTERS	To show what the characters sound like when they are speaking
Kevin Henkes	Repeats words and sentences	To show that an idea is important

Confer

▶ During independent writing, move around the room to confer briefly with as many individual children as time allows. Sit side by side with them and invite them to talk about trying an author's technique in their own writing. Use prompts such as the following if needed.

- *What are you writing about today?*
- *Would you like to try something new today in your writing?*
- *Look at the chart. Which of these things would you like to try?*
- *Is there a place in your story where you could add a speech bubble?*
- *What new thing did you try today? Why did you try that?*

Share

Following independent writing, gather children in the meeting area to share their writing.

> Who tried something new today in your writing?

> What did you try?

You Will Need

- several books with different illustrators, such as the following:

  - *Big Blue Whale* by Nicola Davies, from Text Set: Nicola Davies: Exploring the Animal World

  - *"Let's Get a Pup!" Said Kate* by Bob Graham, from Text Set: Bob Graham: Exploring Everyday Life

  - *Lilly's Big Day* by Kevin Henkes, from Text Set: Kevin Henkes: Exploring Characters

- chart paper and markers

Academic Language/ Important Vocabulary

- decision
- illustrator
- illustration

Continuum Connection

- Notice craft decisions that the author or illustrator has made and try out some of these decisions in one's own writing with teacher support (p. 251)

- Try out techniques other writers and illustrators have used (p. 257)

- Talk about oneself as a writer (p. 257)

GOAL

Notice the craft decisions illustrators make and try them out.

RATIONALE

When children notice the craft decisions that illustrators make, they realize that they can try the same techniques in their own illustrations. They are more likely to experiment with new creative techniques.

ASSESS LEARNING

- Listen to children as they talk about books. Can they identify interesting examples of illustrator's craft?

- Notice whether children try out techniques that they have noticed other illustrators using.

- Observe for evidence that children can use vocabulary such as *decision*, *illustrator*, and *illustration*.

MINILESSON

To help children think about the minilesson principle, guide them to notice illustrators' craft decisions in books they know. Children do not need to be familiar with the books in order to study the illustrations. Here is an example.

- Show the cover of *Big Blue Whale* and read the title. Show pages 6–7.

  Look closely at this illustration. What do you notice?

  Why do you think the illustrator, Nick Maland, drew the animals and person next to the whale?

  Nick Maland decided he could help readers understand how big a whale is by showing how small the animals and people look next to it.

- Add responses to the chart.

- Continue in a similar manner with the illustrations in at least two more books, such as *"Let's Get a Pup!" Said Kate* and *Lilly's Big Day*. You might choose to highlight Bob Graham's use of multiple pictures on one page and Kevin Henkes's carefully drawn facial expressions.

- Add responses to the chart.

Have a Try

Invite children to talk to a partner about techniques they would like to try in their own illustrations.

> Look at the chart. Which of these things would you like to try in your drawings? Turn and talk to your partner about this.

▶ After children turn and talk, invite a few children to share their thinking.

Summarize and Apply

Summarize the learning and remind children that they can use these techniques in their own illustrations.

▶ Write the principle at the top of the chart. Read it aloud.

> During writing time today, start a new book or continue working on one you've already started. Spend some time working on the pictures. Think about something you noticed another illustrator doing. Look for a place to try that out in your book. Bring your book to share when we meet later.

Notice the decisions illustrators make.		
Illustrator	What does the illustrator do?	Why?
Nick Maland	Draws animals and a person next to a whale	To show size
Bob Graham	Draws many pictures on one page	To show everything that happend
Kevin Henkes	Draws faces with expression	To show how characters are feeling

Confer

▶ During independent writing, move around the room to confer briefly with as many individual children as time allows. Sit side by side with them and invite them to talk about trying an illustrator's technique in their own writing. Use prompts such as the following if needed.

- *What are you going to draw on this page?*
- *Would you like to try one of the things we talked about today? Which one?*
- *How is your character feeling? Can you draw that?*
- *What new thing did you try in your drawings? Why did you try that?*

Share

Following independent writing, gather children in the meeting area to share their writing.

> Who tried something new in your illustrations?

> Talk about what you did.

Section 6: Craft

Assessment

After you have taught the minilessons in this umbrella, observe children as they write and talk about their writing. Use the behaviors and understandings in *The Literacy Continuum* (Fountas and Pinnell 2017) to notice, teach for, and support children's learning as you observe their attempts at writing and drawing.

▶ What evidence do you have of new understandings the children have developed related to reading like a writer?

- Do children notice and talk about the decisions that writers and illustrators make?

- Do they try the same techniques in their own writing and illustrations?

- Are they using vocabulary such as *decision*, *writer*, and *illustrator*?

▶ In what other ways, beyond the scope of this umbrella, are children ready to explore author's craft?

- Are they experimenting with different ways of writing story beginnings and endings?

- Do they proofread their writing?

Use your observations to determine the next umbrella you will teach. You may also consult Suggested Sequence of Lessons (pp. 557–571) for guidance.

EXTENSIONS FOR READING LIKE A WRITER

▶ Continue adding to the charts created during these minilessons as children notice more examples of author's and illustrator's craft.

▶ Teach dedicated minilessons about specific techniques the children noticed during these minilessons. Consider using Planning a Writing Minilesson (p. 102) to plan new lessons with a different set of books.

▶ Gather together a guided writing group of several children who need support in a specific area of writing.

Minilessons in This Umbrella

WML1 Start your book with talking.

WML2 Start your book with a feeling.

WML3 Start your book by describing where something happened.

WML4 Start your book with a question.

WML5 Start your book with an interesting fact.

Before Teaching Umbrella 4 Minilessons

Prior to teaching these minilessons, provide opportunities for children to read, talk about, and write their own books in a variety of fiction and nonfiction genres. These minilessons invite children to notice and try out ways that books can begin. For these lessons, the class text from IW.8: Writing a Memory Story will be used as an example.

The focus of this umbrella is to help children understand that writers make choices about how they begin books and that there are different ways books can start. Help children realize that some types of beginnings may be better suited for fiction and some for nonfiction. Use the books listed below from *Fountas & Pinnell Classroom™ Interactive Read-Aloud Collection* text sets, or choose books from the classroom library.

Living and Working Together: Community

Mama Panya's Pancakes: A Village Tale from Kenya by Mary and Rich Chamberlin

Blackout by John Rocco

Mo Willems: Having Fun with Humor

Elephants Cannot Dance!

Using Numbers: Books with Counting

Jake's 100th Day of School by Lester L. Laminack

Kevin Henkes: Exploring Characters

Chrysanthemum

Nicola Davies: Exploring the Animal World

One Tiny Turtle

Just Ducks!

Exploring Nonfiction

Water: Up, Down, and All Around by Natalie M. Rosinsky

What If You Had Animal Teeth!? by Sandra Markle

What Do You Do When Something Wants to Eat You? by Steve Jenkins

Interactive Writing Lessons

IW.8 Writing a Memory Story

As you read and enjoy these texts together, help children

- notice the choices authors make about the beginning of a book, and
- think about alternative ways a book might begin.

Community

Mo Willems

Using Numbers

Kevin Henkes

Nicola Davies

Exploring Nonfiction
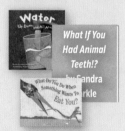

Interactive Writing

Section 6: Craft

Writing Minilesson Principle
Start your book with talking.

Exploring Different Ways Authors Start Books

You Will Need

- several familiar books that begin with talking, such as the following:

  - *Mama Panya's Pancakes* by Mary and Rich Chamberlin, from Text Set: Living and Working Together: Community

  - *Elephants Cannot Dance!* by Mo Willems, from Text Set: Mo Willems: Having Fun with Humor

- class-made story from IW.8: Writing a Memory Story

- chart paper and markers

Academic Language / Important Vocabulary

- book
- beginning
- talking

Continuum Connection

- Use a variety of beginnings to engage the reader (p. 254)

GOAL

Understand that writers can begin a book with someone talking.

RATIONALE

When children understand that writers make choices about how to begin a book, they understand that they can make decisions and vary the way they begin their own books. A character's dialogue is just one way that a book can begin.

ASSESS LEARNING

- Observe whether children recognize that writers make choices about how they begin a book.
- Look for evidence that children choose to begin a book with someone talking.
- Observe for evidence that children can use vocabulary such as *book*, *beginning*, and *talking*.

MINILESSON

Use familiar books and modeling to engage children in noticing that a book can start with someone talking. Here is an example.

- Show the cover and read the first two pages of *Mama Panya's Pancakes*.

  What do you notice about the way the writers, Mary and Rich Chamberlin, decided to start this book?

- Support the conversation to help children identify that the authors begin with Mama Panya and Adika talking to each other.

  Mama Panya tells Adika to hurry up because it is time to go to the market, and Adika says she is all ready to go.

- Show the cover and read the first few pages of *Elephants Cannot Dance!*

  What do you notice about the way Mo Willems decided to start this book?

- Guide children to recognize that Piggie is talking to Gerald.

  What do you notice about how these authors decided to start their books?

Have a Try

Invite children to turn and talk about starting a book with someone talking.

▶ Show a class-made story, such as the memory story from IW.8. Reread the beginning of the story.

> **How could you begin this story with talking? Think about who the people in our memory story are and what each person might say. Turn and talk to your partner about that.**

▶ As needed, support the conversation to get it started. Then provide discussion time. Ask several volunteers to make suggestions, and record responses on the chart paper.

Summarize and Apply

Help children summarize the learning. Invite them to begin a book with someone talking.

> **What did you notice today about how some authors start their books?**

▶ Write the principle at the top of the chart.

> **Today, you can begin a new book or continue one you are working on. Think about whether you want to start your book with talking. If you do, add that to your book. Bring your writing to share when we meet later.**

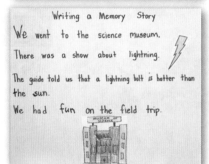

Start your book with talking.

"Welcome to the science museum!" said the guide.

"I can't wait for the field trip," said Michael.

"I hope we see the light show," said Emma.

"Class, line up by the door so we can go to the science museum."

Writing a Memory Story

We went to the science museum.

There was a show about lightning.

The guide told us that a lightning bolt is hotter than the sun.

We had fun on the field trip.

Confer

▶ During independent writing, move around the room to confer briefly with as many individual children as time allows. Sit side by side with them and invite them to talk about their decisions for how to start their books. Use the prompts below as needed.

- *How could you start your book with someone talking?*
- *What is something the characters might say to each other?*
- *What else could they say?*

Share

Following independent writing, gather children in the meeting area. Ask several children to share the beginning of a book they are working on.

> **Did anyone decide to start a book with someone talking? Share how you started your book.**

Exploring Different Ways Authors Start Books

You Will Need

- several familiar books that begin with a feeling, such as the following:
  - *Jake's 100th Day of School* by Lester L. Laminack, from Text Set: Using Numbers: Books with Counting
  - *Chrysanthemum* by Kevin Henkes, from Text Set: Kevin Henkes: Exploring Characters
- class-made story from IW.8: Writing a Memory Story
- chart paper and markers

Academic Language / Important Vocabulary

- book
- beginning
- feeling

Continuum Connection

- Use a variety of beginnings to engage the reader (p. 254)

GOAL

Understand that writers can start a book with a feeling.

RATIONALE

When children learn different ways to begin writing a book, they expand their thinking about the independent decisions they can make about their writing. You may want to point out to children that starting a book with a feeling may be better suited for fiction books.

ASSESS LEARNING

- Observe whether children recognize that writers make choices about how they begin a book.
- Look for evidence that children choose to begin a book with a feeling.
- Observe for evidence that children can use vocabulary such as *book*, *beginning*, and *feeling*.

MINILESSON

Use familiar books and modeling to engage children in noticing that a book can start with a feeling. Here is an example.

- Show the cover and read the first page of *Jake's 100th Day of School*.

  What do you notice about the way the writer, Lester L. Laminack, decided to start this book?

- Support the conversation to help children discover that the book begins with showing that the class is excited about the hundredth day of school. Help them understand that being excited is a feeling.

  As a reader, the first thing you learn is that Mr. Thompson's class feels excited. Lester Laminack started his book with a feeling.

- Show the cover and read the first page of *Chrysanthemum*.

  What do you notice about the way that Kevin Henkes decided to start this book?

- Guide children to recognize that the book begins with words about how Chrysanthemum's parents are feeling.

  What do you notice about how these authors started their books?

Have a Try

Invite children to turn and talk about starting a book with a feeling.

▶ Show a class-made book, such as the memory story from IW.8. Read the beginning of the story.

> Think about how you could start this story with a feeling. How were you feeling before we went to the science museum? Turn and talk to your partner about that.

▶ As needed, support the conversation to get it started. Then provide discussion time. Ask several volunteers to make suggestions, and record responses on the chart paper.

Summarize and Apply

Help children summarize the learning. Invite them to started a book with a feeling.

> What did you notice about how some authors started their books?

▶ Write the principle at the top of the chart.

> Today, you can start a new book or continue one you are working on. Think about whether you want to start your book with a feeling. If so, add that to your book. Bring your writing to share when we meet later.

Start your book with a feeling.

We couldn't wait to get on the bus to go to the science museum.

We were so excited to arrive at the science museum!

We were curious about what we would see at the science museum.

Writing a Memory Story

We went to the science museum.
There was a show about lightning.
The guide told us that a lightning bolt is hotter than the sun.
We had fun on the field trip.

Confer

▶ During independent writing, move around the room to confer briefly with as many individual children as time allows. Sit side by side with them and invite them to talk about their decisions for how to start their books. Use the prompts below as needed.

- *How would you like to start your book?*
- *How are the people feeling at the beginning of your book?*
- *How could you show how the people are feeling?*
- *How did you decide to start your book this way?*

Share

Following independent writing, gather children in the meeting area. Ask several children to share the beginning of a book they are working on.

> Did anyone decide to start a book with a feeling? Share how you started your book.

Writing Minilesson Principle

Start your book by describing where something happened.

Exploring Different Ways Authors Start Books

You Will Need

- several familiar books that begin with a description of where something happened, such as the following:

  - *One Tiny Turtle* by Nicola Davies, from Text Set: Nicola Davies: Exploring the Animal World

  - *Blackout* by John Rocco, from Text Set: Living and Working Together: Community

- class-made story from IW.8: Writing a Memory Story

- chart paper and markers

Academic Language / Important Vocabulary

- book
- beginning
- describe
- where

Continuum Connection

- Use a variety of beginnings to engage the reader (p. 254)

GOAL

Understand that writers can begin a book with a description of where something happened.

RATIONALE

When children learn that they can begin a book with a description of where something happened, they understand that they have many choices to make in their writing. You may want to point out to children that the way a place is described might sound different in a fiction book and in a nonfiction book.

ASSESS LEARNING

- Observe whether children recognize that writers make choices about how they begin a book.

- Look for evidence that children choose to start a book with a description of where something took place.

- Observe for evidence that children can use vocabulary such as *book*, *beginning*, *describe*, and *where*.

MINILESSON

Use familiar books and modeling to engage children in noticing that a book can start with a description of where something happened. Here is an example.

- Show the cover and read the first two pages of *One Tiny Turtle*.

  > What do you notice about the way that the writer, Nicola Davies, decided to start this book?

- Support the conversation to help children identify that the writer begins with a description of the place in the ocean where baby sea turtles live.

  > The writer began with a description of a place far out in the ocean where baby sea turtles and other tiny creatures live.

- Show the cover and read the first two pages of *Blackout*.

  > What do you notice about the way that John Rocco decided to start this book?

- Guide children to recognize that the writer began with a description of the city at night in the summertime.

  > What do you notice about how these authors decided to start their books?

  > These authors decided to describe, or tell about, where something is taking place.

Have a Try

Invite children to turn and talk to a partner about starting a book by describing where something happened.

▶ Show a class-made book, such as the memory story from IW.8. Reread the beginning of the story.

> If you wanted to start this story by describing where it happened, what could you write?

▶ Ask several volunteers to make suggestions. Record responses on the chart paper.

Summarize and Apply

Help children summarize the learning. Invite them to begin a book by describing where something happened.

> What did you notice today about how some authors start their books?

▶ Write the principle at the top of the chart.

> Today, you can start a new book or continue working on one you have already started. Think about whether you want to start your book by describing where something happened. If so, add that to your book. Bring your writing to share when we meet later.

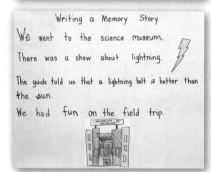

Confer

▶ During independent writing, move around the room to confer briefly with as many individual children as time allows. Sit side by side with them and invite them to talk about their decisions for how to start their books. Use the prompts below as needed.

- *How do you want to start your book?*
- *Where does your story take place?*
- *How can you describe where this is happening?*
- *How did you decide to start your book this way?*

Share

Following independent writing, gather children in the meeting area. Ask several children to share the beginning of a book they are working on.

> Did anyone decide to start a book by describing where something happened? Share how you started your book.

Section 6: Craft

Writing Minilesson Principle
Start your book with a question.

Exploring Different Ways Authors Start Books

You Will Need

- several familiar books that begin with a question, such as the following:
  - *Just Ducks!* by Nicola Davies, from Text Set: Nicola Davies: Exploring the Animal World
  - *Water: Up, Down, and All Around* by Natalie M. Rosinsky, from Text Set: Exploring Nonfiction
- class-made story from IW.8: Writing a Memory Story
- chart paper and markers

Academic Language / Important Vocabulary

- book
- beginning
- question

Continuum Connection

- Use a variety of beginnings to engage the reader (p. 254)

GOAL

Understand that writers can begin a book with a question.

RATIONALE

When children learn that they can begin a book with a question, they think about what questions a reader might have and what a reader might like to know about. You may want to point out that the types of questions may be different in a fiction book and a nonfiction book.

ASSESS LEARNING

- Observe whether children recognize that writers make choices about how they begin a book.
- Look for evidence that children choose to start a book with a question.
- Observe for evidence that children can use vocabulary such as *book*, *beginning*, and *question*.

MINILESSON

Use familiar books and modeling to engage children in noticing that a book can start with a question. Here is an example.

- Show the cover and read the first page of *Just Ducks!*

  What do you notice that the writer, Nicola Davies, decided to do on the first page of her book?

- Support the conversation to help children identify that the author asked a question to get the reader interested in reading the rest of the book.

  The girl asks a question about what is making all of the quacking noises.

- Show the cover and read the first page of *Water: Up, Down, and All Around*.

  What do you notice about the title that Natalie M. Rosinsky put at the beginning of this section?

- Guide children to recognize that it is a question.

  Why do you think authors decide to start their books with a question?

Have a Try

Invite children to turn and talk about starting a book with a question.

▶ Show a class-made book, such as the memory story from IW.8. Reread the beginning of the story.

> **What is a question you could ask at the beginning of this story? Turn and talk to your partner about that.**

▶ As needed, support the conversation to get it started. Then provide discussion time. Ask several volunteers to make suggestions. Record responses on the chart paper.

Summarize and Apply

Help children summarize the learning. Invite them to begin a book by asking a question.

> **What did you notice today about how some authors decide to start their books?**

▶ Write the principle at the top of the chart.

> **Today, you can start a new book or continue working on one you have already started. Think about whether you want to start your book with a question. If so, add that to your book. Bring your writing to share when we meet later.**

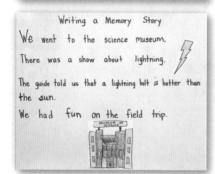

Confer

▶ During independent writing, move around the room to confer briefly with as many individual children as time allows. Sit side by side with them and invite them to talk about their decisions for how to start their books. Use the prompts below as needed.

- *How would you like to start your book?*
- *What question might get the reader interested?*
- *What question could this person ask?*
- *How did you decide to start your book this way?*

Share

Following independent writing, gather children in the meeting area. Ask several children to share the beginning of a book they are working on.

> **Who decided to start a book with a question? Share how you started your book.**

Writing Minilesson Principle
Start your book with an interesting fact.

Exploring Different Ways Authors Start Books

You Will Need

- several familiar books that begin with an interesting fact, such as the following from Text Set: Exploring Nonfiction:
  - *What If You Had Animal Teeth!?* by Sandra Markle
  - *What Do You Do When Something Wants to Eat You?* by Steve Jenkins
- class-made story from IW.8: Writing a Memory Story
- chart paper and markers

Academic Language / Important Vocabulary

- book
- beginning
- interesting
- fact

Continuum Connection

- Use a variety of beginnings to engage the reader (p. 254)

GOAL

Understand that writers can begin a book with an interesting fact.

RATIONALE

When children learn that they can begin a book with an interesting fact, they can think about getting the reader's attention right from the start. You may want to point out that this type of beginning may be more suitable for a nonfiction book than a fiction book.

ASSESS LEARNING

- Observe whether children recognize that writers make choices about how they begin a book.
- Look for evidence that children choose to begin a book with an interesting fact.
- Observe for evidence that children can use vocabulary such as *book*, *beginning*, *interesting*, and *fact*.

MINILESSON

Use familiar books and modeling to engage children in noticing that a writer can start with an interesting fact. Here is an example.

- Show the cover and read page 4 of *What If You Had Animal Teeth!?*

  What do you notice about how the writer, Sandra Markle, decided to start this book?

- Support the conversation to help children identify that the writer began with an interesting fact about beavers.

  The writer wrote an interesting fact in a circle at the bottom of the page.

- Then show the cover and read pages 2–3 of *What Do You Do When Something Wants to Eat You?*

  What do you notice about how Steve Jenkins decided to start this book?

- Guide children to recognize that the information about the octopus is an interesting fact.

  What do you notice about how these authors decided to start their books?

  What kind of book might start with a fact?

The Writing Minilessons Book, Grade 1

Have a Try

Invite children to turn and talk about starting a book with an interesting fact.

▶ Show a class-made book, such as the memory story from IW.8. Read the beginning of the story.

> Think about an interesting fact that we could use to start this story. Turn and talk to your partner about that.

▶ As needed, support the conversation to get it started. Then provide discussion time. Ask volunteers to make suggestions. Record responses on the chart paper.

Summarize and Apply

Help children summarize the learning. Invite them to begin a book with an interesting fact.

> What did you notice today about how some authors decided to start their books?

▶ Write the principle at the top of the chart.

> Today, you can start a new book or continue working on one you have already started. Think about whether you want to start your book with an interesting fact. If so, add that to your book. Bring your writing to share when we meet later.

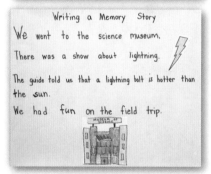

Start your book with an interesting fact.

Lightning bolts are really hot.

Lightning bolts make heat hotter than the sun.

Writing a Memory Story
We went to the science museum.
There was a show about lightning.
The guide told us that a lightning bolt is hotter than the sun.
We had fun on the field trip.

Confer

▶ During independent writing, move around the room to confer briefly with as many individual children as time allows. Sit side by side with them and invite them to talk about their decisions for how to start their books. Use the prompts below as needed.

- *How would you like to start your book?*
- *What is the most interesting fact you learned?*
- *What fact might get the reader interested in reading this book?*

Share

Following independent writing, gather children in the meeting area. Ask several children to share the beginning of a book they are working on.

> Did anyone begin a book with an interesting fact? Share how you started your book.

Section 6: Craft

Assessment

After you have taught the minilessons in this umbrella, observe children as they engage in writing. Use *The Literacy Continuum* (Fountas and Pinnell 2017) to notice, teach for, and support children's learning as you observe their attempts at writing.

▶ What evidence do you have of new understandings children have developed related to ways writers start their books?

- Do children understand that writers make choices about how to start a book?

- Are children choosing to begin books in a variety of ways (e.g., dialogue, a feeling, a description of the setting, a question, or an interesting fact)?

- Is there evidence that children can use vocabulary such as *book*, *beginning*, *talking*, *feeling*, *describe*, *where*, *question*, *interesting*, and *fact*?

▶ In what ways, beyond the scope of this umbrella, are children showing interest in making books?

- Do they show an interest in making both fiction and nonfiction books?

- Are they thinking about different ways books can end?

Use your observations to determine the next umbrella you will teach. You may also consult Suggested Sequence of Lessons (pp. 557–571) for guidance.

EXTENSIONS FOR EXPLORING DIFFERENT WAYS AUTHORS START BOOKS

▶ As you enjoy reading aloud with children, help them notice the way writers began their books. Talk about why the authors might have made those decisions.

▶ Teach children how to punctuate dialogue and questions. (See CNV.U4.WML2 for a minilesson on using question marks.)

▶ Gather together a guided writing group of children who need support in a specific area of writing.

Minilessons in This Umbrella

WML1 End your book by telling your feelings.

WML2 End your book by making the reader think more about the story or topic.

WML3 End your book with something you learned.

Before Teaching Umbrella 5 Minilessons

The focus of this umbrella is to help children understand that writers make choices about how they end books and that there are different ways books can end. Before teaching these minilessons, it would be helpful to teach the previous umbrella (CFT.U4: Exploring Different Ways Authors Start Books). Make sure children have had opportunities to read, talk about, and write their own books in a variety of fiction and nonfiction genres. For these lessons, the class text from IW.8: Writing a Memory Story will be used to try out the minilesson principle.

For mentor texts, use the books listed below from *Fountas & Pinnell Classroom™ Interactive Read-Aloud Collection* text sets, or choose books from the classroom library.

Journeys Near and Far

When This World Was New by D. H. Figueredo

Humorous Stories

That's Good! That's Bad! by Margery Cuyler

Exploring Nonfiction

What Do You Do When Something Wants to Eat You? by Steve Jenkins

Tools by Ann Morris

Sharing Cultures: Folktales

Once a Mouse . . . by Marcia Brown

Mo Willems: Having Fun with Humor

Don't Let the Pigeon Drive the Bus!

Nicola Davies: Exploring the Animal World

Big Blue Whale

Celebrating Diversity

Two Eggs, Please by Sarah Weeks

Interactive Writing Lessons

IW.8 Writing a Memory Story

As you read and enjoy these texts together, help children

- notice the choices authors make about the way they end their books, and
- think about other ways a book might end.

Journeys

Humorous Stories

Exploring Nonfiction

Folktales

Mo Willems

Nicola Davies

Celebrating Diversity

Interactive Writing

Section 6: Craft

Writing Minilesson Principle
End your book by telling your feelings.

Exploring Different Ways Authors End Books

You Will Need

- several familiar books that end with a feeling, such as the following:
  - *When This World Was New* by D. H. Figueredo, from Text Set: Journeys Near and Far
  - *That's Good! That's Bad!* by Margery Cuyler, from Text Set: Humorous Stories
- class-made story from IW.8: Writing a Memory Story
- chart paper and markers

Academic Language / Important Vocabulary

- book
- ending
- feelings

Continuum Connection

- Use an ending that is interesting, leaves the reader satisfied, or gets the reader to think more about a story or topic (p. 254)

GOAL

Understand that writers can end a book by telling their feelings about the topic or an event in the story.

RATIONALE

When children learn different ways to end a book, they expand their thinking about the independent decisions they can make about their writing.

ASSESS LEARNING

- ▶ Observe whether children recognize that writers make choices about how they end a book.
- ▶ Look for evidence that children choose to end a book with a feeling.
- ▶ Observe for evidence that children can use vocabulary such as *book, ending,* and *feelings.*

MINILESSON

Use familiar books and modeling to engage children in noticing how writers end a book with a feeling. Here is an example.

- ▶ Show the cover and read the last few pages of *When This World Was New.*

  What do you notice about how the writer, D. H. Figueredo, decided to end this book?

- ▶ Support the conversation to help children identify that the book ends with how the character feels.

  This writer ended the story with the reader learning that Danilito is still scared, but not as scared as when he first arrived in the United States.

- ▶ Show the cover and revisit the last page of *That's Good! That's Bad!*

  What do you notice about how Margery Cuyler decided to end this book?

- ▶ Guide children to recognize that the book ends with words about how the little boy's parents feel now that he is back with them.

  What do you notice about how these writers decided to end their books?

Have a Try

Invite children to turn and talk about ending a book by telling about feelings.

▶ Show a class-made book, such as the memory story from IW.8. Read the ending.

> Think of another way we could end this story. How were you feeling? Turn and talk about that.

▶ As needed, support the conversation to get it started. Then provide discussion time. Ask several volunteers to make suggestions. Record responses on the chart paper.

Summarize and Apply

Help children summarize the learning. Invite children to end their books by telling their feelings.

> What is one way you could end your book?

▶ Write the principle at the top of the chart.

> Today, you can start a new book or continue working on one you have already started. Think about whether you would like to end your book by telling your feelings. If so, add that to your book. Bring your writing to share when we meet later.

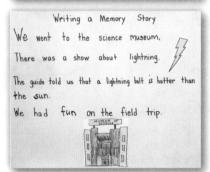

End your book by telling your feelings.

We didn't want to leave the science museum.

We were excited about what we learned about lightning.

We were tired after a whole day at the science museum.

Writing a Memory Story

We went to the science museum.
There was a show about lightning.
The guide told us that a lightning bolt is hotter than the sun.
We had fun on the field trip.

Confer

▶ During independent writing, move around the room to confer briefly with as many individual children as time allows. Sit side by side with them and invite them to talk about their decisions for how to end their books. Use the prompts below as needed.

- *How would you like to end your book?*
- *How are the characters feeling at the end of your book?*
- *What is a word that describes how they are feeling?*
- *How did you decide to end your book that way?*

Share

Following independent writing, gather children in the meeting area. Ask several children to share the ending of a book they are working on.

> Did anyone decide to end a book with a feeling? Share the ending of your book.

Writing Minilesson Principle
End your book by making the reader think more about the story or topic.

Exploring Different Ways Authors End Books

You Will Need

▸ several familiar books that end with something that makes the reader think more about the story or topic, such as the following:

- *What Do You Do When Something Wants to Eat You?* by Steve Jenkins, from Text Set: Exploring Nonfiction

- *Once a Mouse . . .* by Marcia Brown, from Text Set: Sharing Cultures: Folktales

- *Don't Let the Pigeon Drive the Bus!* by Mo Willems, from Text Set: Mo Willems: Having Fun with Humor

▸ class-made story from IW.8: Writing a Memory Story

▸ chart paper and markers

Academic Language / Important Vocabulary

▸ book

▸ ending

▸ think

▸ story

▸ topic

Continuum Connection

▸ Use an ending that is interesting, leaves the reader satisfied, or gets the reader to think more about a story or topic (p. 254)

GOAL

Understand that writers can end their books in a way that makes readers think more about the story or topic.

RATIONALE

When children learn that they can end a book in a way that makes readers think more about the story or topic, they understand that they can make decisions about their own writing and that there are choices they can make about how to end a book.

ASSESS LEARNING

▸ Observe whether children recognize that writers make choices about how they end a book.

▸ Look for evidence that children choose to end a book by leaving the reader with something to think about.

▸ Observe for evidence that children can use vocabulary such as *book*, *ending*, *think*, *story*, and *topic*.

MINILESSON

Use familiar books and modeling to engage children in noticing that a writer can end with something for the reader to think about. Here is an example.

▸ Show the cover and read the last few pages of *What Do You Do When Something Wants to Eat You?*

> What do you notice about the way that the writer, Steve Jenkins, decided to end this book?

▸ Support the conversation to help children identify that the writer ended by leaving the reader thinking about how she would feel if something wanted to eat her, just like the animals in the book.

> The writer ended with a question that asks the reader to think about something.

▸ Show the cover and revisit the last few pages of *Once a Mouse . . . .*

> What do you notice about the way that Marcia Brown decided to end this book?

▸ Guide children to recognize that the writer ended with the hermit thinking about big and little, just like at the beginning of the story. The reader is left wondering what the hermit will do next.

▸ Continue by showing the cover and reading the last few pages of *Don't Let the Pigeon Drive the Bus!* including the drawings on the inside back cover.

> Sometimes, writers decide to end a book by having the reader think more about the story or topic.

Have a Try

Invite children to turn and talk about ending a book with a way to make the reader think more about the story or topic.

▶ Show a class-made book, such as the memory story from IW.8. Read the ending.

Think of another way we could end this story. What could we say to get readers to think more about the field trip? Turn and talk about that.

▶ As needed, support the conversation to get it started. Then provide discussion time. Ask several volunteers to make suggestions. Record responses on the chart paper.

Summarize and Apply

Help children summarize the learning. Invite children to end their books by making the reader think more about the story or topic.

What is a way that you can decide to end your book?

▶ Write the principle at the top of the chart.

Today, you can start a new book or work on one you have started. Think about whether you would like to end your book by making the reader think more about what your book is about. Bring your writing to share when we meet later.

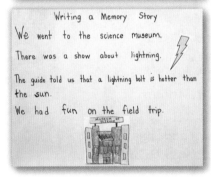

End your book by making the reader think more about the story or topic.

What will we see the next time at the museum?

We saw a sign that said, "Coming soon." What could that be?

Where will we go next?

Writing a Memory Story

We went to the science museum.
There was a show about lightning.
The guide told us that a lightning bolt is hotter than the sun.
We had fun on the field trip.

Confer

▶ During independent writing, move around the room to confer briefly with as many individual children as time allows. Sit side by side with them and invite them to talk about their decisions for how to end their books. Use the prompts below as needed.

- *How will your book end?*
- *How might you make the reader think more about what you have written?*
- *What are some words you might use to end the book in this way?*

Share

Following independent writing, gather children in the meeting area. Ask several children to share the ending of a book they are working on.

Did anyone end a book by making the reader think more about what the book was about? Share how you ended your book.

Writing Minilesson Principle
End your book with something you learned.

You Will Need

- several familiar books (both fiction and nonfiction) that end with something the reader learned, such as the following:

  - *Big Blue Whale* by Nicola Davies, from Text Set: Nicola Davies: Exploring the Animal World

  - *Tools* by Ann Morris, from Text Set: Exploring Nonfiction

  - *Two Eggs, Please* by Sarah Weeks, from Text Set: Celebrating Diversity

- class-made story from IW.8: Writing a Memory Story

- chart paper and markers

Academic Language / Important Vocabulary

- book
- ending
- learned

Continuum Connection

- Use an ending that is interesting, leaves the reader satisfied, or gets the reader to think more about a story or topic (p. 254)

GOAL

Understand that writers can end their books by stating something they have learned.

RATIONALE

When children learn that they can end a book with something they learned, they think about what types of things they want a reader to know after reading their book. You may want to point out that what a reader learns may be different in a fiction book and a nonfiction book.

ASSESS LEARNING

- Observe whether children recognize that writers make choices about how they end a book.
- Look for evidence that children choose to end a book with something they learned.
- Observe for evidence that children can use vocabulary such as *book*, *ending*, and *learned*.

MINILESSON

Use familiar books and modeling to engage children in noticing that authors sometimes choose to end a book with something they learned. Here is an example.

- Read the last few pages of a nonfiction book such as *Big Blue Whale*.

  What do you notice about how the writer, Nicola Davies, decided to end this book?

- Support the conversation to help children talk about the ending.

  The writer ended with the information that even though a whale is very large, it is still small compared to the size of the ocean. That is something that the writer probably learned when she wrote this book, and she shared what she learned with the reader.

- Show the cover and read the last two pages of *Tools*.

  What do you notice about how Ann Morris decided to end this book?

- Guide children to recognize that the writer ends with what was learned about how tools help people and make their lives easier.

- Repeat with a fiction book by revisiting the last two pages of *Two Eggs, Please*.

  This is a story about different animals and how they ordered different eggs. What do the words show about what is learned?

- Make sure children understand that the writer ends the book by showing what readers learned about being both different and the same.

Have a Try

Invite children to turn and talk about ending a book with something they learned.

▶ Show a class-made book, such as the memory story from IW.8. Read the ending.

> Think of another way we could end this story. We could tell something we learned. Turn and talk about that.

▶ As needed, support the conversation to get it started. Then provide discussion time. Ask several volunteers to make suggestions. Record responses on the chart paper.

Summarize and Apply

Help children summarize the learning. Invite children to end their books with something they learned.

> What is one way you can end your book?

▶ Write the principle at the top of the chart.

> Today, you can start a new book or continue working on one you have already started. Think about whether you would like to end your book with something you learned. If so, add that to your book. Bring your writing to share when we meet later.

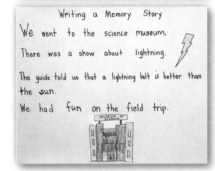

End your book with something you learned.

That is the most important fact about lightning.

You will probably never be struck by lightning.
You should be careful anyway.

The museum was too big to see in one day.

Writing a Memory Story
We went to the science museum.
There was a show about lightning.
The guide told us that a lightning bolt is hotter than the sun.
We had fun on the field trip.

Confer

▶ During independent writing, move around the room to confer briefly with as many individual children as time allows. Sit side by side with them and invite them to talk about their decisions for how to end their books. Use the prompts below as needed.

- *How would you like to end your book?*
- *What do you want your reader to learn?*
- *What lesson do the people in your book learn?*
- *How did you decide to end your book that way?*

Share

Following independent writing, gather children in the meeting area. Ask several children to share the ending of the book they are working on.

> Who ended a book with something you learned? Share how you ended your book.

Assessment

After you have taught the minilessons in this umbrella, observe children as they engage in writing. Use *The Literacy Continuum* (Fountas and Pinnell 2017) to notice, teach for, and support children's learning as you observe their attempts at writing.

▶ What evidence do you have of new understandings children have developed related to how writers end a book?

- Do children understand that writers make choices about how to end a book?

- Are children choosing to end their books in a variety of ways (e.g., by telling their feelings, making the reader think more, or sharing what they learned)?

- Is there evidence that children can use vocabulary such as *book*, *ending*, *feelings*, *think*, *story*, *topic*, and *learned*?

▶ In what ways, beyond the scope of this umbrella, are children showing readiness for making books?

- Do they show an interest in making both fiction and nonfiction books?

- Are they thinking about the words they use in their writing?

Use your observations to determine the next umbrella you will teach. You may also consult Suggested Sequence of Lessons (pp. 557–571) for guidance.

EXTENSIONS FOR EXPLORING DIFFERENT WAYS AUTHORS END BOOKS

▶ As you enjoy reading aloud with children, help them notice the ways writers ended their books. Talk about which endings they like and why.

▶ When children choose a new way to end a story, encourage them to share it with classmates.

▶ Gather together a guided writing group of several children who need support in a specific area of writing.

Minilessons in This Umbrella

WML1 Choose words to match a sound.

WML2 Choose interesting words to describe the way characters talk.

WML3 Choose interesting words to describe actions.

Before Teaching Umbrella 6 Minilessons

Prior to this umbrella, children should have had many opportunities to read and talk about books by writers who use strong words in their writing. Children also should have had many experiences writing stories independently. The goal of these minilessons is to help children recognize the interesting words that writers use and to begin to think about word choice in their own writing.

For mentor texts, use the books listed below from *Fountas & Pinnell Classroom*™ *Interactive Read-Aloud Collection* and *Shared Reading Collection*, or choose books from the classroom library that have sound words, strong verbs, and varied word choices.

Interactive Read-Aloud Collection

Exploring Fiction and Nonfiction

On the Go by Ann Morris

Bob Graham: Exploring Everyday Life

The Silver Button

Shared Reading Collection

The Sweet Mango Tree by Megan K. Smith

The Cactus Hotel by Abbey Grace Moore

Scram! by Julie Reich

As you read and enjoy these texts together, help children

- notice the playful, descriptive, and interesting words that writers use, and

- notice different words for *said*.

Interactive Read-Aloud
Fiction and Nonfiction

Bob Graham

Shared Reading

Section 6: Craft

WML1

Writing Minilesson Principle
Choose words to match a sound.

Making Powerful Word Choices

You Will Need

- several familiar books that have sound words, such as the following from *Shared Reading Collection*:
  - *The Sweet Mango Tree* by Megan K. Smith
  - *The Cactus Hotel* by Abbey Grace Moore
- chart paper and markers
- sticky notes

Academic Language / Important Vocabulary

- writing
- word
- interesting
- sound

Continuum Connection

- Notice a writer's use of playful or poetic language and sound devices: e.g., nonsense words, rhythm, rhyme, repetition, refrain, onomatopoeia (p. 35)
- Write in an expressive way (similar to oral language) (p. 254)
- Learn new words from reading and listening and trying them out in writing (p. 254)
- Try out techniques other writers and illustrators have used (p. 257)

GOAL

Understand that writers use onomatopoeia (sound words) to make writing interesting.

RATIONALE

When children notice the way that writers use sound words to make writing more interesting, they begin to think about ways to imitate the sounds they hear in nature and their own lives and to express those sounds in writing.

ASSESS LEARNING

- Observe whether children notice the sound words that writers use.
- Look for evidence that children are using sound words in their own writing.
- Notice evidence that children can use vocabulary such as *writing*, *word*, *interesting*, and *sound*.

MINILESSON

To help children think about the minilesson principle, engage them in noticing the sound words that authors use. Here is an example.

> Listen as I read some words in this book.

- Show the cover and read the sound words on pages 8–12 of *The Sweet Mango Tree*.

> Turn and talk about what you noticed about the words the author, Megan K. Smith, used.

- After a brief discussion, ask a few volunteers to share what they noticed. Support the conversation to help children recognize that the writer used words that sound like the noises they hear. On chart paper, begin a list of sound words.

> The writer used sound words to help you know the sounds you would hear if you were near this mango tree.

> Listen as I read the words that Abby Grace Moore used in *The Cactus Hotel*.

- Read and show pages 3–5 of *The Cactus Hotel*.

> What sound words did you notice?

- Add to the chart.

> Why do you think the writer used these sound words?

Have a Try

Invite children to turn and talk to a partner about sound words.

▶ Show and read page 12 of *The Cactus Hotel*.

The writer uses *munch, munch, munch* to describe the sounds the bunny makes when it is eating. What are some other sounds an animal or a person makes when eating? Turn and talk about some words you could write to sound like an animal or person eating. You can also make up a word to match a sound.

▶ Support the conversations as needed. After time for discussion, ask a few volunteers to share. Add new sound words to the chart.

Summarize and Apply

Summarize the learning. Invite children to notice and use sound words.

▶ Write the principle at the top of the chart.

Today as you read and write, you might notice other sound words, like *hiss* or *crunch*. If you find one, write it on a sticky note and add it to the chart. As you're working on your book, look to see if there's a place to use a sound word.

Choose words to match a sound.	
crunch	munch
hiss	nam nam
flick	cham cham
squeak	crunch crunch
slurp	slurp
hoo	sip
peep	
buzz	

Confer

▶ During independent writing, move around the room to confer briefly with as many individual children as time allows. Sit side by side with them and invite them to talk about sound words. Use the prompts below as needed.

- *What does that sound like?*
- *What sound word could you write?*
- *How can you help the reader know what that sounds like?*

Share

Following independent writing, gather children in the meeting area to share their writing.

Did anyone add a sticky note to the chart? Tell about that.

Did you use a sound word in your writing today? Share what you wrote.

WML2
CFT.U6.WML2

Writing Minilesson Principle
Choose interesting words to describe the way characters talk.

Making Powerful Word Choices

You Will Need

- several familiar books that use synonyms for *said*, such as *Scram!* by Julie Reich, from *Shared Reading Collection*
- sticky notes
- chart paper and markers

Academic Language / Important Vocabulary

- writing
- word
- interesting
- said

Continuum Connection

- Write in an expressive way (similar to oral language) (p. 254)
- Learn new words from reading and listening and trying them out in writing (p. 254)
- Try out techniques other writers and illustrators have used (p. 257)

GOAL

Understand that writers make their writing more specific and interesting by using different words to describe how characters speak.

RATIONALE

Writers make their writing more specific and interesting by using words for *said* that describe how a character sounds, such as *whispered*, *shouted*, or *cried*. Helping children notice this will help them understand that they, can do the same when they write. Attention to word choice also expands children's vocabulary.

ASSESS LEARNING

- Observe for evidence that children understand why writers use synonyms for *said*.
- Look at children's writing. Do they sometimes use a synonym for *said*?
- Notice evidence that children can use vocabulary such as *writing*, *word*, *interesting*, and *said*.

MINILESSON

To help children think about the minilesson principle, engage them in noticing that authors use different words for *said*. Here is an example.

- Show page 6 of *Scram!* Read the page and point under the word *said*.

  When someone is talking, many times you will see the word *said*.

- Read pages 8 and 10.

  How does the author let you know that someone is talking?

- Guide the conversation to help children identify *shouted* and *yelled*. Begin a list on chart paper of words that can be used instead of *said*.

  Why do you think the writer used *shouted* and *yelled* instead of *said*?

- Help children understand that using words that tell how the person said the words makes the writing not only more interesting to read but also more descriptive.

  As I continue reading, put your thumb up if you hear a word that the writer used instead of *said*.

- Continue reading, pausing to add new words to the list as children identify them.

Have a Try

Invite children to turn and talk to a partner about words that can replace *said*.

▶ Write two simple sentences with *said* on the chart. Leave room for sticky notes to be added beneath the words. Read the sentences aloud.

> Turn and talk about words that could be used instead of *said* to describe how someone might say the sentences.

▶ After discussion, ask a few volunteers to share. Add each word to a sticky note and attach it to the chart. Post the chart so children can add new sticky notes as they notice other synonyms for *said*.

Summarize and Apply

Summarize the learning. Invite children to notice and use synonyms for *said*.

> Why do writers use other words for *said*?

▶ Write the principle at the top of the chart.

> Whenever you notice a word that can be used instead of *said*, write it on a sticky note and add it to the chart. During writing time, look at your writing to see if you can use a word other than *said*. Make sure your pictures match the words you choose. Bring your writing to share when we meet later.

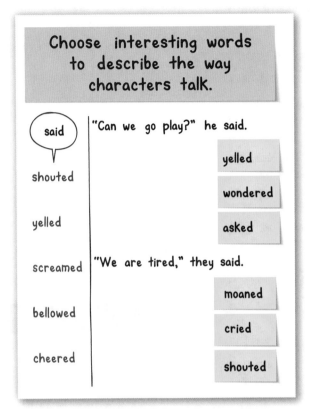

Confer

▶ During independent writing, move around the room to confer briefly with as many individual children as time allows. Sit side by side with them and invite them to talk about how their characters talk. Use the prompts below as needed.

- *Is there a better word to describe how the character says this?*
- *She is talking in an excited voice. What word can you use to show that?*
- *What kind of voice is he using?*

Share

Following independent writing, gather children in the meeting area to share their writing.

> What word did you use instead of *said* in your writing today?

> Did anyone add a sticky note to the chart? Tell about that.

Section 6: Craft

Writing Minilesson Principle
Choose interesting words to describe actions.

Making Powerful Word Choices

You Will Need

- several familiar books with interesting verbs, such as the following:

  - *Scram!* by Julie Reich, from *Shared Reading Collection*

  - *The Silver Button* by Bob Graham, from Text Set: Bob Graham: Exploring Everyday Life

  - *On the Go* by Ann Morris, from Text Set: Exploring Fiction and Nonfiction

- sticky notes

- chart paper and markers

- To download the following online resource for this lesson, visit **resources.fountasandpinnell.com**:

  - chart art (optional)

Academic Language / Important Vocabulary

- writing
- word
- interesting
- action

Continuum Connection

- Learn new words from reading and listening and trying them out in writing (p. 254)

- Use vocabulary appropriate for the topic (p. 254)

- Vary word choice to create interesting description and dialogue (p. 254)

GOAL

Understand that writers make their writing more specific and interesting by using different verbs.

RATIONALE

Writers make their writing more specific and interesting by using verbs that describe how a character is acting or what the character is doing, such as *twirling*, *leaping*, or *sobbing*. Helping children notice this will help them understand that they, can do the same when they write. Attention to word choice also expands children's vocabulary.

ASSESS LEARNING

- Observe for evidence that children understand why writers use specific verbs.

- Look at children's writing. Do they use verbs that describe characters' actions?

- Notice evidence that children can use vocabulary such as *writing*, *word*, *interesting*, and *action*.

MINILESSON

To help children think about the minilesson principle, engage them in noticing that authors use different words for *move*. Here is an example.

- Revisit page 5 of *Scram!* Read the page and point under the word *move*.

  > *Move* is an action word. It tells something you do. As I read, notice the different ways that the family tells the cow to move.

- Read the words in speech bubbles on pages 8, 10, and 12.

  > What did you notice?

- As children identify the words, begin a list on chart paper of synonyms for *move*.

  > These are all words that describe how the family wants the cow to move. Why do you think the writer used *go*, *shoo*, *scram*, and *skedaddle* instead of *move*?

- Talk about how each word tells how the family thinks the cow should move.

- Read and show pages 3–4 in *The Silver Button*.

  > I wonder why the writer used the action words *swayed* and *tilted*. What do you think?

- Guide a conversation about the writer's word choice. Add to the chart.

  > As I continue reading, put your thumb up if you hear an interesting action word that the writer used instead of *move*.

- Read several pages from *On the Go*. As children identify words, add to the chart.

Have a Try

Invite children to turn and talk to a partner about using interesting action words.

▶ Write two simple sentences with common action words on chart paper. Leave room for sticky notes to be added beneath the words. Read the sentences to children. Ask half of the pairs to think of different words for *walk* and the other half to think of different words for *look*.

▶ After discussion, ask a few volunteers to share. Add each word to a sticky note and attach it to the chart. Post the chart so children can add new sticky notes as they read and write.

Summarize and Apply

Summarize the learning. Invite children to notice and use different verbs.

> Why do writers use interesting action words?

▶ Write the principle at the top of the chart.

> Whenever you notice an interesting action word, write it on a sticky note and add it to the chart. During writing time, look at your writing to see if you can use an interesting word to describe a character's action. Show the action in your drawings. Bring your writing to share when we meet later.

Confer

▶ During independent writing, move around the room to confer briefly with as many individual children as time allows. Sit side by side with them and invite them to talk about action words. Use the prompts below as needed.

- *Is there a more interesting word you could use here?*
- *How is he eating? Is there a word you can use to show that?*
- *What action is she doing? Let's talk about some words that you could write.*

Share

Following independent writing, gather children in the meeting area. Ask several children to share their writing.

> Did you use an interesting action word today? Share what you wrote.

> Did anyone add a sticky note to the chart? Tell about that.

Section 6: Craft

Assessment

After you have taught the minilessons in this umbrella, observe children as they engage in writing. Use *The Literacy Continuum* (Fountas and Pinnell 2017) to notice, teach for, and support children's learning as you observe their attempts at writing.

▶ What evidence do you have of new understandings children have developed related to making powerful word choices?

- Are children using words to match sounds in their writing?
- Do you notice children choosing interesting words to describe the way characters say something?
- Are they choosing interesting words to describe actions?
- Do they understand and use vocabulary such as *writing, word, interesting, sound, said,* and *action*?

▶ In what ways, beyond the scope of this umbrella, are children understanding craft choices?

- Are they trying different ways to begin their writing?
- Are they trying different ways to end their writing?
- Do their drawings reflect the words they choose?

Use your observations to determine the next umbrella you will teach. You may also consult Suggested Sequence of Lessons (pp. 557–571) for guidance.

EXTENSIONS FOR MAKING POWERFUL WORD CHOICES

▶ If you are using *The Reading Minilessons Book, Grade 1* (Fountas and Pinnell 2019), the minilessons in this umbrella would pair well with LA.U8: Analyzing the Writer's Craft and LA.U22: Analyzing the Way Writers Play with Language.

▶ Keep the charts from this umbrella posted in the writing center and encourage children to continue to add to them.

▶ Encourage children to make lists of synonyms for overused words that can be posted and used as a writing resource.

▶ Gather together a guided writing group of several children who need support in a specific area of writing, such as making powerful word choices.

Minilessons in This Umbrella

WML1 Use headings to tell what a part is about.

WML2 Use sidebars to give extra information.

WML3 Make a table of contents for your book.

Before Teaching Umbrella 7 Minilessons

It would be helpful to teach IW.14: Writing an All-About Book because the all-about book created during this lesson will be used throughout these minilessons. Consider providing some of the paper templates in the online resources to guide children in adding text features to their books.

Read and discuss engaging nonfiction books with a variety of text features, including headings, sidebars, and tables of contents. Use the following texts from *Fountas & Pinnell Classroom™ Interactive Read-Aloud Collection* and *Shared Reading Collection*, or choose books from your classroom library.

Interactive Read-Aloud Collection
Exploring Nonfiction

Water: Up, Down, and All Around by Natalie M. Rosinsky

Shared Reading Collection

How Animals Eat by Mary Ebeltoft Reid

Interactive Writing Lessons

IW.14: Writing an All-About Book

As you read and enjoy these texts together, help children

- notice headings and talk about what each page or section is about,

- discuss information provided in sidebars, and

- use the table of contents to find information.

Interactive Read-Aloud
Nonfiction

Shared Reading

Interactive Writing

Section 6: Craft

Writing Minilesson Principle
Use headings to tell what a part is about.

You Will Need

- a familiar nonfiction book that has headings, such as *Water: Up, Down, and All Around* by Natalie M. Rosinsky, from Text Set: Exploring Nonfiction

- the class-written text from IW.14: Writing an All-About Book

- chart paper and markers

Academic Language/ Important Vocabulary

- heading

- part

- page

Continuum Connection

- Use illustrations and book and print features (e.g., labeled pictures, diagrams, table of contents, headings, sidebars, page numbers) to guide the reader (p. 251)

- Begin to incorporate illustrations and organizational tools in nonfiction texts: e.g., drawing or photograph with caption or label, map, diagram, table of contents, heading, sidebar (p. 254)

- Place titles and headings in the appropriate place on a page (p. 254)

GOAL

Understand that headings tell the reader what to expect from the section of text.

RATIONALE

When you help children notice headings in books, they begin to understand that nonfiction authors group together related details on a page or in a section. They learn to structure their own nonfiction texts in a similar way and to use headings to help readers know what to expect.

ASSESS LEARNING

- Observe children as they talk about nonfiction books. Do they understand the purpose of headings?

- Notice whether children know how to use headings in their own nonfiction texts.

- Look for evidence that children can use vocabulary such as *heading*, *part*, and *page*.

MINILESSON

To help children think about the minilesson principle, engage them in an inquiry lesson around headings in a familiar nonfiction book. Then demonstrate how to add headings to a text that the class wrote. Here is an example.

- Show the cover of *Water: Up, Down, and All Around* and read the title. Read pages 4–5. Then point to the heading.

    What do you notice about these words at the top of the page?

    How do they look different from the other words?

    This is a heading. A heading is usually bigger than the other words on the page, and it may be in a different color. What does this heading tell you?

    The heading tells you what the part or page is about. This heading tells us that this part is about where raindrops come from.

- Turn to pages 6–7. Invite a volunteer to point to the heading. Read it aloud.

    What is this part of the book about?

    How do headings help you when you read?

- Record ideas on the chart paper.

Have a Try

Invite children to talk to a partner about adding a heading.

▶ Show children the class all-about book or other class writing. Choose one page to which you will add a heading.

> What heading could we write for this page? Turn and talk to your partner.

▶ After children turn and talk, invite several pairs to share their ideas. Agree on a heading and add it to the page. Add headings to the other pages if there is time.

Summarize and Apply

Help children summarize the learning. Remind them to think about using headings when they write nonfiction.

> Why do writers decide to use headings?

▶ Write the principle at the top of the chart. Read it aloud.

> You can use headings when you write your own nonfiction books. If you are working on a nonfiction book today, see if there is a place you could add headings.

Confer

▶ During independent writing, move around the room to confer briefly with as many individual children as time allows. Sit side by side with them and invite them to talk about adding headings to their books. Use prompts such as the following if needed.

- *What is this part/page of your book about?*
- *What heading could you add?*
- *What are you going to write about on this page? You can add a heading now to help you remember to write about that.*

Share

Following independent writing, gather children in the meeting area. Choose several children to share the headings they wrote.

> What is this part of your book about? What is the heading?

> How will the heading help readers?

Use headings to tell what a part is about.

What Headings Do

- They tell readers what the part is about.
- They help readers find information.
- They organize your ideas.

Shark Teeth

Some sharks have three thousand teeth.

Their teeth are in rows.

They are very sharp!

WML2
CFT.U7.WML2

Use sidebars to give extra information.

Adding Text Features to Books

You Will Need

- a familiar nonfiction book that has sidebars, such as *How Animals Eat* by Mary Ebeltoft Reid, from *Shared Reading Collection*

- the class-written text from IW.14: Writing an All-About Book

- chart paper and markers

Academic Language/ Important Vocabulary

- sidebar
- nonfiction
- information
- author

Continuum Connection

- Use illustrations and book and print features (e.g., labeled pictures, diagrams, table of contents, headings, sidebars, page numbers) to guide the reader (p. 251)

- Begin to incorporate illustrations and organizational tools in nonfiction texts: e.g., drawing or photograph with caption or label, map, diagram, table of contents, heading, sidebar (p. 254)

GOAL

Understand that sidebars give extra information about the topic.

RATIONALE

When you help children notice and think about sidebars in nonfiction books, they learn that they, too, can use sidebars to give extra information in their own books. They begin to think about what other information readers might need or want to know about the topic.

ASSESS LEARNING

- Observe children as they talk about nonfiction books. Do they understand the purpose of sidebars?

- Notice whether children include sidebars in their own nonfiction books.

- Look for evidence that children can use vocabulary such as *sidebar*, *nonfiction*, *information*, and *author*.

MINILESSON

To help children think about the minilesson principle, engage them in an inquiry lesson around sidebars in a familiar nonfiction book. Then demonstrate how to add a sidebar to an existing text. Here is an example.

- Show the cover of *How Animals Eat* and read the title. Read pages 4–5. Point to the sidebar on page 5.

    What do you notice about these words? How do they look different from the other words on these pages?

    These words are in a little box called a sidebar. The sidebar is called Animal Facts. What does the sidebar tell you about?

- Read pages 6–7. Invite a volunteer to point to the sidebar.

    What does this sidebar tell you about?

    What does the sidebar have to do with the other information on these pages?

    These pages are about pelicans, and the sidebar gives extra information about the type of pelican shown in the photo.

    Why do you think the author decided to include sidebars in her book?

    Writers use sidebars to give extra information about the topic of the book. In this book, the sidebars tell more about the animals in the photos.

- Guide children to think about using sidebars in their own writing.

    What should you think about when you want to use a sidebar in your own writing?

- Record responses on the chart paper.

Have a Try

Invite children to talk to a partner about what to write in a sidebar.

▶ Display the class-written text from IW.14. Read one page aloud.

> We can add a sidebar to this page in our all-about book about sharks. What extra information might readers want to know about the sizes of sharks? Turn and talk to your partner about what we might write in a sidebar.

▶ Invite several pairs to share their ideas. You might demonstrate writing the sidebar on a separate piece of paper and gluing it in the book.

Summarize and Apply

Help children summarize the learning. Remind them to think about including sidebars when they write nonfiction.

> What did you learn today about using sidebars?

▶ Write the principle at the top of the chart.

> If you work on a nonfiction book during writing time today, try using a sidebar to give extra information. Bring your writing to share when we meet later.

Confer

▶ During independent writing, move around the room to confer briefly with as many individual children as time allows. Sit side by side with them and invite them to talk about adding sidebars to their books. Use prompts such as the following if needed.

- *What else might readers want to know about _____? Do you know any other fun or interesting facts about that?*
- *Do you want to put that in a sidebar?*
- *Where on the page are you going to put the sidebar?*

Share

Following independent writing, gather children in the meeting area to share their writing.

> Did anyone add a sidebar to your book?

> Why did you decide to put that information in a sidebar?

Use sidebars to give extra information.

- Think about what else readers might want to know.

- Use a sidebar to give extra information.

  Did You Know?
  A sidebar looks like this!

- Make sure the sidebar is about the same topic or idea.

Sharks Big and Small

Sharks come in different shapes and sizes.

Some are tiny.

Some are huge!

Fun Fact
The biggest shark is the whale shark. It can be up to 60 feet long!

Adding Text Features to Books

You Will Need

- a familiar nonfiction book that has a table of contents and page numbers, such as *Water: Up, Down, and All Around* by Natalie M. Rosinsky, from Text Set: Exploring Nonfiction
- the class-written text from IW.14: Writing an All-About Book
- chart paper and markers

Academic Language/ Important Vocabulary

- page numbers
- table of contents

Continuum Connection

- Use illustrations and book and print features (e.g., labeled pictures, diagrams, table of contents, headings, sidebars, page numbers) to guide the reader (p. 251)
- Begin to incorporate illustrations and organizational tools in nonfiction texts: e.g., drawing or photograph with caption or label, map, diagram, table of contents, heading, sidebar (p. 254)

GOAL

Understand that writers include a table of contents as an organizational tool for the reader.

RATIONALE

When you help children notice and think about tables of contents in nonfiction books, they begin to understand that a table of contents helps readers find information. They learn that they can include a table of contents in their own nonfiction books.

ASSESS LEARNING

- Observe children as they talk about nonfiction books. Do they understand the purpose of a table of contents?
- Notice whether children know how to make a table of contents.
- Look for evidence that children can use vocabulary such as *page numbers* and *table of contents*.

MINILESSON

To help children think about the minilesson principle, engage them in noticing the characteristics and purpose of a table of contents in a familiar nonfiction book. Then demonstrate how to make one. Here is an example.

- Show the cover of *Water: Up, Down, and All Around* and read the title. Display the table of contents.

  > What is this part of the book called?

  > This is the table of contents. Let's read it together.

- Point to each element as you read it.

  > What does the table of contents tell you?

  > The table of contents is always at the beginning of a book. What information did the author put in the table of contents?

  > She put the name of each part and the page number it starts on.

- Display the class-written text from IW.14.

  > We can make a table of contents for our all-about book about sharks.

- If the pages are not numbered, add the page numbers. Explain that it's important to be sure the pages are in order and numbered before making a table of contents.

- Write *Table of Contents* at the top of a sheet of chart paper.

  > What's the first part of our book? What page is it on?

- Create a table of contents.

Have a Try

Invite children to talk to a partner about how to make a table of contents.

> Think about how we made the table of contents. What do you have to remember to do when you make one? Turn and talk to your partner about this.

▶ After children turn and talk, invite a few children to share their responses. Record responses on the chart paper.

Summarize and Apply

Summarize the learning and remind children that they can include a table of contents in their own books.

> How is a table of contents helpful when you're reading a nonfiction book?

▶ Write the principle at the top of the chart.

> If you are working on a nonfiction book, try making a table of contents for it. If you're not finished with your book, you can add the table of contents later.

Confer

▶ During independent writing, move around the room to confer briefly with as many individual children as time allows. Sit side by side with them and invite them to talk about making a table of contents for their books. Use prompts such as the following to help them make a table of contents if appropriate.

- *What do you need to do first?*
- *Are your pages in the order that you want them in?*
- *Let's add page numbers to your book.*
- *Where will you put the table of contents?*

Share

Following independent writing, gather children in the meeting area to share their writing.

> Who would like to share your table of contents with the class?

> Tell how you made it.

Table of Contents

Sharks Big and Small......1

Shark Teeth.......................2

Shark Skin.........................3

Shark Babies.....................4

Shark Attacks.................5

Make a table of contents for your book.

- Read your writing.

- Make sure the pages are in the right order.

- Number the pages.

- Write the name of each part and the page number in the table of contents.

Assessment

After you have taught the minilessons in this umbrella, observe children as they write and talk about their writing. Use the behaviors and understandings in *The Literacy Continuum* (Fountas and Pinnell 2017) to notice, teach for, and support children's learning as you observe their attempts at writing.

▶ What evidence do you have of new understandings children have developed related to adding text features to their books?

- Do children use headings to tell what each part of a book is about?
- Do they use sidebars to give extra information?
- Do they understand how to make a table of contents?
- Is there evidence children can use vocabulary such as *heading*, *sidebar*, and *table of contents*?

▶ In what other ways, beyond the scope of this umbrella, are children ready to expand their bookmaking skills?

- Are they ready to learn about making different types of books?
- Are they ready to learn how to add more details to their writing?
- Are they experimenting with different illustration techniques?

Use your observations to determine the next umbrella you will teach. You may also consult Suggested Sequence of Lessons (pp. 557–571) for guidance.

EXTENSIONS FOR ADDING TEXT FEATURES TO BOOKS

▶ Gather together a guided writing group of several children who need support in a specific area of writing.

▶ Teach children how to revise a table of contents if they make substantial changes to a book after making the table of contents.

▶ Guide children to notice subheadings in books and invite them to use them in their own books.

▶ Teach children how to make headings, sidebars, a table of contents, and other text features using word-processing software.

▶ Some children might be interested in making a glossary for their all about-books. To plan a new minilesson, you can use the online resource Planning a Writing Minilesson (p, 102).

Minilessons in This Umbrella

WML1 Write a letter to someone.

WML2 Write your name and the name of the person you are writing to in the letter.

WML3 Write the important information in your letter.

Before Teaching Umbrella 8 Minilessons

Engaging children with lessons about functional writing helps them understand that people write for authentic purposes. Functional writing includes labels, lists, directions, and letters. Friendly letters are used to give information, to invite, and to give thanks. In addition to traditional letters, friendly letters can take the form of notes, cards, invitations, and emails.

Prior to teaching these minilessons, teach IW.17: Writing an Invitation and use the class-made letter from that lesson throughout this umbrella. If you use *The Reading Minilessons Book, Grade 1* (Fountas and Pinnell 2019), it would also be helpful to teach WAR.U5.RML5: Write a letter to share your thinking. You may also choose the following from *Fountas & Pinnell Classroom™ Interactive Read-Aloud Collection*, or you might use other examples of letters from the classroom.

Interactive Read-Aloud Collection

Journeys Near and Far

Dear Juno by Soyung Pak

Celebrating Diversity

The Name Jar by Yangsook Choi

Mo Willems: Having Fun with Humor

I Am Invited to a Party!

The Importance of Friendship

Wallace's Lists by Barbara Bottner and Gerald Kruglik

Interactive Writing Lessons

IW.17: Writing an Invitation

As you read and enjoy these mentor texts together, help children

- notice details in the letters, and
- notice the different reasons why people write letters.

Interactive Read-Aloud
Journeys

Celebrating Diversity

Mo Willems

Friendship

Interactive Writing

Section 6: Craft

Writing Minilesson Principle

Write a letter to someone.

Writing a Friendly Letter

You Will Need

- several mentor texts that show friendly letters, such as these:
    - *Dear Juno* by Soyung Pak, from Text Set: Journeys Near and Far
    - *The Name Jar* by Yangsook Choi, from Text Set: Celebrating Diversity
    - *I Am Invited to a Party!* by Mo Willems, from Text Set: Mo Willems: Having Fun with Humor
    - *Wallace's Lists* by Barbara Bottner and Gerald Kruglik, from Text Set: The Importance of Friendship
    - class letter from IW.17: Writing an Invitation
- chart paper and markers
- To download the following online resource for this lesson, visit **resources.fountasandpinnell.com**:
    - chart art (optional)

Academic Language / Important Vocabulary

- friendly letter
- invite
- thanks
- information
- opinion

Continuum Connection

- Write notes, cards, invitations, and emails to others (p. 250)
- Write with a friendly tone (conversational language) (p. 250)
- Understand how to learn about writing notes, cards, and invitations by noticing the characteristics of examples (p. 250)

GOAL

Understand that there are different types of letters and that friendly letters have a conversational tone.

RATIONALE

When children understand why people write letters, they begin to think about what they could write in a letter and understand that they can write with purpose and authenticity.

ASSESS LEARNING

- Notice evidence that children realize that letters can be written for a variety of purposes.
- Observe for evidence that children can use vocabulary such as *friendly letter*, *invite*, *thanks*, *information*, and *opinion*.

MINILESSON

To help children plan and begin writing letters independently, provide examples of different forms of friendly letters (e.g., notes, cards, letters, invitations, emails) and help them think about why people write friendly letters. Here is an example.

- Show examples of a variety of types of friendly letters such as the following. Ask children what they notice.
    - Letter: *Dear Juno* (cover) and *The Name Jar* (page 21)
    - Invitation: *I Am Invited to a Party!* (pages 4–5) and IW.17
    - Note: *Wallace's Lists* (page 13)

- Guide children to identify similarities in the letters (possibilities: they are written from one person to another, have a friendly tone, involve a practical task, and include important information).

- Revisit page 14 in *Dear Juno*.

    Think about this letter that Juno's grandmother wrote to him. Turn and talk about why you think Grandma wrote this letter.

- After time for a brief discussion, guide children in a conversation about Grandma's purpose. Generalize the purpose of the letter and define *friendly letter*.

    Grandma wrote to say hello to Juno and to share information about her life because Juno lives far away. This is an example of a friendly letter because it sounds like Grandma is talking to Juno.

- Begin a list on chart paper of reasons people write letters.

- Continue with several other examples, adding to the list as children identify additional reasons for writing letters.

Have a Try

Invite children to turn and talk about an idea they have for writing a letter.

> Think about why you might write a letter. Turn and tell your partner.

▶ After time for discussion, ask a few children to share. Add new ideas to the chart.

Summarize and Apply

Summarize the learning. Have children begin writing a letter during independent writing.

▶ Write the principle at the top of the chart. Read it aloud.

> You can write a letter for different reasons. When you write to someone you know, you are writing a friendly letter.

> During writing time, choose a reason for writing a letter. Go ahead and begin writing if you are ready. You can write about something you did recently or someplace you visited. You can write about family news or what you thought about a book you read. Look at the chart if you need ideas. Bring your writing to share when we meet later.

Write a letter to someone.

* Say hello and share some news
* Give information
* Say thank you
* Invite to an event
* Ask how someone is feeling
* Tell an opinion
* Email to plan an activity
* Recommend a book or movie to a friend

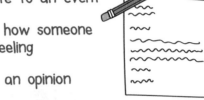

Confer

▶ During independent writing, move around the room to confer briefly with as many individual children as time allows. Sit side by side with them and invite them to talk about writing letters. Use the following prompts as needed.

- *Whom will you be writing a letter to?*
- *What would you like your letter to be about?*
- *What are some things you might write in your letter?*
- *Let's look at the chart for some ideas.*

Share

Following independent writing, gather children in the meeting area to share their friendly letters.

> Who would like to share the letter you wrote today?

> How did you decide what to write?

Umbrella 8: Writing a Friendly Letter

■ 423

Writing Minilesson Principle

Write your name and the name of the person you are writing to in the letter.

You Will Need

- several mentor texts that show a sample letter, such as the following:

  - *Dear Juno* by Soyung Pak, from Text Set: Journeys Near and Far

  - *The Name Jar* by Yangsook Choi, from Text Set: Celebrating Diversity

  - class letter from IW.17: Writing an Invitation

- projector (optional)

- highlighter tape

Academic Language / Important Vocabulary

- friendly letter
- greeting
- closing
- sender

Continuum Connection

- Understand that the sender and the receiver must be clearly shown (p. 250)

- Write to a known audience or a specific reader (p. 250)

GOAL

Understand that a letter includes the name of the sender and the receiver.

RATIONALE

When children learn how to write friendly letters by looking at examples, they will include important details in the letters they write, such as the name of the receiver in the greeting and the name of the sender in the closing.

ASSESS LEARNING

- Notice evidence that children understand that both the sender's name and receiver's name must be included in a friendly letter.

- Observe whether children are including a greeting and a closing in the letters they write.

- Observe for evidence that children can use vocabulary such as *friendly letter*, *greeting*, *closing*, and *sender*.

MINILESSON

To help children understand that letters include the names of both the sender and the receiver, provide a brief interactive lesson that uses model letters. Here is an example.

- Show page 14 in *Dear Juno*. Read the greeting, pointing under each word as you do.

  This letter from Grandma to Juno starts with *Dear Juno*. Why do you think Grandma started the letter in this way?

  Dear Juno is the greeting. A greeting tells the name of the person you are writing to. Usually the greeting begins with the word *Dear*.

- Read and point to the signature line.

  Grandma ends this letter by writing *Grandma*. Why do you think Grandma ends the letter in this way?

  Grandma is the closing. It tells who is sending the letter. Sometimes the closing says *From* or *Love* or *Yours truly* before the sender's name.

- Repeat with page 21 in *The Name Jar*.

- Show the class invitation from IW.17.

  What do you notice about the way this letter begins and ends?

- Use highlighter tape to assist children in noticing that the greeting is at the beginning and the closing is at the end. Help them recognize where each person's name (sender's and receiver's) is placed on the page. Also help them notice the commas after the greeting and closing.

Have a Try

Invite children to turn and talk about including the names of both the sender and the receiver in a friendly letter.

> Turn and talk about what names you will include in the friendly letter you are writing.

> ❯ After time for a brief discussion, ask a few children to share whose names they will include. Ask them to identify where they will write the names on the page.

Summarize and Apply

Summarize the lesson. Remind children to include a greeting and a closing in their letters.

> During writing time, write a friendly letter or continue working on one you have already started. Remember, you can write about something you did recently or some place you visited. You can write about family news or what you thought about a book you read. Write the name of the person you are writing to in the greeting. Write your name in the closing. Bring your writing to share when we meet later.

March 7

Dear Families,

We invite you to bring a food that is important to your family to our class.

Please bring the recipe so we can make a class recipe book.

When : March 26 at 1 PM
Where: Room 12

Our Recipe Book

Thank you!
From,
Mrs. Webster's Class

Confer

> ❯ During independent writing, move around the room to confer briefly with as many individual children as time allows. Sit side by side with them and invite them to talk about their letters. Use the following prompts as needed.
>
> • *Point to where you will write your name on your letter.*
> • *Whose name will go in the greeting?*
> • *What words will you use for the closing?*
> • *Point to where you will add commas in your letter.*

Share

Following independent writing, gather children in the meeting area to share their experiences writing friendly letters.

> Whose names did you include in your friendly letter?

> Show where you wrote the names on the page.

Writing Minilesson Principle
Write the important information in your letter.

Writing a Friendly Letter

You Will Need

- several mentor texts that show a sample letter, such as the following:
  - *Dear Juno* by Soyung Pak, from Text Set: Journeys Near and Far
  - *The Name Jar* by Yangsook Choi, from Text Set: Celebrating Diversity
- chart paper prepared with a letter that recommends a book
- highlighter tape

Academic Language / Important Vocabulary

- friendly letter
- important
- information

Continuum Connection

- Understand that written communication can be used for different purposes: e.g., to give information, to invite, to give thanks (p. 250)
- Understand that a friendly letter can be written in various forms: e.g., note, card, letter, invitation, email (p. 250)
- Include important information in the communication (p. 250)
- Write with a specific purpose in mind (p. 250)

GOAL

Write important information in a letter.

RATIONALE

When children learn that important information is included in a friendly letter, they will think about a letter's purpose and include important details as they write their own friendly letters.

ASSESS LEARNING

- Notice evidence that children understand that friendly letters include important details.
- Observe whether children add relevant details to their friendly letters.
- Observe for evidence that children can use vocabulary such as *friendly letter*, *important*, and *information*.

MINILESSON

To help children understand that letters include important information, provide a brief interactive lesson that uses model letters. Here is an example.

- Show the letters on page 14 in *Dear Juno* and page 21 in *The Name Jar*. Talk about the information that is in these letters.
- Show and read the prepared book recommendation letter.

  What important information do you notice in this letter that I have written to our class?

- As children discuss the letter, add highlighter tape to words that help children identify and recognize the important information that is included in it. Also note the greeting and the closing.

Have a Try

Invite children to turn and talk about including important information in a friendly letter.

> What important information will you include in the friendly letter you are writing? Turn and talk about that.

▸ After time for a brief discussion, ask a few volunteers to share ideas.

Summarize and Apply

Summarize the lesson. Remind children to include important information in the friendly letters they are working on.

> During writing time, work on your friendly letter. Think about the important information you want to write in your letter. For example, if you are writing about something you did recently, you might tell what you did and how you felt about it. If you are writing about a place you visited, you might tell what you saw and who was there. Bring your letter to share when we meet later.

Dear Class,

I read the book Dear Juno. I loved it! I think you will love it too. My favorite part was the letter that Grandma wrote to Juno. I liked how the pictures showed how the letter looks in Korean. You will find this book in our classroom.

From,

Mr. Sunei

Confer

▸ During independent writing, move around the room to confer briefly with as many individual children as time allows. Sit side by side with them and invite them to talk about their letters. Use the following prompts as needed.

- *What are you writing about in your letter?*
- *What important information will you include in your friendly letter?*
- *Reread your letter to check the important information.*

Share

Following independent writing, gather children in the meeting area to share their experiences writing friendly letters.

> What did you write about in your friendly letter?

Assessment

After you have taught the minilessons in this umbrella, observe children as they write letters. Use *The Literacy Continuum* (Fountas and Pinnell 2017) to notice, teach for, and support children's learning as you observe their attempts at reading and writing.

▶ What evidence do you have of new understandings children have developed related to writing friendly letters?

- Do children understand the reasons for writing friendly letters?

- Do children's letters include the sender's and receiver's names and important information?

- Are they using vocabulary related to writing a friendly letter, such as *friendly letter*, *invite*, *thanks*, *information*, *opinion*, *greeting*, *closing*, and *important*?

▶ In what ways, beyond the scope of this umbrella, are children engaging in functional writing?

- Do they show an interest in writing labels, lists, and directions?

- Do their illustrations reflect their words?

Use your observations to determine the next umbrella you will teach. You may also consult Suggested Sequence of Lessons (pp. 557–571) for guidance.

EXTENSIONS FOR WRITING A FRIENDLY LETTER

▶ Talk about different ways of closing a letter (e.g., *From, Sincerely, Love*) and when each is appropriate.

▶ In small groups, engage children in interactive writing of a thank you, congratulations, or get-well card to a member of the school staff or to a classmate.

▶ Children can write emails or letters to families to invite them to an upcoming class activity.

▶ Have children write a class letter to another class to share their opinion about a book.

▶ Encourage children to write friendly letters to each other for a variety of purposes, such as to give information, to invite, or to give thanks.

Minilessons in This Umbrella

WML1 Poems look and sound different from other types of writing.

WML2 Some poems rhyme, but many do not.

WML3 Observe the world to get ideas for poems.

WML4 Place words on a page to make them look like a poem.

WML5 Use your senses to describe something.

Before Teaching Umbrella 9 Minilessons

Prior to teaching these minilessons, provide opportunities for children to read and talk about many types of poetry, including those with rhyme, repetition, rhythm, and sensory language. These minilessons help children notice characteristics of poems that they can try out when they write poems of their own. The focus of this umbrella is to help children understand that writers make choices when they write poems and that their poems have different characteristics.

Before teaching these minilessons, you may want to teach IW.20: Writing a Poem and CFT.U6: Making Powerful Word Choices. If you are using *The Reading Minilessons Book, Grade 1* (Fountas and Pinnell 2019), the minilessons in this umbrella would pair well with LA.U8: Analyzing the Writer's Craft and LA.U22: Analyzing the Way Writers Play with Language. For mentor texts, use the books listed below from *Fountas & Pinnell Classroom™ Shared Reading Collection*, or choose poetry books from the classroom library.

Shared Reading Collection

Silly and Fun: Poems to Make You Smile

Rain, Sun, Wind, Snow: Poems About the Seasons

As you read and enjoy these texts together, help children

- notice the way the words sound,
- observe the way the words look on the page, and
- notice sensory language.

Section 6: Craft

Writing Minilesson Principle

Poems look and sound different from other types of writing.

Crafting Poetry

You Will Need

- books with poems that show a variety of poetry characteristics, such as the following from *Shared Reading Collection*:
  - *Silly and Fun: Poems to Make You Smile*
  - *Rain, Sun, Wind, Snow: Poems About the Seasons*
- chart paper and markers
- sticky notes
- chart paper prepared with a poem you will be using for this lesson

Academic Language / Important Vocabulary

- poem
- poet
- look
- sound

Continuum Connection

- Understand poetry as a way to communicate in sensory images about everyday life (p. 251)
- Understand that print and space look different in poems and attempt these layouts in approximating the writing of poems (p. 251)
- Understand that poems may look and sound different from one another (p. 251)
- Choose topics that one knows about, cares about, or wants to learn about (p. 256)

GOAL

Notice the characteristics of poems and try writing one.

RATIONALE

Helping children recognize some characteristics of poetry will widen their understanding of the decisions a poet makes when writing a poem—about word choice, rhymes, and layout. Children can then use this information when they write their own poems.

ASSESS LEARNING

- Observe whether children notice different characteristics that poets use in poems.
- Look for evidence that children are trying out some new ideas in their own poems.
- Observe for evidence that children can use vocabulary such as *poem*, *poet*, *look*, and *sound*.

MINILESSON

Use examples of traditional poems that have a variety of poetry characteristics to help children notice the characteristics through inquiry. If possible, show poems in an enlarged format so children can easily see the layout. Here is an example.

> As I share a few poems, think about some things you notice.

- Show the cover of *Silly and Fun*. Show and read "A Little Frog" on pages 11–13.

  > What do you notice about how the poem looks?

  > What do you notice about how the poem sounds?

- As children provide ideas about the characteristics they notice, generalize and write each one on a separate sticky note and place on the chart paper. Guide the conversation as needed.

- Repeat with "A Little Red Apple" on pages 14–15 and then "An Autumn Greeting" on page 16 in *Rain, Sun, Wind*, and *Snow*.

- Do all the poems look and sound the same?

  > A person who writes poems is called a poet. The poets who wrote these poems each made a decision about what kind of poem to write, how to make the poem look on the page, and how to make the poem sound. When you write a poem, you will make those decisions, too.

Have a Try

Invite children to turn and talk about characteristics of poetry.

▸ Display the prepared poem and read it aloud.

 Look at what you noticed about poems. Turn and talk about which of these things you notice in this poem.

▸ After time for discussion, ask a volunteer to choose a sticky note and place it beside the poem. Repeat until all of the sticky notes with relevant characteristics have been placed.

Summarize and Apply

Help children summarize the learning. Invite them to write a poem with some of the characteristics they learned about.

 What did you learn about how poems look and sound?

▸ Write the principle at the top of the first chart. Read it aloud.

 During writing time, think about how you want your poem to look and sound. Bring your poem to share when we meet later.

Confer

▸ During independent writing, move around the room to confer briefly with as many individual children as time allows. Sit side by side with them and invite them to talk about writing a poem. Use the prompts below as needed.

- *Look at the chart. What thing would you like to include in your poem?*

- *Where on the page will you start writing your poem?*

- *Will your poem rhyme or not rhyme?*

Share

Following independent writing, gather children in the meeting area. Choose several children to share a poem they are working on. Invite the other children to notice the characteristics.

 What things do you notice about _____'s poem?

Writing Minilesson Principle
Some poems rhyme, but many do not.

Crafting Poetry

You Will Need

- chart paper prepared with a rhyming poem in one column and a non-rhyming poem in the other column

- two sticky notes, one labeled *Rhyme* and one labeled *No Rhyme*

- highlighters or highlighter tape in several colors

- chart from WML1

Academic Language / Important Vocabulary

- writing
- poem
- rhyme

Continuum Connection

- Understand that poems do not have to rhyme (p. 251)

GOAL

Understand that some poems rhyme and some do not.

RATIONALE

Writing rhyming poems can be a creative endeavor or a frustrating task. When children learn that poems do not have to rhyme, they gain freedom in writing poems and can be creative about different ways to craft poems.

ASSESS LEARNING

- Observe whether children can identify rhyming words in poems.
- Look for evidence that children understand that poems do not have to rhyme.
- Observe for evidence that children can use vocabulary such as *writing*, *poem*, and *rhyme*.

MINILESSON

Use examples of both rhyming and non-rhyming poetry to help children understand that some poems rhyme and some do not. Here is an example.

- Show and read the rhyming poem on the chart paper.

   What do you notice about the words in the poem?

- If needed, reread the poem and guide children to recognize the rhyming words. Add the sticky note that says *Rhyme* to the chart.

   What words do you hear that rhyme?

- As children identify the rhyming pairs, use different colors of highlighters or highlighter tape to indicate the pairs.

- Show and read the non-rhyming poem.

   What do you notice about the words in the poem?

- Guide the children to recognize that there are no rhyming words. Add the sticky note that says *No Rhyme* to the chart.

Have a Try

Invite children to turn and talk about characteristics of poems.

> Turn and talk to your partner about what you have noticed about the words in poems.

▶ After time for discussion, ask children to share their thinking. Help them identify the principle and write it at the top of the chart.

Summarize and Apply

Summarize the learning by inviting children to write either a rhyming poem or a non-rhyming poem.

> During writing time, you can write a poem that rhymes or a poem that does not rhyme. Look at the chart we made before (WML1) and think how you want your poem to look and sound. Bring your poem to share when we meet later.

Some poems rhyme, but many do not.	
Rhyme	**No Rhyme**
What do you see?	Autumn leaves are falling fast.
A pig in a tree.	
Where's your cat?	Autumn leaves are spinning through the air.
Under my hat.	
How do you know?	Autumn leaves are floating down to the ground.
He licked my toe.	

Confer

▶ During independent writing, move around the room to confer briefly with as many individual children as time allows. Sit side by side with them and invite them to talk about their poems. Use the prompts below as needed.

- *Will the poem you are working on have rhyming words?*
- *What is the poem about?*
- *Look at the chart (WML1). What are some things you will include in your poem?*

Share

Following independent writing, gather children in the meeting area. Choose several children to share a poem they are working on. If possible, include an example of a rhyming poem and a non-rhyming poem.

> What did you notice about _____'s poem?

Crafting Poetry

You Will Need

- books with poems with topics that children can observe in their world, such as *Silly and Fun: Poems to Make You Smile*, from *Shared Reading Collection*
- chart paper and markers

Academic Language / Important Vocabulary

- writing
- poem
- observe
- idea

Continuum Connection

- Closely observe the world (animals, objects, people) to get ideas for poems (p. 251)
- Write poems that convey feelings or images (p. 251)
- Look for ideas and topics in personal experiences, shared through talk (p. 256)
- Observe carefully before writing about a person, animal, object, place, action (p. 256)

GOAL

Observe the world to find topics for writing poetry.

RATIONALE

When children learn that writers get ideas for poetry by noticing the world around them, they begin to observe their own environment and think about ideas they may use for writing poems.

ASSESS LEARNING

- Observe whether children recognize that writers get poetry ideas by noticing the world around them.
- Look for evidence that children can observe things in their environments to get ideas for poems.
- Observe for evidence that children can use vocabulary such as *writing*, *poem*, *observe*, and *idea*.

MINILESSON

Use poetry about topics children might notice in their world to engage them in thinking about ideas for poetry writing. Here is an example.

- Show the cover of *Silly and Fun* and read "Bouncing" on pages 2–3.

  The writer might have decided to write this poem after bouncing on a pogo stick or after watching other people do that. Let's think of something you do that could be in a poem.

- As children provide ideas, list them on the chart paper.

- Read "Hop, Hop, Hop" on pages 20–23.

  Where did the writer get the idea for this poem?

  What other things might you see in a garden?

  You can get ideas for poems from things you see in a particular place. What are some places you could write a poem about?

- Record ideas on the chart. Note that children could write about what they see in those places.

Have a Try

Invite children to turn and talk about poetry.

> When you observe something, you look closely at it. Turn and talk to your partner about what else you could observe and write about in a poem.

▶ Prompt children with general categories (e.g., people, nature) as needed. After time for discussion, ask a few children to share. Add responses to the chart.

Summarize and Apply

Help children summarize the learning. Invite them to write a poem with some of the characteristics they have learned about.

> Where can you get ideas for your poems?

> You can get ideas for poems from observing the world around you. Ideas are everywhere.

▶ Write the principle on the chart.

> During writing time, think of something you have observed and write a poem about what you noticed. Bring your poem to share when we meet later.

Observe the world to get ideas for poems.

Things People Do	People
play on the swings	baby
ride a horse	teacher
ride a bicycle	police officer
	grandmother

Places	Nature
garden	sun
store	insects
school	clouds
library	trees

Confer

▶ During independent writing time, move around the room to confer briefly with as many individual children as time allows. Sit side by side with them and invite them to talk about their poems. Use the prompts below as needed.

- *What could you write a poem about? Talk about what you observed.*
- *Is there an idea on the chart that you would like to write a poem about?*
- *What do you observe when you go outside? You can write a poem about that.*

Share

Following independent writing, gather children in the meeting area. Ask several children to share a poem they are working on.

> Who would like to share your poem?

WML4
CFT.U9.WML4

Writing Minilesson Principle
Place words on a page to make them look like a poem.

Crafting Poetry

You Will Need

▸ a book with poetry, such as *Rain, Sun, Wind, Snow: Poems About the Seasons*, from *Shared Reading Collection*

▸ pocket chart

▸ word cards with words from the two poems you will be using for the lesson

▸ sentence strip

Academic Language / Important Vocabulary

▸ poem

▸ poet

▸ pause

▸ line

▸ page

Continuum Connection

▸ Understand that print and space look different in poems and attempt these layouts in approximating the writing of poems (p. 251)

▸ Place words on a page to look like a poem (p. 251)

GOAL

Think about where to place words on the page when writing a poem.

RATIONALE

When children recognize that writers think about where to place words on a page, they understand that they can show the reader how they want their poem to be read by making choices about where the words are placed on the page.

ASSESS LEARNING

▸ Observe whether children recognize that writers make choices about where to place words on a page.

▸ Look for evidence that children are thinking about where to place words on a page to make it look like a poem.

▸ Observe for evidence that children can use vocabulary such as *poem, poet, pause, line,* and *page.*

MINILESSON

Use examples of poetry to help children understand that writers place words on a page so that that they look like poems. If possible, show poems in an enlarged format so children can easily see how the words are placed. Here is an example.

▸ Show and read "Summer Heat" on page 10 of *Rain, Sun, Wind, Snow.*

 What do you notice about the way the writer placed the words on the page?

▸ Read the poem again, emphasizing your pause at the end of lines.

 What do you notice about the way the poem sounds?

▸ Guide the conversation so children notice that you paused at the end of lines. Also help them recognize that the writer has placed the words on the page so they look like a poem.

▸ Repeat by reading and showing "Splish Splash Spring" on page 5.

 When you read stories, you pause when you see a period. When you read a poem, you pause at periods and also at the end of a line. Writers place the words on the page to show you how to read the poem.

▸ Put the first set of poetry word cards in a pocket chart, placed as one long sentence. Read it to the children.

 What do you notice about how the words are placed and how they sound?

▸ Rearrange the word cards so they look like a poem. Read the poem.

 What do you notice about how the words are placed and how they sound now?

Have a Try

Invite children to turn and talk about the way the words in poems are placed on a page.

▸ Replace the word cards for the moon poem with the second set of word cards in the pocket chart as one long sentence. Read the poem as a sentence: *Fresh fried fish, fresh fish fried, fried fresh fish, fish fried fresh.*

> Turn and talk about how the writer placed the words of this poem. Talk about how they could be placed differently to show the reader how to read this as a poem.

▸ After time for conversation, ask for suggestions. Change the position of the word cards so that they are written as a poem (each line ending with punctuation). Read the poem.

Summarize and Apply

Write the principle on a sentence strip and place in the top of the pocket chart to summarize the learning. Invite children to think about how they place the words of a poem on the page.

> Poets think about how they want a poem to be read before they place the words on the page. During writing time, think about how you will place the words on the page so your writing looks like a poem. Bring your poem to share when we meet later.

Confer

▸ During independent writing, move around the room to confer briefly with as many individual children as time allows. Sit side by side with them and invite them to talk about their poems. Use the following prompts as needed.

- *Show where you will begin writing on the page.*
- *What will be the last word on this line?*
- *How do you want your poem to sound when it is read aloud?*

Share

Following independent writing, gather children in the meeting area. Ask several children to share a poem they are working on.

> Who would like to share your poem?

Writing Minilesson Principle
Use your senses to describe something.

Crafting Poetry

You Will Need

▸ a book with sensory language poetry, such as *Rain, Sun, Wind, Snow: Poems About the Seasons*, from *Shared Reading Collection*

▸ several objects or pictures of objects that can be described using one or more senses

▸ chart paper prepared with five columns, each with a heading: *Object, Looks, Sounds, Smells, Feels*

▸ markers

▸ To download the following online resources for this lesson, visit **resources.fountasandpinnell.com**:

  ▪ Senses Chart

  ▪ chart art (optional)

Academic Language / Important Vocabulary

▸ poem   senses
▸ poet   describe

Continuum Connection

▸ Use language to describe how something looks, smells, tastes, feels, or sounds (p. 251)

▸ Understand the importance of specific word choice in poetry and sometimes use these words in talk and writing (p. 251)

▸ Add descriptive words (adjectives, adverbs) and phrases to help readers visualize and understand events, actions, process, or topics (p. 256)

GOAL

Use senses to describe something in a poem.

RATIONALE

When children learn that writers use their senses to describe things when they write poetry, they begin to use their own senses and think about what they observe as they craft their own poems.

ASSESS LEARNING

▸ Observe whether children notice that writers use sensory language in poetry.

▸ Look for evidence that children are using their senses to describe things.

▸ Observe for evidence that children can use vocabulary such as *poem, poet, senses,* and *describe.*

MINILESSON

Use examples of poetry and several objects to help children recognize that poets use their senses to describe things in their poems. Here is an example.

▸ Show the cover of *Rain, Sun, Wind, Snow*.

> **Listen as I read the poem "Autumn Leaves." Notice the way the writer describes the leaves.**

▸ Show and read "Autumn Leaves" on pages 14–15.

> **What did you notice about the words the poet uses to describe the leaves?**

▸ Guide the conversation so children identify the sensory language that shows how the leaves looked. Begin filling in the prepared chart with the item being described (leaves) and the sensory words used.

▸ Repeat with "The Little Snowman" on pages 22–23. Add responses to the chart.

> **Sometimes, writers use just one sense to describe an object in a poem. Other times, they use several senses. Writers get to decide how to describe things in the poems they write.**

The Writing Minilessons Book, Grade 1

Have a Try

Invite children to turn and talk about using their senses to describe something.

▸ Show a familiar object or picture of something that lends itself to being described using multiple senses (e.g., a pencil, ice cream).

> What words can you use to describe how this looks? sounds? smells? feels?

▸ After time for discussion, ask a few volunteers to share. Add responses to the chart.

Summarize and Apply

Help children summarize the learning. Invite them to use sensory language in their poems.

> What do poets use to describe something?

▸ Write the principle at the top of the chart.

> When you write a poem, think what you want to write about. Then use your senses to carefully describe things. You might want to fill in a Senses Chart before you start writing. Bring your poem to share when we meet later.

Object	Looks	Sounds	Smells	Feels
Autumn leaves	falling, spinning, floating, turning dancing, blowing, falling, sleeping			
Snowman's nose	orange pointy	nibble crunch		
Pencil	yellow used pink eraser	scratchy when it writes	woody	smooth sharp

Use your senses to describe something.

Confer

▸ During independent writing, move around the room to confer briefly with as many individual children as time allows. Sit side by side with them and invite them to talk about their poems. Use the prompts below as needed.

- *What does it look (sound, smell, feel) like?*
- *What words can you use to describe that?*

Share

Following independent writing, gather children in the meeting area. Ask several children to share a poem they are working on.

> Who would like to share your poem?

> What senses did you use when you wrote your poem?

Section 6: Craft

Assessment

After you have taught the minilessons in this umbrella, observe children as they engage in writing. Use *The Literacy Continuum* (Fountas and Pinnell 2017) to notice, teach for, and support children's learning as you observe their attempts at writing.

- ▸ What evidence do you have of new understandings children have developed related to writing poetry?
  - Do children recognize that poems look and sound different from other types of writing?
  - Are they aware that poems can rhyme, but they do not have to?
  - Do they observe the world around them to get ideas for writing poetry?
  - Are they able to place words on a page in a way that looks like poetry?
  - Can they use their senses to describe something?
  - Is there evidence that children can use vocabulary such as *writing*, *poem*, *look*, *sound*, *rhyme*, *observe*, *idea*, *page*, *senses*, and *describe*?
- ▸ In what ways, beyond the scope of this umbrella, are children showing readiness for writing poetry?
  - Do they show an interest in independently writing a variety of poetry?
  - Are they willing to revise what they have written?

Use your observations to determine the next umbrella you will teach. You may also consult Suggested Sequence of Lessons (pp. 557–571) for guidance.

EXTENSIONS FOR CRAFTING POETRY

- ▸ Have children add ideas, pictures, or words from their observations in nature on sticky notes. Then use the notes to create a class chart with a list of topics for poems.

- ▸ Place various poems on word cards at the poetry center so that children can move the words around to create new ways of placing words on the page.

- ▸ Repeat the Have a Try activity in WML1 with other poems so that children have an opportunity to notice a variety of characteristics. Add more characteristics to the chart.

- ▸ During interactive read-aloud or independent reading, encourage children to listen for sensory and descriptive language.

Section **7** | **Conventions**

THE MINILESSONS IN this section are designed to strike a
balance between teaching children to write clearly and making
them comfortable about taking risks with their writing. Teach
these lessons whenever you see that children are ready for them.

Minilessons in This Umbrella

WML1 Hold your marker and paper to do your best writing.

WML2 Leave space between words and lines.

WML3 Write your letters clearly.

Before Teaching Umbrella 1 Minilessons

The lessons in this umbrella are designed to expose children to the specific motor movements and techniques for handwriting, helping them become more effective and efficient writers. It is recommended that children in first grade begin using lined paper. Paper with a top and bottom solid line along with a dashed (dotted) middle line is a good choice of paper for independent writing. Other paper choices can be provided, including blank unlined paper (which provides space for children to make their marks) and paper with solid lines (which helps beginning writers divide their focus between the meaning of their writing and the conventions of writing). You can also fold unlined paper, which gives the writer an idea of how to use space for lines of print without visible lines on the page. Please note the dual meaning of *writing in lines*, which includes both writing words left to right so they are set up in a line within a row and writing letters vertically within the horizontal lines on the paper. Online resources, such as Alphabet Linking Chart and Verbal Path for Letter Formation, provide the information needed to teach how to form all the letters.

Because you will want to be responsive in your teaching, you do not need to teach the lessons consecutively; instead, teach them when your observations of children indicate a readiness for a particular lesson. Although we recommend using the verbal path to help children form letters, use the prompts sparingly. For WML2, model word and line spacing using an enlarged text, such as the following from *Fountas & Pinnell Classroom™ Shared Reading Collection*.

Shared Reading Collection

Scram! by Julie Reich

As you read and enjoy texts together, help children

- notice the space between words and lines, and
- notice that the writing starts on the left.

Writing Minilesson Principle
Hold your marker and paper to do your best writing.

You Will Need

- a writing tool for each child (washable markers are recommended)
- a sheet of paper for demonstration
- document camera (if available)
- chart paper and markers
- To download the following online resource for this lesson, visit **resources.fountasandpinnell.com**:
  - chart art (optional)

Academic Language/ Important Vocabulary

- writing
- paper
- marker
- finger
- slanted

Continuum Connection

- Hold pen or pencil with satisfactory grip (p. 255)
- Use a preferred hand consistently for writing (p. 255)

GOAL

Hold writing tool and paper efficiently, consistently using a preferred hand for writing.

RATIONALE

When children are comfortable holding a marker/pencil and paper, they write more efficiently and are better equipped to produce writing that communicates a message to the reader.

ASSESS LEARNING

- Observe children's writing behaviors.
- Notice whether children hold the writing tool and paper to write effectively and efficiently.
- Observe for evidence that children can use vocabulary such as *writing*, *paper*, *marker*, *finger*, and *slanted*.

MINILESSON

Prior to teaching this lesson, provide children with opportunities to try out different writing tools and paper. For this lesson, use your choice of writing tool, although it is recommended that you use a washable marker because you do not want erasures or torn paper. All of children's efforts should be visible. Encourage children to use a preferred hand when they write.

- Ensure that all children have a clear view of your hand and a marker for demonstration. If available, use a document camera.

  Watch carefully to see how I pick up the marker.

- Demonstrate picking up a marker off a table.

  What do you notice about my hand and fingers as I pick up the marker?

  Now I am going to write. Watch how I hold the marker and paper.

- Hold a sheet of paper at an angle against an easel/whiteboard or use a document camera. Write on the paper. With your other hand, point to each finger as you talk about it.

  What do you notice about how I hold the marker? I use my thumb and pointer finger. The marker is resting against my middle finger.

  What do you notice about how I hold the paper? I hold the paper down with one hand and hold my marker in the other hand. I slant the paper a little bit.

- Demonstrate holding the paper vertically, slanted to the left, and slanted to the right. Explain that it may take some practice for each child to find the most comfortable way to hold the paper. Be sure to account for both left-handed and right-handed children.

Have a Try

Invite children to practice using the proper grip when holding a marker.

> Each of you will get a marker. Turn and show your partner which hand you use to write and how you hold the marker.

▶ Hand a marker to each child. Have children practice picking up the marker and holding it with the proper grip and preferred hand. Observe children as they practice, and assist as needed.

Summarize and Apply

Write the principle on the top of the chart paper and read it to the children. Summarize the learning and remind children to think about how they hold a marker when they write.

> What did you learn about holding a marker and paper when you write?

▶ Guide the conversation as needed. Briefly write and sketch children's ideas to help them remember how to do their best writing.

> Today, practice holding your marker and paper the way I showed you.

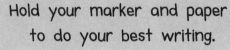

Hold your marker and paper to do your best writing.

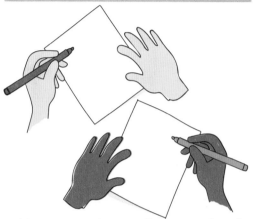

Hold your marker in the same hand every time.

Hold your paper with the other hand.

Try your best.

Confer

▶ During independent writing, move around the room to confer briefly with as many individual children as time allows. Sit side by side with them and invite them to talk about holding a marker and paper. Use the following prompts as needed.

- *Show which hand you write with.*
- *Show how to pick up the marker.*
- *Show how you write your name.*
- *Which fingers do you use to hold the marker?*

Share

Following independent writing, gather children in the meeting area. Ask a few children to share their experiences.

> How did you hold your marker?

> How did you hold your paper?

WML2

CNV.U1.WML2

Leave space between words and lines.

Using Good Handwriting

You Will Need

- a familiar enlarged text, such as *Scram!* by Julie Reich, from *Shared Reading Collection*
- chart paper and markers
- To download the following online resource for this lesson, visit **resources.fountasandpinnell.com**:
  - chart art (optional)

Academic Language / Important Vocabulary

- words
- space
- line
- sentence

Continuum Connection

- Leave appropriate space between words (p. 255)
- Write left to right in lines (p. 255)
- Form upper- and lowercase letters efficiently in manuscript print (p. 255)
- Form upper- and lowercase letters proportionately in manuscript print (p. 255)
- Write letters and words that can be easily read (p. 255)

GOAL

- Leave appropriate space between words and lines.

RATIONALE

- In this lesson, children learn that when they leave a space between words and lines, they help the reader understand what they have written. This knowledge helps children realize that their writing is meant to convey a message.

ASSESS LEARNING

- Look at children's writing to see whether they leave proper space between words and lines.
- Observe for evidence that children can use vocabulary such as *words*, *space*, *line*, and *sentence*.

MINILESSON

For this lesson, children should have a beginning understanding of the concept of a word and a sentence and be able to differentiate between a letter and a word. To help children think about the minilesson principle, use an enlarged text so that they can clearly see the space between words and lines. Here is an example.

- Show and read page 7 of *Scram!* Point under each word as you read.

  Let's count the words in the sentence.

  There are five words. How do you know?

- Guide children to notice that there is always a space between two words.

  After you write a word, leave a space before you write the next word.

- Show and read page 3 of *Scram!* Point under each word as you read it.

  What do you notice about the lines?

- Guide children to notice the space between the first and second lines.

- Using children's suggestions, compose two simple sentences about something they like to do with their families, writing each sentence on a new line.

  Michael, where do you like to go with your family?

- As you write, use two fingers to hold the space between words. Emphasize the clear letters and the space between words and lines.

  What did you notice about the space?

  I left a space before the next word so it is easier to read. I also left a space above each line so it is easier to read.

Have a Try

Repeat the process with two more sentences.

▶ Invite children to turn and talk to a partner about the sentences. After discussion, invite a child to come up and use two fingers to indicate the space before the next word and another child to point to where the next line should start.

> Who can point to the space between the words? the lines?

Summarize and Apply

Write the principle on the chart. Read it to the children. Then remind them to look for the space between words and lines as they read and to leave space between words and lines as they write.

> Why is it a good idea to leave a space before you write the next word? the next line?

> If you read today, look for the space between the words and the lines. When you write today, be sure to leave a space before you write the next word and before you write the next line.

> **Leave space between words and lines.**
>
> Michael likes to go visit his uncle.
>
> Carmen and her family like to go to the store together.
>
> Isaac and his mom go to the library to get books.

Confer

▶ During independent writing, move around the room to confer briefly with as many individual children as time allows. Sit side by side with them and invite them to talk about leaving space between words and lines. Use prompts like the following as needed.

- *Where will you start the next word (line)?*
- *Put the next word (line) here.*
- *Leave a space to help your reader understand what you have written.*

Share

Following independent writing, gather children in the meeting area to share their writing.

> Who would like to share the writing you did today?

> Point to where you left a good space on your paper.

Using Good Handwriting

You Will Need

- chart paper and markers in a variety of colors
- To download the following online resources for this lesson, visit **resources.fountasandpinnell.com**:
  - Alphabet Linking Chart
  - Verbal Path for Letter Formation
  - Letters Made in Similar Ways

Academic Language/ Important Vocabulary

- writing
- direction words
- letter
- left
- right
- clearly

Continuum Connection

- Leave appropriate space between words (p. 255)
- Return to the left margin to start a new line (p. 255)
- Write letters and words that can be easily read (p. 255)

GOAL

Write letters so that others can read the words.

RATIONALE

When you say direction words (the verbal path) for a letter and talk about writing from left to right, you describe the process of forming letters and words clearly.

ASSESS LEARNING

- Notice how well children follow verbal directions for forming a letter.
- Observe for evidence that children are writing words from left to right.
- Notice evidence that children can use vocabulary such as *writing*, *direction words*, *letter*, *left*, *right*, and *clearly*.

MINILESSON

Prior to teaching this lesson, it might be helpful to teach IW.1 and IW.2, which focus on using capital letters and the visual features of letters. To help children think about the writing minilesson principle, model how to use the verbal path to form letters. Here is an example.

- Help children think of one sentence to write, such as *I see a tree*.

  When you write a sentence, it is important to think about writing the letters clearly. The first word in this sentence is an uppercase *I*. To begin writing, start on the left and write in a straight line across the page.

- Use a black marker to write an uppercase *I* on the chart paper as you say the verbal path.

  To write an uppercase *I*, pull down, across, across.

- Invite several volunteers to come up and write an *I* over your writing, using different marker colors to make a rainbow letter. Have the other children repeat the verbal path as they use their fingers to make an uppercase *I* in the air.

  Notice how I place two fingers after the word *I* to know where to start writing the next word.

  The next word is *see*, which begins with a lowercase *s*. Look at the ABC chart. What do you notice about the lowercase *s*?

  It is a short letter with curves. Watch as I write it.

- Continue in this way, using the the verbal path to discuss tall and short letters and letters with straight lines, curves, and circles.

Have a Try

Invite children to practice making the letters in the sentence with a partner.

> Turn and talk to your partner about the way to make the letters in the sentence. Practice with your finger in the air and say the words that help you make the letters.

⬧ As needed, assist with the verbal path language.

⬧ You may decide to write a new sentence to talk about returning to the left margin to begin a new line.

Summarize and Apply

Summarize the learning. Remind children to think about the verbal path when they write.

⬧ Write the principle on the chart and read it aloud.

> Today when you are working on your books, think about how to write each letter clearly. Bring your writing when we meet together later.

Write your letters clearly.

I see a tree.

Confer

⬧ During independent writing, move around the room to confer briefly with as many individual children as time allows. Sit side by side with them and invite them to talk about writing their letters clearly. Use the following suggestions as needed to support letter formation.

- *Can you use your finger to trace the rainbow letters we made?*
- *Is this a short letter or a tall letter? Does it have straight lines, curves, or circles?*
- *Where will you start writing the new line?*
- *Let's talk about how to make the letter _____ [use the verbal path].*

Share

Following independent writing, gather children in the meeting area. Ask a few children to share what they wrote.

> Show a tall (short) letter you made today.

> Show an uppercase (lowercase) letter you made today.

> Did you make any letters with straight lines (curves, circles)?

Assessment

After you have taught the minilessons in this umbrella, observe children as they write. Use *The Literacy Continuum* (Fountas and Pinnell 2017) to notice, teach for, and support children's learning as you observe their attempts at reading and writing.

▶ What evidence do you have that children understand how to use drawing and writing tools?

- Do children hold the marker and paper in a way that helps them write efficiently and comfortably?

- Are they using direction words (the verbal path) to help them write letters?

- Do they leave a space between words?

- Do they start their writing on the left side of the paper and move to the right?

- Do they understand and use vocabulary such as *writing*, *paper*, *marker*, *finger*, *slanted*, *words*, *space*, *line*, *sentence*, *direction words*, *letter*, *left*, *right*, and *clearly*?

▶ In what ways, beyond the scope of this umbrella, are children showing readiness for writing?

- Do they show an interest in writing for a variety of purposes?

- Do they enjoy sharing their writing with others?

Use your observations to determine the next umbrella you will teach. You may also consult Suggested Sequence of Lessons (pp. 557–571) for guidance.

EXTENSIONS FOR USING GOOD HANDWRITING

▶ Provide stencils or plastic forms to have children trace letters.

▶ Have children sort magnetic letters by different visual features (see online resources).

▶ During interactive writing, show children where to start writing on the page and point out space between words. Likewise, during shared reading, highlight how the print starts on the left and continues in a line across the page.

▶ Provide children with a handwriting notebook. Schedule five-minute handwriting lessons during the word study block, and continue these lessons as the year progresses.

▶ Support children who need assistance with clear letter formation by having them make letters in sand or salt on a tray or trace textured letters.

Minilessons in This Umbrella

WML1 Say words slowly to listen for all the sounds.

WML2 Break words into syllables to write them.

WML3 Every word has at least one vowel.

WML4 Use what you know about words to write new words.

WML5 Write words that you know quickly.

Before Teaching Umbrella 2 Minilessons

This umbrella is designed to support children in learning how to write words to develop their independence in writing. Use interactive writing and shared writing to provide a scaffold for children to go from sound to symbol. To build a strong foundation for teaching this umbrella, children should have experienced some interactive writing lessons, especially IW.3: Labeling the Classroom and IW.4: Writing from a Picture. A piece of writing that you and the class have created and that contains some familiar high-frequency words, such as the memory story in IW.8, will be useful when teaching this umbrella. Children will also benefit from familiarity with letter-sound relationships and some work with phonograms.

As you teach these lessons, refer to classroom resources such as a word wall, ABC chart, and/or name chart, as well as items from each child's writing folder, such as a smaller ABC chart, a smaller name chart, and/or a personal word list.

Interactive Writing Lessons

IW.8: Writing a Memory Story

As you read and enjoy texts together, especially shared reading texts,

- use a pointer to help children follow along with the text as you read it,

- have children clap the syllables in a word,

- ask children to point to vowels in words, and

- ask children to point out words that they know.

WML1

CNV.U2.WML1

Writing Minilesson Principle
Say words slowly to listen for all the sounds.

Learning How to Write Words

You Will Need

- picture cards of words that have easy-to-hear sounds
- name chart
- ABC chart
- pocket chart
- blank word cards
- sentence strip
- markers
- To download the following online resources for this lesson, visit **resources.fountasandpinnell.com**:
  - Verbal Path for Letter Formation
  - chart art (optional)

Academic Language / Important Vocabulary

- word
- sounds
- letter
- slowly
- listen

Continuum Connection

- Say words slowly to hear a sound and write a letter that represents it (p. 255)
- Write some words with consonant letters appropriate for sounds in words (beginning and ending) (p. 255)
- Attempt unknown words through sound analysis (p. 255)

GOAL

Say words slowly and listen for all the sounds.

RATIONALE

When you teach children to say words slowly, they learn to isolate and identify the sounds they hear. Making the connection between a letter and the sound it represents is key for both writing and reading.

ASSESS LEARNING

- Observe children's ability to say a word slowly and listen for the first, middle, and ending sounds.
- Notice if children can identify the letter or letters that go with a sound.
- Observe for evidence that children can use vocabulary such as *word*, *sounds*, *letter*, *slowly*, and *listen*.

MINILESSON

To help children think about the minilesson principle, use picture cards of words that have easily identifiable sounds. Here is an example.

- Display a picture card in a pocket chart (e.g., *swim*).

  Look at this picture. What is one word we can write to explain this picture?

  Say the word *swim* slowly with me and listen for all the sounds.

- Ask the children to say *swim* slowly with you again to listen for the first sound. Emphasize /s/.

  What sound do you hear first in *swim*?

  The first sound is /s/. What is the letter that goes with that sound?

- Point to *s* on the ABC chart or name chart. Use the Verbal Path for Letter Formation to describe how to form the first letter in *swim*. Record the letter on a card taped lightly to the easel.

  To make an s, pull back, in, around, and back around.

- Repeat this process for the rest of the word, having children listen for all the sounds in order. It is important that they are the ones who say the word.

- Run your finger underneath the word as you say it slowly, and emphasize all of the letter sounds. Move the card to the pocket chart.

- Repeat the process for a few more picture cards containing words with easy-to-hear sounds, such as *plum* and *clap*.

Have a Try

Invite children to work with a partner to listen for and identify the sounds in another word, such as *sports*.

> These are things you use to play sports. Say *sports* slowly. Now say it slowly to your partner. Tell the sounds you hear and the letters that stand for those sounds.

- Ask volunteers to share the sounds they heard in the correct order. Write the word on a card.
- Check the word by running your finger underneath it and saying all of the sounds slowly. Place the card in the pocket chart.

Summarize and Apply

Summarize the learning. Remind children to listen carefully for all the sounds in words as they write.

- Write the principle on a sentence strip and add it to the top of the pocket chart.

> When you write a word, make sure to say it slowly to listen for all the sounds before you write it. Be sure to write the letters in the order that you heard them.

Confer

- During independent writing, move around the room to confer briefly with as many individual children as time allows. Sit side by side with them and invite them to talk about writing words. Use prompts like the ones below as needed.
  - *You can say the word slowly and listen for the sounds [model].*
  - *What do you hear first? next? after that?*
  - *You can think about the sound and write the letter.*

Share

Following independent writing, gather children in the meeting area. Invite individual children to share their writing.

> Who would like to share your writing?
>
> Point to a word you wrote. How did you know which letters to write?

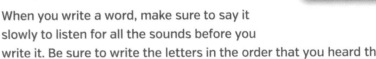

WML2

CNV.U2.WML2

Break words into syllables to write them.

Learning How to Write Words

You Will Need

- pocket chart
- picture cards of two-syllable words that have easy-to-hear sounds and syllable breaks
- blank word cards
- a word card or whiteboard for each pair of children
- sentence strip
- markers
- To download the following online resource for this lesson, visit **resources.fountasandpinnell.com**:
  - chart art (optional)

Academic Language / Important Vocabulary

- parts
- word
- syllable
- clap

Continuum Connection

- Say words to break them into syllables to spell them (p. 255)
- Hear, say, clap, and identify syllables in one- or two-syllable words: e.g., *big, frog; lit/tle, mon/key* (p. 368)
- Understand and talk about the concept of a syllable (p. 368)

GOAL

Clap syllables and listen for sounds to help write words.

RATIONALE

When you teach children to say words slowly, they hear the syllables in words and begin to understand that some words are short (one syllable) and other words are longer (two or more syllables). Clapping syllables emphasizes the breaks in words and makes writing multisyllabic words more manageable.

ASSESS LEARNING

- Observe children's ability to say and clap syllables in words.
- Notice if children can recognize and use syllables to break apart words when writing.
- Observe for evidence that children can use vocabulary such as *parts, word, syllable,* and *clap.*

MINILESSON

To help children think about the minilesson principle, use picture cards representing words with easily identifiable syllable breaks. Here is an example.

- Display a picture card of a two-syllable word and place it in a pocket chart (e.g., *basket*).

  Look at this picture. This is a basket.

  When you say a word, you can clap the parts you hear. Each part is called a syllable.

- Demonstrate saying and clapping *basket.*

  Clap *basket* with me. How many parts, or syllables, do you hear?

  Basket has two syllables, so you clapped twice.

  To write the word *basket,* say the first syllable slowly and write the letters for the sounds you hear. Say *bas* with me slowly. What sound do you hear first? next? last?

- Record the letters for the first syllable on a word card attached lightly to the easel. Then have children clap the syllables in *basket* again, this time stressing the second syllable, and listening for the sounds in *ket.*

- Record the second syllable and place the card in the pocket chart. Run your finger underneath the word as you emphasize all of the letter sounds.

- Repeat this process for additional picture cards for words that have easy-to-hear syllables, such as *kitten* and *wagon.*

Have a Try

Invite children to work with a partner to clap the syllables in a two-syllable word.

▶ Give each pair a blank word card or whiteboard.

Say the word *cactus* slowly with your partner and clap the syllables you hear. Turn and talk to your partner about the number of parts you hear. Say the parts slowly and talk about the sounds you hear and the letters that stand for those sounds. Write the word on your word card (whiteboard).

▶ Invite volunteers to clap the parts of the word and show what they have written. Place a correctly spelled word card, if used, in the pocket chart.

Summarize and Apply

Summarize the learning. Remind children to break apart words into syllables to help them spell them during writing time.

▶ Write the principle on a sentence strip and place it at the top of the pocket chart.

When you write a word that has more than one syllable, clap the syllables. Then say each syllable slowly so that you can listen for the sounds and write the letters.

Confer

▶ During independent writing, move around the room to confer briefly with as many individual children as time allows. Sit side by side with them and invite them to talk about writing words. Use prompts like the ones below as needed.

· *Listen for the parts. Clap the parts you hear.*

· *Listen for the sounds you hear in the first (last) part.*

· *You can say the part slowly and listen for the sounds you hear (model).*

Share

Following independent writing, gather children in the meeting area. Invite individual children to share their writing.

Who would like to share what you wrote today?

Did you write a word that has more than one part? What did you do?

Umbrella 2: Learning How to Write Words

Writing Minilesson Principle
Every word has at least one vowel.

You Will Need

- chart paper and marker
- highlighter or highlighter tape
- sticky note labeled *Vowels*

Academic Language / Important Vocabulary

- sound
- consonant
- word
- letter
- vowel

Continuum Connection

- Include a vowel in each word (p. 255)
- Write a letter for easy-to-hear vowel sounds (p. 255)
- Understand and talk about the fact that some letters represent vowel sounds (p. 368)

GOAL

Understand that every word has at least one vowel.

RATIONALE

Understanding the terms *consonant* and *vowel* allows children to talk about letters and how letters make words. When you teach children which letters are vowels, and that every word has at least one vowel in it, they begin to understand the role of vowels in spelling patterns and are ready to explore how the relationship between vowel sounds and letters is influenced by the letters around them.

ASSESS LEARNING

- Look at children's writing to see whether they include at least one vowel in each word.
- Observe for evidence that children can use vocabulary such as *sound*, *consonant*, *word*, *letter*, and *vowel*.

MINILESSON

To help children think about the minilesson principle, begin by ensuring they are familiar with the terms *vowel* and *consonant*. Then discuss identifying and writing vowels in words. Here is an example.

- Write the vowels *a, e, i, o, u,* and *y* on chart paper.

  Say the letters with me as I point underneath each one.

  Does anyone know what these letters are called?

  These are vowels. All of the other letters in the alphabet are called consonants.

- Write about four simple words on the chart.

  Read each word with me as I point to it.

  What are you noticing about the letters in these words?

- Guide the children to discover that each word has a vowel. Highlight the vowel in each word.

  Every word has at least one vowel. This will help you when you write words. You know that you have to write at least one vowel when you write a word.

- Write another simple word on the chart, this time with the children.

  Let's write the word *fog* together. Say it slowly with me. What letter comes first? What letter comes next? What other letter do you hear?

- Record the word on the chart. Invite a child to come up and point to the vowel.

- Add the sticky note labeled *Vowels* next to the list of vowels on the chart.

The Writing Minilessons Book, Grade 1

Have a Try

Invite children to work with a partner to listen for and identify the letters for the sounds they hear.

> Say the word *cup* slowly with your partner. Turn and talk to your partner about the sounds you hear and the letters that stand for those sounds.

▶ Invite volunteers to share what sounds they hear, guiding them to think about the sounds in the correct order. Record what the children say. Check the word by running your finger underneath the letters as they say the sounds. Ask a volunteer to come up and point to the vowel. Highlight it.

Summarize and Apply

Help children summarize the learning. Remind them to use what they know about vowels to write new words during writing time.

▶ Write the principle at the top of the chart. Read it aloud.

> When you write a word, make sure it has at least one vowel. Write consonants and vowels for the sounds you hear in the order you hear them.

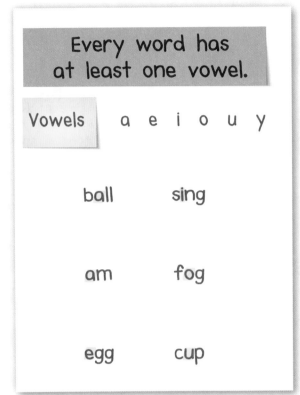

Every word has at least one vowel.

Vowels   a e i o u y

ball   sing

am   fog

egg   cup

Confer

▶ During independent writing, move around the room to confer briefly with as many individual children as time allows. Sit side by side with them and invite them to talk about writing words. Use prompts like the ones below as needed.

   • *You can say the word slowly and listen for the sounds (model).*

   • *You need a vowel next in that word.*

   • *Write the letter for the first (next, last) sound you hear.*

Share

Following independent writing, gather children in the meeting area. Invite individual children to share their writing.

> Who would like to share your writing?

> Can you point to a new word you wrote? What vowel is in that word?

Writing Minilesson Principle
Use what you know about words to write new words.

Learning How to Write Words

You Will Need

▸ chart paper and markers

Academic Language / Important Vocabulary

▸ letter
▸ word
▸ ending
▸ beginning
▸ sound

Continuum Connection

▸ Use known words to help spell an unknown word (p. 369)

▸ Use phonogram patterns and letter patterns to help spell a word (p. 369)

▸ Change the beginning sound or sounds to make and solve a new word: e.g., *he/me* (change /h/ to /m/); *more/shore* (change /m/ to /sh/); *bright/might* (change /b/ /r/ to /m/) (p. 369)

▸ Use onset and rimes in known words to read and write other words with the same parts: e.g., *thr-ow, thr-ee; thr-ow, gr-ow* (p. 369)

▸ Change the ending sound or sounds to make a new word; e.g., *in/it* (change /n/ to /t/); *them/ then* (change /m/ to /n/); *rest/red* (change /s/ /t/ to /d/) (p. 369)

GOAL

Use knowledge of known words to write unknown words.

RATIONALE

Teaching children to read and write all of the individual words in a language would be a huge, time-consuming, and impossible task. A more efficient approach is to teach children to use what they know (known words or parts of words, such as a letter, a cluster of letters, or a phonogram pattern) to understand something new. This equips them with tools to solve new words when they read and write.

ASSESS LEARNING

▸ Observe for evidence that children can use what they know to write unknown words.

▸ Notice if children use parts of words (e.g., a letter, cluster of letters, or a phonogram pattern) to help write new words.

▸ Observe for evidence that children can use vocabulary such as *letter, word, ending, beginning,* and *sound.*

MINILESSON

To help children think about the minilesson principle, choose words that children know well (from the word wall if you have one) and demonstrate using them to write new words. Here is an example.

▸ Write the word *and* on chart paper.

> This is a word that you know well. Say it with me slowly: *and.*

▸ Write the word *hand* on the chart directly below *and.*

> What do you notice about these two words?

> I added a letter to the beginning of the word, but I left the last three letters the same.

> How do you think I knew how to write *hand*?

> I used the word *and* and put an *h* at the beginning to make the word *hand.*

▸ Point under the letters as you guide children to understand that you used what you knew about the sound of the letter *h* and the word *and* to figure out the word *hand.*

▸ Repeat this process with the phonogram *and* to make more words, such as the words *land, band, sand,* and *stand* (connecting the *st* in *stand* to *stop*).

▸ Across the next several days, repeat this process with other known words. Try using words where you add a letter to the end. For example, *the, them, then.* Or you could use words where you alter the middle letter, such as *will, well;* then build additional words such as *spell/smell.*

Have a Try

Invite children to talk to a partner about using the word *will* to write other words.

> This is the word *will*. Turn and talk to your partner. How can you use *will* to spell *pill*?

▶ Ask a volunteer to spell the word. Write it on the chart. Talk about what they knew that helped them to spell the word. Repeat with the words *spill*, *still*, *grill*, and *thrill*.

Summarize and Apply

Help children summarize the lesson. Remind children to use what they know about words to write new words during writing time.

> What is something you can do to help you write new words?

▶ Write the principle at the top of the chart. Read it aloud.

> When you want to write a new word, think about words you already know to help you write the new word.

Use what you know about words to write new words.

and	will
hand	pill
land	spill
band	still
sand	grill
stand	thrill

Confer

▶ During independent writing, move around the room to confer briefly with as many individual children as time allows. Sit side by side with them and invite them to talk about using known words to write new words. Use prompts like the ones below as needed.

- *What can you do if you don't know how to write a word?*
- *Do you know a word that starts like that?*
- *Do you know a word that sounds like that?*
- *Is that like a word you know?*

Share

Following independent writing, gather children in the meeting area. Invite individual children to share their writing.

> Who would like to share your writing?

> Can you point to a new word you wrote? How did you know what letters to write?

WML5

Writing Minilesson Principle
Write words that you know quickly.

Learning How to Write Words

You Will Need

- chart paper prepared with a piece of writing with familiar high-frequency words, such as from IW.8: Writing a Memory Story
- highlighter or highlighter tape
- several word cards prepared with familiar high-frequency words (e.g., *we, went, to, the, there, was, that, is, had, on*)
- chart paper and markers
- To download the following online resource for this lesson, visit **resources.fountasandpinnell.com**:
  - High-Frequency Word List

Academic Language / Important Vocabulary

- word
- quickly
- write
- spell

Continuum Connection

- Spell approximately one hundred high-frequency words conventionally and reflect spelling in final drafts (p. 255)
- Use simple resources to help in spelling words or check on spelling (word walls, personal words lists) (p. 255)
- Recognize and use high-frequency words with one, two, or three letters: e.g., *a, I, in, is, of, to, and, the* (p. 368)
- Spell known words quickly (p. 369)

GOAL

Write known high-frequency words quickly and accurately.

RATIONALE

When you teach children to write high-frequency words quickly and accurately, they can share their thoughts in writing more fluently and begin to use these words as anchors to monitor and check their writing and reading. It also allows them more time to devote to unknown words, often by connecting new words to the familiar words using the beginning letter, sound, or part.

ASSESS LEARNING

- Observe for evidence that children can write high-frequency words quickly and accurately.
- Notice if children refer to resources around the room (such as the word wall) to help write and/or check high-frequency words.
- Observe for evidence that children can use vocabulary such as *word, quickly, write,* and *spell*.

MINILESSON

To help children think about the minilesson principle, identify high-frequency words in a piece of class interactive writing, such as that from IW.8: Writing a Memory Story. If you have a class word wall, refer to it in the lesson.

- Display a page from the class book.

  Remember when we wrote about our class field trip? We wrote about what we learned at the science museum.

- Read the page aloud while pointing under the words.

  You know some of the words that we wrote because they are on our word wall and you see them in the books that we read. You might even have them on your personal word list. You really know them well.

- Help a volunteer highlight the words they know well (e.g., *we, went, to, the, there, was, that, is, had, on*).

  Who would like to come up and highlight the words you know well?

  Who can point to these highlighted words on the word wall?

- Invite children to write the high-frequency words in the air or on the carpet.

  You can write these words quickly because you know them very well. You didn't need to spend a lot of time thinking about how to write them.

  Let's practice writing these words in the air.

Have a Try

Invite children to practice writing words they know quickly.

▶ Display one of the word cards (e.g., *went*).

What word is this?

What are the letters in *went*?

How many letters are in *went*?

▶ Ask a volunteer to write *went* on a clean sheet of chart paper. Remind him to write quickly but keep it legible. The other children can practice writing the word in the air or on the carpet.

▶ Repeat for the other word cards.

Summarize and Apply

Summarize the learning. Remind children to write the words they know quickly when they write.

When you do your own writing and you write a word that you have seen and used a lot, remember to write it quickly the way you know how. Look at the word wall (personal word list) if you need to remember how to write a word.

Writing a Memory Story

We went to the science museum.

There was a show about lightning.

The guide told us that a lightining bolt is hotter that the sun.

We had fun on the field trip.

Museum of Science

Confer

▶ During independent writing, move around the room to confer briefly with as many individual children as time allows. Sit side by side with them and invite them to talk about writing words they know quickly. Use prompts like the ones below as needed.

· *What are you going to write about today?*

· *Read this page aloud. Is there a word that you were able to write quickly?*

· *Find the word _____ on the word wall.*

· *Write the word _____ quickly.*

Share

Following independent writing, gather children in the meeting area. Invite individual children to share their writing.

Who would like to share your writing?

Is there a word that you were able to write quickly?

Umbrella 2: Learning How to Write Words

Assessment

After you have taught the minilessons in this umbrella, observe children as they write and talk about their writing. Use the behaviors and understandings in *The Literacy Continuum* (Fountas and Pinnell 2017) to notice, teach for, and support children's learning as you observe their attempts at writing.

▶ What evidence do you have that children are learning how to write words?

- Are children saying words slowly and listening for all the sounds?
- Do they break apart words and listen for sounds to help write words?
- Do they understand that every word has at least one vowel?
- Is there evidence that children use what they know about words to write new words?
- Can they write known words quickly?
- Do they understand and use vocabulary such as *letter*, *word*, *parts*, *syllable*, *consonant*, *vowel*, *ending*, *beginning*, and *sounds*?

▶ In what other ways, beyond the scope of this umbrella, are the children learning how to write words?

- Would they benefit from learning how to use classroom resources to write words?
- Are they ready to learn when to use capital letters?

Use your observations to determine the next umbrella to teach. You may also consult Suggested Sequence of Lessons (pp. 557–571) for guidance.

EXTENSIONS FOR LEARNING HOW TO WRITE WORDS

▶ To help children listen for sounds, use an audio device and have them record and then listen to several easy-to-hear sounds.

▶ Continue to use interactive writing to demonstrate articulating unknown words and slowly writing predominant sounds in sequence.

▶ Place games in the word work center to practice recognizing and writing high-frequency words, understanding syllables, or building words from a phonogram.

▶ As children read, support them by pointing out known parts of words during shared reading.

▶ Gather together a guided writing group of several children who need support in a specific area of writing.

Minilessons in This Umbrella

WML1 Use the name chart and ABC chart to help you write words.

WML2 Use the word wall to help you write words.

WML3 Use your own word list to help you write words.

Interactive Writing

Before Teaching Umbrella 3 Minilessons

The goal of this umbrella is to help children learn how to use a variety of resources to help themselves write new words. These lessons use the text and photo from IW.4: Writing from a Picture, so if you wish to use this example be sure to teach that lesson beforehand. However, this is only one possibility. You could also choose to write simple sentences about a familiar book or about anything. When you write sentences with the children, be sure to decide what to say and how to say it with the children instead of deciding yourself. When the children co-construct the language, they will be able to read it more successfully.

The chart for this umbrella is built cumulatively across the three minilessons, but the lessons can be completed in any order. Before teaching the first two minilessons, children should already be familiar with the name chart, ABC chart, and word wall. WML3 shows children how to use a personal word list (available in online resources; see also MGT.U4.WML3) as another resource for writing. Write some easy high-frequency words (about ten, e.g., *and, can, him, in, is, like, the, to, we, will*) on the word list prior to attaching it to children's folders. The words should be ones that children are learning and use frequently in their writing. The list is stored in the writing folder (see MGT.U2.WML3). Work with children to add words to their word lists during writing conferences.

Interactive Writing Lessons

IW.4: Writing from a Picture

WML1

Writing Minilesson Principle

Use the name chart and ABC chart to help you write words.

Using Classroom Resources to Write Words

You Will Need

- photo and class-made text from IW.4: Writing from a Picture
- name chart
- chart paper and markers
- To download the following online resource for this lesson, visit **resources.fountasandpinnell.com**:
  - Alphabet Linking Chart

Academic Language / Important Vocabulary

- sound
- letter
- name chart
- ABC chart

Continuum Connection

- Use simple resources to help in spelling words or check on spelling (word walls, personal word lists) (p. 255)
- Use beginning reference tools: e.g., word walls or personal word collections or dictionaries (p. 257)
- Use one's name to learn about words and to make connections to words (p. 367)
- Use the initial letter in a name to make connections to other words: e.g., *Max*, *Maria*, *make*, *home*, *from* (p. 369)
- Use the initial letter in a name to read and write other words: e.g., *Tom*, *toy*, *town*, *stop*, *cat* (p. 369)

GOAL

Use the name chart and ABC chart as resources to help write words.

RATIONALE

When children learn to use classroom resources for writing, they become independent problem solvers who are responsible for their own writing because they can find solutions on their own.

ASSESS LEARNING

- ▶ Notice evidence that children understand that the name chart and ABC chart are two classroom resources they can use for writing.
- ▶ Observe whether children are using classroom resources to help them write new words.
- ▶ Observe for evidence that children can use vocabulary such as *sound*, *letter*, *name chart*, and *ABC chart*.

MINILESSON

Prior to teaching this lesson, children should be familiar with the name chart and ABC chart. Compose and write a simple sentence about a picture (any interesting picture or the example) with the children so you can model how to use the name chart and ABC chart to help with writing. Here is an example.

- ▶ Show the picture and writing from IW.4 and reread it.

  Today, we can add more sentences to what we wrote about this picture. What else could we write?

- ▶ Once you and the children have decided what the sentence will be, say it together. Then write the sentence together.

  Our sentence is *One cow was black and one cow was brown.*

- ▶ Model how to use the name chart and ABC chart to help children write the words. Say and write *One* (a high-frequency word). Then pause. Accentuate /k/ when you say *cow*.

  What is the next word? Say *cow* slowly to listen for the first sound.

  Cow starts with /k/. On the ABC chart, what begins with the same sound?

  What letter do you see with *cat*?

  Cat begins with /k/, and *cat* begins with the letter *c*. *Cow* also starts with *c*.

- ▶ Invite a child to write the *c*. Then finish writing the word *cow*. Say and write *was* yourself. Write the word *black* together. Use the resources to help children write the letters for the first sounds they hear (*b*, *l*, *a*). Write the *ck*.

  How did you find out which letters to write?

Have a Try

Invite children to turn and talk about using the name chart and ABC chart to write words in another sentence.

> What should we write next? We will write *They stood next to each other*. *They* starts like *the*. Who can write *the*? Now add a *y* to make it say *they*. What word is next? With a partner, say *stood* slowly and listen for all the sounds. Use the name chart or ABC chart to help you decide what letters stand for those sounds.

▶ After time for partners to talk, ask volunteers to write some of the letters in the sentence.

Summarize and Apply

Help children summarize the lesson. Remind children to use the name chart and ABC chart when they write.

> Where can you look to think about the sounds that go with a letter?

> Where can you look to know what a letter looks like?

▶ Make a chart to remind children to use classroom resources to write words. Save the chart for WML2.

> During writing time, use the name chart and ABC chart to help you write words.

Ways to Help Yourself Write New Words
• Name chart
• ABC chart

Confer

▶ During independent writing, move around the room to confer briefly with as many individual children as time allows. Sit side by side with them and invite them to talk about how they use classroom resources to write words. Use the following prompts as needed.

- *Say the word slowly and listen for the first (second, next, middle, last sound).*
- *How can the ABC chart (name chart) help you write the letter?*
- *What name do you see on the name chart that can help you write this word?*

Share

Following independent writing, gather children in the meeting area. Ask children to share their experiences using the name chart and ABC chart.

> Who used the name chart or ABC chart for writing today? Tell about that.

Umbrella 3: Using Classroom Resources to Write Words

Using Classroom Resources to Write Words

You Will Need

- class-made text from IW.4: Writing from a Picture
- word wall
- chart paper and markers
- chart begun in WML1

Academic Language / Important Vocabulary

- sound
- letter
- word
- word wall

Continuum Connection

- Use simple resources to help in spelling words or check on spelling (word walls, personal word lists) (p. 255)

GOAL

Understand that the word wall can help you write some words quickly and easily.

RATIONALE

When children learn to use a word wall as one resource for writing, they make the connection that their knowledge of some words can help them write unfamiliar words. It can also help them learn to write high-frequency words quickly.

ASSESS LEARNING

- ▶ Notice evidence that children understand that a word wall can help them with writing.
- ▶ Observe whether children are using classroom resources such as the word wall for writing.
- ▶ Observe for evidence that children can use vocabulary such as *sound, letter, word,* and *word wall.*

MINILESSON

Prior to teaching this lesson, a word wall should be set up and functioning in the classroom. This minilesson builds on the previous minilesson, but you and the children can compose and co-construct a sentence about any interesting picture. Here is an example.

- ▶ Show the picture and writing from IW.4 and reread it.

  What sentence could we add to what we wrote about the picture?

- ▶ Once you and the children have decided what the sentence will be, say it together. Then write the sentence together. If needed, model how to slowly articulate the words and use the word wall.

  Our sentence will be *The cows are standing still.*

  I want to write the word *The.* Who can find *the* on the word wall? Sometimes the word that you want to write is on the word wall. Other times you can use words on the word wall to help you write a word.

- ▶ Children can use the word wall to help them write high-frequency words quickly and easily. They can also use the word wall to help them write new words. For example, they might use *and* to write *standing* or *will* to write *still.*

- ▶ Continue writing the sentence, pausing before any words that connect to a word on the word wall.

Have a Try

Invite children to turn and talk about using the word wall to write new words.

> Turn and talk about how you can use the word wall to help you when you write.

▶ After time for a brief discussion, ask volunteers to share their experiences and ideas for using the word wall as they write.

Summarize and Apply

Help children summarize the lesson. Remind children that the word wall is one place to look when they need help writing new words.

> Where can you look to help you write words you don't know how to write?

▶ Continue the chart from WML1 by adding *Word wall*. Save the chart for WML3.

> Remember that you can use a whole word or part of a word from the word wall to help you write a new word.

Ways to Help Yourself Write New Words

- **Name chart**

- **ABC chart**

- **Word wall**

Confer

▶ During independent writing, move around the room to confer briefly with as many individual children as time allows. Sit side by side with them and invite them to talk about using classroom resources to write words. Use the following prompts as needed.

- *Look at the word wall. What word can help you write what comes next?*
- *How can the word wall help you when you write?*
- *What word sounds like that at the beginning (middle, end)?*

Share

Following independent writing, gather children in the meeting area to share how they used the word wall.

> Who used the word wall to write a new word today? Tell about that.

> Did anyone use anything else to help you write a word?

Writing Minilesson Principle
Use your own word list to help you write words.

Using Classroom Resources to Write Words

You Will Need

- class-made text from IW.4: Writing from a Picture
- chart paper and markers
- chart from WML2
- a personal word list with a few words on it, including some words you will use in the lesson
- children's writing folders with their personal word list inside
- To download the following online resource for this lesson, visit **resources.fountasandpinnell.com**:
  - My Words

Academic Language / Important Vocabulary

- writing folder
- personal word list

Continuum Connection

- Use simple resources to help in spelling words or check on spelling (word walls, personal word lists) (p. 255)

GOAL

Understand what a personal word list is and how to use it.

RATIONALE

When children learn to create and use a personal word list, they understand that the words they learn can be used again and again in their writing, and they learn how to keep track of words so they can refer to them as needed. If children have writing folders, the personal word lists can be fastened inside along with other reference tools.

ASSESS LEARNING

- Notice evidence that children understand how to refer to a personal word list.
- Look for evidence that children are creating and using personal word lists.
- Observe for evidence that children can use vocabulary such as *writing folder* and *personal word list*.

MINILESSON

To help children think about the minilesson principle, demonstrate how to use a personal word list as a resource for writing. This lesson builds on WML2, but you and the children can compose and co-construct a sentence about any interesting picture. Here is an example.

- Ahead of time, prepare a sample word list on chart paper. Include several words that will be used in the model writing you will do during this lesson.
- Post the word list and the writing from IW.4 side by side with a blank piece of chart paper. Reread IW.4.

  What is another sentence we could write about the picture?

  Our sentence is *Cows have long tails that sway back and forth.*

- Once you and the children have decided what the sentence will be, say it together. Then write the sentence together. Model using your word list to write several words in the sentence, such as *long*, *sway*, and *forth*.

  The next word is *long*. Say it slowly. The word *long* rhymes with *song*, which is on my word list.

- Point to the word *song* on the word list and write the word *long*.

  What did I do to change the word *song* to *long*?

- Repeat this process for the word *sway*, connecting it to *day*.

  What part of the word *day* can help you write *sway*?

- Make connections between other words or word parts on your list and the words in the rest of the sentence.

The Writing Minilessons Book, Grade 1

Have a Try

Invite children to turn and talk about personal word lists.

> Turn to your partner and read two words you have on your personal word list.

▶ After time for a brief discussion, ask a few children to share. Suggest that their writing folders would be a good place to keep their personal word lists.

Summarize and Apply

Summarize the lesson. Remind children to use their personal word lists when they write and keep adding to it.

▶ Add the final bullet to the chart from WML2.

> These are all places you can look to help you write words. The next time we talk about your writing, I will suggest some words for you to add to your personal word list. Your word list is in your writing folder so you can find it. Bring your writing to share when we meet later.

Ways to Help Yourself Write New Words

• **Name chart**

• ABC chart

• **Word wall**

• Personal word list

Confer

▶ During independent writing, move around the room to confer briefly with as many individual children as time allows. Sit side by side with them and invite them to talk about using resources to write words. Use the following prompts as needed.

- *What words do you have on your word list so far?*
- *What new word would you like to add to your word list?*
- *Which word on your list will help you write this new word?*

Share

Following independent writing, gather children in the meeting area to share their writing.

> When you were writing, did you use your word list to help you write a word?

> Did anyone look anywhere else to get help to write a new word?

Assessment

After you have taught the minilessons in this umbrella, observe children as they write. Use *The Literacy Continuum* (Fountas and Pinnell 2017) to notice, teach for, and support children's learning as you observe their attempts at reading and writing.

▶ What evidence do you have of new understandings children have developed related to using classroom resources for writing?

- Are children using the name chart or ABC chart to help them write new words?

- Do you notice children using the word wall as they write?

- Has each child added words to a personal word list?

- Do they understand how to use a personal word list to write words?

- Are they using vocabulary related to using classroom resources, such as *writing folder, sound, letter, name, name chart, ABC chart, word, word wall,* and *word list*?

▶ In what ways, beyond the scope of this umbrella, are children using classroom resources?

- Do they use the ABC chart or name chart to help write capital letters?

Use your observations to determine the next umbrella you will teach. You may also consult Suggested Sequence of Lessons (pp. 557–571) for guidance.

EXTENSIONS FOR USING CLASSROOM RESOURCES TO WRITE WORDS

▶ As you use shared reading books and other big books with children, from time to time have them make connections between the words they see and the name chart or ABC chart.

▶ Use the word wall in a variety of ways throughout the day (e.g., "I spy a word that begins with *th* and rhymes with *hen*. What is it?").

▶ Encourage children to add content words to their personal word lists, such as after completing a science project or after attending a field trip.

Minilessons in This Umbrella

WML1   Use a period to end a sentence.

WML2   Use a question mark to end a question.

WML3   Use an exclamation point to show something exciting or surprising.

Before Teaching Umbrella 4 Minilessons

Punctuation falls in the category of conventions, but it is also part of the author's craft. Writers carefully choose the punctuation that best expresses the message they are communicating. Prior to teaching these minilessons, children should have had experiences reading and discussing books with a variety of punctuation marks, including periods, question marks, and exclamation points. The minilessons in this umbrella use the following books from *Fountas & Pinnell Classroom™ Interactive Read-Aloud Collection* and *Shared Reading Collection*. However, you can use other books from the classroom library. As much as possible, use big books so that children can clearly see and identify the punctuation marks.

Interactive Read-Aloud Collection

Mo Willems: Having Fun with Humor

Don't Let the Pigeon Drive the Bus!

Shared Reading Collection

The Big, Green, Scary Monster by Judith E. Nayer

As you read and enjoy these texts together, help children

• notice punctuation marks in the text,

• notice the way your voice changes when you read a sentence that ends with a period, question mark, or exclamation point, and

• talk about the writer's intention in choosing a particular end mark.

Writing Minilesson Principle
Use a period to end a sentence.

Learning About Punctuation

You Will Need

- several familiar books with short sentences ending in periods, such as the following:

  - *Don't Let the Pigeon Drive the Bus!* by Mo Willems, from Text Set: Mo Willems: Having Fun with Humor

  - *The Big, Green, Scary Monster* by Judith E. Nayer, from *Shared Reading Collection*

- highlighter tape (optional)
- chart paper
- colored markers

Academic Language / Important Vocabulary

- writing
- sentence
- period

Continuum Connection

- Notice the use of punctuation marks in books and try them out in one's own writing (p. 255)

- Use periods, exclamation marks, and question marks as end marks (p. 255)

GOAL

Understand that writers put a period at the end of a statement.

RATIONALE

When children recognize how periods at the end of sentences convey meaning, they learn to use punctuation to interpret a writer's intention and begin adding periods to the end of the sentences they write.

ASSESS LEARNING

- Notice evidence that children understand the significance of a period at the end of a sentence.

- Observe whether children are beginning to add periods to the end of sentences when they write.

- Look for evidence that children can use vocabulary such as *writing*, *sentence*, and *period*.

MINILESSON

To help children understand the minilesson principle, engage them in discussion about why writers use periods and how they can use them in their own writing. Here is an example.

- Show and read pages 2 and 6 of *Don't Let the Pigeon Drive the Bus!* making sure your voice goes down and stops after the periods.

  What do you notice at the end of these sentences?

- As children identify each period, point underneath it.

  Why do you think the writer decided to add a period at the end of the sentences?

- Guide the conversation, helping them recognize that the period shows the end of a sentence, or one complete idea. Use the following prompts as needed.

  - *When do writers use this mark?*
  - *What does this mark tell the reader?*
  - *When will you write a period?*

- Show and read page 8 of *The Big, Green, Scary Monster*. Have children reread the sentences with you, pointing under each word and the periods as you read.

  Who would like to come and point to (highlight) the period in these sentences?

  You write a period at the end of a sentence. When you are reading and you come to a period, your voice goes down.

Have a Try

Invite children to add periods to sentences by having them make statements about something they are working on (e.g., something they made in the creation station).

> What sentence could we write about something you created?

▶ Ask a volunteer to suggest a statement. Write the sentence on the chart paper.

> Who can add a period to this sentence?

▶ Read the sentence together as you point under the words. Emphasize making voices go down at the end. Repeat with several more volunteers.

Summarize and Apply

Help children summarize the lesson. Remind children to add periods to the sentences they write.

> Where does the period go in a sentence?

▶ Write the principle at the top of the chart.

> Writers add a period to show where a sentence ends. During writing time, write a period at the end of each sentence. Bring your writing to share later.

> Use a period to end a sentence.
>
> I made a ship.
>
> This is a house.
>
> I built a car.

Confer

▶ During independent writing, move around the room to confer briefly with as many individual children as time allows. Sit side by side with them and invite them to talk about using periods. Use the following prompts as needed.

- *Read this aloud. Can you hear where the sentence ends? Write a period there.*
- *What will you add to the end of the sentence you are writing?*
- *Show me where you will write a period on this page.*
- *How does a period help the reader?*

Share

Following independent writing, gather children in the meeting area to share their writing.

> Who would like to share what you wrote today?

> Tell about how you decided where to put the period in this sentence.

WML2

CNV.U4.WML2

Writing Minilesson Principle
Use a question mark to end a question.

Learning About Punctuation

You Will Need

- several familiar books that have question marks, such as the following:
  - *Don't Let the Pigeon Drive the Bus!* by Mo Willems, from Text Set: Mo Willems: Having Fun with Humor
  - *The Big, Green, Scary Monster* by Judith E. Nayer, from *Shared Reading Collection*
- chart paper
- colored markers
- highlighter tape (optional)

Academic Language / Important Vocabulary

- writing
- question
- question mark

Continuum Connection

- Notice the use of punctuation marks in books and try them out in one's own writing (p. 255)
- Use periods, exclamation marks, and question marks as end marks (p. 255)

GOAL

Understand that writers put a question mark at the end of a question to show that something is being asked.

RATIONALE

When children recognize that question marks at the end of sentences convey meaning, they learn that they can include questions in their own writing by adding question marks to show the reader that something is being asked.

ASSESS LEARNING

- Notice evidence that children understand that a question mark indicates that something is being asked.
- Observe whether children are using question marks in their own writing.
- Look for evidence that children can use vocabulary such as *writing*, *question*, and *question mark*.

MINILESSON

To help children understand the minilesson principle, engage them in discussion about why writers use question marks and how they can use them in their own writing. Here is an example.

- Show and read pages 4 and 5 of *Don't Let the Pigeon Drive the Bus!* making sure your voice goes up at the end of each question.

  What do you notice about the end of these questions?

- As children identify each question mark, point underneath it.

  Why do you think the writer decided to add a question mark at the end?

- Guide the conversation, helping them recognize that the question mark shows that a question is being asked. Use the following prompts as needed.

  - *When do writers use this mark?*
  - *What does this mark tell the reader?*
  - *When will you write a question mark?*

- Show page 11 of *The Big, Green, Scary Monster* and read the first two sentences. Have children reread the question with you, pointing under each word and the question mark as you read.

  Who would like to come and point to (highlight) the question mark?

  Be sure to write a question mark at the end of a question. When you are reading and you come to a question mark, your voice goes up.

The Writing Minilessons Book, Grade 1

Have a Try

Invite children to add question marks by having them ask questions about something their partners are working on (e.g., something in the creation station).

What question could you ask about a classmate's creation?

▶ Ask a volunteer to suggest a question. Write the question on the chart paper.

Who can come up and add a question mark?

▶ Read the question together as you point under the words. Emphasize making voices go up at the end. Repeat with several more volunteers.

Summarize and Apply

Help children summarize the lesson. Remind children to add question marks appropriately when they write.

When do you use a question mark?

▶ Write the principle at the top of the chart.

Writers add a question mark at the end of a sentence to show that they are asking something. When you write, add question marks to the end of questions you write. Bring your writing to share when we meet later.

Confer

▶ During independent writing, move around the room to confer briefly with as many individual children as time allows. Sit side by side with them and invite them to talk about using punctuation. Use the following prompts as needed.

- *Read this aloud. Can you hear where the question ends? Write a question mark there.*
- *What question could you ask?*
- *Where will you write the question mark?*
- *Show me how to make a question mark in the air with your finger.*

Share

Following independent writing, gather children in the meeting area to share their writing.

Who used a question mark in your writing today? Share what you wrote.

Use a question mark to end a question.

What did you make?

How does this work?

Will you show me how it works?

Writing Minilesson Principle
Use an exclamation point to show something exciting or surprising.

You Will Need

- several familiar books that have exclamation points, such as the following:

  - *Don't Let the Pigeon Drive the Bus!* by Mo Willems, from Text Set: Mo Willems: Having Fun with Humor

  - *The Big, Green, Scary Monster* by Judith E. Nayer, from *Shared Reading Collection*

- chart paper and markers

- highlighting tape (optional)

Academic Language / Important Vocabulary

- writing
- exclamation point
- exciting
- surprising

Continuum Connection

- Notice the use of punctuation marks in books and try them out in one's own writing (p. 255)

- Use periods, exclamation marks, and question marks as end marks (p. 255)

GOAL

Understand that writers put an exclamation point at the end of a sentence to show something exciting or surprising.

RATIONALE

When children recognize that exclamation points convey meaning, they learn that they can show emphasis in their own writing by adding exclamation points to the end of sentences.

ASSESS LEARNING

- Notice evidence that children understand that an exclamation point signifies something exciting or surprising.

- Observe whether children are using exclamation points in their own writing.

- Look for evidence that children can use vocabulary such as *writing*, *exclamation point*, *exciting*, and *surprising*.

MINILESSON

To help children understand the minilesson principle, engage them in a discussion about why writers use exclamation points and how they will use them in their own writing. Here is an example.

- Show and read pages 14–16 of *Don't Let the Pigeon Drive the Bus!* making sure to read each sentence with emphasis.

  What do you notice about the end of these sentences?

- As children identify each exclamation point, point underneath it.

  This is an exclamation point. Say that with me: *exclamation point*.

  Why do you think the writer decided to add an exclamation point at the end of this sentence?

- Guide the conversation, helping children recognize that the exclamation points show that the pigeon is using a strong voice. Use the following prompts as needed.

  - *When do writers use this mark?*

  - *What does this mark tell the reader?*

  - *When will you write an exclamation point?*

- Show and read page 3 of *The Big, Green, Scary Monster*. Have children reread the sentences with exclamation points, pointing under each word as you read.

  Who would like to point to (highlight) the exclamation points?

  Write an exclamation point at the end of a sentence when you want to show something exciting or surprising. When you are reading and you come to an exclamation point, use a strong voice.

Have a Try

Invite children to add exclamation points by having them make exclamations about something they are working on (e.g., something they made in the creation station).

> What is something surprising or exciting you could say about something you made?

▶ Ask a volunteer to suggest an exclamation. Write it on the chart paper.

> Who can add an exclamation point?

▶ Read the exclamation together as you point under the words. Emphasize using strong voices. Repeat with several more volunteers.

Summarize and Apply

Help children summarize the lesson. Remind children to add exclamation points to show excitement or surprise when they write.

> When do you use an exclamation point?

▶ Write the principle at the top of the chart.

> When you are writing, look for a sentence that tells something exciting or surprising. Write an exclamation point at the end of that sentence. Bring your writing to share when we meet later.

> Use an exclamation point to show something exciting or surprising.
>
> Look what I made!
>
> You won't believe how this works!
>
> Listen to the funny noise! Slurp! Slurp!

Confer

▶ During independent writing, move around the room to confer briefly with as many individual children as time allows. Sit side by side with them and invite them to talk about using punctuation. Use the following prompts as needed.

- Is there a sentence about something exciting or surprising?
- Where will you put the exclamation point?
- Show me how to use your finger to make an exclamation point in the air.
- How will this exclamation point help the reader?

Share

Following independent writing, gather children in the meeting area to talk about their writing.

> Did anyone write an exclamation point today? Share what you wrote.

Assessment

After you have taught the minilessons in this umbrella, observe children as they write. Use *The Literacy Continuum* (Fountas and Pinnell 2017) to notice, teach for, and support children's learning as you observe their attempts at reading and writing.

> What evidence do you have of new understandings children have developed related to punctuation?
>
> - Do children understand the use of periods, question marks, and exclamation points?
> - Is there evidence children can use vocabulary related to punctuation, such as *writing, sentence, period, question, question mark, exclamation point, exciting,* and *surprising*?
>
> In what ways, beyond the scope of this umbrella, are children understanding the purpose of punctuation?
>
> - Are they ready to revise or proofread their writing?

Use your observations to determine the next umbrella you will teach. You may also consult Suggested Sequence of Lessons (pp. 557–571) for guidance.

EXTENSIONS FOR LEARNING ABOUT PUNCTUATION

> Teach minilessons that relate to punctuation marks that children notice while reading. If you use *The Reading Minilessons Book, Grade 1* (Fountas and Pinnell 2019), see SAS.U3: Maintaining Fluency.

> Working with small groups, write the same sentence three times (e.g., *We go to the library today*), each with a different punctuation mark at the end. Read the sentences. Then have children talk in the small group about how the sentence changes meaning depending on which punctuation mark is used.

> Help children understand that punctuation is also part of the writer's craft. As you read with children, encourage them to notice periods, question marks, and exclamation points and talk about what message the writer sends by choosing each type of end mark.

> Use shared writing to make other statements, questions, or exclamations related to content children are learning. Post each chart and encourage children to continue adding to it.

Minilessons in This Umbrella

WML1 Notice the difference between uppercase and lowercase letters.

WML2 Capitalize the first letter of a name.

WML3 Capitalize the first letter of the first word in a sentence.

WML4 Capitalize the important words in a title.

Before Teaching Umbrella 5 Minilessons

Before teaching this umbrella, ensure that your children have a good understanding of the difference between letters, words, and sentences and of the concept of *first* in relation to words and sentences (first letter in a word, first word in a sentence).

Read and discuss simple books that the children will enjoy. Use the following texts from *Fountas & Pinnell Classroom™ Shared Reading Collection*. You can also choose books from your classroom library. As much as possible, use enlarged texts such as published big books or class-made big books so that children can see the print.

Shared Reading Collection

Monster ABCs by Finnoula Louise

Not Now! by Miriam Glassman

The Elephant by Cordelia S. Finn

Scram! by Julie Reich

Boomer's Checkup by Aaron Mack

Animal Surprises by Nicole Walker

Lots of Snow by Joan Silver

Food Store in the Woods by Reese Brooks

The Hungry Fly by Hannah Cales

Interactive Writing Lessons

IW.7: Writing About Who We Are

As you read and enjoy these texts together, help children

*   identify and talk about different letters,

*   notice names in the text, and

*   identify the first letter in a word and the first word in a sentence.

Shared Reading

Interactive Writing

Using Capital Letters

You Will Need

- a familiar alphabet book, such as *Monster ABCs* by Finnoula Louise, from *Shared Reading Collection*
- whiteboard prepared with a two-column chart
- dry-erase markers
- uppercase and lowercase magnetic letters
- To download the following online resources for this lesson, visit **resources.fountasandpinnell.com**:
  - masking cards
  - Alphabet Linking Chart

Academic Language/ Important Vocabulary

- uppercase (capital)
- lowercase (small)
- letter

Continuum Connection

- Demonstrate knowledge of the use of upper- and lowercase letters of the alphabet (p. 255)
- Recognize and point to the distinctive features of letter forms (p. 367)
- Recognize and point to uppercase letters and lowercase letters: e.g., *B, b* (p. 367)
- Distinguish and talk about the differences between the uppercase and lowercase forms of a letter (p. 367)

GOAL

Understand the difference between upper- and lowercase letters.

RATIONALE

Before children can begin using uppercase (capital) and lowercase letters correctly in their own writing, they must first learn to recognize and differentiate between the uppercase and lowercase form of each letter.

ASSESS LEARNING

- Look for evidence that children understand the idea of tall and short lowercase letters.
- Notice whether children can identify uppercase and lowercase letters and talk about their differences.
- Look for evidence that children can use vocabulary such as *uppercase (capital)*, *lowercase (small)*, and *letter*.

MINILESSON

Use magnetic letters and an alphabet book (or an ABC chart) to help children notice the differences between upper- and lowercase letters. Use the term (*uppercase* or *capital*; *lowercase* or *small*) that you prefer.

- Show an uppercase and a lowercase magnetic *A*.

  What letter is this?

- Ask children what they notice about how the two letters are different. Add both the uppercase and lowercase *A* to the chart (see example chart).

- Show an uppercase and lowercase *B*. Ask children to identify which one is uppercase and which one is lowercase. Write the letters on the chart.

- Continue in a similar manner with a few more letters. Put tall and short lowercase letters in separate sections of the chart.

- Show the cover of *Monster ABCs* and read the title. Turn to page 9.

  Who can find an uppercase *F* on this page? Who can find a lowercase *F*?

- Have volunteers use a masking card to show the letters. Write the uppercase and lowercase *F* on the chart.

- Continue in a similar manner with several more letters.

  What do you notice about lowercase letters? Are they tall or short?

  Some lowercase letters are tall, and some are short.

- Write *Tall* and *Short* in the two sections, as appropriate.

Have a Try

Invite children to talk to a partner about the uppercase letters.

> On our chart, there are some lowercase letters that are tall and some that are short. Look at the uppercase letters. Turn and talk to your partner about what you notice about them. Are they tall or short?

▷ Guide children to understand that all uppercase letters are tall. Write *Tall* on the chart.

Summarize and Apply

Help children summarize the learning and remind them to think about uppercase and lowercase letters when they write.

> What did you notice today about uppercase and lowercase letters?

> When you are writing today, remember the differences between uppercase and lowercase letters. You can look at our ABC chart to help you remember how to write them. Bring your writing to share when we meet later.

Uppercase and Lowercase Letters	
Uppercase	**Lowercase**
B D F H K L — Tall	b d f h k l — Tall
A C E G I J —	a c e g i j — Short

Section 7: Conventions

Confer

▷ During independent writing, move around the room to confer briefly with as many individual children as time allows. Sit side by side with them and invite them to talk about their writing. Use prompts such as the following if needed.

- *Can you read aloud what you wrote?*
- *What letters are in that word?*
- *Is that an uppercase or a lowercase _____?*
- *Can you point to an uppercase letter in your book?*

Share

Following independent writing, gather children in the meeting area to share their writing. Support children's oral language by providing a sentence frame, such as *I wrote an uppercase (a capital) letter _____.*

> Did you write any uppercase letters in your book today? Which ones?

WML2

CNV.U5.WML2

Writing Minilesson Principle
Capitalize the first letter of a name.

Using Capital Letters

You Will Need

- the class-created text from IW.7: Writing About Who We Are
- a familiar book that contains characters' names, such as *Not Now!* by Miriam Glassman, from *Shared Reading Collection*
- chart paper and markers
- highlighter

Academic Language/ Important Vocabulary

- capitalize
- uppercase (capital)
- letter
- name

Continuum Connection

- Use a capital letter at the beginning of a familiar proper noun (p. 255)
- Demonstrate knowledge of the use of upper- and lowercase letters of the alphabet (p. 255)
- Show awareness of the position of capital letters at the beginning of some words (p. 255)

GOAL

Understand that names begin with capital letters.

RATIONALE

When you help children notice that names are always capitalized, they begin to understand that certain types of words need to be capitalized. Later, they will learn that all proper nouns are capitalized.

ASSESS LEARNING

- Observe whether children capitalize the first letter of names.
- Look for evidence that children can use vocabulary such as *capitalize, uppercase (capital), letter,* and *name.*

MINILESSON

Use mentor texts to help children notice that names are capitalized. Use the term (*uppercase* or *capital*) that you prefer.

- Show the class-created text from IW.7: Writing About Who We Are. Read one page aloud.

  What do you notice about the *J* in Juste's name? Is it uppercase or lowercase?

- Write the name on chart paper, highlighting the first letter.
- Show the cover of *Not Now!* Read page 13. Point to the names Luke and Maggie.

  What do you notice about the first letters of the names Luke and Maggie?

- Add *Luke* and *Maggie* to the chart.
- Read page 16.

  What names are on this page?

  What kind of letter do they start with?

- Add *Bella* to the chart.

  What do you notice about the first letter of someone's name?

- Point out that names always start with an uppercase letter, no matter where they are in the sentence.

Have a Try

Invite children to talk to a partner about how they would write their own names.

> Turn and talk to your partner about how you would write your name. What letter comes first? What kind of letter would you start with?

Summarize and Apply

Help children summarize the learning. Remind them to capitalize the first letter of a name.

> What kind of letter do you need to write at the beginning of a name?

❯ Write the principle on the chart.

> When you write an uppercase letter in a name, you capitalize it. Say it with me: *capitalize*. During writing time today, if you write your own name or the names of any characters in your story, remember to capitalize the first letter. Bring your writing to share when we meet later.

Capitalize the first letter of a name.

Juste

Maggie

Luke

Bella

Confer

❯ During independent writing, move around the room to confer briefly with as many individual children as time allows. Sit side by side with them and invite them to talk about writing names. Use prompts such as the following as needed to support children in capitalizing the first letter of names.

- *What is that character's name? Can you write it?*
- *Should this letter be uppercase or lowercase?*
- *Remember that names always start with an uppercase letter, no matter where they are in the sentence.*
- *Did you write any names in your book? How did you write the first letter?*

Share

Following independent writing, gather children in the meeting area to share their writing. Support children's oral language by providing a sentence frame, such as *I wrote the name _____.*

> Raise your hand if you wrote any names in your book today.

> What names did you write? How did you write the first letter?

Writing Minilesson Principle
Capitalize the first letter of the first word in a sentence.

You Will Need

- a familiar book with only one sentence per page, such as *The Elephant* by Cordelia S. Finn, from *Shared Reading Collection*

- familiar books with two or more sentences per page, such as *Scram!* by Julie Reich and *Boomer's Checkup* by Aaron Mack, from *Shared Reading Collection*

- chart paper prepared with sentences from the lesson but without the first letters

- markers

- highlighter

Academic Language/ Important Vocabulary

- capitalize
- uppercase (capital)
- letter
- word
- sentence

Continuum Connection

- Use a capital for the first word of a sentence (p. 255)

- Locate the first and last letters of words in continuous text (p. 367)

GOAL

Understand that sentences begin with capital letters.

RATIONALE

When children notice that sentences in books begin with uppercase (capital) letters, they begin to understand that they, too, should capitalize the first word in a sentence. Children should have a solid understanding of the concepts of *first, letter, word,* and *sentence* before this lesson is taught.

ASSESS LEARNING

- Observe whether children begin sentences with capital letters.

- Look for evidence that children can use vocabulary such as *capitalize, uppercase (capital), letter, word,* and *sentence*.

MINILESSON

Use mentor texts to help children notice that sentences begin with capital letters. Use the term (*uppercase* or *capital*) that you prefer.

- Show the cover of *The Elephant* and read the title. Read page 2. Point to the *T* in *The*.

    What do you notice about the first letter of the first word in this sentence?

    The *T* in *The* is an uppercase letter.

- Write or have a child write uppercase *T* on the prepared chart paper.

- Show the cover of *Scram!* and read the title. Read page 4. Point to the *B* in *But* and the *W* in *Why*.

    What do you notice about the first letter in these sentences?

- Fill in (or have a child fill in) the uppercase *B* and *W* on the chart.

- Repeat with page 6 of *Boomer's Checkup*.

- Fill in (or have a child fill in) the uppercase *N* and *S*.

    What do you notice about the first letter of each sentence?

- Ask a child to highlight the initial letter in each sentence.

Have a Try

Invite children to talk to a partner about how to write the first letter in a sentence.

> How should you write the first letter of the first word in a sentence? Turn and talk to your partner about this.

▶ After a brief time for discussion, point out that uppercase letters are used for different reasons. Ask children to tell what other uppercase letters they see on the chart and how they are used.

Summarize and Apply

Summarize the learning and remind children to capitalize the first letter in a sentence.

> What did you notice today about uppercase letters? When are they used?

▶ Write the principle on the chart and read it aloud.

> When you write today, remember to capitalize the first letter of the first word in every sentence you write. Also remember to capitalize any names that you write. Bring your writing to share when we meet later.

Capitalize the first letter of the first word in a sentence.

The elephant has a big head.

But then Mom stopped the car.
"Why are we stopping?" asked Molly.

Next the vet looked in Boomer's mouth.
She checked his teeth and gums.

Confer

▶ During independent writing, move around the room to confer briefly with as many individual children as time allows. Sit side by side with them and invite them to talk about the capitalization of letters as needed. Use prompts such as the following to support children in capitalizing the first letter in a sentence.

- *What is the next sentence you're going to write?*
- *What's the first word in that sentence?*
- *What's the first letter in that word?*
- *Can you point to the first letter of that sentence? Is it uppercase or lowercase?*

Share

Following independent writing, gather children in the meeting area to share their writing.

> When you wrote today, how did you write the first letter of each sentence?

Writing Minilesson Principle
Capitalize the important words in a title.

You Will Need

- several familiar books with titles of varying lengths, such as the following from *Shared Reading Collection*:
  - *Animal Surprises* by Nicole Walker
  - *Lots of Snow* by Joan Silver
  - *Food Store in the Woods* by Reese Brooks
  - *The Hungry Fly* by Hannah Cales
- chart paper and markers
- highlighter

Academic Language/ Important Vocabulary

- capitalize
- uppercase (capital)
- lowercase (small)
- title

Continuum Connection

- Use uppercase letters in a title (p. 255)

GOAL

Understand that writers capitalize the important words in a title.

RATIONALE

When children notice that the important words in published book titles are capitalized, they will begin to capitalize the important words in their own book titles.

ASSESS LEARNING

- Observe whether children capitalize the important words in book titles.
- Look for evidence that children can use vocabulary such as *capitalize*, *uppercase (capital)*, *lowercase (small)*, and *title*.

MINILESSON

Use mentor texts to help children notice that important words in titles are capitalized. Use the term (*uppercase* or *capital*; *lowercase* or *small*) that you prefer.

- Show the cover of *Animal Surprises* and read the title. Point to the *A* and the *S*.

  What do you notice about the *A* in *Animal* and the *S* in *Surprises*? Are they uppercase or lowercase?

- Write the title on chart paper, highlighting (or inviting a child to highlight) the uppercase letters.

- Show the cover of *Lots of Snow* and read the title.

  Which words have uppercase letters in this title?

- Add the title to the chart.

- Continue in a similar manner with *Food Store in the Woods*.

  What do you notice about how book titles are written?

  Do *all* the words in a title begin with uppercase letters?

  Only the important words are capitalized. Little words like *of*, *in*, and *the* are usually not capitalized in titles.

- Show the cover of *The Hungry Fly* and read the title.

  Which words are capitalized in this title?

- Add the title to the chart. Point out that the word *The* is capitalized in this case because it is the first word in the title.

  The first word in a title is always capitalized, no matter what it is!

Have a Try

Invite children to talk to a partner about which words to capitalize in a title.

> I'm working on a book called *Fun in the Sun* about my summer vacation. Which words should I capitalize when I write the title *Fun in the Sun*? Turn and talk to your partner about this.

▸ After children turn and talk, invite a few pairs to share their thinking. Ensure that children understand which words need to be capitalized, and add the title to the chart.

Summarize and Apply

Help children summarize the learning and remind them to capitalize the important words in a title.

> What did you learn today about how to write book titles?

▸ Write the principle at the top of the chart. Read it aloud.

> When you write the title of your book on the cover, remember to capitalize the important words. Bring your writing to share when we meet later.

> ### Capitalize the important words in a title.
>
> Animal Surprises
>
> Lots of Snow
>
> Food Store in the Woods
>
> The Hungry Fly
>
> Fun in the Sun

Confer

▸ During independent writing, move around the room to confer briefly with as many individual children as time allows. Sit side by side with them and invite them to talk about writing titles. Use prompts such as the following as needed.

- *What is the title of your book?*
- *Which words should be capitalized?*
- *Remember to always capitalize the first word in your title, no matter what it is.*

Share

Following independent writing, gather children in the meeting area to share their book titles.

> What is the title of your book?

> Which words did you capitalize? Why?

Assessment

After you have taught the minilessons in this umbrella, observe children as they write and talk about their writing. Use *The Literacy Continuum* (Fountas and Pinnell 2017) to notice, teach for, and support children's learning as you observe their attempts at writing.

▶ What evidence do you have of new understandings children have developed related to using capital letters?

- Do children understand the difference between uppercase and lowercase letters?
- Do they capitalize the first letter of names?
- Do they capitalize the first letter of the first word in a sentence?
- Do they capitalize the important words in titles?
- Is there evidence children can use vocabulary such as *uppercase*, *lowercase*, and *capitalize*?

▶ In what other ways, beyond the scope of this umbrella, are children ready to expand their writing skills?

- Are they noticing different types of punctuation?

Use your observations to determine the next umbrella you will teach. You may also consult Suggested Sequence of Lessons (pp. 557–571) for guidance.

EXTENSIONS FOR USING CAPITAL LETTERS

▶ Encourage children to reread their writing to make sure they have used capital letters correctly. (See WPS.U6: Proofreading Writing.)

▶ Help children notice that all proper nouns begin with capital letters, not just the names of people (names of places, schools, companies, etc.).

▶ Teach children that the word *I* is always capitalized.

▶ Help children notice that sometimes authors use all caps to indicate yelling or for emphasis.

▶ If children type their writing on a computer, teach them how to use the Shift key to make capital letters.

Section 8 | Writing Process

CHILDREN LEARN TO write by writing. As they write, they engage in some aspect of the writing process. They plan what to write, make a draft and make changes to improve it, check their work to be sure others can read it, and publish it by sharing it with an audience. Not all aspects of the writing process will happen at one time, and they won't always happen in the same order. Writers tend to move back and forth. But over time, each writer will experience the full writing process. The lessons in this section will help you guide the children in your class through the writing process.

Minilessons in This Umbrella

WML1 Think about your purpose.

WML2 Think about your audience.

WML3 Think about the kind of writing you want to do.

Before Teaching Umbrella 1 Minilessons

The purpose of this umbrella is to help children choose the type of writing they want to do by having them think about why they are writing and for whom they are writing. The first lesson focuses on writing to tell a story and writing to give information. You may want to revisit the lesson when you introduce different purposes for writing. If you are using *The Reading Minilessons Book, Grade 1* (Fountas and Pinnell 2019), the minilessons in this umbrella would pair well with LA.U7: Thinking About the Author's Purpose.

Prior to teaching these minilessons, it will be helpful to teach IW.8: Writing a Memory Story, IW.14: Writing an All-About Book, and IW.15: Writing a Question-and-Answer Book. It will also be helpful for children to have explored making books that tell stories (e.g., MBK.U3: Making Memory Books) and books that give information (e.g., MBK.U5: Making All-About Books and MBK.U6: Making Question-and-Answer Books). Children should also have read a variety of genres and talked about the choices that the writers made. For mentor texts, use the books listed below from *Fountas & Pinnell Classroom™ Interactive Read-Aloud Collection*, or choose fiction and nonfiction books from the classroom library.

Interactive Read-Aloud Collection
Taking Care of Each Other: Family

The Relatives Came by Cynthia Rylant

A Birthday Basket for Tía by Pat Mora

Papá and Me by Arthur Dorros

Exploring Nonfiction

Water: Up, Down, and All Around by Natalie M. Rosinsky

Tools by Ann Morris

Nonfiction: Questions and Answers

What Do You Do With a Tail Like This? by Steve Jenkins and Robin Page

Animals Black and White by Phyllis Limbacher Tildes

Interactive Writing Lessons

IW.8: Writing a Memory Story

IW.14: Writing an All-About Book

IW.15: Writing a Question-and-Answer Book

As you read and enjoy these texts together, help children

- notice the writer's purpose, and
- think about what audience the book is intended for.

Interactive Read-Aloud
Family

Exploring Nonfiction

Questions and Answers

Interactive Writing

Section 8: Writing Process

Writing Minilesson Principle
Think about your purpose.

Thinking About Purpose and Audience

You Will Need

- several familiar books that tell a story and several that give information, such as these:
  - *The Relatives Came* by Cynthia Rylant and *A Birthday Basket for Tía* by Pat Mora, from Text Set: Taking Care of Each Other: Family
  - *Water: Up, Down, and All Around* by Natalie M. Rosinsky, from Text Set: Exploring Nonfiction
  - *What Do You Do With a Tail Like This?* by Steve Jenkins and Robin Page, from Text Set: Nonfiction: Questions and Answers
- class-made texts from IW.8: Writing a Memory Story, IW.14: Writing an All-About Book, and IW.15: Writing a Question-and-Answer Book
- chart paper and markers

Academic Language / Important Vocabulary

- reason
- purpose
- tell a story
- give information

Continuum Connection

- Draw and write for a specific purpose (p. 255)
- Think about the purpose for writing each text (p. 255)
- Write to inform the audience and also to engage or interest others (p. 255)
- Think of what to work on next as a writer (p. 257)

GOAL

Understand that writers have a purpose for writing.

RATIONALE

When children understand that writers have a purpose for writing, they begin to think about why and what they want to write and realize that they have choices in their own writing. Giving children a choice in the topics they write about leads to both increased motivation for writing and to more authentic writing.

ASSESS LEARNING

- Notice evidence that children understand that writers have a purpose for writing.
- Observe for evidence that children are talking about different purposes for writing.
- Notice evidence that children can use vocabulary such as *reason, purpose, tell a story,* and *give information.*

MINILESSON

To help children think about the minilesson principle, use familiar texts (including class-made writing) to get them thinking about their own purposes for writing. Here is an example.

- Show the cover of a familiar story, such as *The Relatives Came*.

  Think about the reason that Cynthia Rylant decided to write this book.

- Engage children in a conversation about the author's purpose, guiding them to recognize that the writer's purpose is to tell a story.

  A purpose is the reason for doing something. Before you write something, think about your purpose for writing. Think about why you are writing.

- Show the cover of a familiar all-about book, such as *Water: Up, Down, and All Around*.

  I wonder what Natalie M. Rosinsky's purpose was for writing *Water: Up, Down, and All Around*. What do you think?

- Guide children to understand that the purpose is to give information.

- Begin a two-column chart with *To tell a story* in the first column and *To give information* in the second column. Write the title or draw a picture to record *The Relatives Came* in the first column and *Water: Up, Down, and All Around* in the second column.

- Repeat with *A Birthday Basket for Tía* and *What Do You Do With a Tail Like This?* and the class-made texts from IW.8, IW.14, and IW.15. Add to the chart after discussion about the author's purpose for writing each.

The Writing Minilessons Book, Grade 1

Have a Try

Invite children to turn and talk about different purposes for writing.

> What is something you might like to write about? Will you tell a story or give information? Talk to your partner about that.

▶ After time for discussion, ask several volunteers to share. Using the children's ideas, model a few examples of how the topic might be used to write for different purposes. Here is an example.

> Jacinta wants to write about horses. She could tell a story about the first time she rode a horse. Or, she could make a book about how to take care of horses.

▶ Add to the chart.

Summarize and Apply

Summarize the lesson. Remind children to think about their purpose for writing.

> Today you learned that writers think about their purpose for writing before they begin. When you write today, make a list of things you could write about. Think about ways you might write about each idea.

▶ Write the principle at the top of the chart.

Confer

▶ During independent writing, move around the room to confer briefly with as many individual children as time allows. Sit side by side with them and invite them to talk about their purpose for writing. Use the following prompts as needed.

- *Why are you writing? What kind of writing will you do?*
- *What is your purpose for writing?*
- *Do you want to tell a story, or do you want to give information?*

Share

Following independent writing, gather children in the meeting area to share their lists of topics.

> What are some things you put on your list to write about?

> Tell about some different ways you might write about your topic.

Think about your purpose.

To tell a story	To give information
The Relatives Came	Water: Up, Down, and All Around
A Birthday Basket for Tía	What Do You Do With a Tail Like This?
Writing a Memory Story	All About Sharks
	Taking Care of Animal Babies

| first time riding a horse | how to take care of a horse |

Writing Minilesson Principle
Think about your audience.

Thinking About Purpose and Audience

You Will Need

- a familiar book that gives information and a familiar book that tells a story, such as the following:
  - *Tools* by Ann Morris, from Text Set: Exploring Nonfiction
- chart paper and markers
- To download the following online resource for this lesson, visit **resources.fountasandpinnell.com**:
  - chart art (optional)

Academic Language / Important Vocabulary

- writing
- reader
- audience

Continuum Connection

- Think about the people who will read the writing or might like to read it and what they will want to know (p. 255)
- Actively seek an audience for sharing writing and drawing (p. 255)
- Include important information and details in the drawing or writing that the audience needs to know (p. 255)
- Write with an understanding that it is meant to be read by others (p. 255)
- Think of what to work on next as a writer (p. 257)

GOAL

Understand that writers think about their intended audience.

RATIONALE

When children think about the audience for a piece of writing, they begin to think about their readers, for example, what the audience needs to know. This thinking will help them understand what to include in their writing.

ASSESS LEARNING

- Notice evidence that children recognize that writers think about their intended audience.
- Look for evidence that children are thinking about what the audience needs to know.
- Observe for evidence that children can use vocabulary such as *writing*, *reader*, and *audience*.

MINILESSON

To help children understand that writers think about their intended audience, use mentor texts as examples and interactively model the process. Here is an example.

- Show the cover of *Tools* and flip through a few pages.

  When Ann Morris wrote this book, *Tools*, who do you think she expected to read the book?

- Engage children in conversation about the intended audience, guiding them to realize that the author wrote this book for children.

  Looking at the words and pictures, Ann Morris probably wanted to teach children about tools. She wrote for an audience of children. She probably thought about tools children would be interested in and used familiar words to explain them. When you write, think about who will read your writing and what the audience needs to know.

- On chart paper, start a list of ways to consider the audience when writing. Prompt children to think about how to help the audience read their writing.

  - *What kind of writing will help you tell your audience what you want them to know? For example, if you wanted to share a memory, what could you write? If you wanted to teach someone how to do something, what could you write?*

  - *What kind of writing would your audience like to read?*

  - *How can you make sure your audience can read what you have written?*

  - *Is there anything you can add to your writing that would help explain the story or the information?*

Have a Try

Invite children to turn and talk to a partner about how they would write for different audiences.

> If you were going to write for a parent (caregiver) about your day at school, what are some things that person might want to know? What type of writing could you do? Turn and talk about that.

▶ After time for discussion, ask a few volunteers to share. Guide them to understand that since the person is not part of the classroom, they would need to add more information.

▶ Repeat for several other audiences, such as the principal and children in the class.

Summarize and Apply

Write the principle at the top of the chart to summarize the lesson. Remind children to think about their intended audience when they write.

> When you write today, think about who your audience is and what they will need to know. If your audience doesn't know much about your topic, you will need to include more information. Bring your writing to share when we meet later.

Think about your audience.

Think about what the readers need to know.

Choose a type of writing.
- memory story
- how-to book
- all-about book

Check to make sure the writing is clear.

Add pictures.

Who is my audience?

Confer

▶ During independent writing, move around the room to confer briefly with as many individual children as time allows. Sit side by side with them and invite them to talk about how they are writing for their audience. Use the following prompts as needed.

· *Who is going to read this writing?*
· *Who is your audience?*
· *What would your reader want to know?*
· *What can you do to make sure your audience can read what you have written?*

Share

Following writing time, gather children in the meeting area to share their writing.

> What audience did you think about as you wrote?

Writing Minilesson Principle
Think about the kind of writing you want to do.

Thinking About Purpose and Audience

You Will Need

- a familiar nonfiction book and a familiar fiction book, such as the following:
  - *Animals Black and White* by Phyllis Limbacher Tildes, from Text Set: Nonfiction: Questions and Answers
  - *Papá and Me* by Arthur Dorros, from Text Set: Taking Care of Each Other: Family
- chart paper and markers

Academic Language / Important Vocabulary

- writing
- topic
- choice
- purpose
- audience

Continuum Connection

- Consider how the purpose affects the kind of writing (p. 255)
- Select from a variety of forms the kind of text that will fit the purpose: e.g., poems, stories with pictures, books with words and illustrations; books with illustrations only; ABC books; label books; poetry collections; question and answer books (p. 256)
- Think of what to work on next as a writer (p. 257)

GOAL

Understand that writers choose what type of writing to do.

RATIONALE

When children choose what type of writing they want to do by thinking about purpose and audience, they gain energy and motivation for writing and write with authenticity.

ASSESS LEARNING

- Observe for evidence that children recognize that thinking about purpose and audience can help them decide what type of writing they want to do.
- Notice evidence that children can use vocabulary such as *writing*, *topic*, *choice*, *purpose*, and *audience*.

MINILESSON

To help children think about the type of writing they want to do, provide an interactive lesson. Here is an example.

- Show the cover and flip through a few pages of *Animals Black and White*.

  When Phyllis Limbacher Tildes decided that she wanted to write, what are some things she might have thought about before beginning?

- Guide the conversation to help children think about the topic, the purpose for writing, and the intended audience. You may want to use these prompts.
  - *What topic did she want to write about?*
  - *What was her purpose, or reason, for writing?*
  - *Whom did she want the reader, or audience, to be?*

- Repeat with *Papá and Me*.

  Just like the writers of these books, you can think about your purpose and audience and then decide on the best type of writing.

- Guide children through the process for deciding the type of writing to do by suggesting a topic, purpose, and audience and having children make suggestions for what they could write. Record responses on chart paper.

  What would you write to teach children how to make cookies?

  What would you write to describe how you felt doing something for the first time?

  What would you write to thank someone (grandparents) for a gift?

  What would you write to teach a kindergarten class about snow?

Have a Try

Invite children to turn and talk about the type of writing they want to do.

> What kind of writing do you want to do? Think about your topic, purpose, and audience. Turn and talk to your partner about that.

▶ After time for discussion, ask several volunteers to share what they talked about. Add new ideas to the chart.

Summarize and Apply

Summarize the lesson. Remind children to think about the kind of writing they want to do.

> You have been talking about the kind of writing you want to do by thinking about topics, your purpose for writing, and your audience.

▶ Write the principle at the top of the chart.

> During writing time, choose the kind of writing you want to do and begin writing. Bring your writing to share when we meet later.

Think about the kind of writing you want to do.

Topic	Purpose	Audience	Type of Writing
Cookies	Teach how to make them	Children	How-to book
Doing something for the first time	Describe	Class	Memory story
A gift	Thank	Grandparents	Thank you card
Snow	Give information	Kindergarten class	All-about book

Confer

▶ During independent writing, move around the room to confer briefly with as many individual children as time allows. Sit side by side with them and invite them to talk about choosing the kind of writing to fit the audience and purpose. Use the following prompts as needed.

- *What is your purpose, or reason, for writing?*
- *Who will your reader, or audience, be?*
- *What type of writing are you thinking about doing today?*

Share

Following independent writing, gather children in the meeting area to share their writing. Support children's oral language by providing a sentence frame, such as *I decided to write _____ because _____.*

> What type of writing did you decide to do today? Why?

Assessment

After you have taught the minilessons in this umbrella, observe children as they write. Use *The Literacy Continuum* (Fountas and Pinnell 2017) to notice, teach for, and support children's learning as you observe their attempts at reading and writing.

▶ What evidence do you have of new understandings children have developed related to purpose and audience?

- Is there evidence that children think about their purpose for writing?

- Are children thinking about their audience when they write?

- Do children think and talk about the kind of writing they want to do?

- Do they understand and use vocabulary related to purpose and audience, such as *writing, reason, purpose, tell a story, give information, reader, audience*, and *choice*?

▶ In what ways, beyond the scope of this umbrella, are children understanding purpose and audience?

- Are they ready to learn about different ways to write beginnings and endings?

- Do they proofread their writing?

Use your observations to determine the next umbrella you will teach. You may also consult Suggested Sequence of Lessons (pp. 557–571) for guidance.

EXTENSIONS FOR THINKING ABOUT PURPOSE AND AUDIENCE

▶ Share other types of writing with children, for example, a recipe, a comic strip, an instruction manual, advertisements, and road signs. Talk about how each type of writing has a purpose and an audience.

▶ Revisit WPS.U2: Getting Ideas for Writing and have children talk about purpose and audience for different writing ideas.

▶ Gather together a guided writing group of several children who need support in a specific area of writing.

Minilessons in This Umbrella

WML1   Get ideas from things you collect.

WML2   Get ideas from other writers.

WML3   Go back to ideas you love.

Before Teaching Umbrella 2 Minilessons

We recommend teaching STR.U1: Learning About Self and Others Through Storytelling before teaching these minilessons. It is not necessary to teach the minilessons in this umbrella consecutively. Rather, they can be used whenever you feel your children need some inspiration for their writing. They can also be repeated as needed.

Give children plenty of opportunities to write and draw freely and without constraints. Read and discuss books from a variety of authors and genres that the children will enjoy. For this umbrella, use the following texts from *Fountas & Pinnell Classroom™ Interactive Read-Aloud Collection*, or choose books from your classroom library.

Kevin Henkes: Exploring Characters

Chrysanthemum

Julius, the Baby of the World

Lilly's Big Day

Sheila Rae, the Brave

As you read and enjoy books together, help children

- discuss, whenever possible, how the author got the idea for the book (using the author's note, if applicable),
- notice when an author writes repeatedly about the same topic, idea, or characters, and
- talk about their own ideas for writing about a similar topic or theme.

Kevin Henkes

Section 8: Writing Process

WML1

Writing Minilesson Principle
Get ideas from things you collect.

Getting Ideas for Writing

You Will Need

- several interesting objects
- Me Box for each child (see STR.U1.WML4) or objects children can write about
- chart paper and markers

Academic Language/ Important Vocabulary

- idea
- collect
- objects

Continuum Connection

- Think of topics, events, or experiences from own life that are interesting to write about (p. 250)
- Generate and expand ideas through talk with peers and teacher (p. 256)
- Gather information for writing: e.g., objects, books, photos, sticky notes, etc. (p. 256)
- Observe carefully before writing about a person, animal, object, place, action (p. 256)
- Think of what to work on next as a writer (p. 257)

GOAL

Understand that writers can get ideas from collected objects that are connected to important ideas or memories.

RATIONALE

When children learn that they can get ideas for writing from collected objects, they are likely to write about things that are meaningful and important to them. They will therefore have the motivation and confidence to continue their writing journey.

ASSESS LEARNING

- Observe children as they write.
- Notice whether children get ideas for their writing from collected objects.
- Observe for evidence that children can use vocabulary such as *idea*, *collect*, and *objects*.

MINILESSON

To help children think about the minilesson principle, demonstrate writing about an object. Here is an example.

- Show several objects that are meaningful to you (for example, a teacup, a shell, a train ticket, and a trophy).

  All of these objects are special to me in some way. They all make me think of a special memory. I can get lots of ideas for my writing from these objects.

- Pick up one of the objects and look at it carefully. Then discuss your ideas for writing about it.

  Here's a train ticket from when I took a train to New York City when I was seven years old. I could write about my memories of that trip. I could also write a story about a character who rides a train for the first time. Or I could write an all-about book about trains. First, I'm going to write about the trip I took.

- On chart paper, write a few sentences inspired by the object. Read them aloud as you write them.

Have a Try

Invite children to talk to a partner about their ideas for writing.

> Look carefully at the objects in your Me Box. You told stories about some of them. What other ideas do they give you for writing? Turn and talk to your partner about your ideas.

▶ After children turn and talk, invite a few children to share their ideas.

Summarize and Apply

Summarize the learning. Remind children to think about objects they collect to get ideas for writing.

> What is one way you can get ideas for writing?

▶ Write the principle at the top of the chart. Read it aloud.

> During writing time today, write about one of the objects in your Me Box. You could also write about a different object. For example, you might have a special object at home that you want to write about. Bring your writing to share when we meet later.

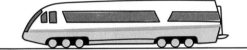

Get ideas from things you collect.

I rode a train for the first time when I was seven.

I went to New York City with my family.

We saw lots of tall buildings and went to museums.

It was so much fun!

Confer

▶ During independent writing, move around the room to confer briefly with as many individual children as time allows. Sit side by side with them and invite them to talk about their ideas for writing. Use prompts such as the following if needed.

- *Which object would you like to write about today?*
- *How could you write about that object? What ideas does it give you?*
- *What does it make you think about?*
- *Do you have any special memories of _____?*

Share

Following independent writing, gather children in the meeting area to talk about their writing.

> What object did you write about today?

> What did you write about it?

Getting Ideas for Writing

You Will Need

- two or more familiar fiction books, such as the following by Kevin Henkes, from Text Set: Kevin Henkes: Exploring Characters:
  - *Chrysanthemum*
  - *Lilly's Big Day*
- chart paper and markers

Academic Language/ Important Vocabulary

- idea
- unique
- writer

Continuum Connection

- Think of topics, events, or experiences from own life that are interesting to write about (p. 250)
- Understand that writers get help from other writers (p. 256)
- Talk about oneself as a writer (p. 257)
- Think of what to work on next as a writer (p. 257)

GOAL

Understand that writers get ideas from other writers.

RATIONALE

When children understand that they can get ideas from other writers, they find it easier to decide what to write about and write more diverse texts.

ASSESS LEARNING

- Observe children as they talk about their ideas for writing.
- Notice whether they get ideas from other writers.
- Observe for evidence that children can use vocabulary such as *idea*, *unique*, and *writer*.

MINILESSON

Use mentor texts to engage children in an inquiry around getting ideas from other writers. Here is an example.

- Show the cover of *Chrysanthemum* and read the title.

  We read this story about a girl named Chrysanthemum who is teased about her long name. This story gave me lots of ideas for my own writing. For example, I could write a story about my first day of school. Or I could write about what my name means and why my parents chose it for me. Or I could write a story about something else that makes me unique.

- Write each idea in a general way on chart paper.

  Does this book give you any ideas for your writing? What does it make you think about?

- Add children's ideas to the chart.

Have a Try

Invite children to talk to a partner about their ideas for writing.

❯ Show the cover of *Lilly's Big Day* and read the title.

> We read this story about a girl named Lilly who really wants to be the flower girl at her teacher's wedding. What ideas does this story give you for your own writing? Turn and talk to your partner about your ideas.

❯ After children turn and talk, invite several children to share their ideas. Record them on the chart.

Summarize and Apply

Help children summarize the learning. Remind them to think about books they have read when they are deciding what to write about.

> What is another way to get ideas for your writing?

❯ Write the principle at the top of the chart.

> During writing time today, work on some writing that you have already started or start something new. You might use an idea from our chart or from a book you have read. Bring your writing to share when we meet later.

Confer

❯ During independent writing, move around the room to confer briefly with as many individual children as time allows. Sit side by side with them and invite them to talk about getting ideas for writing. Use prompts such as the following as needed.

- *What would you like to write about today?*
- *Would you like to write about one of the ideas on our chart?*
- *What is your favorite book? Does it give you an idea to try in your writing?*
- *Have you experienced something similar in your own life?*

Share

Following independent writing, gather children in the meeting area to talk about their writing.

> What did you write about today?

> Where did you get that idea?

Get ideas from other writers.

First day of school

Meaning of your name

Something that makes you special

A time you felt sad

Something that happened to you

Someplace you went

A time you were disappointed

A time you made a new friend

Something that makes you happy

Writing Minilesson Principle
Go back to ideas you love.

Getting Ideas for Writing

You Will Need

- several familiar books by the same author, such as those in Text Set: Kevin Henkes: Exploring Characters

- a simple text you have written, such as the text created for WML1

- chart paper and markers

Academic Language/ Important Vocabulary

- writing

- idea

Continuum Connection

- Generate and expand ideas through talk with peers and teacher (p. 256)

- Look for ideas and topics in personal experiences, shared through talk (p. 256)

- Have a list or notebook with topics and ideas for writing (p. 257)

- Think of what to work on next as a writer (p. 257)

GOAL

Understand that writers often return to the same idea or topic for different writing pieces.

RATIONALE

When children understand that they can write about the same idea or topic many times in different ways, they will find it easy to think of things to write about and will be motivated and excited to continue writing about their favorite topics.

ASSESS LEARNING

- Notice whether children have difficulty thinking of what to write about.

- Observe for evidence that children can use vocabulary such as *writing* and *idea*.

MINILESSON

Use several books by the same author to demonstrate that authors can write about the same idea more than once. Here is an example.

- Show several books by Kevin Henkes (or another familiar author). Read the titles.

  When you read a lot of books by the same author, you learn what he or she likes to write about. What does Kevin Henkes like to write about?

  Kevin Henkes writes about mouse children that have the same experiences as many real children, like going to school for the first time, being teased, and having a baby brother or sister. The character Lilly is in more than one of his books. Do you think he likes this character a lot?

- Display the text written for WML1 or another simple text you have written. Read it aloud.

  Remember when I wrote this? What did I write about?

  I wrote about taking a train to New York City when I was a child. I'm going to write something new now. Watch what I do.

- Write another simple text about another aspect of the same topic. Read it aloud.

  How is this similar to what I wrote before?

  How is it different?

  Instead of writing about my trip to New York when I was seven years old, I wrote facts about the city. I wrote different pieces about the same idea or topic. If there is an idea you love writing about, you can write about it in different ways.

Have a Try

Invite children to talk to a partner about their ideas for writing.

> Think about a topic or idea you've written about. What did you write about it? Could you write about it again in a different way? Turn and talk to your partner about your ideas.

▶ After children turn and talk, invite a few children to share their ideas with the class.

Summarize and Apply

Summarize the learning. Remind children that they can return to ideas they love writing about.

> What is another way to get ideas for your writing?

▶ Write the principle at the top of the chart. Read it aloud.

> During writing time today, work on some writing you have already started or start something new. You might want to go back to an idea or topic you've written about before. You can write about the same idea in a different way.

Confer

▶ During independent writing, move around the room to confer briefly with as many individual children as time allows. Sit side by side with them and invite them to talk about their ideas for writing. Use prompts such as the following as needed.

  • *Let's look at some books you've already written.*
  • *What did you write about in that book?*
  • *Do you want to write about that again?*
  • *What else could you write about that topic [idea]?*

Share

Following independent writing, gather children in the meeting area to share their writing.

> Raise your hand if you wrote about a topic or idea that you've written about before.

> How did you write about it in a different way?

Get ideas from things you collect.

I rode a train for the first time when I was seven.

I went to New York City with my family.

We saw lots of tall buildings and went to museums.

It was so much fun!

Go back to ideas you love.

New York City is a big city in the state of New York.

More than eight million people live there.

The Statue of Liberty is in New York City.

Assessment

After you have taught the minilessons in this umbrella, observe children as they draw and write. Use the behaviors and understandings in *The Literacy Continuum* (Fountas and Pinnell 2017) to notice, teach for, and support children's learning as you observe their attempts at reading and writing.

▶ What evidence do you have of new understandings children have developed related to getting ideas for writing?

- Can children independently think of ideas for writing?
- Do they understand that they can get ideas from different sources, such as a Me Box, other writers, and favorite topics?
- Are they using vocabulary such as *idea*, *writing*, and *story*?

▶ In what other ways, beyond the scope of this umbrella, are children ready to expand their writing and illustrating skills?

- Are they ready to learn about editing and revising their writing?
- Are they ready to learn new techniques for creating interesting illustrations?

Use your observations to determine the next umbrella you will teach. You may also consult Suggested Sequence of Lessons (pp. 557–571) for guidance.

EXTENSIONS FOR GETTING IDEAS FOR WRITING

▶ Use the charts developed during STR.U1: Learning About Self and Others Through Storytelling to help children remember ideas from their oral storytelling.

▶ In the books you read aloud, look to see if the authors reveal (for example, in an author's note) where they got their ideas. If so, share this information with the children.

▶ Gather together a guided writing group of several children who need support in a specific area of writing, such as thinking of what to write about.

▶ After reading aloud a book, invite children to write their own text that is inspired in some way by the book—for example, the same story with a different ending, the same characters in a different situation, or the same writing or illustration style.

Minilessons in This Umbrella

WML1 Write what you think is going to happen.

WML2 Sketch what you observe.

WML3 Write down your observations.

WML4 Write questions and wonderings from your observations.

Before Teaching Umbrella 3 Minilessons

Before teaching the minilessons in this umbrella, you will need to choose, plan, and gather materials for a science experiment that you will do with your children over the course of these lessons. These minilessons are based on an experiment in which children place one plant in the dark and one in direct sunlight and observe what happens. The minilessons assume that the seeds have already sprouted. However, you can use any multiday experiment that is relevant to your class's science curriculum.

You might also want to read and discuss nonfiction books related to the science topic you have chosen. If you choose an experiment related to plants, you might use the following texts from *Fountas & Pinnell Classroom™ Interactive Read-Aloud Collection.*

Understanding the Natural World: Planting and Growing

The Dandelion Seed by Joseph Anthony

This Year's Garden by Cynthia Rylant

Jack's Garden by Henry Cole

Plant Packages: A Book About Seeds by Susan Blackaby

From Seed to Plant by Gail Gibbons

As you read and enjoy these texts together, help children

- make predictions and inferences,

- notice and discuss details in the illustrations, and

- pose questions and wonderings about the topic.

Writing Minilesson Principle
Write what you think is going to happen.

Observing and Writing Like a Scientist

You Will Need

- materials for a science experiment (e.g., two identical plants that the children planted)
- chart paper and markers
- To download the following online resource for this lesson, visit **resources.fountasandpinnell.com**:
  - chart art (optional)

Academic Language/ Important Vocabulary

- science
- experiment
- predict
- prediction

Continuum Connection

- Use vocabulary appropriate for the topic (p. 254)
- Generate and expand ideas through talk with peers and teacher (p. 256)
- Take notes or make sketches to help in remembering information (p. 256)

GOAL

Write a prediction related to a science project.

RATIONALE

When you help children write a prediction for a science experiment, they learn that scientists use what they already know about a topic to make an educated guess about what will happen. They also learn that scientists record their predictions in order to have a permanent, written record of their scientific process.

ASSESS LEARNING

- Observe children as they talk about science experiments. Do they draw on their existing knowledge to make an educated guess about what will happen?
- Notice whether children can write a prediction for a science experiment.
- Observe for evidence that children can use vocabulary such as *science*, *experiment*, *predict*, and *prediction*.

MINILESSON

Introduce the science experiment that the children are going to conduct (see Before Teaching for more information) and help them make predictions. Here is an example.

- Display two identical plants that the children planted.

  We planted seeds in these pots. When we planted them, what did you think would happen?

  You thought the seeds would grow into plants. That was your prediction. When you make a prediction, think about what you already know about a topic and use that to think about what might happen.

  When you planted the seed, did you say, "I think the seed will grow" or "I'm guessing the seed will grow"? How might you say a prediction?

- Help children think about how they can state a prediction. Record on chart paper the language they use (e.g., *I think . . .*).

The Writing Minilessons Book, Grade 1

Have a Try

Invite children to talk to a partner about their predictions.

> What do you think will happen to the plant in the sun? Turn and talk to your partner about this.

▸ After children turn and talk, invite a few pairs to share their predictions.

Summarize and Apply

Help children summarize the learning. Remind them to record their predictions.

> What did you learn today?

▸ Write the principle at the top of the chart.

> It's important to write your prediction so that you will remember it. At the end of the experiment, read your prediction to see if what you thought would happen is what actually happened!

> Today during writing time, write your prediction about the two plants. If you finish before writing time is over, continue working on a book you've already started or start a new one.

▸ You might want to provide sentence frames for the children's writing, such as the following: *I think the plant in the sun (dark) is going to _____.*

Write what you think is going to happen.

- I think . . .
- I'm guessing that . . .
- I wonder if . . .
- I predict that . . .
- My prediction is that . . .

Confer

▸ During independent writing, move around the room to confer briefly with as many individual children as time allows. Sit side by side with them and invite them to talk about their predictions. Use prompts such as the following if needed.

- *What do you think will happen to the plant in the sun?*
- *What do you predict will happen to the plant in the dark?*
- *What words will you use to start your prediction?*

Share

Following independent writing, gather children in the meeting area to share their predictions.

> Who would like to share your predictions?

> These two predictions start with different words, but they mean the same thing.

Writing Minilesson Principle
Sketch what you observe.

Observing and Writing Like a Scientist

You Will Need

- materials for a science experiment (e.g., two identical plants that the children planted)
- chart paper and markers

Academic Language/ Important Vocabulary

- sketch
- observe

Continuum Connection

- Observe carefully to detect and describe change (growth, change over time in plants or animals, chemical changes in food), and talk about observations (p. 256)
- Observe in the environment to notice details or changes (p. 256)
- Use drawings to show how something looks, how something works, or the process or change (p. 256)
- Sometimes label drawings (p. 256)

GOAL

Use drawings to show what has been observed.

RATIONALE

When you help children sketch their scientific observations, they learn to look closely at a subject and observe its many different aspects. They begin to understand that drawings convey meaning.

ASSESS LEARNING

- Notice the details children include in their sketches of scientific observations.
- Observe for evidence that children can use vocabulary such as *sketch* and *observe*.

MINILESSON

To help children think about the minilesson principle, model sketching scientific observations and engage children in an inquiry around what they noticed. Here is an example.

- Display the two plants used in the science experiment, side by side.

  It has been two weeks since we put one plant in the sun and one plant in the dark. We can now observe, or look closely at, the plants to see if and how they have changed. Watch what I do.

- Model sketching the two plants on chart paper. Think aloud as you draw your observations.

  I see that the plant that was in the sun has bright, round, green leaves. It is bigger than the plant that was in the dark. Some of the leaves on the plant that was in the dark look yellow and limp. Some of them have fallen off.

- Label the plants *Sun* and *Dark* and write the date.

  What did you notice about what I did?

  What kinds of things did I think about when I observed and sketched the plants?

  What did I write?

- Record children's responses on chart paper.

  Scientists make many observations over days, weeks, months, or even years. It's important to write the date so you remember when you made each observation.

Have a Try

Invite children to talk to a partner about their observations.

> Look closely at the two plants. Do you notice anything else about them? Is there anything you think I should add to my sketches? Turn and talk to your partner about this.

▶ After children turn and talk, invite a few pairs to share their ideas. Add to the sketches as appropriate.

Summarize and Apply

Write the principle at the top of the chart to summarize the learning. Remind children to sketch their scientific observations.

> When scientists do science experiments, they sketch what they observe. Why is that important?

> Today during writing time, look closely at the two plants and sketch what you observe. Remember to add labels. Bring your sketches to share when we meet later.

Sketch what you observe.

- Look closely.

- Think about size, color, and shape.

- Draw what you notice.

- Label your pictures.

- Write the date.

April 9 — Sun

April 9 — Dark

Confer

▶ During independent writing, move around the room to confer briefly with as many individual children as time allows. Sit side by side with them and invite them to talk about their sketches. Use prompts such as the following if needed.

- *What do you notice about the plant that was in the sun?*
- *What are the plant's leaves like? What color are they?*
- *How is the plant that was in the dark different?*
- *What details could you add to your drawings?*

Share

Following independent writing, gather children in the meeting area to share their sketches.

> Who would like to share a sketch?

> What did you notice about the two plants? How are they different?

Observing and Writing Like a Scientist

You Will Need

- materials for a science experiment (e.g., two identical plants that the children planted)
- chart paper and markers

Academic Language/ Important Vocabulary

- observation
- scientist

Continuum Connection

- Use vocabulary appropriate for the topic (p. 254)
- Observe carefully to detect and describe change (growth, change over time in plants or animals, chemical changes in food), and talk about observations (p. 256)
- Record information in words or a drawing (p. 256)

GOAL

Observe carefully and record important information about the observations.

RATIONALE

When you help children record their scientific observations, they learn to look closely at a subject and observe its many different aspects. They understand the importance of keeping an ongoing record of scientific observations to capture changes over time.

ASSESS LEARNING

- Notice whether children use writing to record their scientific observations.
- Observe for evidence that children can use vocabulary such as *observation* and *scientist*.

MINILESSON

Model recording scientific observations. Then engage children in an inquiry around what they noticed. Here is an example.

- Display the two plants used in the science experiment, side by side.

  It has now been three weeks since we put one plant in the sun and one in the dark. Last week you looked closely at the plants and sketched what you observed. Today we will observe the plants again, but this time we will do something a little different. Watch what I do.

- Model observing the plants and writing your observations on chart paper. Read aloud your writing as you write it.

  What did you notice about what I did? How did I record my observations this time?

  What kinds of things did I write about?

  What did I write at the top of the piece of paper?

- Record children's responses on chart paper. Review why it's important to write down the date when the scientific observations were made.

Have a Try

Invite children to talk to a partner about their observations.

> Do you notice anything else about the two plants? Is there anything else you think I should add to my writing? Turn and talk to your partner.

▶ After children turn and talk, invite a few pairs to share their ideas. Add to the chart as appropriate. Save the chart for WML4.

Summarize and Apply

Write the principle at the top of the chart to summarize the learning. Remind children to write their scientific observations.

> You've been learning about how to write like scientists. What did you learn today about how scientists write their observations down?

> During writing time today, look closely at the two plants and write your observations. You can also add sketches, if you like. Remember to write down the date. Bring your observations to share when we meet later.

<table>
<tr><td colspan="2">Write down your observations.</td></tr>
<tr><td colspan="2" align="right">April 16</td></tr>
<tr><td>Sun</td><td>Dark</td></tr>
<tr><td>The plant is big.</td><td>The plant is small.</td></tr>
<tr><td>The leaves are bright green.</td><td>Many of the leaves are yellow or brown.</td></tr>
<tr><td>They feel smooth and soft.</td><td>Some of the leaves fell off.</td></tr>
</table>

- Look closely.
- Think about size, color, shape, and feel.
- Write what you notice.
- Write the date.

Confer

▶ During independent writing, move around the room to confer briefly with as many individual children as time allows. Sit side by side with them and invite them to talk about their observations. Use prompts such as the following if needed.

- *What do you notice about the plant that was in the dark?*
- *What color are the leaves?*
- *What could you write about the size of the plants?*
- *Do you want to add some sketches of the plants?*

Share

Following independent writing, gather children in the meeting area to share their observations.

> How have the plants changed since last week?

> What do you think the plants will look like next week?

Writing Minilesson Principle
Write questions and wonderings from your observations.

Observing and Writing Like a Scientist

You Will Need

- the chart made during WML3
- chart paper and markers
- To download the following online resource for this lesson, visit **resources.fountasandpinnell.com**:
  - chart art (optional)

Academic Language/ Important Vocabulary

- question
- wondering
- observation

Continuum Connection

- Use vocabulary appropriate for the topic (p. 254)
- Ask questions and gather information on a topic (p. 256)
- Observe carefully to detect and describe change (growth, change over time in plants or animals, chemical changes in food), and talk about observations (p. 256)
- Record information in words or a drawing (p. 256)

GOAL

Use your observations to write questions and wonderings.

RATIONALE

When you make children aware that their scientific observations can lead to questions and wonderings, you engage them in a process of critical thinking. They learn that thinking (and science) doesn't stop when a task is completed. There is always more to think about and learn.

ASSESS LEARNING

- Observe children as they talk about their scientific observations.
- Notice whether children record questions and wonderings based on their observations.
- Observe for evidence that children can use vocabulary such as *question*, *wondering*, and *observation*.

MINILESSON

To help children think about the minilesson principle, model posing questions and wonderings based on scientific observations and invite children to pose their own. Here is an example.

- Display the chart from WML3.

  Yesterday, we wrote our observations about the two plants we've been studying for our science experiment. We noticed that the plant that was in the sun has green leaves and that the plant that was in the dark has yellow and brown leaves. I wonder why plants that get more sun have greener leaves.

- Write *I wonder why . . .* on a clean sheet of chart paper.

  What do our observations make you think about? Does anyone have any questions about plants? Are you wondering anything about plants?

- Invite a few children to share. Record the general language that they use to share questions and wonderings.

  Scientists think carefully about what they observe and use their observations to pose questions and wonderings. Why do you think they do this?

  This helps scientists decide what to work on next. They might look in a book or online to find the answers to their questions, or they might do another experiment.

Have a Try

Invite children to talk to a partner about their questions and wonderings.

> Turn and talk to your partner about any other questions or wonderings you have from your scientific observations. What has this experiment made you think about?

▶ After children turn and talk, invite a few more children to share their thinking. Add to the chart as appropriate.

Summarize and Apply

Write the principle at the top of the chart to summarize the learning. Remind children to record their questions and wonderings.

> Today during writing time, look at the observations you wrote yesterday. Think about the questions and wonderings you have about the experiment. Write them down and bring them to share when we meet later.

Write questions and wonderings from your observations.

- I wonder why . . .
- Why does . . .?
- How long . . .?
- When . . .?
- I wonder what would happen if . . .
- What is . . .?

Confer

▶ During independent writing, move around the room to confer briefly with as many individual children as time allows. Sit side by side with them and invite them to talk about their questions and wonderings. Use prompts such as the following if needed.

- *What are you wondering about the plants?*
- *What questions do you have?*
- *What would you like to find out next?*
- *You noticed that _____. What does that make you wonder?*

Share

Following independent writing, gather children in the meeting area to share their questions and wonderings.

> Who would like to share the questions and wonderings you wrote?

> What experiment could we do next to answer some of your questions?

Assessment

After you have taught the minilessons in this umbrella, observe children as they write and talk about their writing. Use the behaviors and understandings in *The Literacy Continuum* (Fountas and Pinnell 2017) to notice, teach for, and support children's learning as you observe their attempts at writing.

▶ What evidence do you have of new understandings children have developed related to observing and writing like a scientist?

- Can children write a prediction for a science experiment?
- Do they sketch their scientific observations?
- Do they record their scientific observations?
- What kinds of questions and wonderings based on their scientific observations do children have?
- Do children understand and use vocabulary such as *scientist*, *observe*, and *observation*?

▶ In what other ways, beyond the scope of this umbrella, are children ready to write like scientists?

- Are they ready to write different kinds of books about scientific topics (e.g., all-about books, question-and-answer books)?

Use your observations to determine the next umbrella you will teach. You may also consult Suggested Sequence of Lessons (pp. 557–571) for guidance.

EXTENSIONS FOR OBSERVING AND WRITING LIKE A SCIENTIST

▶ Conduct some research to answer some of the questions that arose from the scientific observations.

▶ Teach children how to record and present scientific data and observations in tables, charts, and/or graphs.

▶ Help children write conclusions about a science experiment.

▶ Encourage children to write how-to books about how to do a science experiment or all-about books about a science topic.

Minilessons in This Umbrella

WML1 Add details to your drawings.

WML2 Use a caret to add words.

WML3 Use a strip of paper to add information.

WML4 Use connecting words to add information.

WML5 Add a page to give more information.

Before Teaching Umbrella 4 Minilessons

These minilessons help children progress in the writing process by expanding ideas for revising their writing. It is not necessary to teach the lessons consecutively. Instead, you might choose to teach them throughout the year because revision is a high-level concept and children will need multiple exposures to these lessons. Continue to have children tell stories orally because they often include details that they omit from their writing. These details can be added during the revision process.

Build the chart from WML1 across the umbrella. Post it in the writing center as a resource. Use the same mentor texts throughout to model how writers reread and revise repeatedly to improve their writing and how children can do the same. These lessons use a piece of class interactive writing and a piece of teacher writing to model how to look back at your work to find areas for improvement. Also use the following texts from *Fountas & Pinnell Classroom™ Interactive Read-Aloud Collection* and *Shared Reading Collection*, or choose books from the classroom library that the children will enjoy.

Interactive Read-Aloud Collection

Kevin Henkes: Exploring Characters

Sheila Rae, the Brave

The Importance of Friendship

Mr. George Baker by Amy Hest

Learning and Working Together: School

First Day Jitters by Julie Danneberg

Shared Reading Collection

Scram! by Julie Reich

Interactive Writing Lessons

IW.8: Writing a Memory Story

As you read and enjoy these texts together, help children

- think about the author's process to write and revise the book, and
- discuss what makes the book interesting or exciting.

Interactive Read-Aloud
Kevin Henkes

Friendship

School

Shared Reading

Interactive Writing

Section 8: Writing Process

Writing Minilesson Principle
Add details to your drawings.

Adding Information to Your Writing

You Will Need

- a familiar text with detailed illustrations, such as *Sheila Rae, the Brave* by Kevin Henkes, from Text Set: Kevin Henkes: Exploring Characters

- chart paper prepared with the title *Adding Information*

- a book you have made

- books the children have made

- markers

Academic Language/ Important Vocabulary

- detail
- add
- illustration
- revise/revising
- reread

Continuum Connection

- Review a drawing to revise by adding or deleting information (p. 256)

- Add or remove details to drawings to revise information (p. 257)

- Create drawings that employ careful attention to color or detail (p. 257)

GOAL

Understand how to add details to a drawing.

RATIONALE

By observing and discussing details in pictures, children learn that the details make a difference in what the reader understands about a story. Children learn that the details in their own pictures matter and that it is a good idea to look closely at them to decide if more details are needed. This serves as an introduction to revising, part of the writing process.

ASSESS LEARNING

- Listen to children as they talk about their drawings. Do the drawings reflect what they say?

- Notice whether children are willing to revise (add details to) their drawings.

- Observe for evidence that children can use vocabulary such as *detail*, *add*, *illustration*, *revise/revising*, and *reread*.

MINILESSON

The chart you begin in this minilesson will be added to in the following minilessons. To help children think about the minilesson principle, use a familiar text to engage children in a discussion about details in illustrations. Here is an example.

- Show the cover of *Sheila Rae, the Brave* and read the title. Show the illustration on page 2 of Sheila Rae sleeping.

  What do you notice about this illustration?

  What details did the illustrator include in the picture to help you understand that?

- Help children to restate their answers to be more generative and add them to the prepared chart paper.

  Kevin Henkes shows Sheila in bed, so you know where she is. Look how the flashlight is shining. That's how you know it is dark in the room. Who is holding the flashlight?

  Kevin Henkes includes details about who is in the story, where they are, and even the time of day.

- Demonstrate thinking aloud about how to add details to a book you wrote.

  I will look carefully at each illustration to be sure it has all the details the reader needs to understand that part of the story.

- Quickly add a detail to an illustration.

  Going back to look at writing and making changes to the pictures or the words is called revising.

Have a Try

Invite children to talk to a partner about their own drawings.

▶ Have children look at a book they have already written or are currently working on.

> Look at your illustrations. What details could you add to help people understand more about the story? Turn and talk to your partner about this.

Summarize and Apply

Help children summarize the learning and remind children to add details to their drawings.

> What is a way to make sure your readers will understand your writing?

▶ Write the principle in the first row of the chart.

> Today during writing time, continue to reread your writing and ask yourself if you have put enough details in your drawings. Make the changes. Bring your writing to share when we meet later.

▶ Save the chart for WML2.

Adding Information

• Add details to your drawings.	• Where • Who • Time of day

Confer

▶ During independent writing, move around the room to confer briefly with as many individual children as time allows. Sit side by side with them and invite them to talk about adding to their drawings. Use prompts such as the following as needed.

- *What is happening in this part of the story? What details could you add to your drawing to help the reader understand more about that?*

- *Where were you during this part of the story? What could you add to the illustrations to help the reader know that?*

- *Who was with you during this part of the story? Did you include them in the illustrations?*

Share

Following independent writing, gather children in the meeting area to share their drawings. Ask a few children to share their work, or ask pairs to share while you listen in and then share a child's work that supports the principle.

> Talk about the details you added to your pictures. Why did you add those details?

Writing Minilesson Principle
Use a caret to add words.

Adding Information to Your Writing

You Will Need

- a familiar picture book with examples of descriptive language, such as *Mr. George Baker* by Amy Hest, from Text Set: The Importance of Friendship
- the class writing from IW.8: Writing a Memory Story
- the chart from WML1
- books the children have made
- markers

Academic Language/ Important Vocabulary

- caret
- details
- revise
- word

Continuum Connection

- Reread writing to be sure the meaning is clear (p. 256)
- Add words, phrases, or sentences to make the writing more interesting or exciting for readers (p. 256)
- Add words, phrases, or sentences to clarify meaning for readers (p. 256)
- Add letters, words, phrases, or sentences using a caret, a strip of paper, or a sticky note (p. 257)

GOAL

Understand that writers can use a caret to add words to make the writing more interesting, clear, or exciting.

RATIONALE

When you teach children to use a caret mark to efficiently revise and edit their writing, they learn how to use a caret as a tool to improve their writing.

ASSESS LEARNING

- Observe children as they revise and talk about their writing.
- Notice whether children can elaborate on their stories orally and then transfer the oral elaboration to writing using a caret mark to add a word or words.
- Observe for evidence that children can use vocabulary such as *caret*, *details*, *revise*, and *word*.

MINILESSON

Use a mentor text to engage children in an inquiry around how descriptive language makes a text more interesting, clear, or exciting. Use a piece of class writing to demonstrate how to use a caret to add interesting details to a sentence. Here is an example.

- Show the cover of *Mr. George Baker*. Show and read pages 6–7.

  What did the author tell us about what George is wearing? What are some of the exact words the author used to describe George's clothes?

  Writers include descriptive words like these to help make the story more interesting.

  When you write books, you can reread what you wrote and think about adding or changing words to make your writing more interesting or exciting.

- Display the class writing from IW.8. Read it aloud. Prompt children to think about expanding specifically upon the ideas that are already written on the page. (Subsequent lessons will focus on adding new ideas.)

  What words could we add to this part to make the writing more interesting?

  What else could we say about the location?

  We could say that the museum was in Chicago to give the reader more information.

- Demonstrate using a caret to add words to the writing.

  A caret looks like an upside-down *V* (or the beginning of a capital *A*). You place it right where you want a word to go. Then you write the added word right above the caret. Let me show you.

Have a Try

Invite children to talk to a partner about adding words to their writing.

▶ Have children look at a book they have already written or are currently working on.

> Read what you have written. Is there a place that you could add a word to make the writing more interesting? Turn and talk to your partner.

▶ After they turn and talk, ask for a pair's suggestions.

Summarize and Apply

Help children summarize the learning. Remind them that they can use a caret to add words to their writing.

> How can you revise your writing to make it better?

▶ Write the principle on the chart.

> Today during writing time, reread your writing. Think about what words you could add to make your writing more interesting, clear, or exciting. Try using a caret to show where the new words go.

▶ Save the chart for WML3.

Adding Information

| • Add details to your drawings. | • Where
• Who
• Time of day |
| • Use a caret to add words. | • We went to the science museum in Chicago. |

Confer

▶ During independent writing, move around the room to confer briefly with as many individual children as time allows. Sit side by side with them and invite them to talk about adding to their writing. Use prompts such as the following as needed.

- *Talk about _____. What word or words could you add to tell the reader more?*
- *Where will you put the caret to add the word?*
- *What could you say about the _____? What did it look (sound, smell, feel, taste) like?*
- *You used a caret to add the word _____.*

Share

Following independent writing, gather children in the meeting area to share their writing.

> Who would like to share a spot where you used a caret to add a word?

> What word did you add? Why did you add that?

WML3

WPS.U4.WML3

Writing Minilesson Principle
Use a strip of paper to add information.

Adding Information to Your Writing

You Will Need

- the class writing from IW.8: Writing a Memory Story
- books the children have made
- the chart from WML2
- markers
- strips of paper and tape

Academic Language/ Important Vocabulary

- details
- sentence
- revise
- word

Continuum Connection

- Reread writing to be sure the meaning is clear (p. 256)
- Add words, phrases, or sentences to make the writing more interesting or exciting for readers (p. 256)
- Add words, phrases, or sentences to clarify meaning for readers (p. 256)
- Add letters, words, phrases, or sentences using a caret, a strip of paper, or a sticky note (p. 257)

GOAL

Use a strip of paper as one technique to revise and add on to writing.

RATIONALE

When you teach children to use a strip of paper, called a "spider leg," to efficiently add on to their writing, they learn how to add information to make their writing more interesting.

ASSESS LEARNING

- Observe children as they revise and talk about their writing.
- Notice whether children can elaborate on their stories orally and then transfer the oral elaboration to writing using a strip of paper.
- Observe for evidence that children can use vocabulary such as *details*, *sentence*, *revise*, and *word*.

MINILESSON

Use a piece of class writing to engage children in an inquiry around revising a book by adding a sentence on a strip of paper. You might decide to use the term *spider leg* with the children. Here is an example.

- Display the class writing from IW.8. Prompt children to think about expanding upon the writing with a full sentence.

  What might the reader be wondering about after reading this page? What more can we tell the reader about this part?

  What else could we say about the lightning show?

  We could add *It was dark and loud during the show*.

- Guide children to understand that they can write additional words on a strip of paper and add it to their writing.

  Sometimes you want to add to your writing, but there isn't enough room. What can you do?

  You can get a strip of paper from the writing center and write the sentence on it. This is called a spider leg. This is one way writers revise their work and add to their writing. Let me show you.

  I will write our sentence on this strip of paper. I am going to get a small piece of tape and attach the strip of paper to the page. Where should I place the strip?

- Read the whole page, running your finger underneath all of the words to show how one reads the additional words on the strip of paper.

  After you write on a spider leg and attach it to your writing, be sure to fold it in.

Have a Try

Invite children to talk to a partner about their own books.

▶ Make sure children have one of their own books.

> Read a page in your book to your partner. Think about what is happening in that part of the story. Tell your partner more about that. Then talk about a sentence you could add with a spider leg to help the reader understand more.

Summarize and Apply

Help children summarize the learning and remind them to think about adding more information.

> What is another way to revise, or add information to, your writing?

▶ Write the principle on the chart.

> Today during writing time, reread your writing. Think about what to add to make your writing on a page better. Try using a spider leg to add the words. Remember to fold it in when you are done.

▶ Save the chart for WML4.

Adding Information

• Add details to your drawings.	• Where • Who • Time of day
• Use a caret to add words.	• We went to the science museum in Chicago.
• Use a strip of paper to add information.	

Confer

▶ During independent writing, move around the room to confer briefly with as many individual children as time allows. Sit side by side with them and invite them to talk about adding to their writing. Use prompts such as the following as needed.

- *Read what you wrote on this page. Talk a little more about _____. What could you add to tell the reader more?*

- *Where will you put the spider leg?*

- *What could you say about the _____? What did it look (sound, smell, feel, taste) like?*

- *You used a spider leg to add _____.*

Share

Following independent writing, gather children in the meeting area to share their writing.

> Who would like to share how you used a spider leg to add to your writing?

> What sentence did you add? Why did you add that?

Adding Information to Your Writing

You Will Need

- familiar texts with examples of connecting words, such as:
  - *First Day Jitters* by Julie Danneberg, from Text Set: Learning and Working Together: School
  - *Scram!* by Julie Reich, from *Shared Reading Collection*
- document camera (optional)
- the chart from WML3 with connecting words added in red
- the class writing from IW.8: Writing a Memory Story
- strip of paper (optional)
- markers

Academic Language/ Important Vocabulary

- revise
- connecting words

Continuum Connection

- Add words, phrases, or sentences to make the writing more interesting or exciting for readers (p. 256)
- Add words, phrases, or sentences to provide more information to readers (p. 256)

GOAL

Understand that writers use connecting words (e.g., *and, but, so, because, before, after*) to add information to improve their writing.

RATIONALE

When you teach children to reread their work and to use connecting words to add more information to their writing, they learn a way to revise and make their writing clearer and more interesting.

ASSESS LEARNING

- Notice whether children can identify connecting words in mentor texts.
- Look for evidence in children's writing that they understand how to use connecting words.
- Observe for evidence that children can use vocabulary such as *revise, connecting words,* and specific connecting words (e.g., *and, but, so, because, before, after*).

MINILESSON

To help children think about the minilesson principle, use familiar texts to engage them in a discussion about using connecting words to add to their writing. Use a document camera (if available). Here is an example.

- Show the cover of *First Day Jitters*. Display pages 2–3 and read the first sentence, pointing to the connecting word *and*.

  What word is this?

  Why would the author use that word here?

  Using the word *and* connects two things that are happening. Sarah talks and then she pulls the covers over her head.

- Repeat this process with the second sentence on the page, emphasizing the connecting word *and*.

  How many things is Mr. Hartwell doing? How do you know that?

- Repeat this process with other texts, such as *Scram!* (using the connecting word *so*).

  The words I have written on the chart in red are connecting words; they connect two things. When you go back to look at your writing, think about adding a connecting word to add more information to your writing.

Have a Try

Invite children to talk to a partner about using connecting words to add to a piece of class writing.

▶ Have children look at the writing from IW.8.

Let's look at the story about our class trip. Turn and talk to your partner. How can you use the word *and* or *so* to add information to our writing? Try this: *The guide told us that a lightning bolt is hotter than the sun and. . . .*

▶ Ask a few partners to share. Demonstrate using either a caret (if there is enough room) or a spider leg to add the connecting word and the new information.

Summarize and Apply

Help children summarize the learning and remind them to think about using connecting words in their writing.

What did you learn about revising or adding information to your writing?

▶ Add the principle to the chart.

As you reread your writing, think about how you might use connecting words like *and*, *but*, or *so*. Bring your writing to share when we meet later.

▶ Save the chart for WML5.

Adding Information

• Add details to your drawings.	• Where • Who • Time of day
• Use a caret to add words.	• We went to the science museum in Chicago.
• Use a strip of paper to add information.	
• Use connecting words to add information.	• and • but • so • because

Confer

▶ During independent writing, move around the room to confer briefly with as many individual children as time allows. Sit side by side with them and invite them to talk about adding to their writing. Use prompts such as the following as needed.

- *How might you use the word* and, but, *or* so *to add more information to this part?*
- *Will you use a caret or a spider leg to add that to your writing?*
- *[Read aloud one of the child's sentences, adding the word* and, but, *or* so *at the end. Pause to allow the child to add on to the sentence orally and then in writing.]*

Share

Following independent writing, gather children in the meeting area to share their writing with a partner. Read one child's writing that supports the principle to the whole class.

_____ added _____ to her writing. Did anyone else add information?

Writing Minilesson Principle

Add a page to give more information.

Adding Information to Your Writing

You Will Need

- a book you have made to which a page could be added
- books the children have made
- the chart from WML4
- markers

Academic Language/ Important Vocabulary

- page
- information
- add
- revise

Continuum Connection

- Reread writing to be sure the meaning is clear (p. 256)
- Add words, phrases, or sentences to clarify meaning for readers (p. 256)
- Add words, phrases, or sentences to make the writing more interesting or exciting for readers (p. 256)
- Add pages to a book or booklet (p. 257)

GOAL

Add pages to a book to give more information to readers.

RATIONALE

When children reread their writing and think about what information to add to help the reader understand more about the topic or story, they learn to make their writing more complete. Teaching children to add more pages and information to their books is a revision strategy they will use as writers.

ASSESS LEARNING

- Notice whether children can elaborate on their stories orally and then transfer the oral elaboration to writing.
- Notice whether children add pages to give more information in their books at the beginning, the middle, or the end.
- Observe for evidence that children can use vocabulary such as *page*, *information*, *add*, and *revise*.

MINILESSON

Use a book you wrote to engage children in an inquiry around revising a book by adding pages. Discuss what additional information might be added to give more information. Here is an example.

▶ Discuss how writers revise to add more information on a new page.

> Writers go back to their writing many times to think about what they can add to make parts of their book clearer for the reader. Sometimes they have so much more to add to their writing that they need to add a whole new page. You can add a page to your writing, too.

> Listen as I read this book I wrote. Think about if there is anything you are wondering about.

▶ Read the book and discuss adding a page. Following the children's suggestions, write the page and add it to the book in the right place.

> When you tell me you are wondering about something, I realize I am missing something in my writing. Writers add pages wherever more information is needed so that readers know every important thing that happens in a story.

Have a Try

Invite children to talk to a partner about their own books.

▶ Have children look at a book they have already written or are currently working on.

> Read your book to your partner. Ask your partner if it would help to add a new page to your book. What could you write? Where would the page go? Turn and talk to your partner about this.

Summarize and Apply

Help children summarize the learning and remind them to think about whether their readers need more information.

> How can you add more information to your writing?

▶ Add the principle to the chart.

> As you write today, think about what the reader might be wondering or what might not be clear.
> You might want to add more pages to give more information. Bring your writing to share when we meet later.

Adding Information

• Add details to your drawings.	• Where • Who • Time of day
• Use a caret to add words.	• We went to the science museum in Chicago.
• Use a strip of paper to add information.	
• Use connecting words to add information.	• and • but • so • because
• Add a page to give more information.	

Confer

▶ During independent writing, move around the room to confer briefly with as many individual children as time allows. Sit side by side with them and invite them to talk about adding to their writing. Use prompts such as the following as needed.

- *Read your story. I understand _____. I wonder _____.*
- *What else might your reader want to know?*
- *Write that on a new page and add that to your book.*
- *You added a new page to your book. What did you decide to add?*

Share

Following independent writing, gather children in the meeting area to share their writing. Have partners share pages they added to their book. Use one child's writing as an example for the whole class.

> What did the new page help the reader to understand more about?

Assessment

After you have taught the minilessons in this umbrella, observe children as they draw, write, and talk about their writing. Use the behaviors and understandings in *The Literacy Continuum* (Fountas and Pinnell 2017) to notice, teach for, and support children's learning as you observe their attempts at drawing and writing.

▶ What evidence do you have of new understandings children have developed related to adding to writing?

- Do children understand that they can (and show a willingness to) revise their books to make them better?
- What kinds of details do they add to their drawings to give more information?
- Do children understand how to use a caret, strip of paper, or additional page to add to their writing?
- Do they use connecting words to add more detail to their writing?
- Are they using vocabulary such as *add*, *detail*, *page*, *book*, and *information*?

▶ In what other ways, beyond the scope of this umbrella, are children showing an interest in drawing and writing?

- Do they write with details?
- Are they using classroom resources to write words?

Use your observations to determine what you will teach next. You may also consult Suggested Sequence of Lessons (pp. 557–571) for guidance.

EXTENSIONS FOR ADDING INFORMATION TO YOUR WRITING

▶ Pull together a small group of children who would benefit from guided instruction on adding to their writing.

▶ Teach children how to use a number to identify a place in their writing to add information and an additional page with a corresponding number to write the information for insertion. You could also teach how to use an asterisk and a note at the bottom of the page.

▶ Provide a lesson on how to use writing tools such as the tape dispenser and staple remover (see MGT.U3 for model minilessons and Planning a Writing Minilesson (p. 102) for writing your plan).

▶ Revisit WML4 to teach the connecting words *because*, *before*, and *after*.

Minilessons in This Umbrella

WML1 Cross out a word that does not fit or make sense.

WML2 Take out a page that does not fit or make sense.

WML3 Read your writing to make sure the order makes sense.

WML4 Group similar ideas together.

Before Teaching Umbrella 5 Minilessons

Help children build a habit of rereading their writing aloud (in a whisper voice) each day before they begin writing more. This will help them hear how their writing sounds and consider what to revise. It is not necessary to teach these minilessons consecutively. Instead, you might choose to teach them throughout the year as needed. Revision is a high-level concept and children will need multiple exposures to these lessons.

Children should know how to use headings, write more complex nonfiction texts, and use scissors before you teach WML4. Also give them plenty of opportunities to read texts that are organized with similar ideas grouped together and that may also use headings. If you decide to teach WML4 late in the year and you use *The Reading Minilessons Book, Grade 1* (Fountas and Pinnell 2019), refer to reading minilessons about grouping similar information together and using headings (LA.U12.RML3 and LA.U14.RML1).

WML1–WML3 use the same two pieces of related teacher writing to model the revising process for children. Also use the following texts from *Fountas & Pinnell Classroom™ Interactive Read-Aloud Collection* and *Shared Reading Collection*, or choose similar books from the classroom library.

Interactive Read-Aloud Collection

Learning and Working Together: School

> *First Day Jitters* by Julie Danneberg

Taking Care of Each Other: Family

> *Max and the Tag-Along Moon* by Floyd Cooper

Shared Reading Collection

> *Garden Helpers* by Charlotte Rose
>
> *How Animals Eat* by Mary Ebeltoft Reid

As you read aloud and enjoy these texts together, help children notice that

- the words and sentences on a page are connected to the same idea, and

- the pages in a book are in an order that makes sense.

Interactive Read-Aloud
School

Family

Shared Reading

Section 8: Writing Process

Writing Minilesson Principle
Cross out a word that does not fit or make sense.

Deleting and Organizing Writing

You Will Need

- chart paper prepared with the cover and several pages of a book you wrote in advance, with words that do not fit
- marker
- document camera (optional)
- To download the online resource for this lesson, visit **resources.fountasandpinnell.com**:
  - chart art (optional)

Academic Language / Important Vocabulary

- sentence
- reread
- make sense
- cross out
- fit
- fix

Continuum Connection

- Reread writing each day (and during writing on the same day) before continuing to write (p. 256)
- Reread writing to be sure the meaning is clear (p. 256)
- Delete words or sentences that do not make sense or don't fit the topic (p. 256)
- Delete text to better express meaning and make more logical (p. 256)
- Cross out words or sentences with pencil or marker (p. 257)

GOAL

Understand that writers cross out words that do not fit or make sense.

RATIONALE

When children understand that writers reread their writing and listen to make sure it makes sense, they learn to revise parts (by crossing out words) that do not fit or could be confusing to the reader.

ASSESS LEARNING

- Look for evidence that children reread their writing to determine whether it makes sense.
- Observe whether children are willing to reread their writing and make changes.
- Observe for evidence that children can use vocabulary such as *sentence*, *reread*, *make sense*, *cross out*, *fit*, and *fix*.

MINILESSON

To help children think about the minilesson principle, demonstrate rereading a piece of your own writing to determine if there are parts that do not make sense. Here is an example.

- Attach the cover and first page of your book to chart paper so that everyone can see it.

  > You know to reread your writing each day before you write more. Listen as I reread my writing. Does the writing make sense? Do all the words fit together? I will use a voice you can hear, but when you reread to yourself you will use a whisper voice.

- Read aloud the cover and first page, including the extraneous word.

  > Wait a minute. Something didn't sound quite right. Did you hear it? Listen again.

- Reread the sentence. Guide children to notice the word that does not make sense.

  > I have a word that doesn't fit. When that happens, I can just cross it out.

- Reread the sentence, modeling how you can cross out (not erase) the part you want to delete.

  > I drew one line through the word. I didn't erase it or scribble over it to make a mess or take more time. That way I can still see what the word was in case I want to think about it later.

- Read the sentence correctly, skipping the crossed-out word.

Have a Try

Invite children to use the same procedure to discuss the next two pages of your writing.

> Do all the words fit and make sense? Turn and talk to your partner about that.

▶ After time for a brief discussion, ask a volunteer for suggestions. Model how to cross out the word that does not make sense. Repeat with the next page.

▶ Save your book pages for WML2.

Summarize and Apply

Summarize the lesson. Remind children to reread their writing to make sure it makes sense.

> What should you do if you find a word that does not fit or make sense in your writing?

▶ Write the principle at the top of the chart.

> When you reread your writing, make sure all the parts fit. If you find that a word or even a whole sentence that doesn't make sense, draw one line through the word or the whole sentence.

Confer

▶ During independent writing, move around the room to confer briefly with as many individual children as time allows. Sit side by side with them and invite them to talk about finding and fixing any words that don't fit or make sense. Use the following prompts as needed.

- *Read this page aloud. Is there a word (sentence) that does not make sense? Draw a line through that word (sentence). Now reread it. Does it make sense?*

- *(If a child doesn't recognize an error) Listen as I read this part of your book aloud. What do you notice? Draw a line through that word. Now reread it. Does it make sense?*

Share

Following independent writing, gather children in the meeting area to share their writing. Not all children will have an example of having crossed out a word or sentence. Children may have difficulty reading a sentence with a crossed-out word. If so, read the child's writing, including errors. Then ask the child to reread the sentence correctly. Use a document camera, if available.

> Who would like to share your writing?

WML2

Writing Minilesson Principle
Take out a page that does not fit or make sense.

You Will Need

- a familiar book to model a well-written story, such as *Max and the Tag-Along Moon* by Floyd Cooper, from Text Set: Taking Care of Each Other: Family

- chart paper prepared with the book from WML1 and a new page that does not fit

- sticky note

- marker

- document camera (optional)

- To download the online resource for this lesson, visit **resources.fountasandpinnell.com**:
    - chart art (optional)

Academic Language / Important Vocabulary

- writing
- reread
- take out
- pages
- make sense

Continuum Connection

- Reread writing each day (and during writing on the same day) before continuing to write (p. 256)

- Reread writing to be sure the meaning is clear (p. 256)

- Delete pages when information is not needed (p. 256)

- Remove pages from a book or booklet (p. 257)

GOAL

Understand that writers remove pages that do not fit or make sense.

RATIONALE

When children understand that writers make sure each page of their writing communicates their ideas clearly, they learn to revise their own writing and delete pages that do not fit or make sense.

ASSESS LEARNING

- Look for evidence that children can determine if each page in their book fits with the other pages.

- Observe whether children understand how to remove pages of their own writing that do not make sense.

- Observe for evidence that children can use vocabulary such as *writing*, *reread*, *take out*, *pages*, and *make sense.*

MINILESSON

To help children think about the minilesson principle, read a familiar text and discuss how the pages all fit and make sense. If appropriate, model how to use a stapler and staple remover (see MGT.U3.WML4 and the extension activities for WPS.U4, one of which is related to using a staple remover). Here is a sample lesson.

- Show and read a few pages from *Max and the Tag-Along Moon*. Discuss how all of the pages relate to the topic of the whole book.

    What is this whole book about?

    All of the pages tell the story of Max's journey back home after visiting his grandfather. His grandfather tells him that the moon they see at Granpa's house is the same moon Max will see on his way home and at his home once he is back.

    When the author wrote this book he reread it to make sure all of the pages and illustrations fit and made sense. You can do this when you write, too.

The Writing Minilessons Book, Grade 1

Have a Try

Invite children to turn and talk about how to fix a page in a book that does not seem to make sense.

▶ Read each page of a book you attached to chart paper. Point under the words as you read them.

> Here's my book. Do all of the pages make sense together? Turn and talk about that.

▶ After time for a brief discussion, ask a child to indicate which page does not make sense. Remove the page or cover it with a sticky note indicating that it will be used elsewhere. Reread the book to show that it makes sense now.

> I am going to put the page that doesn't fit back in my writing folder. It could make a great page in another book, just not in this book.

Summarize and Apply

Summarize the lesson. Remind children to reread their writing and remove pages that do not fit or make sense.

▶ Write the principle at the top of the chart.

> During writing time, reread your writing to make sure all the pages make sense together. If they don't, use the staple remover to take out the page. Place it in your writing folder. Staple your book back together and continue writing.

Confer

▶ During independent writing, move around the room to confer briefly with as many individual children as time allows. Sit side by side with them and invite them to talk about whether they need to remove pages from their books. Use the following prompts as needed.

- *Your first page is about _____. This page is about _____. Do these pages fit together?*
- *You took that page out of your book. Why did you decide to do that?*
- *You can make a new book with the page you took out. What will the new book be about?*

Share

Following independent writing, gather children in the meeting area to share their writing. Use a document camera, if available, so that everyone can see the writing.

> Who found a page that did not make sense in your book? Share how you fixed it.

WML3

WPS.U5.WML3

Writing Minilesson Principle
Read your writing to make sure the order makes sense.

Deleting and Organizing Writing

You Will Need

- a familiar book to model a well-written story, such as *First Day Jitters* by Julie Danneberg, from Text Set: Learning and Working Together: School

- chart paper prepared with several pages of a book you wrote attached lightly and out of order

- marker and tape

- To download the online resource for this lesson, visit **resources.fountasandpinnell.com**:
  - chart art (optional)

Academic Language / Important Vocabulary

- writing
- reread
- make sense
- order

Continuum Connection

- Present ideas in a logical sequence (p. 254)

- Reread writing each day (and during writing on the same day) before continuing to write (p. 256)

- Reread writing to be sure the meaning is clear (p. 256)

- Rearrange and revise writing to better express meaning or make the text more logical (reorder drawings, reorder pages, cut and paste) (p. 257)

- Reorder pages by laying them out and reassembling them (p. 257)

- Reorganize and revise the writing to better express the writer's meaning or make the text more logical (p. 257)

GOAL

Understand that writers reread their writing to be sure the order makes sense.

RATIONALE

When you teach children to reread their writing to check that the order makes sense, they begin to see themselves as writers who have a responsibility for communicating clearly and meaningfully.

ASSESS LEARNING

- Look for evidence that children reread their own writing to determine if the order makes sense.

- Observe whether children are willing to reorder their writing to put pages in chronological order.

- Observe for evidence that children can use vocabulary such as *writing*, *reread*, *make sense*, and *order*.

MINILESSON

To help children think about the minilesson principle, read a familiar text and discuss how the order of events makes sense. Here is an example.

- Show and read a few representative pages that span across *First Day Jitters*. Help children notice that the author wrote the story in the order the events occurred. You may need to prompt children by asking what happened first, next, after that, and at the end.

  What happened in this story?

  First, she is in bed and doesn't want to get up to go to her new school. Next, they are in the car and she doesn't want to get out of the car. After that, we find out that she isn't a student at all. She is the teacher! At the end, she is introduced to her new class.

  Julie Danneberg, the author, thought about the order the story took place and put the pages in that order so the story would make sense to the reader and so the reader would be surprised. You can do this when you write, too.

Have a Try

Invite children to turn and talk about the order of the pages in your book.

> This is a book I wrote using the page that didn't fit in my other story. What do you notice about the order of the pages? Turn and talk about that.

▶ Read the pages aloud if needed. Allow time for a brief discussion.

> Turn and talk to your partner about how I can fix my book to put the pages in order.

▶ Show children how to reorder the pages. Read the book and ask a few children to talk about whether it makes sense now.

Summarize and Apply

Summarize the lesson. Remind children to reread their writing to make sure the pages are in the correct order.

▶ Write the principle at the top of the chart.

> During writing time, reread the book you are making to check that the pages are in the right order. If they are not in the right order, use the staple remover to take apart the pages. Lay them out in front of you so you can put them in the right order. Then use the stapler to put the book back together in the right order. If the pages are in the right order, you can keep working on your book.

Confer

▶ During independent writing, move around the room to confer briefly with as many individual children as time allows. Sit side by side with them and invite them to talk about checking the order of their pages. Use the following prompts as needed.

- *Does the order of the pages make sense with your story? How can you fix that?*
- *Reread your story to be sure it is in that order.*

Share

Following independent writing, gather children in the meeting area to share their writing. Use a document camera, if available.

> Did anyone reorder the pages in your book? Share how you fixed it.

Section 8: Writing Process

Writing Minilesson Principle
Group similar ideas together.

Deleting and Organizing Writing

You Will Need

- familiar nonfiction texts, with and without headings, such as the following from *Shared Reading Collection*:
  - *Garden Helpers* by Charlotte Rose
  - *How Animals Eat* by Mary Ebeltoft Reid
- chart paper prepared with a nonfiction book you wrote attached lightly to chart paper, one fact out of order
- marker, scissors, and tape
- To download the online resource for this lesson, visit **resources.fountasandpinnell.com**:
  - chart art (optional)

Academic Language / Important Vocabulary

- topic
- similar
- heading
- reread
- details

Continuum Connection

- Put together the related details on a topic in a text (p. 254)
- Tell one part, idea, or group of ideas on each page of a book (p. 254)
- Reread writing each day (and during writing on the same day) before continuing to write (p. 256)
- Reread writing to be sure the meaning is clear (p. 256)

GOAL

Organize writing so that similar ideas are grouped together.

RATIONALE

When you teach children to reread their writing to check that similar ideas are grouped together, they begin to see themselves as writers who have a responsibility for communicating clearly and meaningfully.

ASSESS LEARNING

- Look for evidence that children reread their own writing to evaluate if it makes sense.
- Observe whether children are willing to reorganize their writing.
- Observe for evidence that children can use vocabulary such as *topic*, *heading*, *details*, *similar*, and *reread*.

MINILESSON

To help children think about the minilesson principle, use familiar nonfiction texts with and without headings to discuss how the authors grouped similar ideas together. If possible, use a document camera so everyone can see the pages. Here is an example.

- Show a book that groups ideas using headings, such as *Garden Helpers*. Show and read pages 8–9, including the headings and labels. Discuss what the pages are about. Point to the headings and labels as children name them.

  Why do you think the author grouped all of these ideas together?

  These ideas are all about tomatoes and the insects that hurt them and help them. Another way we know that is because the author wrote a heading on this page, *Tomatoes*. Notice the details. She used pictures of tomatoes, too.

- Repeat this process with pages 10–11.

  Are these pages about tomatoes?

  These pages are about peppers. Why do you think the author grouped these ideas together on a different set of pages?

  Authors reread their writing to check that similar ideas are grouped together.

- Repeat this process with a book that does not use headings, such as *How Animals Eat*. Show and read pages 4–5.

  There are no headings in this book. These ideas are all about apes, so the author grouped all of the ideas about apes together on these pages.

- Repeat this process with pages 6–7.

Have a Try

Invite children to turn and talk about whether similar ideas are grouped together in your writing.

> This is a nonfiction book I wrote about whales. What are these pages about? Do the ideas on each page belong there? Turn and talk about that.

▶ After time for a brief discussion, ask a child to identify the sentence out of place.

> How I can fix the writing to make sure similar ideas are grouped together? Turn and talk to your partner.

▶ Circle the sentence. Then cut the text and tape it on the correct page. Reread the book and ask a few children whether it makes sense now.

Summarize and Apply

Add the principle to the top of the chart to summarize the lesson. Remind children to reread their writing.

> During writing time, reread the book you are making to check that similar ideas are grouped together. If your book doesn't have headings, you can still make sure you have similar ideas together. If you find an idea you want to move, circle it. Use the scissors to cut it out. Then tape the writing where it belongs in your book.

Confer

▶ During independent writing, move around the room to confer briefly with as many individual children as time allows. Sit side by side with them and invite them to talk about organizing their writing. Use the following prompts as needed.

- *Listen to find out if similar ideas are grouped together. If not, how can you fix it?*
- *What kind of information do you want to have with the heading on this page?*
- *What heading could you write on this page?*

Share

Following independent writing, gather children in the meeting area to share their writing. If only a few children reordered their writing, ask individual children to share what they did to be sure that similar ideas were grouped together. Use a document camera, if available.

> Did anyone reorder the ideas in your book? Talk about that.

Assessment

After you have taught the minilessons in this umbrella, observe children as they draw, write, and talk about their writing. Use *The Literacy Continuum* (Fountas and Pinnell 2017) to notice, teach for, and support children's learning as you observe their attempts at drawing and writing.

- What evidence do you have of new understandings children have developed related to drafting and revising writing?
  - Are children building the habit of rereading their writing before they write more?
  - Do they notice words that do not fit and cross them out?
  - Are they willing to remove a page from their writing?
  - Do they understand how to reorder pages?
  - Do they group similar ideas together under headings?
  - Are they using vocabulary such as *writing, words, pages, reread, make sense, order, fix,* and *fit*?
- In what ways, beyond the scope of this umbrella, are children taking part in the writing process?
  - Are they writing different kinds of books?
  - Do they include illustrations in their nonfiction?

Use your observations to determine the next umbrella you will teach. You may also consult Suggested Sequence of Lessons (pp. 557–571) for guidance.

EXTENSIONS FOR DELETING AND ORGANIZING WRITING

- Gather together a guided writing group of several children who need support in a specific aspect of writing, such as deleting parts that do not fit or reorganizing parts that are out of order.

- Reteach WML2 as children write all-about books and how-to books.

- Reteach WML3 as children write how-to books.

Minilessons in This Umbrella

WML1 Make sure there is space between your words.

WML2 Make sure your letters are easy to read.

WML3 Make sure you wrote the words you know correctly.

Before Teaching Umbrella 6 Minilessons

The goal of this umbrella is to help children understand how to edit and proofread their own writing. A basic checklist for proofreading will be built as a chart across the three minilessons to model for children how to use their own checklists (available from the online resources). Decide whether you will have children use the proofreading checklist during these minilessons or after the minilessons have been presented. Children should keep the proofreading checklist in their writing folders. Fasten it inside the folder along with other reference tools, such as a personal word list.

Before teaching these lessons, make sure children have had many experiences writing and reading their work. It would be helpful to have taught minilessons about conventions (CNV.U1–CNV.U5) and the writing process (WPS.U1–WPS.U5). Use a variety of familiar mentor texts as examples to show that authors edit and proofread their work. Include samples of class-made writing as well as examples from the *Fountas & Pinnell Classroom™ Shared Reading Collection*. Some suggestions are below.

Shared Reading Collection

Squawk by Nicole Walker

Captain Brock, Firefighter by Andrea Delbanco

The Hungry Fly by Hannah Cales

Interactive Writing Lessons

IW.8: Writing a Memory Story

IW.14: Writing an All-About Book

As you read and enjoy these books, help children notice

- space between words, and

- print that is correct and can be read.

Shared Reading

Interactive Writing

Section 8: Writing Process

Writing Minilesson Principle
Make sure there is space between your words.

Proofreading Writing

You Will Need

- several familiar books that show clear spacing between words, such as the following:
  - *Squawk* by Nicole Walker and *Captain Brock, Firefighter* by Andrea Delbanco, from *Shared Reading Collection*
- class writing from IW.14: Writing an All-About Book or other class writing
- chart paper and markers
- highlighting tape (optional)
- children's writing (one per child or pair of children)
- To download the following online resource for this lesson, visit **resources.fountasandpinnell.com**:
  - Proofreading Checklist (optional)

Academic Language / Important Vocabulary

- writing
- proofread
- space
- between
- words

Continuum Connection

- Use space between words (p. 254)
- Understand that the more accurate the spelling and the clearer the space between words, the easier it is for the reader to read it (p. 257)
- Cross out words or sentences with pencil or marker (p. 257)

GOAL

Reread writing to check for space between words so the reader can understand the message.

RATIONALE

When children learn to edit their work by checking the space between words, they understand that their writing needs to be understood by the reader. They also gain independence and confidence in their own writing.

ASSESS LEARNING

- Look for evidence that children understand that writers proofread their writing.
- Observe whether children are proofreading work by checking the space between words.
- Observe for evidence that children can use vocabulary such as *writing*, *proofread*, *space*, *between*, and *words*.

MINILESSON

To help children learn to proofread their work, provide examples of mentor texts with proper spacing between words and lines. We recommend using enlarged texts or a document camera so that everyone can see the text clearly. Decide whether children will start using a checklist now or after you have taught the minilessons in this umbrella. Here is an example lesson.

- Show and read sentences from several familiar books, such as *Squawk* and *Captain Brock, Firefighter*. Point under each word as you read.

  Take a look at the words as I read them. How can you tell where one word ends and the next word begins?

- Guide the conversation to help children notice the space between words and between lines. Emphasize the space with highlighter tape or ask two or three children to point to the space.

- Show the class-made writing from IW.14 and read the text.

  Is there space between the words and the lines we wrote in this book? Who can point to a space?

  How does space between words and lines help the reader?

  When you do your own writing, proofread to make sure you put space between the words and lines so that your reader will understand what you wrote.

- Begin a proofreading checklist on chart paper. Show children how to make a check mark in the box after they proofread their writing.

Have a Try

Invite children to turn and talk about proofreading their own work.

▶ Give children a sample of their writing (or one sample per pair).

> Look at the writing. Turn and tell your partner if there are any words that need better space between them and how you could fix the problem.

▶ Refer to the chart to remind children to cross out the words that are not properly spaced and rewrite them clearly above.

▶ Save the chart for WML2.

Summarize and Apply

Summarize the lesson. Remind children to check word spacing when they proofread their writing.

> Today you learned to proofread by checking for space between words. When you are writing today, check for space between words by reading what you have written. Bring your writing to share when we meet later.

> ### Proofreading Checklist
>
> ☑ Make sure there is space between your words.
>
> to the
>
> ~~tothe~~

Confer

▶ During independent writing, move around the room to confer briefly with as many individual children as time allows. Sit side by side with them and invite them to talk about proofreading their writing. Use the following prompts as needed.

- *Show how you check to make sure there is space between each word (line).*
- *Take a look at this sentence. Is there a space between all the words?*
- *How can you fix these words that are too close together?*
- *You proofread your work. Show how you put a check mark in the box.*

Share

Following independent writing, gather children in the meeting area to share their writing.

> Who would like to share your writing?

> When you proofread your writing, did you check for space between words in your writing and fix any that were too close together? Talk about what you did.

WML2

Writing Minilesson Principle
Make sure your letters are easy to read.

Proofreading Writing

You Will Need

▸ class-made book from IW.8: Writing a Memory Story or other class writing

▸ chart from WML1

▸ markers

▸ children's writing (one per child or pair of children)

▸ To download the following online resource for this lesson, visit **resources.fountasandpinnell.com**:

  ▪ Proofreading Checklist (optional)

Academic Language / Important Vocabulary

▸ writing

▸ proofread

▸ letters

Continuum Connection

▸ Form upper- and lowercase letters efficiently in manuscript print (p. 255)

▸ Form upper- and lowercase letters proportionately in manuscript print (p. 255)

▸ Check and correct letter formation or orientation (p. 257)

▸ Cross out words or sentences with pencil or marker (p. 257)

GOAL

Reread writing to check for correct letter formation and orientation so the reader can understand the message.

RATIONALE

When children understand that letter formation is important because it allows the reader to understand what they have written, they begin to pay attention to the legibility of their writing.

ASSESS LEARNING

▸ Observe children when they write. Do they proofread, or check, their work?

▸ Notice whether children check for correct letter formation and orientation when proofreading their work.

▸ Observe for evidence that children can use vocabulary such as *writing*, *proofread*, and *letters*.

MINILESSON

To help children learn to proofread, or check, their work, provide examples of mentor texts with proper letter formation and orientation. Model how writing can be corrected when letters are not formed properly. Decide whether children will start using a checklist now or after you have taught the minilessons in this umbrella. Here is an example lesson.

▸ Show the class writing from IW.8.

  What do you notice about how the letters are written?

▸ Guide the conversation to help children notice that the letters are written so that they are easy to read and they go from left to right.

  When you do your own writing, make your letters the best that you can so that your reader will understand what you wrote. When you proofread your writing, check to make sure that your letters are clear and easy to read.

▸ Add to the proofreading checklist you began in WML1.

▸ Show children how to cross out the word, and then rewrite it above instead of erasing.

The Writing Minilessons Book, Grade 1

Have a Try

Invite children to turn and talk about proofreading their writing.

▶ Give children a sample of their writing (or one sample per pair).

> Look at the writing. Turn and tell your partner about any letters that should be fixed and how you can fix them.

▶ Refer to the chart to remind children to cross out the word that has a letter that could be made better and rewrite it clearly above.

▶ Save the chart for WML3.

Summarize and Apply

Summarize the lesson. Remind children to proofread their writing.

> During writing time, read your writing to make sure that you have written each letter so that it is easy to read. If you find a letter that needs to be fixed, cross the word out neatly and write the word above. Bring your writing to share when we meet later.

Proofreading Checklist

☑ Make sure there is space between your words.

☑ Make sure your letters are easy to read.

to the

~~tothe~~

see

~~see~~

Confer

▶ During independent writing, move around the room to confer briefly with as many individual children as time allows. Sit side by side with them and invite them to talk about proofreading their writing. Use the following prompts as needed.

- *Are there any letters that you could write differently so a reader can read them better?*
- *Where can you look to know how to make a letter?*
- *Show how you can fix this letter.*
- *Show how you used the proofreading checklist.*

Share

Following independent writing, gather children in the meeting area. Have them bring their writing from today.

> Who would like to share your writing?

> Did you fix any letters after you proofread your writing? Show what you did.

Proofreading Writing

You Will Need

- a book with familiar high-frequency words, such as the following:
  - *The Hungry Fly* by Hannah Cales, from *Shared Reading Collection*
- chart paper and markers
- To download the online resources for this lesson visit **resources.fountasandpinnell.com**:
  - High-Frequency Word List
  - Proofreading Checklist (optional)

Academic Language / Important Vocabulary

- writing
- words
- proofread
- spelling

Continuum Connection

- Understand that a writer uses what is known to spell words (p. 257)
- Understand that the more accurate the spelling and the clearer the space between words, the easier it is for the reader to read it (p. 257)
- Edit for spelling errors by making another attempt (p. 257)
- Notice words that do not look right and spell by saying them slowly to represent as much of the word as possible (p. 257)
- Cross out words or sentences with pencil or marker (p. 257)

GOAL

Reread writing to check for correct spelling so the reader can understand the message.

RATIONALE

When children learn to proofread by checking for misspelled words, they understand that it is the writer's responsibility to spell words they know correctly.

ASSESS LEARNING

- Observe children when they write. Do they proofread their writing?
- Notice evidence that children proofread their work by making sure that the words they know are spelled correctly.
- Observe for evidence that children can use vocabulary such as *writing*, *proofread*, *words*, and *spelling*.

MINILESSON

To help children learn to proofread their work, display mentor texts with examples of proper spellings of words that the children know. Model how writing can be corrected when words they know are spelled incorrectly. Decide whether children will start using a checklist now or after you have taught the minilessons in this umbrella. Here is an example lesson.

- Show the cover of *The Hungry Fly*. Read the title and page 5.

  There are some words you know on this page. What words do you know?

- Help children notice familiar words that are spelled correctly.

  You know the words *she* and *it*. Notice that they are spelled here the same way you would spell them. That's how you know what those words are.

- Guide the conversation to help children understand that words are spelled the same way each time they are written.

  When you do your own writing, it's important to write the words you know correctly so that your reader will understand what you wrote.

- Make sure children understand to cross out (not erase) the word and then rewrite it above.

  When you proofread your writing and find a word that you think is not written correctly, where can you look to check the spelling?

- Remind children to look at the word wall, personal word list, or another source.

- Add to the proofreading checklist from WML2.

Have a Try

Invite children to turn and talk about how to correct their spelling.

▶ Give children a sample of their writing (or one sample per pair).

> Look at the writing. Turn and tell your partner about a word you know that needs to be fixed. How can you fix it?

▶ After time for a brief discussion, ask a few volunteers to share how they can fix any words that are misspelled.

Summarize and Apply

Summarize the lesson. Remind children to proofread their writing and to check off the items on the checklist as they do them.

> Today you learned to proofread by checking to make sure the words you know are spelled correctly. During writing time, check for spelling by reading what you have written. Bring your writing to share when we meet later.

Proofreading Checklist

☑ Make sure there is space between your words.

to the

~~tothe~~

☑ Make sure your letters are easy to read.

see

~~see~~

☑ Make sure you wrote the words you know correctly.

was

~~wuz~~

Confer

▶ During independent writing, move around the room to confer briefly with as many individual children as time allows. Sit side by side with them and invite them to talk about proofreading their writing. Use the following prompts as needed.

- *Read this sentence to make sure the words you know are spelled correctly.*
- *What do you notice about this sentence?*
- *How can you fix the spelling of this word?*
- *Show how you used the proofreading checklist.*

Share

Following independent writing, gather children in the meeting area. Have them bring their writing from today.

> Who would like to share your writing?

> When you proofread, did you find any words that were not spelled correctly? Show what you did to fix them.

Assessment

After you have taught the minilessons in this umbrella, observe children as they write. Use *The Literacy Continuum* (Fountas and Pinnell 2017) to notice, teach for, and support children's learning as you observe their attempts at reading and writing.

> ▶ What evidence do you have of new understandings children have developed related to proofreading?
>
> > • Are children checking for space between words and correcting errors by crossing out and rewriting?
> >
> > • Are they able to proofread to make sure that they have made letters the best they can?
> >
> > • Do they proofread to make sure that the words they know are spelled correctly?
> >
> > • Are they using vocabulary such as *writing*, *proofread*, *space*, *between*, *words*, *letters*, and *spelling*?
>
> ▶ In what ways, beyond the scope of this umbrella, are children taking part in the writing process?
>
> > • Do they reread their work to add and delete information?

Use your observations to determine the next umbrella you will teach. You may also consult Suggested Sequence of Lessons (pp. 557–571) for guidance.

EXTENSIONS FOR PROOFREADING WRITING

▶ Have children add other things to check to the proofreading checklist, such as correct use of capital letters and punctuation.

▶ Gather together a guided writing group of several children who need extra support in proofreading their writing.

▶ Revisit CNV.U3: Using Classroom Resources to Write Words. Reinforce that children can use the name chart, the word wall, and their personal word lists to help with proofreading.

▶ From time to time when you are using big books, ask children to point out the space between words and lines.

Minilessons in This Umbrella

WML1 Get ready to share a book or poem you want to celebrate.

WML2 Make your book or poem ready for others to read.

WML3 Celebrate something new you tried.

Before Teaching Umbrella 7 Minilessons

We recommend teaching MBK.U2: Expanding Bookmaking before teaching the minilessons in this umbrella. It would also be helpful for you to make a simple book to use for demonstrating this umbrella's principles.

The purpose of the minilessons in this umbrella is to prepare children to choose pieces they are proud of to publish and share. Some ways that children can share their books include reading them aloud to the whole class or a small group, inviting the children's parents or guardians to a class celebration in which children share their books, or sharing with another classroom or grade level. Some children might enjoy "publishing" their work by typing it on a computer, with an adult's help. However, we recommend that this process be reserved for special occasions, as children's work should generally speak for itself. We want children's writing to look like children's writing!

As you read aloud and enjoy books together, help children

- be aware of how you read aloud to them (look at them, speak so they can understand), and

- talk about how authors make their books ready for others to read.

WML1

WPS.U7.WML1

Writing Minilesson Principle
Get ready to share a book or poem you want to celebrate.

Celebrating Writing

You Will Need

▶ a book that you have made as an example

▶ chart paper and markers

Academic Language/ Important Vocabulary

▶ book

▶ poem

▶ celebrate

▶ share

▶ read

Continuum Connection

▶ Select best pieces of writing from own collection (p. 257)

▶ Share a text with peers by reading it aloud to the class (p. 257)

▶ When finished with a piece of writing, talk about it to others (p. 257)

GOAL

Choose books to celebrate and prepare to share with an audience.

RATIONALE

Before children can share their work with an audience, they must first choose which piece to share and then practice sharing it. This lesson helps them think about the criteria they can use to evaluate their work. When children think carefully about choosing pieces, they are more likely to select work that they are truly proud of and confident about sharing.

ASSESS LEARNING

▶ Listen to children's reasons for choosing pieces to celebrate.

▶ Notice whether children read aloud their work in a consistent manner.

▶ Look for evidence that children can use vocabulary such as *book*, *poem*, *celebrate*, *share*, and *read*.

MINILESSON

To help children think about the minilesson principle, share why you have chosen to celebrate a particular book and help them generate a list of criteria for evaluating pieces to share. Here is an example.

> You have written many wonderful books and poems this year. Sometimes you might want to celebrate a special piece of writing by sharing it.

▶ Display the example book that you prepared.

> This is a book that I wrote and illustrated and that I'd like to share with you. I'm very proud of it! I worked hard on it, and I reread my writing carefully to make sure that it shows my best work. It's about a topic that is important to me, and I think other people will be interested, too.

> What do you notice about why I chose this book to celebrate?

▶ Use children's responses to begin a list of how to get ready for sharing a piece of writing.

> Now that I've chosen what book I want to share, I need to get ready to share it. I will get ready by practicing reading it aloud. Watch how I read it.

▶ Read a few pages of the book aloud.

> What are these pages of my book about?

> If I were to read these pages to you again tomorrow, would I say the same things?

> I will read it the same way each time I read it aloud because the words and the pictures are always the same. To get ready to share your book with someone, practice reading it the same way each time.

Have a Try

Invite children to talk to a partner about a book or poem they would like to celebrate.

> Think about the books or poems you have written lately. Which one would you like to celebrate by sharing with other people? Why? Turn and talk to your partner about your reasons.
>
> Now talk about how you will get ready to share it.

Summarize and Apply

Write the principle at the top of the chart. Summarize the learning and invite children to get ready to share a book or poem they want to celebrate.

> Today you learned about how to choose a book or poem to celebrate and how to get ready to share it. During writing time today, think more about which book or poem you'd like to celebrate and practice sharing it.

> Get ready to share a book or poem you want to celebrate.
>
> - Choose a book or poem that makes you proud.
>
> - Make sure your writing shows your best work.
>
> - Read it the same way each time.

Confer

▶ During independent writing, move around the classroom to confer briefly with as many individual children as time allows. Sit side by side with them and invite them to evaluate their books/poems and practice sharing them. Use prompts such as the following as needed.

- *Which book makes you feel proud? Why?*
- *What do you like about this poem?*
- *Can you explain why you chose this book to celebrate?*
- *How should you read aloud your book to others?*

Share

Following independent writing, gather children in the meeting area to share their writing.

> Who would like to share a book or poem?
>
> Why are you proud of that book (poem)?

Writing Minilesson Principle
Make your book or poem ready for others to read.

Celebrating Writing

You Will Need

- an example book that has been typed and printed and has a cardboard cover
  - a typed poem that has been framed or mounted
  - chart paper and markers
- To download the following online resource for this lesson, visit **resources.fountasandpinnell.com**:
  - chart art (optional)

Academic Language/ Important Vocabulary

- type
- computer
- label
- cover
- title
- author

Continuum Connection

- Select a poem, story, or informational book to publish in a variety of appropriate ways: e.g., typed/printed, framed and mounted or otherwise displayed (p. 257)
- When finished with a piece of writing, talk about it to others (p. 257)

GOAL

Learn different ways to "publish" a piece of writing and make it accessible to others.

RATIONALE

When you teach children different ways to make their writing accessible to others, they begin to understand that writing is a process that may involve several steps beyond writing the words and drawing the pictures. They also begin to conceptualize the idea of writing not just for themselves, but also for an audience.

ASSESS LEARNING

- Observe what children do to make their books and poems ready for others to read.
- Notice whether children experiment with different ways of making their writing accessible to others (e.g., adding a cover, framing or mounting a poem).
- Look for evidence that children can use vocabulary such as *type, computer, label, cover, title,* and *author.*

MINILESSON

To help children think about the minilesson principle, engage them in a discussion about different ways to make their books and poems accessible to other people. Here is an example.

- Display the example book you prepared and draw attention to the cover.

  What do you notice about my book?

  I put a cardboard cover on my book so that it won't tear easily. I am proud of my book and I want to keep it safe. What did I write on the cover?

  The cover helps readers know what the book is about and who the author is.

  What could I add to the illustrations in my book to help readers learn more about the topic?

  I could add labels to my illustrations.

- Read aloud the author page and dedication, if applicable, and ask children what they notice.

- Add to the chart as you discuss each way of getting work ready to share.

- Display the framed or mounted poem.

  How did I get my poem ready for others to read?

  I typed my poem and put it on a piece of construction paper to make it look nice.

- Children are not expected to type their own stories or poems. An adult should assist.

Have a Try

Invite children to talk to a partner about how they would like to make their books and poems ready for others to read.

> Think about a special book or poem that you would like to share. How would you like to get it ready for others to read? Turn and talk to your partner about this.

Summarize and Apply

Write the principle at the top of the chart to summarize the learning. Remind children to think about different ways of making their books or poems ready for others to read.

> Today we talked about different things you can do to make your books and poems ready for others to read. During writing time, I would like you to get one of your books or poems ready to share. I can help you.

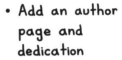

Make your book or poem ready for others to read.

- Add a cardboard cover.

- Write the title and author.

- Add labels to the illustrations.

Cactus

- Add an author page and dedication  To my family.

- Type it.

- Frame it.

Confer

> During independent writing, move around the room to confer briefly with as many individual children as time allows. Sit side by side with them and invite them to talk about preparing their writing to share. Use prompts such as the following as needed.
>
> - *What are you going to do to get your book/poem ready for people to read?*
> - *Would you like to have your poem typed?*
> - *Where on the page will you put the words? Where will you put the illustration? Why?*
> - *Would you like to add a dedication to your book? What will the dedication say?*

Share

Following independent writing, gather children in the meeting area to talk about getting books ready to read.

> Who would like to share the book/poem you worked on today?
>
> What did you do to get your book/poem ready for others to read?

Writing Minilesson Principle
Celebrate something new you tried.

Celebrating Writing

You Will Need

▸ several examples of children's work that show something new the writer tried (e.g., speech bubbles, rhyming words, collage)

▸ chart paper and markers

▸ To download the following online resource for this lesson, visit **resources.fountasandpinnell.com**:

  ▪ chart art (optional)

Academic Language/ Important Vocabulary

▸ celebrate

▸ book

▸ poem

Continuum Connection

▸ Self-evaluate writing and talk about what is good about it and what techniques were used (p. 257)

GOAL

Identify and celebrate trying new writing techniques.

RATIONALE

Encouraging children to share the new things they have tried in their writing makes it more likely that other children will try similar things. Identifying the risks children have taken in their writing makes that writing worth celebrating!

ASSESS LEARNING

▸ Observe children's attempts at trying something new in their writing and illustrating.

▸ Notice whether children identify and celebrate new writing or illustrating techniques they have tried.

▸ Look for evidence that children can use vocabulary such as *celebrate*, *book*, and *poem*.

MINILESSON

To help children think about the minilesson principle, engage them in talking about trying new techniques in their writing and illustrating. Here is an example.

▸ Display one of the examples of children's work that you selected before class.

  _____ worked very hard on this poem. She tried something new in this poem. What did you try, _____ ?

▸ Record the example on chart paper.

▸ Continue sharing examples of new things that children have tried in their writing and illustrating. Add words and/or sketches to the chart to represent them.

Have a Try

Invite children to talk to a partner about something new they have tried in their writing or illustrating.

> Turn and talk to your partner about something new you have tried recently in your writing or illustrations.

> ▶ After children turn and talk, ask several volunteers to share with the class. Add any new ideas to the chart.

Summarize and Apply

Write the principle at the top of the chart to summarize the learning. Remind children to celebrate new techniques they have tried.

> Today during writing time, spend some more time thinking about new things you have tried in your writing or illustrations. If you are proud of something new you tried, you might want to choose that piece to celebrate by sharing with others.

Confer

> ▶ During independent writing, move around the room to confer briefly with as many individual children as time allows. Sit side by side with them and invite them to talk about something new they tried in their writing. Use prompts such as the following if needed.

> • *What new thing did you try in your book/poem? How do you feel about that?*

> • *You tried collage for the first time in this book. Would you like to celebrate this book with others?*

> • *Which piece of writing would you like to share? Why?*

Share

Following independent writing, gather children in the meeting area to share the new things they tried in their writing.

> Who would like to share something new you tried in your writing or illustrating?

Assessment

After you have taught the minilessons in this umbrella, observe children as they draw, write, and talk about their writing. Use the behaviors and understandings in *The Literacy Continuum* (Fountas and Pinnell 2017) to notice, teach for, and support children's attempts at drawing and writing.

▶ What evidence do you have of new understandings children have developed related to celebrating writing?

  • Do children celebrate their books and poems with an audience?

  • Do they read their writing the same way and accurately each time?

  • How do they make their books and poems ready for others to read?

  • What new writing and illustrating techniques have they tried?

  • Do they understand and use vocabulary such as *book*, *poem*, *share*, and *celebrate*?

▶ In what other ways, beyond the scope of this umbrella, are children exploring the writing process?

  • Are they revising, editing, and proofreading their writing?

Use your observations to determine the next umbrella you will teach. You may also consult Suggested Sequence of Lessons (pp. 557–571) for guidance.

EXTENSIONS FOR CELEBRATING WRITING

▶ Help children identify and talk about different text features in published books (e.g., title page, table of contents, glossary). Invite them to add the same features to their own books (see CFT.U7: Adding Text Features to Books).

▶ Dedicate a section of the classroom library or area of the school (e.g., hallway or lobby) to displaying and celebrating children's own books.

▶ Teach children how to put books or stories together into an anthology or collection.

Appendix:
Suggested Sequence of Lessons

The Suggested Sequence of Lessons is also available in the Fountas & Pinnell Online Resources site (**resources.fountasandpinnell.com**).

Suggested Sequence of Lessons

This sequence shows when you might teach the interactive writing lessons and writing minilessons across the year. It also aligns these lessons with the texts from *Fountas & Pinnell Classroom™ Shared Reading Collection* and *Interactive Read-Aloud Collection*, as well as the reading minilesson umbrellas from *The Reading Minilessons Book, Grade 1*. You do not need these other resources to teach the lessons in this book, but this comprehensive sequence helps you see how all these pieces can fit together and think about how you might organize reading and writing across the year. Note that the number of days refers to approximately how long it will take to teach the lessons. It does not indicate how long your students might spend applying new ideas or experimenting with new kinds of writing.

Suggested Sequence of Lessons

Months	Texts from *Fountas & Pinnell Classroom™ Shared Reading Collection*	Text Sets from *Fountas & Pinnell Classroom™ Interactive Read-Aloud Collection*	Reading Minilessons (RML) Umbrellas	Interactive Writing (IW) Lessons*	Writing Minilessons (WML) Umbrellas	Teaching Notes
Months 1 & 2	Monster ABCs The Elephant The Hippo The Giraffe The Flamingo In My Bag Silly and Fun: Poems to Make You Smile	Learning and Working Together: School	MGT.U1: Working Together in the Classroom MGT.U2: Using the Classroom Library for Independent Reading	**IW.1: Making a Name Chart (1 day)** **IW.2: Writing About Our Classroom (1 day)** **IW.3: Labeling the Classroom (1–3 days)** **IW.4: Writing from a Picture (1 day)**	**MGT.U1: Working Together in the Classroom, WML1–WML5 (5 days)**	If you are using *The Reading Minilessons Book, Grade 1*, you do not need to teach MGT.U1. Both RML and WML establish the same routines. However, be sure to take time to build community in your classroom by asking children to draw and write about themselves as they practice these new routines. The opening page of the writing minilessons umbrella MGT.U1 provides specific suggestions. IW.2 can be taught as a culminating activity. Teach IW.3 in conjunction with RML.MGT.U2.

*Interactive writing lessons can be taught on the same day as a writing minilesson or in place of a writing minilesson.

Key

MGT: Management   STR: Telling Stories   MBK: Making Books   DRW: Drawing
CFT: Craft   CNV: Conventions   WPS: Writing Process

Months	Texts from *Fountas & Pinnell Classroom*™ *Shared Reading Collection*	Text Sets from *Fountas & Pinnell Classroom*™ *Interactive Read-Aloud Collection*	Reading Minilessons (RML) Umbrellas	Interactive Writing (IW) Lessons*	Writing Minilessons (WML) Umbrellas	Teaching Notes
Months 1 & 2 (cont.)	Rain, Sun, Wind, Snow: Poems About the Seasons	Having Fun with Language: Rhyming Texts	MGT.U3: Engaging in Classroom Literacy Work, RML1–RML4, RML10	IW.5: Innovating on a Rhyming Text (1 day)	STR.U1: Learning About Self and Others Through Storytelling, WML1–WML2 (2 days)	STR.U1 helps children get to know one another and build classroom community while allowing them to orally rehearse their stories before writing. Teach the minilessons in STR.U1 over time so that children have more time to tell stories. Provide time each day for children to tell stories while you teach the next few writing umbrellas.
	Creep, Crawl, Fly: Poems About Bugs					
	The Big Mix-Up	The Importance of Friendship		IW.6: Making a Story Map (1–2 days)	MGT.U1: Working Together in the Classroom, WML6–WML9 (4 days)	WML.MGT.U1 provides specific examples for how to encourage children to share who they are. The lessons in RML.WAR.U1 also provide ways for children to write about themselves, their family, their friends, things they like to do in school and out of school. This writing can be revisited over time to inspire other writing ideas.
	The Big, Green, Scary Monster					
	Tap, Tap, Tappity-Tap!	Taking Care of Each Other: Family	LA.U1: Thinking and Talking About Books		MGT.U3: Using Drawing and Writing Tools (4 days)	Children can apply these minilessons while making books. You may want to wait to teach WML3 (Choose your paper) along with MBK.U1: Getting Started Making Books because paper choice can impact the layout of a book.
	Clippity Clop					
	Not Now!				DRW.U1: Making a Self-Portrait (2 days)	Teach DRW.U1 before IW.7 so you can use children's self-portraits in the class big book.
	The Right Spot		WAR.U1: Introducing a Reader's Notebook	IW.7: Writing About Who We Are (5–7 days)	MBK.U1: Getting Started with Making Books (5 days)	Invite and encourage children to make books about anything they want. Suggest that they draw and write stories they have been sharing orally. The class writing from IW.5 and IW.7 can be used to model bookmaking.

The Writing Minilessons Book, Grade 1

Months	Texts from *Fountas & Pinnell Classroom™ Shared Reading Collection*	Text Sets from *Fountas & Pinnell Classroom™ Interactive Read-Aloud Collection*	Reading Minilessons (RML) Umbrellas	Interactive Writing (IW) Lessons*	Writing Minilessons (WML) Umbrellas	Teaching Notes
Months 1 & 2 (cont.)	The Broken Ladder The Strawberry Hunt Lots of Snow	Kevin Henkes: Exploring Characters		**IW.8: Writing a Memory Story (1–2 days)**	**MGT.U2: Establishing Independent Writing (7 days)**	Once children are comfortable with the routine of making books at an established time of day, it will be easy to establish the routines of independent writing. We suggest introducing MGT.U2 after children have had time to experiment with bookmaking so they understand one way to use their time during independent writing.
			LA.U2: Studying Authors and Illustrators, RML1	**IW.9: Studying an Author's Writing (1–2 days)**		Interactively write about the characteristics of Kevin Henkes's writing in IW.9. Use this lesson in conjunction with LA.U2.RML1 or in its place. You can also repeat this lesson to write about the characteristics of his illustrations.
					CNV.U1: Using Good Handwriting (3 days)	Repeat the lessons in this umbrella as needed across the year.
					STR.U1: Learning About Self and Others Through Storytelling, WML3–WML4 (2 days)	The remaining minilessons in this umbrella will infuse new life into the storytelling happening in your classroom. The stories children tell as part of these lessons become resources for making books.
					WPS.U2: Getting Ideas for Writing (3 days)	The minilessons in this umbrella can be taught all at once or one at a time over the course of the year. Consider revisiting WPS.U2 whenever children need support generating ideas. Children choose their topics as well as the kind of writing they will do during independent writing.
			LA.U19: Understanding Characters and Their Feelings		**MGT.U4: Introducing Writing Folder Resources (3 days)**	Introduce writing folder resources whenever you think children will find them helpful. Children are more likely to use the resources once they are comfortable with the routines of independent writing and bookmaking.

Months	Texts from *Fountas & Pinnell Classroom™ Shared Reading Collection*	Text Sets from *Fountas & Pinnell Classroom™ Interactive Read-Aloud Collection*	Reading Minilessons (RML) Umbrellas	Interactive Writing (IW) Lessons*	Writing Minilessons (WML) Umbrellas	Teaching Notes
Months 1 & 2 (cont.)					**CNV.U2: Learning How to Write Words (5 days)**	Teach this umbrella all at once or teach each lesson based on need. Revisit the minilessons later in the year as needed.
					STR.U2: Learning How to Present Ideas (4 days)	STR.U2 will support children as they continue to tell their stories orally. The last two lessons in STR.U2 help them start thinking about how they will structure their ideas when they begin to write.
Months 3 & 4	Splash, Plop, Leap! Woof! Woof! Boomer's Checkup Scram!	Using Numbers: Books with Counting Exploring Fiction and Nonfiction	WAR.U3: Writing About Fiction Books in a Reader's Notebook, RML1–RML3 LA.U4: Getting Started With Book Clubs SAS.U1: Monitoring, Searching, and Self-Correcting LA.U5: Studying Fiction and Nonfiction	Revisit **IW.8: Writing a Memory Story (1–2 days)**	**DRW.U2: Learning to Draw (5 days)**	The five lessons in DRW.U2 support children in making representational drawings as well as in learning new drawing techniques.
						We recommend revisiting IW.8 and interactively writing a few class memory stories before teaching MBK.U3 to give children a rich background in composing memory stories before writing them independently.
					MBK.U3: Making Memory Books (5 days)	Use the class writing from IW.8 as a mentor text in MBK.U3. Encourage children to revisit stories they have told to get ideas for their memory books (STR.U1). Invite children to write several memory books over a couple of weeks.
					CFT.U1: Writing with Details (3 days)	Children can apply the minilessons in CFT.U1 to their memory books.

Suggested Sequence of Lessons (cont.)

Months	Texts from *Fountas & Pinnell Classroom™ Shared Reading Collection*	Text Sets from *Fountas & Pinnell Classroom™ Interactive Read-Aloud Collection*	Reading Minilessons (RML) Umbrellas	Interactive Writing (IW) Lessons*	Writing Minilessons (WML) Umbrellas	Teaching Notes
Months 3 & 4 (cont.)					**WPS.U4: Adding Information to Your Writing (5 days)**	Use WPS.U4 to teach practical ways to add details (e.g., use a caret mark, attach a strip of paper). You may decide it is helpful to teach minilessons from CFT.U1 and WPS.U4 together (e.g., alternating between the two umbrellas). Children can apply these lessons to the memory books they are working on or to any other writing they want to improve.
				Revisit **IW.4: Writing from a Picture (1 day)**	**CNV.U3: Using Classroom Resources to Write Words (3 days)**	This umbrella will help children expand their ability to write words in their memory books or in any of their other writing. The minilessons build on the writing from IW.4 to demonstrate how to apply the writing principles introduced in this umbrella.
	A Pig Tale	Mo Willems: Having Fun with Humor			**MBK.U2: Expanding Bookmaking (3 days)**	Teach this umbrella any time you think children are ready. Suggest that they apply these minilessons to the memory books they would like to "publish" and celebrate with the class.
	Antonio and the Firefly		LA.U2: Studying Authors and Illustrators, RML1–RML2	Revisit **IW.9: Studying an Author's Writing (1–2 days)**	**WPS.U7: Celebrating Writing, WML1–WML2 (1–2 days)**	Teach WPS.U7 throughout the year to celebrate writing. You might choose to use the minilessons in this umbrella to finish and celebrate children's work on memory books.
			SAS.U2: Solving Words			Revisit IW.9 whenever you are studying several books by the same author. If you are using *Fountas & Pinnell Classroom™ Interactive Read-Aloud Collection*, consider conducting a study of Mo Willems's writing and illustrations.
			LA.U20: Knowing Characters Inside and Out		**STR.U3: Presenting with a Purpose, WML1 (1 day)**	Teach the minilessons in this umbrella over time to give children opportunities to try out new learning. When children use puppets to act out a familiar story, they begin to pay more attention to dialogue. This lays the foundation for adding dialogue to their own writing.

Appendix: Suggested Sequence of Lessons

Months	Texts from *Fountas & Pinnell Classroom™ Shared Reading Collection*	Text Sets from *Fountas & Pinnell Classroom™ Interactive Read-Aloud Collection*	Reading Minilessons (RML) Umbrellas	Interactive Writing (IW) Lessons*	Writing Minilessons (WML) Umbrellas	Teaching Notes
Months 3 & 4 (cont.)					Revisit **WPS.U2: Getting Ideas for Writing** (1–3 days)	Revisit any of the minilessons in WPS.U2 as needed. Substitute different mentor texts to inspire new ideas. Children choose their topic and the kinds of writing they want to do.
				IW.10: Writing with Speech Bubbles (1 day)	**CFT.U2: Adding Dialogue to Writing** (3 days)	Use the class writing from IW.10 as a mentor text in CFT.U2. Invite children to add dialogue to their current writing if fitting. If not, ask them to revisit one of their memory books to try adding dialogue.
		Living and Working Together: Community		**IW.11: Labeling a Map** (1 day) **IW.12: Writing Interview Questions** (1 day)		IW.11 and IW.12 demonstrate other purposes for writing. They also connect nicely with a study of community. IW.12 supports the work you are doing with dialogue. You can invite children to interview someone they know well and write down what the person says.
	The Camping Trip				**CNV.U4: Learning About Punctuation** (3 days)	CNV.U4 builds on children's experiences of using punctuation in interactive writing (e.g., question marks in IW.12; periods and exclamation points in IW.10). If children are ready to learn about punctuating dialogue, teach them as an extension to this umbrella.
	Not Ladybugs!	The Importance of Kindness	LA.U18: Understanding Simple Plot: Problem and Solution	**IW.13: Making Kindness Signs** (1 day)	**WPS.U5: Deleting and Organizing Writing, WML1–WML3** (3 days)	Teach the minilessons in this umbrella to respond to a need you observe in children's writing. We recommend waiting to teach WML4 until children are engaged in writing all-about books.
	Garden Helpers		WAR.U2: Using a Reader's Notebook		**WPS.U7: Celebrating Writing, WML3** (1 day)	Invite children to celebrate the risks they have taken in their writing.

Months	Texts from *Fountas & Pinnell Classroom™ Shared Reading Collection*	Text Sets from *Fountas & Pinnell Classroom™ Interactive Read-Aloud Collection*	Reading Minilessons (RML) Umbrellas	Interactive Writing (IW) Lessons*	Writing Minilessons (WML) Umbrellas	Teaching Notes
Months 5 & 6	Bigger and Bigger and Bigger Captain Brock, Firefighter Up, Up, and Away How Animals Eat	Exploring Nonfiction	MGT.U3: Engaging in Classroom Literacy Work (RML5–RML9, RML10–optional) LA.U11: Studying Nonfiction		**STR.U3: Presenting with a Purpose, WML2 (1 day)**	STR.U3.WML2 allows children to rehearse for informational writing. When they practice oral presentations, they learn to stay on topic and to answer questions. This sets the stage for them to experiment with writing their own all-about informational books.
				IW.14: Writing an All-About Book	**MBK.U5: Making All-About Books (4 days)**	Use the class writing from IW.14 as a mentor text in MBK.U5.
	Going on a Bear Hunt Squawk	Humorous Stories	SAS.U3: Maintaining Fluency		**DRW.U4: Illustrating Nonfiction, WML1–WML2 (2 days)**	Invite children to apply the first two minilessons in DRW.U4 to the all-about books they are making. We recommend teaching WML3 later in the year. If you do choose to teach it at this point of the year, it will be helpful to make diagrams together in interactive writing before introducing WML3.
	Animal Surprises Zoom In and Out Inventions and Nature Bone Riddles	Nonfiction: Questions and Answers	WAR.U4: Writing About Nonfiction Books in a Reader's Notebook		**CFT.U7: Adding Text Features to Books (3 days)**	If children are ready, teach CFT.U7 and have them apply the minilessons to the all-about books they are writing. Alternatively, wait until you revisit all-about books later in the year or when you teach RML.LA.U14: Adding Text Features to Gain Information.
					WPS.U5: Deleting and Organizing Writing, WML4: revisit as needed: **WML1–WML3 (1–4 days)**	Revisit the first three minilessons in WPS.U5 as needed. Introduce WML4, and encourage children to apply the minilesson to their all-about books.

Months	Texts from *Fountas & Pinnell Classroom*™ *Shared Reading Collection*	Text Sets from *Fountas & Pinnell Classroom*™ *Interactive Read-Aloud Collection*	Reading Minilessons (RML) Umbrellas	Interactive Writing (IW) Lessons*	Writing Minilessons (WML) Umbrellas	Teaching Notes
Months 5 & 6 (cont.)	Ripples in the Sea Zip, Zip, Zip The Sweet Mango Tree The Cactus Hotel The Hungry Fly Food Store in the Woods	Nicola Davies: Exploring the Animal World			Revisit **WPS.U7: Celebrating Writing, WML1–WML2 (2 days)**	Revisit WPS.U7 and invite children to celebrate one of their all-about books.
				IW.15: Writing a Question-and-Answer Book (2–3 days)	**MBK.U6: Making Question-and-Answer Books (5 days)**	Use the class writing from IW.15 as a mentor text when you teach the minilessons in MBK.U6.
			LA.U2: Studying Authors and Illustrators, RML4	Revisit **IW.9: Studying an Author's Writing (1–2 days)**		Revisit IW.9 to study the writing of Nicola Davies. Consider repeating the lesson to write about the characteristics of her illustrations as well.
					DRW.U5: Making Pictures Interesting (3 days)	Encourage children to apply these minilessons to their question-and-answer books or to any writing they are doing. Allow time between minilessons for children to experiment with using different materials.
			LA.U3: Giving a Book Talk		Revisit **WPS.U7: Celebrating Writing, WML3 (1 day)**	Invite children to celebrate the risks they have taken to try something new in writing their question-and-answer books.
				IW.16: Making a Shopping List (1 day)		Teach IW.16 around the hundredth day of school to make a shopping list for snack mix. If you have *Fountas & Pinnell Classroom*™ *Interactive Read-Aloud Collection*, reread *Jake's 100th Day of School* from the text set Using Numbers: Books with Counting before you teach IW.16.

Months	Texts from *Fountas & Pinnell Classroom™ Shared Reading Collection*	Text Sets from *Fountas & Pinnell Classroom™ Interactive Read-Aloud Collection*	Reading Minilessons (RML) Umbrellas	Interactive Writing (IW) Lessons*	Writing Minilessons (WML) Umbrellas	Teaching Notes
Months 5 & 6 (cont.)	Snail's Big Adventure	Journeys Near and Far			Revisit **STR.U1: Learning About Self and Others Through Storytelling** and **WPS.U2: Getting Ideas for Writing**	Help children tell new stories and revisit ways to get ideas for their writing. Children need opportunities throughout the year to choose both their topics and the kind of writing they are excited about.
					CFT.U4: Exploring Different Ways Authors Start Books (5 days)	Children can apply these lessons to any type of writing they are drafting or revising, or they can revisit old pieces of writing to try out new beginnings.
					CNV.U5: Using Capital Letters (4 days)	Ask children to apply these minilessons to any writing they are doing. You may have to revisit these minilessons several times during the year. Read children's writing frequently for evidence of their understandings about captilization.
					WPS.U6: Proofreading Writing (3 days)	The minilessons in WPS.U6 help children develop independence in checking their own writing so that it makes sense to their readers.
			WAR.U5: Writing Opinions About Books		**CFT.U3: Reading Like a Writer, WML1 (1 day)**	Use books by any familiar author to teach this minilesson. When you teach children to notice the decisions writers make, you teach them to read like writers. Reading like a writer becomes a habit that they will carry into all of their reading and writing experiences.
					Revisit **WPS.U7: Celebrating Writing, WML3 (1 day)**	Ask children to celebrate risks they have taken in their writing. You may want to extend this minilesson by asking children to share ways they have tried writing like the writers they have studied.

Months	Texts from *Fountas & Pinnell Classroom™ Shared Reading Collection*	Text Sets from *Fountas & Pinnell Classroom™ Interactive Read-Aloud Collection*	Reading Minilessons (RML) Umbrellas	Interactive Writing (IW) Lessons*	Writing Minilessons (WML) Umbrellas	Teaching Notes
Months 7 & 8	Home Sweet Home	Celebrating Diversity	LA.U22: Analyzing the Way Writers Play with Language	**IW.17: Writing an Invitation (1 day)**	**CFT.U8: Writing a Friendly Letter (3 days)**	Use the class writing from IW.17 as a mentor text in CFT.U8. Invite children to write their own friendly letters. This umbrella builds on RML.WAR.U5, which invites children to write about their reading in a letter. Consider having children write letters to you and to each other about the books they are reading.
	The Donkey and the Farmer: An Aesop Fable	Sharing Cultures: Folktales	LA.U9: Looking Closely at Print	**IW.18: Taking a Survey (1 day)**		IW.17, CFT.U8, and IW.18 introduce examples of functional writing—writing that is done for practical purposes. Children learn the value of writing when they see it being used for authentic purposes. In IW.18, they learn that writing can be used in all subject areas, including math and social studies.
	Emily: The Cat Who Thought She Was a Dog					
	Scrunch, the Caterpillar		LA.U7: Thinking About the Author's Purpose		**WPS.U1: Thinking About Purpose and Audience (3 days)**	WPS.U1 builds on children's understanding that writing is used for various purposes. This umbrella teaches children how to choose the kind of writing they want to do to fit their purpose and audience. WPS.U1 works well with RML.LA.U7 and RML.LA.U6.
	The Farmer and the Crow					
	The Creaky House: A Tale from Europe		LA.U6: Thinking About the Author's Message			
	The Singing Wolf: An Aesop Fable					
	Goldilocks and the Three Bears					

Months	Texts from *Fountas & Pinnell Classroom™ Shared Reading Collection*	Text Sets from *Fountas & Pinnell Classroom™ Interactive Read-Aloud Collection*	Reading Minilessons (RML) Umbrellas	Interactive Writing (IW) Lessons*	Writing Minilessons (WML) Umbrellas	Teaching Notes
Months 7 & 8 (cont.)	Little Bear and the Three Campers

The Three Little Pigs

Chicken Licken

Jumping into the Leaves

The Gingerbread Girl: A European Folktale

Three Billy Goats Gruff: A Tale from Norway | Folktales: Exploring Different Versions | | | **CFT.U5: Exploring Different Ways Authors End Books (3 days)** | Children can apply the minilessons in CFT.U5 to the writing they are currently working on, or they can revisit finished pieces to try new endings. |
			LA.U16: Studying Folktales	**IW.19: Writing an Alternative Ending (1 day)**		After you have introduced IW.19, invite children to write their own alternative endings to familiar tales.
					Revisit **WPS.U4: Adding Information to Your Writing** and/or **WPS.U5: Deleting and Organizing Writing (1–3 days)**	Help children revise their writing by teaching any of the minilessons in these umbrellas.
					Revisit **WPS.U6: Proofreading Writing, CNV.U4: Learning About Punctuation,** and/or **CNV.U5: Using Capital Letters (1–3 days)**	Revisit any of the minilessons in these umbrellas to help children edit their writing.
					Revisit **STR.U3: Presenting with a Purpose, WML1 (1 day)**	Invite children to use puppets to act out the new endings they have written for familiar tales.

Months	Texts from *Fountas & Pinnell Classroom™ Shared Reading Collection*	Text Sets from *Fountas & Pinnell Classroom™ Interactive Read-Aloud Collection*	Reading Minilessons (RML) Umbrellas	Interactive Writing (IW) Lessons*	Writing Minilessons (WML) Umbrellas	Teaching Notes
Months 7 & 8 (cont.)	The Frog Who Couldn't Jump Oh, Good! The Great Detective	Bob Graham: Exploring Everyday Life			Revisit **MBK.U3: Making Memory Books (1–4 days)**	Revisit the minilessons in MBK.U3 as needed. Memory stories allow children to think about writing and drawing with details as they learn to focus on a small moment from their own experience.
					Revisit **CFT.U1: Writing with Details (3 days)**	Revisit CFT.U1 as needed. The minilessons in this umbrella provide a foundation for children to think more deeply about adding details to illustrations to convey meaning (DRW.U3).
			LA.U2: Studying Authors and Illustrators, RML1–RML2	Revisit **IW.9: Studying an Author's Writing (1–2 days)**		Revisit IW.9 to study the writing and illustrations by Bob Graham.
					CFT.U3: Reading Like a Writer, WML2 (1 day)	In CFT.U3.WML2, you will help children to look at the decisions that illustrators make to convey meaning. This umbrella supports the minilessons in the next umbrella, DRW.U3.
			LA.U17: Thinking About Where Stories Take Place		**DRW.U3: Adding Meaningful Details to Illustrations (4 days)**	Building on CFT.U1 and CFT.U3, DRW.U3 teaches children to make decisions about the illustrations in their books. Ask children to apply these lessons to their memory books. Revisit these ideas in reading minilessons later in the year when you teach RML.LA.23: Looking Closely at Illustrations.
	Dance and Twirl Run, Jump, Swim: Poems About Animals	Poetic Language	Revisit Writing About Reading and Strategy and Skills minilessons as needed.		**CFT.U6: Making Powerful Word Choices (3 days)**	Just as illustrators make decisions about the details they add to their illustrations, writers make important decisions about their word choices. Children can apply these lessons to their memory books or to any of their writing.

Months	Texts from *Fountas & Pinnell Classroom™ Shared Reading Collection*	Text Sets from *Fountas & Pinnell Classroom™ Interactive Read-Aloud Collection*	Reading Minilessons (RML) Umbrellas	Interactive Writing (IW) Lessons*	Writing Minilessons (WML) Umbrellas	Teaching Notes
Months 7 & 8 (cont.)					Revisit **WPS.U7: Celebrating Writing, WML3** (1 day)	Invite children to celebrate some of the risks they have taken with their illustrations or their choice of words.
				IW.20: Writing a Poem	**CFT.U9: Crafting Poetry** (5 days)	This umbrella continues to build on children's understandings of writer's craft. Use the class writing from IW.20 as a mentor text in CFT.U9.
Months 9 & 10	Old to New	Understanding the Natural World: Planting and Growing	LA.U10: Noticing Text Resources		**STR.U3: Presenting with a Purpose, WML3** (1 day)	STR.U3 will allow children to orally rehearse how to teach someone to do something before they try writing a procedural text (how-to book).
				IW.21: Writing a How-to Book (2–3 days)	**MBK.U4: Making How-to Books** (4 days)	Use the class writing from IW.21 as a mentor text in MBK.U4.
			LA.U23: Looking Closely at Illustrations	**IW.22: Making a Life-Cycle Diagram** (1 day)	**DRW.U4 Illustrating Nonfiction, WML3** (1 day)	Teach DRW.U4.WML3 after teaching IW.22. Feel free to revisit any of the other lessons in DRW.U4 that would benefit your students.
	The Big Surprise	Using Your Imagination			Revisit **CFT.U4: Exploring Different Ways Authors Start Books** (1–3 days)	You may want to revisit CFT.U4 using nonfiction mentor texts to support children in trying different ways to start their how-to books.
			LA.U8: Analyzing the Writer's Craft		Revisit **CFT.U6: Making Powerful Word Choices** (1–3 days)	Revisit CFT.U6 to help children apply the principles to nonfiction writing. These minilessons build on understandings developed in RML.LA.U8.
					Revisit **WPS.U6: Proofreading Writing** (1–3 days)	Repeat any minilessons from this umbrella that you think would be helpful in supporting children in editing their own writing

Months	Texts from *Fountas & Pinnell Classroom™ Shared Reading Collection*	Text Sets from *Fountas & Pinnell Classroom™ Interactive Read-Aloud Collection*	Reading Minilessons (RML) Umbrellas	Interactive Writing (IW) Lessons*	Writing Minilessons (WML) Umbrellas	Teaching Notes
Months 9 & 10 (cont.)		Standing Up for Yourself			Revisit **WPS.U7: Celebrating Writing (1 day)**	Revisit any of the lessons in WPS.U7 to celebrate the how-to books children have written.
		Understanding the Natural World: Oceans		**IW.23: Making Scientific Observations (1 day)**	**WPS.U3: Observing and Writing Like a Scientist (4 days)**	Teach IW.23 before WPS.U3. The minilessons in WPS.U3 will help children write about their scientific experiments and inspire ideas for future nonfiction writing.
					Revisit **MBK.U5: Making All-About Books** or **WPS.U1: Thinking About Purpose and Audience (3–5 days)**	Revisit MBK.U5 or have children choose the type of writing they would like to do based on their purpose.
			LA.U12: Noticing How Authors Organize Nonfiction			If you are using *The Reading Minilessons Book, Grade 1*, you may observe children experimenting with different ways to organize nonfiction (LA.U12). Children will learn about these different organizational structures in writing minilessons in later grades. For now, encourage their attempts and willingness to experiment with their writing.
			LA.U13: Learning Information from Illustrations and Graphics	**IW.24: Making an Ocean Mural (1–2 days)**	**Revisit DRW.U4: Illustrating Nonfiction**	IW.24 builds on understandings introduced in RML.LA.U13. Invite children to add their own labeled drawings to their work. Revisit any lessons in DRW.U4 that will support this work.

Months	Texts from *Fountas & Pinnell Classroom*™ *Shared Reading Collection*	Text Sets from *Fountas & Pinnell Classroom*™ *Interactive Read-Aloud Collection*	Reading Minilessons (RML) Umbrellas	Interactive Writing (IW) Lessons*	Writing Minilessons (WML) Umbrellas	Teaching Notes
Months 9 & 10 (cont.)			LA.U14: Using Text Features to Gain Information		Revisit **CFT.U7: Adding Text Features to Books (1–3 days)**	Revisit the minilessons in CFT.U7 as needed. Children can apply these lessons to an all-about book or to any writing they are doing.
			LA.U15: Understanding Realistic Fiction vs. Fantasy	**IW.25: Writing a Letter**	Revisit **CFT.U8: Writing a Friendly Letter (1–3 days)**	Use IW.25 to teach children how to write a letter to convince someone to do something. This lesson plants seeds for future persuasive writing. Revisit the minilessons in CFT.U8 that will support children in writing their own letters.
		Vera B. Williams: Celebrating Family and Community	LA.U21: Understanding That Characters Can Change		Revisit any of the umbrellas in the **Conventions** or **Writing Process** sections as needed. **(1–3 days)**	As children write more complex texts, they may need to revisit minilessons in the Conventions or Writing Process umbrellas. Read children's writing to determine which lessons would help you respond appropriately.
			LA.U2: Studying Authors and Illustrators (RML1–RML3: Vera Williams)	Revisit **IW.9: Studying an Author's Writing (1–2 days)**		Revisit IW.9 to study Vera B. Williams as a writer and illustrator. Invite children to experiment with writing fiction stories like Vera Williams. In later grades, children will experience explicit minilessons about writing fiction. For now, encourage them to experiment and learn from the authors they study.
					Revisit **WPS.U7: Celebrating Writing (1 day)**	Finish the year with a writing celebration. Children can choose to share a piece they are proud of or a piece that they think shows their growth as a writer.

Glossary

active learning experience A meaningful experience, such as reading and talking about books, making something, or going somewhere, prior to interactive writing.

all-about book A nonfiction book that tells about only one subject or topic.

alphabet book/ABC book A book that helps children develop the concept and sequence of the alphabet by pairing alphabet letters with pictures of people, animals, or objects with labels related to the letters.

alphabet linking chart A chart containing upper- and lowercase letters of the alphabet paired with pictures representing words beginning with each letter (*a*, *apple*, for example).

assessment A means for gathering information or data that reveals what learners control, partially control, or do not yet control consistently.

audience The readers of a text. Often a writer crafts a text with a particular audience in mind.

behaviors Actions that are observable as children read or write.

bold / boldface Type that is heavier and darker than usual, often used for emphasis.

book and print features (as text characteristics) The physical attributes of a text (for example, font, layout, and length).

character An individual, usually a person or animal, in a text.

choice time An essential part of the preschool learning experience in which children make their own decisions regarding which activities to do.

chronological sequence An underlying structural pattern used especially in nonfiction texts to describe a series of events in the order they happened in time.

compose Think about the message and how to say it.

concepts of print Basic understandings related to how written language or print is organized and used—how it works.

construct Write the message that has been composed together; includes sharing the pen.

conventions In writing, formal usage that has become customary in written language. Grammar, usage, capitalization, punctuation, spelling, handwriting, and text layout are categories of writing conventions.

counting book A book that teaches counting in which the structure follows numeric progression.

craft In writing, how an individual piece of writing is shaped. Elements of craft are organization, idea development, language use, word choice, and voice.

dialogue Spoken words, usually set off with quotation marks in text.

directionality The orientation of print (in the English language, from left to right).

directions (how-to) Part of a procedural nonfiction text that shows the steps involved in performing a task. A set of directions may include diagrams or drawings with labels.

drafting and revising The process of getting ideas down on paper and shaping them to convey the writer's message.

drawing In writing, creating a rough image (i.e, a drawing) of a person, place, thing, or idea to capture, work with, and render the writer's ideas.

editing and proofreading The process of polishing the final draft of a written composition to prepare it for publication.

elements of fiction Important elements of fiction include narrator, characters, plot, setting, theme, and style.

elements of poetry Important elements of poetry include figurative language, imagery, personification, rhythm, rhyme, repetition, alliteration, assonance, consonance, onomatopoeia, and aspects of layout.

English learners People whose native language is not English and who are acquiring English as an additional language.

family, friends, and school story A contemporary realistic text focused on the everyday experiences of children of a variety of ages, including relationships with family and friends and experiences at school.

fiction Invented, imaginative prose or poetry that tells a story. Fiction texts can be organized into the categories realism and fantasy. Along with nonfiction, fiction is one of two basic genres of literature.

figurative language An element of a writer's style, figurative language changes or goes beyond literal meaning. Two common types of figurative language are metaphor (a direct comparison) and simile (a comparison that uses *like* or *as*).

font In printed text, the collection of type (letters) in a particular style.

form A kind of text that is characterized by particular elements. Mystery, for example, is a form of writing within the realistic fiction genre. Another term for form is *subgenre*.

friendly letter In writing, a functional nonfiction text usually addressed to friends or family that may take the form of notes, letters, invitations, or email.

functional text A nonfiction text intended to accomplish a practical task, for example, labels, lists, letters, and directions with steps (how-to).

genre A category of written text that is characterized by a particular style, form, or content.

graphic feature In fiction texts, graphic features are usually illustrations. In nonfiction texts, graphic features include photographs, paintings and drawings, captions, charts, diagrams, tables and graphs, maps, and timelines.

high-frequency words Words that occur often in spoken and written language (for example, *the*).

illustration Graphic representation of important content (for example, art, photos, maps, graphs, charts) in a fiction or nonfiction text.

independent writing A text written by children independently with teacher support as needed.

informational text A nonfiction text in which a purpose is to inform or give facts about a topic. Informational texts include the following genres: biography, autobiography, memoir, and narrative nonfiction, as well as expository texts, procedural texts, and persuasive texts.

innovate on a text Change the ending, the series of events, the characters, or the setting of a familiar text.

interactive read-aloud An instructional context in which students are actively listening and responding to an oral reading of a text.

interactive writing A teaching context in which the teacher and students cooperatively plan, compose, and write a group text; both teacher and students act as scribes (in turn).

italic (italics) A styling of type that is characterized by slanted letters.

label A written word or phrase that names the content of an illustration.

layout The way the print and illustrations are arranged on a page.

learning zone The level at which it is most productive to aim one's teaching for each student (the zone of proximal development).

lowercase letter A small letterform that is usually different from its corresponding capital or uppercase form.

main idea The central underlying idea, concept, or message that the author conveys in a nonfiction text. See also *message*.

memory story A story about something experienced personally.

mentor texts Books or other texts that serve as examples of excellent writing. Mentor texts are read and reread to provide models for literature discussion and student writing.

message An important idea that an author conveys in a fiction or nonfiction text. See also *main idea*.

modeled writing An instructional technique in which a teacher demonstrates the process of composing a particular genre, making the process explicit for students.

nonfiction Prose or poetry that provides factual information. According to their structures, nonfiction texts can be organized into the categories of narrative and nonnarrative. Along with fiction, nonfiction is one of the two basic genres of literature.

organization The arrangement of ideas in a text according to a logical structure, either narrative or nonnarrative. Another term for organization is *text structure*.

organizational tools and sources of information A design feature of nonfiction texts. Organizational tools and sources of information help a reader process and understand nonfiction texts. Examples include tables of contents, headings, indexes, glossaries, appendices, author bios, and references.

picture book An illustrated fiction or nonfiction text in which pictures work with the text to tell a story or provide information.

planning and rehearsing The process of collecting, working with, and selecting ideas for a written composition.

plot The events, action, conflict, and resolution of a story presented in a certain order in a fiction text. A simple plot progresses chronologically from start to end, whereas more complex plots may shift back and forth in time.

poetry Compact, metrical writing characterized by imagination and artistry and imbued with intense meaning. Along with prose, poetry is one of the two broad categories into which all literature can be divided.

principle A generalization that is predictable. It is the key idea that children will learn and be invited to apply.

print feature In nonfiction texts, features that include the color, size, style, and font of type, as well as various aspects of layout.

procedural text A nonfiction text that explains how to do something. Procedural texts are almost always organized in temporal sequence and take the form of directions (or how-to texts) or descriptions of a process.

prompt A question, direction, or statement designed to encourage the child to say more about a topic.

publishing The process of making the final draft of a written composition public.

punctuation Marks used in written text to clarify meaning and separate structural units. The comma and the period are common punctuation marks.

purpose A writer's overall intention in creating a text, or a reader's overall intention in reading a text. To tell a story is one example of a writer's purpose, and to be entertained is one example of a reader's purpose.

question and answer A structural pattern used especially in nonfiction texts to organize information in a series of questions with responses. Question-and-answer texts may be based on a verbal or written interview or on frequently arising or logical questions about a topic.

repetition Repeated words or phrases that help create rhythm and emphasis in poetry or prose.

rhyme The repetition of vowel and consonant sounds in the stressed and unstressed syllables of words in verse, especially at the ends of lines.

rhythm The regular or ordered repetition of stressed and unstressed syllables in poetry, other writing, or speech.

sequence See *chronological sequence* and *temporal sequence*.

setting The place and time in which a fiction text or biographical text takes place.

share the pen At points selected by the teacher for instructional value, individual children take over or "share the pen" with the teacher.

shared reading An instructional context in which the teacher involves a group of students in the reading of a particular big book to introduce aspects of literacy (such as print conventions), develop reading strategies (such as decoding or predicting), and teach vocabulary.

shared writing An instructional context in which the teacher involves a group of students in the composing of a coherent text together. The teacher writes while scaffolding children's language and ideas.

sidebar Information that is additional to the main text, placed alongside the text and sometimes set off from the main text in a box.

speech bubble A shape, often rounded, containing the words a character says in a cartoon or other text. Another term for *speech bubble* is *speech balloon*.

story A series of events in narrative form, either fiction or nonfiction.

story map A representation of the sequence of events from a text using drawings or writing.

style The way a writer chooses and arranges words to create a meaningful text. Aspects of style include sentence length, word choice, and the use of figurative language and symbolism.

survey Asking a question and recording the responses.

syllable A minimal unit of sequential speech sounds composed of a vowel sound or a consonant-vowel combination. A syllable always contains a vowel or vowel-like speech sound (e.g., *pen/ny*).

temporal sequence An underlying structural pattern used especially in nonfiction texts to describe the sequence in which something always or usually occurs, such as the steps in a process or a life cycle. See also *procedural text*.

text structure The overall architecture or organization of a piece of writing. Another term for text structure is *organization*.

thought bubble A shape, often rounded, containing the words (or sometimes an image that suggests one or more words) a character thinks in a cartoon or other text. Another term for *thought bubble* is *thought balloon*.

tools As text characteristics, parts of a text designed to help the reader access or better understand it (tables of contents, glossaries, headings). In writing, references that support the writing process (dictionary, thesaurus).

topic The subject of a piece of writing.

uppercase letter A large letterform that is usually different from its corresponding lowercase form. Another term for *uppercase letter* is *capital letter*.

verbal path Language prompts paired with motor movements to help children learn to form letters correctly.

viewing self as writer Having attitudes and using practices that support a student in becoming a lifelong writer.

word boundaries The space that appears before the first letter and after the last letter of a word and that defines the letter or letters as a word. It is important for young readers to learn to recognize word boundaries.

wordless picture book A form in which a story is told exclusively with pictures.

writers' workshop A classroom structure that begins with a whole-group minilesson; continues with independent writing, individual conferences, and small-group instruction; and ends with a whole-group share.

writing Children engaging in the writing process and producing pieces of their own writing in many genres.

writing about reading Children responding to reading a text by writing and sometimes drawing.

writing process Key phases of creating a piece of writing: planning and rehearsing, drafting and revising, editing and proofreading, and publishing.

Credits

Cover image from *Animals Black and White* by Phyllis Limbacher Tildes. Copyright © Charlesbridge Publishing, Inc. All rights reserved. Used with permission of Charlesbridge Publishing, Inc. www.charlesbridge.com.

Cover image from *Best Foot Forward* by Ingo Arndt. Copyright © 2013. All rights reserved. Used with permission from Holiday House.

Cover image from *Big Blue Whale*. Text copyright © 1997 by Nicola Davies. Illustrations copyright © 1997 by Nick Maland. Reproduced by permission of the publisher, Candlewick Press, Somerville, MA, on behalf of Walker Books, London.

Cover image from *A Birthday Basket for Tia* by Pat Mora with illustrations by Cecily Lang. Text copyright © 1992 by Pat Mora. Illustrations copyright © 1992 by Cecily Lang. Reprinted with the permission of Simon & Schuster Books for Young Readers, an imprint of Simon & Schuster Children's Publishing Division. All rights reserved.

Cover image from *Blackout* by John Rocco. Jacket illustration © 2011 by John Rocco. Reprinted by permission of Hyperion Books for Children, an imprint of Disney Book Group, LLC. All rights reserved.

Cover image from *Chester's Way* by Kevin Henkes. Copyright © 1988 by Kevin Henkes. Used by permission of HarperCollins Publishers.

Cover image from *Chrysanthemum* by Kevin Henkes. Copyright © 1991 by Kevin Henkes. Used by permission of HarperCollins Publishers.

Cover image from *The Dandelion Seed* by Joseph Anthony, illustrated by Cris Arbo. Copyright © 1997 by Dawn Publications. All rights reserved. Used with permission of Dawn Publications.

Cover image from *David's Drawings* by Cathryn Falwell. Copyright © 2006 Cathryn Falwell. Permission arranged with Lee & Low Books, Inc., New York, NY 10016.

Cover image from *Don't Let the Pigeon Drive the Bus!* Copyright © 2003 by Mo Willems. First published by Hyperion Books for Children, an imprint of Disney Book Group, LLC. Used with permission. All rights reserved.

Cover image from *A Fine, Fine, School* by Sharon Creech. Copyright © 1998 by Sharon Creech. Jacket art copyright © 2001 by Harry Bliss. Used by permission of HarperCollins Publishers.

Cover image from *Elephants Cannot Dance!* by Mo Willems. Copyright © 2009 by Mo Willems. First published by Hyperion Books for Children, an imprint of Disney Book Group, LLC. Used with permission. All rights reserved.

Cover image from *Elizabeti's School* by Stephanie Stuve-Bodeen, illustrated by Christy Hale. Copyright © 2002 Stephanie Stuve-Bodeen and Christy Hale. Permission arranged with Lee & Low Books, Inc., New York, NY 10016.

Cover image from *First Day Jitters* by Julie Danneberg, illustrated by Judith Love Dufour. Copyright © Charlesbridge Publishing, Inc. All rights reserved. Used with permission of Charlesbridge Publishing, Inc. www.charlesbridge.com.

The Writing Minilessons Book, Grade 1

Works Cited

Anthony, Joseph P. 1997. *The Dandelion Seed*. Nevada City, CA: Dawn Publications.

Blackaby, Susan. 2003. *Plant Packages: A Book About Seeds*. Mankato, MN: Picture Window Books.

Fountas, Irene C., and Gay Su Pinnell. 2019. *The Reading Minilessons Book, Grade 1*. Portsmouth, NH: Heinemann.

———. 2018. *Fountas & Pinnell Classroom™ Interactive Read-Aloud Collection*. Portsmouth, NH: Heinemann.

———. 2018. *Fountas & Pinnell Classroom™ Shared Reading Collection*. Portsmouth, NH: Heinemann.

———. 2018. *The Literacy Quick Guide: A Reference Tool for Responsive Literacy Teaching*. Portsmouth, NH: Heinemann.

———. 2017. *Fountas & Pinnell Literacy Continuum: A Tool for Assessment, Planning, and Teaching*. Portsmouth, NH: Heinemann.

———. 2017. *Guided Reading: Responsive Teaching Across the Grades*, 2nd ed. Portsmouth, NH: Heinemann.

———. 2017. *Phonics, Spelling, and Word Study System, for Grade 1*. Portsmouth, NH: Heinemann.

Gardner-Neblett, Nicole. "The Conversation." September 2015. https://theconversation.com/why-storytelling-skills-matter-for-african-american-kids-46844.

Gibbons, Gail. 1993. *From Seed to Plant*. New York: Holiday House.

Glover, Matt. 2009. *Engaging Young Writers, Preschool–Grade 1*. Portsmouth, NH: Heinemann.

Heard, Georgia. 2016. *Heart Maps: Helping Students Create and Craft Authentic Writing*. Portsmouth, NH: Heinemann.

Johnston, Peter, Kathy Champeau, Andrea Hartwig, Sarah Helmer, Merry Komar, Tara Krueger, and Laurie McCarthy. 2020. *Engaging Literate Minds: Developing Children's Social, Emotional, and Intellectual Lives, K–3*. Portsmouth, NH: Stenhouse.

McCarrier, Andrea, Irene C. Fountas, and Gay Su Pinnell. 2000. *Interactive Writing: How Language and Literacy Come Together, K–2*. Portsmouth, NH: Heinemann.

Ray, Katie Wood, and Matt Glover. 2008. *Already Ready: Nurturing Writers in Preschool and Kindergarten*. Portsmouth, NH: Heinemann.

Resnick, Lauren B., and Catherine E. Snow. 2009. *Speaking and Listening for Preschool Through Third Grade*. Revised Edition. University of Pittsburgh and The National Center on Education and the Economy. Published under license. The New Standards® trademark is owned by the University of Pittsburgh and The National Center on Education and the Economy at 2121 K Street, NW, Suite 700, Washington, DC 20037.

Vygotsky, Lev. 1979. *Mind in Society: The Development of Higher Psychological Processes*. Cambridge, MA: Harvard University Press.